COMPUTER GRAPHICS

BOOK SALE

Tools for *Visualization*

MORRIS W. FIREBAUGH
University of Wisconsin–Parkside

WCB   **Wm. C. Brown Publishers**

Dubuque, Iowa · Melbourne, Australia · Oxford, England

Book Team

Editor Earl McPeek
Developmental Editor Linda M. Meehan

Wm. C. Brown Publishers
A Division of Wm. C. Brown Communications, Inc.

Vice President and General Manager *Beverly Kolz*
Director of Sales and Marketing *John W. Calhoun*
Advertising Manager *Janelle Keeffer*
Director of Production *Colleen A. Yonda*
Manager of Visuals and Design *Faye M. Schilling*
Design Manager *Jac Tilton*
Art Manager *Janice Roerig*
Publishing Services Manager *Karen J. Slaght*
Permissions/Records Manager *Connie Allendorf*

Wm. C. Brown Communications, Inc.

President and Chief Executive Officer *G. Franklin Lewis*
Corporate Vice President, President of WCB Manufacturing *Roger Meyer*
Vice President and Chief Financial Officer *Robert Chesterman*

Cover design by Jeff Storm

Cover image by Morris Firebaugh

A Times Mirror Company

Library of Congress Catalog Card Number: 92–75103

ISBN 0–697–11646–8

Manuscript editing and page layout done with Microsoft Word and
printed on a LaserMaster® 1000 dpi printer. Illustrations produced with
THINK Pascal, Visual Basic, Canvas®, Swivel-3D®, VersaCAD®,
COSMOS/M, RenderMan®, Mathematica®, Interactive Physics®,
NCSA Image, VIRTUS WalkThrough®, and the Spyglass® series of
visualization programs.

Printed in the United States of America by Wm. C. Brown Communications, Inc.,
2460 Kerper Boulevard, Dubuque, IA 52001

10 9 8 7 6 5 4 3 2 1

Credits

Figure 1.1: Reprinted by permission of PWS-Kent Publishing Company.
Figure 1.7: Smarr, Larry; Bernstein, David; Hobill, David.
Figure 1.9: Portions developed at the National Center for
Supercomputing Applications at the University of Illinois at Urbana–
Champaign.
Figure 1.15: PixelPaint® images provided by Pixel Resources, Inc., 1993.
Figure 1.17: Based on "Meltdown," Apple® Science CD-ROM, volume 1.
Figure 2.17: Based on Figure 5, "Mouse Mechanism," page III-28,
Inside Macintosh, © 1985, Apple Computer, Inc.
Figure 5.2d: Courtesy of Harrell Sellers, University of Illinois.
Figure 10.13: Image of HP Personal VRX Workstation reprinted
courtesy of Hewlett-Packard Co.
Figure 11.40: "Iris before/after" copyright © Iterated Systems, Inc,
1991 (404) 840–0633. This image was compressed and decompressed
using Iterated Systems, Inc's fractal image compression products.
Figure 13.33: "Gear" image from Sample Files folder of Canvas® 3.0.
Courtesy of Deneba Software.

Figures 13.34 and 13.37: VersaCAD® drawing courtesy of
Computervision.
Figure 14.15: Klein bottle by Stewart Dickson, visualized using
Mathematica®.
Figure 14.16: Images created by Alfred Gray, University of Maryland.
Figure 15.2a: Michael Norman (University of Illinois), Jack Burns
(New Mexico State University), and Martin Sulkanen (NASA).
Figure 15.2b: "MRI Brain Scan," Apple® Science DC-ROM, volume 1.
Figure 15.6: Based on Washington.151 and Lincoln.151, from the
samples folder of Morph®, Gryphon Software Corporation.
Figure 15.17: "Still life/JPEG" from the Samples folder, PicturePress®
Demo disk. Courtesy of Storm Technology.
Figure 16.1: M. Norman, University of Illinois, and P. Hardee,
University of Alabama.
Figure 16.2: M. Moseley, I. Rampil, et. al., University of California,
San Francisco.
Figure 16.10: "Rowing Crew," Sample Disk 1, Adobe Premiere®.

Contents

Section 2

N-Dimensional Graphics 87

Chapter 4

One-Dimensional Graphics 89

Chapter 5

Two-Dimensional Graphics – Representation 113

Chapter 6

Two-Dimensional Graphics – Implementation 139

Chapter 7

Three-Dimensional Graphics – Fundamentals 167

Chapter 8

Three-Dimensional Graphics – Geometric Modeling and Visibility 197

Chapter 9

Three-Dimensional Graphics – Visual Realism and Color 229

Chapter 16

Visual Realities 467

Appendix A

Vectors and Matrices 499

Appendix B

FIGS
Fundamental Interactive Graphics
System 507

Index 527

Preface

This text is the culmination of more than fifteen years of teaching and over twenty years of research in computer graphics. It is built on the author's conviction that computer graphics provides the foundation for a new paradigm in computing that is revolutionizing the ways in which humans interact with computers. The tools are finally here, in the forms of personal workstations and astounding arrays of applications programs, to provide everyone who has an interest and a modest budget with a computer graphics system that has high-quality, integrated tools for visualization. The goals of this book are to provide students with the algorithmic tools of traditional computer graphics and to introduce them to tools for visualization and image processing.

The production of this book, itself, illustrates the concepts of integration and visualization in computer graphics systems. It was designed and built from initial prospectus through camera-ready copy on the author's Macintosh and MS-DOS workstations. All graphics appearing in the text were generated by the algorithms, application programs, and image sources described in the text. All images and image processing results shown in the text were generated, transformed, and embedded in the text on the same machine. This text is unique among books in the field because it is a product of the graphical systems and processes that it describes. By demonstrating to students the graphical capabilities of systems widely available on their own campuses, we hope to inspire them to explore and extend the graphics paradigm in their own programs.

Many of the advanced graphics tools described, such as digital image scanners, digital video protocols, image libraries of 3D clip-art and movies, and animation tools, were simply not available on earlier personal workstations at any price. The present text demonstrates not only the graphical capabilities of such tools but also illustrates how graphical information from diverse hardware and software systems can be integrated in one document. Our objective in this project was to produce a book distinguished by its emphasis on visualization, integration, and authenticity.

Visualization

Our basic assumption is that most students of computer graphics are interested in tools for visualization, that is, algorithms, software, and hardware systems that will enable them to generate, manipulate, and present visual information. Such tools greatly improve one's ability to understand complex data and complicated systems and to communicate this understanding to others. The power of the visual paradigm is now widely recognized and is the foundation for graphics-based systems such as Apple's Macintosh, Microsoft's Windows, and MIT's X Window System development environment for UNIX. Confirmation of the significance of the graphical paradigm is evident by the speed and unanimity with which computer companies have adopted the window/icon/-menu/pointer (WIMP) interface. While "user-friendly" graphical interfaces do not necessarily guarantee quality in application programs, one of the most obvious and universal hallmarks of modern, high-quality software is an elegant graphical interface.

Visualization also provides the key for solving one of the most severe problems posed by supercomputers and present-day, high-capacity instrumentation for measurement and data collection. This is the problem of the *information explosion*. Weather satellites, seismic sensors, and medical scanners produce data far more rapidly than trained humans can analyze it. By offering tools for visualization, computer graphics provides a highly efficient technique for data representation and reduction that helps humans extract meaning from the "fire hose" of raw data produced by modern instrumentation.

Integration

The second theme running through this textbook is the concept of *integration* of the *synthetic* and *analytic* aspects of computer graphics. Traditional texts in computer graphics have stressed the synthetic aspect—the representation and rendering of graphical models—with little or no attention to the analytical aspect. Image processing and analysis is the complementary area to image synthesis and constitutes an essential component of computer graphics. All of the mathematics and algorithmic techniques developed for image synthesis apply equally well to image analysis.

Image processing and analysis represents a rapidly growing field with applications in surveillance, automation, robotics, pattern recognition, and pen-based operating systems. In this text, we attempt to integrate these two complementary areas by recognizing images generated by electronic transducers (video, scanners, and so on) as graphical objects equivalent to those generated by algorithmic techniques. Images of real objects are used throughout the book to illustrate graphics concepts, and a whole chapter is devoted to special techniques for image processing and analysis.

This integration approach is possible through the multimedia capabilities of modern workstations. Integration occurs at the application program level through the ability to capture photographic, video, and screen images and transfer them throughout many programs via the cut and paste option available on graphics-based operating systems. Thus, graphical data from Pascal programs, painting and drawing programs, and various image digitizers are readily transferred from image enhancement programs to word processors, for example. The integration of applications programs is essential for the production of effective and attractive visual media in all fields of human communication. The advent of dynamic data types, such as the *QuickTime*™ protocol, has extended the domain of multimedia integration to include sound, animation, and video information.

Another level of integration in which computer graphics plays a key role is at the multitasking and network level. Examples of this integration are provided by Macintosh System 7 and Microsoft Windows NT which allow multiple windows to be open, each of which is actively processing an application program. Through networking, individual workstations become nodes of a massive, parallel architecture. Computer graphics provides the key for understanding and controlling such complex operating systems that would be virtually impenetrable if implemented on old-fashioned, command-line systems.

The final level of integration explored and demonstrated in this text is that of *interoperability* between computer systems. Standards such as the X Window protocol have simplified the communication of graphical information between heterogeneous networked workstations. Perhaps even more important are the *de facto* standards for data

exchange between major workstation manufacturers like Sun, Apple and IBM. Already most major software manufacturers offer word processing, spread sheets, database, desktop publishing, and CAD programs for the Macintosh and IBM-PC lines which write data files accessible on both systems.

This interoperability at the data level has greatly reduced the risk factor for prospective buyers of workstation systems—and for textbook authors—considering the optimum platform. The advantages of standards for interoperability are apparent in the success of the *PostScript* page description language, AutoCAD's *DFX* file format, and the *TIFF* image file format. One of the goals of the Apple/IBM consortium is that of *program* interoperability. That level of integration will encourage graphics users to focus on the capabilities of visualization software (the important stuff) rather than the peculiarities of individual platforms (a moving target).

Authenticity

The advent of personal workstations and the software inspired by these computers makes possible the final feature distinguishing this book from previous efforts—*authenticity*. By authenticity, we simply mean that essentially all graphics presented in the book have been *produced* by the programs and tools described, rather than *reproduced* from the work of others. While many previous computer graphics texts contain excellent discussions of the principal algorithms used in computer graphics, the convincing, realistic graphics they present were rendered on expensive commercial systems not generally available to college students. Most computer graphics texts are, in fact, illustrated by some combination of three modes: a) low-resolution, bit-mapped raster graphics, b) artist renderings illustrating graphics concepts, or c) reproductions of output from expensive, dedicated graphics workstations, which frequently come with attribution credits reading "Courtesy of Evans and Sutherland."

Previous graphics books have also frequently been limited to algorithms implemented in FORTRAN, BASIC, Pascal, or C with limited graphics capabilities. Significant application examples such as image processing and CAD, if presented at all, were drawn from a fragmented assortment of graphics workstations, mainframe computers, and special-purpose machines. We finally have computers available with substantial computing power, excellent graphics rendering features, and a remarkable range of image generation and processing capabilities. A principal objective of this text is to demonstrate the breadth and depth of computer graphics tools available on the major personal workstations. By restricting the examples and illustrations to those readily available on low-cost machines—rather than relying on reproductions of output from a hodgepodge of specialized systems)—we have tried to produce a *truly authentic* computer graphics book. Students of this text need not gaze wistfully at "Courtesy of …" reproductions, but rather can plunge into the excitement of creating their own graphics masterpieces using the tools and techniques described.

A final aspect of authenticity is the theme of *model authenticity* developed throughout the book. The success of ray tracing and radiosity rendering models is interpreted as a direct result of incorporating the physics of light and energy. Model authenticity represents the key to realistic simulation of the behavior of physical objects interacting with their environment. This principle has been used to produce realistic graphical simulations of fractal landscapes, draped garments, human smile formation, and somersaulting Luxo lamps. Model authenticity is demonstrated by numerous detailed examples, including the simulation of a chaotic pendulum motion and the use of finite element analysis for visualizing beam deflection. Such techniques will play a critical role in the emerging field of virtual reality.

A Note to the Instructor

As a university instructor with many years experience, I know better than to tell other instructors how to use this book. However, the following note may help prospective instructors understand the motivation for the book's organization and how it might be used in various courses.

Organization

The purpose of Section One (Chapters 1–3) is to provide background and motivation for the subsequent two sections. Chapter 1 is intended to explain how visualization offers a coherent theme which provides the rationale for computer graphics and unifies its many aspects. Chapters 2 and 3 provide background on hardware, software, standards, and environments available for computer graphics. All three chapters are independent of each other, and none is required to understand the algorithmic development in Section Two.

Section Two (Chapters 4–11) presents the material of a standard computer graphics course through a systematic development and elaboration on the theme of N dimensions. A somewhat unique aspect of this approach, which I have found very helpful in my own courses, is to introduce homogeneous coordinates and transformations in one dimension. This simplifies the mathematical treatment and is easily extended to 2D and 3D in later chapters. Several styles of presentation graphics (pie charts, bar charts, and so on) are presented in a 1D context as examples of representing scalar quantities.

The section devotes increased attention to the increasing complexity involved with representing and rendering images of 2D and 3D scenes. Ray tracing and radiosity are presented as effective approaches for achieving visual realism, and detailed examples of realistic rendering are presented using the REYES architecture of *RenderMan*. The section concludes with an in-depth discussion of fractals as objects of fractional dimension and great visual appeal. Several fractal algorithms are presented, and the chapter concludes with a discussion of iterated function systems as a promising technique for image compression. The material in this section is highly interdependent, and the chapters should be studied in order.

Section Three (Chapters 12–16) summarizes some of the most impressive software tools available for visualization. All of the languages and examples presented illustrate the important computer graphics concepts and algorithms of Section Two. Starting with the development of graphical user interfaces (GUIs) in Chapter 12, it spans the fields of design, engineering, mathematics, physics, image processing, and the design of virtual realities. Real visualization examples are presented, using such outstanding tools as *Visual Basic*, *Mathematica*, and the *Spyglass* series. The chapters of Section Three are independent of each other and may be used to provide material to illustrate the graphics concepts of Section Two.

Course Structure

Three possible course configurations in which this text could be used include the following:

    i) A ten-week, undergraduate computer graphics course. Recommended syllabus: Chapters 4–9.

    ii) A fifteen-week, undergraduate computer graphics course. Recommended syllabus: Chapter 1, sections of Chapters 2 and 3, and Chapters 4–10.

iii) A fifteen-week, upper-level undergraduate or lower-level graduate course in image processing (Prereq: Introduction to Computer Graphics). Recommended syllabus: Chapters 7–11 and Chapters 14–16.

A final comment on "reinventing the wheel" is appropriate at this point. Most of the algorithms described in the first two sections of the book have been effectively incorporated into many commercial computer graphics applications programs. So why do we sweat through the mathematics of matrix multiplication to implement these algorithms when applications programs have already solved our problem?

There are two points to consider when deciding whether to "build or buy." One is that, for most one-shot graphics applications, there probably exists an excellent commercial program capable of performing the graphics functions you require. In such cases, intelligent project management suggests that you purchase and utilize the appropriate application program.

The second point that should be stressed is that the hallmarks of modern, user-friendly software are graphical user interfaces and extensive use of computer graphics throughout. Software engineers and even casual programmers need some awareness of the underlying graphical data structures, transformations, and algorithms in order to implement graphics in the programs they build. The formalism of the first two sections is intended to develop this understanding of fundamental concepts essential for effective graphics programming. Because the commercial programs demonstrated in the text all incorporate fundamental graphical concepts, students will gain insight into the concepts themselves and inspiration for their own programming through exposure to well-written application programs.

Acknowledgments

A number of colleagues and institutions have contributed to the production of this textbook. First, I want to thank Earl McPeek, Linda Meehan, and Carla Kipper of Wm. C. Brown Publishers for their enthusiastic support of this project. My colleague Yong Auh contributed greatly to the conceptualization and critical review of the text and to the production of the *Vectors and Matrices* Appendix. I greatly appreciate the careful reading and creative word-smithing by Theodora Gottstein and Sue Hess. Particular thanks are due my former student, colleague, and fellow biker, David Siegler,

for his contributions in algorithm development, operating system details, and stimulating conversations. Dan Knudson, PHIGS guru and fellow climber, contributed greatly by writing the *Fundamental Interactive Graphics System*, FIGS, and developing examples of graphical user interfaces. I also appreciate the effort of former student, Scott Singer, in writing the *Simulator* GUI example. Debra Schroeder also deserves much thanks for appearing like an angel to enter proofreader corrections in the final stages of publication.

I owe a considerable debt to the professional computer graphics community, primarily SIGGRAPH, for the stimulation its publications, short courses and conferences provided. In particular, I want to thank Donald Greenberg, Brian Barsky, Craig Upson, Benoit Mandelbrot, Robert Wolff, Loren Carpenter, Richard Voss, and Alva Ray Smith for inspiring me with the beauty of their graphics and revealing the importance of visualization. Michael Barnsley and Dale Snider were particularly helpful in their reviews of the fractal chapter. Brad Horn of Wolfram Research made valuable corrections and improvements to the *Mathematica* discussion. V. I. Weingarten, President of Structural Analysis and Research Corporation, contributed to the accuracy of the discussion of finite element analysis. Brand Fortner, of Spyglass, Inc., supported the effort on volume visualization with his programs, *Transform* and *Dicer*.

Outside evaluation and critical review were of great assistance throughout the development of the book. In particular, I want to thank the following reviewers: J. D. Robertson, Daniel Lamet, Marc Armstrong, Rosalee Nerheim-Wolfe, Mark Measures, Nan Schaller, Richard Detmer, Jeff Spears, John Lowther, J. Eugene Ball, and Evelyn Rozanski.

Finally, I want to thank the University of Wisconsin-Parkside for a sabbatical year during which the structure of the project emerged and serious writing began. I am indebted to my colleagues Russell Ashdown, Phil Charest, Steven Dolins, Steven Firebaugh, Tim Fossum, Ben Greenebaum, Ron Gutkowski, Tony Larsen, Bill Moy, Bill Ogden, George Perdikaris, Rabah Rennane, Jim Wick, and my computer graphics students for their interest and feedback throughout the development of the book.

M. W. F.

Section 1

Foundations of Visualization

The goals of this section are:

Chapter 1
Justify visualization as a new computational paradigm by examining its physiological basis, the analysis tools it provides, and applications of visualization to understanding both real and imaginary worlds.

Chapter 2
Discuss the technological basis for computer graphics and its central importance in the paradigm shift in computer operating systems.

Chapter 3
Interpret some of the elemental interactive graphics functions on which all interactive computer graphics systems are based in the language of object-oriented programming.

Chapter 1

Visualization: A New Paradigm

The psychical entities which seem to serve as elements of thought are certain signs and more or less clear images which can be voluntarily reproduced and combined ... The above-mentioned elements are, in my case, of visual and some muscular type. Conventional words or other signs have to be sought for laboriously only in a secondary stage ...
Albert Einstein

There are many approaches to the study of computer graphics. They range on a spectrum from highly abstract formal mathematical processes to informal impressionistic artistic techniques. The mathematical approach emphasizes the power of abstraction for achieving maximum flexibility in transforming one graphical object into another. The artistic approach stresses the generation of interesting patterns while holding the level of mathematical sophistication to a minimum. Most courses in computer graphics fall midway on this spectrum with an emphasis on sufficient mathematical formalism to enable students to generate and manipulate realistic graphical images. The goals of this text are to introduce students to the fundamental concepts of computer graphics, to demonstrate many of the powerful new graphics tools which have recently become available, and to establish visualization as the unifying principle for all of computer graphics.

The underlying theme in computer graphics is *visualization*. Computer graphics provides a tool without equal for helping achieve a clear mental image of the object under study. Whether we are interested in an abstract mathematical transformation, US census data, or a cleanly rendered CAD part, computer graphics allows us to see the object of our interest more clearly than we could by other techniques.

Traditionally, computer graphics authors have focused almost exclusively on computer graphics as a tool for the *synthesis* of graphical images. Synthetic images may be generated two ways. First, by using graphical primitives for curves, surfaces, and elementary 3D objects it is possible to generate almost any graphical image by the proper synthesis of these more primitive elements. Second, data from real world phenomena can be plotted as charts, scatter plots, or contour plots in either 2D or 3D to help the observer discover interesting patterns. Both of these techniques feature the use of computer synthesized output images for visualizing either synthetic models or real physical data.

However, we believe that a visualization approach to computer graphics requires an expansion of the definition to include image *analysis* as well as image synthesis. New tools make it possible for the computer to collect visual data directly. These, in effect, give the computer the power to "see." The extraction of meaning from such images is generally referred to as *image processing* or *computer vision*. In image processing, the image itself is the object of analysis. This synthesis/analysis distinction is determined by the direction of information flow: synthetic images are generated as *output* by the computer; image analysis requires transducers for collecting data and generating an image as *input* to the computer.

Many of the tools available on computer graphics systems provide valuable operations for both the synthesis and analysis of images. These tools perform many of the same operations on graphical data that spreadsheets and data bases perform on numeric data—object selection, integration, arithmetic operations on single objects, and Boolean operations between objects. It is useful to introduce the *graphical data flow* paradigm for describing this integration and manipulation of graphical data in a manner parallel to that widely used for numerical and symbolic data. This book illustrates numerous examples of graphical data flow between programs on a single machine and across hardware platforms.

Seeing and Understanding

Computer graphics provides potent tools for *seeing*, and hence *understanding*, objects of interest. Remember as a child when the light bulb of understanding suddenly flashed on in your mind and you exclaimed "I see!"? In order to truly understand objects, whether they are abstract mathematical functions or intriguing artistic designs, it is tremendously important to see them. Computer graphics allows us to accomplish this visualization.

Visualization involves cognitive functions such as recognition, learning, and memory. It is the basis for the concept of "the mind's eye," an abstract mental representation of our physical experience. The clearer we visualize an object in our mind's eye, the more effectively we can relate to it and ultimately understand it. Our own visual system is the shortest path to the mind's eye.

Other authors have noted the effectiveness of graphics as aids in understanding and communication. Tufte[1] presents an excellent discussion on the history of pre-computer graphics and the elements of good graphics design. Shu[2] considers the importance of the visual paradigm in her book on visual programming. The role of visualization in scientific computing was emphasized in a special issue of *Computer Graphics* reporting on an NSF workshop cochaired by McCormick, DeFanti, and Brown.[3]

The Physiological Basis for Visualization

Other senses besides sight provide valuable clues for understanding the world around us. The sense of smell is a very powerful determinant in the behavior of many mammals, fish, and insects, but is less critical as a survival tool in human beings. The sense of touch is still vitally important, particularly in the cognitive development of young children. Watch a young child and note how she refines her psychomotor movements while batting an object with her hand and observing its subsequent behavior. Much of the child's sense of "objectness" is developed by the

tactile sensations resulting from grasping, punching, and poking objects.

The sense of hearing is another highly developed communication channel by which we interact with the world around us. While the sense of hearing does not provide as large an information bandwidth as sight, it is a sense with a huge range of sensitivity (we can comfortably hear sound intensities ranging from 1 Watt/m^2 down to 10^{-12} Watt/m^2.) The lower limit of hearing cuts off just above the energy of individual molecules—a fact for which we can be grateful! In fact, many individuals with losses of both sight and hearing report that they consider hearing the more important of the two senses for functioning in society.

The physiological basis of visualization is grounded on the fact that vision is the most highly developed sense in humans and many animals. Many textbook depictions of the brain, in fact, include the eyes as an integral part of this vital organ. Evolutionary development has produced an organ, the brain/eyes, in which *approximately half* of the neurons are dedicated to the processing of visual information. Vision is the complex process of transforming an optical image registering on the retina of the eye into meaningful information. Such information provides the basis for understanding and action.

Motivated by the goal of putting machine vision on a sounder theoretical basis, David Marr emphasized the necessity for understanding the human vision system and using the information-processing insights it offers.[4] Some understanding of the power and complexity of the human vision system may emerge by considering the following facts:

- The eye contains over 100 million receptors, accommodates an intensity range of 10^9, detects intensity changes of 2 percent over most of this range, distinguishes nearly one million hues, and is limited in visual acuity only by the diffraction limit of light waves. The eye itself does considerable computation on the incoming image, including pattern analysis for edge detection. Certain animals have even developed specialized retinal pattern detectors—frogs have a retinal bug filter, and rabbits have a hawk detector built into their retinas.

- The brain component of the brain/eye system is even more impressive in its statistics—it contains between $10^{12} - 10^{13}$

neurons (nerve cells) which, while constituting only 2 percent of the body's mass, use 20 percent of its oxygen. The time required for a human to recognize a face in a photograph is about 200 ms – 300 ms. While this appears slow compared to the μs – ns cycle time of computers, Churchland and Sejnowski point out that even the brain of the common housefly processes information one hundred times faster than the fastest digital computer.[5] In addition, the brain is *7 – 8 orders of magnitude* more energy efficient in processing information than the best silicon chips.

- Great progress has been made in mapping the senses and motor control functions onto various regions of the brain. Studies of lesions (well-defined changes caused by injury or disease) in both animals and humans have provided scientists with great detail in determining which parts of the brain process sensory information from the various organs. New, non-intrusive techniques such as PET (positron emission tomography) allow even more precision in such mapping.

- The psychology of vision is as intriguing as its physiology. The mind interprets very subtle cues from shading, texture, stereopsis (visual disparity from two eyes), and relative motion during the process of visualization. The study of the effectiveness of various visual cues can help us design better techniques for computer graphics visualization. Churchland presents a wealth of information on our present understanding of the psychology and physiology of the brain in her book *Neurophilosophy*.[6]

The human vision system is an extremely powerful tool for information processing and analysis. It operates at a relatively low level on the hierarchy of cognitive functions (processing takes place even in the retina of the eye), and the large portion of the brain devoted to visual processing suggests the importance of vision in the evolutionary process.

Highly symbolic cognitive processes such as language and number processing arrived relatively recently on the evolutionary time scale compared to our highly developed vision. This may explain, in part, why no regions of the brain have been identified exclusively for carrying out these functions. They tend to be distributed throughout the brain as a whole. This evolutionary development is replayed in the development of the individual child. A child's vision arrives long before the ability to use language or compute.

Historically, the development of computer systems, particularly the representations used for languages and operating systems, has occurred in precisely the *opposite* order from the evolution of these representations in human beings. That is, the first communication with computers was through numbers, binary and decimal. Then alphabetic mnemonics and, later, natural language instructions appeared. Finally, in the 1980s, visualization arrived with its emphasis on representing objects and actions by semantic icons and the display of data in functional and geometric form. In retrospect, it is quite remarkable that it took the computer science community so long to recognize the power and efficiency of the visual paradigm in computing.

Effective Communication through Visualization

The reason visualization has assumed such an important role in computer graphics is the enhanced communication it provides at the human/machine interface. We illustrate the power of communication through visual images with four examples, including side-by-side comparison of visual/image/icon representations with more traditional alphanumeric forms. The examples include:

- Public signs,
- Operating systems,
- Correlations in data,
- Computer simulations.

This set of examples begins by illustrating the power and efficiency of icons for communicating meaning about ordinary experiences in everyday life. The second example, operating systems, illustrates how the power of icons increases when they become "intelligent," that is, when they represent not only objects but also the functions of which objects are capable. Next, we look at the added insight that graphics provides for studying the relationship of (x,y) data sets interpreted as y = f(x). Finally, we indicate how computer graphics and image processing tools can help interpret the output from computer simulations of complex systems.

Public Signs

In Table 1.1, we illustrate several iconic signs that are becoming fairly standardized in international usage, along with an approximation of their meaning in English. Note how the signs convey information in a culture- and language-free mode. Note also how the eye is instinctively drawn to the iconic symbols and only later browses back to the natural language interpretation. The iconic symbols often relate at a *primitive* level to one or more of our other senses such as hearing, touch, and smell which also require low-level cognitive processing. Meaningful alphanumeric symbols, on the other hand, are *compound* symbols (words and sentences) comprising strings of more elementary symbols (letters) that require a higher level of cognitive processing to extract their meaning.

Some educators are beginning to voice concern that the ease and simplicity of communication via computer graphics and visual icons will result in reduced reading ability on the part of students in general. When the electronic calculator came into widespread use, educators expressed concern that students would lose their ability to do arithmetic by hand (How many of us can calculate the square root of a number by longhand?). The counter argument, in both cases, is that the computer has provided a valuable extension of our cognitive processes, allowing us to perform functions more rapidly than otherwise possible.

Operating Systems

Computer operating systems and programming environments provide a classic example of the extremes possible on the textual/visual spectrum. On the one end, we have traditional command-line languages such as JCL (or MS-DOS or UNIX, for that matter), an example of which is shown in Figure 1.1. On the other end of the extreme, we have windows/icons/menus/pointer (WIMP) interfaces exemplified by the Macintosh operating system and Microsoft *Windows* on MS-DOS systems.

Consider the Job Control Language (JCL), shown in Figure 1.1, required to run a finite element analysis job on an IBM mainframe.

The primary advantage of textual operating systems and environments is the power and flexibility they provide to perform any conceivable task. The price one pays for this power is the effort to master exceedingly complex systems with arcane commands, a task that frequently requires

years to develop real expertise. Then, just as you have fully mastered one operating system, Murphy's Law requires you to learn a completely new and equally arcane system as the old computer is retired. One attractive feature of UNIX is that it is relatively machine-independent, so that the learning curve need not be repeated as a new system is installed.

Alan Kay and his colleagues at the Xerox Palo Alto Research Center (PARC) conceived of the basic windows/icons/menus/pointer concepts which form the WIMP paradigm. The basic principles underlying this paradigm are:

- Windows associated with several user tasks are simultaneously visible,

- Switching between task windows requires only a mouse button push,

- Information is not lost in the process of switching,

- Screen space can be used economically

Table 1.1
Comparison of Natural Language vs. Iconic Signs

English Representation (symbolic)	Iconic Representation (visual)
Fuel Available at this Exit	
This Parking Space Reserved for the Handicapped	
Women's Restroom, Men's Restroom	
No Smoking	

```
//UOX608 JOB (1,X60800S,2N01),'MAGSQN94 RUN',
// MSGLEVEL=(2,0),CLASS=N,MSGCLASS=S
/*ROUTE PRINT R15
//A EXEC TSMAGSQN,RUNNAME=HUGE,REGION.MAG=2800K,RESEQ=HUGE,
// USERID=UOX608,PLTNAME=HUGE,PROS=MAGSTA94,PROG=MAGNET94
//START.STEPLIB DD DSN=AOS1.GRP23.TLOAD1,DISP=SHR
//MAG.STEPLIB DD DSN=AOS1.GRP23.TLOAD1,DISP=SHR
//MAG.FT08F001 DD UNIT=SYSDA,SPACE=(18144,300)
//MAG.FT09F001 DD UNIT=SYSDA,SPACE=(18144,300)
//MAG.FT07F001 DDUNIT=SYSDA,DCB=(RECFM=FB,LRECL=1440,BLKSIZE=1440),
// SPACE=(1440,5000)
```

Figure 1.1
Example of Job Control Language. This segment of JCL is listed directly from the author's finite element analysis runs on a mainframe computer. The difficulty of translating such language into English rivals that of natural language translation. The main difference is that this problem is the result of conscious design. (*Reprinted from Firebaugh[7] by permission of PWS-Kent Publishing Company.*)

through the use of overlapping windows.

These concepts were first implemented in 1972 in the Xerox *Alto*, the first "personal computer" with 256 KB memory, a 600×800 pixel full-page, bit-mapped graphic display, a mouse, and a 2.5 MB removable hard disk pack (floppies had not yet been invented). The enormous popularity of the Alto within the Xerox Corporation led to the development of the Xerox *Star*, the first commercial WIMP system. The Star used a Xerox 8010 workstation to deliver a very powerful networked windows/icons/menus/pointer operating system. This system provided e-mail through Ethernet, an office automation system through *OfficeTalk*, and contained many object-oriented features derived from the *SmallTalk* language, another product of Alan Kay's PARC group. An excellent history of the development of the WIMP paradigm as it was implemented in the Xerox *Star* has been given by Jeff Johnson *et al.*[8]

Because of inattentiveness to the personal computer revolution occurring outside of Xerox and the company's choice to keep the Star's technologies proprietary, the system failed to become an industry standard. It had, however, a tremendous influence on the development of the Apple *Lisa*, another benchmark computer. The Lisa was another ground-breaking technological success that resulted in a commercial failure. Two contributing reasons for its lack of success were its closed architecture and excessive price. The primary contribution of the Lisa was to give birth to the *Macintosh*, a miniaturized version of the Lisa with all of its functionality at one-fifth the cost.

Consider the operation of a common, garden-variety Macintosh. In Figure 1.2, we show an example of the author's Mac Plus desktop environment as this was being written. The original desktop contained the icon for a 45-MB hard drive labeled "Morris_Rodime," a floppy disk labeled "CG-Text," and the icon of a trash can. By double clicking the mouse cursor (shown as an arrowhead near MS Dictionary) on the hard drive icon, the contents are opened to reveal a hierarchical filing system containing sixteen files and folders headed by the "System Folder." Double clicking on the "Applications" folder reveals its contents, eight folders labeled "WORD4.0," "Graphics," "WINGZ," and so on. After selecting the WORD4.0 folder by pointing at it and double-clicking, the next level of the filing system opens revealing applications programs such as "Microsoft Word," documents such as "Word 4 ReadMe," and ancillary files such as "MS Dictionary."

Objects such as files and folders may be deleted by selecting them with a single click of the mouse and dragging them into the trash can. Objects may be copied onto other objects by simply selecting them (single click) and dragging them onto the desired object. When more complex operations are required, the user simple scans the contents of the pull-down menu bar at the top of the screen for the desired function.

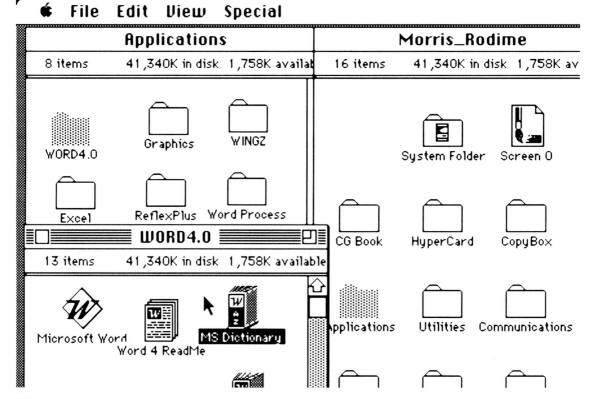

Figure 1.2
Example of a WIMP Operating System, showing three overlapping w̲indows (W), multiple i̲cons of folders, applications, and documents (I), the m̲enu (M), and the cursor arrow p̲ointer (P) near MS Dictionary.

The operation of WIMP operating systems may be summarized by the following three simple rules:

1. Single click to select an object,
2. Double click to open an object,
3. When in doubt, scan the menu for the appropriate function or help.

The beauty of a WIMP system is the intelligence built into it. That is, the knowledge of how to interact with and operate such systems is an intrinsic part of the system itself. In conventional command-line operating systems, this knowledge is archived in reference manuals that often approach a thousand pages or more. Since the intelligent machine *knows* the commands and functions of which it is capable and can explain them to the user, the user doesn't have to memorize or painfully reference the operating manual. As the advertisers of WIMP operating systems correctly claim, "It's better to teach machines to think like humans than to train humans to think like machines."

The desk top environment—consisting of nested folders and files—is a paradigm with which most knowledge workers are already familiar. It is remarkably simple to transfer this intuition for creating, moving, copying, and trashing paper documents to the computerized desk top. Personnel unfamiliar with computers can learn to operate and become productive with WIMP systems in a matter of hours or days compared to the weeks or months of training required for more conventional command-line systems. Experienced WIMP power-users take great pride in exploiting the full capabilities of a totally unfamiliar software system *without having to open the user's manual.* And they do so without ever having to memorize arcane mnemonics like "MKDIR", "COPY A:*.* C:", or "grep."

Power users of command-line systems used to huffily protest that "Real programmers don't use a mouse," and that they could easily type out their

Table 1.2
Comparison of Command-line and WIMP Systems

Applications Program	Keystrokes on PC (Command-line)	Keystrokes on Mac (WIMP)
Word Processor MS-Word 2.0 on PC MS-Word 1.0 on Mac	**16** (5 functions)	**13** (5 functions)
Drawing Program DR Draw 1.0 on PC MacDraw 1.7 on Mac	**42** (7 functions)	**15** (7 functions)

complex, arcane commands and beat any WIMP system in performance. However, the figures from careful, side-by-side studies of systems with nearly identical capabilities but differing only in user interface (command-line Vs WIMP) show the much greater efficiency of WIMP systems. One of the earliest studies indicates the relative efficiency of a typical command-line system (IBM PC) compared to a WIMP system (MAC).[9] The results of this study in which similar word processing and drawing programs were compared on the two systems are shown in Table 1.2.

The combination of an intelligent operating system with an intuitive, easy-to-visualize desk top environment has resulted in dramatic decreases in training time and expenses with corresponding increases in productivity. These practical, "bottom-line" results have led, in turn, to a complete rout of command-line operating systems (with the notable exception of UNIX systems) and the triumph of the mouse. The success of this revolution is evident in the rush to Microsoft Windows, X Windows, and other graphical user interface environments.

The success of the visual paradigm for computer operating systems has encouraged considerable effort in extending the visual paradigm to programming languages themselves. Achievements in this area have been well documented in a special issue of *IEEE Computer* on "Visualization in Computing."[10] Application programs written in one of the leading graphical programming languages, *Visual Basic*™, are presented in the chapter on Designing Graphical User Interfaces.

Correlations in Data

Assume we make four sets of measurements on the dependence of variable Y on the independent parameter, X. These measurements are shown as $(X_i, Y_i, i = 1$ to $4)$ in Table 1.3.[11]

A cursory examination of these sets of numbers reveals nothing at all, or at least nothing unusual, except for the constancy of X4 for all values except the eighth one.

To better understand how X and Y are correlated within each data set and how such correlations differ between the four sets, we can apply some standard statistical tests. First, we can calculate the mean of both X and Y, ($<X>,<Y>$), for each set and find that they are identical across sets. To compare the scatter of the points, we can compute the sum of the square of $(X - <X>)$ and find that that, too, is identical in all four cases. Assuming a simple linear relationship of the form $Y = mX + b$ between the variables, a least squares fit of the data (i.e., a linear regression analysis) yields m = 0.5 and b = 3.0 for all four sets of data. Continuing the linear regression analysis, we obtain identical results for all relevant statistical parameters such as t, r^2, the standard error of estimate of slope, the

Table 1.3
Four Sets of Measurements

X1	Y1	X2	Y2	X3	Y3	X4	Y4
10.00	8.04	10.00	9.14	10.00	7.46	8.00	6.58
8.00	6.95	8.00	8.14	8.00	6.77	8.00	5.76
13.00	7.58	13.00	8.74	13.00	12.74	8.00	7.71
9.00	8.81	9.00	8.77	9.00	7.11	8.00	8.84
11.00	8.33	11.00	9.26	11.00	7.81	8.00	8.47
14.00	9.96	14.00	8.10	14.00	8.84	8.00	7.04
6.00	7.24	6.00	6.13	6.00	6.08	8.00	5.25
4.00	4.26	4.00	3.10	4.00	5.39	19.00	12.50
12.00	10.84	12.00	9.13	12.00	8.15	8.00	5.56
7.00	4.82	7.00	7.26	7.00	6.42	8.00	7.91
5.00	5.68	5.00	4.74	5.00	5.73	8.00	6.89

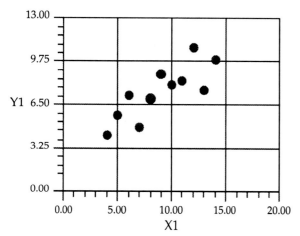

Figure 1.3
The functional relationship between X1 and Y1.

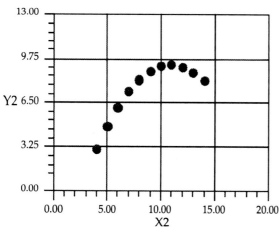

Figure 1.4
The functional relationship between X2 and Y2.

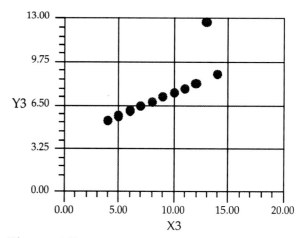

Figure 1.5
The functional relationship between X3 and Y3.

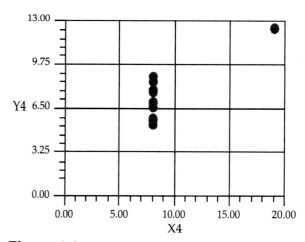

Figure 1.6
The functional relationship between X4 and Y4.

regression sum of squares, and the correlation coefficient.

At this point we would be sorely tempted to conclude that all four sets of data somehow "represent the same thing" since they have identical linear correlations (with the possible exception of set 4 in which the numbers themselves obviously "look funny"). A graphical analysis, however, shows us just how wrong we would be!

If we view these data sets on a 2D scatter plot, we can see patterns emerge which, in fact, tell us a great deal about the functional relationship between X and Y. Consider, for instance, the relationship between X1 and Y1 shown in Figure 1.3.

From this graph it appears that Y is strongly dependent on X in approximately a linear fashion,
but with significant statistical spread, possibly due to measurement errors.

Next, consider the dependence of Y2 on X2. In Figure 1.4 there appears to be an obvious quadratic dependence of Y on X, with virtually no statistical scatter or measurement error.

Figure 1.5 indicates that Y3 is clearly a precise linear function of X3 for all points except the tenth one. Because nature tends to be well-behaved, we can probably conclude that a measurement error was involved in point 10 of Figure 1.5. If this is experimental data, it would probably be wise to repeat measurement 10.

The only conclusion we can draw from Figure 1.6 is that Y is essentially independent of X as long as X remains at 8 but increases sharply as X increases to 19. This apparently strange behavior closely resembles the temperature/pressure curves of certain materials as they change state (e.g. freeze or boil).

The graphical display of these data sets reveals dependencies and behavior that is totally masked by the raw numerical data and standard statistical tests. Visualizing this data with simple 2D graphics reveals such important relationships.

Computer Simulations

Supercomputers provide "artificial laboratories" for simulating the behavior of complex physical systems. Simulations are valuable as research tools for modeling physical system properties that are too difficult, too dangerous, or too expensive to measure. In some cases, such as an exploding neutron star or molten fluid flow at the center of the earth one can model systems on which measurements are impossible.

Computer simulations are also of tremendous value to engineers in modeling mechanical, thermal, and electromagnetic systems by the techniques of finite element analysis. Hundreds of finite element models may be designed, built, and tested for the same cost as building and testing a single laboratory model. The behavior of such computer models may be examined under conditions of stress and temperature unavailable in most laboratories.

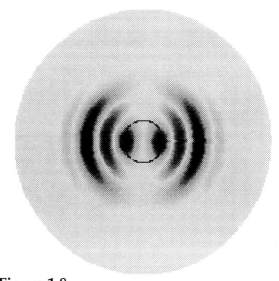

Figure 1.8
Shading enhanced version of simulated gravity waves generated by a black hole. Regions of stronger gravity (crests) are shown in red and those of weaker gravity (troughs) are shown in blue in the original color enhancement.

As an example of physical simulations of systems totally inaccessible to laboratory measurement, consider the simulation of a gravity wave on the surface of a black hole shown in Figure 1.7.[12] The oscillating mass in the black hole is seen to generate gravity waves (regions of greater and lesser gravity) that propagate away from the surface of the black hole at the speed of light.

Special features of the process under study may be highlighted by processing the computed image. In Figure 1.8, we show the same image using color, shown as shading, to emphasize the crests and troughs of the gravity wave.

Prior to the development of supercomputers it was necessary to build expensive wind tunnels, wave tanks, and scale models of local topography in order to predict the flow of fluids over airplane wings, ship hulls, and drainage basins. Such physical models suffered from the disadvantages of high cost, slow production, and inaccuracies in the final results due to uncertainties in the scaling laws. Supercomputers allow us to solve complex hydrodynamic equations in order to predict fluid flow in arbitrary environments.

In Figure 1.9, we show the results of computing the development of a vortex such as one might observe in the drain in a sink. Note that some of the artifacts introduced by the finite grid

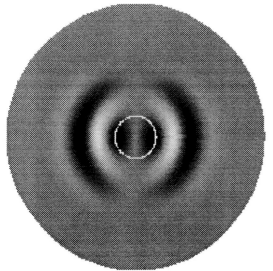

Figure 1.7
Computer simulation of gravitational waves generated on the surface of a black hole. The classical radius (Schwartzshield radius) is shown as a white circle.

on which the model is computed are even more apparent in the shading enhanced version (Figure 1.12).

These four examples demonstrate the power of visualization as an effective new paradigm in computing. The effectiveness of this paradigm arises from the excellent coupling between the graphical output of the computer and the visual system of humans. The human visual system has an enormous bandwidth for information, and the computer acts as a transformer to convert indigestible numeric results into a form that optimizes communication with humans.

Visualization in Scientific Computing

Since the original NSF study of *Visualization in Scientific Computing* there has been a tremendous upsurge of interest in visualization by scientists and engineers.[13,14,15] As Robert Wolff stated in the issue of *Computers in Physics* devoted completely to scientific visualization,

> "Visualization is not new, but its awareness by the general scientific community is."[16]

Motivation for Visualization

In addition to the improved communication at the human/computer interface discussed previously, a primary motivation for visualization in scientific computing concerns the huge amount of data with which scientists and engineers must contend. The sources of this data glut include:

- Supercomputer calculations and simulations,

- Experimental data from improved transducers and telemetry systems, including:

    ➢ Orbiting satellites,

    ➢ Planetary and interplanetary spacecraft,

    ➢ Earth-based radio astronomy,

    ➢ Geophysical transducers (seismic, volcanic,)

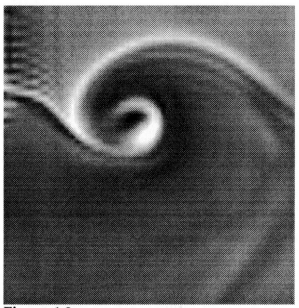

Figure 1.9
Computer simulation of vortex development in fluid flow.

    ➢ Medical scanners,

    ➢ Direct video and scanner input.

Improved transducers and telemetry systems generate data at such tremendous rates that it is impossible for individual scientists to process and make sense of it by conventional techniques. It is estimated that less than one part in a million of this data receives careful analysis by researchers using standard analysis and plotting techniques.

Supercomputers, instead of solving this problem, aggravate it by producing additional vast amounts of data through computer simulations of systems. For instance, Robert Wolff reported on a supercomputer simulation of the magnetohydrodynamic interaction of the solar wind with Venus. A single simulation on a 2D grid of 300×300 points required 20 hours on a Cray X-MP and generated over 30 GB of data. For purposes of our discussion on visualization we consider the simulations generated by supercomputers as equivalent to the experimental data generated by standard measurement techniques.

Modes of Visualization

While discussing visualization in scientific computing, it is helpful to distinguish the following categories of computer graphics applications:

1. Imaginary World Information,
2. Real World Information.

Imaginary World Information

We have already described two applications classed as imaginary world applications of computer graphics. All simulation calculations fall into this category, and it is a big one indeed! Problem areas include population dynamics, turbulent flow, fission and fusion processes and reactors, racing hull design, and finite element analysis of mechanical and electromagnetic systems. In addition, the elegant functional analysis of programs such as *Mathematica* and the beautiful patterns generated by fractal programs may be considered as projections of an imaginary world.

The computer provides to researchers in mathematics and the theoretical side of the physical world the advantage of not being bound by the constraints of the real world. As long as a concept of some imaginary reality can be expressed in definite algorithmic language, one can explore the behavior of the theoretical system and its ramifications until the subject (or the researcher) is exhausted.

Real World Information

Tools are evolving for examining real world phenomena with much greater resolution and detail. Present earth satellites, for instance, are providing photographic resolution one hundred times that of a few years ago. Not only do the new satellites produce several orders of magnitude more data than did the older ones, but the older ones continue to produce data at a slower rate. The sheer volume of this data has overwhelmed space scientists who are simply "warehousing" the data in hopes of newer and more efficient analysis techniques.

Several examples illustrate the success of visualization techniques in recent years. The first is the extraordinarily effective reporting on national weather conditions provided by newspapers carrying the colored weather map service. In one 10-second glance you can get an accurate overview of the temperature and weather conditions through-out a whole continent. The author receives two major metropolitan newspapers. One carries the daily color-coded weather map and the other carries a plain black and white weather map with a greater number of weather service symbols encoded. The color-coded map is incomparably more efficient in communicating the global weather picture to all but trained meteorologists.

The second prime example of scientific visualization is the outstanding work done by NASA and the Jet Propulsion Laboratory in communicating the results of space exploration from our spacecraft. It is quite remarkable that the visual images transmitted from an obsolete spacecraft built fifteen years earlier can reach the press and general public within hours of their reception.

A final example of an area in which visualization techniques are critical for studying real world information is medical imaging. New techniques in magnetic resonance imaging (MRI) and positron emission tomography (PET) produce large quantities of data which are most effectively displayed graphically. Frequently the scanning is performed as a series of 2D slices that can be combined graphically to yield 3D images. These techniques allow the doctor to use volume visualization for "seeing into" the patient in a non-invasive manner for the early detection of medical problems.

Applications of Visualization— Scientific and Otherwise

While the awakening of interest in visualization by the scientific community is an important and relatively recent phenomenon, other segments of society have long recognized the importance of computer graphics and have accepted visualization as an effective mode for communication. The aspect of visualization changing most rapidly is the ease of creating striking graphics and the hardware for transmitting images to computers and representing them on a variety of hardware devices. These new technologies are examined in detail in Chapter 2.

Here we summarize very briefly some major areas of society in which computer graphics plays an important role. The list is not exhaustive, and the student is urged to become aware of the use of graphics and observant as to its effectiveness.

2D Graphics in Magazines and Newspapers

Many national news magazines, particularly those with a business orientation such as *U. S. News & World Report*, make extensive and effective use of graphics. The format usually consists of bar graphs or pie charts to show trends and distributions. Many daily newspapers have followed suit and present at least one graph on the front page, several in the business section, and a graphical weather map.

If used properly, these graphics can quickly convey the relative sizes or trends of the topic under discussion. There is a tendency, however, for some graphics designers to become too "cute" in the design of their graphics. The availability of huge catalogs of clip art on personal workstations facilitates the use of decoration and design in ways which often confuse the eye and hide the meaning of the numbers being plotted. The availability of drawing programs capable of image manipulation and transformation has made it even easier to distort graphical data and create false impressions (sometimes intentionally). Tufte[17] describes these tendencies as graphics with a "richness of design and a poverty of information" and characterizes them as "chartoons" and "schlock."

Business and Presentation Graphics

Presentation graphics has become one of the most influential forces driving the development of new and sophisticated graphical software and hardware. The business community was quick to recognize the effectiveness of sharp, simple, colorful graphics for sales meetings, training sessions, employee meetings, annual reports, and so on. The almost universal acceptance of the graphics medium for communication in the business community is built on the principle:

> The average person in business, whether the company CEO or the newest hire, does not have the time or inclination to sit down and read detailed text and study columns of numbers describing the object of communication. Graphics does it better.

Three observations may be relevant here. First, the efficacy of presentation graphics is beyond dispute. There is no need to sell businesses on this medium—they have already bought it. Second, a wealth of extremely capable software has been developed for the presentation graphics

market. The final section of this text will describe several of these software packages, and the middle section will help you understand how they work. Finally, the main challenges in presentation graphics involve access to data (database query systems) and communication of data between systems (networking); e.g., "What was the sales of garden tractors to Kenya in 1978?"

Art and Design

A growing area of computer graphics application involves art and design. Specific applications include:

- Movie animation,
- Video animation ("flying logos"),
- Advertising,
- Packaging,
- Textile pattern design,
- Architectural design,
- City planning.

Two examples illustrate the application of computer graphics in art and design. The pseudopod water creature in the film, *The Abyss,* was created purely by computer graphics, making this the most technically advanced motion picture filmed up to that point. The pseudopod required six months to design on some of the most powerful workstations running Pixar's *RenderMan* rendering system and a host of other animation, modeling, and image processing tools.[18] In addition, the project used two Macintosh IIs running 3D animation and image processing programs for creating hard copy of the "story boards," the scripts from which the special effects people worked.

The second example is *Modadrape*, a fabric design program that can map various textile fabric designs onto models of the human figure. The program correctly models the clinging, wrinkling, and draping behavior of real textiles on real human models. The program contains over 2,000 images and libraries of fabrics and flat block patterns. Productivity increases over conventional techniques of clothing design are estimated to be as high as 400 percent.[19]

Note how the examples of visualization in art and design blend smoothly from art to design. It is very difficult to classify a particular area of computer graphics as purely "art" or purely "design" or purely "scientific visualization." Some of the most artistic achievements of the movie makers' art are outstanding examples of scientific visualization, and some of the graphics generated in research on scientific visualization are works with tremendous visual appeal, i. e., art. The next section moves further along the art – science continuum by examining how computer graphics is applied to engineering design.

Engineering Design

Two major areas in which computer graphics plays central roles in engineering design are CAD (Computer Aided Design) and FEA (Finite Element Analysis). In fact, CAD has been probably the most influential force in the development of sophisticated computer graphics techniques. It was the first area to make widespread use of graphics workstations in a production environment. Design shops found the high cost of early CAD graphics workstations more than offset by the enormous productivity increases made possible. Many of the interactive pointing, selection, and dragging techniques which we now take for granted were first used routinely on CAD systems.

CAD systems are now essential tools for the design of integrated circuits, manufactured parts, complex mechanical systems, and architectural plans. In addition to the drawing and drafting tools found on all systems, some systems provide for inclusion of material properties, the calculations of volumes and masses, the specification of bill of materials, and the estimation of costs. Advanced systems even permit the direct connection of the CAD design phase to the CAM (Computer Aided Manufacturing) phase. Design parameters from the CAD program are used directly for the numerical control of machine tools. This eliminates the intermediate stage of hard copy blueprints and provides an additional increase in productivity.

FEA models are essentially CAD models to which physical properties have been assigned in order to predict their behavior under condition of stress or excitation. CAD models, at least in their first stage, are purely geometric in nature, i.e. the designer uses drawing and drafting tools to build the model in 2D or 3D space. The first phase of finite element analysis is also purely geometrical—a geometric model of the object under study is created, often with a standard CAD program. Next the material properties of the model are assigned to each element. Then the boundary conditions are defined, that is, the designer specifies which parts of the model bridge are clamped and which parts are free to move. Finally, the forces acting on

various parts of the model are specified and the program "turned loose" to calculate the resulting displacements and oscillations of all parts of the structure.

Finite element analysis, because of its power, flexibility, and incorporation of physical law, is becoming the standard design tool in many areas of engineering. It is widely used in modeling of automotive parts, electromagnetic devices such as motors and generators, and the thermal properties of many physical systems. While FEA was born on mainframes, it is now routinely implemented on personal workstations.

Cartography

Cartography, the production, analysis, and display of maps, is a natural application of computer graphics. The official maps of the United States Geological Survey (USGS) have recently become available in computer format, and one company has converted every 7.5 minute quadrangle map to *AutoCAD* format.[20] Various layers provided by these maps include:

- Enhanced Digital Line Graphs (DLG,)
- Geographic Names Information System (GNIS,)
- Digital Elevation Model Terrain Relief Grid (DEM,)
- Section Lines,
- State, County, and Township Boundaries,
- Municipal Boundaries,
- XYZ Elevation Points,
- DEM Contours.

The powerful *AutoCAD* computer aided design program allows the user to display water features, roads, railroads, airports, pipelines, power lines, elevation contours, and names of cities, towns, and other landmarks. In the 3D mode of AutoCAD it is possible to display a terrain relief grid, providing the user with an actual 3D image of the terrain covered by the map.

The USGS maps available for a variety of workstations permit professionals in civil engineering, utility management, surveying, and real estate planning to turn the tedious task of cartographic research into a creative design experience.

Real-Time Control

Most routine data collection and control operations are accomplished by interfacing the experiment or controlled process directly to the computer. There are a host of laboratory control software programs that provide great flexibility in designing application-specific graphical control panels complete with meters, monitors, warning lights and other indicators of the status of the experiment or process. Graphical representations of panel meters, chart recorders, push-buttons, switches, and variable potentiometers allow the user to manipulate the experiment or process just as she/he would a real control panel lined with switches and pots.

The advantages of such simulated control systems are immediately obvious. The user has complete flexibility in design and may modify the design repeatedly until just the right combination of sensitivity, intuition, simplicity, and control is achieved. These control systems frequently go under the names "work benches," "data stations," and, when combined with data logging and report generations routines, "Laboratory Information Management Systems" (LIMS).

One of the chief lessons learned in the melt down at the Three Mile Island Unit II nuclear reactor in Pennsylvania was the importance of a good machine/user control interface. One of the causes of that accident was the profusion of outdated, irrelevant, and misleading indicators which gave the operators a totally misleading picture (image?) of what was happening in the reactor. The Kemeny Commission, which studied the causes of the accident, recommended that on all reactor control panels, the archaic mechanical controls and indicators be replaced by modern graphical systems to help the operators quickly verify the true status of the system and take appropriate action.

The above summary of important visualization areas, although far from complete, gives some idea of the breadth and value of computer graphics. Computer graphics in scientific visualization is an area of particularly rapid growth of interest.

Visualization Tools for Image Processing

Anyone introduced to the concept of spreadsheet analysis of numerical data is soon struck by the power and flexibility of the spreadsheet model of programming. Simply put, any cell or block of cells of the matrix may be any function of any other cell, row, column, or block of cells. For example, the spreadsheet program, *Wingz™* provides a matrix of 32,000 × 32,000 cells and approximately 150 functions to transform the information contained in these cells. Most spreadsheet programs also include graphics capabilities for displaying the contents of the data matrix. Wingz, for instance, has 20 chart styles for displaying data in 2D or 3D, including sophisticated wire frame and contour plotting.

Just as spreadsheet transformation transforms one set of numerical data into another set, so image processing transformations transform one image into another image. Such image processing transformations provide valuable tools for exploring the nature of the information contained in an image and for searching for the most effective form for presenting the graphical information. We have already hinted at one of the more effective transformations, that of mapping shading into color. The following are also techniques that have proven effective.

Contour Map of z = f(x,y)

The image shown in Figure 1.9 simulates a photograph of the vortex in a real liquid. Our eyes interpret the brightness of the image as the level of the fluid.

Any 2D image may be represented as $I(x,y)$ where I is the intensity (or "brightness") of the image at pixel (x,y). The intensity, in this case, plays the same role as the z elevation on a relief map of the geographic region in which $z = f(x,y)$. And,

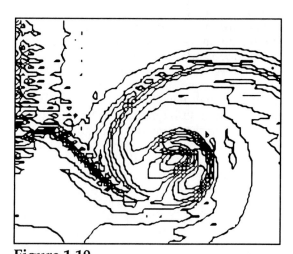

Figure 1.10
A 10-level contour map of the eye of the vortex
(*Contour mapping done by NCSA Image.*)

just as relief maps may be compressed into contour maps of lines of constant elevation, the intensity map of Figure 1.9 may be contoured to show lines of constant density. Such a map is shown in Figure 1.10.

Wireframe and 3D Histograms

The data on which the previous Figure 1.9 is based may also be represented as a *wireframe model* and viewed as a 3D object. Wireframe models may either be "pure" as that shown in Figure 1.11 or be depicted with hidden lines removed, producing a more realistic image at the expense of removing some information. Wireframe models are particularly effective in clarifying the surface structure of functions of two variables and the geometric structure of objects. Their usefulness is enhanced by providing graphical "handles" or controls for rotating the model in 3D space. This provides the sensation of flying around the object and looking at it from many angles. Variations of wireframe models include 3D histograms and elevation plots.

Pseudo-Color Transformations

Another particularly effective image processing technique involves pseudo-color transformations. In its most general form, a pseudo-color transformation involves mapping one set of colors (called a *palette*) into another set of colors. By mapping the gray scale image shown in Figure 1.9 into a particular color palette, we get the color enhanced image shown in grayscale in Figure 1.12. The word *pseudo* is used to remind us that the image does not represent a real color photograph but rather some arbitrary set of colors chosen to aid in interpreting the image. Pseudo-color is frequently used in infrared photography to show the color of dense foliage as red, while other image colors more closely approximate their real hues. Pseudo-color is also widely used in medical imaging to emphasize a particular organ or growth by mapping its shade into a vivid hue.

Geometric Transformations

The standard geometric transformations include translation, scaling, and rotation. More complex transformations involve skewing, warping, projecting, and image mapping onto arbitrary surfaces. Consider the diagram of a "button box" containing two circular buttons in Figure 1.13.

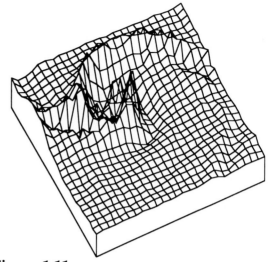

Figure 1.11
A 3D relief map of the eye of the vortex (*Wireframe model done by NCSA Image.*)

Note that the left side of the box was generated by a simple 180° rotation of the right side. To build the box, the right side was designed first, then duplicated, and the duplicate was then rotated by 180° and dragged into the correct position adjacent to the original. Thus, fifty percent of the final design was accomplished by three simple mouse actions.

Geometric transformations are very important for applications such as CAD in which the final object may be constructed by replicating more primitive objects and transforming them into the

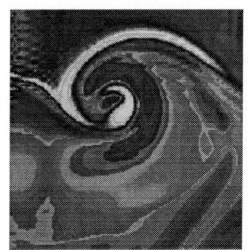

Figure 1.12
Color enhanced version shown in grayscale (*Pseudo-color map by NCSA Image.*)

positions and shapes required.

As a curious sidelight related to visual cueing, note how the right button appears to be convex while the left button appears to be concave. Why should a simple rotation also appear to cause an inversion of the buttons? (*Hint: How does the shading cue correlate with the "normal direction of the sun's rays"?*)

Edge Detection

Computer vision is an area of visualization in which we attempt to train the computer to visualize an image from an external transducer such as a video camera. It is particularly important for robotics, autonomous land vehicles, and any application requiring the automatic scanning of large numbers of photographs.

The essential function of this visualization process is to extract meaning from the incoming image. Computer vision requires pattern recognition, and the first step in nearly all pattern recognition tasks is edge detection. The simplest method in edge detection involves calculating the contours for which the second spatial derivative of the intensities goes to zero. Some edge detectors first smooth the edges by some spatial scale factor (called the convolution integral) and then calculate the contour lines where the second derivative of the smeared intensity pattern crosses zero.

Applying an edge detection algorithm to the button box, we get the pattern shown in Figure 1.14.

Smoothing and Filtering Transformations

Our intuition tells us that the sharper the image, the more realistic or life-like it will be. But this is not necessarily so. Our eyes are optical instruments with the pupil acting like the aperture of a camera. Because of diffraction effects, the images formed on the retina are not precisely sharp but rather diffused diffraction patterns. The eye, however, "knows" about diffraction effects and performs a Fourier analysis of the diffracted image to extract a sharper image of the object which it sends on to the brain.

To explore this effect, consider the two images shown in Figures 1.15 and 1.16. The first is a portion of the "Architect's House" image from *PixelPaint*™. Note the extremely sharp detail down to the pixel level.

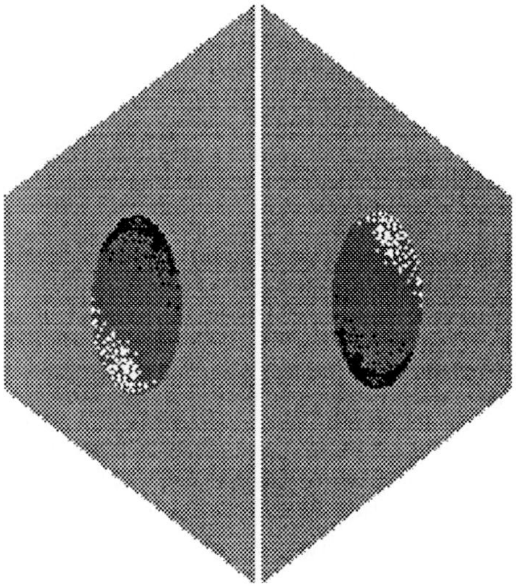

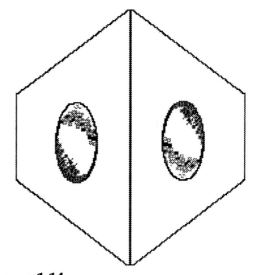

Figure 1.13
Button box in which the left side is generated by a simple 180° rotation of the right side. Which button appears to be convex? Why? (*Figure generated using Canvas*™.)

Figure 1.14
Results of edge detection algorithm applied to Figure 1.13. Note how the boundaries between different intensities produce edges while regions of constant intensity produce no signal at all. (*Edge detection by PixelPaint*™.)

Next, we apply a smoothing transformation which in effect averages each pixel with pixels in its immediate vicinity. The effect of this operation is to slightly blur the image, an effect that we might expect to degrade the image. Let's see what it looks like (Figure 1.16).

The interesting result is that the image appears somewhat more realistic than the original. Notice at least three effects which enhance the realism of the smoothed image. First, the patterned shadow of the original averages out to a smooth shadow in the processed image. Second, the light-colored ends of the tiles on the roof average out to a less conspicuous and more natural shade in the processed image. Finally, the detailed dark lines in the tree average to a more realistic shadow effect, and the "jaggies" in the awning support above the door are blurred into a smoother appearance.

The conclusion of this experiment is that, in certain circumstances, the loss (or degradation) of image information may actually enhance visual realism. This discovery was first proposed by the French Impressionist painters in the late 1800s:

> *Photo realism is not necessary for creating the desired impression on the viewer, and highly non-realistic images at the micro level may be integrated by the eye to produce very realistic impressions.*

Volume Visualization and Transparency Mapping

The ability to render surfaces of objects realistically is well developed and available on many drawing and CAD programs. However, the science of "seeing inside" objects for which we know the composition at each point in space is still new and undergoing rapid development. One useful approach for visualizing the interior of objects for which we know the properties at each voxel

Figure 1.15
"Pixel perfect" original image of architect's house (*Figure by Pixel-Paint™.*)

(volume element) is to gradually turn intervening materials transparent and, in effect, "dissolve" our way through the object. An example of this technique is shown in the Figure 1.17, a simulated melt down of fuel rods in a power reactor.

Computer Animation

Animation techniques were perfected in the pre-computer era by Disney Studios and culminated in the exquisite, hand-crafted *Fantasia*. Even the sophisticated synthesis of real images and cartoon characters in *Who Framed Roger Rabbit* was primarily hand-crafted. However, the potential of computer animation became apparent in movies such as *The Abyss, Beauty and the Beast, Lawnmower Man,* and *Alladin*.

Some of the earliest and best work in scientific visualization was done by Evans and Sutherland in designing flight simulators. The Evans and Sutherland machines use powerful, dedicated graphics processing hardware to provide the high-

Figure 1.16
Smoothing function applied to Figure 1.15. Note the greater realism achieved by slight blurring and reliance on the eye to reconstruct the original image. (*Image processed by PixelPaint™.*)

to this principle of *model authenticity* for achieving visual realism.

Interactivity

The goal of researchers in scientific visualization is to provide a system that enables the user to interact directly with the simulation or analysis which they are observing. At present, most simulations on supercomputer systems are run in batch mode—the user sets the experimental parameters at her terminal, sends the job off to the supercomputer, and examines the results after the run is completed. Because really interesting results and directions for further investigation are often not known at set-up time, this mode provides less than the optimal environment for creative and serendipitous discovery. What is needed is a transparent system in which the investigator can monitor the progress of a simulation experiment, visualize partial results as soon as they are computed, and interact with the experiment in progress.

speed processing required for real-time graphics and animation. For simulation of complex systems, e.g., turbulence in fluid flow and vibrational modes in structural mechanics, animation provides valuable insight unavailable from any other technique.

Programs are now available for performing animation on personal workstations. Capabilities include *tweening* for automatically filling in missing animation frames *between* two user supplied images. This significantly reduces the amount of tedious handcrafting required of the user. In scientific visualization, on the other hand, the emphasis is on the behavior of the system model, and the computer animation consists of "filming" the model's behavior. Physical models incorporate the physics of force, inertia, momentum and energy. As a result, the realism of animated sequences of physical models greatly exceeds that of 2D animations not grounded in physical law. Throughout this book frequent reference is made

By visually displaying the progress of the computation and providing user interrupt options, a system with *interactivity* allows the user to *steer the course of the investigation*. The improvement in research and design productivity provided with interactivity is comparable to that achieved when program debugging moved from batch to interactive mode. The rapid increase in network bandwidth and improved postprocessing capabilities of personal workstations form the basis for the implementation of interactivity in visualization.

The IBM supercomputer, called the *POWER Visualization System*, represents a direct industry response to the need for interactivity and computational steering.[21] This system uses up to thirty-two parallel processors to provide a peak computational rate of 1,280 double-precision megaflops (million floating point operations per second). Simulation results are displayed as 3D animations on a $1,920 \times 1,536$ pixel screen.

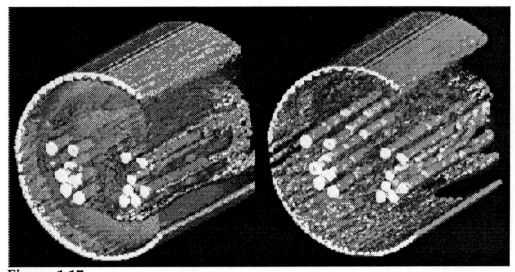

Figure 1.17
Volume visualization of melt down of fuel rods in a nuclear reactor.[22] On the left, fuel rods immersed in coolant; on the right, fuel rods with coolant gone. (*Figure rendered by NCSA Image.*)

Conclusions

In this chapter, we have attempted to show that the power of the visualization paradigm in computing has a solid physiological basis. The first two examples of visualization in communication (signs and operating systems) suggested that graphical systems are the *best mode* of communications in many applications. The next two examples (correlations and simulations) indicated that the *only mode* for understanding complex systems is frequently through visualization.

Visualization is generating great interest in the scientific community because of the tools it provides for reducing and analyzing the mountains of data produced by modern instrumentation and supercomputers. The survey of the applications of visualization indicated the wide range of human activity in which computer graphics plays an important role. Many of these activities would be practically impossible without computer graphics. Finally, several image processing tools were demonstrated for transforming images and enhancing our ability to visualize more clearly what they represent.

Exercises

1.1 Describe three examples from your study this past year in which a graphic (sign, meaningful nonalphabetic symbol, sketch, graph, diagram, or picture) helped you understand a concept which was not clear from its textual description.

1.2 Terrence Sejnowski has computed that the eye/brain neural network "computes" at the rate of about 10^{15} bits/second while interpreting a visual image. Assume that the "clock rate" of neurons firing is 50 Hz and that only 1 percent of the brain's 10^{12} neurons are processing at any one time. Use dimensional analysis to compute the interconnectivity, N, which is the average number of neurons to which a given neuron is connected. (Hint: assume the processing rate is given by the number of active neurons × interconnectivity × frequency.)

1.3 List three public signs (other than those from the text), rank them in order of their effectiveness for communications, and discuss your reasoning.

1.4 From your own experience working with both command-line oriented operating systems and WIMP systems, describe two functions each can do which the other can not do or, at best, does badly. If you have not had experience with both systems, discuss the issue with one of your colleagues to obtain background information.

1.5   Verify that the four sets of data listed in Table 1.3 does, in fact, have the same statistical values for the mean of X, the mean of Y, and the standard deviations of both X and Y.

1.6   Perform a least squares fit to the equation Y = m X + b for each data set of Table 1.3, and verify the claim that they yield identical results for m and b. What type of least squares fit would you propose to distinguish between the four sets of data?

1.7   The virtue of computer simulations is that they allow us to "run experiments" which would be too difficult, too dangerous, too expensive, or simply impossible to do in the laboratory. List an example of each of these four categories of computer simulations, different from those cited in the text.

1.8   Most computer graphics applications fall cleanly into one of the two categories of "real world" or "imaginary world." Give an example (other than those from the text) illustrating each class and a third example from the boundary region between the two classes where the distinction is not so sharp.

1.9   Locate and photocopy from your daily newspaper or news magazine two examples illustrating the extremes on the good design-bad design spectrum. The following sketch of criteria may help:

- *Good design* – Crisp, clean graphics clearly representing the data; axes, bars, or pie slices clearly labeled; icons effective in enhancing intended image,

- *Bad design* – Data cluttered, obscured, or overwhelmed by cute design or overdecoration (you'll know it when you see it); axis scales not clearly labeled or with offsets not obviously labeled; icons distracting from intended image.

1.10   Identify and photocopy one graphical example from each of the six application areas starting with *2D Graphics in Magazines and Newspapers* through *Real-Time Control.* What additional application areas would you suggest be added to the list?

1.11   From your other college textbooks or reference books, locate and photocopy an example of a *contour map.* What are three common applications for contour maps? What advantages do contour maps have over other 3D representations?

1.12   From your other college textbooks or reference books, locate and photocopy an example of a *Wireframe or 3D histograms.* What are three common applications for Wireframe and 3D histograms? How do Wireframe graphs differ from 3D histograms?

1.13   From your other college textbooks or reference books, locate and photocopy an example of a *geometric transformation* graphic. What are three common applications for geometric transformations in graphics?

1.14   Volume visualization is a technique unique to computer graphics. We discussed its application to the study of meltdown of fuel rods. What are three additional areas in which volume visualization could be or is being usefully applied?

1.15   Write a brief, critical analysis of the underlying theme of this text:

A visualization approach to computer graphics requires study of the tools for both the synthesis and analysis of images.

Endnotes

1. Tufte, Edward R., *The Visual Display of Quantitative Information*, Graphics Press, Cheshire, CN (1983). See also: Tufte, Edward R., *Envisioning Information*, Graphics Press, Cheshire, CN (1990).

2. Shu, Nan C., *Visual Programming*, Van Nostran Reinhold Company, New York, NY (1988).

3. McCormick, Bruce H., DeFanti, Thomas A., and Brown, Maxine D., (eds), Special issue on "Visualization in Scientific Computing," *Computer Graphics* **21**, No. 6, November (1987).

4. Marr, David, *Vision*, W. H. Freeman and Company, New York (1982).

5. Churchland, Patricia S. and Sejnowski, Terrence J., *The Computational Brain*, The MIT Press, Cambridge, MA (1992).

6. Churchland, Patricia Smith, *Neurophilosophy – Toward a Unified Science of the Mind/Brain*, A Bradford Book, The MIT Press, Cambridge, MA (1986).

7. Firebaugh, Morris W., *Artificial Intelligence – A Knowledge-Based Approach*, PWS/Kent Publishing Co., Boston, MA (1988).

8. Johnson, Jeff, Roberts, Teresa L., Verplank, William, Smith, David C., Irby, Charles H., Beard, Marian, and Mackey, Kevin, "The Xerox Star: A Retrospective," *Computer* **22**, No. 9, pp. 11–26, September (1989).

9. Burns, Diane and Venit, S., "PC vs. MAC: An Unfair Match?," *PC Magazine* Cover Story, pp. 110–131, July 23, (1985).

10. Special Issue on "Visualization in Computing," *IEEE Computer* **22**, No. 10, pp. 9–65, October (1989).

11. Anscombe, F. J., "Graphs in Statistical Analysis," *American Statistician* **27**, pp. 17–21, February (1973).

12. Smarr, Bernstein and Hobill, (1989). For information write to either David Bernstein or David Hobill, NCSA, 605 E. Springfield Ave. Champaign, Il. 61820. Bitnet address: 10537@NCSAVMSA.bitnet (Bernstein) or 10932@NCSAVMSA.bitnet (Hobill). Phone (217) 244-1980.

13. Upson, Craig, Faulhaber, Thomas, Jr., Kamins, David, Laidlaw, David, Schlegel, David, Vroom, Jeffrey, Gurwitz, Robert, and van Dam, Andries, "Scientific Visualization," *IEEE Computer Graphics and Applications* **9**, No. 4, pp. 30–42, July (1989).

14. Special Issue, "Scientific Visualization – Bringing Data into Focus," *IEEE Computer* **22**, No. 8, pp. 10–101, August (1989).

15. Rapaport, Dennis, "Visualizing Physics,"*Computers in Physics* **3**, No. 5., pp. 18–29, Sept/Oct (1989).

16. Wolff, Robert S., "Visualization in the Eye of the Scientist," *Computers in Physics* **2**, No. 3, pp. 28–35,May/June (1988).

17. Silverstone, Stuart, "Why today's graphics fail," Interview with Edward Tufte, *MacWEEK*, pp. 49–50, Sept. 26, (1989).

18. Vasilopoulos, Audrey, "Exploring the Unknown," *Computer Graphics World* **12**, No. 10, pp. 76–82, October (1989).

19. Neal, Margaret, "Keep it Simple," *Computer Graphics and Applications* **9**, No. 5, pp. 3–5, September (1989).

20. American Digital Cartography, 715 W. Parkway Blvd., Appleton, WI 54914.

21. For information on the *POWER Visualization System*, contact:
    IBM Scientific Visualization Systems
    T. J. Watson Research Center
    P.O. Box 704
    Yorktown Heights, NY 10598
    (800)388-9820.

22. The authors of this image are Chuck Mosher and Ruth Johnson of Sun Microsystems, Research Triangle Park, NC. The image is a shaded surface volume rendering of 128 CT scans of data from Sandia National Laboratories. Image used with permission of the authors. Source: Apple Science CD Volume 1.

Chapter 2

The Technological Basis of Visualization

The purpose of [scientific] computing is insight, not numbers.
Richard Hamming

A number of technological developments and economic trends emerged in the early 1990s that resulted in the integration of visualization tools into capable multimedia workstations. In this chapter, we discuss the technology widely available in computer graphics laboratories and consider the economic and institutional forces that have shaped the computer graphics industry. An appreciation of these forces will help computer graphics students prepare themselves for this maturing industry.

The primary drivers of technological growth in computer graphics can be classified as:

- Hardware,
- Software and Firmware,
- Standards.

All three areas are in a rapid state of flux, and to follow developments in the industry requires essentially a full-time effort reading journals and scanning trade magazines. Some of the most useful sources are listed in the *Endnotes*.[1]

In addition to the purely technological developments listed above, there are a number of interesting cultural/institutional forces at work in shaping present and future graphics workstations. These include:

- Increasing performance/price ratios,

- The rise of the desktop publishing and multimedia industry,

- The decline of centralized control of computing services,

- The increased availability of broad bandwidth networks,

- Trends toward increased interoperability of files, operating systems, and machines.

It should be stressed that no *single* one of these technological or institutional forces is responsible for the rapid development of visualization capability. Rather, we are observing a synergistic effects of all these factors.

The following example illustrates this synergy. The National Center for Supercomputer Applications (NCSA) of the University of Illinois at Urbana-Champaign has developed a network of supercomputers linked to Sun and Macintosh workstations for the use of researchers in scientific visualization.

Consider these four elements. The *workstations* provide excellent computer graphics and image processing capability for analyzing the computations performed on the supercomputer. In an hour, the *supercomputer* can number crunch complex simulations that would take days or weeks on the workstations. To port the supercomputer results to the workstations requires a high bandwidth *network* to handle the large data flow and, eventually, to interactively control the simulation experiment. The image processing task requires sophisticated *image processing software* running on the workstations for the interactive analysis of graphical data. As isolated components, none of these four elements are particularly noteworthy—working together they constitute a system of exceptional power and capacity.

Increasing Performance/Price Ratios

The computer industry, and in particular the personal computer industry, seems to be governed by two immutable laws:

1) *The cost of the leading-edge products remains constant;*

2) *Their performance doubles every 1–3 years.*

These observations stem from the author's personal experience. In 1980, he paid $2,700 for an Apple II Plus (1 MHz clock rate, 64 KB memory). This was followed four years later by a Zenith 158 (IBM XT clone) for the same price. It runs at 8 MHz and has 640 KB of memory. About the same time, the original Mac 128 (8 MHz, 128 Kb) was purchased for almost exactly the same price. After a series of upgrades, this initially weak machine has evolved into a 4 MB Mac Plus running at 16 MHz.

Two years after this system enhancement, a new machine, the Mac IIcx, was added. This unit, with 1 MB memory and a 16 MHz 32-bit 68030 processor, cost almost precisely the same as the original Apple II had 9 years previously. Taking into account nine years of inflation, the cost of adding a 16 inch color monitor, 7 MB of RAM, and a 200 MB hard drive to this system brought its cost in constant dollars equivalent to that of the original Apple II. The present Mac IIcx system has 48 times the speed, 125 times the RAM memory, 20 times the ROM operating system memory, and 1,200 times the disk storage capacity of the original Apple II Plus.

The latest addition, a 33 MHz 486 system with 8 MB of memory, 200 MB hard drive, and 1024 × 786 resolution VGA screen, continues this trend. Such systems are available from a number of vendors at well under $3,000 in 1993 dollars.

Exponential Growth

What we are describing is a classic example of exponential growth in the ratio of the performance to the price. Whenever the doubling time of a quantity remains constant, the result is exponential growth in that quantity over time. To illustrate this growth, the performance trend of the CPU clock speed of typical personal computers is indicated schematically in Figure 2.1

Additional anecdotal evidence on the rapid growth of the performance/price ratios emerged

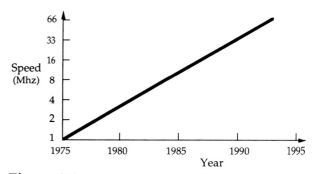

Figure 2.1
Growth of clock speed for PCs over the years. Note logarithmic scale on ordinate.

during the process of building the personal workstations used in the preparation of this book. Uncompressed colored computer graphics images require vast amounts of storage. To accommodate colored images, a 45 MB removable hard drive was added to the system. In the three years since the arrival of the $799 drive, prices have fallen to less than $400. The media for this system costs about $65 per 45 MB cartridge as this is being written and most likely costs less than $1 per MB as this is being read. Such systems provide hard drive performance (25 ms average access time) at floppy drive prices.

Even the cost of floppy disk storage reflects exponential behavior. The original Apple II disks cost $5 for 0.140 Mb, while high density disks now cost $.50 for 1.4 Mb, a performance/price increase of one hundred in ten years. CD-ROM (compact disc read-only memory) provide Gb memories at a price of $.50/Mb.

The area of graphics displays has shown similar improvements. The original Apple II Plus displayed 280 × 192 pixels in 8 colors.[2] Standard Macs and PCs feature 640 × 480 pixels in 256 colors, and *true color* (24-bit) monitors are now available in 1024 × 768 pixels in 16 million colors. Color scanners capturing an 8 × 10 inch picture at 300 dots per inch (dpi) in true color generate an image with over 20 MB of information. Thus, the information content of graphical images has grown by a factor of more than a thousand in about ten years. This corresponds to a doubling time of almost exactly one year.

The total throughput of a computer depends just as importantly on availability of high-speed RAM as it does on clock speed. In Figure 2.2, we show the trends in addressable memory capacity of standard personal computers over the last few years.

The list continues. If we plotted the number of MIPS (million instructions per second), MFLOPS (million floating point operations per second), size of the resident ROM operating system, the storage capacity of hard drives per dollar, the resolution of output hardcopy devices, or most any other measure of performance of graphics workstations, the curves would all exhibit the exponential growth in performanceprice ratios. The only variation would occur in the doubling time (slope) of the curves.

Emerging Applications

A remarkable aspect of exponential growth in any area of technology is that, if the performance you want is not yet available, just wait, and it will be very shortly. Two applications from engineering design illustrate this point. First is in the area of computer aided design (CAD), and the second is in finite element analysis (FEA). Both of these applications are heavily computation-bound and require high-resolution graphics interfaces. As a result, conventional wisdom has maintained that these applications prove that mainframes (or at least powerful minicomputers) will always be required for "serious work."

Two of the real number crunching tasks of 3D CAD programs are the hidden line removal problem and the generation of realistic shading. Recently, a number of CAD products with these features have emerged for personal workstations. In Figure 2.3, the output of one such system is shown for the design of an automobile camshaft.

While the finite screen resolution is still apparent in Figure 2.3, the image resulting from the application of hidden line removal and shading

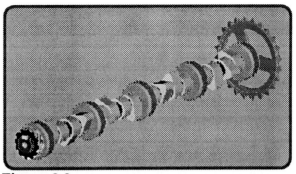

Figure 2.3
Design for an automobile camshaft illustrating the use of solid modeling and shading.

algorithms is a great improvement over more conventional wire-frame models. Until recently, constructive solid geometry and shading features were available only on mainframe-based CAD systems costing in the $100,000 range.

The second application that has recently migrated from mainframe to personal workstations is finite element analysis. FEA may be considered an extension of CAD in which material properties are added to the model and the resulting physical system subjected to user-specified forcing functions and boundary conditions. The system's response to the applied forces are then computed and displayed graphically. The heart of FEA programs consists of algorithms for discretizing the model into simple polygons (for 2D models) or volume elements (for 3D models) and applying physical laws to generate a set of equations relating the elements to each other and the forcing function. The FEA program then solves the resulting set of coupled differential equations and presents the user with a solution, typically in the form of displacements or electromagnetic potentials at each node of the finite element model.

Postprocessing modules are available for viewing the resulting field solution using several of the visualization modes described in the previous chapter, including contour maps, wire-frame topographic maps, pseudo-color images, and animation sequences of such representations. Postprocessors also provide the user with global problem solution parameters, often through integration over components of the model, including information such as the stored field energies and frequencies of the normal modes of vibration. Figure 2.4 illustrates a typical FEA problem, the displacement of a beam under an applied force .

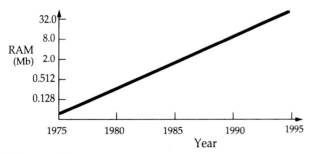

Figure 2.2
The growth of addressable random access memory (RAM) for standard PCs over the years. Note exponential scale on ordinate.

The advantages of porting applications such as FEA from mainframes graphics workstations are the flexibility and interactivity obtained by local control. One might expect to pay a serious penalty in performance as the price of these advantages. However, benchmark tests indicate that personal workstations perform very well against larger computers. In Figure 2.5, the results of running the same FEA model with the same program on a variety of minicomputers and personal workstations are compared.

The benchmark problem consisted of two intersecting pipes that were modeled by 1020 3D solid finite elements. The program *COSMOS/M*™ was run on a variety of computers, and some of the timing results are shown in Figure 2.5. Of the computers shown in Figure 2.5 all, except the VAX and Mac IIx, were running at 25 MHz and used math coprocessors whenever possible.

The most remarkable performance was turned in by a garden-variety 25 MHz 386 PC equipped with a 4-node, 25 MHz transputer. This machine ran the benchmark in 254 seconds compared to the 3452 seconds required for the VAX 750. This same problem required 22 seconds running on a CRAY XMP/416 with the *ANSYS*™ finite element system. Thus, a standard 386 PC equipped with a transputer parallel processor (system cost, $10K–$15K) performs finite element analysis at about one-tenth the speed of a multimillion dollar supercomputer. Since over 50 percent of the CPU time used on supercomputers is devoted to some kind of finite element analysis, this result has significant implications.

With this background in some of the cultural/institutional forces shaping the computer graphics marketplace, let us turn specifically to the hardware and software readily available in most computer graphics laboratories.

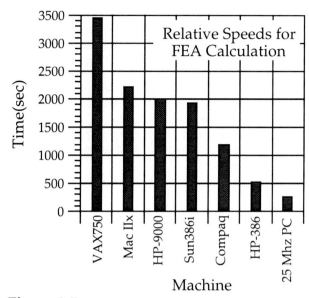

Figure 2.5
Benchmark test of COSMOS/M FEA program running on several computers. The model consisted of 1020 3D solid elements representing the junction of two mechanical pipes.

Hardware Systems

A modern integrated graphics workstation consists of one or more hardware components from each of the following categories:

- Graphical input devices,
- Workstation processor (with network options),
- Graphics output devices.

The general architecture of a graphics workstation is diagrammed in Figure 2.6.

The general pattern of data flow in a graphics workstation deserves some comment. At the lowest level, graphical information may be generated by the stand-alone workstation, using the keyboard to type in a program which calls the built-in graphics capabilities of the workstation to display graphical output on the workstation monitor. The next higher level of integration involves using interactive devices such as the mouse or data tablet to control a graphics program (possibly a paint or CAD program) resident in the workstation, displaying the graphical results on the monitor and printing a copy on a dot matrix, inkjet, or laser printer. The third level of graphics system integration involves obtaining image

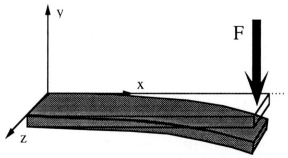

Figure 2.4
Prototype finite element analysis problem—displacement of a beam subjected to the force **F**.

information directly from an image transducer or storage device (scanner, video, or CD-ROM), transforming the image to solve the problem, and routing it to any of the output devices listed.

The highest level of graphical system integration involves embedding the workstation in a network which provides access to additional graphics processing resources such as file servers and supercomputers. File servers allow access by multiple work stations to common graphical data bases. The role of the supercomputer is to provide additional processing power for solving problems infeasible on the workstation. The supercomputer serves as an analysis engine. Let's look at the properties and capabilities of workstations in a little more detail.

Graphics Workstations

We define a graphics workstation as a computer with associated high resolution imaging screen, keyboard, and pointer device, whose purpose is to process graphical information. By this definition, the SAGE air-defense system of the 1950s probably qualifies as the first large scale implementation of graphics workstations.[3] The purpose of the SAGE system, a precursor of modern air traffic control systems, was to map radar signals onto a cathode ray tube (CRT) in order to represent the positions and velocities of the planes under observation.

The primary graphics workstations during the 1960s were *vector display devices*. Given the (x,y) location of the two end points, these expensive terminals would draw precision, continuous lines on the face of CRTs. However, this period preceded the arrival of minicomputers and microprocessors, and so the cost of a system capable of computing anything interesting and refreshing the screen fast enough to generate a stable image was in the $100K range.

A breakthrough in technology occurred in 1968 when Tektronix invented the direct view storage tube CRT. This device used two independent electron guns, one to write the initial image on a finely-meshed storage grid and the second to read the stored image and display it on the output screen. These devices had severe limitations, which included among others: (i) selective object erase could not be done, ruling out the possibility of animation, (ii) full screen erase required the greater part of a second, (iii) the terminal screen displayed only one color—green, (iv) the early versions were dumb terminals—that is, they contained no independent computer and had to be used in a network containing a minicomputer or main frame.

However, in spite of these weaknesses, Tektronix terminals had a number of attractive features and contributed greatly to progress in computer graphics.

- The graphics memory was built into the CRT itself, thus eliminating the need for RAM memory to store images and display processors to continuously update the display. This provided a stable, flicker-free image.

- The screen retained many of the advantages of a vector display; that is, lines appeared smooth although their end points were fixed by the discrete addressing of the storage mesh. This resulted in excellent, high-resolution images that opened the way to computer-aided design.

- Probably the most important contribution of the Tektronix direct view storage tube terminals was to break the important $10K price barrier. These terminals, in effect, opened up high resolution computer graphics to the average computer user on a network system.

The road to the present high-resolution, color-graphics workstation was paved by the introduction of personal microcomputers. These computers initially used ordinary B/W or color television monitors to display alphanumeric and graphic information. The breakthrough occurred when low-cost memory became available and the enormous advantages of bit-mapped displays were recognized. Bit-mapped graphics involves assigning the bits in a particular region of memory to corresponding pixels on the screen. Image display then simply involves mapping this portion of memory directly to the screen. A "1" in memory means "turn the pixel ON"; a "0" means "turn it OFF." By hardwiring this mapping process, great efficiency and speed may be obtained. This advance has led to steady progress towards greater resolution both spatially and chromatically. Because bit-mapped graphics has become the standard of the computer graphics industry, we will restrict our discussion of display devices to bit-mapped displays.

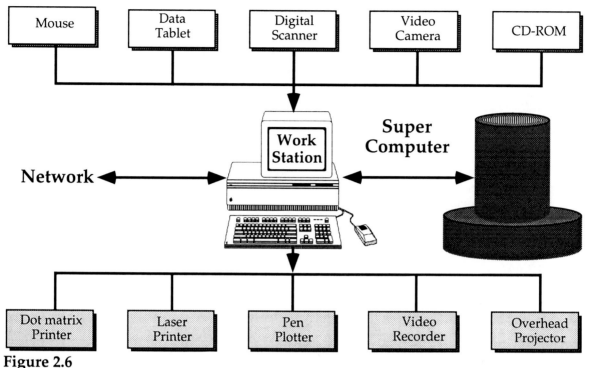

Figure 2.6
Graphics Workstation Architecture. The top line indicates the range of input devices. The bottom line shows possible output devices. The supercomputer and network provide additional resources for computationally intensive applications.

Computer graphics is a unique area in computer science in which at least one aspect of the performance goal is well defined and already in our grasp. The goals of traditional computer design have involved a never-ending search for faster computation, larger word size, and larger memories. In computer graphics, on the other hand, when the screen or some other output device produces a "picture perfect" image, we have reached our goal. Present displays of 1,000 × 1,000 pixels in sixteen-million colors come very close to achieving that goal.

Display Devices

Although the cathode ray tube (CRT) is the oldest of all display devices, it is still the best and most cost-effective. The only serious competitors are plasma-display devices and liquid crystal display devices (LCDs). Both of these have a number of features that make them very attractive as graphical output devices, and we shall return to them shortly. Meanwhile, consider the operation of a typical CRT. The mechanism for displaying information on a CRT screen is shown in Figure 2.7.

The basic elements of a CRT are an electron gun, a deflection system, and a fluorescent screen which emits light when it is struck by electrons. Two kinds of deflection systems are commonly used—magnetic and electrostatic. Magnetic deflection systems use two current-carrying coils to create magnetic fields that force the electrons either up and down or right and left. More easily understood are electrostatic systems in which deflection plates are charged by external voltage drivers.

By applying the proper voltage waveforms to the horizontal and vertical deflection plates (in principle, a sawtooth to the horizontal plates and a stairstep wave to the vertical plates), the electron beam traces out a pattern on the screen as shown in Figure 2.8. On the path AB in Figure 2.8, the voltage on the vertical deflection plates remains constant while the horizontal voltage is a linear ramp.

On the flyback path, BC, a blanking signal cuts off the beam, while the vertical deflection voltage is incremented by a step. The cycle repeats from CD down to E, where another blanking signal

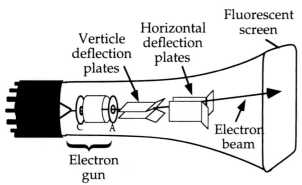

Figure 2.7
Cathode Ray Tube. The basic elements are an electron gun for accelerating a beam of electrons, a deflection system for bending the beam, and a fluorescent screen that emits light when struck by the electron beam.

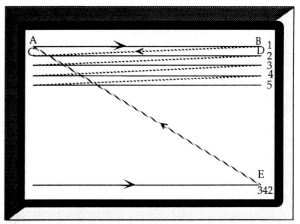

Figure 2.8
Beam Pattern of a CRT Display. The electron beam follows the path ABCD...E once every 1/30 second or less. Dotted/dashed lines indicate blanked beam; solid line means beam is active, plotting a pixel, either white or black.

turns off the beam on the flyback path EA. This whole process must occur in under 1/30 second to avoid irritating flicker. Typical frequencies for the complete screen refresh cycle are 60–70 Hz.

On the B/W Macintosh (SE30 and Classic), for example, the full screen display consists of 342 horizontal scan lines, each composed of 512 pixels. The detailed specifications for these displays are given as:[4]

f = 15.6672 MHz = pixel clock rate (frequency at which pixels are displayed),

F = 60.15 Hz = full screen display frequency,

t_{AB} = 32.68 μsec = time to draw 512 pixels,

t_{BC} = 12.25 μsec = horizontal blanking interval,

t_{EA} = 1258.17 μsec = vertical blanking interval,

d = 1/72 inch = distance between pixels, horizontally and vertically,

M = 21,888 bytes = RAM needed for a single bit-mapped frame buffer.

On color monitors, the complexity increases by the requirement of three independent electron guns and three independent phosphors at each pixel, one each for red, green, and blue. The structure of the electron guns, phosphors, and the color

mask that controls the geometry is shown schematically in Figure 2.9.

As we show in the chapter discussing color, the proper mixture of red, green, and blue light can reproduce any color, according to the *additive RGB model*, and in practice the model works very well. A black pixel is generated by turning off all three beams at the electron gun; the three primary colors are generated by turning on a single gun; and intermediate hues are generated by mixing red, green, and blue in various proportions. To get yellow, we mix roughly equal intensities of red and green light while violet is generated by mixing red and blue. By mixing approximately equal intensities of red, green, and blue light, white light is produced. You can verify this statement experimentally when sitting in front of a color terminal displaying a white screen by wetting your finger with your tongue and lightly touching the screen. The droplets of liquid act as tiny magnifying glasses and sparkle brightly of red, green, and blue.

A second device that continues to capture an increasing share of the graphics display market is the LCD (liquid crystal display). The reason for this rapid growth is the improvement in the devices price/performance ratio, both through falling prices and greatly improved performance. The introduction of LCDs with color capability has accelerated this trend.

LCD displays are the standard output device for essentially all calculators and are found on many children's games. The heart of the device

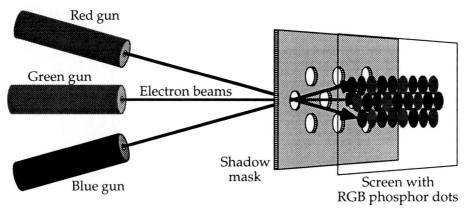

Figure 2.9
Shadow mask color CRT. Color registration is achieved by use of a physical mask with holes or vertical slots through which each color beam is focused on its respective color phosphor. Note: the electron gun angles are exaggerated for purposes of illustration.

consists of a *smectic liquid* whose long chain molecules exhibit polarization properties which can be controlled by an electric field. By segmenting the fluid into tiny cells (pixels), each of which can be switched electrically from transparent to opaque, we have the basis for a high-resolution graphics display. Black-and-white LCDs are now available with resolutions comparable to CRT monitors. Essentially all laptop and portable computers are equipped with LCDs as their display monitor. The advantages to LCD displays include:

- Their image is absolutely stable because it is determined by the intrinsic geometry of the device. The image of an LCD device will never waver, expand, collapse, or be distorted by magnetic fields—all problems that plague CRTs.

- The geometry of LCDs lends itself to thin, light-weight displays which are ideal for portable computers. Thus, the Toshiba T6400 portable weighs under 13 pounds and provides a 10.4 inch (diagonal) LCD screen with a resolution of 640 × 480 in 256 colors. A high resolution RGB CRT monitor in the 16″– 19″ range alone typically weighs 50 pounds or more.

- The power consumption of LCDs is extremely small. This feature allows the construction of portable computers that will work for several hours on a single battery charge.

With attractive features such as these, what has kept LCDs from sweeping away the ancient CRT? There have been two serious drawbacks. The first is well on the way to being solved, and the second problem is slowly receding.

- **The problem of screen visibility** – Early LCD displays using reflected light required good illumination and viewing at a particular angle. This was an annoying feature that caused fatigue after an extended period in front of the screen. However, this problem has been mainly overcome with backlighting and the use of new "super twist" displays that provide excellent contrast. Color LCDs have also largely eliminated the problem of poor screen visibility.

- **Price** – The better quality LCD displays actually incorporate a transistor at each pixel. If even one transistor of the 300,000 contained on the LCD panel is defective, the whole unit must be discarded. Thus, the production cost is high, resulting in a price of portable and lap top computers two to three times that of desk top machines with equivalent performance. As manufacturing techniques improve, the price of LCD devices will decline.

The final display device we discuss is the *plasma display*. This device had its origin in the Nixie tubes of Burroughs Corporation and was developed as a graphical output device by Donald Bitzer and Hiram Slottow of the PLATO Project of the University of Illinois.[5] It has been marketed at various times by Owens-Illinois, Magnavox,

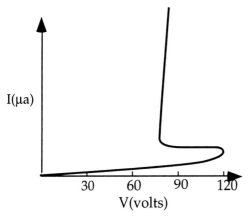

Figure 2.10
Voltage–current characteristic curve for a neon glow lamp, the heart of the plasma display terminal. An applied voltage of > 120 v. will flip an OFF state ON, while a voltage of ~90 v. will maintain a state in its status quo.

Control Data, Fujitsu, Toshiba, and IBM. It shares many of the advantages and the disadvantages of LCDs and is becoming a standard display device on high-end portable computers.

A plasma display screen is essentially a square matrix of tiny neon glow lamps, each individually addressable. Neon glow lamps have an "L" shaped current–voltage characteristic curve similar to that shown in Figure 2.10.

In the region below 120 volts, the neon lamp is OFF, that is, nonconducting and not glowing. As the voltage is raised above the threshold of 120 volts, an autocatalytic discharge occurs and the lamp begins conducting and giving off light. A voltage of approximately 90 volts is then required to maintain conduction, and the discharge continues until the voltage is driven below this value.

The architecture of a plasma display panel is shown in Figure 2.11. By maintaining a voltage of about 3/4 of the threshold voltage, all OFF cells will remain OFF and all ON cells ON. When a pixel needs to be turned on, the voltage on the two lines addressing its cell, e.g. B2, are both increased to just over one-half the threshold voltage and with opposite polarity. Thus, the voltage across cell B2 exceeds the threshold voltage and it turns ON. However, no other cells along line B or along line 2 received more than the threshold voltage. Therefore, no other cells are turned on.

Some very attractive features characterize plasma display panels.

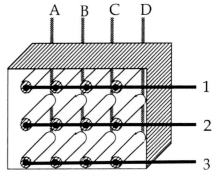

Figure 2.11
Plasma Display Panel. A clear plastic panel with neon-filled cells is addressed by the solid horizontal conductors and the vertical shaded conductors.

- The cell provides its own memory. The role of the display processor is simply to address each pixel to *change* its state, not to *maintain* its state.

- The display geometry is *hardwired* by the structure of the neon cells. As such, it is absolutely stable over time and immune from the nonlinearity and oscillation problems of CRTs.

- Plasma display panels are thin, rugged, light-weight, and transparent. Screens of the PLATO project, in fact, serve as rear-view projection screens on which standard slides may be projected.

There are two serious limitations of plasma displays.

- They have limited gray-scale capabilities. Initially, a pixel cell could be in one of only two possible states, OFF and ON. More recently, companies such as Toshiba have introduced plasma displays with sixteen gray scale levels.

- Your choice of colors is limited to neon orange, although progress is being made on colored plasma displays. This limitation is a serious drawback when competing with CRTs and LCDs.

Table 2.1
Levels of Graphics Workstations

Level	Microprocessor (No. bits)	Typical Machine	Clock rate (MHz)[MIPS]	Typical Memory
1	I8088, 80286(8–16) M68000 (16)	IBM PC, XT,AT Mac Plus, Classic	4.8 – 16 MHz 7.8 MHz	640 Kb 1 Mb
2	I80386 (16–32) M68030 (16–32)	IBM PS/2 Line Mac II Series Sun, Apollo	16 – 33 MHz	4 – 16 Mb
3	I486 (32) M68040 (32)	IBM PS/2, Clones Mac Quadras NextStation HP-Apollo 9000	25 – 66 MHz [25 MIPS]	8 – 64 Mb
4	Sparc RISC M88000 RISC MIPS R3000 RISC RISC	Sun Sparcstation Tektronix SGI Iris Indigo IBM 6000	25–66 MHz	8 – 256 Mb
5	MIPS Proprietary ASIC MIPS R4000SC RISC	Stardent 3000 IBM 6090 SGI Iris Crimson	[128 MIPS] [85 MIPS]	32 Mb 32 Mb 16–256 Mb

Processors

The two main classes of microprocessors which have made high quality graphics readily available are the "sixes" and the "eights" manufactured by Motorola and Intel, respectively. The genealogy of the sixes originated with the MOS-6502 (Apple II, Atari, Commodore 64), and includes the Motorola M6800, the M68000, the M68020, M68030, and M68040 (Macintosh, Next, HP-Apollo, and Sun). The eights genealogy includes the I8088 (IBM PC and XT), the I80286 (IBM AT), I80386, and I80486 (IBM PS/2 and clones).

For purposes of developing some understanding of the evolution of microcomputers and their various strengths and weaknesses as graphics systems, the following classification system may be helpful.

In this text, we will confine ourselves primarily to the discussion of level 1, 2, and 3 systems because of their performance/price advantage and value as instructional tools. Level 4 and 5 systems provide exceptionally powerful graphics workstations, but their improved performance comes at a price ranging from a factor of two to more than ten times that of Level 1–3 systems. Level 1 systems are available in the $0.5K – $1.5K price range and are capable of carrying out most of the algorithmic computer graphics of the first two sections of the book. Level 2 and 3 systems cost $1.5K – $15K and are capable of all algorithmic calculations plus the image processing and higher level graphics applications in the rest of the book. The final advantage of orienting the text for level 1–3 systems is their plentiful supply—most laboratories are well stocked with PCs or Macs or both.

Another consideration on Level 2–3 machines: new technologies are becoming available to enhance the performance of these machines as graphics workstations into direct competition of Level 4 and 5 machines. These technologies include special graphics accelerator cards and networking systems for harnessing workstations as parallel graphics processors. Sluggish graphics display behavior is a particularly serious problem for machines like the Macintosh in which a single microprocessor CPU must handle all interrupts and graphical display tasks in addition to its main computing assignments. Application Specific Integrated Circuits (ASICs), such as the Texas Instruments TI34010, are designed specifically to speed the processing of graphical information display. The Radius Quickcad board for the Mac II is an example of the improvement achieved through the use of special graphics cards. This board reduced the time required to display an AutoCAD file of 110,000 vectors from 83 seconds to three seconds.[6]

Clever networking technology is available to convert unused machines into parallel graphics processors. One particularly impressive example is *NetRenderMan*, a UNIX-based workstation enhancement of *MacRenderMan*, the high-quality rendering system we study in the chapter on realistic rendering of 3D graphics. In one test, a rendering task that took 35 minutes on a Macintosh Quadra using *MacRenderMan* was completed in four minutes and thirty seconds using *NetRenderMan* in a network containing the Quadra, a Sun Sparcstation, and an Iris Indigo workstation.

A final note on Level 2–3 machines—the richness and variety of software available for level 1–3 machines far surpasses that available on Level 4-5 machines. For the same functionality, the price of software running on level 1–3 machines is typically one half to one tenth that of the level 4-5 equivalent. In particular, in a multi-station instructional environment, the software price advantage may outweigh the hardware price advantage as the critical consideration.

Level 1 Example – I8088 System

These machines, when equipped with standard EGA or VGA color adapters and monitors, provide medium resolution color graphics capabilities at a low price. A typical setup built around a Zenith 158 XT with NEC MultiSync monitor and a PC Mouse is shown in Figure 2.12.

The chief drawbacks of 8088-based systems are:

- They are slow because of small word length and low clock speed.

- They suffer from a plethora of adapter cards, monitors, and drivers making software development cumbersome.

- They are limited to 640 KB of addressable memory. This severely restricts the sophistication of applications which may be developed.

- They do not support graphics user interfaces at the hardware level. Thus, for instance, mouse support does not come naturally, and all graphics user interfaces must be added as a second layer of operating system piggy-backing the resident MS-DOS. This exacts a severe price in speed performance and interapplication communication.

In spite of these handicaps, some very elegant application programs have been developed for PCs, XTs, and their clones. Many of these problems have been overcome in the M68000-based Macintosh level-1 systems.

M68000-Based Machines

By moving to a 16-bit memory bus and 32-bit register structure, these machines achieve a factor of two in processing power over the 8–16 bit 8088-based machines. In addition, the Macintosh Classic implementation runs at 7.8 MHz, another factor of nearly two improvement over the 4.77 MHz PC. However, this theoretical factor of 4 in speed advantage is not realized in practice because of the heavy work load assigned the 68000 Mac processor.

The chief advantage of the Macintosh implementation for graphics applications is in the firmware (ROM). The Macintosh User Interface Toolbox firmware consists of the following tools:

- Resource manager
- Font Manager
- Window Manager
- Menu Manager
- Dialog Manager
- Package Manager
- QuickDraw
- Control Manager
- Text Edit
- Toolbox Utilities

The Toolbox provides high-level functions and procedures for performing complex tasks. For instance, the task of opening a window which lists all files available in a folder and the control buttons necessary for selecting and opening a

Figure 2.12
A Zenith 158 Computer. The system contains 640 KB of RAM and runs at 4.77 or 8 MHz. It has one 5.25" floppy, a 40 MB hard drive (segmented as two 20-MB partitions), a NEC MultiSync EGA monitor, and a PC mouse. (*Video image captured with Computer Eyes*™.)

given file from the list is performed by a single function call. In addition to saving programmers much time in building such tools from scratch, the toolbox routines ensure familiarity and consistency of application programs for the user.

The Toolbox tools of most interest for users of this text are the QuickDraw routines. QuickDraw tools are provided to specify graphical objects such as rectangles, circles, and polygons; graphical attributes such as cursor, pen, and text characteristics and transfer modes; and drawing environments with its GrafPort routines for creating and manipulating independent graphical windows. There are, for instance, five routines for handling the cursor, fifteen for manipulating GrafPorts, thirteen for pen and line drawing, twelve for text drawing, five each for operating on rectangles, ovals, arcs, and rounded-corner rectangles, and so on.

The key concept to the effectiveness of the toolbox paradigm is that all of these tools are built into the system at the hardware level through firmware. As we will see shortly, they permit quite sophisticated graphics to be generated by short and elegant programs. In the chapter on designing GUIs, the features of graphical toolkits are discussed in detail and several application programs are developed using them.

What are the problems with the Macintosh Plus/Classic?

- The nine-inch screen with its 512×342 pixel resolution feels rather confining, particularly after experience on larger screens.

- The whole Mac Plus/SE/Classic line supports only black and white on its built-in monitor. The SE does provide a slot for adding a color driver board and external color monitor.

- The Macintosh is not as fast as one might expect from its 68000 processor. This one processor is assigned all control, I/O, and computing tasks. Other vendors of 68000-based computers (e.g., Atari and Commodore) achieve increased performance by assigning application-specific chips for tasks such as I/O, thereby freeing the 68000 CPU for computationally intensive work.

Even with these handicaps, the Mac Plus/SE/Classic line of computers has played an important role in computer graphics as the first low-cost, widely available system supporting a windows/icon/menus/pointer operating system. The popularity and acceptance it won for the graphical user interface (GUI) concept may be its single most important contribution.

Level 2 Examples

Next consider the two leading classes of Level 2 systems. By solving most of the problems of Level 1 systems, these machines have demonstrated that personal computers can serve as serious graphics workstations.

I80386-Based Machines

IBM and Compaq introduced the fast and capable Intel 80386 line of computers and many companies have followed suit. These machines have broken the 640K memory limits of earlier PCs and support a wealth of B/W and color monitors which match the requirements of many user application programs. The addition of Microsoft Windows or the OS/2–Presentation Manager operating system makes the 80386 computer a credible graphics workstation.

Although I80386 machines offer considerable computing power per dollar invested, they are not without problems. These include:

- The lack of a hardware-based graphical user interface makes the development of application programs and interapplication information transfer more difficult than it is with systems with firmware GUIs.

- The proliferation of "standards" has led to a proliferation of devices and drivers which makes application programs bulky and cumbersome. There remain numerous graphics adapters, each with differing spatial and chromatic resolution. This proliferation is highlighted by the split in communication bus protocols between Micro Channel Architecture (MCA – supported by IBM and NCR) and Extended Industry Standard Architecture (EISA – supported by almost everyone else).

Although the problems presented here make the development of application programs more complex for developers and the selection of system components more problematic for users, there are real advantages to open architectures. The flood of application programs running under Windows demonstrates the potential of the 386 machines as graphics workstations.

M68030-Based Machines

The Motorola 68030 has become a popular microprocessor and is used in the HP, Apollo, Sun, Next and several models of the Macintosh. It is a full 32-bit processor which runs at 16, 25, 40, and even 50 MHz. Next we consider the Mac IIcx, IIsi, and IIci line as examples of 68030-based machines.

The whole Macintosh II line has returned to the open architecture pioneered by the Apple II and adopted by the IBM PC. As with the PC, the CPU comes as a chassis in which a hard drive, additional memory, and a variety of peripheral cards may be installed. Cards are available for such functions as color monitor drivers, video frame grabbers, and experimental control modules.

The Mac IIcx–IIci line supports all of the toolbox routines of the Mac Plus and additional color QuickDraw functions to support color graphics manipulation. The author's Mac IIcx workstation is shown in Figure 2.13.

The components of this workstation consist of the following elements.

1) Mac IIcx with 8 MB RAM/14 MB virtual memory and 200 MB hard drive,
2) E-Machines monitor, 16M colors, 832 × 624 pixel resolution, 72 dpi,
3) Cirus 80 MB hard drive,
4) Toshiba 680 MB CD-ROM,
5) Syquest 45 MB removable hard drive,
6) Apple Extended Keyboard,
7) Mouse,
8) Computer Eyes B/W Video Transducer,
9) HP-DeskWriter, 300 dpi, with *Freedom of Press* PostScript.

This system has all of the elements of the general graphics workstation shown in Figure 2.6 except the data tablet and video recorder. The digital scanner, dot matrix printer, and laser printer are not shown but available on a network. A modem provides access to a VAX minicomputer and Cray supercomputers.[7]

The principal limitation of the Mac IIcx–IIci line of workstations is speed—or lack thereof. Because the 16–25 MHz processor must handle all interrupts and I/O as well as computation, speed of processing becomes a problem for applications such as CAD and finite element analysis. One solution to this problem is to add 40–50 MHz

Figure 2.13
Macintosh IIcx workstation with peripherals.
(*Video image captured with Computer Eyes™.*)

accelerator boards based on both M68030 and M68040 processors. With or without accelerators, the Mac IIcx, IIsi, and IIci line provides very capable and flexible workstations. All of the graphics in this text were generated or reproduced by this computer graphics system.

Level 3 Machines

Machines built around the i486 and M68040 resemble their lower model number counterparts but have accelerated processing capability. This is primarily through the use of ingenious caching schemes for fetching and storing locally those items from memory on which the processor will operate in the immediate future. The caching scheme helps overcome one of the big bottlenecks in sequential von Neumann machines—the fetching and storing of information to and from memory.

For purposes of this text we consider the i486 and M68040 as high speed, downwardly compatible versions of the I80386 and M68030, respectively. They represent the state-of-the-art processors for the current generation of standard personal workstations. The author's 486/33 machines is shown in Figure 2.14.

There are a number of innovations which will greatly enhance the power available on graphics workstations. These include:

- *The trend toward ever higher clock speeds –* While the industry is presently pushing the 50–66 MHz limit on processor clock rate, some analysts predict that clock speeds of

Figure 2.14
Gateway 2000/486/33C Computer. The system contains 8 MB of RAM and runs at 33 MHz. It has one 5.25″ floppy, one 3.5″ floppy, a 200 MB hard drive, a 1024 × 768 Super VGA monitor, and a Microsoft mouse. (*Figure scanned from a photograph using Microtek 300G.*)

100–150 MHz will be available within the next few years. This advance may occur through the use of emitter-coupled logic (ECL) and closer packing of devices on printed circuit boards. Gate delays of 160 ps on nine-layer boards are now proven technology.

• *The move towards greater word length* – The present standard for personal workstations is 32-bit word length. Many analysts predict, however, that the next major advance will occur as workstations move to 64-bit address space—in the footsteps of their mainframe and supercomputer ancestors.

• *The trend towards parallel processing* – As greater experience and insight on the operation of parallel processors is achieved, this technique for breaking the von Neumann bottleneck will emerge. By incorporating INMOS's transputer cards into conventional PC workstations, 100 MIP/20 MFLOP performance can be achieved.

Input Devices

Every stand-alone graphics workstation has at least the following two input devices: a pointing device and a keyboard. In addition, it is essential to have a sizable hard drive for intermediate storage of images and image processing programs. In order to build an integrated graphics workstation, however, additional graphical input and output devices are desirable. That is, at least some components from the top and bottom row of Figure 2.6 must be available to the workstation for capturing and exporting images. Below we consider standard input devices in detail and discuss briefly additional transducers for capturing images.

Mice

Pointing devices have evolved from light pens and joysticks to data tablets, track balls, and touch-sensitive screens. Except for certain specialized applications such as cartography and some areas of CAD requiring data tablets, the pointing device of choice for graphics workstations is the mouse. It was invented at Xerox PARC and has the sensitivity, accuracy, and intuitiveness to make it an ideal pointing device. In Figure 2.15 we show three different mice. The mouse on the right is, in fact, alive and controlling the shutter on the video camera which took its picture.

Mice can be classified by two modes of operation: *optical* and *mechanical*. The PC Mouse, on the left in Figure 2.15, works in the optical mode with a reflective pad beneath it. The pad has

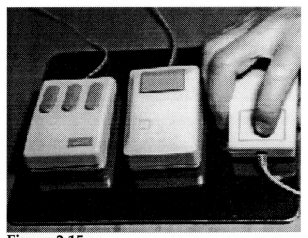

Figure 2.15
Three mice: PC Mouse on left, Apple Mouse, old style, in center, and Apple Mouse, new style, on right. (*Video image captured with Computer Eyes™.*)

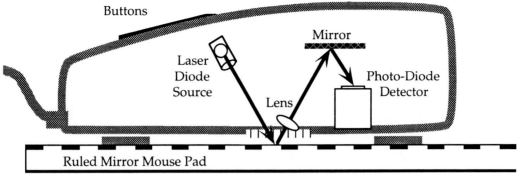

Figure 2.16
Internal construction of optical mouse. As the mouse moves right or left, the intensity of the reflected light is modulated by the ruled mirror mouse pad, and the photo-diode produces a train of square waves.

a square grid of lines ruled at 1 mm intervals imposed on its reflective surface. The horizontally ruled lines are of a different color (and hence reflectivity) from the vertically ruled lines. Mounted internally is an LED light source and a lens which focuses light reflected from the ruled mouse pad and an internal mirror onto a photodetector.

Figure 2.16 shows the physical arrangement of the active elements on the PC Mouse. As the mouse is moved, a series of pulses is generated as the alternate silvered and darker colored bands reflect the beam into the detector. By appropriate interpretation of the train of pulses generated, the computer can interpret the mouse motion as up, down, right, or left.

The advantage of the optical PC Mouse is that it has no moving parts to wear out or gum up. The only disadvantages are that it must be used

with the reflective mouse pad, and the system has a fairly coarse resolution.

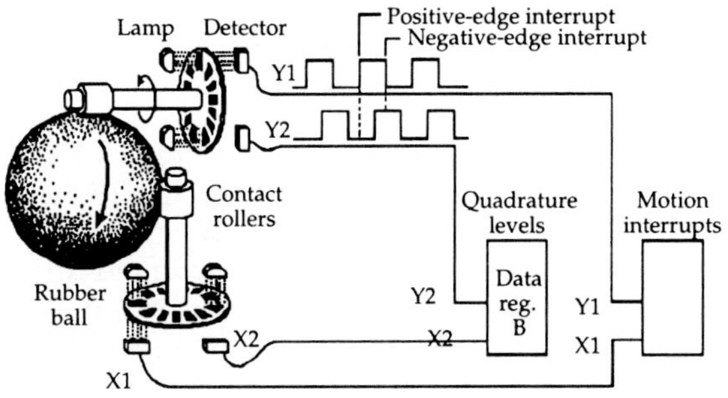

The two mice on the right of Figure 2.15 work in a coupled mechanical/optical mode. A weighted, rubber ball protrudes slightly from the bottom and rolls as the mouse is moved on any surface. Inside the mouse, the ball bears against two mutually perpendicular rollers that drive shafts on which are mounted slotted shutter disks as shown in Figure 2.17. On one side of the disk are mounted two LED light sources and opposite them on the other side are two photodetectors. As the mouse ball rolls, the shafts turn rotating the slotted shutter which produces a train of square-wave voltages from the photodetectors. By properly interpreting the number and relative phases of the four wave trains generated by the mouse, the computer can compute the direction and distance it has moved.

The advantage of the mechanical mouse is that it can be used on almost any smooth surface and has a very smooth, precise action. The disadvantage is that the internal rollers tend to get dirty and behave erratically. As a mechanical device it is more prone to problems than purely optical mice.

Keyboards

A consensus is evolving among users of graphics workstations on the value of extended keyboards. Keyboards with 101 or 105 keys provide function keys in which complex but repetitive operations may be encoded. The first six function keys on the keyboard in Figure 2.13, for instance, are encoded with the operations: *undo, cut, copy, past, information,* and *select all.* Many second source suppliers are now producing keyboards with more keys and functions than the original equipment.

Figure 2.17
Mechanical mouse assembly. As the mouse is moved, the rubber ball protruding from the bottom turns, causing one or both contact rollers to turn. As they turn the shaft on the optical shutter detector, a train of square electrical pulses is generated which can be decoded to read motion.

Hard drives

One or more large hard drives is essential for any workstation on which serious computer graphics work is contemplated. The COSMOS/M finite element program specifies that at least 8 MB of hard disk space must be available for loading the program. B/W video images, such as those in Figures 2.12, 2.13, and 2.15, require 300 KB – 1.5 MB for storage. A workstation performing image processing operations will require 30 MB – 50 MB for system and application programs. Since it is useful to have at least that much disk space available for temporary storage of images, a hard drive of at least 100 MB – 300 MB is recommended.

Figure 2.13 illustrates an optimal configuration of graphics workstation hard drives. The 200 MB internal hard drive contains all of the basic systems, languages, graphics, and word processing tools. The removable drives provides individualized cassettes for specialized programs and their associated data files. A second important function that the removable drives provides is rapid backup of the internal drive. Backup is performed at hard disk I/O speeds.

Digital Scanners

One of the most useful graphics input devices is the digital scanner. Two main applications of digital scanners include scanning text for conversion into ASCII character files (i.e., reading text), and capture of images (paintings, drawings, photographs, and so on) for subsequent use in advertisements, documents, papers, and books.

Scanners are available in both B/W and color with spatial resolution of 200 dpi – 600 dpi and color resolution from 1 bit – 24 bits. Several models are now available that offer 24-bit, 300 dpi resolution at a price comparable to B/W scanners.

Video Scanners and Digitizers

The marriage of video media with computer image processing has spawned a whole new generation of multimedia technology. Sources of graphical information in a video format include:

- Television sets,
- Video Cassette Recorders (VCRs),
- Video cameras,
- Video camera/recorders ("camcorders"),
- Video snapshot cameras.

Video input devices typically operate in one of two distinct modes: frame grabbers and scanning digitizers. Frame grabbers capture whole video frames and save them for later image processing. Some frame grabbers can even capture and store sequential frames, turning the workstation, in effect, into a video recorder for short sequences. The *Moonraker*™ system, for instance, can capture and play back video frames at 30 frames per second with a resolution of 645 × 484 pixels in 8-bit color. At 15 fps, it can display up to four separate windows from four distinct video sources simultaneously. Since frame grabbers must transfer large amounts of information rapidly, they are typically packaged as boards plugged into the internal bus structure which provides for parallel data flow.

Scanning digitizers such as *Computer Eyes* shown in Figure 2.14 operate on a somewhat different principle. The standard NTSC (National Television System Committee) composite video signal consists of 480 horizontal scan lines. A scanning digitizer samples each of the scan lines at a number of evenly spaced intervals along it (640 for *Computer Eyes*), sending the digitized values to the computer which gradually builds up a complete video image. The process takes about 20 seconds to scan and generate a complete image. At each of the 307,200 sample points the analog video signal is digitized to 8-bits of precision. Control of the scanning process is exercised by a program resident in the workstation.

CD ROMs

Because of their large storage capacity, CD ROMs have become a popular medium for archiving graphics images. A number of public domain CD ROMs are available which contain a vast amount of graphical data. Commercial clip art disks are marketed specifically for artists and desktop publishers. Finally, some very significant scientific visualization images are available on CD ROM.

For the purposes of this book, we consider CD ROMs as a sizable resource of prepackaged images that are available for downloading into the workstation, transferring to other media (floppies and hard drives), integrating into new images, and providing raw data for the many image processing programs. For instance, the detailed workstation subimage in Figure 2.6 was downloaded from a public domain disk and edited by the addition of input devices, output devices, and a supercomputer by the program *Canvas* to produce the final figure. Archival graphics libraries such as this are a valuable resource to graphics artists and designers.

The specifications and features of the Toshiba TXM-3201-A1-Mac include:

- Storage capacity = 600/680 MB (depending on format),
- Average access time = 400 ms,
- Data transfer speed (average) = 175 Kb/sec,
- Data transfer speed (Maximum, from buffer) = 1.4 Mb/sec,
- Data buffer capacity = 64 Kb,
- Rotation speed = 200 – 530 RPM,
- Hard read error $< 10^{-12}$ (in mode 1),
- SCSI interface,
- Built-in error correction code,
- Reads formats: High Sierra, HFS Macintosh, ISO 9660, and Audio CDs,
- Audio reproduction with headphone jack and volume control.

The last two features add another pleasant medium to the multimedia workstation—high quality stereo sound. When the user is not busy examining graphical data from the CD ROM, she/he can eject the disk, select a musical CD, and play it uninterrupted in background mode while computing on the workstation with no degradation in either musical quality or computational performance.

The only two problems with CD ROMs are their relatively slow speed compared to magnetic media and the "read only" nature of the media. Although the read only nature of CD ROMs restricts the range of applications, it does provide iron-clad security for information resources such as encyclopedias, the collected works of William Shakespeare, and Roget's Thesaurus.

Output Devices

Since most readers are already familiar with several of the output devices listed in Figure 2.6 we will not discuss them individually. Instead, we now present a few observations on the technology and its economics.

First, all the output devices are available in both B/W and color. In general, one pays somewhere in the range of 50 percent to 300 percent premium in moving from B/W to color. However, the market is moving very rapid toward better color output devices at ever lower prices. As more color devices become available, the advantages of color as an aid to visualization are becoming more widely recognized. When color output becomes

the norm, the pressure will build to produce low-cost effective copying devices, the lack of which is the last remaining obstacle to the widespread use of color.

The second observation is that a range of resolution is available on color devices, both in color resolution and spatial resolution. At the low end, one can add 144 dpi, 8-color capability to the ImageWriter II dot matrix printer for the cost of a 4-color ribbon (~$5.00). Color inkjet printers with 200–300 dpi resolution in 16 M colors are available in the $1K – $2K range. Three hundred dpi thermal transfer printers cost $5K – $10K, and 6,000 dpi slide recorders are becoming available in the same price range.

Software/Firmware Systems

One logical way to analyze the software/firmware technology of computer graphics is to categorize it into the following classes.

- System software,
- Programming languages,
- Level 1 graphics software,
- Level 2 image processing software.

System Software

GUI operating systems such as Microsoft Windows and the Macintosh OS provide a rich repertoire of functions for controlling the graphics interface and building application programs. Windows is a graphical extension to MS-DOS which provides an elegant graphical user interface to Windows compatible applications and a graphical shell for calling non-Windows applications. More importantly from the graphics programmer's point of view is that Windows provides an object-oriented programming environment with access to graphical objects such as windows, icons, menus, and mouse events through high-level languages such as *C, Turbo Pascal for Windows*, and *Visual Basic*. Similarly, the Macintosh utilizes ROM firmware containing the operating system and the Macintosh User Interface Toolbox. Of particular interest to the graphics programmer are the Menu Manager, Window Manager, Control Manager, Event Manager, and QuickDraw routines.

Menu Manager give the programmer full control over the creation of menus, their contents, the "pull down" feature, and the highlighting of individual menu actions. Window Manager and

Control Manager give the programmer the tools for creating windows with title bar, scroll bars, size box and close box, controls the selection and shuffling of overlapping windows, and tracks window pointers and *WindowRecord* data types. Event Manager builds event queues for recording events such as mouse button action, keyboard entry, and disk drive insertions, and properly integrates them with the Menu Manager, Window Manager, and operating system.

Programming Languages

Numerous dialects of all major high-level programming languages are available for both the PC and Mac computer lines. Many of these, such as Turbo Pascal (for both the PC and Mac) support an extensive set of graphical routines. Traditionally, the most common languages used to write graphics applications are *FORTRAN*, *Pascal*, and *C*. The rich, graphical environment of GUI systems has inspired object-oriented graphical languages like *Visual Basic* in which the programmer can create sophisticated multiple-window user interfaces without writing any code. Other languages such as *LISP*, *Scheme*, *Prolog*, *Forth*, and *SmallTalk* also offer strong graphics support, but have not been as widely adopted for graphical application programming.

We have selected *Pascal* to introduce graphics programming concepts, and later will introduce *Visual Basic* to illustrate the concept of an event-driven graphical language. The reasons for emphasizing *Pascal* are the following:

- Its syntax closely resembles various pseudocode languages in widespread use for teaching both computer science and computer graphics.

- It is the language most familiar to college students in computer science.

- Its design encourages the use of good programming style, of particular importance in graphics program design, such as structured, modular, top-down design.

- *Turbo Pascal for Windows* provides a Windows-hosted environment with an extensive GUI library, resource editing tools, and a debugger for windows.

- The Macintosh User Interface Toolbox routines are written in *Pascal* and the formats for most of the Toolbox and QuickDraw routines are specified in *Pascal* format.

- The *Pascal* dialects chosen both support object-oriented programming.

A number of excellent *Pascal* compilers are available for both the PC and the Macintosh. *Turbo Pascal for Windows* and *THINK Pascal* for the Macintosh share the features of a fast compiler and linker, an integrated text editor, and an object-oriented development environment. Their intelligent compilers understand the relationships between program modules, and, when sections are changed, they will recompile only the necessary dependent code. This greatly improves program debugging and development efficiency. The debuggers provide breakpoints, single stepping, and variable window for observing and changing the value of variables while the program is running.

Level 1 Graphics Software– Spreadsheet Graphics

Two software tools of great value for computer users in general and technical analysts in particular are graphical spreadsheets and paint/draw programs. Several excellent graphical spreadsheets are on the market, including MS-Excel, Quatro Pro, Full Impact, MS-Works, and WINGZ. We have selected WingZ as the illustrative spreadsheet for this text because of its speed, capacity, power, and graphics capability. It is one of the fastest spreadsheets available anywhere. It has a capacity of 32,768 rows by 32,768 columns and offers over three hundred special functions for performing operations on data with twenty

Table 2.2
WINGZ™ Special Functions

Category	Number of Functions
Business	18
Database	10
Date/Time	23
HyperScript	161
Logical	9
Numeric/Trig	34
Spreadsheet	18
Statistical	10
Text	24
Total	**307**

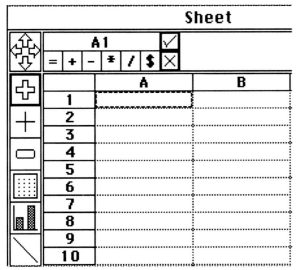

Figure 2.18
Segment of WINGZ spreadsheet. Rows range from
1 – 32,768 and columns range from A – AVLH.
Tools for creating graphical objects are shown as
icons on the left.

Figure 2.19
Image of final spreadsheet that was pasted into the
text. Operations needed to build the spreadsheet
included reformatting, data entry, and executing
the "sum" function in B-12.

	A	B
1		Number of
2	Category	Functions
3	Business	18
4	Database	10
5	Date/Time	23
6	HyperScript	161
7	Logical	9
8	Numeric/Trig	34
9	Spreadsheet	18
10	Statistical	10
11	Text	24
12	Total	307

different graph types for plotting it.

The breakdown of the functions by logical category is presented in Table 2.2.

Table 2.2 was created by WINGZ itself. Spreadsheets employ the very powerful metaphor that every cell in a 2D matrix array may be any function of any other cell or cells.

To illustrate the ease of operation with spreadsheets, consider the following simple steps used in creating this table and computing the total given in the last line. WINGZ opens as a blank spreadsheet shown in Figure 2.18. The next step in creating the spreadsheet is to use the cursor to widen column A to accommodate the category text. After this formatting is done, the text and numbers are entered as shown. Pull-down menu commands are issued to center the heading and column B, convert the numbers into integers, and change the heading to bold face.

The total is computed by moving the cursor to B-12 and entering the function command, "=sum(", then by dragging the cursor from B-3 to B-11, and finally by typing a ")". The contents of cell B-12 then reads "=sum(B3..B11)." Upon hitting a <cr> the total, 307, magically appears in cell B-12. The final spreadsheet is shown in Figure 2.19. This table was selected by dragging the cursor from A-1 to B-12, executing "COPY" from the pull-down menu, switching to the word

processor on which the text was written, and executing "PASTE" into a 12 × 2 table.

The beauty of graphical spreadsheets is the ease with which complex functions can be evaluated and visualized. Consider, for example, the following equation which corresponds to a damped, circular cosine wave.

$$z = cos(4\pi r)\, e^{-r} \qquad [2.1]$$

where
$$r = \sqrt{x^2 + y^2}$$

   = radial distance from impact

   z = height of wave

   e^{-r} = exponential damping term

Two design decisions must be made in order to map this function onto a spreadsheet.

1) Select a 51 × 51 cell array. This gives reasonable resolution without excessive computation.

2) Let cell A-1 correspond to (x,y) = (−1,−1) and cell AY-51 correspond to (1,1). The

| A1 | ✓ | =cos(4*((sqrt(((row()-26)/25)^2+((col()-26)/25)^2))*pi()))) |
| = | + | − | * | / | $ | ✗ | *exp(-sqrt(((row()-26)/25)^2+((col()-26)/25)^2)) |

	A	B	C	D	E	F
1	0.12	0.04	-0.05	-0.14	-0.21	
2	0.04	-0.06	-0.14	-0.22	-0.26	
3	-0.05	-0.14	-0.22	-0.27	-0.29	
4	-0.14	-0.22	-0.27	-0.29	-0.27	
5	-0.21	-0.26	-0.29	-0.27	-0.22	

Figure 2.20
Spreadsheet calculation of damped circular cosine wave shown in Figure 2.21.

center of the matrix (r = 0 impact point) then occurs in cell Z-26.

To compute Equation 2.1, we position the cursor in cell A-1 and type in Equation 2.1 in spreadsheet syntax. This equation is shown in the upper entry box in Figure 2.20, along with a small segment of the resulting spreadsheet.

The equation uses three resident WINGZ routines, "row()" to report the numerical value of the row in which the computational cell resides, "col()" to do the same thing for the column, and "pi()" to return the numerical value of pi. The numbers 26 and 25 are, respectively, the center offset and the normalization factors to implement the scaling described above. After hitting <cr>, the resulting number, 0.12, appears in cell A-1.

The second step in the process is to sweep the cursor from cell A-1 to AY-1, selecting the first 51 cells in the top row. Then, the menu command, "copy right," duplicates this equation in each of the selected cells. Finally, we select the first row through cell AY-1 and drag the cursor down to select all cells to row 51. The "copy down" command copies the key equation into all 51 × 51 cells. After a fraction of a minute, the numbers shown in Figure 2.20 appear. These numbers correspond to the z values of the wave equation 2.1 at all 2601 points in the (x,y) grid.

Three steps are required to generate a 3D graph from the numbers. First, we select (or leave selected) all 2601 cells. Second, we click on the graph tool (shown left of row 8 in Figure 2.19). Third, we create a graph box by dragging the cursor. The program does the rest. After minor adjustment of the vertical scale divisions and color key, the shade-encoded surface plot of Figure 2.21 appears. Notice the very sophisticated processing represented in this figure. It includes:

- Automatic height-encoding by shading,

- Automatic 3D perspective projection,

- Automatic hidden-line and surface removal.

These nontrivial operations will, in fact, be among the topics covered in Section 2 of this text. The graphics processing incorporated in this one application program constitutes approximately 95 percent of the subject matter covered in most conventional graphics textbooks.

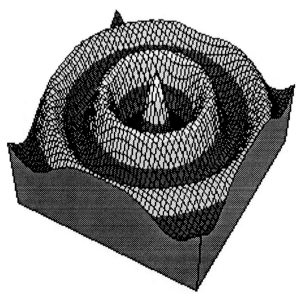

Figure 2.21
WINGZ 3D surface plot of damped cosine wave.

Level 1 Graphics Software – Painting/Drawing Programs

MacPaint is the program that created the most interest and captured the imagination of creative artists and programmers alike at the unveiling of the original Macintosh. It is really a bit-mapped reincarnation of Ivan Sutherland's historic 1963 program, *Sketchpad*.[8]

Users totally unfamiliar with computer languages could now create original designs and poster art with minimum effort and have total flexibility in manipulating the bit-mapped screen. In addition to a simple etch-a-sketch-like capability, MacPaint offers graphics functions for drawing lines, rectangles, polygons, and ovals. By applying constraints to these functions, fixed angle lines (45° increments), squares, and circles are easily constructed. The program also offers a variety of pen shapes and patterns, a spray can for special effects, and a paint option for filling areas with shades of gray or special patterns. The tool palette and the result of applying some of these functions are shown in Figure 2.22.

The message, "Hi there!," in this figure was written with the paintbrush tool and mouse. The rectangle, rounded rectangle, oval, and irregular object were created with the respective tools in the left hand column. The little house was created with the lower left hand polygon tool to draw the end of the house and the line drawing tool to draw the roof and side. They were then filled using the paint can tool and appropriate patterns from the pattern palette shown at the bottom of the screen. The whole screen painting operation took about two minutes.

The most intriguing feature of MacPaint is its fast bit-mapped editing functions. These include the *lasso, marquee, hand, pencil,* and *eraser* tools near the top of the tool palette, and the *duplicate* function under the edit pull-down menu. Using the images in Figure 2.22 as the starting point, the edited image in Figure 2.23 was easily generated.

First, the upper right hand *marquee tool* was used to select and *cut* the word "there!." It was also used to select the word "Hi" and slide it to the right. The word "there!" was then *pasted* from the clipboard and dragged into its present position. Next, the rounded rectangle was selected by the lasso and dragged on top of the rectangle, and this process was repeated for the oval and the irregular figure. The figure was then painted by the speckled pattern. Finally, the house was selected by the lasso tool and duplicated two times. The right-hand copy was generated by selecting one of the

copies with the marquee tool and calling the menu function *Flip Horizontal* to draw the house shown.

Although it is a simple and easy to use program, MacPaint has some very sophisticated image processing functions. These include an *edge detector* and the *fat bits* editing option in which the user can easily edit individual pixels to refine the image to the limit of the screen resolution (72 pixels/inch).

The second major class of level 1 paint/draw programs are the drawing programs exemplified by *MacDraw*™ which is marketed by Claris Corporation. While some of the palette tools have the same shape and function as painting programs, drawing programs differ in a very fundamental way. This distinction can best be understood by distinguishing bit-mapped images from object-oriented images.

- **Bit-mapped images** – Once the image element is painted or pasted on the bit-mapped screen, it becomes part of the composite image and loses all of its individual identity. All "objectness" of the element is lost once it is drawn or pasted. If an image element is manually selected by the marquee or lasso tool and dragged elsewhere, it leaves behind blank white space where it formerly resided. That is, it is no longer a graphical object, but rather just a (possibly incomplete) pattern of pixels.

- **Object-oriented images** – Images created by the tools in object-oriented drawing programs maintain their identity and "objectness" throughout the lifetime of the scene of which they are a part. Individual objects may be grouped to construct more complex objects, and complex objects may be disassembled into their individual parts and the parts edited or deleted. Objects are selected by simply clicking on them and may be moved, re-sized, and manipulated in any number of ways.

Figure 2.22
MacPaint tool palette and sample output.

Figure 2.23
An edited version of Figure 2.22.

A little reflection on these two differing graphical paradigms suggests that each is most appropriate for certain classes of tasks. Painting programs are best suited for creating artistic images involving shading, complex patterns, and impressionistic effects. Drawing tools are best suited to engineering and design applications in which geometric objects form the basis and precision gridding and dimensioning are important.

A number of excellent programs have emerged which combine the best features of both painting and drawing programs. Among these are *SuperPaint*™ and *Canvas*™. Figures 2.6–2.9, 2.11, 2.16, and 2.17 were created using Canvas. By providing accurate dimensioning options and the capability of stacking objects on top of other objects, programs such as Canvas really qualify as 2D CAD tools. We will return to these tools in more detail in the applications section.

Level 2 Image Processing Software

The integration of computer graphics, image processing, pattern recognition, and scientific visualization has led to a whole new class of image processing software. While no single program is capable of all possible functions, some program generally provides the required feature. The most common image processing operations include: brightness and contrast adjustment, color palette selection and manipulation, image smoothing and sharpening, blurring and edge detection, dithering and halftoning, and the negative transformation.

In addition to the mathematical operations on images themselves, a host of programs are available for the generation and realistic rendering of 3D images. These programs fall under the category of 3D drafting, CAD, and rendering applications. We examine them in greater detail in the applications section.

Standards

The issue of standards is problematic in computer science and, in particular, in computer graphics. The benefits derived from the adherence to standards include transportability, simplicity, and efficiency. Data files adhering to standard formats are easily transportable between applications programs, and programs written in standard languages are easily transported between different machines.

The "down side" of standards is that they are made to be broken. That is, a strict adherence to the standard(s) in effect at a given point in time forbids the introduction of innovative new techniques and extended capabilities. To the extent that the standards are "dynamic" in adapting to new hardware and software capabilities, their value as standards is lost. In a rapidly expanding field such as computer graphics, standards are particularly problematic.

Before turning to case studies and the discussion of graphics standards, two classes of standards should be distinguished. They include:

- **Professional standards** – Standards promulgated by widely recognized and respected professional organizations are defined here as professional standards. Organizations such as the American National Standards Institute (ANSI), Association for Computing Machinery (ACM), the Institute for Electrical and Electronic Engineering (IEEE), International Standards Organization (ISO), and the Deutsches Institut für Normung (DIN) play an important role in standardization by establishing committees to study a particular problem, evaluate competing proprietary solutions, incorporate academic generalizations, and finally produce a compromise that attempts to include the best features and minimize the drawbacks of competing systems.

- **De facto standards** – Standards emerging from a particular company, group of companies, or other proprietary sources are defined as *de facto* standards. The widespread acceptance of such standards may result from the standard's intrinsic value and appeal or may result from the desire to "follow the leader" of dominant trends in the industry. Examples include AT&T's UNIX operating system, IBM's EGA, VGA, and XGA graphics cards, Apple's desktop metaphor, and Adobe's POSTSCRIPT page description language.

Case Studies

Consider the following case studies which illustrate both the advantages and difficulties with standards.

- **Standard character codes** – The American National Standards Institute has specified the American Standard Code for Information

Interchange (ASCII) as the standard 7-bit collating sequence for representing the alphanumeric character set. This standard has been nearly universally accepted by hardware manufacturers. As a result, communication between machines of different types is painlessly accomplished by the exchange of ASCII text files. The primary deviation from this standard was IBM's Extended Binary Coded Decimal Interchange Code (EBCDIC), an 8-bit code of which ASCII is a subset.

• **Standard Pascal** – The accepted standard for the Pascal language is the American National Standard Pascal (ANS Pascal).[9] Since the establishment of this standard, many new Pascal implementations have appeared which keep ANS Pascal as a subset but extend the language by the addition of useful data types and graphics functions. Both Turbo Pascal and THINK Pascal, for example, have relaxed some ANS Pascal restrictions and added various useful extensions, among them:

➤ New data types: *longint, double, computational*, and *extended,*
➤ *String-types* and string handling functions,
➤ *Units* for modular construction and compilation of programs,
➤ *Object Pascal* to support object-oriented programming,
➤ Access to the *Macintosh Toolbox* of graphical functions.

By adhering to ANS Pascal as a subset, these dialects have retained the advantage of import compatibility, i.e., both Turbo Pascal and THINK Pascal will run programs written in ANS Pascal. However, by adding extensions, they have lost export compatibility—Turbo and THINK Pascal programs making use of extensions most likely will not run under other Pascal dialects.

• **Graphical Display Standards** – Perhaps the prime example of the value and problem of standards is the history of the *de facto* graphics display standards established by IBM for its PC line and adhered to in varying degree by PC clones. The first standard was the *Color Graphics Adapter* (CGA) giving 320 × 200 pixel resolution in 4 colors. The first significant deviation (extension ?) to this standard was the Hercules monochrome card which provided 720 × 350 pixel resolution in black and white. This was particularly welcomed by users doing word processing. Next came the IBM *Enhanced Graphics Adapter* (EGA) card which provides 640 × 350 pixel resolution in 16 colors. This standard was challenged by IBM's own *Professional Graphics Controller* (PGC) card which gave 640 × 480 pixel resolution in 256 colors. Both EGA and PGC were soon displaced as the state-of-the-art standard by the *Video Graphics Adapter* (VGA) giving 640 × 480 resolution in 16 or 256 colors, depending on card memory. The VGA standard is rapidly giving away to *Super VGA* with a resolution of 1024 × 768 pixels.

The establishment of these *de facto* standards has served a very useful function in providing specifications for second source hardware manufacturers. However, it has also caused headaches for software houses which had to write interface modules for a nearly infinite number of combinations of CPU/interface card/monitors. As a result, software was bulky and cumbersome, and incompatibilities quite common. A typical graphics-dependent application program requires the user to run a "twenty questions" installation program to specify the system configuration. The Macintosh has cleverly avoided such compatibility problems by establishing the Macintosh User Interface Guidelines, enforcing them, and interpreting the hardware configuration invisibly at the system level.[10]

What can we learn from these case studies of standards? The first lesson is that standards achieve their maximum value to the extent that they are widely adhered to and stable over time. The experience with ASCII character codes illustrates this lesson. The second lesson is that standards in dynamic areas of technology are made to be broken. A slavish acceptance of standards can actually impede technological development. The dynamic field of IBM graphics standards demonstrates this. Finally, the value of standards in relatively static areas such as high-level language may be to provide a stable base on which to build powerful extensions.

Graphics Standards

We finish this chapter with a discussion of graphics standards and the role they play in the technological basis of visualization. While the above three case studies of standards are all of interest to computer graphics programmers, of even more immediate concern are the standards for graphics image file formats and graphics implementation languages.

Graphics Image File Formats

Just as the ASCII standard permitted the smooth flow of alphanumeric data between various application programs and various machines, the goal of graphics image file format standards is to facilitate the flow of graphical data between machines and among application programs on a given machine. To the extent that standard graphics image file formats are developed and widely accepted, we can manipulate complex graphics files as easily as we now do text files.

Two general classes of image file formats have emerged with differences which reflect the distinct nature of the images they represent. These two classes can be labeled as pixel-mapped and object-oriented.

- **Pixel-mapped formats** – Pixel-mapped file formats reflect the MacPaint-like nature of the image. That is, if each of the 512×342 pixel values (= 0 or 1) of a B/W Macintosh is specified, the image is completely specified. For color displays, each pixel requires 1, 2, or 3 bytes depending on whether you are encoding 8-, 16-, or 24-bit color. Pixel-mapped formats are of particular value in storing video and digital scanner generated images. We discuss here the *GIF* and *TIFF* formats.

- **Object-oriented formats** – Just as drawing and CAD programs generate their images from precisely defined geometric objects, files used to represent the resulting images are most efficiently encoded by recording commands for generating the objects themselves. Unless the drawing is extremely complex, this scheme should be more economical in use of disk space than simply recording the color of each pixel as do pixel-mapped formats. Another advantage of object-oriented formats is that they accommodate the difference between screen resolution and output device resolution, optimizing the image for

both. The object-oriented file formats of interest to graphics programmers include *DXF*, *EPS*, *IGES*, *NAPLPS*, and *PICT*.

GIF – Graphics Interchange Format

The GIF *de facto* standard is a device independent format developed by the CompuServe Information Service and H&R Block Company for the distribution and exchange of images over the network. It supports 8-bit color images up to 64K pixels on a side. Multiple images may reside on a file, and GIF provides very efficient packing and unpacking of files using the Lempel-Ziv & Welch compression algorithm.[11] This is a valuable feature for transmitting files over a network or by modem.

The field format of GIF files starts with a signature/version block followed by a logical screen descriptor block which specifies the screen height and width, whether or not a global color map exists, the color resolution, background color, pixel size, and aspect ratio. Next come two optional fields, the global color map and an extension block (tag field) which may be used for comments identifying the software or scanning equipment used to create the image.

An image descriptor block follows which defines the top and left coordinates of the image and its height and width along with some control flags. Following this comes an optional local color map and a requisite raster data block containing a block byte count and the actual data bytes defining the image. The final data structures consist of optional extension blocks and a terminator. The actual byte assignment of each field in a GIF file is shown in Figure 2.24 and described by Graef.[12]

Although few image processing application programs support the GIF format, it is a convenient, fast, and efficient format for exchanging graphics files between graphics platforms. The display programs *FastGif* (on the PC) and *Giffer*[13] (on the Mac) are in the public domain. File transfer between the PC and Mac is accomplished simply by connecting their serial ports and running any file transfer program or by reading and writing DOS-compatible files on the Macintosh.

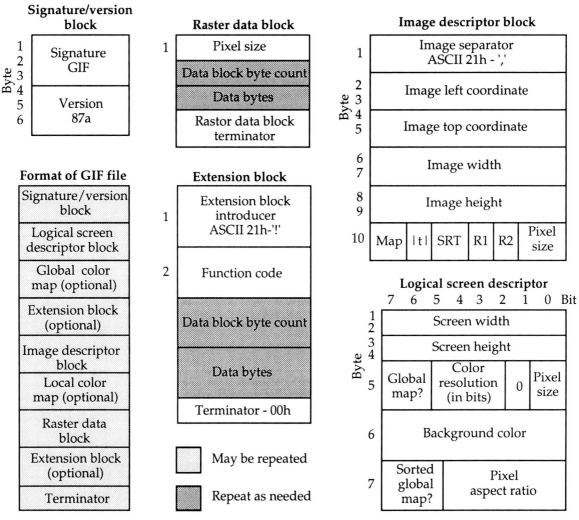

Figure 2.24
GIF Image File Format.

TIFF – Tag-based Image File Format

This *de facto* standard was conceived through a joint venture between Aldus Corporation and Microsoft to support digital scanner manufacturers and desktop publishing systems. The purpose of TIFF is to describe and store raster image data. Its features include the following:

- Capability of describing bilevel, grayscale, palette-color, and full-color image data in several color spaces.

- Support for a number of compression schemes that allow developers to choose the best space or time tradeoff for their applications.

- Independent of specific scanners, printers, or computer display hardware.

- Portability. It does not favor particular operating systems, file systems, compilers, or processors.

- Extensibility to evolve gracefully as new needs arise.

- Inclusion of an unlimited amount of private or special-purpose information.

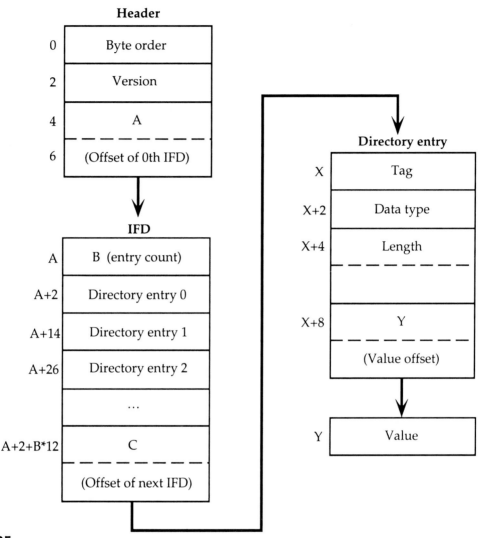

Figure 2.25
Tag-based Image File Format (TIFF). One or more Image File Directories (IFDs) contain pointers to image objects. Offsets are measured in bytes to the referenced element. Details of the TIFF format are given in *TIFF – Rev 6.0*.[14]

As the name implies, TIFF files consist almost exclusively of tag data fields. Tag fields are blocks of data whose first element is a 2-byte *tag*, a unique identifying code which labels the field. The tag-field data structure provides a flexibility and extensibility that is helping TIFF become a standard for image storage and communication. The file format is independent of specific operating systems, processors, compilers, and filing systems. The only assumption is that the system storage medium supports files defined as a sequence of 8-bit bytes numbered from 0 to N. TIFF files may be as large as 2^{32} bytes. Figure 2.25 presents the details of the file format.

The only positional field in TIFF is the 8-byte header which specifies the ordering of the bytes, the version number, and the offset to the first *Image File Directory* (i.e., how many bytes further down the file the directory starts). Next comes the first Image File Directory containing 12N +2 bytes for a TIFF file with N tag-fields. Then additional directories appear for multiple image files following tag-fields which may be included in any order. Each entry in the directory contains the tag, a specification of the data type, the length of data in the tag-field and a pointer to the tag-field location on the file. Version 5.0 of TIFF supports up to 45 tag-fields for storing all essential and informational data concerning the image. In addition to the essential information on image dimensions, color palette, and pixel map, TIFF records information on the specifications of the machine on which the image was generated, the software used to generate it, and the image aspect ratio.

As users and developers extend the tag-image fields to enhance the image or incorporate new image specifications, they are encouraged to register the new tags with Aldus to preserve the uniqueness of the tag-field information.

CAD File Formats

Standard computer-aided design formats include:

- DXF/AutoCAD – Drawing Exchange Files

- IGES – Initial Graphics Exchange Specifications

- NAPLPS – North American Presentation-Level Protocol Syntax

For object-oriented graphics applications, it is frequently more efficient to store a *description of how to draw the image* rather than the image itself. This becomes obvious when considering an image of a single line from the lower left hand corner of the screen to the upper right hand corner. A naive pixel-mapped B/W image would require storing a "1" or "0" for each pixel of the image; an object-oriented file would simply specify the object type ("LINE" as a DXF object) and the (x,y) coordinates of the beginning and end points of the line. Thus, instead of specifying 640 × 480 pixel values to represent the line, an object-oriented file can store its image as a short string and four numbers—a great savings in file space!

A second advantage of object-oriented representations of well-defined graphical objects is that they are screen and output-device independent. This enhances the transportability of object-oriented files and exploits the full resolution capabilities of the current output device. For all of these reasons, object-oriented files are the preferred standard for drawing and CAD programs. Three of the most widely used object-oriented CAD file formats are the ANSI standards, NAPLPS and IGES, and the *de facto* industry standard, DXF.

NAPLPS offers a wide range of graphical commands for encoding features such as geometric shapes, text scaling and rotation, color palettes, and mosaic graphics. Because graphical objects are encoded in a simple, straight-forward way, they may be decoded rapidly. This speed allows NAPLPS to be used as a format for simple animation displays. However, since video and digitally scanned images contain no well-defined mathematical objects, NAPLPS is not an appropriate format for storing such images.

IGES is another ANSI industry standard widely used by workstation, minicomputer, and mainframe-based CAD applications. DXF is the file format widely used for exchanging CAD files between *AutoCAD*, the leading CAD system, and other CAD programs. A number of translator programs have emerged for converting between various CAD file formats. One of the first programs available for the Mac was *CADMOVER* by Kandu Software. The Apple Computer spin-off company, Claris, has released *Claris Graphics Translator* (CGT) for interconversion between MacDraw, PICT, IGES, and DXF files. International Microcomputer Software, Inc. markets the *Graphics Transformer* program which runs on MS-DOS machines and is capable of interconversion between essentially all graphics file formats on both DOS and Mac machines.

PICT – The Macintosh Object/Image File Format

Apple Computer Corporation has developed a proprietary file format for handling both object-oriented images and images from scanners and video digitizers. The first version of this format, *PICT*, encoded bit-mapped images in terms of *QuickDraw* commands; version 2, called *PICT2*, has a virtually identical format but encodes the images in *Color QuickDraw* commands. A convenient mental image of a PICT file is that of a recording of the QuickDraw commands required to draw an image. If the series of commands is issued directly to the computer, a standard QuickDraw image appears. If the series of commands is saved to a file and played back later, the same image appears. The file in which these commands are stored is the PICT file.

In Figure 2.26, the general structure of a PICT file is illustrated. The file structure consists of a fixed length header containing application-specific information including size, scaling and version. Following the 512-byte informational header comes a 2-byte picture size field and an 8-byte picture frame field ([x,y] for top, left, bottom, and right corner). The main body of the PICT file is a sequence of op-codes and arguments for encoded

QuickDraw commands to reconstruct the image. Op-codes are 2-byte (4-digit hexadecimal) commands such as: *fill pattern* = $000A, *Line* = $0020. and *paintOval* = $0051. Immediately following each op-code command is its argument, shown in the figure as *picture data*. Depending on the complexity of the data, arguments range from 0 – 12 bytes in length. The final field of a PICT file is the *opEndPic* = $00FF command. Byte-level details of the PICT file structure are given in *Inside Macintosh, Vol. V.*[15]

Clearly PICT files can range greatly in their complexity and length. PICT files are opened by the QuickDraw *OpenPicture* routine, closed by the *ClosePicture* routine, and displayed using *DrawPicture*. PICT files are very efficient formats for encoding object-oriented images and, a bit surprisingly, also efficient for storing general image information from scanners. They share the device-independent, high-resolution advantages of strictly object-oriented file standards and retain the generality of pixel-mapped standards such as TIFF files. PICT is a proprietary Apple format that has become the *de facto* standard within the Macintosh community.

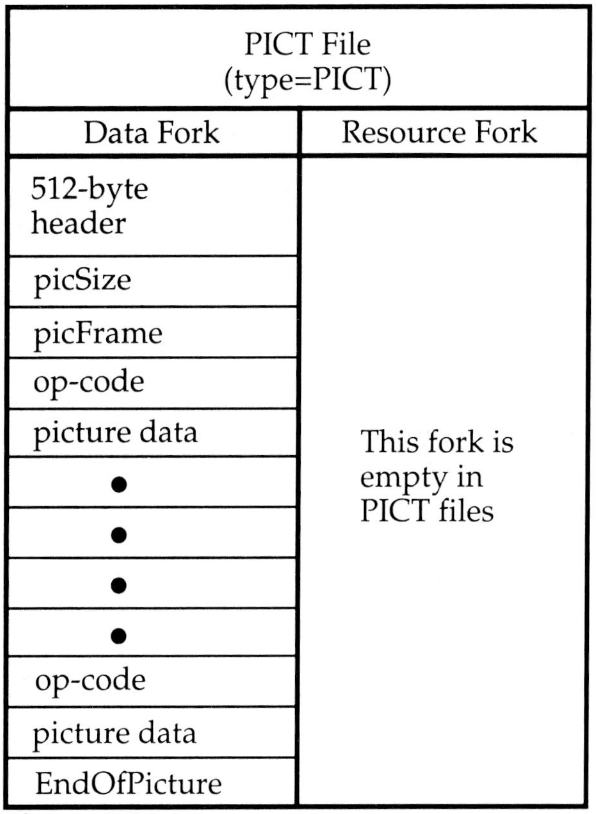

EPS – Encapsulated PostScript Files

POSTSCRIPT by Adobe Systems has become one of the most successful graphics languages. We examine some of its features in the next section. Just as PICT files encode a sequence of QuickDraw routines which generate an image, so EPS files encode a sequence of PostScript commands to generate an image. Since EPS commands are machine- and device-independent and supported by all PostScript equipped printers, the PostScript language has become a new *de facto* standard. And since EPS files are essentially "recordings" of PostScript commands, we turn next to the subject of graphics language standards.

Graphics Implementation Languages

The goal of a graphics implementation language (GL) is to provide a standard set of graphics functions and procedures which span the range of hardware and software systems. The objectives of an ideal GL standard should include:

- **Input device independent** – It should support mice, data tablets, light pens, joy sticks, track balls, and buttons in a uniform and logically consistent fashion.

PICT File (type=PICT)	
Data Fork	**Resource Fork**
512-byte header	This fork is empty in PICT files
picSize	
picFrame	
op-code	
picture data	
●	
●	
●	
●	
op-code	
picture data	
EndOfPicture	

Figure 2.26
PICT File Format. Note the "macro-like" structure of op-code followed by image data. Opening a PICT file corresponds to playing back the sequence of graphics commands encoded in QuickDraw op-code commands.

- **Processor independent** – It should run efficiently on machines ranging from micros to supercomputers with word lengths from 8 to 64 bits.

- **Output device independent** – It should drive and optimize the output on all devices, including dot matrix, inkjet, laser, and typesetting printers, electrostatic and pen plotters, and film and video recorders.

- **Language independent** – It should provide transparent access to all routines and system functions from any programming or applications language.

- **System integration** – It should support effective communication within network architectures and with image I/O devices, including video and digital scanners.

Building a GL standard which satisfies this set of enormously difficult goals has proven insurmountable to date. First, we consider some of the problems, then some of the technological breakthroughs which are helping resolve these problems, and finally a discussion of the major standard GLs and their features.

The problems which have bedeviled the attempts at implementing a GL standard include:

- **Proprietary hardware differences** – The hardware emerging from IBM, DEC, HP, Apple, Sun, Tektronix, Calcomp, and a host of other computer and peripheral manufacturers have historically been based on different processors, operating systems, and communications protocols. Graphics support for a given system was proprietary and designed to optimize the performance of the particular processor, operating system, and display device.

- **Rapid evolution of devices** – The evolution and multiplicity of pointing devices, for instance, makes standardization difficult. The basic difference between vector-oriented and bit-mapped storage and display of graphical information requires different techniques for optimizing storage and display algorithms. The evolution of color from 1-bit through 24/32-bit has provided a moving target for any standards specification committee.

- **Lack of system integration** – As second sources supplied graphics adapter boards, display boards, and printers, the number of possible configurations of a given graphics workstation exploded. Since new devices appear daily on the market, the problem of developing a "standard" which optimizes the performance of such dynamic and variable systems is indeed huge. The initial lack of device drivers for Microsoft/IBM's *OS/2* and *Presentation Manager* systems illustrates this problem.

A number of technological breakthroughs promise to resolve many of the most serious problems and facilitate the development of a standard graphics language. The most promising of these include:

- **Emergence of standard processor and graphics coprocessor families** – Both Intel and Motorola have been careful to build downward compatibility into their respective 80X86 and 680X0 lines of processors. These processors, particularly those with X ≥ 3, are very capable graphics engines and are assuming the role of standards, at least in low-end graphics workstations. The widespread use of graphics coprocessor chips across a range of manufacturers' workstations will also simplify GL standard development.

- **Emergence of standard display devices** – High-resolution raster (pixel-mapped) displays are rapidly emerging as the display device standard. A raster terminal with resolution > 1,000 in both dimensions and 16M colors is capable of displaying photo-realistic images which are more than adequate for the vast majority of all graphics applications. The widespread recognition of this fact is building pressure for a new standard in display device.

- **Standardization of page description languages** – The widespread acceptance of POSTSCRIPT as a *de facto* page description language standard has proven to be a huge step towards the goal of GL standardization. More and more output devices are supporting POSTSCRIPT or one of its "look-alike" clones.

- **Emergence of interoperability** – The consortium between Apple and IBM has formalized an emerging trend – the interoperability between these two major platform builders. Application programs such as MS-Word, MS-Excel, WingZ, Pagemaker, dBASE, and Lotus 123 were already advertising file compatibility between their nearly identical products for the Macintosh and IBM platforms. A specific goal of the Apple/IBM consortium is to provide program as well as file interoperability between these two major systems.

To understand the present state of affairs one should know something of the history of GL standards. Some of the major languages which have been proposed and, in some cases, adopted as graphics standards are summarized below.

Additional information on the history and features of computer graphics languages is presented by Rankin.[16]

CORE System

By 1977 the proliferation of graphics systems and the complete lack of any graphics language standards led ACM's *Special Interest Group on Computer Graphics* (SIGGRAPH) to propose the CORE standard.[17] In 1979 the graphics standardization activities started by SIGGRAPH were turned over to ANSI which formed committee ANSI X3H3 with considerable membership overlap from the original SIGGRAPH committee.

The CORE standard never received final approval as an international graphics standard language. However, much of the logical framework and syntax proposed in CORE survives as the basis for subsequent approved standard languages. For instance, CORE proposed the classification of logical input devices: *button, pick, keyboard, valuator, locator,* and *stroke* – the scheme subsequently adopted by the international standard GKS. Many of the CORE commands (e.g., *setwindow, lineabs2, moverel2*) provided the model for subsequent graphics languages from Borland's PC Turbo Graphix Toolbox to the Macintosh QuickDraw routines.

Since CORE is a very large system encompassing both 2D and 3D graphics, many graphics authors have chosen a simpler subset of the language for illustrating their texts. However, because it was issued before the advent of bit-mapped color graphics, CORE does not support any of the fill and pattern commands widely available on modern workstations. It also does not support the high-level arc, oval, and spline commands which many systems provide as intrinsic functions. Students of graphics should be aware of the contributions CORE has made to the standardization enterprise, but we shall not consider it further in this book since it is not supported on graphics workstations.

GKS – Graphics Kernel System

The initial design of GKS began in Germany in 1975, about the same time that work began on the CORE system. After 7 revisions, an enormous amount of work by an active core of about thirty people, and the participation of about 100 experts from sixteen nations, the GKS standard was accepted by the ISO and published ten years later in 1985.[18] José Encarnação was the chairman of the

first DIN-GKS committee and prime mover in the early development of GKS. The fascinating history of this development and some considerations which went into the design of the GKS are spelled out in detail by Enderle, Kansy, and Pfaff.[19]

Some of the design issues which were considered include:

- **Should GKS support 3D primitives?** The decision was made to define GKS as a 2D graphics standard, primarily to make the problem of reaching a consensus easier. A later extension, GKS-3D, defined the 3D standard based on the earlier CORE 3D work.

- **Should GKS support a "current position" (CP) register?** A CP register is standard practice for many graphics systems and simplifies commands involving relative motion. However, it also complicates issues of text and fill primitives and to which coordinate system the CP refers. The CP register concept was discarded.

- **Should GKS provide "high-level primitives"** such as arc, circle, and spline? Some workstations already support these functions in hardware, and any graphics language should allow access to such intrinsic functions. However, for systems without such functions, adding them would have increased the work of implementing the standard and increased its size. The issue was resolved by a compromise which added a *Generalized Drawing Primitive* function giving the user access to machine-dependent functions.

- **Should GKS support hierarchical segment structure?** Segmentation in computer graphics offers the same advantages as do modules in structured programming. Complex graphical objects are constructed more simply by assembling previously defined primitive objects (segments). The GKS compromise on this issue was to offer segmentation, but only at one level. Hierarchical segmentation is not supported.

This brief glimpse at the issues confronting those defining the GKS graphical language standard illustrate the problematic nature of standards. By homogenizing the language so that it becomes acceptable to everyone and runs on all machines, you must make compromises which discard some of the highest-level graphics options available. The result lacks the innovative features of "cutting-edge" technologies.

In addition, to implement GKS on any given system, it is necessary to write the GKS functions in terms of the intrinsic system functions, many of which may be equivalent to, or even more powerful than, the corresponding GKS function. This adds another layer of code to any graphics application with the inevitable result of system degradation. Since many graphics algorithms are already compute bound, this may be an unacceptable price to pay for the transportability that a standard language offers.

These comments are not meant to disparage the great accomplishment that GKS represents. The language meets most of the criteria set out earlier in this chapter as ideals for any standard. One of the most important contributions of GKS was the careful study of issues influencing the design of graphics standards and languages. It also strongly influenced the design of subsequent graphics standards (e.g., PHIGS) which emerged to overcome some of the limitations of GKS.

PHIGS – Programmer's Hierarchical Interactive Graphics Standard

PHIGS is the reincarnation of CORE with special attention to hierarchical segmentation and full 3D functionality. It was developed by a committee of the American National Standards Institute and has been approved as an ANSI standard.[20] Several features distinguish PHIGS. Its object-oriented segmentation structure contains graphical primitives, attributes, and transformations, all of which may be edited interactively. Segments may be referenced or copied from other segments, thus requiring only one copy of the original segment. Attributes of a supersegment are placed on a stack when a subsegment is executed and restored when the lower-level execution is completed. This hierarchical segmentation structure provides for great flexibility and efficiency of image storage.

PHIGS takes great care to distinguish the *building* and *manipulation* of graphical objects, on the one hand, from their *display*, on the other. The creation of graphical objects, called modeling, is done in a device-independent way, and the GKS-like functions used to model the data are placed in a *centralized structure store* (CSS). When the modeling is complete, the modeled structure is *posted*, i.e., sent to a display or output device. Thus the machine-dependent device drivers may be completely isolated and confined to the posting function. This paradigm closely resembles that used by the POSTSCRIPT language.

A somewhat more controversial feature of PHIGS is the monolithic nature of the system. It does not permit the "tool box" metaphor of assembling small, efficient, special-purpose systems by pulling functions from the toolbox. Thus, it is difficult to build a simple 2D subset of the PHIGS language. We have attempted, however, to use the PHIGS nomenclature and philosophy in the construction of FIGS (Fundamental Interactive Graphics System), a subset of PHIGS used to build a GUI application program in the chapter on designing graphical user interfaces. Appendix B specifies the FIGS routines and calling sequence in detail.

The design criteria in building PHIGS explicitly specify that it is to be a super-set of GKS. That is, for all features with similar functionality, PHIGS defaults to the syntax and behavior of GKS. Thus, nearly one hundred of PHIGS's three hundred functions have identical names and functionality as the GKS 2D functions. This is good judgment not only from a standards engineering perspective—it also served to enhance its acceptability to the ISO committee which recently approved it as a standard. The attempts to harmonize the PHIGS and GKS standards are discussed at some length by Encarnação, the guru of GKS.[21]

PHIGS PLUS is a proposed extension which provides more advanced graphical modeling and rendering capabilities.[22] It is under consideration as an international standard by the ISO. Some of the additional features offered by PHIGS PLUS include:

- **Advanced data structures:** triangle strip for organizing connected triangles and quadrilateral mesh for organizing quadrilateral facets.

- **Curve and surface representation:** nonuniform B-splines (NURBS) for manipulation of curves and surfaces.

- **Better rendering capabilities:** illumination source definition, color specification, and shading parameter controls.

Neither PHIGS nor PHIGS PLUS is yet capable of producing photorealistic images since they lack features for rendering shadows, reflections, transparency, and surface textures. However, the extensions of PHIGS PLUS generate much more pleasing and useful output for practical applications in design and engineering. An excellent introduction to PHIGS and PHIGS PLUS is given in Howard *et al.*[23] A commercial version of PHIGS, called FIGARO+, is described in an extensive manual and is available for a variety of graphics and UNIX workstations.[24]

POSTSCRIPT

Of the examples considered here, POSTSCRIPT comes the closest to the criteria for the ideal graphical language. John Warnock, its author, describes the evolution of the language through three stages: its origin as the *Design System* from his work at the Evans & Sutherland Computer Corporation beginning in 1976, its development as *JaM* (for "John and Martin") from his work with Martin Newell at Xerox PARC beginning in 1978, and its culmination as *POSTSCRIPT* in 1982 when he and Charles Geschke incorporated Adobe Systems to market the language.[25]

Through the cooperation of Warnock and Steven Jobs of Apple Computer, POSTSCRIPT was selected as the printer driver for the Apple LaserWriter. The combination produced printed output of near typeset quality, and the desktop publishing industry was born. Soon POSTSCRIPT drivers were available for Linotronic printers as the output device for the Macintosh, thereby making available true type-set quality and extremely high-resolution graphics. POSTSCRIPT has spread to many other computer systems and is rapidly becoming the *de facto* standard graphics language.

Let's look at some of its features.

- POSTSCRIPT is a complete programming language, not just a graphics language. It is a FORTH-like interpreter with standard data types (real, Boolean, array, and string), variables, operators, operands, control primitives (conditionals, loops, and procedures), and recursion.

- POSTSCRIPT is a high-level, device-independent graphics language. One-third of the language is devoted to graphics, with functions ranging from simple primitives (*moveto, lineto, rmoveto*) to object-oriented transformations (*translate, rotate, scale*). Its sophisticated *clipping path* permits clipping to arbitrary shaped windows.

- POSTSCRIPT's imaging model consists of a *current page* on which one paints *text, geometric figures,* and *sampled images*. The user works in *user space* on the current page and POSTSCRIPT automatically maps the completed current page to the particular output device's *device space*. Text is mapped to the device space as graphical objects and, as such, may be positioned, scaled, rotated, and otherwise manipulated just as any other graphical object.

- POSTSCRIPT's programming model consists of a last in, first out (LIFO) *stack* on which any POSTSCRIPT object may be pushed. Objects include numbers, variables, arrays, strings, composite graphical objects, and dictionaries.

- POSTSCRIPT dictionaries are unique POSTSCRIPT objects that are stored on a dictionary stack. The first object pushed onto the stack is the *system dictionary* containing operator-name/action pairs. The second object pushed onto the stack is the *user dictionary* which associates names with the procedures defined by the program.

- POSTSCRIPT solves the problem of output device independence by requiring that the output device be intelligent enough to interpret and properly print the POSTSCRIPT commands sent it by the host computer. Thus, each POSTSCRIPT printer is really another computer, typically with a M680X0 processor and 1 – 4 MB of memory, dedicated to nothing but decoding and printing POSTSCRIPT.

It is interesting that POSTSCRIPT has achieved such phenomenal success as a *de facto* standard, while the major international graphics standards are "lumping along." POSTSCRIPT is well ahead of the other standards in its total flexibility in handling text and its capability for processing sampled images. However, it is not yet the complete answer to the graphics programmer's needs. Missing features include:

- Interactive graphical device input is not supported. POSTSCRIPT doesn't even know that the mouse exists.

- With the exception of the Next Machine which uses Display POSTSCRIPT on the screen, output is limited to POSTSCRIPT-compatible printers. That is, the user cannot visualize on the screen the elegant POSTSCRIPT output s/he is about to get on hard copy. With POSTSCRIPT, WYSINWYG (what you see is *not* what you get).

X Windows

While it is neither strictly a graphics language nor a graphics file format, X Windows has become one of the most important standards in computer graphics. It can perhaps best be described as a system for the communication and manipulation of graphical information in a network environment.[26] The X Windows system grew out of MIT's Project Athena, an experiment in the use of networked graphics workstations as a teaching aid. The Athena team released X Windows into the public domain, and it was so successful that Hewlett-Packard and DEC designed new workstations around it.

In 1988, a consortium was formed, including MIT, Apollo, Apple, AT&T, DEC, HP, IBM, Sun, Tektronix, and other leading manufacturers, to establish X Windows as an ANSI standard. The X Consortium froze the X Windows specifications through 1991 at the X11 level in order to fix its bugs, add 3D extensions to support the PHIGS standard, and obtain ANSI approval.

What are some of the features of the X Windows System that has led to this success?[27]

- **System Independence** – X Windows defines graphics protocols which enable it to run on a variety of machines under a variety of operating systems. In this way it resembles UNIX and, in fact, serves as the primary graphical interface to UNIX systems.

- **Network Support** – The daunting task of communicating across different machines and operating systems simultaneously within a given network has been effectively solved by the X Windows System. X Windows supports a client-server model within a multiple-window, multitasking environment under UNIX.

- **GUI Tools** – X Windows provides a hierarchy of graphical user interface tools for assisting the programmer in designing new applications. At the lowest level is *Xlib*, a C-based interface to the X protocol. Built on top of this are the *Xt Intrinsics*, a

library of more abstract routines performing the Xlib functions. The Athena *widget set*, in turn, is a set of generic user interface objects built from Xt Intrinsics and used for constructing graphical objects such as windows and menus.

- **Open Architecture** – Rather than enforcing a rigid "look and feel" for applications developed under X Windows, the system encourages freedom and flexibility in developing customized toolkits and interface formats. Commercial application developers, for instance, have written alternate widget sets including OSF.Motif and Open Look Toolkit for greater functionality and ease of development.

X Windows is not designed for stand-alone workstations running a limited number of commercial application programs. To the extent that workstations connect to networks of heterogeneous platforms, however, X Windows demonstrates the value of standards by offering a proven system for integration and communication of graphical information.

Conclusions

The power of modern computer graphics workstations is optimized through the careful integration of hardware, software, and graphics standards. As a result of the exponential improvement in performance/price ratio, high-performance workstations are readily available for less than $10K and capable instructional systems cost well under $2K. The technological basis of computer graphics is caught up in a three- stage positive feed-back loop: The surge in high-performance hardware has led to the development of a plethora of excellent drawing, drafting, CAD, image processing, and desktop publishing software, which has, in turn, driven the evolution of graphics file and language standards. The acceptance and use of *de facto* standards such as PICT, TIFF, and EPS files and the POSTSCRIPT language has resulted in widespread generation and dissemination of graphical data. This, in turn, increases the demand for more and better hardware—and the cycle continues. This survey of the technological basis of visualization should help the reader understand the graphics industry and better evaluate the professional opportunities it offers.

Exercises

2.1 Exponential growth in any quantity exhibits two easily recognizable features: (a) a straight line on a logarithmic plot of the quantity vs. time, and (b) a constant doubling time. From the straight line growth curve in Figure 2.2, estimate the doubling time in RAM memory available on PCs.

2.2 Plot the two data points on the cost of floppy disk storage given in the text on semi-log paper and estimate the doubling time in the performance/price ratio. What assumptions are necessary to make this a valid conclusion?

2.3 Scan some issues of the journals and trade magazines listed in the reference section for advertisements of PC/Mac-based software packages for accomplishing some of the "hard tasks" previously reserved for larger computers. These may include CAD, finite element analysis, and cartographic mapping programs. Write a brief description summarizing the features of two such programs.

2.4 The architecture of a theoretical graphics workstation is shown in Figure 2.6. Can you spot a logical inconsistency in the figure? What is it? What devices would you suggest to augment the input device list? What additional output devices would you suggest? How could the system be integrated into a workstation network?

2.5 CRT monitors were one of the earliest and remain the most common output display device (see Figure 2.7). They maintain this position in spite of many drawbacks. List the major disadvantages of CRT displays and indicate the extent to which LCDs have solved these problems.

2.6 From the detailed specifications given for the Macintosh screen display frequency, blanking intervals, and so on, plot a graph of the horizontal sweep voltage, $V_h(t)$, applied to the horizontal deflection plates for a time interval of 89.86 µs. Scale the ordinate to a maximum voltage V_{max}.

2.7 From the screen display information, plot the vertical sweep voltage, $V_v(t)$, over the time interval of 33.25 ms.

2.8 Even with a shadow mask, the image on CRT monitors sometimes "shimmies" because of stray fields and can become very distorted in the presence of external magnets and motors. What common feature of LCDs and plasma display panels prevents these problems?

2.9 Assuming bit-mapped or pixel-mapped images, compute how much storage is required for each of the following image formats:
   a) $512 \times 342 \times 1$-bit B/W
   b) $640 \times 350 \times 4$-bit color
   c) $640 \times 480 \times 8$-bit color
   d) $1024 \times 768 \times 16$-bit color
   e) $8'' \times 10''$ 24-bit @ 300 dpi [scanner image]
What do these numbers suggest to you in terms of specifications for graphics workstation hard disk or other storage requirements?

2.10 When mice began to become commonplace, arguments raged over the 1-button mouse (Mac format) vs. the 3-button mouse (PC-format). Discuss the pros and cons of each format. What is your personal preference?

2.11 Optical drives with storage capacities of 300MB – 1,000 MB come in three varieties: CD-ROM (read only), WORM (write once, read many), and erasable read/write CDs. From a perusal of the computer magazine trade literature, list the prices for comparable capacity disks from each of these classes. What are the relative advantages and disadvantages of each?

2.12 Two of the three phases of high-resolution color image processing (generation/input and display) are now economically available. The bottleneck to full low-cost color image processing is in the output phase. From a study of the literature, describe three color output devices (spatial resolution, color resolution, size and format of image, system compatibility, and cost).

2.13 Operating systems can generally be classified as command line-oriented (textual) or icon-oriented (graphical). UNIX and MS-DOS are examples of the first, and the Mac and NEXT machines are examples of the second. Write a brief comparison of the two operating systems from your personal experience. (If you have not yet done so, run a couple of application programs on each type.)

2.14 From the computer lab library obtain a copy of the reference manual for some version of Pascal for either the Macintosh or IBM PC and scan it for graphics routines. List four primitive graphics functions (*lineto*, etc.) and four high-level routines (*drawRectangle*, etc.) along with their arguments and calling sequence, and indicate which Pascal dialect you found.

2.15 Using a graphical spreadsheet (e.g., WINGZ, Excel, or Quatro Pro), key in the two-column special function distribution of Table 2.1 and plot it out as a pie chart. What does this chart tell you that is not immediately obvious from the table?

2.16 Using a paint program (MacPaint or SuperPaint on the Mac or WindowsPaint on the PC) reconstruct a painting similar to Figure 2.22. Then manipulate it to reproduce Figure 2.23. Finally, from the university phone directory, create an organizational chart of the campus' top administrators.

2.17 Using your favorite paint program create the most imaginative, original art work you can, using as many of the palette tools as possible. Your instructor will judge the class efforts as an art contest and announce and display the top three winners.

2.18 Standards have served a very important role in the development of computer science. Discuss five advantages which the adoption of a good standard offers and rank them in decreasing order of importance. Give two examples of successful standards in computer science.

2.19 Standards also have their "down side." Discuss five possible problems of adopting a standard, and list them in decreasing order of importance.

2.20 In the Conclusions section we interpreted the hardware/software/standards synergy as a positive feedback loop driving the industry. The opposite side of the coin is the negative feedback or "chicken and egg" problem often facing newly released hardware and software. (e.g., Why is no one buying computer X? Well, because there is no software out there which will run on it. Why is there no software? Well, who would build software for a computer no one is buying?) From the trade journals, locate and summarize a story on a particular product which illustrates this problem.

Endnotes

1. The following is a useful, but by no means complete, list of journals and trade magazines providing information on new visualization tools in computer graphics:

> *Computer Graphics*, ACM SIGGRAPH
> *Computer Graphics and Applications*, IEEE, Los Alamitos, CA
> *Computer Vision, Graphics, and Image Processing*, Academic Press, San Diego, CA 92101
> *Scientific Computing and Automation*, Gordon Publications, Inc., P. O. Box 650, Morris Plains, NJ 07950-0650
> *Computers & Graphics – An International Journal of Applications in Computer Graphics*, Pergamon Press, Inc., Maxwell House, Fairview Park, Elmsford, NY, 10523
> *Computer Graphics World*, PennWell Publishing Company, Westford, MA 01886
> *GRAPHIS – The International Journal of Visual Communication*, 141 Lexington Ave., New York, NY 10016
> *BYTE*, A McGraw-Hill publication, One Phoenix Mill Lane, Peterborough, NH 03458
> *Info World*, 1060 Marsh Road, Suite c-2000, Menlo Park, CA 94025
> *PC Magazine*, A Ziff-Davis publication, One Park Ave., New York, NY 10016
> *PC World*, P. O. Box 51833, Boulder, CO 80321-1833
> *Mac World*, P. O. Box 54529, Boulder, CO 80322-4529
> *Mac Week*, P. O. Box 5821, Cherry Hill, NJ 08034.

2. Graphics display screens are typically described by citing their horizontal and vertical dimensions in *pixels*. Pixel is the mnemonic for *picture element*, and is the smallest addressable graphical object. On black-and-white screens each pixel has a

binary value: 0 for white and 1 for black. On colored screens, the color of each pixel is defined by an N-bit word where N = 3, 4, 8, 16, or 24 bits.

3. Machover, Carl, "A Brief, Personal History of Computer Graphics", *IEEE Computer*, November (1978).

4. Apple Computer Company, *Inside Macintosh, Vol. III*, Addison-Wesley Publishing Company, Inc., pp. 18–19 (1985).

5. Slottow, Hiram Gene, "Plasma Displays," *IEEE Transactions on Electron Devices* **ED-23**, No. 7, July (1976).

6. Wohlers, Terry, "A Mac Test Drive – Evaluating the new Mac IIci as a CAD platform," *Computer Graphics World* 13, pp. 69–74, January (1990).

7. Free access to supercomputers is available for academic purposes from:
   Janice Friedland
   User Administration Coordinator
   JvN National Supercomputer Center
   P.O. Box 3717
   Princeton, NJ 08593
   On e-mail, contact *friedland@jvnca.csc.org*.

8. Sutherland, I. E., "Sketchpad: A Man-Machine Graphical Communication System," *AFIPS* **23**, pp. 329–346 (1963).

9. *An American National Standard IEEE Standard Pascal Computer Programming Language*, ANSI/IEEE770X3.97-1983, IEEE, Wiley-Interscience (1983).

10. Apple Computer, Inc., *Inside Macintosh* **I**, pp. 27–70 (1985).

11. Welch, Terry A., "A Technique for High-Performance Data Compression," *IEEE Computer* **17**, No. 6, June (1984).

12. Graef, Gerald L., "Graphics Formats – A close look at GIF, TIFF, and other attempts at a universal image format," *BYTE* **14**, No. 9, pp. 305–310, September (1989).

13. According to its author, Steve Blackstock, *Giffer* is officially Beerware™. If you use it and like it you are invited to send $20 for a case of beer to the author at 40 Bartlett Ave, Lexington, MA 02173. You then become a registered user and receive *Giffer* updates.

14. Aldus Developers Desk, "TIFF™ – Revision 6.0." Final – June 3, 1992. Available from:
   Aldus Corporation
   411 First Avenue South
   Seattle, WA 98104-2871
   (206)628-6593.

See also: "TIFF Access and Creation Library," available from:
   Image Software Associates
   P. O. Box 1634
   Danville, CA 94526.

15. Apple Computer, Inc., *Inside Macintosh* **V**, pp. 84–105 (1986).

16. Rankin, John R., *Computer Graphics Software Construction*, pp. 456–480, Prentice Hall, New York, NY (1989).

17. "Status Report of the Graphics Standards Planning Committee of ACM/SIGGRAPH," *Computer Graphics* **11**, No. 3, Fall (1977). See also same title, *Computer Graphics* **13**, No. 3, Fall (1979) and *Computer Graphics*, Special GKS Issue, February (1984).

18. Hopgood, F. R. A., Duce, D. A., Gallop, J. R., and Sutcliffe, D. C., *Introduction to the Graphical Kernal System*, Second Edition, Academic Press, 250 p., (1986).

19. Enderle, G., Kansy, K., and Pfaff, G., *Computer Graphics Programming: GKS – The Graphics Standard*, Second Edition, Springer-Verlag, Berlin (1987).

20. American National Standards Institute, *PHIGS Baseline Document*, Document ANSI/X3H3/85-21 (1985). See also International Organization for Standardization, *Information Processing – Computer Graphics – Programmer's Hierarchical Interactive Graphics Standard (PHIGS)*, TC97 SC21/N819 (June, 1986).

21. Encarnação, José, "R & D Issues and Trends Consequent Upon GKS and Related Standards," in *Techniques for Computer Graphics*, David F. Rogers and Rae A. Earnshaw (eds), Springer-Verlag, pp. 443–454, New York, NY (1987).

22. van Dam, Andries, "PHIGS+ – Functional Description, Revision 3.0," *Computer Graphics* **22**, No. 3, July (1988).

23. Howard, T. L. J., Hewitt, W. T., Hubbold, R. J., and Wyrwas, K. M., *A Practical Introduction to PHIGS and PHIGS PLUS*, Addison-Wesley Publishing Company, Wokingham, England (1991).

24. Template Graphics Software, Inc., *Using PHIGS with Figaro+*, TGS, 3510 Dunhill Street, San Diego, CA 92121 (1990).

25. Adobe Systems, Incorporated, *POSTSCRIPT Language Reference Manual*, Addison-Wesley Publishing Company, Reading, MA (1985) See also Adobe Systems, Incorporated, *POSTSCRIPT Language Tutorial and Cookbook*,

Addison-Wesley Publishing Company, Reading, MA (1985).

26. Clifford, H. B. J., Satchell, Stephen T., and King, Peggy, "Graphics under UNIX," *Personal Workstation* **2**, No. 10, pp. 52–56, October (1990). See also: Lainhart, Todd, "Intrinsics of the X Toolkit," *Dr. Dobb's Journal* **16**, No. 2, pp. 94–100, February (1991).

27. Smith, Jerry, *Object-oriented Programming with the X Window System Toolkits*, John Wiley & Sons, Inc., New York, NY (1991)

Chapter 3

Tools for Interaction –
Object-Oriented Programming

I think of a computer display as a window on Alice's Wonderland in which a programmer can depict either objects that obey well-known natural laws or purely imaginary objects that follow laws he has written into his program.
Ivan Sutherland

In the first two chapters we attempted to establish the key role computer graphics plays in helping users visualize their work, and the technological tools which make this visualization possible. In this chapter we jump right in and demonstrate the interactive techniques on which modern computer graphics is based. First, we discuss a *programming environment* in which we will build our applications. Next, we introduce the concept of *graphical objects* from an object-oriented programming point of view. Then, *event handling techniques* are discussed and demonstrated with some simple algorithms. Finally, *interactive graphics techniques* are surveyed, and an algorithm for one of the more useful techniques is presented.

One definition of computer graphics is the *creation and manipulation of graphical objects*. While this statement may appear intuitively obvious or even trivial, the essential nature of computer graphics is almost completely determined by the design decisions involved in representing graphical objects and the operations available for their creation and manipulation. The objectives of this chapter are to examine these design issues in detail and to create tools for interaction with graphical objects.

Programming Environments

Artificial intelligence research has emphasized the importance of the development environment in the productivity of programmers and system developers. The programming environment is at least as important as language features in

determining the quality of code and speed with which it is generated. Elements of a an integrated development environment include:

- Program hierarchy structure ,
- Integrated editor with syntax checking,
- Object-oriented class library,
- Incremental, high-speed compiler,
- Powerful debugging tools,
- Access to Application Programming Interface (API) routines,
- Online, context sensitive help,
- Integration with other languages and applications.

Several supportive integrated development environments have emerged that provide many or all of these features.[1] We demonstrate several features of one such programming environment, THINK Pascal, manufactured by a Symantec, company with deep roots in the artificial intelligence enterprise.[2]

A Pascal Programming Environment Implementation

The abstract programming environment concepts summarized above are best understood by observing them in action, that is, by studying an actual implementation. The example environment provides all of the elements of a supportive programming environment listed above. In addition, it includes a number of language extensions such as the object-oriented features of

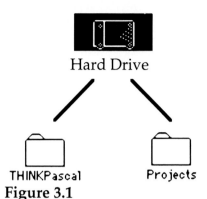

Figure 3.1
Overall file structure for the Pascal application folder and the user project folder.

Object Pascal, an object-oriented extension of Standard Pascal. Some of the most important features are now summarized.

Hierarchical Structure

Among the more useful hierarchical features of this language are *projects*, *units*, and *libraries*. Units and libraries are fairly common Pascal extensions for building modular programs through top-down design. Our model environment adds the *project* as a hierarchical structure containing the main program and all associated units and libraries. A suggested file structure for the Hierarchical File System on the Macintosh is shown in Figure 3.1.

The Pascal application folder contains the integrated Pascal editor-linker-compiler, libraries, units, and utilities folders as shown in Figure 3.2.

The *Projects* folder is a HFS structure containing individual project folders, such as *Project1*, *Project2*, and *Project3* as shown in Figure 3.3. The contents of a typical project, *Project 2*, are also shown.

The project file, *Project2.π*, is the focus of the programming environment. You can think of the project file as the collection of all the essential elements of your completed program—the object code into which your source code is compiled, the library routines called by your program, all units used by your program, and the bookkeeping records indicating how they should all be linked together. The Pascal editor provides a *Project* menu which contains the following options:

- New Project,
- Close Project,
- Add File,
- Build Library,
- Remove Objects,
- Compile Options,
- Open Project,
- Add Window,
- Remove,
- Build Applications,
- Set Project Type,
- View Options.

The *Project* menu contains the necessary tools for assembling all the elements into a complete, stand-alone program. In addition to standard application programs, special applications programs called *desk accessories*, *device drivers*, and *code resources* may be created by use of the *Set Project Type* option. The next figure shows the contents of the *Project2.π* file.

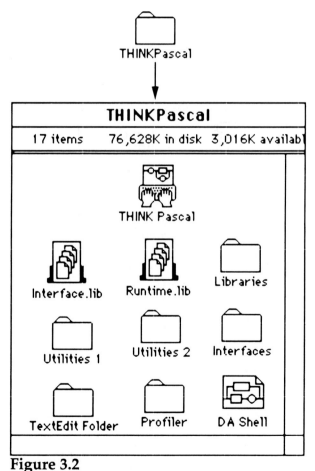

Figure 3.2
Internal structure of the Pascal folder, showing integrated Pascal editor-linker-compiler (keyboard icon), libraries, and folders containing additional libraries and utilities.

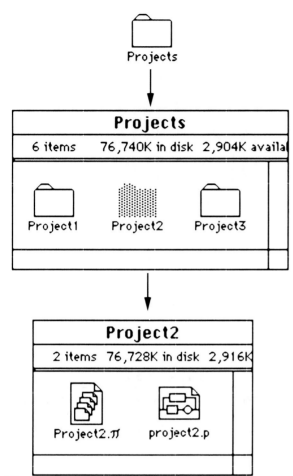

Figure 3.3
Hierarchical structure of *Projects* folder. The
Project2 folder contains two files: the project file,
Project2.π and the source code file, *project2.p*.
Details on their contents are shown in subsequent
figures.

The last element of the hierarchical structure is
the Pascal program itself. In Figure 3.5 a simple
Pascal program is shown along with the graphics
it produced in the **Drawing** window.

To summarize the steps required to create and
execute a Pascal project:

1. Create a project folder using the **New
   Folder** command under the desktop **File**
   menu. Pick a helpful mnemonic, *Name*.

2. Enter the Pascal editor/compiler by double
   clicking on its icon, and create a new
   project by selecting the **New Project**
   command under the **Project** menu. Use the
   suggested convention, *Name.π*, in naming
   the project file.

3. Under the editor's **File** menu, use **New** to
   create a source code file for your main
   program.

4. Write your program, using the editor, and
   save it as *Name.p*.

5. Use the **Add File** option under the **Project**
   menu to add *Name.p* to the *Name.π* project.

6. Use the **Add File** option to add any additional required libraries and units to
   Name.π. Note that the order of appearance
   of libraries and units follows standard
   Pascal protocol—an element must be
   declared before it is called.

7. When all program elements have been
   assembled in the project file, *Name.π*, use
   the **Run** menu to compile, link, and execute
   it. The three execution options include **Go**

The *Runtime.lib* library contains all standard
Pascal routines such as writeln and sqrt. The
Interface.lib library contains the "glue code" for all
Macintosh Toolbox routines marked *[Not in ROM]*.
Since routines from these two libraries are
commonly used in almost all Pascal programs on
the Macintosh, they are automatically included in
the project file. The *project2.p* source file is
included by an **Add File** command under the
Project menu. Upon compilation the corresponding object code is included and properly linked
to the appropriate routines from the libraries and
units included in the project file.

Project2.π		
Options	**File (by build order)**	**Size**
	Runtime.lib	18256
	Interface.lib	8104
D N V R	project2.p	214

Figure 3.4
Contents of *Project2.π* project file. The runtime and
interface libraries are listed automatically when a
project file is created. The *project2.p* source file is
included by an *Add File* command.

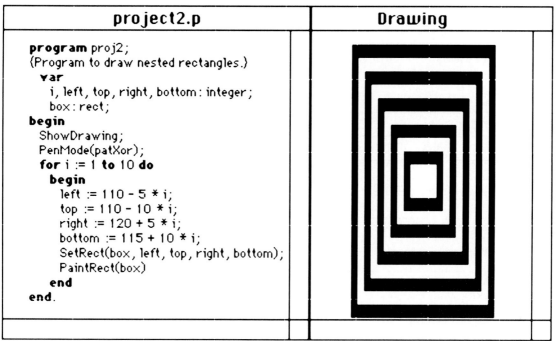

project2.p	**Drawing**
| ```
program proj2;
(Program to draw nested rectangles.)
  var
    i, left, top, right, bottom: integer;
    box: rect;
begin
  ShowDrawing;
  PenMode(patXor);
  for i := 1 to 10 do
    begin
      left := 110 - 5 * i;
      top := 110 - 10 * i;
      right := 120 + 5 * i;
      bottom := 115 + 10 * i;
      SetRect(box, left, top, right, bottom);
      PaintRect(box)
    end
end.
``` | |

Figure 3.5
Source code in *project2.p* file and resulting graphics in **Drawing** window. The loop causes ten rectangles to be drawn, each 10 pixels wider and 20 pixels higher than the previous one. The *patXor* mode causes a color inversion of each pattern as it is painted over by a larger rectangle.

for the fastest execution, **Step Into** and **Step Around** for the manual single-step mode, and **Trace** for a slow-motion, automatic execution.

Integrated Editor

Pascal programs may be prepared by any editor, but most modern programming environments provide intelligent, integrated editors to simplify the coding phase and assure syntactically correct,

```
  begin
    ShowDrawing;
    PenMode(patXor);
☞  for i ▤ 1 ▨ 1▨ ▨
    begin
      left := 110 - 5 * i;
```

Figure 3.6
Thumbs down symbol indicating the line containing the error. The highlighted erroneous code follows the missing ":" in the ":=" assignment symbol.

properly formatted code. Think Pascal offers the programmer considerable flexibility in designing the pretty-printing style. The **Source Options** selection under the **Edit** menu provides four sub-windows for customizing *Fonts, Keywords, Indentation,* and *Parameters*. The pretty-printing default options produce the output shown in Figure 3.5.

The intelligent model Pascal editor "knows" Pascal syntax and will flag any deviations from non-standard usage. For instance, if the programmer had forgotten the colon in the Pascal loop in Figure 3.5, the system would ring the bell and display the helpful hint shown in Figure 3.6.

Such intelligent editors make writing incorrect syntax virtually impossible, but even intelligent editors cannot detect *semantic errors* (errors in meaning).

The model Pascal editor is described as *integrated* because the system includes the linker and compiler in the same application. The user can move smoothly from the editing phase to the compilation phase without ever leaving the program. If an error occurs during compilation, the program "bounces back" to the editing phase for debugging.
```

Intelligent, High-Speed Compiler

Think Pascal compiles many thousand lines of code per minute which is faster than most time-shared minicomputers. In addition to its high speed, this Pascal is "intelligent" in keeping track of which routines have been modified since the last compilation and then recompiling and relinking only those routines in which changes have been made.

Compiler options allow for generation of code for the M68020 (rather than the M68000) and for the MC68881 floating point coprocessor. It also allows for range options on the set of integers. Additional system options are indicated by letter under the *Options* column in Figure 3.4. This user-controlled option code signifies the following:

D → Debug. Allows stepping, stopping, stack checking, and observing.

N → Names. Insert *Macsbug* (debugger) names into the code.

V → Integer arithmetic overflow checking.

R → Range checking compiler switches.

The combination of compilation and runtime options with the high-speed, integrated compiler provides a truly supportive, integrated environment for program development.

Debugging Tools

The Pascal *syntax* you generate with the editor is guaranteed to be correct. However, programs may be syntactically correct but still contain *semantic errors*, that is, errors in logic or meaning. You may mean to do one thing, but the program does something else.

The easiest semantic errors to detect are *run-time errors*. These include such common errors as dividing by zero or setting the index of an array dimensioned [1..100] to 101. The model Pascal detects such errors at run time and flags the offending line of code with the "thumbs down" icon. Usually the error indication and line identification is sufficient information for correcting the bug.

For the most difficult errors, those in which the program runs flawlessly but produces flawed results, the system supplies six powerful debugging tools with which the programmer can rapidly identify and eliminate errors of logic. These include:

- The **Step Into** and **Step Around** command with execution finger – Upon selecting the **Step** option under the **Run** menu, an execution finger appears at the starting point in the program (see Figure 3.7). Hitting the appropriate control keys single steps you through the program with the execution finger always pointing at the line about to be executed. Options are available for stepping into or around called functions and procedures. The combination of this mode with observation of the **Text** and/or **Drawing** window output is often sufficient for debugging your program.

- The **Trace** command with *execution finger* – This mode closely resembles the **Step** mode in which the computer, rather than the user, does the stepping. It runs slowly enough that the programmer can follow the control of flow, but , al;so runs rapidly enough to reduce the tedium of single stepping.

- Setting *break points* with *Stop Signs* and **Go-Go** – For large programs, both the **Step** and **Trace** modes may become slow and awkward. In such cases, you may select the **Stops In** option under the **Debug** menu and drag the stop sign icon into your program where ever you wish a break point (see Figure 3.7). Upon running with the **Go-Go** command, the program will run full speed up to the stop sign and then pause, allowing you to check the value of output and program parameters.

- Parameter monitoring via the **Observe** window – The **Observe** window is the most useful tool for monitoring the value of expressions and variables as the program executes in one of the above three debug modes. One simply selects the **Observe** item under the **Windows** menu and an empty **Observe** window appears. Next, the variables we wish to monitor are entered, one per line. As the program is executed line by line, the present values of the parameters under observation are displayed. Figure 3.8 shows the status of the **Observe** window after two loops of the for statement. In addition to debugging programs, the **Observe** window is useful in demonstrating the concept of scope and

project2.p	Observe	
| ```
program proj2;
(Program to draw nested rectangles.)
  var
  i, left, top, right, bottom : integer;
  box : rect;
begin
 ShowDrawing;
 PenMode(patXor);
 for i := 1 to 10 do
  begin
   left := 110 - 5 * i;
   top := 110 - 10 * i;
   right := 120 + 5 * i;
   bottom := 115 + 10 * i;
   SetRect(box, left, top, right, bottom);
   PaintRect(box)
  end
end.
``` | 2 | i |
	100	left
	90	top
	130	right
	135	bottom

Figure 3.7
Source code window, **Observe** window, and portion of **Drawing** window after two executions of the for loop. The Observe window indicates the value of the parameters as the code is executed line by line. The stop sign at SetRect will halt execution at this point in the fullspeed **Go** mode.

lifetime of parameters. Scope is the physical extent in a program for which the parameter is defined; lifetime is the temporal duration of a parameter's definition.

- Modifying parameters with the **Instant** window – The **Instant** window enables you to modify any parameter of the program without actually modifying the program itself. If, for instance, we wish to reassign left the value of 50 just before SetRect is called, we open the **Instant** window, type in the desired code segment

as shown in Figure 3.8, and click **Do It**.

- Detailed probing of the program with the **LightsBug** code view debugger – The three debug modes and two debug windows described above are sufficient for detecting the vast majority of program bugs. If, however, a particularly pesky bug requires examining the compiled program at the machine language level, the appropriate tool is the **LightsBug** debugger. This tool resides under the **Windows** menu and provides access to all variables, the system registers, the heap zone, memory, and compiled code. The **LightsBug** window, shown in Figure 3.9, consists of four user-resizable panes for viewing the system status and nine probe tools for selecting and modifying system parameters.

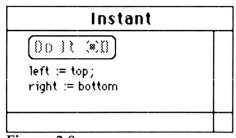

Figure 3.8
Modification of code segment to produce a square.
Do It is pressed when the pointer is on SetRect.
```

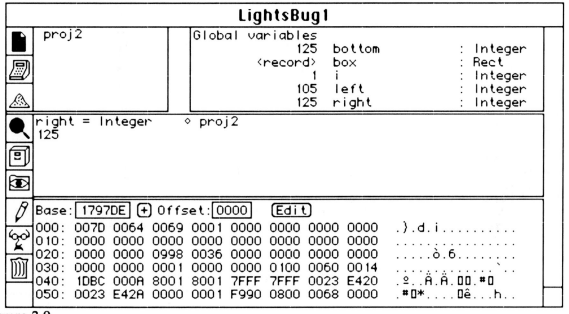

Figure 3.9
LightsBug debugger window showing panes for viewing the system status and the probe tools for selecting and modifying system parameters.

Access to High-Level Routines

More than six hundred routines of the User Interface Toolbox are written in Pascal and readily callable from THINK Pascal. Data types used by the routines are described as Pascal records, pointers, and arrays. The details of their calling sequence and parameter specifications are given in *Inside Macintosh*.[3] As various routines are required for building graphical applications, they will be listed and demonstrated.

We conclude this discussion of integrated development environments by noting that many other excellent programming environments are available. Some of the most noteworthy include UNIX, X Windows, and Turbo Pascal. They all provide powerful editors and debugging tools to facilitate the rapid development of error-free code. Rather than survey the features of all of them, we felt the reader would gain most from the fairly thorough summary of the features of the system used to build graphical objects and introduce graphical algorithms in this chapter.

Graphical Objects and OOP

In the broadest sense, all graphical images are graphical objects. They all share common attributes such as height, width, pixel depth (color resolution), creator, file type (PICT, TIFF, EPS, and so on), and operations to which they respond. The image file structures discussed in the previous chapter specify graphical objects in the traditional procedural programming paradigm. However, graphical objects also provide examples of the techniques and advantages of the more modern *object-oriented programming* (OOP) paradigm.[4] Consider the following OOP concepts and their icon-based, graphical user interface representations (GUIs).

Object-Oriented Programming Concepts

Graphical user interface design rests firmly on the foundation of OOP and illustrates its power and elegance. Some of the most important OOP concepts are listed below.

Figure 3.10
System response when command "trash this application program" is issued with the mouse by dragging its icon to the trash can. To suppress this warning, the *Option* key may be pressed during the drag command.

- **Objects** – These are defined as data and the closely associated actions which operate on the data. This integration of data and operations into a single object is called *encapsulation*. In GUI design, objects are abstracted as icons and menus which represent folders, files, application programs, processes, and operations.

- **Messages** – These are defined as the requests sent to an object to execute the actions of which it is capable. Different objects may support different messages and may respond identically or differently to the same message. In GUI design, messages may be sent by the mouse in performing actions such as *selection, launching, copying, restructuring, trashing,* and *ejecting*. Messages commanding actions of *saving, duplicating, printing, cutting, copying,* and *pasting* may be sent via either the mouse or keyboard. The same message may cause different actions in different icons—a single click selects some icons and opens others.

- **Methods** – These are the routines and algorithms for implementing messages. In GUI design, methods are implemented by high-level routines supported by the event manager, windows manager, menu manager, and so on.

- **Class hierarchy** – Each object belongs to a *class* and is called an *instance* of the class. Class hierarchy provides for *superclasses* and *subclasses*. All objects of a subclass *inherit* the data and behavior defined by the superclass of which they are members. The class without a superclass is called the *root class*. A given class supports certain methods common to all members of the class. In GUI design, classes exist for data files, applications programs, menu headers, and menu selection items.

- **Inheritance** – Membership in a class provides *inheritance* of data and methods for all members of the class. Members of a subclass inherit all the instance variables and methods of its superclass unless it chooses to *override* them with local variables and/or methods. Inheritance provides advantages of reducing data redundancy and action code duplication. In GUI design, all data icons share the method of examining their own *creator* slot and searching for the application program it points to when they are opened. However, the subclass of WINGZ data files differs significantly from the subclass of MS-Word data files in its icon style, creator designation, internal file structure and so on.

- **Polymorphism** – Literally *multiple forms*, this feature of OOP means that the same message may be sent to objects of different classes. The response from members of distinct classes may be identical to, similar to, or completely distinct from each other, depending on the method chosen by each class for implementing the message. In GUI design, for instance, all members of the *data file* class may meekly vanish without trace when dragged to the trash can, whereas icons from the more important *application program* class will bravely challenge the user with the warning shown in Figure 3.10, and disk icons will interpret the same message as "eject yourself."

Computer graphics has served as the test bed for many of the original OOP concepts. *SmallTalk*, the seminal OOP language, was written at Xerox PARC, the origin of the WIMP GUI. It should not come as a surprise to students of computer graphics that the most successful GUIs rely most heavily on OOP. We shall find OOP concepts helpful and natural tools for developing graphics algorithms throughout the remainder of this book.

Graphical Object Types

Just as with other complex data structures, graphical objects may themselves be composed of more elementary graphical objects. A useful analysis of graphical objects can be made in terms of their type and hierarchical structure. A straightforward classification of graphical object types may be given as:

- **Primitive objects** – Single QuickDraw routine calls,

- **Complex objects** – Composite of primitives,

- **Undifferentiated objects** – Pixel level information.

Consider these in more detail.

Primitive Objects – Pens, Points, and Lines

In principle, the only absolutely essential graphics primitive, assuming a raster display is a routine to draw a point at pixel (x,y). Algorithms exist for constructing lines and curves from points. Routines for more complex figures are easily built from the line and curve routines. However, almost all languages support graphical routines for constructing primitive objects at least as complex as rectangles and ovals.

The most elementary Pascal primitive objects and their calling sequence are the *pens*, *points*, and *lines* shown in Table 3.1.

These elementary graphics functions are suffi-

Table 3.1
Graphics Primitives – Pens, Points, and Lines

Object	Pascal Syntax	Example Call	Description
Pen	Procedure PenSize(width, height:INTEGER);	PenSize(2,2);	Sets the size of the plotting pen, in pixels
Pen– move absolute	Procedure MoveTo(h,v: INTEGER);	MoveTo(100,50);	Moves pen (invisibly) to pixel (h,v) (absolute coordinates)
Pen- move relative	Procedure Move(dh,dv: INTEGER);	Move(10,10);	Moves pen (invisibly) dh pixels horizontally and dv pixels vertically (relative coordinates)
Point	Procedure DrawLine(x1,y1, x1,y1:INTEGER);	DrawLine(50,100,50,100);	Draws a line from point (x1,y1) to the second point, (x1,y1), i.e. a point
Point	Procedure MoveTo(x1,y1: INTEGER); Procedure LineTo(x1,y1: INTEGER);	MoveTo(50,100); LineTo(50,100);	Moves to pixel (x1,y1) and draws a line to (x1,y1), i.e. a point
Point	Procedure Line(dx,dy: INTEGER);	Line(0,0);	From the present position of the pen, draw a line a distance (0,0)
Line – absolute	Procedure DrawLine(x1,y1, x2,y2:INTEGER);	DrawLine(50,100,200,300);	Draws a line from point (x1,y1) to the second point, (x2,y2)
Line – absolute	Procedure MoveTo(x1,y1: INTEGER); Procedure LineTo(x2,y2: INTEGER);	MoveTo(50,100); LineTo(200,300);	Moves to pixel (x1,y1) and draws a line to (x2,y2)
Line – relative	Procedure Line(dx,dy: INTEGER);	Line(100,200);	Draw a line a distance (dx,dy) relative to the present pen position
Text	Procedure WriteDraw(p1 [,p2…, pn]);	WriteDraw('Pen at:',x,y);	The WriteLn equivalent procedure for the drawing window
Drawing Window	Procedure ShowDrawing;	ShowDrawing;	Opens the Drawing Window

cient for writing our first complete Pascal program, Primitives. In Primitives, three different procedures are used for drawing three different sized *points*. Then, three different procedures are used for drawing three *lines* of different widths. All points and lines are labeled using the **WriteDraw** command, the **Drawing** window equivalent to WriteLn.

Pascal Program Primitives

```
program Primitives;
{Program to demonstrate Pascal point & line primitives.}

begin
   ShowDrawing;           {Opens Drawing Window}

{First draw three points by three different functions}

   PenSize(1, 1);     {Sets pen size to 1 x 1 pixels}
   DrawLine(50, 50, 50, 50);
   WriteDraw(' Point at (50,50) using DrawLine');

   PenSize(2, 2);
   MoveTo(100, 75);       {Absolute move}
   LineTo(100, 75);
   WriteDraw(' Point at (100,75) using LineTo');

   PenSize(3, 3);
   MoveTo(150, 100);      {Absolute move}
   Line(0, 0);
   WriteDraw(' Point at (150,100) using Line');

{Now Draw three lines by three different functions}

   MoveTo(150, 175);        {Absolute move}
   WriteDraw('Line drawn with DrawLine');
   DrawLine(150, 125, 50, 225);

   PenSize(2, 2);
    Move(0, 25);           {Relative move}
   LineTo(150, 250);
   WriteDraw('Line drawn by LineTo');

   Pensize(1, 1);
   Move(0, 25);            {Relative move}
   Line(-100, 50);
   WriteDraw('Line drawn by Line');

end.
```

The output generated by running Primitives is shown in Figure 3.11.

A close examination of Figure 3.11 reveals several features of THINK Pascal graphics on the Macintosh.

- The unit of measure is the *pixel*. This is the "natural" unit corresponding to the smallest addressable object on the screen.

- *Pixels are square.* On the Macintosh, each pixel is approximately 1/72 inch on a side, equivalent to one point in typesetting notation. This fortunate choice of pixel dimension has simplified the tasks surrounding typesetting and avoids the complexity of *aspect ratios* inherent in the nonsquare pixels used by many other display devices.

- The coordinate system is *local* to the **Drawing** window, that is, pixel measurements are made relative to the window rather than the overall display screen. This OOP feature greatly simplifies the task of locating the image within the window—in OOP language all objects in the window are subclasses of the window object and inherit its coordinate system.

- The *origin* of the coordinate system is located at the *upper left corner*, with increasing x measured to the right and increasing y measured downward. While this seems to go against our intuition, it conforms closely to the format for scanning the CRT screen and for writing text to a page. The task of memory-mapping images to the screen is greatly simplified by adopting this protocol, and, as a result, it has become the standard for most graphics systems.

- Both *absolute* and *relative* pen-move and line commands are supported. Absolute commands refer to actual pixel coordinates, (x,y). Relative commands refer to incremental motions, (dx,dy), relative to the present pen position.

- The *output line* generated by the **WriteDraw** command begins at the *present pen position* which is at the lower left-hand corner of the message. Judicious use of **WriteDraw** for labeling graphics output is valuable to programmer and user alike in interpreting graphical output.

Although pens, points and lines are the most elementary of all graphical objects, they form the basis for much more complex objects. For many applications they provide the natural building block object for constructing intricate and complex patterns. Consider, for instance, the program, Pattern, which uses the relative line function, *line(x,y)*, in a recursive function, Spiral, to draw a square, spiral pattern.

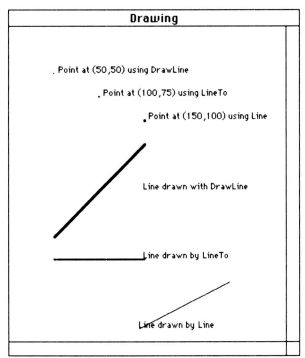

Figure 3.11
Output generated by Primitives program.

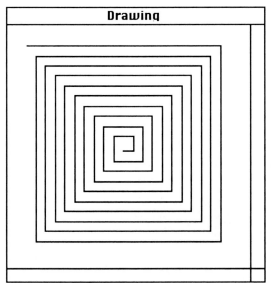

Figure 3.12
Output of recursive spiral generator. The main program moves the pen to (20,20) and then calls Spiral which continues to call itself, plotting as it shrinks to nothing. It halts when the relative moves in both x and y fall below 10 pixels.

The basic algorithm of Pattern can be stated as:

1. Move to the starting point,
2. Draw a line relative to this point,
3. Shorten the relative line ,
4. Turn 90° to the right by a combination of $x \leftrightarrow y$ exchanges and sign changes,
5. Repeat from step 2, using recursion, until the relative move size drops below some threshold.

In systems supporting *Turtle Graphics* from the LOGO language, the Pattern program could be reduced to a tight, recursive loop containing two commands, right(90) and move(r-5). In whatever language, however, it is clear that a line command is the natural and essential command for creating such patterns.

Pascal Program Pattern

```
program Pattern;
{Program to build spiral pattern, using}
{relative line routine in a recursive loop}

 procedure Spiral (x, y, sign: integer);
{Procedure to spiral into limbo}
    var
       temp: integer;
  begin
    sign := (-1) * sign;
    if (abs(x) < 10) and (abs(y) < 10) then
       halt             {Done recurring - ground case}
    else                {Spiral still sizable}
       begin
       line(x, y);      {Plot relative line}
{Reduce magnitude of relative move by 5 pixels}
       if abs(x) > abs(y) then
          x := x - (x div abs(x) * 5)
       else
          y := y - (y div abs(y) * 5);
{Exchange x<--> y}
       temp := x;
       x := y;
       y := temp;
{On even calls, change sign}
       x := sign * x;
       y := sign * y;
       Spiral(x, y, sign);    {Recur}
     end;
  end;

begin
  sign:=1;
  ShowDrawing;
  MoveTo(20, 20);
  Spiral(200, 0, -1);
end.
```

The second program illustrates an algorithm in which the natural object is a point. Consider the Fractal program which implements the "Chaos Game" algorithm for constructing the Sierpinski fractal shown in Figure 3.13.

Pascal Program Fractal

```
program Fractal;
{Program to play the Chaos Game                      }
{Algorithm:                                          }
{  1.  Pick a point in a triangle at random & plot it }
{  2.  Pick a vertex of the triangle at random       }
{  3.  Move 1/2 way from present point to this vertex }
{  4.  Plot point and loop from (2) until mouse pressed.}

  var
    xp, yp, i: integer;
    x, y: array[1..3] of real;

  function Rndint (n: integer): integer;
  {Function to return random integer on range 1 --> n}
    var
      rr: longint;
      r: real;
    begin
      rr := random;                    {Intrinsic routine}
      r := (rr + 32767) / (32767 + 32768);
      Rndint := trunc(n * r) + 1;
    end;

begin
  ShowDrawing;
{Set corners of triangle centered at (110,125),}
{with sides 200 pixels long}
    x[1] := 110 - 100;
    y[1] := 125 + 57.73503;
    x[2] := 110;
    y[2] := 125 - 115.470;
    x[3] := 110 + 100;
    y[3] := y[1];
{Pick first point at random in box containing triangle}
    xp := Rndint(200) + 10;
    yp := Rndint(173) + 10;
    DrawLine(xp, yp, xp, yp);                {Plot point}

  repeat     {until Mouse button is pressed}
    i := Rndint(3);               {Pick random corner}
    xp := round((x[i] - xp) / 2 + xp);  {Go half way}
    yp := round((y[i] - yp) / 2 + yp);  {Go half way}
    DrawLine(xp, yp, xp, yp);            {Plot point}
  until button;
end.
```

The Chaos Game algorithm is described in detail by Barnsley and his co-workers.[5] Two features introduced in this program include:

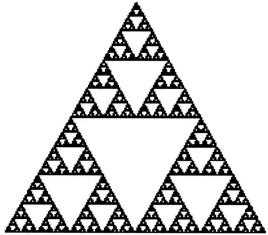

Figure 3.13
Output of Fractal program. This pattern demonstrates *self-similarity* and *scaling* (no atomic size) which are features of fractal objects. It is remarkable that an iterative, random-number-based algorithm can generate such a symmetric and regular object.

- The use of the system routine, Random, which returns an integer in the range from -32768 through 32767 to build a more useful function, RndInt(n), which returns a pseudo-random integer on the range 1 → n. This process of giving an object a name and generalizing it is called *abstraction*.

- The use of interactive programming for program control. The intrinsic Button procedure remains *false* until the mouse button is pressed at which point it becomes *true*.

Primitive Objects – Geometric Figures

The next level in data abstraction is the definition of common geometric objects – *squares, rectangles, rounded rectangles, circles, ovals, arcs,* and *wedges*. All seven of these geometric objects may be considered special instances of the four basic QuickDraw objects: *Rectangles, Ovals, Rounded-Corner Rectangles,* and *Arcs*. These four QuickDraw objects are all based on the special data type, *Rect*, consisting of the four integers, *left, top, right,* and *bottom* defining the bounding-box containing the object. Messages are sent to the bounding-box rectangles by a set of ten rectangle manipulation procedures, including *SetRect, OffsetRect, Union-Rect, EqualRect,* and *EmptyRect*. Each of the

QuickDraw object types has a standard set of messages to which it responds. Table 3.2 presents a summary of the Messages/Objects procedures available for geometric figures.

These procedures will be demonstrated in the program GeomFig. While the procedure names and arguments are fairly obvious from their mnemonics, the following clarifications may be helpful:

• Bounding boxes are defined with the SetRect procedure whose syntax is:

procedure SetRect(**var**
r:Rect;left,top,right,bottom:integer);

To build a 200 × 100 pixel shoe box called box1, whose upper left-hand corner was located at (50,50), we would make the procedural call:

SetRect(box1,50,50,250,150);

• The default value of the pen pattern is black, but at any point in the program a new pattern may be defined and used in subsequent messages. This is particularly useful for the filling commands. The syntax for setting a pen pattern is given as:

procedure PenPat(pat:Pattern);

Predefined choice of patterns include: *white, black, gray, ltGray,* and *dkGray*. To redefine the pattern, we would call:

PenPat(gray);

• The Rect bounding box for defining ovals specifies the boundary within which the oval is inscribed. To draw a circle, for instance, one specifies a square Rect.

• The ovalWidth and ovalHeight used in defining rounded-corner rectangles are simply dimensions in pixels of the ovals which specify the shape of the corners of the rounded-corner rectangles.

• The startAngle and arcAngle parameters used in defining arcs and wedges specify exactly what their names imply, with angles measured in degrees.

With this background, let's build the program GeomFig to demonstrate the response of each of these object types as it receives various messages.

Table 3.2
Graphics Primitives – Geometric Figures

Object→ ↓Message	Rectangles (Squares)	Ovals (Circles)	Rounded-Corner Rectangles	Arcs and Wedges
Frame	Procedure FrameRect(r:Rect)	Procedure FrameOval(r:Rect)	Procedure Frame Round Rect (r:Rect; oval Width, ovalHeight:Integer)	Procedure FrameArc (r:Rect;startAngle,arcAngle:Integer)
Paint	Procedure PaintRect(r:Rect)	Procedure PaintOval(r:Rect)	Procedure Paint Round Rect(r:Rect; oval Width, ovalHeight:Integer)	Procedure PaintArc (r:Rect;startAngle,arcAngle:Integer)
Erase	Procedure EraseRect(r:Rect)	Procedure EraseOval(r:Rect)	Procedure Erase Round Rect(r:Rect; oval Width, ovalHeight:Integer)	Procedure EraseArc (r:Rect;startAngle,arcAngle:Integer)
Invert	Procedure InvertRect(r:Rect)	Procedure InvertOval(r:Rect)	Procedure Invert Round Rect(r:Rect; oval Width, ovalHeight:Integer)	Procedure InvertArc (r:Rect;startAngle,arcAngle:Integer)
Fill	Procedure FillRect(r:Rect; pat:Pattern)	Procedure FillOval(r:Rect; pat:Pattern)	Procedure FillRound Rect(r:Rect; ovalWidth, ovalHeight:Integer; pat:Pattern)	Procedure FillArc (r:Rect;startAngle,arcAngle:Integer; pat:Pattern)

Pascal Program GeomFig

```
program GeomFig;
{Program to build each of the four basic geometric
figures:                                          }
{      rectangle                                   }
{      oval                                        }
{      rounded-corner rectangle                    }
{      arc                                         }
{and demonstrate the five messages to which these
objects respond:                                  }
{      Frame, Paint, Erase, Invert, and Fill.      }

  var
     windowBox, rectBox, ovalBox, rcBox, arcBox: Rect;
     row, col, dh, dv, A: integer;
begin
{First, define the Drawing Window for a large screen
Mac}
   SetRect(windowBox, 400, 100, 832, 604);  {A 6" x 7"
window}
   SetDrawingRect(windowBox);
   ShowDrawing;

{Next, use FrameRect in a loop to draw frames for
subsequent figures}
   setRect(rectBox, 18, 18, 196, 160);
   PenSize(2, 2);
   dv := 0;
   dh := 0;
   for col := 0 to 1 do
     begin
       for row := 0 to 2 do
       begin
         OffsetRect(rectBox, dh, dv);
         FrameRect(rectBox);
         dv := 160;
       end;
       OffsetRect(rectBox, 200, (-2 * 160));
       dv := 0;
     end;

{Paint a square in the upper left frame}
   SetRect(rectBox, 65, 40, 145, 120);
   PaintRect(rectBox);
   MoveTo(45, 150);
   WriteDraw('A Paint Message to a Square');

{Draw an oval frame in the upper right frame}
   setRect(ovalBox, 240, 30, 380, 130);
   PenSize(8, 3);
   FrameOval(ovalBox);
   MoveTo(245, 150);
   WriteDraw('A Frame Message to an Oval');

{Draw a circle and paint it gray}
   setRect(ovalBox, 55, 190, 155, 290);
   PenPat(Gray);
   PaintOval(ovalBox);
   MoveTo(45, 310);
   WriteDraw('A Paint Message to a Circle');

{Draw a Rounded-Corner Rectangle and fill it with
ltGray}
   setRect(rcBox, 240, 190, 380, 290);
   PenSize(10, 10);
   PenPat(Black);
   FillRoundRect(rcBox, 40, 30, ltGray);
   FrameRoundRect(rcBox, 40, 30);
   MoveTo(227, 310);
   WriteDraw('A Fill/Frame Message to a Rnd-Rect');

{Draw a 270° arc}
   setRect(arcBox, 40, 355, 170, 445);
   PenSize(1, 1);
   FrameArc(arcBox, 0, 270);
   MoveTo(45, 470);
   WriteDraw('A Frame Message to an Arc');

{Draw a Pie-Chart from wedges}
   setRect(arcBox, 255, 350, 355, 450);
   PenSize(2, 2);
   A := 15;
   FillArc(arcBox, A, A, White);
   FillArc(arcBox, 2 * A, 2 * A, dkGray);
   FillArc(arcBox, 4 * A, 4 * A, ltGray);
   FillArc(arcBox, 8 * A, 8 * A, Black);
   FillArc(arcBox, 16 * A, 9 * A, Gray);
   InvertArc(arcBox, 12 * A, A);
   EraseArc(arcBox, 20 * A, 2 * a);
   FrameArc(arcBox, 0, 360);
   MoveTo(245, 470);
   WriteDraw('Fill Messages to Wedges');
end.
```

The GeomFig program demonstrates a number of interesting features. First is that the increased abstraction achieved by named objects with attributes and methods results in increased programming power and expressiveness. Each of the six frames in Figure 3.14 required 5–6 commands on the average. To achieve the same results using more primitive point and line commands would have required several times as much code.

The second observation is that reasonably complex graphics (e.g., the frame rectangles and piecharts) are readily produced by variations on these geometric primitives.

Higher-level graphical languages like PHIGS and FIGS extend the concept of abstraction by providing routines for manipulating 3D objects. Most toolkits like *TurboPascal for Windows* and the Macintosh QuickDraw routines are limited to 2D objects and manipulations.

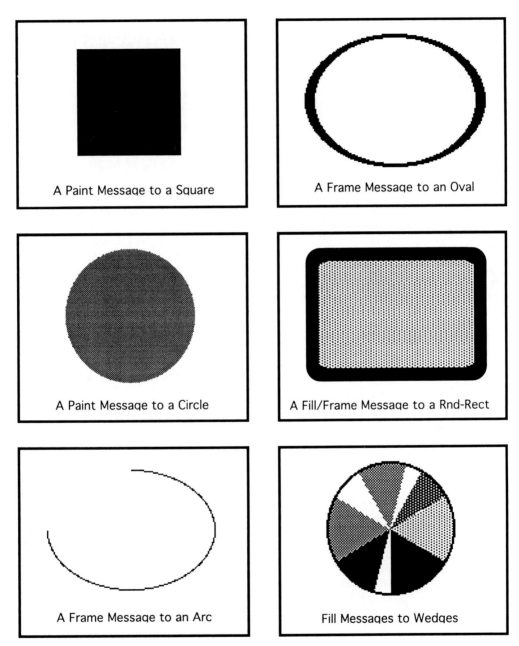

Figure 3.14
Output from **GeomFig** program. The program displays seven geometric objects (*rectangle, square, oval, circle, rounded-rectangle, arc,* and *wedge*) through five messages sent to four object types (*Rectangle, Oval, Rounded-Corner Rectangle,* and *Arc*).

Interaction Algorithms

The secret of good graphical user interface design is *interactivity*. In an application supported by a good GUI, users will frequently find themselves deeply involved in the application and doing productive work before ever touching the keyboard.

Features of Good GUIs

There are three indicators of systems with good GUIs and their users.

- The *User Reference Manual* for a given application is still shrink-wrapped months after the user has become an expert with the application. All possible program options are instantly available under one or more levels of menu selection, and an encapsulated, context-sensitive Reference Manual in the form of a **HELP** file is only a button click away.

- The mouse becomes, in effect, a powerful extension of the user. After a few months of intensive use of a WIMP system, users find themselves frustrated and a bit embarrassed when they try to point at off-screen objects with the mouse cursor which hangs up on the edge of the screen. This is a particularly noticeable phenomena in a large group programming environment in which programmers frequently highlight some program element for their colleagues by pointing at it with the mouse cursor rather than their finger.

- The measure of a good GUI is the extent to which the user is totally unaware of the *system* and conscious only of the *work*. Programs ported over from command-line interface systems are detected instantly (actually, it may take a minute or two), because of their lack of a good GUI.

Now that we have become acquainted with graphics primitives such as points, lines, and geometric objects, the only missing ingredient we must explore before we begin building interactive graphics user interfaces is a set of event handling routines. While Standard Pascal does not support interactive graphics, most of the extended Pascal dialects do include routines for sensing mouse cursor position and detecting events such as button presses. Without such event handling rou-

tines, it is virtually impossible to build a good GUI.

Basic Event Handling Routines

The three logical functions necessary for building a graphical user interface include (1) *pointing*, (2) *position sensing*, and (3) *action sensing*. We are assuming the availability of a WIMP system shell in which case the pointing device is the mouse/cursor. The mouse sensing interrupt on systems such as the Macintosh and PC Windows operates at the highest priority level. That is, the mouse is "alive" and the cursor responds to mouse motion even when other processes are in operation. In fact, on such systems the quickest test for system failure is an unresponsive mouse. So the first function, *pointing*, is automatically available on all WIMP systems.

The second and third functions, *position* sensing and *action* sensing, are provided through functions at the language or systems level. Additional Pascal routines are available for event handling, timing purposes, and sound generation. A summary of the basic interactive functions is presented in Table 3.3.

A quick scan of Table 3.3 suggests that these functions from the Event Manager are more than adequate for handling the interactive dialog for GUIs and graphics applications. The next step, therefore, is to implement several of these functions in the simple demonstration programs, ButtonEvents and ReadPosition.

Button Messages Algorithm

In ButtonEvents the use of two interactive routines, *Button* and *TickCounts*, is illustrated. These procedures are used to detect the three messages:

- Button down message,
- Button up message,
- Double-click message.

Here is a simple algorithm which accomplishes these tasks.

Pascal Program ButtonEvents

```
program ButtonEvents;
{Program to demonstrate detection of button events  }
{and use of button for program control.             }

    var
       tic1, tic2: longint;

begin
{Open Drawing Window and label screen.}
   ShowDrawing;
   MoveTo(20, 20);
   TextSize(18);
   WriteDraw('Button Event Test');
   MoveTo(35, 40);
   TextSize(12);
   WriteDraw('Double-Click to QUIT');
   MoveTo(40, 70);
   WriteDraw('Now the Button is: ');

{Use XOR pattern to erase and rewrite output}
   TextMode(srcXor);
   MoveTo(80, 100);
   TextSize(24);
   TextFace([bold]);

   repeat                    {Until we double-click}
     while button do         {Button down message
                              detector}
        begin
           WriteDraw('down');
           MoveTo(80, 100);
           repeat            {Tight loop until button up}
           until not Button;
           WriteDraw('down');     {Erase "down" text}
           MoveTo(80, 100);
           tic1 := TickCount;     {Sample system clock: }
        end;                      {1/60 sec ticks}

     while not button do       { Button up message
                                 detector}
        begin
           WriteDraw('up');
           MoveTo(80, 100);
           repeat            {Tight loop until button down}
           until button;
           WriteDraw('up');   {Erase "up" text}
           MoveTo(80, 100);
           tic2 := TickCount;     {Sample system clock}
        end;

   until abs(tic2 - tic1) < 30;    {Double click message
                                    detector}
end.
```

The main features and new concepts introduced in ButtonEvents include:

- A formatting section in which the **Drawing** window is opened, font sizes selected (in points), and the figure labeled.

- The pen mode set to *exclusive or* (Xor) for purposes of carrying out the erase text function. Text erase is accomplished simply by writing the text a second time in the

Table 3.3
Event Handling Routines

Object	Pascal Syntax	Example Call	Description
Button	Function Button:Boolean	if Button then … else…	The Button function returns *True* if the mouse button is down; *False* otherwise
Button	Function StillDown: Boolean	if StillDown then… else…	Returns *True* if the button is still down from the original press; *False* if it has been released or released and repressed (i.e., mouse event on event queue)
Button	Function Wait-MouseUp:Boolean	if WaitMouseUp then… else…	Same as StillDown, but removes previous mouse event from queue before returning False
Mouse cursor	Procedure GetMouse(**var** mouseLoc:point)	GetMouse(p);	Returns the present mouse cursor position in local coordinates as a Point type
Keyboard	Procedure GetKeys(**var** theKeys:KeyMap)	GetKeys(key);	Reads the current state of the keyboard and returns a keyMap, a Packed Array[1..127] of Boolean
Clock	Function TickCount:LongInt	if TickCount<60 then…	Returns the elapsed time in ticks (1/60th sec) since last TickCount call
Event	Function GetNextEvent (eventMask:Integer;**var** theEvent:EventRecord): Boolean	if GetNextEvent(2,Rec) then… else…	A logical function which returns *True* if an event of the requested type exists on the event queue; *False* otherwise. If *True*, it also returns a descriptive record of the event. (type, location, time, conditions, etc)

```
┌──────────────────────────────────┐
│           Drawing                │
│ ┌──────────────────────────┐     │
│ │                          │     │
│ │  Button Event Test       │     │
│ │                          │     │
│ │  Double-Click to QUIT    │     │
│ │                          │     │
│ │  Now the Button is:      │     │
│ │                          │     │
│ │      down                │     │
│ │                          │     │
│ └──────────────────────────┘     │
│                                  │
└──────────────────────────────────┘
```

Figure 3.15
Output of program, ButtonEvents. It responds to
ButtonUp, *ButtonDown*, and *DoubleClick* messages
with methods which acknowledge the button state
or exit the program.

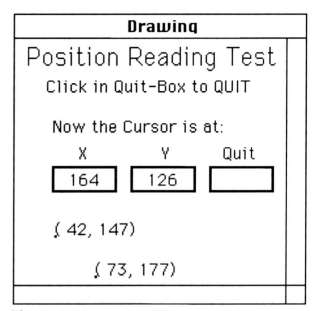

Figure 3.16
Output of Read_Position program. As the user
moves the cursor about the screen, the X and Y
"odometer" panels continuously monitor its
location. The present cursor position, (x,y), is reported upon pressing the mouse button. Clicking
in the **Quit** box causes program termination.

same location. The Xor function changes
the previous black pixels of the text to
white, effectively erasing what was written
the first time.

- A **repeat** block designed to be exited by
double-clicking the mouse button. The
difference between tic2 and tic1 is the
number of (1/60)ths of a second (ticks)
between the release of the mouse button
and the next press of the button. This
number is an effective measure of how
rapidly the mouse button is double-clicked.
By setting the limit to 30 we determine that
the double-click message will be recognized
if the time between clicks is shorter than
about 1/2 second.

- Two **while** loops corresponding to the two
logical possibilities—*button-down* or *button-
up*. When the button-down message is
received, it is acknowledged by writing
"down" to the **Drawing** window and
waiting for the button state to change with
the **not** Button test. The *Button-up* loop is
identical to the *Button-down* loop with the
interchange of the **not** Button ↔ Button
tests.

The result of this algorithm is a button interpreting program which displays the current state
of the mouse button, precisely tracking button
presses and releases. In addition, it provides

double-click recognition and uses it for a graceful
exit of the program. Figure 3.15 shows the
program output when the button is pressed.

Cursor Position Algorithm

Frequently, it is as important to know *where* an
event has happened as it is to know *that* it has
happened. This logical function of pointing is
carried out on most graphics workstations with
the mouse cursor, although earlier systems used
light pens, joy sticks, data tablets, and even human
fingers for this purpose. The essential function of
all such devices is to provide an interactively controlled cursor, along with software routines for
reading its (x,y) position on the screen.

The next algorithm, Read_Position, demonstrates the use of the mouse cursor with the
routine, GetMouse, for performing the cursor
reading operation and using the results of this
operation for program control as shown in Figure
3.16.

Pascal Program Read_Position

```
program Read_Position;
{Program to demonstrate the GetMouse procedure  }
{and use it to implement a position measuring    }
algorithm  and for program control via the Quit box  }
  var
    x, y: integer;
    xrect, yrect, QRect: rect;
    Pt: Point;
begin
{Open Drawing Window and label screen.}
  ShowDrawing;
  MoveTo(20, 20);
  TextSize(18);
  WriteDraw('Position Reading Test');
  MoveTo(35, 40);
  TextSize(12);
  WriteDraw('Click in Quit-Box to QUIT');
  MoveTo(40, 70);
  WriteDraw('Now the Cursor is at: ');
{Now draw the "speedometer boxes" for x & y position}
{and the Quit box to terminate program operation    }
  MoveTo(40, 90);
  WriteDraw('   X        Y        Quit');
  SetRect(xRect, 40, 95, 90, 115);
  SetRect(yRect, 100, 95, 150, 115);
  SetRect(QRect, 160, 95, 210, 115);
  FrameRect(QRect);
  PenSize(2,2);
  repeat
    GetMouse(Pt);        {This reads the cursor position}
    x := Pt.h;           {as a 2 component vector of }
    y := Pt.v;           {type POINT  = (v,h)  }
    MoveTo(52, 110);
    WriteDraw(x : 3);    {x value in pixels}
    MoveTo(112, 110);
    WriteDraw(y : 3);    {y value in pixels}
    if button then       {If button pressed, then}
      begin              {Plot and label point}
        MoveTo(x, y);
        DrawLine(x,y,x,y);
        WriteDraw('(', x : 3, ', ', y : 3, ')');
      end;
    EraseRect(xRect);    {Must erase rectangles}
    EraseRect(yRect);    {to avoid overwriting all}
    FrameRect(xRect);    {values of measurements}
    FrameRect(yRect);    {then redraw rectangles}
  until (PtInRect(Pt, QRect) and Button);  {Click}
end.                     {in Quit Box}
```

Figure 3.16 illustrates some of the output possible with the Read_Position program. Several novel features introduced in this program include:

- Dynamic, continuous read-out "odometer" type displays of the *x* and *y* coordinates of the cursor throughout the lifetime of the program. These are very useful in exploring

the pixel dimensions of the **Drawing** window and even regions outside of this window. Note that in this application the required erase-before-writing function is performed by the EraseRect procedure.

- Option for measuring any point within the **Drawing** window, plotting its point permanently, and recording the coordinates of the plotted point next to it on the screen in an (x,y) format. The message to measure and display the present cursor position is sent by clicking the mouse button.

- Program control via a menu box labeled **Quit**. To gracefully exit the program, the user simply moves the cursor into the **Quit** box and clicks the mouse button. The exit message is detected by the elegant combination of PtInRect (Point in rectangle) and Button functions.

ButtonEvents and ReadPosition should suggest to the reader the enormous potential of even simple routines like Button and GetMouse for interactive GUI design. Once the user can point to any object on the screen and signal an action based on the object to which she/he is pointing, a whole new world of possibilities opens up. In fact, it can be shown, as we suggest in the next section, that all six of the CORE input device classes can be implemented almost trivially by combinations of these two functions.

CORE Input Device Classification

As we indicated in the previous chapter's discussion of standards, the ACM CORE graphics system proposed the following six classes of logical input devices.

1. **Button device** – indicates a choice, returning an integer, or selecting a menu item. Logical button devices are typically implemented using mouse buttons or function keys. A PC mouse provides two or three unique buttons, and the Macintosh mouse has a single button which can simulate additional button commands through double and triple clicking. Both systems can simulate additional button commands through picking virtual buttons drawn on the screen.

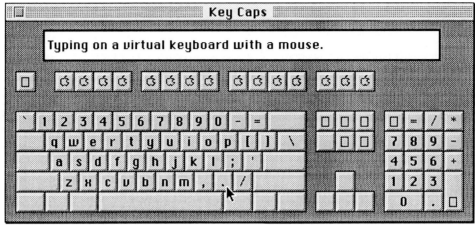

Figure 3.17
Generating a character string using a mouse to type on a virtual keyboard. Using the mouse to implement a *keyboard* logical device is somewhat like using keyboard cursor arrows to implement a *locator* device.

2. **Pick device** – selects user-defined objects on the screen. Typically, a logical pick device is implemented by a combination of continuously reading the cursor position plus event selection by pressing the button when the cursor is near or on the desired object. The **Quit** box in Read_Position illustrates the use of a *pick device*.

3. **Keyboard device** – returns a character string. Typically this logical device is implemented through a real keyboard, generally including function keys and keypad. However, this logical function can also be readily performed by using the mouse/cursor to select keys from a virtual keyboard. An example familiar to every Macintosh user is the *Key Caps* desk accessary shown in Figure 3.17. Typing on this keyboard with the mouse generates the string of characters shown in the window at the top of the keyboard.

4. **Valuator device** – returns numerical values. This logical device is readily implemented, for example, by drawing a horizontal scale along which the user slides the cursor. Other valuator devices may be implemented by dragging meter needles and twisting control knobs graphically.

5. **Locator device** – returns the (x,y) coordinates of a point on the graphics screen. This logical functions is implemented precisely with the GetMouse function

demonstrated in Read_Position. What else is there to say?

6. **Stroke device** – returns a sequence of (x,y) coordinates. This logical function was implemented by the x and y "speedometer" boxes on the **Drawing** window in Read-Position.

A number of graphics text writers have observed that any of these logical interactive devices may be "mapped onto"—or implemented by)—any real input device.[6] For instance, a keyboard with cursor arrow keys may be used to perform these logical functions for languages and platforms not supporting mice (such as pre-Windows *Turbo Pascal*). This is roughly equivalent to—and about as convenient as—using the mouse for generating a character string, a feat neatly accomplished in Figure 3.17.

Interactive Construction Techniques

Now that we have built up a repertoire of interactive techniques, the tools are at hand for writing useful interactive programs. A large class of interactive graphics programs involves the use of interactive devices such as the mouse to construct graphical objects on the screen. This class includes all painting, drawing, drafting, CAD, and finite element programs. A useful set of interactive techniques have evolved for making the task of constructing objects simpler, faster, and more accurate. Most of these interactive construction techniques involve use of the logical devices and interactive techniques demonstrated above.

Four of the most general interactive construction techniques include:

- **Gridding** – Most construction applications include a grid option. When the grid option is turned on, lines are constrained to start and stop at the grid points, and the bounding box of more complex graphical objects snap from one grid point to the next. This assures physical continuity of the object and provides size and location accuracy limited only by the precision of the machine. The grid option usually provides a sub-option for displaying or hiding the grid points.

- **Constraints** – Construction application programs usually provide constraint options for constructing graphics primitives such as lines, squares, and circles. A typical constraint applied to a line (e.g., by holding down the *Option* key while drawing it), restricts the angle it makes with the horizontal to modulo 45°. Constraining a rectangle produces a square, and constraining an oval produces a circle. Such constraints greatly simplify the construction process.

- **Snaps** – The snap option resembles an object-based grid constraint. That is, when the snap option (also known as "gravity field") is turned on, the end point of a line being drawn in the vicinity of an already existing line "snaps" to the end of the existing line to assure continuity. Typically, objects can be selected as the "snap-to" object so that a line drawn near a snap-to circle will be drawn in so as to be tangent to it. Snaps are particularly important in applications such as finite element analysis to assist in eliminating gaps, cracks, holes, and other embarrassing drafting artifacts.

- **Rubber banding** – Lines are the basic graphical primitive of all construction programs, and any technique for simplifying and making line drawing more intuitive is highly desirable. One of the most useful techniques for constructing lines is the *rubber band* algorithm. Rubber banding involves sending a message via

input device to select the anchor point (first point) of the line, moving the cursor to the terminal point of the line and sending another message to signal the end point. During the motion to the final point position, the rubber band algorithm draws, erases, and redraws the line repeatedly between the anchor point and the present cursor position to provide highly effective feedback to the designer on what the final result will look like.

Rubber Banding Algorithm

A rubber banding algorithm is presented in the program RubberBand, and its output is shown in Figure 3.18.

The minimalist philosophy used in building RubberBand was: write a labeled, rubber banding construction program in the minimum number of lines of code. All of the procedures used in RubberBand have been described previously.

The first section, down to repeat, opens the **Drawing** window, labels it, lists the program options, and sets the pen mode to *Xor* to facilitate the line erase process. The repeat loop performs the repetitive line drawing operations and is exited only by double clicking on the left-hand side of the **Drawing** window. The repeat loop does nothing until the button is pressed. Then, the anchor point is read as $(x1,y1)$ and the program enters a loop which continues as long as the button remains down. This is the key rubber banding loop which reads the current cursor position, $(x2,y2)$, draws a line from $(x1,y1)$ to $(x2,y2)$, and immediately erases it by the second DrawLine command in *Xor* mode. Without the erase operation, the screen soon becomes cluttered with a "sun burst" of lines radiating from the anchor point. When the button is released, program control drops down to the final DrawLine command which draws a permanent line between the desired points. The exit procedure is an inelegant shortcut to terminate the program without introducing any more variables or defining new menu boxes.

In spite of its simplicity, RubberBand offers nearly the same functionality as the *Line* mode of many commercial painting and drawing programs. Its primary weakness is that the *Xor* pen mode causes the intersection of two lines to revert to a white pixel.

Pascal Program RubberBand

```
program RubberBand;
{Program to demonstrate Rubber Band technique}
{for constructing graphical objects          }

    var
      x1, y1, x2, y2: integer;
      p:point;

begin
    ShowDrawing;          {Open Drawing Window}
    MoveTo(20, 20);          {Label graph and options}
    TextSize(18);
    WriteDraw('Rubber Band Program');
    TextSize(10);
    MoveTo(30, 40);
    WriteDraw('• Button down to draw line');
    MoveTo(30, 50);
    WriteDraw('• Double-click left of window to QUIT');
    PenMode(patXor);       {Set Pen Mode to Xor}
                           {to erase and redraw line}
    repeat                 {Keep working until exit}
      if Button then       {executes once/line}
        begin
          GetMouse(p);     {Read first point on line}
          x1:=p.h;         {horizontal element of point}
          y1:=p.v;         [vertical element of point]
          while Button do  {Loop until button released}
            begin
              GetMouse(p);      {Read second point}
              x2:=p.h;       {horizontal element}
              y2:=p.v;       [vertical element}
              DrawLine(x1, y1, x2, y2);   {Draw line}
              DrawLine(x1, y1, x2, y2);   {Erase line}
            end;     {Now redraw  permanent line }
          DrawLine(x1, y1, x2, y2);
        end;
    until (x1 < 0) and Button     {Exit by clicking left}
end.                              {of Drawing Window}
```

Figure 3.18
Output of program, RubberBand. The program
provides a simple but intuitive drawing tool. After
about fifteen minutes of practice, the user can
create sketches such as this in about five minutes.

Conclusions

An important element in developing graphical
applications programs is a supportive programming environment. Such environments provide an
integrated editor-linker-compiler-debugger with
helpful windows for observing variables in single
step or trace modes. Object-oriented programming
(OOP) is a particularly effective paradigm for
designing, building and manipulating graphical
objects. WIMP graphical user interfaces illustrate
all the essential features and advantages of OOP.
Interaction with objects on a graphics screen
require the capabilities for pointing, position
sensing, and action sensing. Procedures for
performing these three functions may be
combined to implement all six logical input device
functions. These, in turn, form the basis for
interactive construction techniques such as
constraints and rubber banding on which painting,
drawing, and CAD applications are built.

Exercises

3.1 Compare the integrated editor-linker-compiler-debugger programming environment of THINK Pascal with the programming environment in which you learned Pascal. Indicate the name of that system and the steps required for developing a program. What aspects of an integrated development environment do you feel help increase productivity the most?

3.2 What advantages does the hierarchical, project-based structure of THINK Pascal have over more conventional "flat-file" program structures?

3.3 The proj2 program in Figure 3.5 is a Standard Pascal framework with several embedded QuickDraw extensions for doing graphics. Make a photocopy of the program and highlight the extended Pascal (QuickDraw) syntax. Why are such extensions necessary for doing graphics in Pascal?

3.4 Key in the proj2 program, open an *Observe* window as shown in Figure 3.7, and screen dump the *Observe* and *Drawing* windows for i = 1 → 3. How do you explain the alternating color of the inner rectangle?

3.5 How is greater programming efficiency achieved by the *inheritance* property of objects in object-oriented programming?

3.6 Polymorphism in OOP was defined as different objects receiving, and possibly responding differently to, the same message. Give three other examples from your programming experience in which polymorphism is being or could be used effectively.

3.7 The program primitives demonstrated both *absolute* move (MoveTo) and *relative* move (Move) procedures. Explain the different behavior of these two functions and give an example in which each would have an advantage over the other.

3.8 Does WriteDraw more closely resemble the Standard Pascal Write or Writeln? Write a procedure, WriteLnDraw, which simulates on the Drawing Window the function of Writeln on the text screen.

3.9 In Figure 3.11, use a ruler to determine the following properties of pixels and coordinates on the Drawing Window:
- Aspect ratio: are Macintosh screen pixels square?
- Scale: How many pixels are there in an inch?
- Origin position in the **Drawing** window.
- Location of "plotting point" on extended (multi-pixel) point.

3.10 In Figure 3.11, use two of the (x,y) coordinates specified in the figure to compute the equation of the straight line going through all three points using the two-point formula for a line, convert the equation into the slope/intercept formula for a line and plot the resulting straight line. Does the line go through the three points?

3.11 Interpret the *local* coordinate system of the **Drawing** window in OOP terms. What advantages does a local system provide compared to using the *global* screen coordinates? Are negative coordinates possible with a global system?

3.12 For historic and technological reasons, the origin of the screen coordinate system for most graphics systems is in the upper left-hand corner of the screen (or window for systems supporting windows). What are some of the reasons for this? What problems do you foresee arising for this non-conventional choice?

3.13 The spiral program, Pattern, with output shown in Figure 3.12 was written as a recursive program. Rewrite the program using straight interation. Which version is more efficient? Why?

3.14 The Fractal1 program was a "quick and dirty" implementation of the *Chaos Game* in as few lines of code as possible. One abstraction which would generalize the program would be to replace the code generating the (x_i,y_i)s with a procedure Triangle which, given the center coordinates and length of side, would return the three (x,y) coordinates of its vertices. Write Triangle and verify its operation.

3.15   Another "quick and dirty" fault of Fractal1 is that it contains no instructions for the user. Modify the program to write the user a short message on the **Drawing** window listing the program's name, function, and method of exit.

3.16   Table 3.2 lists five messages which may be sent to each of the four basic geometric figure types (*rectangles, ovals, rounded-corner rectangles,* and *arcs*). Assume you have a system which does not support these messages, but rather has only the pen, point, and line primitives of Table 3.1. Write a procedure `PaintRect`, using only these primitive procedures and lines one pixel wide.

3.17   Write a program, Histogram, which uses user-supplied data and the PaintRect procedure to plot a histogram of the data. Label the chart and axes.

3.18   Write a program, PieChart, which uses user-supplied data and the FillArc procedure to plot a pie chart of the data. Label the chart and pie segments.

3.19   Write a program, BlackBox, which draws two boxes on the screen and blacks out the one most recently clicked, leaving the other one white.

3.20   Write a program, Ruler, which draws a rectangle, triangle, and oval on the screen and provides a measuring function to measure the pixel distance between any two points selected by clicking the mouse cursor. Report the results in three "odometer" boxes labeled (*x1,y1*), (*x2,y2*), and *MeasDist*.

Endnotes

1. Borland International, *Turbo Pascal for Windows,* Language amd Five Volume set of manuals.
2. The primary language used to demonstrate an integrated development environment is *THINK Pascal* by Symantec Corporation.
3. Apple Computer, Inc., *Inside Macintosh Vol 1–5,* Addison-Wesley Publishing Company, Reading, MA (1985–1986).
4. Schmucker, Kurt J., *Object-Oriented Programming for the Macintosh,* Hayden Books, Indianapolis, IN (1986).
5. Barnsley, M. F., Devaney, R. L., Mandelbrot, B. B.,Pietgen, H-O., Saupe, D., and Voss, R. F., *The Science of Fractal Images,* p. 223, Springer-Verlag, New York, NY (1988).
6. Foley, James D. and Wallace, Victor L., "The Art of Natural Graphic Man-Machine Conversation," *Proceedings of the IEEE,* April (1974), Reprinted in *Computer Graphics Tutorial,* John C. Beatty and Kellogg S. Booth (eds), IEEE Computer Society, pp. 315–324 (1982).

Section 2

N-Dimensional Graphics

The goals of this section are:

Chapter 4
To understand *one-dimensional graphics* and transformations such as translation and scaling which can be done with simple matrix mathematics using homogeneous coordinates. Important graphics concepts of windows, viewports, and clipping are introduced.

Chapters 5 and 6
To study *two-dimensional graphics* as a natural extension of 1D graphics within the homogeneous coordinate representation. Chapter 5 deals explicitly with issues involved with representing 2D objects and the transformations of which they are capable. Chapter 6 deals with implementation issues involved with drawing, clipping, and viewing 2D objects. Examples of bit-mapped and object-oriented graphics are presented.

Chapters 7, 8, 9, and 10
To describe *three-dimensional graphics* within the mathematical framework developed for 1D and 2D graphics. The importance of representation and modeling is emphasized as the basis for techniques for 3D transformations, hidden surface removal and shading. The concept of model authenticity is introduced as the key to visual realism, with ray tracing and radiosity presented as examples.

Chapter 11
To explore fractals as objects of *fractional dimensionality*. Algorithms are presented for generating the major classes of fractals. Fractal geometry is crucial for model authenticity of natural scenes, and the first practical application of fractal geometry—image compression—is described in detail.

Chapter 4

One-Dimensional Graphics

...of all methods for analyzing and communicating statistical information, well-designed data graphics are usually the simplest and at the same time the most powerful..
Edward Tufte

T he first section of this book presented the technological basis for computer graphics visualization. In our definition of computer graphics as the *creation and manipulation of graphical objects*, the source of graphical objects is not specified. The most general definition of computer graphics encompasses the whole field of image processing, including images originating from video sources, digital scanners, and image libraries. A more restrictive view of computer graphics—one adopted by most textbook authors—defines graphical objects exclusively in terms of those generated algorithmically. In fact, classification of graphical objects as *natural* vs. *artificial objects* makes a fairly clean distinction between these two types.

Natural objects are those *transferred into the machine* from some external source. Some of the most common examples include: weather satellite photos, images from medical tomography, video, and scanner input. Artificial objects are those springing from the mind of the user and need not have any physical realization. Images created by painting, drafting, drawing, CAD, and all other *generative programs* fall into this category. As in all classification schemes, there are ambiguous and borderline cases. What is a scanned image of a computer generated blueprint? Is a perfectly rendered industrial part with all the dimensions and properties of the real part (and indistinguishable from a photograph), natural or artificial?

Whether we deal with natural or artificial objects, there are a host of object manipulation functions which we need in order to analyze and refine existing objects or create new ones. A few of these functions were demonstrated explicitly in Chapter 1, but many others were implicit in much

of the other illustrative material presented to this point. For instance, the **Drawing** window object simply appears magically on the screen when the ShowDrawing command is issued in the algorithms of Chapter 3, but we have left it up to the student to carry out the operations of positioning the window conveniently (translation) and dragging the corner to size it appropriately (scaling). Both of these functions may be accomplished under program control but were omitted to simplify the programs. We will deal explicitly with window systems in the chapter on graphical user interface design.

So beneath the smooth facade of any program with a well-designed graphical user interface, there is a lot "going on." The casual user of such programs need not be aware of all the graphical algorithms and their mathematical basis. Students of computer graphics, however, will gain a much keener appreciation of the beauty of these programs and the skills required for building their own graphics applications through knowledge of the graphics fundamentals.

Because many fundamental graphics concepts are basically geometric, we take an N-dimensional approach in which N starts at one and increases throughout the section. For instance, the concept of translation is much simpler in one dimension than in two or three. Manipulations possible in 1D correspond to those from arithmetic—the operations possible on scalars. Moving into 2D and 3D we need to introduce vectors and vector operations, and new possibilities in rotation operations open up. This N-dimensional approach, with N = 1 → X, should be familiar since it parallels our

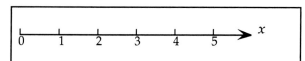

Figure 4.1
A 1D coordinate system.

experience of learning mathematics in elementary school.

Though an N-dimensional approach has the instructional advantage of corresponding to our mathematical development, it also introduces some interesting problems. Chief among these are the intriguing phenomena encountered in scaling from dimension one to higher dimensions.[1] A popular discussion of these issues is given in the book *Flatland*.[2] A more rigorous treatment is presented by Barnsley in *Fractals Everywhere*.[3]

Translation and Scaling Transformations in 1D

What do we mean when we speak of objects in one dimension? Perhaps we should step back one dimension and discuss objects in 0D. In zero dimensional space, the only object is the primitive object, the *point*. A mathematical point is a dimensionless object. The nearest computer graphics analog to a mathematical point is the *pixel*. The analogy is a bit misleading, however, since unlike points, pixels do have a physical size (e.g., 1/72 inch) and other attributes such as color and brightness. Pixels also have another property, location, which is important to their status as computer graphical objects but completely non-essential to their status as mathematical objects. Their only status as mathematical objects is their existence or non-existence, and the only operators are the creation and annihilation operators.

Now consider what happens when we turn the dial on our dimension meter from $0 \rightarrow 1$. Three important phenomena are worthy of note.

- The primitive object(s) present in dimension (N–1) continue to exist.

- New primitive object(s) of dimension N emerge, in this case, the *line segment*, hereafter referred to as the *line*.

- A new set of transformations, undefined in dimension (N–1), appear.

Specifying Points and Lines

The newly emergent 1D object, the *line*, has the mathematical property of length. As a measure of length, it helps to establish a 1D coordinate system as shown in Figure 4.1.

The establishment of the 1D coordinate system provides two useful functions: a) length determination, and b) position specification. These operations are indicated graphically in Figure 4.2.

Note that both the position of points and the length of lines are scalars (objects specified by a single number) in a 1D coordinate system. To completely specify a line, both its position and length must be given. Two conventions are possible:

$$(X,L) \qquad\qquad [4.1]$$

where X = left hand end point position
         L = length.

or, alternatively,

$$(X_1,X_2) \qquad\qquad [4.2]$$

where X_1 = left hand end point position
         X_2 = right hand end point position.

Thus line (a) is specified by (0,4) in either convention, and line (b) is specified as (2.5,5.0) in the two-point convention.

Note that the *point-length* and *two-point* conventions are equivalent in their information content. Each is easily derivable from the other:

$$X_1 = X$$
$$X_2 = X + L. \qquad\qquad [4.3]$$

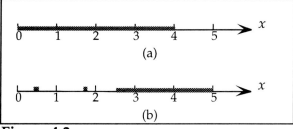

Figure 4.2
Using 1D coordinate systems for functions:
   a)   Length: Line is 4 units long,
   b)   Position: Points at 0.5, 1.75, line starts at 2.5 units.

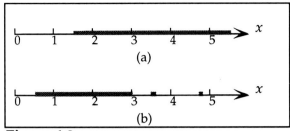

Figure 4.3
Translations applied to objects of Figure 4.2.
   a) $T = +1.5$
   b) $T_1 = +3$ (points)
       $T_2 = -2$ (line).

Translating Points and Lines

Perhaps the most widely used transformation in computer graphics is that of translation—moving graphical objects around the screen. In 1D, translation is restricted to sliding objects along the X axis. Translating an object at point X a distance T moves the object to point X'. The equation relating these quantities is:

$$X' = X + T. \qquad [4.4]$$

Because the length of a line remains unchanged under translation, we can specify the translation of a line as:

$$(X,L) \rightarrow (X',L) = (X + T,L), \qquad [4.5]$$
or
$$(X_1,X_2) \rightarrow$$
$$(X_1',X_2') = (X_1 + T, X_2 + T). \qquad [4.6]$$

Applying several translation operations to the objects shown in Figure 4.2 produces the configurations shown in Figure 4.3.

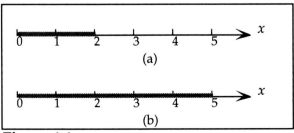

Figure 4.4
Scaling operation with $S = 2.5$.
   a) Original line,
   b) Scaled line.

Note that both points and lines behave similarly under the translation operation. Also, conceptually, the translation, T, of a line may be considered the translation of the infinitely many points composing the line, each by the amount T. Computationally, it is much simpler to simply translate both end points and assume the intermediate points "ride along." Good OOP style suggests defining the line as an object and sending it the message "*Move T.*"

Scaling of Points and Lines

Perhaps the next most important transformation in computer graphics is that of *scaling*. This operation frequently goes under the names of *magnification/-demagnification* and *zoom in/zoom out*. Since points have zero dimension, there is nothing to magnify except their position. Therefore, the behavior of an individual point under scaling is indistinguishable from its behavior under translation.

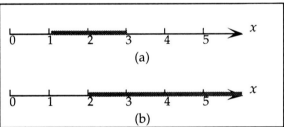

Figure 4.5
Scaling operation with S = 2 applied to line not including the origin.
   a) Original line,
   b) Scaled line.
Note both magnification and shift of line.

The equation for scaling is a simple multiplication of each coordinate, X, by the scale factor, S. This operation transforms each point into a new location, X'.

$$X' = S X. \qquad [4.7]$$

This appears to be quite an intuitive idea, and our intuition is borne out in Figure 4.4 in which a line of length $L = 2$ starting at the origin grows to length $L' = 5$ when scaled by a factor of $S = 2.5$. Scaling of a line involves scaling the two end points, connecting the scaled end points with a line, and interpreting this line as the collection of scaled points connecting the end points.

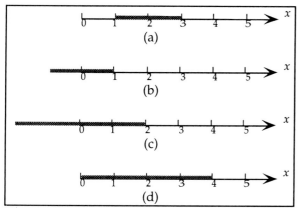

Figure 4.6
Scaling of an object about a point at location 2:
  a) The original line   b) Translated by T = –2
  c) Scaled by S = 2   d) Translated by T = +2.

An interesting phenomena appears when scaling is performed on objects located away from the origin. In Figure 4.5 we show what happens when we scale an L = 2 line located one unit from the origin with a scale factor S = 2.

Scaling of an Object about a Point

Note that the scaling operation performed on objects not located at the origin result in both a *magnification* by the scale factor and a *translation*. The translation may or may not be a desired side effect of the scaling operation. In many instances, the objective of scaling is simply to magnify the object "in place." This is called *scaling of an object about a point*. This objective may be achieved by the introduction of a new concept—*a sequence of operations*. Suppose, for instance, that the goal is to magnify the line shown in Figure 4.5(a) while keeping its center located at location 2.0. This is easily accomplished by the following three-operation sequence of transformations:

1. Translate the line by T = –2 to move its center point to the origin,

2. Scale the line by S = 2,

3. Translate the line back using T = +2 to return its origin to location 2.

The results of this sequence of operations are shown schematically in Figure 4.6.

Reflection Transformation

A final transformation of great utility in graphics synthesis programs is that of *reflection*. We are all familiar with reflection from our daily experience with mirrors. The 1D representation of reflection is given simply by the scaling operation with S = –1. That is, each point on an object with coordinate X maps into coordinate X′ = –X as shown in Figure 4.7.

Two observations may be helpful in better understanding reflections. A quick glance at Figure 4.7 might suggest that the transformation of the line (X_2, X_3) into line $(X_2′, X_3′)$ could equally well be accomplished by the translation, T = –7. This is clearly not the case, however, as a check on the mapping of X_2 proves. A translation of T = –7 would map X_2 onto $X_3′$ rather than $X_2′$ as it ought. So the reflection operation involves primarily an *inversion* of all objects as well as a translation of objects not centered at the origin.

The second observation is that the operation of *reflection about a point* may be accomplished by a sequence of operations just as the scaling about a point was. The three-step sequence for reflection about a point at location *P* includes:

1. Translate the object by $T = -P$

2. Scale the resulting object by $S = -1$

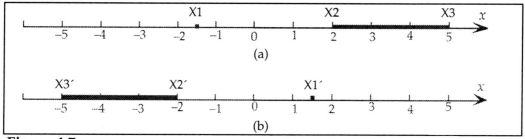

Figure 4.7
Reflection transformation given by S = – 1. Note that X′ = – X.

3. Translate the resulting object by $T = +P$.

Figure 4.8 shows that these three steps do, indeed, reflect the original object by a mirror at point P.

Homogeneous Coordinates and Transformations

The reader may have noticed that scaling and translation are fundamentally different kinds of transformations. One is multiplicative, and one is additive. As we turn the dimension dial up to $N \geq 2$, we shall encounter additional multiplicative transformations for performing rotations and perspective transformations. It would be highly desirable to devise a mathematical formalism capable of representing all of these transformations in a coherent and systematic manner. Early computer graphics researchers recognized the need for such a uniform representation and proposed a system we call the homogeneous matrix representation.[4]

The fundamental idea of a homogeneous coordinate system is that for representing points in an N-dimensional system, we use an N+1 dimen-sional representation. Thus, the scalar representation of a point (X) is represented in a homogeneous system as the vector, (x,w). Since w is simply an arbitrary over-all scale factor, the customary definition is w = 1. This results in the relationship:

$$(X) \rightarrow (wX,w) \rightarrow (x,w) \qquad [4.8]$$

where (x,w) are the homogeneous coordinates of the point X.

Normalizing the homogeneous coordinates by dividing by w gives:

$$(x/w,w/w) \rightarrow (x/w,1) \rightarrow (x,1) \qquad [4.9]$$

after applying the convention that $w = 1$.

Note that the relationship between the conventional coordinate X and the homogeneous coordinate, x, is given by

$$X = x/w \qquad [4.10]$$

where w is arbitrary (but not 0).

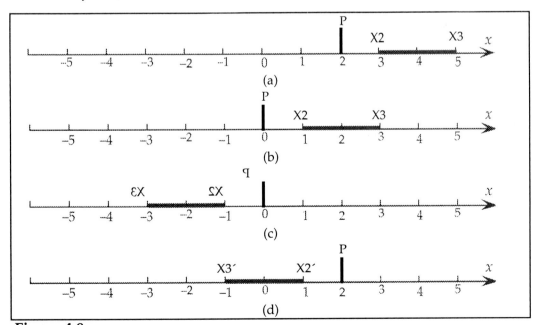

Figure 4.8
Reflection about a point, P. The reflection through a mirror at location P (original configuration (a) is performed by the sequence: (b) translation by $T = -P$, (c) scaling by $S = -1$, followed by (d) translation by $T = +P$. Note that reflection (b) → (c) really does invert the scene.

Therefore, the 1D point $X = 4$ may be represented by the equivalent homogeneous coordinate pairs $(x,w) = (4,1)$, $(8,2)$, or $(20,5)$. This redundancy can be eliminated by selecting the convention, $w = 1$, for which $X = x$. Blinn has pointed out that this convention is equivalent to the projection of the (x,w) 2D point onto the $w = 1$ line along a line from the point through the origin.[5] This geometric interpretation is shown in Figure 4.9.

Matrix Formalism for Transformations

Note that the combination of the scaling and translation transformation may be written as:

$$X' = S\,X + T. \qquad [4.11]$$

The combination of such transformations, that is, a linear scaling followed by a translation, is called an *affine* transformation. One property of affine transformations is that the operators performing the transformation must be one dimension larger in rank than the dimensionality of the objects on which they operate. To perform affine transformations on our 1D objects, we shall need 2D operators, that is, matrices of rank 2. When we transform 2D objects, we will use 3D operators. Barnsley discusses the properties of affine transformations in more rigorous detail.[6]

Matrix Conventions

The general formalism for operating on object X with operator O to transform it into object X' is given as:

$$X' = O\,X. \qquad [4.12]$$

The objects in this case are two, three, and four dimensional vectors representing points in 1D, 2D, and 3D space, and the operators are 2×2, 3×3, and 4×4 matrices. The conformality requirement for matrix multiplication in Equation 4.12 requires that X be a column vector. This is the standard convention for matrix operations in physics, mathematics, and engineering. For reasons lost in the historical mist, but possibly related to the ease of writing row vectors compared to column vectors, the computer graphics community has generally chosen to work with row vectors rather than column vectors. Thus, the computer graphics

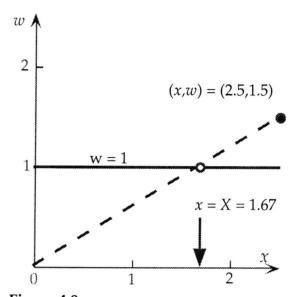

Figure 4.9
Geometric interpretation of transformation of homogeneous coordinates, (x,w), into conventional coordinate, X. The X coordinate is the intersection of the ray from the origin to the (x,w) point with the w = 1 line. Note that all equivalent homogeneous coordinate pairs such as $(1.67,1)$, $(2.5,1.5)$, $(5,3)$, etc. would all project to $x = X = 1.67$ by this projective technique.

convention requires reformulating equation 4.11 as:

$$X' = X\,O. \qquad [4.13]$$

Matrix Representation of Affine Transformations

With this background in matrix conventions and homogeneous coordinates, the affine transformation representing an arbitrary scaling by S and translation by T may be written:

$$X' = X \cdot M, \qquad [4.14]$$

where
$\quad X' = [x'\ 1]$ (2×1 row vector),
$\quad X = [x\ \ 1]$ (2×1 row vector),
and

$$M = \begin{bmatrix} S & 0 \\ T & 1 \end{bmatrix} \qquad (2 \times 2 \text{ matrix}).$$

Note the boldface convention: vectors and matrices (i.e., objects with internal elements) are written in **boldface**. To verify that Equation 4.14 is, in fact, equivalent to Equation 4.11, we can multiply the vector X by matrix M to get:

$$[x' \ 1] = [x \ 1] \begin{bmatrix} S & 0 \\ T & 1 \end{bmatrix}. \qquad [4.15]$$

Doing the matrix multiplication (remember the two-finger, row/column rule?) gives:

$$\begin{aligned} x' &= x\,S + T\,, \\ 1 &= 1 \end{aligned} \qquad [4.16]$$

The first equation in 4.16 agrees with 4.11 when we substitute the identity $X = x$, and the second equation is a trivial solution corresponding to the redundant nature of the homogeneous representation.

Several points are worth noting about this matrix formalism. First is that the affine transformation given by Equation 4.11 may be decomposed into its constituent transformations, scaling and translation, within the formalism. Thus, the scaling transformation may be written:

$$X' = X \cdot S\,, \qquad [4.17]$$

and the translation transformation as:

$$X' = X \cdot T\,, \qquad [4.18]$$

where

$$S = \begin{bmatrix} S & 0 \\ 0 & 1 \end{bmatrix} \ \text{and} \ T = \begin{bmatrix} 1 & 0 \\ T & 1 \end{bmatrix}. \qquad [4.19]$$

Secondly, complex transformations, such as the reflection through a point described in Figure 4.8, may be performed by a single matrix, M, which is the *composed* transformation obtained by multiplying together the matrices of the individual transformations. For instance, in Figure 4.8, consider the three transformations:

1. Translation by $T_1 = -2$,

2. Scaling by $S = -1$,

3. Translation by $T_2 = +2$.

The concatenated matrix, M, is simply

$$M = T_1 \cdot S \cdot T_2 \qquad [4.20]$$

$$= \begin{bmatrix} 1 & 0 \\ -2 & 1 \end{bmatrix} \begin{bmatrix} -1 & 0 \\ 0 & 1 \end{bmatrix} \begin{bmatrix} 1 & 0 \\ 2 & 1 \end{bmatrix},$$

$$= \begin{bmatrix} -1 & 0 \\ 4 & 1 \end{bmatrix}.$$

Interpreting this result as the affine transformation, $X' = S\,X + T$, we see that the mirror reflection about point $P = 2$ is accomplished by the combination of scaling by $S = -1$ followed by a translation of $T = +4$.

Finally, consider the power and elegance of the matrix formalism on homogeneous coordinates. The transformation matrix, M, given in Equation 4.20 is just a taste of things to come. When we derive the transformation matrix for rotation about an arbitrary axis in 3D, we must perform SEVEN distinct transformations. By concatenating the seven transformation matrices into a single matrix, we achieve tremendous computational efficiency. Since all transformations of interest in computer graphics may be expressed as a single transformation matrix, M, the formalism provides a simplicity and elegance of great value in generating program code. So rather than writing a separate matrix multiply routine for scaling, translation, rotation, perspective, and viewing, a single routine will solve all transformations.

One last observation is in order on the pedagogical rationale for introducing rather abstract concepts such as homogeneous coordinates and matrix algebra for solving the almost trivial transformations allowed in 1D. Isn't this really killing a gnat with a sledgehammer? If we were to stop at 1D graphics, the answer is certainly "yes." However, the formal mathematics from this section will transfer smoothly to our studies of 2D and 3D transformations. Illustrating the concepts using 2×2 matrices from 1D is four times more efficient than using the 4×4 matrices of 3D. Not only do the equations appear simpler (because, numerically, they are), but we also save typing and paper. This is one of the main reasons we have chosen an N-Dimensional approach and started with N = 1.

Windows, Viewports, and Clipping in 1D

Since 1D examples have proven useful to illustrate the concept of transformations, let's see what they can tell us about the concepts of windows, viewports, and clipping. Until now, we have dealt only with fairly abstract concepts of mathematical transformations which are completely independent of any real graphical display system. However, the viewing transformation concepts of windows, viewports, and clipping involve the process by which the image of real-world objects are projected on a real-world screen. Therefore, we must become more specific.

First, what do we mean by a real-world 1D object? And what would a 1D, real-world screen look like? One 1D object of interest (actually, there are not too many) would be a graph of a Morse code message. One such message that hopefully will never be sent is shown above. When translated, this means *SOS JOY OF RACINE*, the international signal indicating the author's boat is in distress. In International Morse code, the space between parts of the same letter is equal to one dot, the space between two letters is three dots, the space between two words is five dots, and a dash is equal to three dots.

Viewing Transformation Nomenclature

The 1D "screen" for displaying such a message might consist of a linear row of LEDs or LCDs similar to the "peak detector" indicators on most audio tape decks. An interesting problem is: How many picture elements (pixels) would be required to display this image clearly on the 1D screen? Now that we can visualize what a 1D object might look like and the type of screen we might display it on, we can better understand the viewing transformation, the process by which we map the object into an image on the screen. Before defining the viewing transformation, however, it is necessary to define some terms which will be used frequently throughout the book.

- **Scene** – The collection of real-world objects we wish to visualize. The first step in displaying the scene is to represent it in terms of numbers corresponding to the size,

shape, and locations of the objects in the scene. This process is called building a *model of the scene* and involves issues of *representation*. It is accomplished by building a numerical database, computing the numbers algorithmically, or capturing video or scanned images in image files.

- **Object space** – The space in which the original object exists. The 1D object space of Morse code is the space of dots and dashes. The 2D object space of an integrated circuit chip design consists of the arrangement of component gates and connecting leads. The 3D object space of a motor consists of the physical arrangement of its components. Note that object space is completely independent of computers, screens, and how we look at the objects.

- **World coordinates** – The coordinates for specifying the positions and shapes of objects in object space. The coordinates are given in natural units of the object space. In our 1D example the natural unit of the world coordinates would be one dot. The world coordinate units of a 2D IC chip would be in microns or thousandths of an inch. The natural units for specifying the 3D arrangement of components of a motor would be inches or centimeters.

- **Image space** – The image space is the screen on which an image of the object is to be projected. The natural unit for describing image space on raster scan devices is the pixel. On our 1D display, pixels would be labeled from 0 to 255, for example. The image space of 2D displays such as VGA screens is a 640 × 480 pixel array. At present, we have no 3D image display devices, but the goal of research on holographic techniques is to project 3D objects into 3D image space.

- **Normalized device coordinates** – These are coordinates on the range 0 → 1 designed to eliminate the device dependence of screen coordinates. Thus, a NDC = 0.5 would refer to pixel 127 of our linear 0 – 255 pixel display. Most images in computer graphics are specified in terms of NDC. In actual practice, drivers must be written for each device to convert NDC into pixel coordinates of the screen.

- **Window** – That portion of the scene selected for observation, specified in terms of world coordinates. In our 1D example the window would be specified by the two numbers, W_L and W_R, the left-most and right-most dot spaces we wish to display. Rectangular windows on 2D scenes are specified by the four world coordinates, W_{x_L}, W_{x_R}, W_{y_T}, and W_{y_B}, appropriate to the scene (e. g., centimeters, feet, or miles).

- **Viewport** – That portion of the display device selected to show the image, specified in terms of NDC. On our linear display, the viewport would be specified by V_L and V_R, the left-hand and right-hand edges of the viewport. A typical, rectangular viewport on a 2D screen is specified by V_{x_L}, V_{x_R}, V_{y_T}, and V_{y_B}. Although the nomenclature seems a bit inconsistent, the "windows" of windows operating systems such as Microsoft Windows, X Windows, and the Macintosh OS are really viewports by computer graphics definition and usage.

- **Viewing transformation** – The operations required to map world coordinates of the model of a scene contained within a window onto the image space viewport. Three transformations required to perform the viewing transformation include:

  1. Translating one corner of the window to the origin in world coordinates.
  2. Scaling the window to conform to (fit) the viewport.
  3. Translating the scaled image to the desired viewport location.

- **Clipping** – It is clearly unnecessary to apply the viewing transformation to those portions of the scene which lie outside of the window. The process of discarding any unwanted information is called clipping.

From efficiency considerations, clipping should be applied in object space rather than image space. This is particularly important for high-magnification viewing transformations, that is, when viewing a complex scene with a very small window.

The Morse code Example – 1D

Now let us use the Morse code example to illustrate as many of these concepts as we can. The scene, in this case, is the collection of dots and dashes making up the message, *SOS JOY OF RACINE*. The object space unit is the dot, in terms of which the dash, character separation, and word separation are defined. World coordinates are specified in terms of the count of dot spaces, with the origin starting at the first dot or dash of the message. Image space consists of the row of LCD pixels on which we will map the image. The normalized device coordinates, X_N, are real numbers on the range 0 – 1 and are obtained from pixel number coordinate, X, by the operation:

$$X_N = X/N \qquad [4.21]$$

where N = Number of pixels in display.

Suppose, as the boat is filling with water, we wish to examine only the essential portion of the message, *SOS JOY*. We apply the window, $(W_L W_R) = (1,75)$, to bracket this submessage as shown in Figure 4.10.

To make the mapping as simple as possible, we select a viewport as the leftmost 75 LEDs of the linear display. Assuming the display has 100 LED pixels, this corresponds to $(V_L V_R) = (0,0.75)$ in NDC. This selection provides a one-to-one mapping of the dot structure of the message to the LED pixels. In terms of the viewing transformation, this can be stated as a window translation of zero, followed by a scale factor of 1, followed by a viewport translation of zero. Clipping is done on the original scene by the simple test:

> if $X \geq 1$ and $X \leq 75$
> then PLOT
> else SKIP.

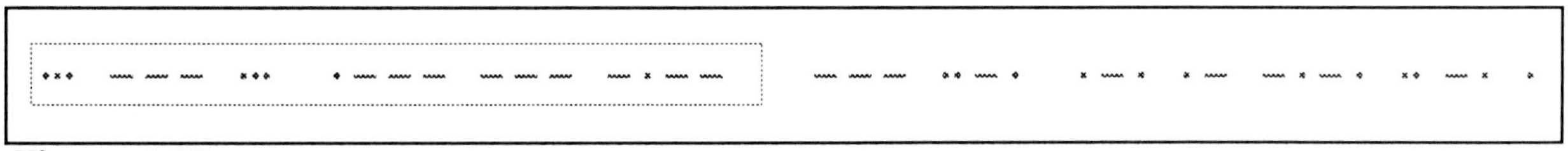

Figure 4.10
Morse code "image" with linear window bracketing *SOS JOY*.

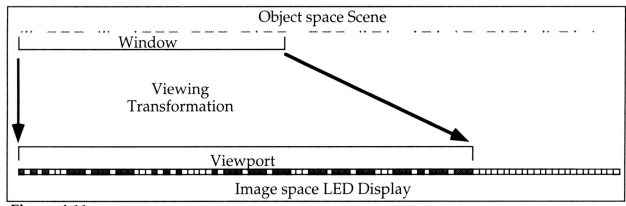

Figure 4.11
Image of Morse code segment, *SOS JOY*, displayed on LED indicator.

Applying this viewing transformation with clipping produces the image shown in Figure 4.11.

Suppose we are now up to our neck in water and want to display a large *SOS* in the center of the indicator screen until the last gurgle is heard. We narrow our window down to $(W_L, W_R) = (1,27)$ to bracket just the *SOS*, set the scale factor $S = 2$, and set the viewport translation to $T = 23$. Since the scaled message is 54 dots long, its center is at dot 27. We want to move this dot to LED pixel 50 of the 100-pixel screen, requiring a translation of 23 dots (pixels). In terms of the viewport, since the image is 54 pixels in size and we want it centered on the screen, we need $(V_L, V_R) = (0.23, 0.77)$. The resulting magnified, centered *SOS* distress call is shown in Figure 4.12.

The Viewing Transformation

Since the viewing transformation is a sequence of translation and scaling transformations, it should be possible to represent it by a general affine transformation of the form:

$$X_d = a\, X_w + b \qquad [4.22]$$

where
X_d = display device coordinate,
X_w = world coordinates.

As indicated above, the viewing transformation consists of the translation, T_1, of the left "corner" of the window to the origin, followed by a scaling, S, to map the window onto the viewport,

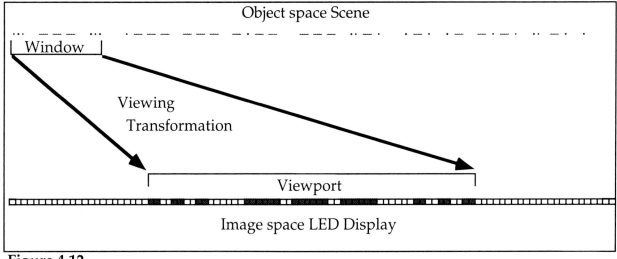

Figure 4.12
Image of (1,27) dot window transformed to (0.23,0.77) viewport.

followed by a translation, T_2, to shift the scaled image to the correct viewport location. In terms of the specified parameters, W_L, W_R, V_L, and V_R, it is apparent that these three transformations are given by:

$$T_1 = -W_L \qquad [4.23]$$

$$S = \frac{V_R - V_L}{W_R - W_L} \qquad [4.24]$$

$$T_2 = +V_L. \qquad [4.25]$$

In the matrix representation, the concatenated transformation, M, is given as:

$$M = T_1 \cdot S \cdot T_2 \qquad [4.26]$$

$$= \begin{bmatrix} 1 & 0 \\ T_1 & 1 \end{bmatrix} \begin{bmatrix} S & 0 \\ 0 & 1 \end{bmatrix} \begin{bmatrix} 1 & 0 \\ T_2 & 1 \end{bmatrix}. \qquad [4.27]$$

Multiplying our Equation 4.27 gives:

$$M = \begin{bmatrix} S & 0 \\ (ST_1 + T_2) & 1 \end{bmatrix}. \qquad [4.28]$$

The homogeneous coordinate representation of the viewing transformation can be written:

$$X_d = X_w M \qquad [4.29]$$

where
$$X_d = [x_d \ 1] \ and \ X_w = [x_w \ 1]$$
(Row vectors).

Substituting 4.28 into 4.29 and multiplying out yields:

$$x_d = S\, x_w + (S\, T_1 + T_2) \qquad [4.30]$$

which is indeed of the form shown in 4.22. Expressing 4.30 in terms of the viewing transformation parameters given in 4.23 – 4.25, we get:

$$x_d = S\,(x_w + T_1) + T_2$$

$$= \frac{V_R - V_L}{W_R - W_L}\,(x_w - W_L) + V_L. \qquad [4.31]$$

Equation 4.31 is the final result, the equation of the viewing transformation in 1D.

Alternative 1D Coordinate Systems

The objective of 1D coordinate systems is the unique representation of scalar information, i.e., numbers. A number of other coordinate systems and visualization techniques have been developed for displaying scalar information. These include angular and polar coordinates and volume visualization techniques. While scalars can be correctly displayed on the linear, 1D coordinate system discussed above, it is often more effective and convenient to use one of the alternate coordinate systems.

Angular Coordinates

One of the most common, nearly universal, instruments for measuring electrical and physical quantities electrically is the d'Arsonval galvanometer. In this instrument, an electric current creates a magnetic force on a spring-loaded, mechanical indicator needle. By careful design, the needle movement shows a nearly linear response to current over a wide range of angular deflection. Since many quantities of physical interest (e.g., speed, temperature, pressure, flow rates, and so on) are easily transduced into electrical signals, electrical galvanometers remain in widespread use and will continue to do so for the foreseeable future. They remain extremely effective instruments for conveying information on stability, noise, oscillations, and other signal properties which are difficult to convey through a digital voltmeter output.

Because of the attractive features of d'Arsonval meters and widespread experience with them, designers of graphical user interfaces, graphical tool kits, and graphical instrument simulation programs frequently supply a "meter" object for displaying scalar information. The user specifies the variable for display on the meter and the full-scale reading. The meter then provides a continuous display of the variable of interest. Figure 4.13 shows one possible application for angular coordinates displayed on a simulated meter.

Since angular-measure "meters" display only single scalars, they are not capable of displaying a linear image such as the Morse code message. However, other 1D graphical concepts, such as object space, world coordinates, and image space carry over directly to angular coordinates. The window on world coordinates is typically $(0, X_{fs})$, where X_{fs} is the full scale calibrated meter reading. The viewport is specified in terms of the angular range, $(0, \theta_m)$, where θ_m is the maximum angular deflection. A given world coordinate, X, is mapped to the appropriate angular coordinate, θ, by the transformation:

$$\theta = S\,X \qquad\qquad [4.32]$$

where

$$S = \frac{\theta_m}{X_{fs}} \qquad \text{(scale factor)}.$$

Polar Coordinates

The limitations of the angular meter capable of displaying only angular points can be overcome by using more generalized polar coordinates. Polar coordinates can represent both angular points (as the angular meter did) and angular intervals (the angular equivalent of a line with

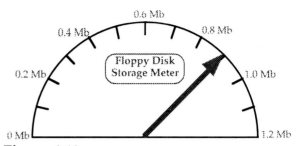

Figure 4.13
Analog meter for displaying scalar information. Here the needle indicates that the 1.2 Mb disk is about 3/4 full of data.

length). In Figure 4.14, two examples of 1D polar coordinate representations are shown.

It is important to take note of certain constraints imposed by 1D polar coordinates. First is that the "viewport" in almost all cases corresponds to θ on the range 0°–360°. This is not necessarily *always* the case, however. Consider the polar coordinate indicator shown in Figure 4.14(a) which we all recognize as a clock. Although probably the most commonly used measuring indicator, the reading and correct interpretation of clock information is a non-trivial task. The difficulties of mapping the scalar called time of a 24-

(a)

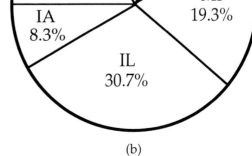

(b)

Figure 4.14
Two examples of polar coordinate displays. In (a), the two hands indicate two angular points which we interpret as hours and minutes; in (b), the pie segments indicate angular intervals equivalent to line segments in 1D linear displays.

Table 4.1

Shale Oil Resources of the World[7]

Region	Total Estimated Resources (10^9 bbl)
Africa	4000
Asia	5500
Australia/New Zealand	1000
North America	3000
South America	2000

hour day onto a clock face can be summarized as:

- There is a two-fold redundancy in a given reading, a.m. and p.m., which can only be resolved by "keeping track of time" or looking out the window.

- The indicator system is a hybrid digital-analog system. The small hand indicates the hour digitally. The large hand gives an analog minute reading unless there is a second hand, in which case the minute hand becomes digital and the second hand is analog.

- A clock face generally provides two super-imposed polar coordinate scales, neither of which is labeled, with the hour scale numbered and the minute scale simply marked by tick marks. Full rotation of one hand corresponds to 12 units and that of the other, 60 units.

- One complete "clock cycle" of the small hand is two complete revolutions or 720°. That of the large hand is 24 revolutions or 8,640°. Thus, the "viewport" may be considered as 2 layers or 24 layers of a 360° basis.

These complexities explain why reading time is one of the major subjects of the first few years of primary education.

Perhaps the most common usage of polar coordinates in graphics is the so-called "pie chart" shown in Figure 4.14(b). Pie charts are generally used to display the relative sizes of the components of some whole object, in this case, the *Midwest Sales* of a fictitious company by state. If the size of the whole object is represented by the window, X_t, and each component of the window is X_i, then the appropriate size of each angular pie, θ_i, is given by:

$$\theta_i = S X_i \qquad [4.33]$$

where

$$S = \frac{360}{X_t} \qquad \text{(scale factor)}.$$

Volume Visualization

A final 1D application, widely used and often abused, is the representation of scalar quantities as volumes. For example, to represent automobile exports by country, auto icons are used with sizes scaled to represent the volume of export. Analyses of natural resources frequently use volume visualization techniques with, for instance, the size of a coal pile representing coal production by state and the size of an oil barrel representing oil imports by country.

Consider, for instance, using volume visualization to represent the data of Table 4.1 on estimated shale oil resources of the world.

The temptation in using volume visualization to represent these scalar numbers is to construct the barrel for Australia/New Zealand and simple scale it by two times to generate South America's resource, three times for North America, and so on, to produce the graph shown in Figure 4.15.

In Figure 4.16, the correct representation of the volumes is presented, with a scaling of the linear dimension by the cube root of the raw data. Thus, the Asian barrel in Figure 4.16 would hold 5.5 times as much oil as the Australian/New Zealand barrel—as it ought—rather than 166 times as much which the misleading Figure 4.15 would suggest.

Volume visualization, correctly used, can be an effective presentation technique. Care must be taken, however, not to map scalars to the display screen with a linear mapping if the image icons represent areas or volumes. If the original scalars are interpreted as volumes, V_i, then the mapping of the linear dimension, X_i', of the display icon should scale as:

$$X_i' \propto \sqrt[3]{V_i}. \qquad [4.34]$$

Some authors caution against using 2D and 3D techniques for displaying 1D data because of the difficulty of design and the ambiguity in perception.[8]

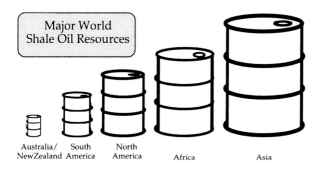

Figure 4.15
Misleading volume visualization of data from
Table 4.1. Here the linear dimensions have been
scaled by the numbers shown which results in a
gross misrepresentation of the data.

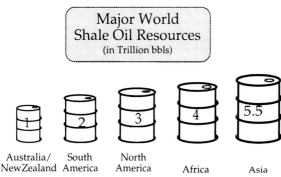

Figure 4.16
Correctly scaled volume representation of Table
4.1 data. The linear dimensions have been scaled
by the cube root of the data. Note also the labeling
of the graph which enables the reader to make use
of the data.

Presentation Graphics in 1D

The graphical mode for communicating numerical
and conceptual information has become so
pervasive that it has achieved its own designation,
presentation graphics. Presentation graphics, using
the media of overhead transparencies, slides, computer-generated video, or live computer output,
has become the standard mode for reporting
company earnings, market trends, organizational

structure, and even presenting difficult concepts
such as goals and strategy. A large share of
presentation graphics efforts deal with effective
techniques for representing and presenting 1D
information.

We have already been introduced to two of
the most important modes for scalar data display.
These two modes include:

- *Bar charts* – a special case of the general 1D
  linear LED indicator,

- *Pie charts* – several variations on the polar
  coordinate theme.

The user has two options for generating high-
quality presentation graphics—commercial programs or homegrown programs. Because of their
generality, power, and convenience, commercial
presentation graphics programs will in most cases
be the preferred option. However, we shall demonstrate both options in order to give the reader
a better feeling for the techniques and programming effort incorporated in commercial programs and problems the programmer must
resolve.

Presentation Graphics Techniques

For converting scalar information efficiently into
convincing bar and pie charts, graphical spreadsheets such as *Lotus 123*™, *Quatro Pro*™, *Excel*™,
and *WingZ*™ are hard to beat. Consider the
following steps for displaying data from Table 4.1.

1. Open *WingZ* by a single menu select.

2. With the mouse, select the ten items from
    the table in the word processed text by
    sweeping from "Africa" to "2000," and
    select *Copy* from the *Edit* menu.

3. In the *WingZ* screen select a conformal
    region of the spread sheet (5 rows × 2
    columns), and select *Paste* from the *Edit*
    window.

4. Click on the "graph" icon, and drag a box
    on the screen for the graph.

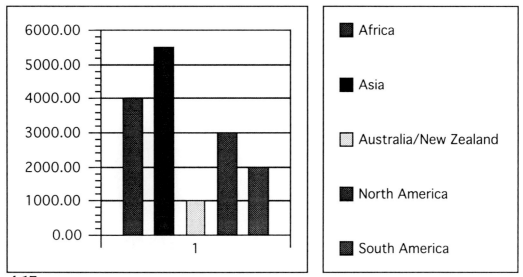

Figure 4.17
Bar chart of Table 4.1 data copied into and displayed by *WingZ*.

These seven mouse operations, which require about 20 seconds, generate the graph shown in Figure 14.17. Note that this shaded bar chart has been produced without typing a single key.

Next, we restructure and label the bar chart of Figure 4.17 to produce Figure 4.18. The changes made include:

1. Type a Title ("Shale Oil Resources") and Legend ("Trillion bbls") at the top of the two data columns and change fonts and sizes to those shown.

2. Position the Title and Legend at the top of the graph by menu selection under *Graph/Title* and *Graph/Legend*.

3. Select *Vertical Parsing* under *Graph/General* to label the x-axis.

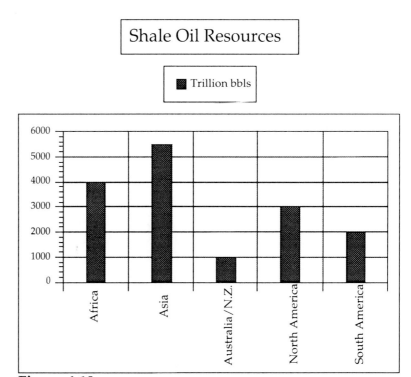

Figure 4.18
Reformatted and labeled bar chart of Table 4.1 data.

Note that this reformatted graph did, in fact, require typing the *Title* and *Legend* and shortening up the "Australia/New Zealand" name. This typing, plus five selections with the mouse, reformatted Figure 4.17 into Figure 4.18.

The stacked format provides a final variation of bar chart. Making two mouse selections from the *Graph/General* menu, *Vertical Stacking* and *Horizontal Parsing*, converts Figure 4.18 → Figure 4.19.

A single mouse select of *Pie* from the *Graph/Gallery* menu converts this into Figure 4.20.

And, finally, the visually appealing but somewhat overworked 3D pie chart of Figure 4.21 is obtained by selecting this format under *Graph/Gallery*. The only other change made was to turn off the *Automatic Layout* feature under the *Graph/General* menu in order to manipulate the title and legend. These were dragged into their final position in order to compress the figure and save space.

The purpose of Figures 4.17 – 4.21 is to demonstrate the ease and versatility with which modern, graphical spreadsheets can be used to produce presentation graphics of scalar data in the form of 1D bar charts or pie charts. The user need only key in or copy data into the spreadsheet, open a viewport on the spreadsheet, and the graph

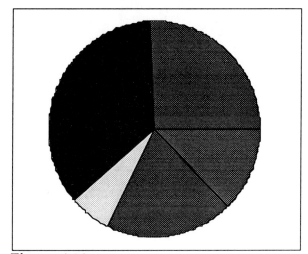

Figure 4.20
Pie chart of Table 4.1 by *WingZ.*

magically appears. With a few more mouse clicks, the user can rearrange the display into any desired format.

A final advantage of the graphics produced by programs such as *WingZ* is their object-oriented structure. That is, the 3D pie shown in Figure 4.21 is really composed of individual graphical elements which may be grouped and manipulated by any drawing program. So, for instance, Figure 4.21 may be copied into Canvas™ and partially "exploded" as shown in Figure 4.22 by selecting and dragging the component pie slices into any desired location. The OOP nature of the elements of the graphical pie object supports messages such as "select yourself," "join a group," "move to this location," and "go to front" or "go to back" layers. Such object-oriented features provide graphics designers with maximum flexibility.

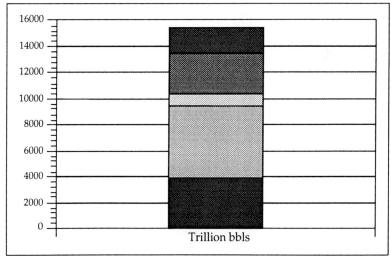

Figure 4.19
Vertically stacked shaded bar chart of Table 4.1 data.

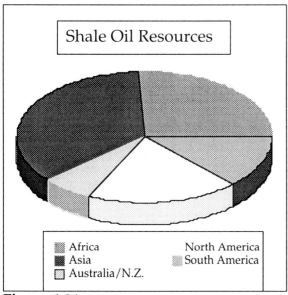

Figure 4.21
3D Pie Chart of Table 4.1 data.

Figure 4.22
Results of manipulating the graphical elements of
the pie object of Figure 4.21. By copying the image
of Figure 4.21 into a drawing program, the graphics designer has complete freedom to manipulate the component elements as desired.

Bar Charts in Pascal

To help readers understand and appreciate some
of the algorithms employed in commercial graphics programs, it is useful to write a program to
implement one of the simpler graphical functions
of *WingZ*. The design criteria for the Pascal
program, BarCH, will be to provide modest
capability with minimal programming effort.

To be more specific, let's design BarCH with
the following features:

- The user can select an existing data file to
  plot or choose to enter data from the
  keyboard.

- The format for data entry will be an
  arbitrary series of (X_i, ID_i) pairs, where X_i is
  the numerical value of the scalar to be
  plotted and ID_i is the identifier.

- The program will count the number of data
  entries and scale the axes automatically to
  accommodate the data.

- The user will be queried for the graph title
  and labels for two axes.

Pascal Program BarCH

```
program BarCH;
{Program to automatically plot BAR CHART based on }
{user supplied graph title, axes labels, and data.    }
{Data may be supplied as existing file or keyed in    }
{directly.                                             }

   const
      left = 50;
      right = 450;
      top = 40;
      bottom = 340;
      XaxisB = 50;
      XaxisE = 350;
      YaxisB = 255;
      YaxisE = 5;

   var
      Title, OrdLab, AbsLab: string;
      DataFile: text;
      ID, OutLine: string;
      npoints, ScMax, ScMin, tens, Dy: integer;
      Max, Min, x: real;
      Sy, Dx: real;

   procedure GetInformation;
   {Routine to open interactive query viewport to input }
   {essential information.                               }
      var
         TextPort: rect;
         i: integer;
         ans: string;
      begin              {Set up text window and open it.}
```

```
    SetRect(TextPort, left, top, right, bottom);
    setTextRect(TextPort);
    ShowText;
    WriteLn;
    WriteLn('    Bar Chart Grapher');
    Writeln;
    Writeln('How shall we title this graph?  (enter
    string)');
    Readln(title);
    Writeln;
    Writeln('Ordinate Label?  (enter string)');
    Readln(OrdLab);
    WriteLn('Abscissa Label?  (enter string)');
    Readln(AbsLab);
    Writeln;
    Writeln('Is data in table (T) or from keyboard (K)?
    Enter T or K');
    Readln(ans);
                {If data file exists, query for its name.}
    if (ans = 't') or (ans = 'T') then
                {Use file query function, "OldFileName"}
        Reset(DataFile, OldFileName('DataFile for Bar
        Chart?'))
    else      {Otherwise, create it from the keyboard.}
        begin
            ReWrite(DataFile, 'BarCH.dat');      {Open for
                                                   writing.}
            Writeln;
            Writeln('Please key in data in format (Xi _ IDi)
            <cr>');
            Writeln('Terminate with message (n _ end)
            <cr>');
            Writeln('   where _ = space, n = number, "end"
            = sentinal to stop');
            Readln(x, ID);
            repeat    {Read and write data points until end.}
                Writeln(DataFile, x, ID);
                Readln(x, ID);
            until ID = ' end';
        end;
end;

procedure Normalize;
{Routine to scan data to count points and set Min and
Max.}
{Round to nearest single digit inclusive number and}
{extract power of ten for correct scaling.}
    var
        i, n, b: integer;
        a: real;

    function sign (z: real): real;
    {Returns the sign as a real number.}
    begin
        sign := z / abs(z)
    end;

    procedure Reduce (xin: real; var a: real; var b:
    integer);
    {Procedure to read a real x and return it in the form
    a x 10**b}
    var
        x: real;
    begin
        x := abs(xin);
        if x < 1e-10 then  {Test if number ≈ o;  set a,b =0}
            begin
                a := 0.0;
                b := 0;
            end
        else if x < 1 then    {Scale small numbers up by
                                powers of 10}
            begin
                b := 0;
                repeat
                    x := 10 * x;
                    b := b - 1;
                until x > 1;
            end
        else  {Case:  x>1}  {Scale large numbers down
                             by powers of 10}
            begin
                b := -1;
                repeat
                    x := x / 10;
                    b := b + 1;
                until x < 1
            end;
        a := sign(xin) * exp(ln(abs(xin)) - b * ln(10))
    end;        {End Reduce}

begin
    reset(DataFile);        {Reset data file and open it for
                             reading.}
    Max := -1e30;
    Min := -Max;
    npoints := 0;
    repeat
        Readln(DataFile, x, ID);
        npoints := npoints + 1;
        if x > Max then
            Max := x;
        if x < Min then
            Min := x;
    until eof(DataFile);
    Reduce(Max, a, b);          {Convert Max to power
                                 of 10 notation.}
    ScMax := Trunc(a + 1);      {Round single digit up.}
    Tens := b;
    Reduce(Min, a, b);      {Convert Max to power of 10
                             notation.}
    if b < Tens then
        ScMin := 0
    else
        ScMin := Trunc(a - 1);{Round single digit down.}
end;                            {End Normalize}

procedure PlotAxes;
{Routine to plot and label abscissa & ordinate axes.}
    var
        ViewPort: rect;
        i, n: integer;
```

```
begin
                    {Open Drawing window as viewport.}
  SetRect(ViewPort, left, top, right, bottom);
  setDrawingRect(ViewPort);
  ShowDrawing;
            {Draw Ordinate axis (Y), with arrowhead.}
  DrawLine(XaxisB, YaxisB, XaxisB, YaxisE);
  Line(5, 10);
  Line(-10, 0);
  Line(5, -10);
                        {Draw Abscissa axis.}
  DrawLine(XaxisB, YaxisB, XaxisE, YaxisB);
                    {Compute Dx, width of bar.}
  Dx := (XaxisE - XaxisB) / (2 * Npoints);
          {Compute Sy, the ordinate scale factor.}
  Sy := (YaxisB - YaxisE) / (ScMax - ScMin);
  if tens > 0 then            {Scale by appropriate
                                    power of 10}
    for i := 1 to tens do
      Sy := Sy / 10
  else if tens < 0 then
    for i := tens to -1 do
      Sy := 10 * Sy;
  Dy := Round((YaxisB - YaxisE) / (ScMax - ScMin));
  n := 0;
          {Draw tick marks and label ordinate axis.}
  for i := ScMin to (ScMax - 1) do
    begin
      MoveTo(XaxisB - 15, YaxisB - n * Dy + 4);
      WriteDraw(i : 1);
      MoveTo(XaxisB, YaxisB - n * Dy);
      Line(5, 0);
      n := n + 1;
    end;
  MoveTo(XaxisB + 50, YaxisE + 10);{Write Title}
  TextSize(18);
  WriteDraw(Title);
  MoveTo(XaxisB + 150, YaxisB + 25);      {Label
                                       abscissa}
  TextSize(12);
  WriteDraw(AbsLab);
                              {Label ordinate}
  MoveTo(XaxisB - 45, (YaxisB + YaxisE) div 2);
  WriteDraw(OrdLab);
                        {Write scale factor}
  MoveTo(XaxisB - 48, (YaxisB + YaxisE) div 2 +
  15);
  TextSize(9);
  WriteDraw('(X10');
  Move(3, -5);
  WriteDraw(Tens : 1);
  Move(0, 5);
  WriteDraw(')');
end;                        {End PlotAxes}

procedure PlotData;
{Routine to plot data bars.}
  var
    i, L, R, T, B: integer;
    Bar: rect;

begin
  B := YaxisB;
  reset(DataFile);
  for i := 1 to Npoints do
    begin        {Read point and build Bar rectangle}
      Readln(DataFile, x, ID);
      T := B - Round(Sy * x) + Dy * ScMin;
      L := XaxisB + Round((2 * i - 1) * Dx);
      R := XaxisB + Round((2 * i) * Dx);
      SetRect(Bar, L, T, R, B);
      PaintRect(Bar);{Plot bar by painting rectangle}
      MoveTo(L, B + 12);{Label each bar with its ID}
      WriteDraw(ID);
    end;
end;                        {End PlotData}

begin                        {Main program}
  GetInformation;
  Normalize;
  PlotAxes;
  PlotData;
end.
```

Program Operation

The overall structure of the program is indicated by the mnemonics of the four worker routines called by the main program. Rather than passing variables through the argument lists of procedures (the generally preferred style), the simpler option of making most variables global for processing by worker routines was selected. The only two items which may appear mysterious are:

- The use of *OldFileName* – This routine opens a query window labeled by the prompt supplied as its argument and allows the user to scan through volumes and scroll through file names to select and open the file of their choice. It is an operating system routine which provides the application programmer an efficient shortcut to this repetitive task.

- The scaling performed by *Normalize* – The task of mapping the window (range of X_i data values) to the viewport (250 pixels along the y-axis) is essentially trivial. The problem with this straightforward scaling is that the y-axis scale readings will range from $X_{min} = 2385$ to $X_{max} = 7592$, for example, in five evenly spaced but odd-ball numbers spanning the range. The purpose of *Normalize* is to map the window onto a slightly demagnified window that has edges are $W_L = 2 \times 10^3$ and $W_R = 8 \times 10^3$. The algorithm is designed to round the

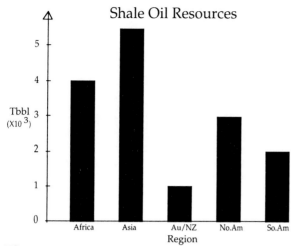

Figure 4.23
Output of **BarCH** operating on Table 4.1 data.

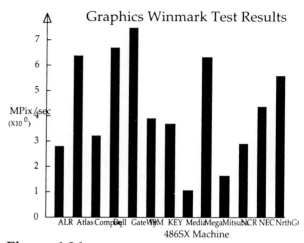

Figure 4.24
BarCH output on another data file.[9]

most significant figure of X_{min} downward and the most significant figure of X_{max} upward and extract the power of ten for graph labeling purposes. Only the most significant figure is used to label the y-axis intervals. This algorithm generally works well, failing only in cases such as Figure 4.24 in which X_i data values vary only in the second significant figure.

Program Features and Output

Let us see how **BarCH** handles the data of Table 4.1. Figure 4.23 shows the results of selecting the properly formatted data file, *BarCH.Oil*.

Although **BarCH** is not a model of elegant programming, the program does have certain attractive features. These include:

- Flexibility in selecting data from existing file or direct interactive input.

- Automatic scaling of data over all ranges of real number magnitude.

- Capability of handling negative numbers. (What is a negative bar chart?)

- Rounding to give simple 1 digit coordinates on y-axis.

- Automatic offset of closely compacted data.

- Arbitrary number of data points handled automatically without arrays.

Some of these features were fairly difficult to program, particularly with Pascal's poor support of mathematical functions such as *log* and *x.y*

Even with these nice features, **BarCH** is extremely weak compared to the presentation graphics of programs such as *WingZ* and *Excel*. Some of these limitations become apparent in the final figure, Figure 4.24.

The limitations of this program illustrate the problems inherent in building completely general graphics programs. These problems include:

- Difficulty of accommodating arbitrary length titles and labels,

- Limited amount of data before clutter becomes overwhelming.

Two other observations are appropriate at this point. First is that the orientation of the bars selected for **BarCH** is sometimes called a *column graph* rather than a bar chart. A horizontal bar chart has several intrinsic advantages over the column graph shown. The programming is simpler, and it is easier to label the bars both by ID and numerical value. A serious shortcoming of **BarCH** is the lack of numerical labels on each bar.

Conclusions

Many of the basic concepts of higher-dimensional graphics are clearly illustrated by a careful study of 1D graphics. Graphical transformations of translation, scaling, reflection, and viewing have concise and simple definitions in 1D that transfer smoothly into higher dimensions. The rationale for the matrix formalism and homogeneous coordinate systems can be made as convincingly in 1D and demonstrated more economically than in 2D or 3D. The definitions of windows, viewports, and clipping have precise 1D analogs which extend seamlessly to higher dimensions. The viewing transformation concepts are illustrated with the Morse code example. Scalar quantities may be represented by coordinate systems other than the linear Cartesian axis. For instance, scalar data is frequently displayed on meters (angular coordinates), pie charts (polar coordinates), and as volumetrically scaled icons. Finally, valuable tools for 1D presentation graphics were illustrated with bar charts and pie charts. The considerable programming effort involved in elegant presentation graphics programs is better appreciated by the contrast with results from a modest Pascal bar chart program.

Exercises

4.1 The chapter was introduced by distinguishing between *natural objects* and *artificial objects* of computer graphics. List three examples which clearly fall into each class and three more examples that are borderline and could be interpreted either way. Is this a useful distinction?

4.2 In examples from previous chapters, there was a lot "going on" in terms of viewport sizing and position in which default values were modified interactively by the user. Give three examples of transformations you performed on the windows and illustrate them with screen dumps.

4.3 As the dial on the dimension meter was turned from $0 \to 1$, some new transformations (e.g., translation and scaling) appeared which were undefined in the lower dimension. What new transformations can you think of that appear when we turn the dimension dial from $1 \to 2$?

4.4 As the dimension meter is turned up, new objects appear. As N goes from $0 \to 1$, lines appear which may be considered as generated by sweeping the lower dimensional object, the point, along the new axis. What are the analogous new objects and generation mechanisms which appear as N goes from $1 \to 2$ and $2 \to 3$?

4.5 Lines have an intrinsic mathematical property, length, which is useful for operations such as ordering them, plotting bar charts, and so on. Do points have any intrinsic mathematical property? What is the closest computer graphics representation of a point? Does this representations have any attributes? If so, what are they?

4.6 Scaling has a simple, intuitive meaning when applied to lines, to wit, magnification or demagnification. What does scaling of a point mean? If the size of a mathematical point is zero, how can it be scaled? (*Hint: Consider its position.*)

4.7 Write a program to draw and label a 1D coordinate system such as that shown in Figure 4.1.

4.8 Extend the program of problem 4.7 to interactively request and plot points along the x-axis. Show an example of the interactive dialog along with your plotted results.

4.9 Extend the program of problem 4.8 to interactively request and plot lines along the the x-axis. Use this extended program to reproduce Figures 4.2 through 4.8.

4.10 Summarize briefly the problem solved by the introduction of homogeneous coordinates.

4.11 Suppose we want to scale a 1D object about the point $X = 7$ by a scale factor $S = 5$. Write down the three 2×2 matrices, T_1, S, and T_2 required for this operation and the single, concatenated matrix, $M = T_1 \cdot S \cdot T_2$ which will perform the desired scaling about a point.

4.12 Derive the single transformation, $M = T_1 \cdot S \cdot T_2$, required to reflect an object about the point $X = -3$. Show the numerical values for the three component matrices.

4.13 A bit of poetic license was required to interpret the Morse code message as a 1D object. Think about the problem, and list three additional examples to which we could apply the 1D transformation presented is this chapter.

4.14 Consider the design of a high-resolution, 1D display device. What technology would you propose? What would be its resolution? Does the concept of gray-scale and color make sense for a 1D display? How would it be helpful? Is the "MultiPeak Indicator" on your hi-fi a true linear display or a bar chart plotter? What is the difference?

4.15 Define the terms *window, viewport, clipping,* and *viewing transformation* in your own words, and indicate with sketches the process of applying the viewing transformation to a 2D scene.

4.16 Suppose the task is to center the Morse code message, JOY, on the 100-LED display of Figure 4.11 with a magnification of 2. This may be accomplished by the three-step viewing transformation: clipping, translation, and scaling. Write the clipping algorithm, the translation matrix, **T**, and the scaling matrix, **S**, to perform this task.

4.17 Express the solution to the task of problem 4.16 in terms of the viewport parameters, (W_R, W_L), and viewport parameters, (V_R, V_L), using the viewing transformation equation, 4.31.

4.18 List three applications for which 1D angular coordinates (simulated meter) would be particularly effective. What would the advantages of such meters for monitoring these signals over more conventional output like digital displays?

4.19 Scan your local newspaper or news magazine for five examples of 1D presentation graphics in the form of pie charts and make photocopies of them. Rank them for the effectiveness of the presentation they make, and comment on why the top-ranked pie chart is better than the bottom-ranked one.

4.20 Scan your local newspaper or news magazine for three examples of 1D presentation graphics in the form of volume visualization icons, and make photocopies of them. Have the authors used them correctly? If so, why? If not, why not?

4.21 Write a program for producing a straight bar chart, with the bars lying along the x-axis. The program should read data from a file, label each bar with both an ID and the value of X_i, label the x-axis, and write a title for the graph. It is not necessary to struggle with the rounding problem unless you are so inclined.

4.22 Write a program for reading in scalar data from a file and generating a pie chart. You should label each slice of the pie with the appropriate ID and compute and print the percentage of each slice outside the graph near the perimeter of the slice. Write the title at the top of the graph.

4.23 Consider the problems encountered in problem 4.22 and compare the output format with the "Legend" approach of Figure 4.20. Which is more "bomb-proof" and which more prone to clutter and why?

4.24 Some authors have decried the 3D display of 1D data such as shown in Figure 4.21 as "chart junk." A strong case can be made for this position on the grounds of over-kill. However, a strong case can also be made for visual effectiveness of such renditions in terms of conveying the sense of a real, 3D object sitting there in space with real 3D components making up the whole. Take a position on this issue, and make the best case you can for your position.

4.25 On Figures 4.15 and 4.16 use a ruler to measure the oil barrel icon heights, H_i, and compute the ratios, H_2/H_1, H_3/H_1, etc. for both graphs from your measured values. Compute the theoretical values expected from scaling linearly (Figure 4.15) and volumetrically (Figure 4.16). Finally, compute the percentage difference between the measured and theoretical values and attempt to explain the difference.

Endnotes

1. Dewdney, A. K., *The Planiverse – Computer Contact with a Two-dimensional World*, Poseiden Press, New York, NY (1984).
2. Abbott, Edwin, *Flatland - A Romance of Many Dimensions* , 6th Edition, Oxford University Press, NY, 102 pp., (1950).
3. Barnsley, Michael, *Fractals Everywhere*, Academic Press, Boston, MA (1988).
4. Roberts, Lawrence G., "Homogeneous Matrix Representation and Manipulation of N-Dimensional Constructs," *MIT Lincoln Laboratory, MS 1405*, July (1966).
5. Blinn, J. F., "A Homogeneous Formulation for Lines in 3-Space," *Computer Graphics* **11**, No. 2, pp. 237–241 (1977). See also: Blinn, James F. and Newell, Martin E., "Clipping Using Homogeneous Coordinates," *Computer Graphics* **12**, No. 3, pp. 245–251 (1977).
6. Barnsley, *op cit.*
7. Ruedisili, Lon C. and Firebaugh, Morris W. (eds), *Perspectives on Energy*, Third Edition, Oxford University Press, New York, NY p.227 (1982)
8. Tufte, Edward R., *The Visual Display of Quantitative Information*, Graphics Press, Cheshire, CN , p. 71 (1983).
9. "Benchmark Tests: 25-MHz 486SX PCs," *P C Magazine* **11**, No. 17, p. 168, October 13 (1992).

Chapter 5

Two-Dimensional Graphics – Representation

The real task of computer graphics is that of describing graphical entities.
J. W. Wendorf

As we move from 1D to 2D graphics, we would like to do so in the context of representation issues. Representation is at the heart of computer science. Finding the optimal representation for a problem is often the key to its solution. By representation, we mean the description of graphical objects. "Graphical objects" implies an object-oriented description— both the data structures themselves as well as the operations allowable on the data must be defined. Representation occurs at various levels of abstraction. At the highest level, we have the purely mathematical representation of vectors, X_i, transformation matrices, M_j, and the relationships between them. The next lower-level of abstraction is the algorithmic level in which the sequence of operations required to solve the problem is specified. Finally, at the lowest level, we have the program which implements the algorithm. At this level actual data structures must be specified and specific plotting routines called.

We start the discussion of 2D graphics by introducing the more abstract, mathematical representations of graphical objects and conclude it with a chapter on issues of implementation. However, before looking at how points, lines, and so on are represented, it helps to note how a 2D environment differs from that of 1D.

Efforts to put computer graphics on a firm mathematical foundation constitute much of the academic research in computer graphics. A particularly good summary of these efforts is given by Eugene Fiume in the book based on his thesis research.[1]

Moving from 1D to 2D

In the preceding chapter, a 1D environment was used to develop the representation of graphical objects and the operations which are possible on them. Matrix techniques for operating on homogeneous coordinates were introduced for combining scaling and translation transformations, and the method was shown to be easily extensible for more complex transformations such as scaling about a point and reflection about a point. The viewing transformation for mapping a scene onto a screen was described in terms of windows, viewports, and the clipping operation.

In the next two chapters, we extend these ideas to two dimensions. However, as suggested in Chapter 4, when we turn the dimension meter up from $1 \rightarrow 2$, we expect to observe the following:

- Objects present in dimension 1 should continue to exist. That is, points and lines should be well-defined graphical objects in 2D.

- New objects of dimension N = 2 should emerge. The simplest 2D primitive is the *plane*, an object generated by sweeping a lower-dimensionality primitive (line) along the new axis.

- New transformations appear which were undefined in dimension N–1. The important new transformation is the *rotation* group, θ.

Other complexities arise as we click the dimension dial from N = 1→ 2. Lines are no longer constrained to lie along a single axis, but instead can wander about the whole x-y plane, requiring the description of a new object, the *curve*. Objects, which in 1D required *n* numbers to specify, now require *2n* numbers. In a Cartesian coordinate system, points are specified by the pair, (x,y). Straight line segments require the 4-tuple, (x_1,y_1,x_2,y_2). Finally, increased complexity appears in the clipping algorithm since line segments may now be totally inside, totally outside, or straddling the edge of the clipping window.

The beauty of the matrix representation will become apparent as we attempt to specify the operations (transformations) allowed on 2D objects. Just as 2 × 2 matrices were required to handle the general 1D transformation, the affine transformations possible in 2D require 3 × 3 matrices. It is a relatively simple task to determine the appropriate matrix.

Representation of 2D Objects

Before looking at what operations are allowed on objects in 2D space, we ought to consider just what classes of objects we are interested in and how they can be represented. A little thought leads to the following categories:

- **Primitive** → point, line, polygon, curve

- **Composite** → design diagrams, laboratory data, scanner data, video signals.

In Figure 5.1, we show the four primitive objects and the parameters that specify them. Note that points are no longer simple 1D scalar objects but rather *vectors* requiring the 2D coordinate pair, (x,y), as shown in (a). To understand the term *vector*, imagine an arrow with a head at point (x,y) and a tail at $(0,0)$. Clearly, a line is well-specified by giving the coordinate pairs of its end points as shown in (b).

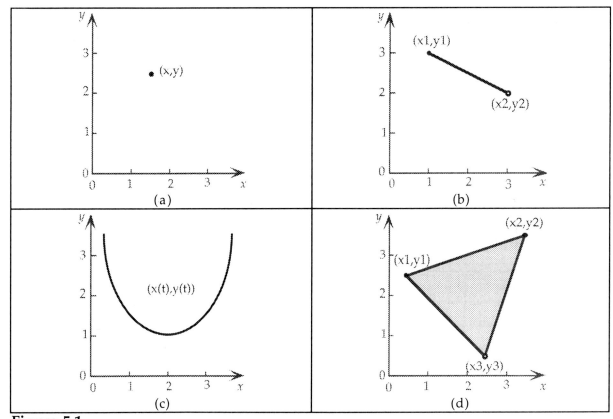

Figure 5.1
Some 2D graphics primitives. (a) point defined as (x,y) pair, (b) line defined as the (x,y) coordinates of its end points, (c) curve defined as x and y as a function of the parameter, t, and (d) polygon defined as vertex points.

Curves are somewhat more problematic to specify. If y is a single-valued function of x, such as that shown in (c) (i.e., no loops, circles, and so on), the generally accepted representation is to give $y = f(x)$, where $f(x)$ is some mathematical function of x. However, a more general representation, which we discuss below, is to specify both x and y as a function of a third, independent parameter, t. This *parametric representation* has the virtue of generality—circles, ellipses, spirals, and loops are represented with the same formalism as simple functions of x.

Planar regions may be represented in 2D by a variety of techniques. They may be generated as the interior surface bounded by analytic functions such as circles, ellipses, and lines. They may be specified as the interior surface of a

closed polygon bounded by a set of lines; primitives we already know how to specify. They may be specified as the interior surface of a closed figure bounded by a series of connected parametric curve segments such as that shown in (c). Finally, they may be specified by the interior surface of a polygon bounded by lines connecting a set of points as shown in Figure 5.1 (d).

In Figure 5.2, four composite 2D images are shown.

Note the increasing complexity of the composite objects in Figure 5.2. Graph (a) is composed essentially from lines and text with a *round-cornered rectangle* pasted on as title. Image (b) is an electronic reproduction of a photographic reproduction of a real mountain scene. It is a PICT file generated by a color

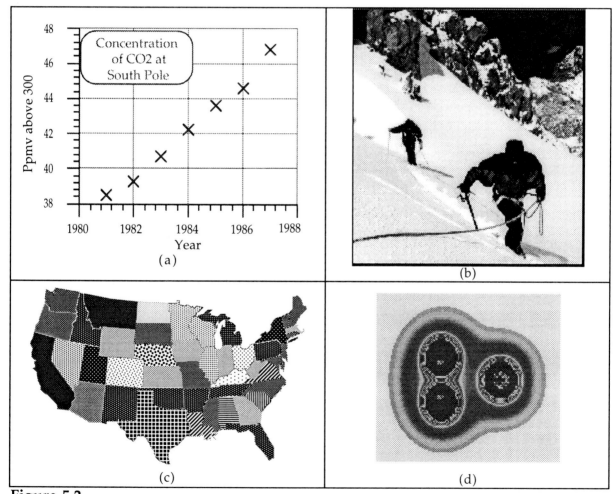

Figure 5.2
Four composite 2D graphical objects. (a) A scatter plot of the concentration of CO_2 in parts per million (volume) in excess of 300 vs year[2], (b) Scanned image of FIGS author climbing Glacier Peak, c)US Map[3], and d) Electron density plot of Niobium trimer[4].

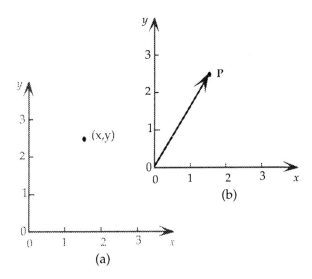

Figure 5.3
Two equivalent representations of a point in 2D. The scalar representation, (a), requires an n-tuple (n = 2) of scalar numbers. The vector representation, (b), defines the point more abstractly as the vector, **P**, whose components must be specified before any computation.

scanner. Map (c) is a collection of objects (states), each of which is drawn as a polygon filled with a color. Finally, synthetic image (d) is a supercomputer simulation of the electron density of three Niobium atoms in the process of ionization. Although both (b) and (d) represent 3D objects at a fundamental level, we consider (b) to be a simple 2D photograph and (d) to be a 2D slice through a 3D object.

Mathematical Representations

Two levels of abstraction are available for representing 2D graphical primitives. The first we shall call a *scalar* representation; the second is called a *vector* representation. Another way of distinguishing these two representations is by considering the scalar representation as *algebraic* and the vector representation as *geometric*.

Points

Figure 5.3 illustrates both the scalar and vector representation of a point. Note that the scalar representation does require a pair of scalars to represent the point in 2D, and the abstract position vector, **P**, requires specification of its two

components for any implementation. (Note: vectors are designated by boldface characters.)

The homogeneous coordinate system representation equivalent to both of these representations is the 3-element row vector

$$P = [x, y, w] \qquad [5.1]$$

where
  $w = 1$ (conventional choice of scale factor, w).

Lines

Lines may be defined in several ways. Two familiar algebraic schemes include the *slope-intercept* form:

$$y = m\,x + b \qquad [5.2]$$

where
  m = slope,
  b = intersection of line with y-axis,

and the *two-point* form:

$$y = \frac{(y_2 - y_1)}{(x_2 - x_1)}(x - x_1) + y_1 \qquad [5.3]$$

where
  (x_1,y_1) and (x_2,y_2) are any two points on the line.

Note that both Equations 5.1 and 5.2 may be rewritten in the more general form,

$$A\,x + B\,y + C = 0 \qquad [5.4]$$

where, for instance,
$$m = \frac{-A}{B} \quad \text{and} \quad b = \frac{-C}{B}.$$

The parameters, m and b, of the slope-intercept representation are shown in Figure 5.4(a).

The general algebraic form, [5.4], may be generated by setting to zero the scalar product of the row vector, **P**, with a column vector whose elements are the A, B, C coefficients of [5.4]. Using row vector, $P = [x, y, 1]$, and column coefficient vector, **C**, given as

$$C = \begin{bmatrix} A \\ B \\ C \end{bmatrix}$$

Equation 5.4 is the 1×1 scalar product of these row and column vectors:

$$P \cdot C = 0 \qquad [5.5]$$
or
$$A\,x + B\,y + C = 0.$$

Thus the algebraic formulation of a line has a very concise vector representation. Points are represented as 3-element row vectors, and lines are represented by 3-element coefficient column vectors.

The *parametric vector* representation of a line assumes that every point on the line is a vector, L, from the origin to that point. The parametric vector equation for L in terms of a vector point P on the line, a tangent vector T parallel to the line, and an arbitrary parameter, t, is given as

$$L = P + t\,T. \qquad [5.6]$$

This parametric vector representation has a very simple geometric interpretation shown in Figure 5.4(b). Equation 5.6 says that you can get to point L on the line by first going to point P on the line and then moving t units along the vector T tangent to the line. For the case shown in Figure 5.4(b), where T is a unit vector, the value

of the parameter, t, would be approximately 2. To get to those points on the line left of P, the value of t would be negative.

Note that the parameter, t, acts like a "control knob" telling us how far away from point P we are on the line. When $t = 0$, we are precisely at point P. As t is turned up to 1, we get to the tip of the T vector in Figure 5.4(b). As it moves on towards 2, we approach the tip of the L vector. As it moves past 2 toward infinity, we move along the line to the right toward infinity.

The parametric vector representation is a convenient way to represent *line segments* as well. If the line segment is defined by two end point vectors, P_1 and P_2, the tangent vector, T, in Equation 5.6 can be replaced by the unnormalized vector, $(P_2 - P_1)$:

$$L = P_1 + t\,(P_2 - P_1). \qquad [5.7]$$

Then, the vector L sweeps uniformly along the line from P_1 to P_2 as the parameter t changes from $0 \to 1$.

The connection between the Cartesian coordinates, (x,y), of vector L and the coordinates and components of the defining vectors, P and T, are given by:

$$\begin{aligned} x &= x_p + t\,T_x, \\ y &= y_p + t\,T_y, \end{aligned} \qquad [5.8]$$

where

(x_p, y_p) = coordinates of vector P,
(T_x, T_y) = components of T.

The advantage of the vector formalism is the ease with which relationships between points and lines may be computed. Consider the following useful tests for classifying points P and lines C.

Inside test: $P \cdot C < 0$

Multiplying $P = [x, y, 1]$ by $C = [A, B, C]^{\mathrm{T}}$ and applying the inequality gives the result

$$A\,x + B\,y + C < 0, \qquad [5.9]$$

which is the algebraic expression for points (x,y) which lie *inside* (i.e., on the same side as the origin) of a line whose coefficients are (A, B, C). Note that the "T" symbol means *transpose*—interchanging rows and columns.

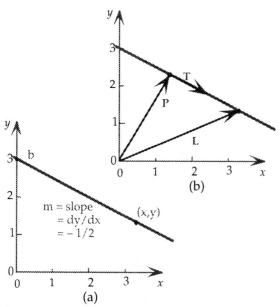

Figure 5.4
Two representations of a line. (a) Slope-intercept algebraic form: $y = mx + b$, (b) Parametric, vector form: $L = P + t\,T$, where t = parameter.

Outside test: $P \cdot C > 0$

Similarly, the test for "outside" points (i.e., those on the other side of the line from the origin) is given by

$$A\,x + B\,y + C > 0 \qquad [5.10]$$

Normal lines test: $T_1 \cdot T_2 = 0$

Recall from geometry that two vectors, V and U, are normal lines (perpendicular to each other) if $U \cdot V = 0$. Writing the vector representation of two lines as

$$L_1 = P_1 + t\,T_1, \qquad [5.11]$$
$$L_2 = P_2 + t\,T_2.$$

A little thought leads to the conclusion that the elements of this representation important for testing perpendicularity are the tangent vectors, T_i. The test for two lines being normal then reduces to the simple expression

$$T_1 \cdot T_2 = 0. \qquad [5.12]$$

In terms of Cartesian components, this product yields:

$$T_{1x}T_{2x} + T_{1y}T_{2y} = 0. \qquad [5.13]$$

This may be rewritten as

$$\frac{T_{1y}}{T_{1x}} = -\frac{T_{2x}}{T_{2y}} \quad \text{(perpendicularity)} \qquad [5.14]$$

which is equivalent, in the slope-intercept form ($y = m\,x + b$), to

$$m_1 = -\frac{1}{m_2} \quad \text{(perpendicularity)} \qquad [5.15]$$

and, since $m = -\frac{A}{B}$ in the $Ax + By + C = 0$ form, the relationship of the coefficients for two perpendicular lines may also be written:

$$A_1 A_2 + B_1 B_2 = 0 \qquad [5.16]$$

Distance from P to C

The distance, d, from a point P to a line C is given by the expression:

$$d = \frac{|P \cdot C|}{\sqrt{A^2 + B^2}}. \qquad [5.17]$$

This result follows from the following arguments. Given the point: $P = [x_p, y_p, 1]$ and the line: $C = [A_0, B_0, C_0]^T$ Equation 5.16 can be used to write the following equation for the line normal to C that contains P:

$$-B_0\,(x - x_p) + A_0\,(y - y_p) = 0. \qquad [5.18]$$

The normal line intersects the original line at point (x_i, y_i), at which point the equation of the original line can be written:

$$A_0\,x_i + B_0\,y_i + C_0 = 0. \qquad [5.19]$$

These last two equations may be solved for the point of intersection to give

$$x_i = \frac{B_0\,(B_0\,x_p - A_0\,y_p) - A_0\,C_0}{\sqrt{A^2 + B^2}}, \qquad [5.20]$$

$$y_i = \frac{A_0\,(-B_0\,x_p + A_0\,y_p) - B_0\,C_0}{\sqrt{A^2 + B^2}}. \qquad [5.21]$$

Since the point of intersection is the point on the line closest to point P, the distance from P to the original line is simply

$$d = \sqrt{(x_i - x_p)^2 + (y_i - y_p)^2}. \qquad [5.22]$$

Substituting Equations 5.20 and 5.21 into 5.22 and doing a bit of algebra yields

$$d = \frac{A_0\,x_p + B_0\,y_p + C_0}{\sqrt{A^2 + B^2}}, \qquad [5.23]$$

which is an expanded form of the desired result, Equation 5.17.

Polygons

The third 2D primitive we discuss in this chapter is the polygon. Polygons are valuable graphical objects for a number of reasons. First, they provide powerful modeling tools with a simple data structure format. That is, *n*-sided polygons can be used to model triangles, squares, pentagons, stars, and even circles and ovals in the limit of $n \to$ large. Very irregular objects, such as the outline of an animal or a human face,

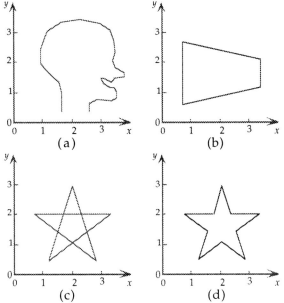

Figure 5.5
Legal and illegal polygons. (a) Although an *n*-sided figure, it is not a polygon because it is not closed. (c) Although constructed from five lines, it is not a polygon because it is not simply-connected. Both (b) and (d) are legal polygons.

may be represented accurately by the appropriate n-sided polygon with *n* sufficiently large.

Secondly, collections of polygons have proven to be extremely effective 3D modeling tools. That is, any solid object may be represented by the seamless conjunction of three- and four-sided polygons (triangles and rectangles). This is an important tool in CAD and the essential tool of finite element analysis. Since these techniques are becoming standard techniques for engineering design and scientific modeling, it is important to study the nature of polygons and their representations.

How might we represent a generalized polygon? First, it helps to define a polygon as a *closed, n-sided, planar, simply-connected geometric figure*. This definition and some of the problems it helps avoid are illustrated in Figure 5.5.

Several schemes are possible for representing polygons. Each has its own particular advantages and drawbacks. Three possible representations of an n-sided polygon include:

1. **An ordered list of n+1 (x,y) vertices (absolute)** – This representation has the virtue of the simplicity of a "dot-to-dot" algorithm, but suffers slight redundancy in that the first and last data pair are identical. This redundancy can be useful, however, in flagging the last point of a general, n-sided polygon.

2. **An ordered list of n+1 (x,y) vertices (relative)** – Here the first vertex is given in absolute coordinates, and all successive vertices are in relative coordinates. This is a more object-oriented structure defined by a single position (coordinates (x_1, y_1)) and internal structure (relative coordinates (x_i, y_i)). It has the advantage of increased efficiency since relative coordinates, as smaller, off-set numbers, generally require fewer bits to represent them. The cost of this scheme is a somewhat increased complexity over absolute schemes.

3. **A set of n lines** – This representation is a higher level of abstraction that correctly reflects our intuition of a polygon consisting of a collection of edges. It has the advantage of flexibility, generality, and extensibility. That is, the lines need not be ordered, and any line, for example, may be deleted and replaced by two or more additional lines which close the figure. These advantages are bought at a dear price in memory requirements, however, since each line requires two vertices for representation. This doubles the storage requirements over schemes (1) and (2).

The particular choice of representation will depend upon the application. In this book, we use both scheme (1) and (3).

Curves

The intuition we developed in calculus suggests that it is possible to represent any geometric object to any desired degree of accuracy by using enough straight line segments, or, at a higher level, by some combination of polygons. This concept, in fact, is the foundation for finite element analysis in which complex objects are decomposed into many primitive polygons or polyhedra. While this intuition is correct and finite element techniques have proven to be powerful analysis tools, from a mathematical point of view these techniques are embarrassingly crude and often computationally inefficient. Curves and curved surfaces have the tremendous advantage of more realistic modeling of graphical objects using far fewer parameters than required by finite element techniques.

Consider, for example, the two contrasting representations of a circle.

- **Finite element** – As a curve, we would need an *n*-sided polygon with *n* probably ≥ 100. As a surface, we would probably need fifty or more pie-shaped triangles, each with three vertices.

- **Mathematical** – All we need is three numbers, x_c, y_c, and r and one relationship, $(x - x_c)^2 + (y - y_c)^2 = r^2$.

Furthermore, many of the objects of nature are smooth curves or have smooth surfaces with well-behaved mathematical properties. Examples include the trajectories of particles moving in force fields, an egg, a raindrop, and the human face. Such smooth, "organic" forms have greatly influenced the design of human artifacts as a survey of silverware, furniture, and automobile design will verify. In fact, the motivation for some of the best work in computer modeling of smooth surfaces was specifically to develop more flexible and powerful tools for automobile hood design. It was at Citroën where P. de Casteljau developed his (unpublished) algorithms for designing and displaying smooth surfaces in the early 1960s. And it was at Renault where Pierre Bézier developed his *UNISURF* CAD system and the curves which bear his name.[5]

Before looking in more detail at the mathematical representation of Bézier curves, it is helpful to consider the question: Why use curves? There are two quite distinct answers which are determined, again, by the all important representation issue.

- *The curve represents points.* In this point of view, widely held in the physical sciences and engineering, the data points themselves are the primary objects, usually the results of careful measurements. The curve is superimposed on the data, often as an aid to visualization to help detect trends and subtle behavior of the data points. Sophisticated techniques, such as least squares fitting, have evolved to put such curve fitting on a firm mathematical basis.[6]

- *Points represent—and control—the curve.* In this point of view, the curve is the primary object, usually as output of the design process, and points serve only as convenient tools for molding the curve into the desired shape. This representational approach is the basis for the field of *Computer Aided Geometric Design* (CAGD).[7]

A final observation concerns the constraints relating points and curves, and it applies equally to both scientific and the design applications. The two classes of constraints are:

- **Approximation** – The curve need not go through each point. In scientific applications this is sometimes called *data averaging*. In design applications, we say the points "pull on the curve," but don't force an intersection.

- **Interpolation** – The curve goes through all points. In scientific applications this constraint requires the use of high-order polynomials or other functions and frequently results in undesirable side-effects such as overshoot and oscillation. In design, this property is essential for the design of critical parts (e.g., piston dimensions), but much less desirable for "free form" design (e.g., fender profile).

Parametric Cubic Polynomial Representations

A number of schemes have been developed for relating curves and points. In scientific curve fitting, the user typically selects some trigonometric or polynomial series as the basis for representing the data. In computer aided geometric design, on the other hand, the choice has consistently been a parametric polynomial representation, generally with polynomials of order two, three, or four. Cubic curves (order 3) provide a compromise between simplicity and computational efficiency on the one hand, and smoothness and sensitivity to points on the other. The major forms of parametric polynomials are the Hermite, Bézier, B-spline, and Beta-spline.[8]

The advantages of a parametric cubic representation include the following.

- **It is parametric.** By this we mean that, instead of writing y as a function of x, we

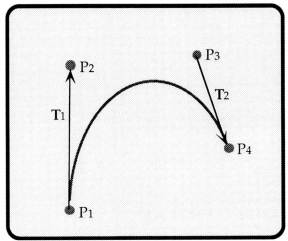

Figure 5.6
Bézier curve with control points. Vector $\mathbf{T_1}$ determines the direction of the curve leaving point $\mathbf{P_1}$. Vector $\mathbf{T_2}$ determines the direction the curve enters point $\mathbf{P_4}$. Longer vectors pull on the curve more than do shorter vectors. Point $\mathbf{P_1}$ corresponds to t = 0, and point $\mathbf{P_4}$ to t = 1.

write both x and y as a function of some third parameter, t. Thus,

$$x = x(t),$$ [5.24]
$$y = y(t).$$

- **It is smooth.**   Both the Hermite and Bézier forms provide continuity of both the curve itself and the first derivative at each control point. B-splines even provide continuity in the second derivative or *curvature*.

- **It is "variation diminishing."**   That is, the curves are *well behaved* and do not overshoot their control points or oscillate. The Bézier curve, for instance, lies within the *convex hull* (polygon envelope) of the set of control points.

- **It provides local control.**   The curve is "pulled" or most strongly effected by those control points closest to it.

Bézier Formulation

We can express x and y as cubic functions of parameter t by writing:

$$x(t) = a_x\, t^3 + b_x\, t^2 + c_x\, t + d_x$$ [5.25]

$$y(t) = a_y\, t^3 + b_y\, t^2 + c_y\, t + d_y$$

for
$$0 \le t \le 1 .$$

Four points are selected to control the curve as follows:

$P_1 \rightarrow$ Constrains curve to pass through it,
$P_2 \rightarrow$ Determines direction of tangent to curve at point P_1,
$P_3 \rightarrow$ Determines direction of tangent to curve at point P_4,
$P_4 \rightarrow$ Constrains curve to pass through it.

The four points and the controlled curve are shown in Figure 5.6.

Note that Equation 5.25 may be represented in vector form as:

$$x(t) = \mathbf{T} \cdot \mathbf{C}_x$$ [5.26]

where
$$\mathbf{T} = [\, t^3 \quad t^2 \quad t \quad 1\,],$$ [5.27]
(parameter vector),

and

$$\mathbf{C}_x \begin{bmatrix} a \\ b \\ c \\ d \end{bmatrix}_x$$ (coefficient vector) [5.28]

and similarly for y.

Now the problem becomes: Given a set of control points, $P_1, P_2, P_3,$ and P_4, how can we express the unknown coefficients, $(a, b, c, d)_x$ and $(a, b, c, d)_y$ in terms of the control point coordinates, (x_1, y_1), (x_2, y_2), (x_3, y_3), and (x_4, y_4). From now on, all arguments applied to x will apply similarly to y, so we shorten the discussion by solving only the x equations.

We need four equations to solve for these four unknowns, and we obtain them by applying boundary conditions to the curve and its derivative at points P_1 and P_4. The derivatives are taken with respect to the parameter, t. Point P_1 corresponds to the parameter $t = 0$, and P_4 is reached when $t = 1$. The derivatives at the two end points are defined in terms of the four points as:

$$x'(0) = 3\,(x_2 - x_1)$$ [5.29]
$$x'(1) = 3\,(x_4 - x_3).$$

The number "3" is chosen as an arbitrary scale factor. The parametric form itself gives:

$$x(0) = x_1 \qquad\qquad\qquad\qquad [5.30]$$
$$x(1) = x_4,$$

and since

$$x'(t) = 3\, a_x\, t^2 + 2\, b_x\, t + c_x, , \qquad [5.31]$$

direct substitution of Equations 5.29 and 5.30 into 5.25 and 5.31 yields:

$$c_x = 3\, x_2 - 3\, x_1 \qquad\qquad\qquad [5.32]$$
$$3\, a_x + 2\, b_x + c_x = 3\, x_4 - 3\, x_3$$
$$d_x = x_1$$
$$a_x + b_x + c_x + d_x = x_4.$$

These four equations in four unknowns are readily solved to give:

$$a_x = -x_1 + 3\, x_2 - 3\, x_3 + x_4 \qquad [5.33]$$
$$b_x = 3\, x_1 - 6\, x_2 + 3\, x_3$$
$$c_x = -3\, x_1 + 3\, x_2$$
$$d_x = x_1.$$

This may be concisely expressed in matrix form as:

$$C_x = M_b \cdot P_x \qquad\qquad\qquad [5.34]$$

where

$$M_b = \begin{bmatrix} -1 & 3 & -3 & 1 \\ 3 & -6 & 3 & 0 \\ -3 & 3 & 0 & 0 \\ 1 & 0 & 0 & 0 \end{bmatrix} \qquad [5.35]$$

(Bézier coefficient matrix)

and

$$P_x = \begin{bmatrix} x_1 \\ x_2 \\ x_3 \\ x_4 \end{bmatrix} \text{(Bézier point vector).} \quad [5.36]$$

Substituting Equation 5.34 back into the original matrix representation, 5.26, gives

$$x(t) = T \cdot M_b \cdot P_x \qquad\qquad [5.37]$$

$$= [\, t^3\ t^2\ t\ 1\,] \begin{bmatrix} -1 & 3 & -3 & 1 \\ 3 & -6 & 3 & 0 \\ -3 & 3 & 0 & 0 \\ 1 & 0 & 0 & 0 \end{bmatrix} \begin{bmatrix} x_1 \\ x_2 \\ x_3 \\ x_4 \end{bmatrix}. \quad [5.38]$$

Equation 5.37 is a very concise parametric form for $x(t)$ in terms of the controlling point coordinates. Note that the parametric form for $y(t)$ would be identical with y's substituted for x's in 5.37 and 5.38. This form is very convenient for implementation in a computer algorithm.

Blending Functions

An equivalent form for representing Bézier curves is through blending functions. This formulation may be written:

$$x(t) = \sum_{i=1}^{4} B_i(t)\, x_i , \qquad\qquad [5.39]$$

$$y(t) = \sum_{i=1}^{4} B_i(t)\, y_i .$$

The $B_i(t)$s are the *Bernstein polynomial blending functions*. Since [5.25] and [5.39] are equivalent representations, we should be able to derive the blending functions directly from equation 5.37. Multiplying it out and simplifying, we get:

$$x(t) = (1-t)^3\, x_1 + 3\, t\, (1-t)^2\, x_2$$
$$+ 3\, t^2\, (1-t)\, x_3 + t^3\, x_4 \qquad [5.40]$$

from which, by comparison to 5.39, we can read off:

$$B_1(t) = (1-t)^3 , \qquad\qquad [5.41]$$
$$B_2(t) = 3\, t\, (1-t)^2 ,$$
$$B_3(t) = 3\, t^2\, (1-t) ,$$
$$B_4(t) = t^3.$$

Note how the blending functions, B_i, act as weighting functions for the four control point coordinates, x_i. That is, at point 1 (where $t = 0$), point 1 controls completely since $B_1 = 1$ and all the other B_i's are zero. As t approaches 0.33, point 2 dominates the curve as the influence of point 1 is dying out and that of point 3 is growing but not yet strong. As we move through $t = 0.67$, point 3 dominates and the influence of points 2 and 1 is dying and dead, respectively. Finally, at point 4, B_4 approaches 1 and all the other blending functions fade away. This behavior can be better visualized by examining the blending function behavior as a function of t as shown in Figure 5.7.

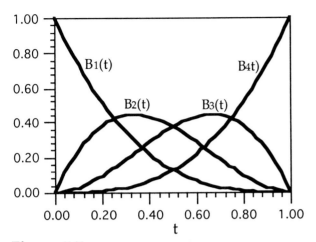

Figure 5.7
Blending functions. These functions, called
Bernstein polynomials, serve as weighting functions to weight points P_1, P_2, P_3, and P_4, respectively.

Pascal Program Bezier

```
program Bezier;
{Program to read in four Bezier control points:    }
{ P1  =  first point                                }
{ P2  =  second point, controlling slope at first   }
{ P3  =  third point, controlling slope at fourth   }
{ P4  =  fourth point, end of section               }
{and compute and plot resulting parametric          }
{cubic curve.                                        }
   type
      mat = array[1..4, 1..4] of real;
   var
      Px, Py, Cx, Cy: mat;
      Tv,Mb,x, y: mat;
      i, j, k, xx, yy: integer;
      window: rect;
      t, dt: real;
      P:point;

{************ MatMlt **************}
   procedure matmlt (var d, a, b: mat; n, m:
               integer);
{ Program to calculate matrix product:    }
{D=A*B, where                             }
{   a = n x 4 input matrix                }
{   b = 4 x m input matrix                }
{   d = n x m output matrix               }
      var
         i, j, k: integer;
         sum: real;
         temp: mat;
   begin
      for i := 1 to n do
         begin
            for j := 1 to m do
```

```
            begin
               sum := 0.0;
               for k := 1 to 4 do
                  sum := sum + a[i, k] * b[k,
                  j];
               temp[i, j] := sum;
            end;
         end;
      for i := 1 to n do
         for j := 1 to m do
            d[i, j] := temp[i, j];
   end;

{+++++++++ Get-Points +++++++++++++}
   procedure getPoints;
      var
         i, x, y: integer;
   begin        {First set up drawing window}
      setRect(window, 30, 30, 400, 300);
      setDrawingRect(window);
      showDrawing;
      penSize(2, 2);
      moveto(40, 20);              {Print heading }
      textSize(18);
      textFont(2);
      writeDraw('Bezier Parametric Cubic
         Curve');
      textSize(12);
      ForeColor(409);              {Set pen to blue.}
      {Loop to read 4 points.}
      for i := 1 to 4 do
         begin
            setRect(window, 90, 30, 255, 50);
            eraseRect(window);
            moveto(100, 45);
            writeDraw('Please click in point', I : 3);
            frameRect(window);
            repeat
               getMouse(P)
            until button;
            repeat
            until (not button);
            Px[i, 1] := P.h;
            Py[i, 1] := P.v;
            setRect(window, (P.h - 2), (P.v - 2), (P.h + 4),
               (P.v + 4));
            {Draw point as 6-pixel diameter circle.}
            paintOval(window);
         end;
   end;

   procedure set_BezMat;
   begin                   {Simplest to go brute force.}
      Mb[1, 1] := -1;
      Mb[1, 2] := 3;
      Mb[1, 3] := -3;
      Mb[1, 4] := 1;
      Mb[2, 1] := 3;
      Mb[2, 2] := -6;
      Mb[2, 3] := 3;
      Mb[2, 4] := 0;
```

```
        Mb[3, 1] := -3;
        Mb[3, 2] := 3;
        Mb[3, 3] := 0;
        Mb[3, 4] := 0;
        Mb[4, 1] := 1;
        Mb[4, 2] := 0;
        Mb[4, 3] := 0;
        Mb[4, 4] := 0;
   end;

{********   MAIN PROGRAM   *************}
begin
   set_BezMat;
   getPoints;
   {Calculate coefficient vector}
   matmlt(Cx, Mb, Px, 4, 1);
   matmlt(Cy, Mb, Py, 4, 1);
   {Now trace out curve in 101 steps }
   t := -0.01;
   xx := round(Px[1, 1]);
   yy := round(Py[1, 1]);
   moveto(xx, yy);
   ForeColor(137);          {Set pen to magenta.}

   for i := 1 to 101 do
      begin
         t := t + 0.01;
         Tv[1, 4] := 1;
         Tv[1, 3] := t * Tv[1, 4];
         Tv[1, 2] := t * Tv[1, 3];
         Tv[1, 1] := t * Tv[1, 2];
         matmlt(x, Tv, Cx, 1, 1);
         matmlt(y, Tv, Cy, 1, 1);
         xx := round(x[1, 1]);
         yy := round(y[1, 1]);
         lineto(xx, yy);
      end;
end.
```

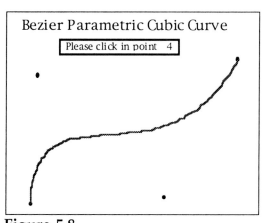

Figure 5.8
Bézier parametric cubic curve. Note how second and third points determine the tangents at points one and four.

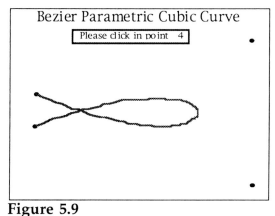

Figure 5.9
Another Bézier curve. Note the capability of loops.

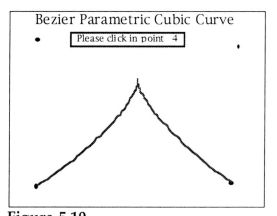

Figure 5.10
Bézier curves are capable of cusps when control points are arranged in an "X."

The purpose of **Bezier** is to illustrate the Bézier control paradigm with a simple but convenient program. The user is prompted for four control points and the program then constructs the resulting cubic curve using the matrix representation developed above.

Let's examine some output from program **Bezier**. In Figure 5.8, the curve starts at point 1 in the lower lefthand corner and heads towards point 2 immediately above it. It then veers off and curve into point 4, approaching it from the direction determined by point 3 near the bottom of the window.

In Figure 5.9, a fish-like object is generated from point 1, the lower, lefthand point, with the curve pulled towards point 2 in the upper, righthand corner. As the influence of point 3 in the lower, righthand corner is felt, the curve loops around and heads for point 4, the upper righthand point. Figure 5.10 demonstrates that Bézier curves are capable of generating sharp cusps as well as smoothly-rounded curves.

These three curves demonstrate the great flexibility and power of Bézier curves as design tools.

More Complex Curves

In actual practice, a designer generally requires curves with more complexity than that possible with a single Bézier segment. Three available approaches include:

- **The use of higher order Bézier curves** – By increasing N the polynomial order, from three to four, five, or higher, the user gets five, six, or more control points with which to mold the curve between the first and last points. The price paid is that of more computational complexity.

- **The joining of multiple cubic Bézier segments** – It is relatively simple to make the first point of a second Bézier segment coincide with the last point of the first segment. This guarantees continuity of the curve itself (called C^0 continuity. By taking care to align point P_3 of the first segment with point P_2 of the second segment and both co-linear with the bracketed point, the user can achieve a smooth join, that is, one with continuity in the slope of the curve at the join point (called C^1 continuity).

- **The use of cubic B-splines** – The B-spline curve can be used to fit n points where n is ≥ 4. It is even smoother than Bézier curves by having continuous curvature (C^2 continuity) as well as C^0 and C^1 continuity. The curve goes through the first and last point but is only *pulled* by the intermediate control points. The mathematical formalism is identical with that of Bézier curves, with M_s replacing M_b and the point vector composed of the elements (P_{i-1}, P_i, P_{i+1}, P_{i+2}). The full matrix representation for the coordinate x is then given as:

$$x(t) = T \cdot M_s \cdot P_{xs} \qquad [5.42]$$

where

$$M_s = \frac{1}{6} \cdot \begin{bmatrix} -1 & 3 & -3 & 1 \\ 3 & -6 & 3 & 0 \\ -3 & 0 & 3 & 0 \\ 1 & 4 & 1 & 0 \end{bmatrix} \qquad [5.43]$$

(B-spline coefficient matrix)

and

$$P_{xs} = \begin{bmatrix} x_{i-1} \\ x_i \\ x_{i+1} \\ x_{i+2} \end{bmatrix} \qquad 2 \leq i \leq n-2 \qquad [5.44]$$

Thus, as t goes from 0 to 1, the set of control points moves from $i = 2$ to $i = n-2$ for an n control-point set. That is, the local control-point set starts at points (1,2,3,4) for $t = 0$ and then moves through (2,3,4,5), (3,4,5,6), and so on until it reaches ($n-3$, $n-2$, $n-1$, n) for $t = 1$. Each set corresponds to a different cubic fit with the four nearest points controlling the curve. An equivalent reresentation applies for $y(t)$.

Representing Actions – Transformations in 2D

As noted in Chapter 4, when we move from N dimensions to N+1 dimensions, new transformations are possible which were undefined and unimaginable in the lower dimension. The most important new transformation, which is undefined in 1D but opens up in 2D space, is *rotation*. The homogeneous matrix formalism previously introduced is easily extended to represent both the familiar translation and scaling operations as well as the new concept of rotation. Let us consider these in sequence.

All 2D homogeneous coordinate transformations are represented by the familiar equation:

$$X' = X M \qquad [5.45]$$

where

$$X' = [x' \; y' \; 1]$$
(homogeneous coordinates of transformed object),

$$X = [x \; y \; 1]$$
(homogeneous coordinates of original object),

where

M = matrix unique to each transformation.

It is useful to distinguish between the following four classes of transformations:

- Primary transformations,
- Secondary transformations,
- Complex or concatenated transformations,
- Inverse transformations.

Primary transformations (translation, scaling, and rotation) are so common and useful that they appear in nearly every drawing and drafting program. Secondary transformations (reflections and shears) are less common and often used for special effects. Finally, complex transformations are concatenated from a series of primary, secondary, or other complex transformations to perform particular operations.

Primary Transformations

The following three transformations perform the operations of shifting, magnification, and rotation of objects.

Translation

For translating an object a distance T_x along the x-axis and T_y along the y-axis, the matrix *M* is the *T* matrix, defined as:

$$T = \begin{bmatrix} 1 & 0 & 0 \\ 0 & 1 & 0 \\ T_x & T_y & 1 \end{bmatrix}.$$ [5.46]

Substituting *T* for *M* in Equation 5.45 and multiplying gives the standard linear translation equations:

$$x' = x + T_x$$ [5.47]
$$y' = y + T_y .$$

Scaling

Generalizing the 1D scaling transformation to 2D involves defining separate scale factors, S_x and S_y, for independent scaling along each axis. The M matrix of Equation 5.45 then becomes the **S** matrix, defined as:

$$S = \begin{bmatrix} S_x & 0 & 0 \\ 0 & S_y & 0 \\ 0 & 0 & 1 \end{bmatrix}.$$ [5.48]

Substituting *S* for *M* in Equation 5.45 and multiplying gives the standard linear scaling equations:

$$x' = S_x x ,$$ [5.49]
$$y' = S_y y .$$

Rotation

A very useful transformation in drawing, drafting, and CAD applications involves rotating an object by some arbitrary, user-defined angle, θ. This transformation is performed by redefining the generalized *M* matrix as the rotation matrix, *R*, where

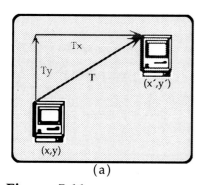 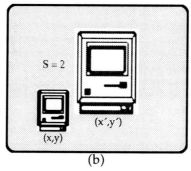 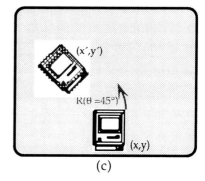

(a)   (b)   (c)

Figure 5.11
Three primary transformations: (a) linear translation by the vector $T = T_x \cdot x + T_y \cdot y$, (b) linear scaling by $S = S_x = S_y = 2$, and (c) rotation about the origin by $\theta = 45°$.

$$R = \begin{bmatrix} \cos\theta & \sin\theta & 0 \\ -\sin\theta & \cos\theta & 0 \\ 0 & 0 & 1 \end{bmatrix} \qquad [5.50]$$

Substituting R for M in equation 5.45 and multiplying gives the standard rotation equations, familiar from trigonometry:

$$x' = x\cos\theta - y\cdot\sin\theta \qquad [5.51]$$
$$y' = x\cdot\sin\theta + y\cdot\cos\theta .$$

These three primary 2D transformations are illustrated in Figure 5.11.

Two items of note are apparent in [5.11]. First is that scaling involves both a magnification (as expected) and a translation (sometimes an unwanted side-effect). Second is that a pure rotation as specified by Equations 5.51 is defined as taking place about the origin, $(x,y) = (0,0)$. Therefore, unless the object to be rotated is already centered on the origin, rotation will cause it to swing in a large circle centered at the origin. The frequently desired *rotation in place* may be accomplished by composing a series of transformations to produce a single *complex transformation*.

Secondary Transformations

Two additional classes of transformations, that may be useful in certain applications, are *reflections* and *shearing*. Reflections are special cases of the scaling transformation with S_x, S_y, or both having the value –1. Shearing may be considered as a special case of scaling in which the scale factor in the direction of one axis is a function of the coordinate of the other axis. Let's look at these two transformations in more detail.

Reflections

We will consider three reflections here. First, an object may be reflected across the x-axis (all $y_i \rightarrow -y_i$). Second, an object may be reflected across the y-axis (all $x_i \rightarrow -x_i$). Third, an object may be reflected through the origin (all $x_i \rightarrow -x_i$ and all $y_i \rightarrow -y_i$). These three reflections are neatly accomplished by the three mirror reflection matrices, M_x, M_y, and M_{xy}, given by:

$$M_x = \begin{bmatrix} 1 & 0 & 0 \\ 0 & -1 & 0 \\ 0 & 0 & 1 \end{bmatrix} \qquad [5.52]$$

(mirror about x-axis),

$$M_y = \begin{bmatrix} -1 & 0 & 0 \\ 0 & 1 & 0 \\ 0 & 0 & 1 \end{bmatrix} \qquad [5.53]$$

(mirror about y-axis),

and

$$M_{xy} = \begin{bmatrix} -1 & 0 & 0 \\ 0 & -1 & 0 \\ 0 & 0 & 1 \end{bmatrix} \qquad [5.54]$$

(reflect through origin).

These three reflection transformations are illustrated in Figure 5.12.

Shearing Transformations

Shearing transformations are a particular form of translation where the offset factor is position dependant. The most common dependencies involve *x-shear* and *y-shear* defined by the following transformation matrices:

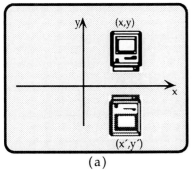 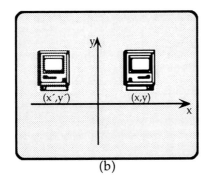 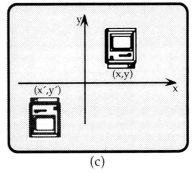

(a) (b) (c)

Figure 5.12
Reflection transformations. (a) Reflection through x-axis, M_x, (b) Reflection through y-axis, M_y, (c) Reflection through origin, M_{xy}.

$$Sh_x = \begin{bmatrix} 1 & 0 & 0 \\ a & 1 & 0 \\ 0 & 0 & 1 \end{bmatrix},$$ [5.55]

(shear along x-axis)

$$Sh_y = \begin{bmatrix} 1 & b & 0 \\ 0 & 1 & 0 \\ 0 & 0 & 1 \end{bmatrix},$$ [5.56]

(shear along y-axis)

where a and b are control parameters specifying how "sharp" the shear is.

When substituted for *M* in Equation 5.45 and multiplied out, these matrices lead to the following sets of transformation equations:

Shear along x-axis –

$$x' = x + ay,$$ [5.57]
$$y' = y,$$

and

Shear along y-axis –

$$x' = x,$$ [5.58]
$$y' = bx + y.$$

In Figure 5.13, the effects of shearing transformations along the two axes are shown. The x-axis shear transformation is easily demonstrated physically by laying a paper-back book on a table, holding the bottom cover stationary with respect to the table top, and pressing the top cover in a direction perpendicular to the binding direction with the other hand. The end view of the book will illustrate the x-axis shearing transformation.

Complex (Composed) Transformations

The final class of transformations considered in this chapter are those complex transformations generated by *composing* (multiplying) two or more elementary transformation matrices. Such complex transformations are required to perform the useful operations of scaling about a point, reflection about a line, and rotation about a point. Consider how we might, for instance, magnify an object in place, i.e., scale it about some internal point.

Scaling About a Point

As Figure 5.11(b) clearly indicates, simple scaling produces not only magnification but also a translation in general (unless the object happens to be at the origin). Since the goal is frequently to simply magnify the object in place, we must introduce more complexity into the transformation process.

To accomplish the goal of scaling about a point, consider the following algorithm which is illustrated in Figure 5.14.

1. Select a center point, (x_c, y_c), about which you want the scaling to occur.

2. Translate the object with $T(-x_c, -y_c)$ to shift the center point to the origin.

3. Scale the object with the desired $S(S_x, S_y)$.

4. Translate the object with $T(+x_c, +y_c)$ to shift back to where we started.

This sequence of operations can be expressed

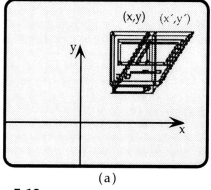

(a)

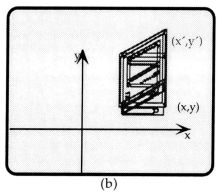

(b)

Figure 5.13

Shearing transformations. (a) along the x-axis; (b) along the y-axis.

very cleanly through the composition of the three transformation matrices within the homogeneous coordinate system. We simply rewrite Equation 5.29 as

$$X' = X\, M_c \qquad [5.59]$$

where the composed matrix, M_c, is computed by

$$M_c = T(-x_c,-y_c)\, S(S_x,S_y)\, T(+x_c,+y_c). \qquad [5.60]$$

Computing this gives the matrix,

$$M_c = \begin{bmatrix} S_x & 0 & 0 \\ 0 & S_y & 0 \\ x_c(1-S_x) & y_c(1-S_y) & 1 \end{bmatrix}. \qquad [5.61]$$

As a concrete example, consider Figure 5.14 where $S_x = S_y = 4$ and we measure (x_c,y_c) to be $(10,5)$. The composed matrix then reduces to

$$M_c = \begin{bmatrix} 4 & 0 & 0 \\ 0 & 4 & 0 \\ -30 & -15 & 1 \end{bmatrix}. \qquad [5.62]$$

Solving Equation 5.59 for the transformed coordinates in terms of the original ones gives the set of transformation equations

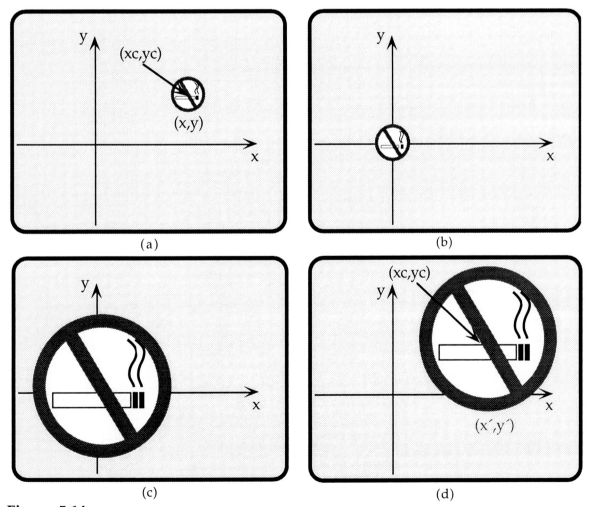

(a)

(b)

(c)

(d)

Figure 5.14
Scaling about a point. To scale the icon shown in (a) by 400 percent about center point, (x_c,y_c), we perform the sequence: (b) translate by $T(-x_c,-y_c)$; (c) scale by $S(4,4)$; finally, translate back by $T(+x_c,+y_c)$.

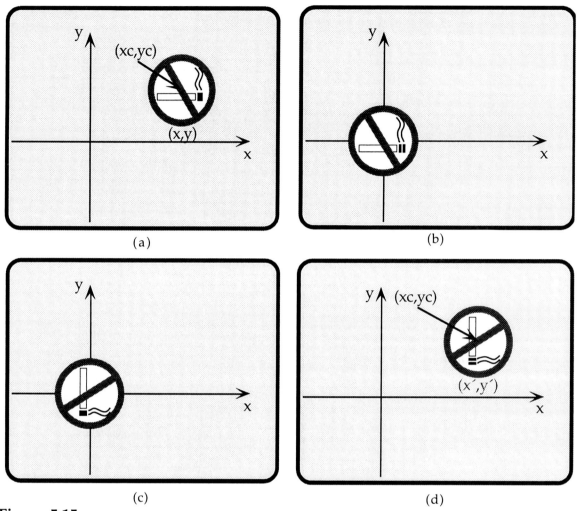

(a)

(b)

(c)

(d)

Figure 5.15
Rotation about a point. Select a point, (x_c, y_c), as in (a). Then, shift the object to the origin by $T(-x_c, -y_c)$ as shown in (b). Next, rotate by desired angle, θ, as shown in (c). Finally, shift back to the original position as in (d).

$$x' = 4x - 30 \qquad [5.63]$$
$$y' = 4y - 15.$$

Rotation About a Point

Nearly identical arguments can be made for the operation of rotation in place or *rotation about a point*.

The algorithm, illustrated in Figure 5.15, becomes:

1. Select a center point, (x_c, y_c), about which you want the rotation to occur.

2. Translate the object with $T(-x_c, -y_c)$ to shift the center point to the origin.

3. Rotate the object by the angle, θ.

4. Translate the object with $T(+x_c, +y_c)$ to shift the center point back to where we started.

The mathematics for the complex transformation of Figure 5.15 closely resembles that for scaling about a point, with the rotation matrix, $R(\theta)$, replacing the scaling matrix, $S(S_x, S_y)$. Rotation about a point may be represented as:

$$M_c = T(-x_c,-y_c)\, R(\theta)\, T(+x_c,+y_c).\quad [5.64]$$

Computing this gives the concatenated matrix,

$$M_c = \begin{bmatrix} \cos\theta & \sin\theta & 0 \\ -\sin\theta & \cos\theta & 0 \\ x_c(1-\cos\theta)+y_c\sin\theta & y_c(1-\cos\theta)-x_c\sin\theta & 1 \end{bmatrix}.$$
$$[5.65]$$

Although this looks a bit forbidding, knowing (x_c,y_c) and θ allows us to quickly compute the composed rotation-about-a-point matrix, M_c, as a simple 3×3 numerical matrix. Again, the reader should appreciate the computational efficiency of representing a complex, composition of three transformation matrices by a single, numerical array.

Inverse Transformations

For each *forward* transformation matrix, M, discussed above, there is an *inverse* transformation matrix, M^{-1}. What M^{-1} means, in a graphical sense, is that whatever transformation M does, M^{-1} "undoes" it. If M shifts an object 4 units to the right, M^{-1} shifts it 4 units to the left; if M magnifies an object by a factor of 2, M^{-1} demagnifies it by a factor of 0.5; and if M rotates an object by 45°, M^{-1} rotates it by –45°. It is apparent that the combined operation of applying M followed immediately by applying M^{-1} will leave an object completely unchanged.

From a matrix algebra point of view, we say that the composition of M and M^{-1} is the identity matrix, I. That is, $M\,M^{-1} = I$. The identity matrix is a square matrix with 1s on the diagonal and 0s elsewhere. Its effect, when multiplied with any other conformal matrix, is to return the original matrix. Therefore, we have $X\,I = I\,X = X$, a result which agrees with the word proof above.

A little thought on the nature of translation, scaling, and rotation leads to the following inverse matrices for the primary and secondary transformations.

Inverse Translation:

$$T^{-1} = \begin{bmatrix} 1 & 0 & 0 \\ 0 & 1 & 0 \\ -T_x & -T_y & 1 \end{bmatrix}. \quad [5.66]$$

Inverse Scaling:

$$S^{-1} = \begin{bmatrix} \frac{1}{S_x} & 0 & 0 \\ 0 & \frac{1}{S_y} & 0 \\ 0 & 0 & 1 \end{bmatrix}. \quad [5.67]$$

Inverse Rotation:

$$R^{-1} = \begin{bmatrix} \cos\theta & \sin\theta & 0 \\ -\sin\theta & \cos\theta & 0 \\ 0 & 0 & 1 \end{bmatrix} \quad [5.68]$$

Inverse Reflection Transformations:

These matrices are their own inverses.

Inverse Shearing Transformations:

$$Sh_x^{-1} = \begin{bmatrix} 1 & 0 & 0 \\ -a & 1 & 0 \\ 0 & 0 & 1 \end{bmatrix} \quad [5.69]$$
(x-axis shear)

$$Sh_y^{-1} = \begin{bmatrix} 1 & -b & 0 \\ 0 & 1 & 0 \\ 0 & 0 & 1 \end{bmatrix} \quad [5.70]$$
(y-axis shear).

The reader may wish to verify that these are correct representations of the inverse transformations by checking that $M\,M^{-1} = I$. The inverse transformation matrix is particularly useful in implementing the **Undo** feature of drafting, drawing, and CAD programs.

Table 5.1
Sailboat Encoded Vertices

x_i	y_i	c_i	x_i	y_i	c_i	x_i	y_i	c_i	x_i	y_i	c_i
4.5	0.35	0	1.85	1.10	1	3.7	2.85	1	6.8	6.0	1
14.75	0.35	1	4.5	0.35	1	11.3	2.85	1	6.3	10.2	0
15.55	0.62	1	11.6	1.50	0	11.1	21.25	1	8.0	9.5	1
16.0	0.85	1	11.2	21.25	1	9.2	17.1	1	7.7	13.7	0
16.65	1.2	1	11.1	21.25	1	1.5	1.35	0	9.5	13.0	1
17.0	1.55	1	11.3	1.5	1	11.1	21.25	1	9.2	17.1	0
17.3	1.90	1	15.55	1.75	0	4.8	1.22	0	10.5	16.7	1
15.0	1.65	1	11.35	16.2	1	5.0	1.6	1	3.7	2.85	0
11.3	1.40	1	11.1	2.65	1	8.6	1.75	1	5.0	6.65	1
8.0	1.325	1	15.55	1.75	1	11.0	1.75	1	6.3	10.2	1
5.0	1.20	1	11.3	2.6	0	11.3	1.4	1	7.7	13.7	1
1.50	1.35	1	3.7	2.6	1	5.0	6.65	0	9.2	17.0	1
	(i = 1 → 12)			(i = 13 → 24)			(i = 25 → 36)			(i = 37 → 48)	

Pascal Example – **TRANSFORM**

To illustrate the role of representation of data structures and the implementation of the matrix transformations, we conclude this section with a Pascal example, **TRANSFORM**. In **TRANSFORM**, we must consider and resolve several important representation issues which greatly influence algorithm design and implementation.

The goal of **TRANSFORM** is to build a minimal system for performing the primary transformations on reasonably complex and general line drawings. The representation issues which arise immediately include:

- What data structure provides an optimum compromise between simplicity, efficiency, and generality in representing line drawings?

- What data structure provides a reasonable compromise between simplicity and power in representing matrices and their manipulation within the program?

- What control structure provides the user with the ability to perform the primary transformations, any arbitrary composition of these transformations, and a few simple utilities in a reasonably friendly environment?

As a realistic object to represent by line drawing, we selected the sail plan from a boat featured in the magazine, *Sailing*. A grid was superimposed on the schematic and the major features of the boat were outlined by a set of vertices connected by straight lines. The (x,y) location of each vertex was measured and tabulated.

At this point, there were several options. We could have used a brute force approach and represented the boat by a set of lines, each specified by the quadruple, (x_1,y_1,x_2,y_2), of its end points. Or, we could have attempted to force some structure on the drawing by representing each feature of the boat by a polygon. However, this would have required re-digitizing the drawing with this structure as a constraint, and the representation would have been unnatural for long, thin elements such as the forestay and backstay.

The compromise data structure chosen was a file of ordered triads, (x_i,y_i,c_i), representing the coordinates of each vertex along with a control code, c_i. The control code is given as:

$c_i = 1$ Move to this point with pen down (use *LineTo*(x_i,y_i))

$c_i = 0$ Move to this point with pen up (use *MoveTo*(x_i,y_i))

This scheme is equivalent to a list of (non-closed) polygons in which one jumps to the first point on a polygon labeled with the $c_i = 0$ code and continues plotting the polygon's sides using vertices labeled with the $c_i = 1$ code. The scheme eliminates the considerable redundancy of points inherent in a set-of-lines representations and quite naturally matches the mapping technique by which the original vertex table was generated. The entire sailboat figure is represented by the 48 vertices listed in Table 5.1.

The natural Pascal data structure selected for representing matrices was the square array of dimension *nd*. The *nd* = 3 arrays required for homogeneous 2D coordinates are easily extended to *nd* = 4 arrays required for 3D transformations. So all of the matrix manipulation routines of TRANSFORM are easily extended to 3D applications.

The one nonstandard matrix algebra shortcut employed in TRANSFORM is based on the observation that all of the primary transformations and complex transformations built up from multiplying them can be represented by the form:

$$M = \begin{bmatrix} a & b & 0 \\ c & d & 0 \\ e & f & 1 \end{bmatrix}. \qquad [5.71]$$

Therefore, the matrix multiplication, $X' = X\,M$, is equivalent to the two algebraic expressions:

$$x' = a\,x + b\,y + e, \qquad [5.72]$$
$$y' = b\,x + d\,y + f,$$

and this is the form used to apply the transformation in routine applyxfn. This allows a somewhat cleaner, more efficient code than possible with vector matrix multiplication.

The control structure selected for TRANSFORM was a user-controlled loop in the routine, Menu, which requires the user to move in any order among the following transformations and utility functions by use of one-letter keyboard commands.

Load: Reads a new graphics object data file at any point of the session,

Translate: Translates the current object by a user-provided (T_x, T_y)

Scale: Scales the current object by a user-provided (S_x, S_y),

Rotate: Rotates the current object by a user-provided angle, θ,

Display: The object being transformed is displayed upon this command,

Clear: Erases the current drawing window,

Quit: Exits the program.

Although this set of operations and utilities is minimal, it is capable of providing *any* transformation possible through composition of the primary transformations.

Pascal Program Transform

```
program Transform;
{ Program to transform graphical objects          }
{ by user-specified translation, scaling, and rotation  }
{and any concatenation of these three transformations.}

const
  nd = 3;          {Dimension of matrices}
  ns = 100;        {Maximum size of object }
                   {(in control points)}
  VxL = 20;        {Viewport left boundary}
  VxR = 450;       {Viewport right boundary}
  VyT = 20;        {Viewport top boundary}
  VyB = 350;       {Viewport bottom boundary}
  Xo = 50;         {X pixel coordinate off-set of origin}
  Yo = 50;         {Y pixel coordinate off-set of origin}

type
  mat = array[1..nd, 1..nd] of real;
var
  dx, dy: real;
  m: mat;
  i, j, k, npts: integer;
  x, y, xp, yp: array[1..ns] of real;
  c: array[1..ns] of integer;
  infile: text;
  pt, xx, yy, cc: integer;
  ViewPort: rect;
{*************************************}
 procedure applyxfn;
{Applies concatenated transform.}
 var
  i: integer;
 begin
 for i := 1 to npts do
   begin
   xp[i] := x[i] * m[1, 1] + y[i] * m[2, 1] + m[3, 1];
   yp[i] := x[i] * m[1, 2] + y[i] * m[2, 2] + m[3, 2];
   end;
 end;
{*************************************}
 procedure diagmat (var xmat: mat);
{Generates the identity matrix}
 var
  i, j: integer;
 begin
 for i := 1 to nd do
   begin
   for j := 1 to nd do
   xmat[i, j] := 0.0;
   xmat[i, i] := 1.0;
   end;
 end;
{*************************************}
 procedure matmlt (var d, a, b: mat);
{Calculate matrix product: D=A*B }
 var
  n, i, j, k: integer;
  sum: real;
  temp: mat;
```

```
begin
 n := nd;
 for i := 1 to n do
  begin
   for j := 1 to n do
   begin
    sum := 0.0;
    for k := 1 to n do
     sum := sum + a[i, k] * b[k, j];
     temp[i, j] := sum;
    end;
  end;
 for i := 1 to n do
  for j := 1 to n do
   d[i, j] := temp[i, j];
 end;
{*************************************}
 procedure display;
{Procedure to draw object in viewport}
 var
  i, xx, yy: integer;
  screen: rect;
 begin
 ShowDrawing;
 applyxfn;         {Apply concatenated matrix to X vector}
 for i := 1 to npts do           {Draw object}
  begin
  xx := VxL + Xo + round(xp[i]);
  yy := VyB - Yo - round(yp[i]);
  if (c[i] = 0) then             {invisible move}
    moveto(xx, yy);
  if (c[i] = 1) then             {draw visible line}
    lineto(xx, yy);
  end;
 end;
{*************************************}
 procedure getobject;           {Procedure to select }
                                {and read in data file.}
  var                           {Format is (xi, yi, ci).}
   infile: text;
   i, pt, cc: integer;
   xx, yy: real;
 begin
 i := 0;
 open(infile, OldFileName('Transform DataFile?'));
 repeat
 i := i + 1;
 readln(infile, xx, yy, cc);
 x[i] := xx;
 y[i] := yy;
 c[i] := cc;
 until eof(infile);
 npts := i;
 end;
{*************************************}
 procedure load;
 begin
 getobject;
 diagmat(m);
 display;
 end;
```

```
{*************************************}
 procedure translate;
{Procedure to translate point by dx,dy}
  var
   t: mat;
  begin                  {Get translation parameters.}
  writeln('Tx, Ty?');
  readln(dx, dy);
  diagmat(t);            {Set up matrix, T }
  t[nd, 1] := dx;
  t[nd, 2] := dy;
  matmlt(m, m, t);       {Now compose with M matrix}
  end;

{*************************************}
 procedure scale;
{Procedure to scale X by SX and Y by SY}
  var
   sx, sy: real;
   s: mat;
  begin                  {Get scaling parameters.}
  writeln('SX, SY?');
  readln(sx, sy);
  diagmat(s);            {Set up matrix, S}
  s[1, 1] := sx;
  s[2, 2] := sy;
  matmlt(m, m, s);       {Now compose with M}
  end;
{*************************************}
 procedure rotate;
{Procedure to set up rotation matrix}
  const
   rad = 57.29578;
  var
   th: real;
   R: mat;
  begin                  {Get rotation angle, th}
  writeln('Angle (deg)?');
  readln(th);
  th := th / rad;
  diagmat(R);
  R[1, 1] := cos(th);
  R[2, 2] := R[1, 1];
  R[1, 2] := sin(th);
  R[2, 1] := -R[1, 2];
  matmlt(m, m, r);       {Concatenate M with R}
  end;
{*************************************}
 procedure clear_viewprt;
 begin
 SetRect(ViewPort, 0, 0, VxR - VxL, VyB - VyT);
 EraseRect(ViewPort);
 end;
{*************************************}
 procedure menu;
  var
   done: Boolean;
   command: char;
 begin
 done := false;
```

```
setRect(ViewPort, VxR - 20, VyT, VxR + 80, VyB);
setTextRect(ViewPort);
ShowText;
setRect(ViewPort, VxL, VyT, VxR, VyB);
setDrawingRect(ViewPort);
repeat
 writeln(' Menu');
 writeln('L)  Load');
 writeln('T)  Translate');
 writeln('S)  Scale');
 writeln('R)  Rotate');
 writeln('D)  Display');
 writeln('C)  Clear');
 writeln('Q)  Quit');
 readln(command);
{Now branch to chosen procedure}
 case command of
 'l', 'L':
  load;
 't', 'T':
  translate;
 's', 'S':
  scale;
 'r', 'R':
  rotate;
 'd', 'D':
  display;
 'c', 'C':
  clear_viewprt;
 'q', 'Q':
```

```
   done := true;
  otherwise
  begin
   writeln('Bad command');
   writeln('Try again . ');
   readln;
  end;
 end;
 until done;
end;
{********** Main Program **************}
begin
 diagmat(m);
 getobject;
 menu;
end.
```

Let's examine three cases of output generated by TRANSFORM.

When the program runs, it requests a data file containing the image. Upon selecting the file SAIL.Dat (Table 5.1) and typing "D", the user observes the tiny object shown in the lower lefthand corner of Figure 5.16. The obvious reaction is "to magnify that thing so we can see what it is." So we type "s" to scale the object and respond with "10 10" when asked for S_x and S_y. Upon displaying this transformation,

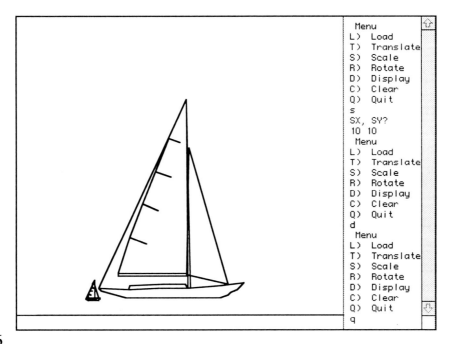

Figure 5.16
Output of TRANSFORM. The small object on the left is generated by displaying the raw data file given in Table 5.1. It is so small because its world coordinates (cm) are plotted out directly as pixels with no scaling. The larger boat is generated by scaling the model by ten times as indicated in the menu transcript. The menu can be scrolled to recall previous transformations.

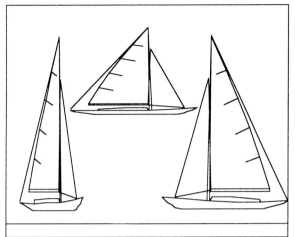

Figure 5.17
Reflections and differential scaling output of
TRANSFORM. By judicious use of the three
primary transformations, interesting special effects are possible.

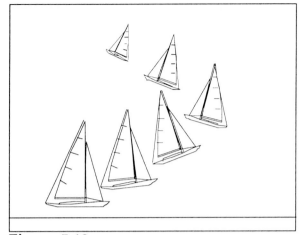

Figure 5.18
Rounding the mark in a sailboat race. The illusion of 3D is achieved by scaling down the size
of each object and giving it a small rotation.

we get the magnified boat shown in Figure 5.16.
Various aspect ratios between height and
width are easily achieved by making S_x different from S_y as demonstrated in Figure 5.17. This
figure also indicates that the ship's direction
can be reversed by the reflection operation: $S_x =$
-1.

Finally, more complex scenes such as the
sailboat race shown in Figure 5.18 may easily be
composed by combining instances of the basic
object under various transformations. The illusion of a 3D scene is created by appropriate
scaling and small rotations.

Note that the screen contains two viewports: a **Drawing** window in which the objects
appear and a **TEXT** window for the control
menu and commands. The scrolling control window provides both a continuous prompt on command options and a complete transcript of preceding commands and transformation parameters. This, frequently, is useful information.

While **TRANSFORM** does provide many
graphics functions in a relatively compact program, it does have its problems. Among these
are the lack of any **Undo** option for erasing the
last object drawn and the use of awkward keyboard control instead of the more natural mouse
menu control. These are easily implemented, but
were omitted because of program length
considerations.

Conclusions

As we move from 1D into 2D, new transformations such as the rotation group become possible.
Within a homogeneous coordinate system representation, the matrix formalism is easily extended to incorporate rotations as well as other
emergent transformations like differential scaling and shearing. The key importance of representation issues becomes apparent in describing
polygons and 2D curves. Considerations in the
selection of representation for polygons and
curves are discussed and example solutions are
presented. Transformations of these graphical
objects are represented elegantly and concisely
with the matrix formalism. Finally, a program
is presented to show an implementation of this
formalism and the ease with which complex
transformation may be generated by a composition of primary transformations. Throughout the
chapter the theme has been the importance of
the correct representation to the solution of any
given problem.

Exercises

5.1   Throughout this chapter, the terms *abstract* and *abstraction* appear several times. Define the term *abstraction* and discuss its advantages and problems.

5.2   In the section, rotations were introduced as new phenomena arising from the move from 1D to 2D. Actually, there are several other transformations possible in 2D which are not in 1D. Which are they and how are they generated?

5.3   In Figure 5.1 we show a curve defined in parametric form, a term used several times in this chapter. What are the advantages of using parametric forms for lines and curves rather than implicit forms such as $y = m x + b$ and $y = x^2$?

5.4   The general implicit forms for circles and parabolas are:

$$(x - x_c)^2 + (y - y_c)^2 - r^2 = 0$$
$$k\, x^2 + (y_o - y) = 0$$

Rewrite each of these equations in parametric form in terms of the parameter, t, with t on the range, $0 \leq t \leq 1$.

5.5   Figure 5.2 illustrates more complex, composite images. Each one poses representation problems with widely different optimal solutions. For each of the four images, develop a data structure which could be used to represent it and similar images of its type. The map, for instance, could be represented by a set of M polygons, each with N sides plus color. (*Hint: the Pascal record type is a useful way of creating objects with elements of different types.*)

5.6   Lines in 2D can be represented by either the algebraic form (Equation 5.2) or the parametric vector form (Equation 5.6). Sketch a diagram and define the parameters of the parametric vector form corresponding to the algebraic equation:

$$y = 5 x + 7.$$

5.7   Sketch a diagram showing the relevant vectors for the parametric vector form of the line segment from point (2,10) to point (8,3). Equation 5.7 will help.

5.8   Categorize the following points with respect to the line $y = 2 x + 8$ into the two classes: inside (origin side of line) and outside (opposite side from origin).

(–6,3)   (5,8)   (–3,20)   (–5,–10)   (30,6)

5.9   In problem 5.8, how far is the last point from the line? What point on the line is closest to the last point?

5.10   Which of the three polygon representation schemes described in this chapter seem to you to be the best and why? What would you suggest as an alternative scheme to the three presented?

5.11   Although the text indicated that parametric curves and patches are much more efficient at representing smooth, curved objects, most modeling and design program still use combinations of polygons or polyhedra (finite element methods). Why do you think this is so?

5.12   Curves can be used to either interpolate or approximate points. Sketch two diagrams of some points and a curve that illustrate each case.

5.13   Verify the steps leading from Equations 5.32 to 5.33 and verify by matrix multiplication that $\mathbf{C}_x = \mathbf{M}_b \cdot \mathbf{P}_x$ is really equivalent to the set of Equation, 5.33.

5.14   The Bézier blending functions, B_i, (Equations 5.41) were derived by setting

$$x(t) = \mathbf{T} \cdot \mathbf{M}_b \cdot \mathbf{P}_x = \sum_{i=1}^{4} B_i(t) \cdot x_i$$

Please fill in the intermediate steps of this derivation.

5.15   Modify the **Bezier** program to superimpose multiple Bézier segments on the screen, and use this more general program to model some complex figures such as human faces. A nice additional feature would be to erase the control points once the Bézier segment has been drawn.

5.16 Modify the **Bezier** program to give it a *dynamic modeling* capability. This would involve specifying the initial four points and drawing the Bézier curve as the present program does, and then adding a loop which allows selection of either point P_2 or P_3 and dragging it to some new position while recalculating and dynamically plotting the resultant Bézier curve as frequently as possible at sampled intermediate positions. This will provide a much more responsive modeling tool than does the present program.

5.17 Modify the **Bezier** program to give it the capability of drawing multiple, connected Bézier segments with smooth joins. For segment n ($n \geq 2$) this will mean making point P_1 identical to point P_4 of segment $n-1$. It will also require constraining point P_2 of segment n to lie along the tangent to points P_3 and P_4 of segment $n-1$. The results of problem 5.9 should help you with this.

5.18 Reflection transformations may be considered as special cases of one of the primary transformations? Which transformation is that?

5.19 Reflection through one axis (mirror reflections) causes what mathematicians refer to as the *parity* operation, changing right-handed objects into left-handed objects and *visa versa*. Sketch the original and y-axis reflection of a clock face and discuss the results. Does a reflection through the origin cause a parity inversion? Why or why not?

5.20 Work out the concatenated numerical matrix which will rotate an object located at $(x_c, y_c) = (10,5)$ in place by an angle of $\theta = 45°$.

5.21 Verify that that the inverse shear matrices, Shx^{-1} and Sh_y^{-1}, given in Equations 5.69 and 5.70 are indeed the inverses of Sh_x and Sh_y given in 5.55 and 5.56.

5.22 Explain the reasoning for the control code, c_i, use to represent the sailboat in the data set of Table 5.1. Why not use just a file of lines?

5.23 Study the structure of program **TRANSFORM** and sketch a flow chart to indicate the control structure. What additional features would make it more useful as a scene design program?

5.24 Rewrite **TRANSFORM** to convert the keyboard menu control to a mouse pointer menu select. Revise the translate command to position the object at a cursor location selected by a user-mouse click.

Endnotes

1. Fiume, Eugene L., *The Mathematical Structure of Raster Graphics*, Academic Press, Inc., Harcourt Brace Jovanovich Publishers, Boston, MA (1989).
2. From Table 1, Tans, Pieter P., Fung, Inez Y., and Takahashi, Taro, "Observational Constraints on the Global Atomspheric CO^2 Budget," *Science* **247**, p. 1432, March 23 (1990).
3. From MegaROM 2.0 CD disk.
4. From *The Apple Science CD*, Vol 1, developed at the National Center for Supercomputing Applications at the University of Illinois at Urbana-Champaign.
5. Bézier, P., *The Mathematical Basis of the UNISURF CAD System*, Butterworths, London (1986). See also: Bezier, P., *Numerical Control: Mathematics and Applications*, John Wiley & Sons, Chichester (1972).
6. Lancaster, Peter and Salkauskas, Kestutis, *Curve and Surface Fitting*, Academic Press, London (1986).
7. Farin, Gerald, *Curves and Surfaces for Computer Aided Geometric Design*, Academic Press, Inc., San Diego, CA (1988).
8. Barsky, Brian A., *Computer Graphics and Geometric Modeling Using Beta-splines*, Springer-Verlag, Hidelberg (1988).

Chapter 6

Two-Dimensional Graphics – Implementation

We are somewhat chagrined that the obvious extension of work on line clipping with which we have been involved... kept us so long from seeing the simplicity of the present approach.
Ivan Sutherland and Gary Hodgman

R epresentation and implementation are very tightly related and interdependent issues in computer science. The proper representation can make the implementation a quick, painless, and satisfying task. A poorly chosen representation, on the other hand, can reduce implementation to an awkward, inefficient, or nightmarish task. The emphasis of the last chapter was on representation issues, with particular stress on the role of the proper mathematical representation in performing important graphical operations easily and efficiently.

In this chapter we turn to some of the techniques and concepts involved in implementation of 2D graphics routines. These are issues that have dominated the discussion in previous texts. However, as the sophistication of graphics hardware and software systems increases, more and more of these techniques move from the "to be proven" category into the "given" category. When the only plotting tool available was the control of an individual pixel, the issue was: Given a pixel control routine, how does one most effectively draw lines? When systems achieved line drawing routines, the issue became: Given the routine, *DrawLine*, how does one most effectively draw polygons? Now that virtually all systems support polygon manipulation routines, the issue becomes: Given polygon manipulation routines, how does one most effectively construct and render 3D solids? High-level graphics languages like PHIGS now supply standard 3D object manipulation and rendering routines.

So a good argument can be made for deleting several of the topics in this chapter altogether as a rehash of already-solved problems. However,

there is value in reviewing the solutions to some of the most important historical problems in computer graphics. Insight on efficiency considerations and algorithm development is gained by study of elegant techniques used in rendering graphical objects. Our compromise on this issue is to present representative algorithms for solving each of the major graphics problems rather than an exhaustive survey of solutions.

As a final observation in this introduction, it is helpful to consider the close parallel of the representation/implementation issue to the abstract/-concrete continuum. Representation issues are generally simplified by defining a new abstract data type for generalizing some object by naming it and giving it an internal structure in which the nitty-gritty details are hidden. This is an effective strategy for conceptualizing and simplifying algorithms. However, the details cannot be "swept under the rug" forever. Eventually the complex data types must be unpacked and data displayed on a real screen. These concrete tasks are at the heart of implementation issues and are the focus of study in this chapter.

Raster Graphics Implementation

In the previous chapter, we developed some mathematical tools for representing points and lines. Real graphics devices, however, do not display mathematical points and lines, but rather some coarser approximations that are limited on raster displays by pixel density and size. The question then becomes: Given a mathematical point at (x,y), or a mathematical line from (x_1,y_1) to

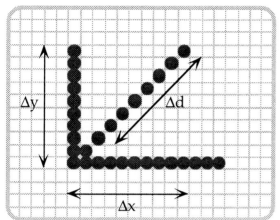

Figure 6.1
The line density problem. Note how the pixel density, $\Delta N/\Delta L$, is 10 along Δx and Δy but only about 7 along the 45° line, Δd.

(x_2,y_2), what is the optimal raster graphics representation?

Raster Graphics Representations

Before we examine algorithms for the efficient mapping of mathematical primitives to real raster graphics displays, two observations are in order. First, very significant design issues are involved in the solution to these problems. Second, system designers for the languages and application programs have, for the most part, solved these problems efficiently, so the reader need not worry about them in practice. However, it is instructive to study the problems and the design considerations used in their solution.

What are the criteria that must be considered when designing an algorithm for drawing graphics primitives on a raster screen? Certainly all line drawing should attempt to optimize the following:

- **Uniform, user-selected density** – This is a nontrivial problem as a quick examination of Figure 6.1 will indicate. Here the simplest algorithm yields a 45° line with a pixel density only 70.7 percent that of a horizontal or vertical line.

- **Straight lines should appear straight** – The quickest test for distinguishing a raster graphics display image from a vector display image is to note the presence of the *jaggies* on raster display devices. Figure 6.2 illustrates why the jaggies occur. Jaggies are an intrinsic side-effect of the discrete, pixel structure of raster screens, but clever programming can minimize the effect.

- **Line end-points should be constrained** – Multiline objects created by user pointer input quickly become very messy due to end-point overshoots and gaps if constraints are not imposed. Straightforward techniques of *grids* and *snaps* have helped solve this problem. However, in some cases, over-constrained systems can even worsen the problem. See Figure 6.3 as an example.

- **Line algorithms should be fast** – The main bottleneck on CAD workstations remains the time required to redraw complex diagrams composed of tens or hundreds of thousands of vectors. Without graphics accelerator cards this task may take the order of minutes on personal workstations. Any tricks to speed the line drawing operations translate directly into productivity increases.

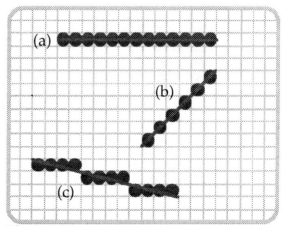

Figure 6.2
The jaggies problem. Line (a) is well represented by the array of pixels. Line (b) is OK, but suffers the obvious density problem and some question as to "where the line really starts." Line (c) has a severe case of the jaggies, a problem inherent in any raster system and particularly distracting for lines nearly horizontal or vertical.

Straight Line Algorithms

Consider the following concrete problem: Your new, raster-screen computer has only the most primitive graphics function, point(x,y), and your job is to write a line function, line(x_1,y_1,x_2,y_2). Assume, further, that you want to follow the design criteria given above as far as possible, and that the pixels on your machine have a value of either 1 (ON) or 0 (OFF), i.e., no gray scale is supported. How will you proceed?

Your first instinct might be to use the two points to compute the parameters of the slope-intercept form of a line, $y = m x + b$, and then simply to step along the x value of pixels, computing y at each point. By rounding the y value you would get the (x,y) pixel pair closest to the line and send it to point(x,y). What is wrong with this approach?

While this method makes good sense conceptually, there are two serious problems, one mathematical and one computational. The mathematical problem is seen most clearly for the special case of a vertical line in which case x is not stepped at all. It is also apparent that the nearly vertical case would also badly violate the *uniform density* criterion. The obvious solution to the mathematical problem is to determine in which angular region the line lies and switch to a $x = f(y)$ representation for the 90° sector centered on the y axis.

The second problem is related to computational efficiency. Note that each slope-intersect calculation involves both a multiplication and an addition. Additions and condition checking are relatively efficient on most computers, but multiplications are not. Multiplications, particularly on computers not equipped with special co-processors, consume many clock cycles compared to the 1–2 cycles of an addition. Therefore, to satisfy the *fast* criteria, we should look for a different algorithm.

Simple DDA Algorithm

The simple Digital Differential Analyzer (DDA) algorithm follows our instinctive approach started above, but cleverly avoids the two problems indicated. The algorithm can be summarized as follows:

1. Compute slope, m, from the two points,

$$m = \frac{\Delta y}{\Delta x} = \frac{y_2 - y_1}{x_2 - x_1}.$$

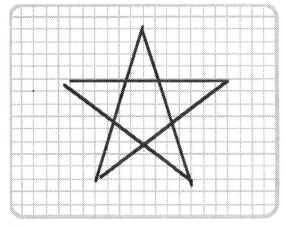

Figure 6.3
The "fighting constraints" problem. Each line of the star was generated by duplicating the horizontal line and rotating it by n × 72° where n = 1→ 4. Then, with "Snap to grid" in force, an attempt was made to drag them into the correct orientation. This was the best we could do. What went wrong?

2. Select a step axis with the test

   if abs(m) < 1 then
   step axis = x-axis
   else
   step axis = y-axis.

3. Select the range for iteration with the test

   range = Max(| Δx |, | Δy |).

4. Set increments and starting points:

   $$dx = \frac{\Delta x}{range}, \qquad dy = \frac{\Delta y}{range}$$
   $$x = x_1 \qquad\quad y = y_1.$$

5. Iterate over range

   point(round(x),round(y))
   x = x + dx
   y = y + dy.

Note that the first two steps are really subsumed by the last three. That is, deleting the first two steps and renumbering steps (3), (4), and (5) as (1), (2), and (3) will accomplish the precise task desired. Below we show a Pascal program, *SimpDDA*, and the output it generates.

Pascal Program SimpDDA

```
program SimpDDA;
{Program to implement simple        }
{Digital Differential Analyzer      }
{for drawing a straight line from (x1,y1) to (x2,y2)    }

   var
      i, irange, xp, yp: integer;
      x1, y1, x2, y2: real;
      dx, dy, x, y, range: real;

begin
{Query the user for two points}
   writeln('Simple DDA Program');
   writeln('Input point 1 (x1,y1):');
   readln(x1, y1);
   writeln('Input point 2 (x2,y2):');
   readln(x2, y2);
   range := abs(x2 - x1);
   if abs(y2 - y1) > range then
      range := abs(y2 - y1);
   dx := (x2 - x1) / range;
   dy := (y2 - y1) / range;
   x := x1;
   y := y1;
   showDrawing;
   irange := round(range);
   for i := 1 to irange do
      begin
         xp := round(x);
         yp := round(y);
         moveto(xp, yp);
         lineto(xp, yp);
         x := x + dx;
         y := y + dy
      end;
end.
```

This program does, indeed, solve the problem. The *point(x,y)* function is implemented through the *moveto + lineto* calls. The only other differences from the algorithmic version are the *showDrawing* call to open the **Drawing** window and the statements converting real to integer numbers.

A variation of the simple DDA, called the *symmetric DDA*, uses scaling the range by powers of 2 to calculate the values of *dx* and *dy*.[1] Since scaling by powers of 2 can be done by right shift operation—very efficiently in machine language—the only two divide operations in this algorithm can be replaced by shift operations for further improving the efficiency of the algorithm.

Bresenham's Algorithm

While registers in the DDA kept track of the true values of (x,y) as the line was being plotted, Bresenham's algorithm uses only the *error* between the true values and the pixel locations.[2] Basically, the algorithm determines along which axis the point plotter will move most rapidly and then plots a point at each pixel along this direction. Along the slower moving axis it keeps track, via an error signal, of the difference between the true line position and the current pixel position. When this error signal becomes positive, the current pixel position is incremented by one, and the error signal is reduced by one. This algorithm can be summarized as:

1. Compute the maximum range of motion:

$$range = Max(\,|\Delta x|\,,\,|\Delta y|\,).$$

2. Initialize error signal and plotting parameters:

$$err = \frac{\Delta y}{\Delta x} - 0.5 \; [\text{assuming } |\Delta x| > |\Delta y|\,]$$

$$x_p = round(x_1) \qquad y_p = round(y_1).$$

3. For each pixel along the x direction:

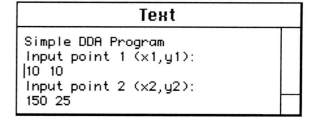

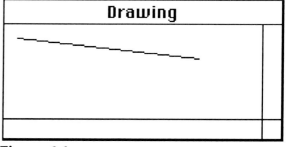

Figure 6.4
Output of SimpDDA program. User control dialog takes place in the **Text** window and the graphical output in the **Drawing** window. Note the jaggies.

$$point(x_p, y_p)$$
$$if\ err > 0\ then$$
$$\qquad y_p = y_p + 1$$
$$\qquad err = err - 1$$
$$x_p = x_p + 1$$
$$err = err + \frac{\Delta y}{\Delta x}.$$

As presented, one might expect that this algorithm would suffer a performance penalty due to the division in steps 2 and (even worse) 3. However, Bresenham noted that the test for incrementing the y pixel location involves the *sign* of the error signal, not its magnitude. We can, therefore, modify *err* with multiplication by the constant, 2 Δx, to get the equivalent error signal, *errp,* defined as:

$$errp = 2\ \Delta x\ err.$$

Old statements in the algorithm are then replaced by the new statements:

Old Statement	New Statement
$err = \dfrac{\Delta y}{\Delta x} - 0.5$	$errp = 2\ \Delta y - \Delta x$
if err > 0 then	*if errp > 0 then*
$err = err - 1$	$errp = errp - 2\ \Delta x$
$err = err + \dfrac{\Delta y}{\Delta x}$	$errp = errp + 2\ \Delta y$

Next, we list a Pascal program that implements Bresenham's algorithm.

Pascal Program Bresenham

```
program Bresenham;
{Program to draw a straight     }
{ line from (x1,y1) to (x2,y2)  }
{using Bresenham's Algorithm    }
   var
      i, irange, xp, yp, dxs, dys: integer;
      x1, y1, x2, y2: real;
      dx, dy, x, y, range: real;
      errp: real;
      axis: char;

   procedure point (x, y: integer);
   {Procedure to plot point at (x,y)}
   begin
      moveto(xp, yp);
      lineto(xp, yp);
```

```
   end;

begin
{Query the user for two points}
   writeln('Bresenham''s Straight-Line Algorithm');
   writeln('Input point 1 (x1,y1):');
   readln(x1, y1);
   writeln('Input point 2 (x2,y2):');
   readln(x2, y2);
   range := abs(x2 - x1);
   axis := 'x';
{Test for axis of more rapid motion}
   if abs(y2 - y1) > range then
      begin
         range := abs(y2 - y1);
         axis := 'y';
      end;
   irange := round(range);
   dx := (x2 - x1);
   dy := (y2 - y1);
   errp := 2 * dy - dx;
   dxs := 1;
{Test for direction of x motion}
   if dx < 0 then
      dxs := -1;
   dys := 1;
{Test for direction of y motion}
   if dy < 0 then
      dys := -1;
   xp := round(x1);
   yp := round(y1);
   showDrawing;
{This part steps along x axis}
   case axis of
      'x':
         begin
            for i := 1 to irange do
               begin
                  point(xp, yp);
                  if errp > 0 then
                     begin
                        yp := yp + dys;
                        errp := errp - 2 * dx *
                           dxs
                     end;
                  xp := xp + dxs;
                  errp := errp + 2 * dy * dys;
               end;
         end;
      'y':     {This part steps along y axis}
         begin
            for i := 1 to irange do
               begin
                  point(xp, yp);
                  if errp > 0 then
                     begin
                        xp := xp + dxs;
                        errp := errp - 2 * dy *
                           dys
                     end;
                  yp := yp + dys;
```

```
            errp := errp + 2 * dx * dxs;
        end;
      end;
   end;
end.
```

The output of program **Bresenham** is shown in Figure 6.5.

Several comments are in order on program *Bresenham*. Two extensions to the algorithm listed were necessary to generalize the program. The first involves testing for the axis of more rapid motion and using the results of this test in a case statement to step along either *x* pixels or *y* pixels. The second recognizes that x_2 may be less than x_1. To handle the direction of the resulting motion, we test on the sign of Δx and set a sign flag, *dxs*, accordingly. These two extensions generalize the program so that it correctly handles lines of any orientation pointing in any direction.

Note, however, that both the simple DDA and Bresenham's algorithms suffer from severe cases of the jaggies. This problem is inherent in drawing pixel-wide lines on B/W raster systems. A more scientific name for the jaggies problem is the *aliasing* problem. That is, the true mathematical line is represented by short horizontal and vertical "alias" segments. Raster displays with gray-scale or pixel shape capabilities can minimize the alias problem by various *antialiasing* techniques.

Antialiasing Algorithms

We shall use two approaches to minimize the aliasing problem. The first involves the *shape* of pixels and the second, their *intensity*. The principle on which the pixel shape antialiasing algorithm is based is illustrated in Figure 6.6.

Though this is a relatively crude antialiasing technique, it has the advantage of working on bi-level monitors—of course, at the expense of line width resolution. The program, Shape_AntiAlias, implements this algorithm.

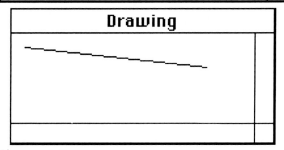

Figure 6.5
Output of **Bresenham** program . Note the similarity to the output of SimpDDA.

Pascal Program Shape_AntiAlias

```
program Shape_AntiAlias;
{Program to implement }
{pixel shape antialiasing}
{in a DDA line generator.}

   var
      dx, dy, steps, k: integer;
      x1, y1, x2, y2, xp, yp: integer;
      sx, sy, x, y, m: real;
begin
   writeln('Antialias DDA program');
   writeln('Input (x1,y1): ');
   readln(x1, y1);
   writeln('Input (x2,y2): ');
   readln(x2, y2);
   showDrawing;
{Calculate appropriate differential.}
   dx := (x2 - x1);
   dy := (y2 - y1);
   m := abs(dy) / (abs(dx) + 1);
{Set anti-aliasing pensize, }
{depending on slope.}
   if m < 0.5 then
      pensize(1, 2);
   if (m > 0.5) and (m < 2.0) then
      pensize(2, 2);
   if m > 2.0 then
      pensize(2, 1);
   if abs(dx) > abs(dy) then
      steps := abs(dx)
   else
      steps := abs(dy);
```

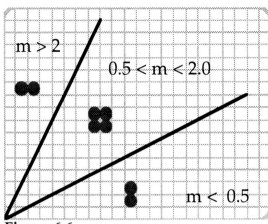
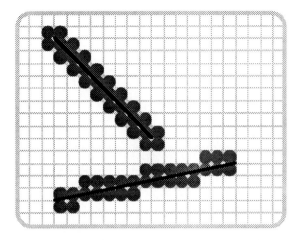

Figure 6.6
Pixel shape antialiasing technique. By using "super pixels" of shape 2 × 1, 2 × 2, or 1× 2 regular pixels, depending on the line direction, the resulting line is heavier but appears smoother. Panel (a) shows the angular regions for each shape. Panel (b) shows two lines and their superpixel representation.

```
    sx := (dx / steps);
    sy := (dy / steps);
{Initialize and draw first point.}
    x := x1;
    y := y1;
    drawline(x1, y1, x1, y1);
{Loop through remaining steps.}
    for k := 1 to steps do
      begin
        x := x + sx;
        y := y + sy;
        xp := round(x);
        yp := round(y);
        drawline(xp, yp, xp, yp);
      end;
end.
```

In Figure 6.7 we show two lines, each with and without shape antialiasing. The results produced by this simple algorithm are surprisingly good.

The second approach to antialiasing is through *shading*. The shade antialias algorithm assumes that a mathematical line is represented by a long, thin rectangle of the same length as the line and n pixels wide. Any pixels totally inside this box are given a maximum shading of $S = 1$. A pixel lying partially within the box is given a shading proportional to the area inside the box. For instance, if only one-quarter of the pixel was within the box, the shading would be set to $S = 0.25$. Figure 6.8 illustrates this shading algorithm.

In Figure 6.9 the results of applying this algorithm to two lines is demonstrated, along with a 400% magnification of one section of the figure.

As can be seen from Figure 6.9, shade antialiasing is effective in reducing aliasing effects and improving the appearance of lines. The price paid for this enhanced appearance is a broadening and blurring of the line. Line broadening is a problem only for lines ~ one pixel wide and is barely noticeable for lines ≥ 3 pixels wide. Note also that this technique is not available on bi-level (B/W) screens. It can be emulated on a B/W screen by using superpixels in which the number of real pixels turned on is proportional to the shading.

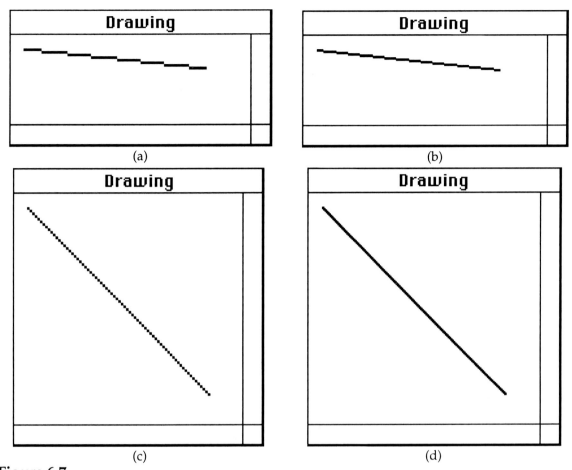

Figure 6.7
Two lines with shape antialiasing off (left) and on (right). All four figures use "superpixels," 2×2 regular pixels for (a) and (c), and shaped as in Figure 6.6a in (b) and (d).

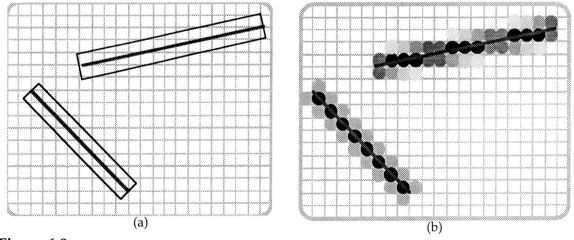

Figure 6.8
Shade antialiasing algorithm. A rectangle of finite width is drawn circumscribing the mathematical line. Each pixel even partially contained within the rectangle is shaded in proportion to that fraction of its area within the rectangle.

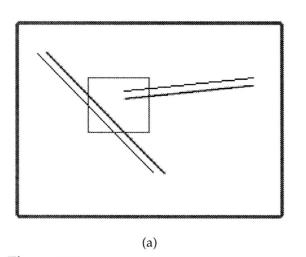

(a)

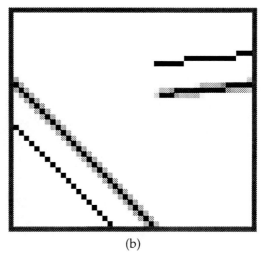

(b)

Figure 6.9
Application of shade antialiasing. (a) Two lines, each with shade antialiasing on and off. (b) Sub-window of (a) magnified 400% to show detail.

Windows and Viewports – 2D

All of the terms and definitions of windows, viewports, and clipping defined in Chapter 4 are easily generalized to 2D. A *window* is that portion of object space selected for visualization. Rectangular windows are specified by the *world coordinates*, W_{xL}, W_{xR}, W_{yT}, and W_{yB}. That portion of the display device on which the window is to appear is called the *viewport*. A rectangular viewport is defined by the parameters, V_{xL}, V_{xR}, V_{yT}, and V_{yB}, generally specified in *normalized device coordinates*, NDC, ranging from zero to one. The process of mapping world coordinates from the scene onto the viewport is called the *viewing transformation*. Matrix composition may be used to derive a simple and elegant representation for this transformation.

The Viewing Transformation

The viewing transformation is illustrated in Figure 6.10 in which a window on a world coordinate scene is mapped onto a viewport on a display screen.

The equations of the viewing transformation are relatively easy to derive with the help of homogeneous coordinates and composed matrices. The three-step algorithm may be written as:

1. Transform the lower left-hand corner of the window to the origin.

2. Scale the window to match the viewport.

3. Transform the lower left-hand corner of the viewport to its desired location.

Written in terms of concatenated matrices, this algorithm becomes:

$$M_v = T_w \cdot S_{wv} \cdot T_v \qquad [6.1]$$

where

$$T_w = \begin{bmatrix} 1 & 0 & 0 \\ 0 & 1 & 0 \\ -W_{xL} & -W_{yB} & 1 \end{bmatrix} \qquad [6.2]$$
(shift window to origin),

$$S_{wv} = \begin{bmatrix} S_x & 0 & 0 \\ 0 & S_y & 0 \\ 0 & 0 & 1 \end{bmatrix} \qquad [6.3]$$
(scale window to viewport),

$$T_v = \begin{bmatrix} 1 & 0 & 0 \\ 0 & 1 & 0 \\ V_{xL} & V_{yB} & 1 \end{bmatrix} \qquad [6.4]$$
(shift out to viewport).

with

$$S_x = \frac{V_{xR} - V_{xL}}{W_{xR} - W_{xL}} \qquad [6.5]$$

$$S_y = \frac{V_{yT} - V_{yB}}{W_{yT} - W_{yB}} . \qquad [6.6]$$

Multiplying these yields the viewing matrix:

$$M_v = \begin{bmatrix} S_x & 0 & 0 \\ 0 & S_y & 0 \\ V_{xL} - S_x \cdot W_{xL} & V_{yB} - S_y \cdot W_{yB} & 1 \end{bmatrix}$$
$$[6.7]$$

With the viewing transformation matrix, M_v, the transformation equations are obtained from $X' = M_v \cdot X$ as

$$x' = S_x \cdot (x - W_{xL}) + V_{xL} \qquad [6.8]$$
$$y' = S_y \cdot (y - W_{yB}) + V_{yB} .$$

Clipping in 2D

An important element in the viewing pipeline is the process of clipping, that is, discarding portions of the scene outside of the window. This process is most efficient when performed at the earliest possible point in the viewing pipeline, since then objects and portions of objects not appearing in the final viewport need not undergo the transformation calculations.

There are two primary approaches to clipping in 2D. First is the very general and elegant line clipping algorithm of Cohen and Sutherland. Second is the more object-oriented polygon clipping algorithm of Sutherland and Hodgman. To quickly appreciate the difference between these two algorithms, consider Figure 6.11.

Line Clipping

Cohen and Sutherland developed a simple, recursive procedure for reducing all lines to the two trivial cases: *in* or *out*. The algorithm for this procedure may be written:

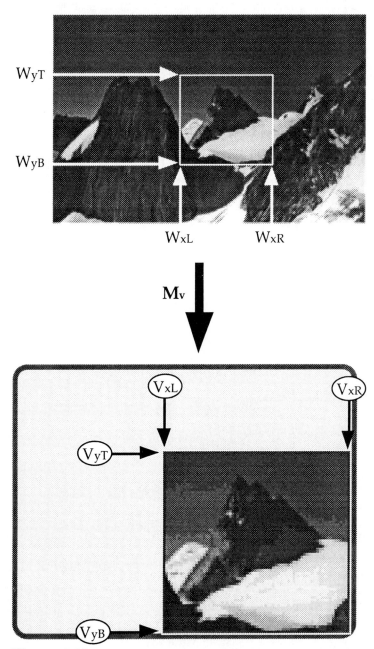

Figure 6.10
The Viewing Transformation. The transformation, M_v, maps a window from the world coordinate scene (top view) onto a viewport on the screen (bottom view).

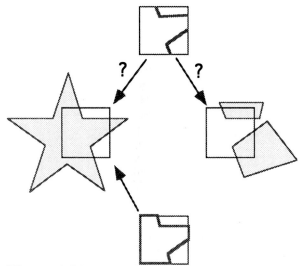

Figure 6.11
Distinction between line clipping and polygon clipping. *Line clipping* results shown at top could equally well represent clipping the right or left figure. *Polygon clipping* shown at bottom uniquely distinguishes between the two possibilities by *edge coding*, thus removing the line clipping ambiguity.

1. Classify_lines

2. Procedure classify_lines
    while lines remain
      If trivially in, plot line and delete from list
      If trivially out, discard line
      If nontrivial
        split at window edge
        discard outer segment
        send inner segment to classify_lines.

Figure 6.12 illustrates how lines are classified by this algorithm.

The second major contribution by Cohen and Sutherland was the efficient test that they developed for determining the trivially in and trivially out cases. The end points of each line are classified by the four-bit code:

  TBRL

where
   $T = 1$ if point is above top of window,
     0 otherwise

   $B = 1$ if point is below bottom of window,
     0 otherwise

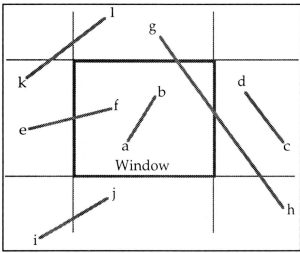

Figure 6.12
Classification scheme for Cohen-Sutherland line clipping algorithm.
   Trivially in: Segment ab
   Trivially out: Segments cd, ij
   Non-trivial: Segments ef, gh, kl
Segments totally above, below, to the right or left of the window are trivially out.

   $R = 1$ if point is right of window,
     0 otherwise

   $L = 1$ if point is left of window,
     0 otherwise.

The nine regions delimited by the extended window boundaries are then identified by the binary code shown in Figure 6.13.
   A line with end-points P_1 and P_2 can be coded by C_1 and C_2, respectively, where:

   $$C_1 = T_1 B_1 R_1 L_1$$

   $$C_2 = T_2 B_2 R_2 L_2.$$

The tests for lines being trivially in and trivially out may then be stated:

Trivially in: $(C_1 = 0000)$ AND $(C_2 = 0000)$

Trivially out: $(C_1$ AND $C_2) < > (0000)$.

The following program, Line_Clip, implements this recursive algorithm.

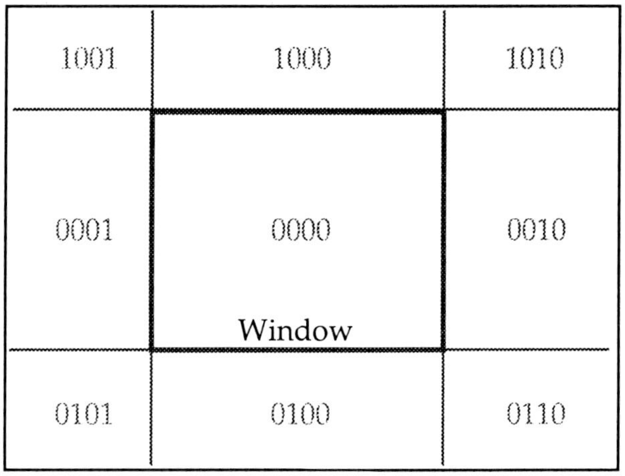

Figure 6.13
Cohen-Sutherland classification regions and binary codes for line end points.

Pascal Program Line_Clip

```
program Line_Clip;
{Program to use Cohen-Sutherland algorithm to     }
{line clip an arbitrary set of lines.             }
{Lines are represented as x1,y1,x2,y2 in a text file. }
   const    {This sets size of window.}
      top = 125;
      left = 200;
      bot = 225;
      right = 350;
   type
      pointArr = array[1..2] of integer;
      CodeFour = ( T, B, R, L );
      CodeType = set of CodeFour;
      PointType = record
           point: PointArr;
           Code: CodeType;
        end;
      LineType = array[1..2] of PointType;
      ClassType = (Tin, Tout, neither);
   var
      line: LineType;
      window: rect;
      x1, y1, x2, y2: integer;
      DataFile: text;

{****************** draw_window *******************}
   procedure draw_window;
   begin
      pensize(2, 2);
      setRect(window, left, top, right + 3, bot +
        3);
      frameRect(window);
   end;
```

```
{********************* Code *************************}
   procedure Code (var P: PointType);
{This procedure tests point P to see if in window.   }
{If in, the LRTB code is returned empty.            }
   begin
      P.Code := [];
      if P.Point[1] < left then
         P.Code := P.Code + [L]
      else if P.Point[1] > right then
         P.Code := P.Code + [R];
      if P.Point[2] < top then
         P.Code := P.Code + [T]
      else if P.Point[2] > bot then
         P.Code := P.Code + [B];
   end;

{***************** classify line *******************}
   function Classify (Line: LineType): ClassType;
{This procedure classifies            }
{ all lines into 3 groups:            }
{     Tin = Trivially in              }
{     Tout = Trivially out            }
{   Neither = Neither trivially in or out. }
   begin
      if ((Line[1].Code = []) and (Line[2].Code = [])) then
         classify := Tin     {Line is in if both
                             code sets are empty.}
      else if (Line[1].code * Line[2].code <> []) then
         classify := Tout    {Line is trivially
                             out if the intersection}
      else                   {of the code sets is
                             NOT empty.}
         classify := neither;
   end;

{***************** clip_lines ***********************}
   procedure clip_line (Line: LineType);
{This routine recurs until line is reduced to       }
{trivially in or trivially out.                     }
{It plots those "in", and ignores those "out".      }
   var
      P1,P2:PointType;
      class: ClassType;
      codeOut: CodeType;
      xp, yp: real;
      done: boolean;
      xt, yt: integer;
   begin
      repeat              {Until done --> totally trivial}
         done := false;
         P1:=Line[1];
         P2:=Line[2];
         Code(P1);
         Code(P2);
         Line[1]:=P1;
         Line[2]:=P2;
         x1 := trunc(P1.Point[1]);
         y1 := trunc(P1.Point[2]);
         x2 := trunc(P2.Point[1]);
         y2 := trunc(P2.Point[2]);
         class := classify(line);
```

```
case class of
  Tout:                {Trivially out case}
    done := true;
  Tin:                 {Trivially in case}
    begin
      PenSize(3, 3);  {Draw clipped lines bold.}
      drawLine(x1, y1, x2, y2);
      done := true;
      PenSize(1, 1);
    end;
  neither: {Neither case - requires segmentation}
    begin
      if (P1.Code = []) then
        codeOut := P2.Code
      else
        codeOut := P1.Code;
      if (L in CodeOut) then
        begin       {Calculate intersection with
                            left edge.}
          yp := y1 + (y2 - y1) *
                (left - x1) / (x2 - x1);
          xp := left;
        end
      else if (R in CodeOut) then
        begin       {Calculate intersection with
                            right edge.}
          yp := y1 + (y2 - y1) *
                (right - x1) / (x2 - x1);
          xp := right;
        end
      else if (T in CodeOut) then
        begin       {Calculate intersection with
                            top edge.}
          xp := x1 + (x2 - x1) *
                (top - y1) / (y2 - y1);
          yp := top;
        end
      else if (B in CodeOut) then
        begin       {Calculate intersection with
                            bottom edge.}
          xp := x1 + (x2 - x1) *
                (bot - y1) / (y2 - y1);
          yp := bot;
        end;
      xt := trunc(xp);
      yt := trunc(yp);
      if (codeOut = P2.Code) then
                {Determine which point is out}
        begin
                    {and reduce line to "in"}
          line[1].Point[1] := x1;
                    {point + intersection point.}
          line[1].Point[2] := y1;
          line[2].Point[1] := xt;
          line[2].Point[2] := yt;
          clip_line(line);
                    {and recur here if P2 out}
        end
      else
        begin
          line[1].Point[1] := xt;
```

```
          line[1].Point[2] := yt;
          line[2].Point[1] := x2;
          line[2].Point[2] := y2;
          clip_line(line);
                            {or recur here, if P1 out}
        end;
      end;
    end;
  until done;
end;

{***************** Main Program *********************}
begin          {by having user select file of lines.}
  ReSet(DataFile, OldFileName('Input Line File?'));
  draw_window;
  repeat        {for all lines in file}
    ReadLn(DataFile, x1, y1, x2, y2);
    pensize(1, 1);       {Draw line as thin, 1-pixel line.}
    DrawLine(x1, y1, x2, y2);
    {Load line record to send to clipper.}
    line[1].Point[1] := x1;
    line[1].Point[2] := y1;
    line[2].Point[1] := x2;
    line[2].Point[2] := y2;
    clip_line(line);
  until eof(DataFile);
end.
```

The results of running this program are shown in Figure 6.14.

Program Line_Clip demonstrates several features of interest.

- It is completely general. It can clip any number of lines and does so without the use of arrays for internal storage. The lines can occur in any order and need not be connected in polygon form. The set of lines to be clipped is selected by the user at run time.

- It uses recursion. This is a natural control structure to use for this application since the problem requires reducing a complex problem to a simpler one with each recursive call until a trivial case is achieved.

- It uses a simple, convenient representation of lines as a file of (x_1,y_1,x_2,y_2) coordinates of end points.

- It uses abstract data types, *LineType* and *PointType*, to simplify passing these graphical objects as arguments to the worker routines.

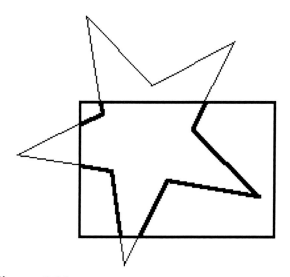

Figure 6.14
Results of Cohen-Sutherland line-clipping algorithm. Original set of lines shown as one-pixel figure, clipping-window as a two-pixel wide figure and clipped lines as three-pixel wide lines.

Polygon Clipping

As Figures 6.11 and 6.14 indicate, the coherence implicit in graphical objects such as polygons is lost in simple line clipping. For distinguishing between the ambiguities inherent in line-clipping closed objects, it is useful to provide visual clues for the viewer. Figure 6.11 suggests two such visual cluing schemes. First is the *edge coding* indicated in the bottom figure. Second, and even more effective, would be *shading coding* in which the shade or color of the object is preserved through the clipping process. Shading coding is possible only on displays supporting shading/color, whereas edge coding works on any display supporting graphics.

For graphical objects represented as polygons, edge coding is accomplished by *polygon clipping*. The best known polygon clipping algorithm is that developed by Sutherland and Hodgman.[3] This elegant algorithm has the virtues of generality, extensibility, and conceptual simplicity. It is not restricted to rectangular windows, but rather is easily applicable to irregular convex windows. Not restricted to 2D windows, it is readily extended to 3D clipping volumes.

In the introductory quote the algorithm's authors themselves express chagrin that it took so long for them to discover the polygon clipping algorithm.

The basic idea in the Sutherland-Hodgman algorithm is that an *n*-sided polygon is represented by a set of *n* input vertices which are clipped successively against each extended edge of the clipping window. On each edge, two tests are applied to each vertex. First, does the line, which the vertex and its precursor vertex defines intersect the edge? If so, add the intersecting point to the output vertex list defining the polygon. Second, is the vertex point itself outside of the edge under test? If so, ignore it. If not, add it to the output vertex list. The output vertex list resulting from testing against edge *i* becomes the input vertex list for testing against edge *i+1*. This re-entrant algorithm is iterated until the dynamic vertex list has been tested against all edges. The resulting output vertex list corresponds to the clipped polygon with edge coding an automatic side-effect.

The Sutherland-Hodgman algorithm may be formally specified as follows:

1. Repeat for all (extended) edges of the window
   1.1 Repeat for all vertices on the current vertex list
       1.1.1 If line between vertex *i* and vertex *i–1* intersects edge
       Add intersection point to output list
       1.1.2 If vertex *i* is "inside" edge
       Add vertex *i* to output list
   1.2 Set current vertex list = output list

The only additional complications in the algorithm arise from handling end points of the polygon. In order for the first vertex, i = 1, to have a predecessor vertex, a new vertex, i = 0, is defined and given coordinates of the last vertex, i = n. Since we want to check the line crossing of the line from vertex n to the starting vertex, i = 1, we extend the polygon "forward" to vertex n+1 and assign it the coordinates of vertex 1. Thus by always carefully maintaining the dynamic polygon as a n-vertex figure but appending vertices 0 and n+1 before re-entering the next edge clip, we automatically handle the problematic end points of the polygon without having to resort to some awkward flag system.

Pascal Program Poly_Clip

```pascal
program Poly_Clip;
{Program to perform polygon clipping       }
{using the Sutherland-Hodgman algorithm.   }
  const
    top = 100;
    left = 150;
    bot = 200;
    right = 300;
  var
    window, viewPort: rect;
    x, y: array[0..100] of real;
    xo, yo: array[0..100] of real;
    nout, npts, n, j: integer;
    DataFile: text;

{************** polygon read routine ***************}
  procedure load_object;
  begin       {Assume n vertices for and n-
                sided polygon.}
    ReSet(DataFile, OldFileName('Input File?'));
    n := 0;
    repeat                       {for all vertices in file}
      n := n + 1;
      ReadLn(DataFile, x[n], y[n]);
      xo[n] := x[n];
      yo[n] := y[n];
    until eof(DataFile);
    npts := n;
    x[0] := x[n];       {Extend backward by one vertex.}
    y[0] := y[n];
    x[n + 1] := x[1];    {Extend forward by one vertex.}
    y[n + 1] := y[1];
  end;

{*****************Plot output polygon *******************}
  procedure plot_out;
    var
      i: integer;
  begin
    eraseRect(0, 0, 300, 500);
    pensize(3, 3);
    xo[n + 1] := xo[1];
    yo[n + 1] := yo[1];
    moveto(round(xo[1]), round(yo[1]));
    for i := 2 to (n + 1) do
      lineto(round(xo[i]), round(yo[i]));
  end;

{***************** draw_window ********************}
  procedure draw_window;
  begin
    pensize(1, 1);
{Use off-sets to accommodate pixel-width of object.}
    setRect(window, left - 1, top - 1, right + 4, bot + 4);
    frameRect(window);
  end;
```

```pascal
{*********Procedure to load output into input**********}
  procedure reload;
  {Re-entrant vertex array loader}
    var
      i: integer;
  begin
    for i := 1 to n do
      begin{Set new vertex array to old output array}
        x[i] := xo[i];
        y[i] := yo[i];
      end;
    x[n + 1] := x[1];    {Extend polygon 1 vertex forward}
    y[n + 1] := y[1];
    x[0] := x[n];       {Extend polygon 1 vertex backward}
    y[0] := y[n];
  end;

{****************** clip_edges ********************}
  procedure edge_clip;
{This procedure clips polygon sequentially }
{on each output window edge and plots the results.}
    var
      i: integer;
  begin
    n := npts;
{Clip against right side, and plot clipped polygon.}
    j := 0;              {Dynamic "in" vertex counter}
    for i := 1 to (n + 1) do
      begin
        if ((right - x[i]) * (right - x[i - 1]) < 0) then
          {Intersect test}
          begin
            j := j + 1;
            yo[j] := y[i-1]+(y[i]-y[i-1])*(right-
              x[i -1]) / (x[i] - x[i -1]);
            xo[j] := right;
          end;
        if x[i] < right then
          {Test if point itself is in}
          begin     {If so, add to output list}
            j := j + 1;
            xo[j] := x[i];
            yo[j] := y[i];
          end;
      end;
    n := j;
    plot_out;
    draw_window;
    reload;

{Clip against top, and plot clipped polygon.}
    j := 0;
    for i := 1 to (n + 1) do
      begin
        if (top - y[i]) * (top - y[i - 1]) < 0 then
          {Intersect test}
          begin
            j := j + 1;
            xo[j] := x[i-1]+(x[i]-x[i-1])*(top-
              y[i -1]) / (y[i] - y[i - 1]);
            yo[j] := top;
```

```
        end;
      if y[i] > top then          {Test if point itself is in}
        begin                     {If so, add to output list}
          j := j + 1;
          xo[j] := x[i];
          yo[j] := y[i];
        end;
    end;
  n := j;
  plot_out;
  draw_window;
  reload;

{Clip against left edge, and plot clipped polygon.}
  j := 0;
  for i := 1 to (n + 1) do
    begin
      if (left - x[i]) * (left - x[i - 1]) < 0 then
      {Intersect test}
        begin
          j := j + 1;
          yo[j] := y[i-1] + (y[i]-y[i-1])*(left-
            x[i-1])/(x[i] - x[i - 1]);
          xo[j] := left;
        end;
      if x[i] > left then          {Test if point itself is in}
        begin                      {If so, add to output list}
          j := j + 1;
          xo[j] := x[i];
          yo[j] := y[i];
        end;
    end;
  n := j;
  plot_out;
  draw_window;
  reload;

{Clip against bottom, and plot final clipped polygon.}
  j := 0;
  for i := 1 to (n + 1) do
    begin
      if (bot - y[i]) * (bot - y[i - 1]) < 0 then
      {Intersect test}
        begin
          j := j + 1;
          xo[j] := x[i-1]+(x[i]-x[i-1])*(bot-
            y[i -1])/(y[i] - y[i - 1]);
          yo[j] := bot;
        end;
      if y[i] < bot then           {Test if point itself is in}
        begin                      {If so, add to output list}
          j := j + 1;
          xo[j] := x[i];
          yo[j] := y[i];
        end;
    end;
  n := j;
```

```
    plot_out;
    draw_window;
    reload;
  end;
{****************** Main Program ********************}
begin
  load_object;
  {Open drawing window}
  setRect(viewPort, 0, 0, 400, 300);
  setDrawingRect(viewPort);
  showDrawing;
  plot_out;
  draw_window;
  edge_clip;
end.
```

Output from Poly_Clip is shown in Figure 6.15.

A number of features distinguish the Sutherland-Hodgman polygon clipping algorithm.

- The algorithm achieves its primary objective—maintenance of polygon coherence by edge coding. This edge coding even extends to tieing together two or more discontinuous sub-polygons of the same parent within the clipping window as a *degenerate* polygon as shown in Figure 6.16.

- The algorithm uses a dynamic, vertex-based representation of the polygon as the basic data structure. Thus the ten vertex object in Figure 6.15 expands to a twelve vertex object after clipping on the right edge and a fifteen vertex object when clipping is finished. Had the window been interior to the object, the ten vertex polygon would have reduced to a four vertex polygon the size of the window.

- The algorithm is re-entrant. That is, the output of one clipping process becomes the input for the next. This feature makes it relatively straightforward to recode the algorithm in recursive form. Once a vertex has made the output list of one edge clip, it immediately becomes valid input for the next edge clip. The appropriate recursive formulation would significantly reduce the need for intermediate storage of the vertex points.

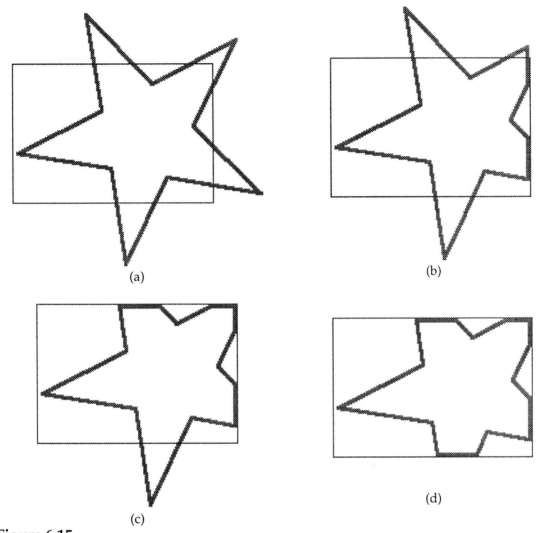

(a) (b)

(c) (d)

Figure 6.15
Poly_Clip output. (a) Original polygon with superimposed clipping window; (b) output after clipping on right edge; (c) output after clipping on top edge; (d) final output after clipping on all four edges.

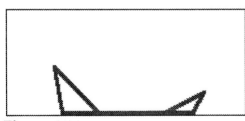

Figure 6.16
Polygon coherence from Sutherland-Hodgman polygon clipping algorithm. The degenerate edge segment connecting the small triangles indicates that they are part of a common figure, the star from Figure 6.11.

Text Clipping

Text-clipping algorithms are classic examples of the compromises the graphics system designer must make between performance and efficiency. Ranked in order of decreasing performance and increasing efficiency, three text-clipping schemes may be listed as:

- **Pixel level** – This level produces the most attractive and intuitive text clipping effect. The algorithm is simply: display all pixels of all characters out to, but not including, the edge of the window. Since this displays the maximum alphanumeric information, it

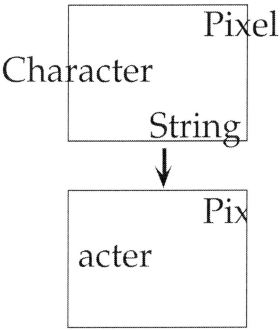

Figure 6.17
Levels of text clipping. Pixel level shows all of the text within the window, down to the pixel level. Character level shows only those characters totally within the window. String level shows only strings that are entirely within the window.

is the highest performance algorithm. However, since it requires testing at the pixel level, it is the least efficient.

- **Character level** – This level produces the next, best-looking clipped output, but is simpler to implement. The algorithm may be stated: draw a box totally enclosing each character and disregard any character whose bounding box lies partially or totally outside of the window.

- **String level** – This level provides the poorest performance but is the simplest to implement. The algorithm is identical to the character level algorithm with *string* substituted for *character*. If even the last period of the string lies outside of the bounding box, none of the string is displayed.

These three text-clipping algorithms are illustrated in Figure 6.17.

Two important observations are relevant to the implementation of text clipping. First, most powerful graphics applications programs which readers are likely to encounter provide automatic clipping of both text and graphical objects for all windows and viewports with which they work. Secondly, the trend in computer graphics is strongly toward outline fonts as the standard display and printer text format. Outline fonts consist of mathematical representation of the character set which, in turn, facilitates pixel level clipping appropriate to the resolution of the output device. Thus, the implementation of text clipping is a task already solved on all but the most primitive systems.

Bit-mapped vs. Object-Oriented Graphics

Successful commercial graphics applications programs are implemented by combining efficient representation schemes with easy-to-use graphics manipulation tools. Most such implementations may be classified as painting programs or drawing programs using bit-mapped or object-oriented representations, respectively. The distinction between these two graphics modes involves fundamental issues of both representation and implementation and illustrates the tight relationship between these two aspects of graphics. Each mode has its own particular strengths and drawbacks, and the choice of mode depends strongly on the particular application.

To summarize the distinction before examining each mode in more detail, the following classification scheme is helpful.

- **Bit-mapped mode** – Generally associated with *painting* programs, bit-mapped graphics represents graphical images and patterns by assigning a block of memory for the direct storage of the intensity patterns that are to be displayed on the screen. On bi-level devices, a 1 bit corresponds to a pixel being turned on and a 0 bit with it off (or *vice versa*). Implementation then corresponds to mapping this block of memory directly to the screen. Note that all "objectness" of a line, polygon, or brush stroke *is lost* the moment it is written to the screen (and hence, the bit-mapped memory).

- **Object-oriented mode** – Generally associated with *drawing* and *CAD* programs, object-oriented graphics involves storing the commands that are used to draw the objects on the screen (or some other output device). This generally involves a mathematical representation in terms of lines, rectangles, ovals, Bézier curves, and so on. Implementation of the drawing functions involves rendering through pixels on the display, but the object's mathematical identity is preserved. Note that the *objectness* of object-oriented graphics *is maintained* throughout the graphics session and preserved in the file storage process.

Next, let's examine the features and tools of each graphics mode in more detail and consider the applications best suited for each. Painting and drawing programs both implement efficiently most of the 2D operations presented so far, and their differences illustrate the critical role of representation on the functionality of graphical systems.

Bit-Mapped Graphics – The *Paint* Mode

The basic concept of raster graphics on which the bit-mapped representation is built was clearly stated by the philosopher L. Wittgenstein in 1922.[4]

> *Let us imagine a white surface with irregular black spots on it. We then say that whatever kind of picture these make, I can always approximate as closely as I wish to the description of it by covering the surface with a sufficiently fine square mesh, and then saying of every square whether it is black or white. In this way I shall have imposed a unified form on the description of the surface. The form is optional, since I could have achieved the same result using a net with a triangular or hexagonal mesh.*

The parallel development of vast, low-cost memory for storing images and high-resolution monitors onto which the images in memory are easily mapped has been the key to the widespread implementation of bit-mapped graphics systems. The principles and advantages of bit-mapped computer graphics had been recognized for several years before Bill Atkinson of Apple Computer Company introduced his revolutionary *MacPaint* program on the newly released Macintosh computer in 1984. This happy marriage of bit-mapped graphics concepts with a toolbox of extremely fast functions for manipulating bit-mapped regions of the screen defines the *paint mode* of raster graphics that has become the standard of the industry.

Bit-mapped graphics remains an active area of research and development. A recent attempt to put bit-mapped graphics on a more formal mathematical foundation has been published by Fiume.[5]

Figure 6.18
Typical tools available on painting programs (*from Canvas 2.0*).

Lasso
Marquee
Spray can
Paint Brush
Paint Bucket
Pencil
Eraser
Bitmap Editor
Hand
Magnifying Glass

Paint Tools

A typical palette of tools available on most painting programs is shown in Figure 6.18.

The functions provided by these icons can be summarized as:

- **Lasso** – Any (irregular) region of the image may be selected by dragging the cursor around its perimeter in a closed loop. This selected region may then be duplicated, dragged to a new location, saved to the clipboard, or operated on by any other painting functions available on the system.

- **Marquee** – Any rectangular region of the image may be selected by dragging a bounding box around it. This selected region may then be duplicated and dragged to a new location, saved to the clipboard, or operated on by any other painting functions available on the system.

- **Spray can** – When the mouse button is pressed, the spray can sprays pixels on the screen in a pattern centered on the cursor. Both the shape of the pattern outline and the pattern itself may be selected from menus by the user. Just as with a real can of spray paint, the longer the button is pressed, the denser becomes the pattern.

- **Paint brush** – When the mouse button is pressed, the paint brush applies paint in a pen pattern and pen shape, both of which are menu selectable. This provides a flexible "etch-a-sketch" painting tool.

- **Paint Bucket** – By dragging the icon so that the tip of the flowing paint is within a white region surrounded by any outline of pixels and by pressing the mouse button, the user can fill (or "flood") the enclosed region with a menu-selectable *fill pattern*.

- **Pencil** – The pencil tool draws a thin (one-pixel) line whenever the mouse button is pushed. It generally operates in an XOR mode, toggling pixel states. In an all white region it draws a line of black pixels; in regions of black pixels, it draws a white line. With a magnified image, the pencil provides an excellent pixel-level editing tool.

- **Eraser** – The eraser functions precisely as a blackboard or pencil eraser does. Any part of the bit-mapped image under the eraser is erased to white when the mouse is pressed.

- **Bitmap Editor** – After this icon is selected, the cursor may be used to select an invisible rectangular region on the screen in which bit-maps may be created. It then automatically selects the Paint Brush tool so painting can begin. Holding the cursor down on this icon brings up a menu allowing the user to select pixel densities from 72 dpi to 300 dpi.

- **Hand** – This intuitive icon allows the user to push the bit-mapped image around on the screen. When the mouse button is pressed, the hand "grabs" the image that then tracks the hand as it is moved about the screen. It serves as a short cut to the more formal screen edge *elevators* for accessing off-screen segments of the image.

- **Magnifying Glass** – After this icon is selected, the cursor turns into a magnifying glass with a symbol in the center. The default value of the symbol is "+" which causes the image to be magnified by a factor of two upon each click of the mouse button. Holding down the *shift* key changes the symbol to a "–" corresponding to demagnification by a factor of 0.5 upon each click of the mouse.

The icon functions give the user the ability to select and edit arbitrary segments of the image ranging from the whole image down to the individual pixels composing it. Included at this level is the translation operation. By simply dragging a selected segment of the image, it may be translated to any new location in the active window. Higher-level transformations such as reflections, shearing, arbitrary rotations, and arbitrary scaling are performed through menu options. We look at some of these next.

Paint Menu Operations

Most painting programs support the following transformations for whole images or any selected segment of an image:

- Rotate (specified in degrees or by dragging a handle),
- Flip horizontal (reflection through y-axis),
- Flip vertical (reflection through x-axis),
- Flip both axes (reflection through origin),
- Skew (shearing along either x- or y-axis),
- Distort (the product of x-shear and y-shear),
- Scale (either by S_x, S_y, or both),
- Perspective (x-dependent y-scaling, or *vice versa*, to create 3D illusion),
- Invert (change all black pixels to white and vice versa),
- Trace edges (draws line at interface between black-and-white regions).

These menu operations, in conjunction with the image-manipulating icons, give the artist/-designer a broad and powerful array of tools for artistic creation. A skilled practitioner with a capable painting program can rapidly create designs and works of art comparable to those created with more traditional media. Note, however, that painting programs are designed for applications requiring free-form expression rather than applications requiring precise numerical accuracy. Such applications require drawing programs.

Next let's study a PICT image and how painting functions can modify it.

Paint Example

Consider the bit-mapped image shown in Figure 6.19 produced by scanning a photograph of Yosemite National Park. The original photo was marred by an unsightly contrail from a passing airplane. Using the photoediting tools available on

Figure 6.19
Bit-mapped image of scene from Yosemite National Park. Note contrail from passing aircraft.

most paint programs it is a simple task to remove this flaw.

The first step is to use the marquee tool to select an area about one-half inch on a side, next to the contrail, but not containing it. This region is duplicated and then dragged on top of the corresponding section of the contrail, thereby hiding it by a section of clear sky. This process is repeated about four times down the length of the contrail, resulting in the restored image shown in Figure 6.20.

The gradient in sky intensity is very apparent as one moves up the y axis. A less apparent gradient is present in the x direction. Using nearby portions of the clear sky to paint over the contrail avoids the artifacts introduced by trying to paint over the contrail with the paintbrush tool.

As an extension of this example, suppose you wished to emphasize the point that glaciers often carved symmetric, U-shaped valleys through the mountains. The geometric transformation tools available on paint programs provide the perfect solution for this task.

Using the restored image of Figure 6.20 as the basis, the first step is to use the marquee tool to select the left-hand half of the image. This is duplicated and the result is flipped horizontally. This mirrored half image is then dragged to the right

side of the image, painting over the existing image. The resulting image of a symmetric valley is shown in Figure 6.21.

Although this example is simplistic, it does illustrate how painting tools may be used to manipulate 2D images. In fact, the ease with which photographs can be altered with photoediting tools has destroyed the concept of *photographic evidence*. Electronic photoediting raises serious issues of journalistic ethics. For instance, should editors authorize the removal of facial blemishes and wrinkles from their reporters' photographs of public officials? If photoediting can be used to enhance a person's appeerence, might it not also be used to distort photographs?

Limitations of Bit-maps

The primary limitation of bit-mapped graphics is a result of "pixel democracy"—all pixels are created equal once they are set in a bit-mapped image. Once a brush stroke or pencil mark has been entered on the image, it becomes a permanent part of the image, overwriting what was there before. The only exception to this rule is the extremely valuable **Undo** option most painting programs provide for reversing the latest painting operation.

Figure 6.20
Yosemite scene with contrail eliminated by photoediting Figure 6.19.

Figure 6.21
Results of editing Figure 6.20 bit-map with *flip horizontal* tool. This illustrates a symmetric, U-shaped valley.

The price one pays for this pixel democracy is that changes in portions of an image must be done by processes which frequently are slow, painstaking, and tedious. The most common image-editing techniques include *painting over* (a brush with the correct pattern and color is used to paint over the flaw), *patching over* (a near-by region of the correct texture and shading is selected, duplicated, and dragged to cover the flaw), and *pixel editing* (the screen is magnified to the level where each pixel can be individually modified).

The second limitation of bit-mapped images is that they generally do not support images requiring precision or numerical dimensioning. Therefore, painting programs are not suitable for drafting or CAD applications.

The final limitation we shall discuss here is that most bit-mapped graphics are device dependent. So, for instance, when a 72 dpi bit-mapped image from a display screen is printed on a 300-dpi laser printer or a 1,200-dpi – 2,400-dpi typesetter, the resolution of the image remains a coarse 72 dpi. As high-quality printers become more readily available, this problem is becoming increasingly bothersome. To solve it, some painting programs are now supporting a user-selected pixel resolution of 300 dpi or more.

Object-Oriented Graphics – *Draw* Mode

Object-oriented graphics is the mode most appropriate for applications requiring accurate detail, numerical dimensioning, and precision. Such applications include electrical engineering circuit board design, mechanical engineering part design, civil engineering construction project design, and architectural design. We designate such object-oriented graphics as working in the *draw mode*. The following features distinguish the draw mode from the paint mode.

- Objects designed in the draw mode retain their identity. This is the single most important distinguishing feature of object-oriented graphics. Such objects can be selected at any stage in the design, can be transformed by all standard operations independent of all other objects, and can be replicated or deleted at will.

- Objects designed in the draw mode may have a hierarchical structure. Primitive objects may be grouped to form more complex objects which in turn may be grouped to form more complex objects, and so on.

Draw programs may provide libraries of basic design elements from which the base of the hierarchy may be efficiently constructed.

- Objects designed with draw programs have a mathematical representation (as opposed to a bit-mapped representation). This is particularly advantageous at the rendering stage. Since the drawing commands themselves are sent to the output device, the resulting image is rendered with the highest resolution of which the device is capable. The 300 dpi or greater resolution of many hard-copy devices produces objects of much greater resolution than is available on the screen on which they were designed.

- Objects designed with draw programs can be easily edited. Lines, rectangles, circles, polygons, and spline curves can be radically altered or fine tuned by clicking on the object to select it and dragging the control points. This permits fluid design strategies and keeps the process reversible.

Now that we have a general overview of the features characterizing drawing programs, let's look at some of the specific functions they provide.

Draw Functions

Drawing programs vary greatly in the range and sophistication of the tools that they provide the designer. The spectrum of programs, in order of increasing cost and power, include:

- Simple drawing programs,
- Drafting programs,
- Low-level 2D CAD programs,
- High-level 2D CAD programs,
- 3D CAD programs.

There is no clear line distinguishing each of these classes, and each release of a new version of a given program often moves it up one class. However, a basic set of drawing tools that every drawing program should contain includes:

- Basic shapes icons
  - ➤ line
  - ➤ rectangle
  - ➤ rounded-corner rectangle
  - ➤ oval
  - ➤ arc

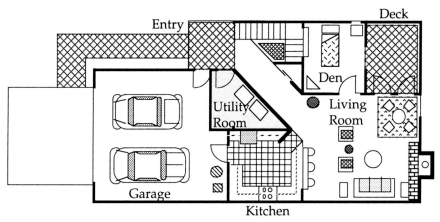

Figure 6.22
Ground level-floor plan of a house

- Generalized shapes
  - ➤ Freeform pen
  - ➤ Polygon tool
  - ➤ Bézier tool

- Transformations
  - ➤ Rotate
  - ➤ Translate
  - ➤ Differential scaling

- Special effects
  - ➤ Fill (closed objects filled with pattern)
  - ➤ Invert
  - ➤ Flip horizontal
  - ➤ Flip vertical
  - ➤ Flip both axes

- Magnification or zoom

- Alignment of objects

- Grid tools
  - ➤ Coordinate readout
  - ➤ Show grid
  - ➤ Snap to grid

- Hierarchy tools
  - ➤ Group
  - ➤ Ungroup

- Ordering (layering) tools
  - ➤ Bring to front
  - ➤ Send to back
  - ➤ Shuffle up one
  - ➤ Shuffle down one
  - ➤ Send to layer

Constraints are particularly valuable tools for drawing programs. The *Snap-to-grid* constraint requires that all lines start and end on grid points. This effectively eliminates the embarrassing 1-2 pixel overshoots or gaps inevitable when drawing by hand in a free form mode.

Another valuable constraint is provided by holding down special keys when in a particular drawing mode or process. For instance, a line drawn in constrained mode lies along multiples of 45°. Constrained rectangles are squares; constrained ovals are circles; and constrained moves and resizing can occur only in the *x*-axis or *y*-axis directions.

Draw Example

Let's examine a typical example of a useful application of a drawing program—the 2D floor plan of the ground level of a home as shown in Figure 6.22. Assume this is one of a library of 50 basic floor plans an architect is showing potential clients.

The clients indicate that the interior was just what they were looking for, but they really wanted a three-car garage. "No problem!" says the architect, and sixteen mouse clicks and keyboard strokes later shows them Figure 6.23.

What steps were required to revise this object-oriented drawing to meet the new specifications?

1. The architect first *ungrouped* the original drawing which had been stored on disk as a grouped hierarchical object labeled *Condo.Des34*.

2. Next she selected the driveway object which was designed as a rectangle and stretched it in constrained mode to the size to accommodate three cars.

3. Then she selected the south wall and southwest garage door frame as a joint object and dragged them in constrained mode to connect to the expanded driveway.

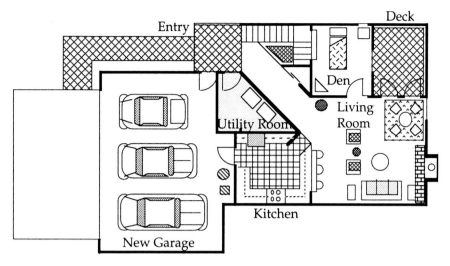

Figure 6.23
Floor plan revised to include three-car garage

4. To complete the garage, the door-frame line was duplicated and dragged into position, and resized to form the southeast wall of the new garage.

5. Then the larger car was selected, duplicated, scaled up a bit along the x-axis, and dragged into the position shown.

6. Finally, the text mode was entered and the word "New" added to "Garage." To return to the top of the hierarchy, all objects were selected and regrouped as a single object, *Condo.Des34G.*

This example demonstrates the ease with which complex objects may be built from more elementary objects and may be arranged in an efficient hierarchical order. It also demonstrates the ease with which object-oriented images may be edited and manipulated. Every object in Figures 6.22 and 6.23 may be selected, reoriented, resized, and relocated at the whim of the designer.

Difficulties of Object-oriented Graphics

Object-oriented graphics achieve much of its power, in comparison to bit-mapped graphics, by using a more abstract representation of an image. In general abstraction is achieved by labeling an object and specifying it to be composed of more primitive objects. In object-oriented graphics, this labeling is achieved by graphical interaction in which the user selects (i.e., "identifies") a set of objects and groups them as a single complex object.

Just as more abstract data types are frequently more difficult to understand than simple, concrete ones, the hierarchy of graphical objects can sometimes be confusing, especially for the novice. The very "objectness" of drawing objects can lead to confusion because some objects may be lying on top of other objects, totally obscuring them from view. Selecting objects totally surrounded by other objects, for example, can be tricky.

A final difficulty with drawing programs is that most do not support any of the more elegant painting tools such as the spray can. Such tools give the artist/designer great freedom in creating realistic images but are intrinsically limited to operating on bit-mapped images rather than objects. Some hybrid paint/draw programs have attempted to resolve this problem by letting the user operate in both modes. S/he can drag a rectangular bit-mapped object, then switch to paint mode, and apply all of the painting tools within this object. This "painted" object then becomes an abstract object and can be grouped with other "real" objects. However, most of the transformations available for draw objects have no effect on the bit-map—it is "frozen" into the original object.

Conclusions

We conclude the discussion of 2D graphics with an examination of some of the implementation issues that must be resolved in order to display graphical objects on real devices. Even such simple primitives as line drawing algorithms for raster graphics displays involve interesting compromises between speed and line quality. Aliasing effects, intrinsic to raster display devices, pose a related set of problems for which some interesting solutions are proposed. Concepts related to the viewing transformation (windows, viewports, and clipping), which were introduced in a 1D context, are easily generalized to 2D. The homogeneous coordinate representation is shown to offer a concise way to derive the equations for the viewing transformation. The clipping process occurs early in the "viewing pipeline" designed to map a world coordinate scene onto a viewport image. Two clipping algorithms, one for lines and one retaining the coherence of polygons, are presented. The two graphical modes in which most applications programs operate are the bit-mapped mode and the object-oriented mode. The chapter concludes with a description of each mode, its major strengths and limitations, and an example illustrating the actual operation of both modes.

Exercises

6.1   Throughout the discussion of 2D graphics a considerable emphasis has been placed on issues of representation and implementation. Define these two terms as they relate to computer graphics and give examples of each.

6.2   List and discuss briefly three problems that the discrete nature of pixels poses for raster displays.

6.3   Discuss four desirable characteristics that any line drawing algorithm should have. How well do the two algorithms presented in the text measure up against these criteria?

6.4   Describe in words the algorithm for the straight line Digital Differential Analyzer (DDA). How does it distinguish between near vertical and near horizontal lines?

6.5   How does Bresenham's straight-line algorithm differ from the DDA? What efficiencies are achieved by this difference?

6.6   Describe what is meant by the "aliasing" problem. Where did this problem get its name? What does "antialiasing" mean?

6.7   In the program, *Shape_AntiAlias*, three differently shaped "super pixels" were used, depending on the slope of the line. What advantage does this have over using a single 2×2 super pixel?

6.8   Shape antialiasing does appear to generate lines smoother than those without antialiasing. However, this is accomplished at a high cost. What is it?

6.9   Explain the advantages of a display supporting gray scale in doing effective antialiasing.

6.10   Aliasing is as much a problem for filled 2D objects such as rectangles and polygons as it is for lines. Sketch by hand or generate computer output illustrating antialiasing on the edges of such 2D objects.

6.11   Consider how the aliasing problem of 6.10 might be alleviated through antialiasing. Write a shade antialias algorithm for filled polynomials.

6.12   Of Figures 6.8 and 6.9 one of them is created with a drawing program to illustrate the principles involved in shade antialiasing and one is generated by doing a screen capture of actual lines drawn with and without aliasing. Which is which, and how can you tell?

6.13   On the 5.5 cm $\times$ 8.5 cm original in Figure 6.10, $W_{xL} = 3.5$ cm, $W_{xR} = 6.0$ cm, $W_{yB} = 1.6$ cm, and $W_{yT} = 4.0$ cm. Calculate the viewing transformation matrix, M_v, to map this window to a viewport defined as $V_{xL} = 400$, $V_{xR} = 910$, $V_{yB} = 700$, and $V_{yT} = 220$ pixels, respectively.

6.14   Work out the end point codes, C_1 and C_2, for the six lines of Figure 6.12 according to the Cohen-Sutherland classification scheme. From these codes, classify each line into one of the three categories:
a)   Trivially in,

b) Trivially out,
c) Nontrivial (neither trivially in nor trivially out).

6.15 Sketch a sequence of frames indicating the action of program Line_Clip on the six lines of Figure 6.12. Sketch the correctly updated image after each clipping action (segment plotted, segment discarded, line intersected by edge).

6.16 Critique the statement: "Since polygons are composed of lines, polygon clipping is equivalent to line clipping."

6.17 Figure 6.14 shows the results of line clipping a star polygon. However, from the line-clipped results alone, the parent figure(s) might have been one, two, or three polygons. Sketch five topologically distinct parent configurations, other than the star, which are consistent with the clipped results shown.

6.18 Recursion always involves two essential elements: a) trivial case(s), and b) reduction of problem size with each recursive call. Demonstrate how Line_Clip satisfies these criteria as a recursive program.

6.19 A second recursive algorithm ivolves successive bisection of each line until it is trivially in or trivially out. Re-write Line_Clip to implement this algorithm.

6.20 An interesting attribute of polygon clipping is that an n-vertex polygon going into a clipping cycle against a given edge emerges as an m-vertex polygon, where m and n may be related as $m > n$, $m < n$, or $m = n$. Draw an initial ten-vertex star plus rectangular window configurations that result in an m-vertex clipped figure for as many cases as you can for m in the range $4 \le m < 10$.

6.21 Using the polygon defining and fill commands available in your Pascal implementation, write a polygon clipping algorithm that preserves polygon coherence (i.e., correctly shades each clipped polygon).

6.22 Explore the features of a paint program on your favorite graphics workstation. Use screen dumps or the Print command to demonstrate as many of the tools from Figure 6.18 as your system supports as well as any additional paint commands not mentioned in the text.

6.23 Use the paint program on your favorite graphics workstation to create a significant work of artistic design. Examples of possible projects include duplication of existing posters or advertisements, original paintings of realistic scenes, and original impressionistic or abstract paintings.

6.24 Explore the features of a drawing program on your favorite graphics workstation. Use screen dumps or the Print command to demonstrate as many of the tools as your system supports as well as any additional drawing commands not mentioned in the text.

6.25 Use the drawing program on your favorite graphics workstation to create a significant architectural design. Examples of possible projects include duplication of existing floor plans, sail plans, industrial designs, or original designs in your area of interest.

Endnotes

1.   Newman, William M. and Sproull, Robert F., *Principles of Interactive Computer Graphics*, Second Edition, p.22, McGraw-Hill Book Company, New York, NY (1979).

2.   Bresenham, J. E.,"Algorithm for Computer Control of a Digital Plotter," *IBM Syst. J.* **4**, No. 1, pp. 25–30 (1965).

3.   Sutherland, I. E. and Hodgman, G. W., "Reentrant Polygon Clipping," *Comm. ACM* **17**, No. 1, pp. 32–42, January (1974) Available also in Beaty, John C. and Kellogg, S. Booth (eds), *Tutorial: Computer Graphics*, Second Edition, IEEE Computer Society, pp. 270-280 (1982).

4.   Wittgenstein, L.,*Tractatus Logico-Philosophicus*, Proposition 6.341, Routledge and Kegan Paul, London, U.K. (1922) Translated by D. F. Pears and F. F. McGuinness (1961).

5.   Fiume, Eugene L., *The Mathematical Structure of Raster Graphics*, Academic Press, Boston, MA (1989).

Chapter 7

Three-Dimensional Graphics – Fundamentals

Visual forms - lines, colors, proportions, etc. - are just as capable of articulation, i.e. of complex combinations, as words. But the laws that govern this sort of articulation are altogether different from the laws of syntax that govern language. . . . They do not present their constituents successively, but simultaneously, so the relations determining a visual structure are grasped in one act of vision.
Suzanne Langer

As we move from two to three dimensions, let us consider several concepts valuable in visualizing the 3D environment. The first involves new geometric considerations and problems posed by the additional dimension. Second is the increased importance of object representation for efficient algorithmic processes in 3D. Finally, we will observe how smoothly the homogeneous coordinate representation allows us to extend 2D transformations to 3D.

Another concept introduced is *visual realism*, which is the theme running through the chapters on 3D. Visual realism has been the Holy Grail of classical computer graphics almost from its inception. As many of the figures in the book demonstrate, great progress has been made toward this goal. The trend in both graphical hardware and software is to provide the programmer with tools for production of realistic visual images.

The goal of visual realism itself remains irresistible, but difficult for all but relatively simple scenes. The science of ray tracing and radiosity and the mathematics of fractal geometry provide powerful tools for rendering realistic scenes. And yet, the trained observer can, in most cases, distinguish a photograph of a given scene from a computer graphics rendering of the same scene. As you scan the computer-generated graphics in the computer science literature, try to detect the subtle clues which distinguish natural from artificial scenes.

As a final observation, we note that, while visual realism remains an important goal of traditional computer graphics, it is definitely not the goal of all computer graphics. Many productions of computer animation (e.g., "flying logos") and computer art (e.g., distortions of color and space) explicitly exploit the computer-origin of the images rather than attempting to model any physical reality. Similarly, the whole area of image processing is intrinsically an artificial process—the manipulation of natural or artificial images to achieve the desired visual effect. So while visual realism is an important aspect of computer graphics, it is not the whole story.

Moving from 2D to 3D

The task of envisioning 3D worlds on 2D devices has been characterized by Tufte as "escaping flatland."[1] Part of the fun in the N-dimensional approach to graphics is to speculate on what new effects will arise as we move from dimension N to dimension N+1 space. The move from 2D to 3D is particularly interesting. Not only do new transformations appear that are related to the dimensionality of the space itself, but also new problems arise related to the *viewing pipeline*—the sequence of steps required to transform a world coordinate scene into an image on the screen.

New Transformations

As we moved from 1D to 2D, certain transformations became possible simply through the addition of another axis. These included the translations and scaling now possible along two axes independently. In moving into 3D these transformations naturally extend to all three axes. In going from 1D to 2D, however, some fundamentally new transformations appeared. These included rotation, a transformation undefined in 1D. In moving to 3D new transformations, undefined in 2D, become possible. Two of the most interesting include rotations about an arbitrary axis, shown in Figure 7.1, and the parity operation, shown in Figure 7.2. The parity operation changes right-handed systems into left-handed systems. *Handedness* (parity) is a concept undefined in 2D.

The viewing transformation is particularly simple in 2D since it involves mapping a window on a 2D scene onto a viewport on a 2D display. In the previous chapter we showed that this transformation involves a single matrix generated by concatenating a scaling, a transla-

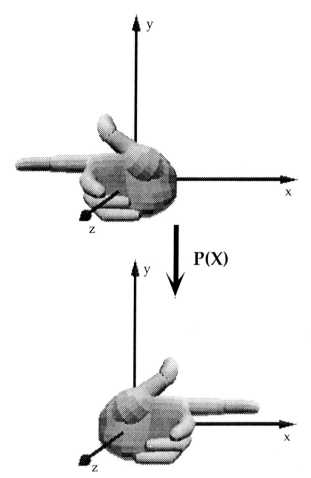

Figure 7.2
The *parity* operation. The operation P(**X**) takes the vector, **X**, into the vector **X**′= –**X**. The effect is to change a right-handed system into a left-handed system. The parity operator applied to the right hand (top view) changes it into a left hand which is shown rotated 180° (bottom view).

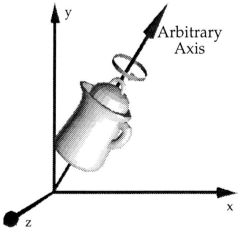

Figure 7.1
Rotation about an arbitrary axis. In 3D, rotations may be performed about any of the three principle coordinate axes or about any arbitrary axis as shown.

tion, and another scaling. In 3D, the viewing transformation is not so simple because the viewing process now involves projecting a 3D scene onto a 2D display surface. The projection transformation involves mapping world coordinate (x,y,z) triplets onto (x',y') display pairs. As we shall see shortly, projection may be a nonlinear function of the newly introduced z-coordinate. This new complexity is considered in the section on projections and viewing in 3D.

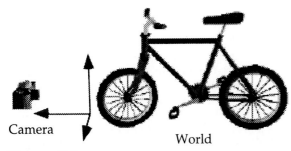

Figure 7.3
Original configuration of camera and world scene.

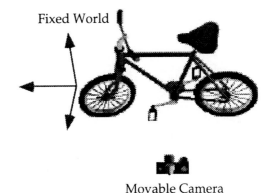

Figure 7.4
Fixed world/movable camera viewing mode.

Two Points of View

There are two completely equivalent modes for performing the projection process of the viewing transformation. It is helpful to present these now since they interrelate the rotation transformation of objects and the projection phase of the viewing transformation. By clearly naming these alternative modes, the basic concepts become apparent. Consider the world scene shown in Figure 7.3.

Now consider the following two options for obtaining a side view of the world coordinate scene:

- **Fixed World/Movable Camera Mode –** In this mode, the world coordinates of objects composing the scene are considered fixed and the camera through which we view the scene may be moved to obtain the desired point of view. This mode has the advantage of an intuitive mental model of the viewing transformation but requires defining three coordinates for camera position and three parameters specifying film plane orientation. Figure 7.4 illustrates this mode.

- **Fixed Camera/Movable World Mode –** In this mode, the camera is considered fixed, generally with the film plane parellel to the plane containing the x- and y-axes. To obtain different points of view of the world coordinate scene, the whole world coordinate system is rotated and translated as a single object. This mode has some computational advantages, and intuition develops quickly by considering the display screen to be the camera film plane. Figure 7.5 illustrates this mode.

A little thought will convince the reader that these two modes are completely equivalent. Since the fixed camera/movable world mode fits so naturally into the transformation matrix formalism, this is the mode we adopt in this chapter.

Representation of 3D Objects

Consider how objects might be represented in 3D space. What are the options available? A range of alternatives exist on the concrete/abstract spectrum. The most concrete geometric representation consists of specifying every (x,y,z) point on the surface of the object. This representation requires no abstract data structure—a single file of points defines the object. But it is also enormously inefficient. A single object would require a megabyte or more of storage space to represent it to the resolution available on most display screens.

The other end of the spectrum involves the abstract representation available through parametric curved surfaces. With a relatively small

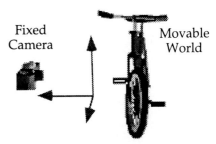

Figure 7.5
Fixed camera/movable world mode.

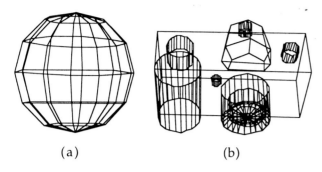

(a)   **(b)**

Figure 7.6
Wire frame representation of two objects.

set of parameters, significant portions of the surface of the object may be accurately modeled. The whole object may, in turn, be represented by smoothly joining a set of parametric patches. The advantages of this representation are efficient storage and a high degree of accuracy independent of the characteristics of the display. The main disadvantages of parametric curved surface representations stem from the difficulties in determining the correct set of curved patches with which to model real objects.

Wire Frame Representation

Most 3D graphics systems represent a compromise along the concrete/abstract spectrum. For certain applications, a *wire frame* representation is adequate. This can be achieved most simply by a file of straight lines, each of which is represented by its two end points, (x_1, y_1, x_2, y_2). Wire frame representations show adequately the skeletal structure of objects, but are not capable of representing surfaces or any other features of a 3D object. Figure 7.6 illustrates the use

of wire frame representations.

For certain applications, wire frame representations have distinct advantages. They allow the user to "see through" objects and visualize the internal structure and shape of normally invisible surfaces. However, wire frames also have definite limitations. The complexity of even relatively simple objects soon overwhelms the observer, with insight into shape being lost in the clutter of lines. Figure 7.6(b) is approaching this limitation. Another severe limitation stems from the inefficiency of the independent-line data structure. For instance, each vertex (except the top and bottom vertices) of Figure 7.6(a) is the end point for four lines. So a simple file of lines would contain a four-fold redundancy of data points, and the top and bottom vertex would appear twelve times!

Polyhedral Representations

The compromise most widely used in computer graphics systems is the polyhedron, a set of smoothly joined polygons. By the appropriate selection of polygon shape and number, polyhedrons are capable of modeling any 3D object to the desired degree of accuracy. Some objects, e.g. tetrahedra and cubes, may be modeled precisely by a set of four equilateral triangles or six squares, respectively. Others, such as spheres and cylinders, may be approximated by combinations of trapezoids, triangles, rectangles, and n-sided polygons. For certain applications a coarse polygon grid may be adequate—for applications requiring greater accuracy, more polygons with a smaller grid spacing may be required. Figure 7.7 demonstrates how a sphere may be approximated with increasing accuracy by polyhedra.

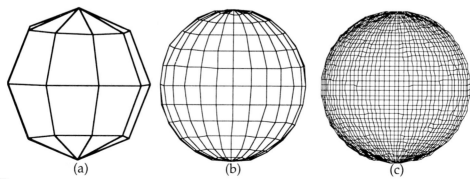

(a)   **(b)**   **(c)**

Figure 7.7
Approximating a sphere by polyhedra. (a) consists of 32, (b) of 288, and (c) of 3200 polygons.

Figure 7.8
Human with Robot scene based on polyhedra. Note how the whole scene is composed of rectangles, trapezoids, or, in the case of the 3D letters, rectangles and n-sided polygons.

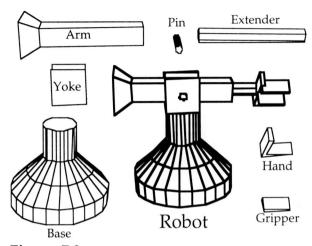

Figure 7.9
Exploded view of hierarchical structure of robot. The robot main object (bold) is constructed by assembling graphical primitive subobjects which are easily generated by CAD systems.

A polyhedra-based 3D scene such as that shown in Figure 7.8 may be represented by the hierarchical data structure shown in Figures 7.9–7.10. The highest level is the *scene*; in the next lower level are *objects* composing the scene; each object is composed of *subobjects* which may contain other subobjects or *geometric primitives*; each geometric primitive is a polyhedron composed of polygons; each polygon, in turn, is composed of vertex points; and finally, each point consists of a (x,y,z) triplet.

An illustration of the hierarchical structure of one of the objects in the Figure 7.8 scene is shown graphically in Figure 7.9 in which the robot is *exploded* into its geometric primitive subobjects. As the figure indicates, the robot has only one level of subobject. However, in general, subobjects may themselves consist of subobjects which, in turn, may consist of subobjects and so on. A useful algorithmic approach is to label the lowest level of sub-object as a 3D geometric primitive and recursively branch down the hierarchical tree until a primitive object is reached. Primitive objects contain, as a minimum, a polygon list pointing to the vertices defining the polygon and a vertex list defining the coordinates in three dimensions. This data structure provides the basis for the complete polyhedral scene.

The polyhedra-based representation of scenes has the advantages of simplicity, generality, and computational efficiency. Objects may be manipulated and transformed by operating on the points composing the polygons. Polygon surfaces have well-defined orientations which simplify computations of visibility and shading. Thus, polygonal representations provide a natural basis for the addition of refinements to increase the visual realism of natural objects. The addition of shading, shadows, and edge antialiasing to the camera polyhedron of Figure 7.6(b) produces the more realistic Figure 7.11. These techniques for enhancing visual realism are discussed in subsequent chapters and continue as areas of active computer graphics research. A serious attempt to establish a mathematical theory for representation of 3D graphical objects and scenes is given in Fiume.[2]

The principal weakness of polyhedral representations is their poor approximation to smooth curved surfaces, complex shapes, and life-like forms. Simply increasing the number of polygons to achieve visually realistic representations of complex scenes will overwhelm the storage and computing capacity of even the largest computers. Efficient algorithms have been developed smoothing the transition from one polygon to the next in order to reduce the discontinuities in color and shading as one moves across a multipolygon surface. Such smoothing techniques can produce visually realistic results with a manageable number of polygons.

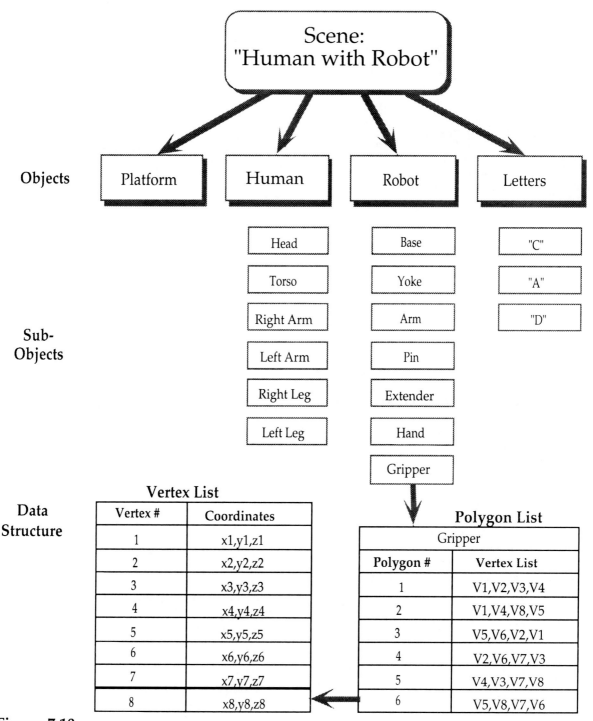

Objects

Sub-Objects

Data Structure

Figure 7.10
Hierarchical structure of polyhedral scene. Note that each subobject will have its own polygon list and associated vertex list. Also, subobjects such as right arm will have its own subobjects such as *upper arm*, *lower arm*, and *hand*. The hand may, in turn, have subobjects such as fingers, and so on.

Figure 7.11
More visually realistic rendering of polyhedral representation of camera. Adding shading, shadows, and edge antialiasing to the polygons of Figure 7.6(b) produces this image.

Transformations of 3D Objects

In the remainder of this chapter we consider two important but conceptually distinct topics—the manipulation of objects in 3D space and the projection of objects from 3D to 2D space. By clearly distinguishing these two concepts the reader will save herself considerable grief.

From our experience to date with the homogeneous coordinate system and the matrix representation, the reader should find the extension to 3D transformations straight-forward, particularly for translation and scaling. Recall that the fundamental transformation equation may be written in homogeneous coordinates as:[3]

$$X' = X \cdot M , \qquad [7.1]$$

where
$X' = [x'\, y'\, z'\, 1]$ (transformed point),
$X = [x\, yz\, 1]$ (original point),
and
$M = 4 \times 4$ transformation matrix.

Primary Transformations

Note that by transforming the points defining the object (wire frame or polygon vertices), the object itself is transformed. The desired transfor-

mation is uniquely determined by setting the transformation matrix, M, appropriately. We can summarize the M matrices for the primary transformations as follows.

Translation

For translating an object a distance T_x along the x-axis, T_y along the y-axis, and T_z along the z-axis, the matrix M is the T matrix, defined as:

$$T = \begin{bmatrix} 1 & 0 & 0 & 0 \\ 0 & 1 & 0 & 0 \\ 0 & 0 & 1 & 0 \\ T_x & T_y & T_z & 1 \end{bmatrix}. \qquad [7.2]$$

Substituting T for M in equation 7.1 and multiplying gives the standard linear translation equations:

$$\begin{aligned} x' &= x + T_x \\ y' &= y + T_y \\ z' &= z + T_z \, . \end{aligned} \qquad [7.3]$$

In vector notation, this transformation may be considered as the addition of a displacement vector, D, to an original position vector, x, to move the object to x'. Mathematically, this is written:

$$x' = x + D \qquad [7.4]$$

where
$x = (x,y,z),$ (original coordinates of object)

$x' = (x',y',z') .$ (object coordinates after translation).

The displacement vector, D, has T_x, T_y, and T_z as its components as illustrated in Figure 7.12.

Scaling

Generalizing the 2D scaling transformation to 3D involves adding the scale factor, S_z, to the previously defined S_x and S_y for independent scaling along the new z-axis. The M matrix of Equation 7.1 is then represented by the S matrix, defined as:

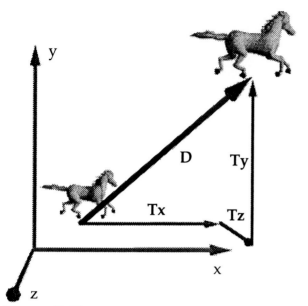

Figure 7.12
Translation of an object by vector *D*.The transformation is performed by the *T* matrix with components T_x, T_y, and T_z whose meanings are shown here.

$$S = \begin{bmatrix} S_x & 0 & 0 & 0 \\ 0 & S_y & 0 & 0 \\ 0 & 0 & S_z & 0 \\ 0 & 0 & 0 & 1 \end{bmatrix}. \qquad [7.5]$$

Substituting *S* for *M* in Equation 7.1 and multiplying gives the standard linear scaling equations:

$$x' = S_x \cdot x, \qquad [7.6]$$
$$y' = S_y \cdot y,$$
$$z' = S_z z.$$

For the commonly used uniform magnification of an object by a scale factor *S*, all three scale factors are set equal to *S*. However, differential scaling also provides a useful tool for object deformations as demonstrated in Figure 7.13.

Rotation

Note how naturally and easily the translation and scaling matrices have expanded to accommodate the third dimension. In fact, comparing with the extension from 1D to 2D, you probably predicted the Equations 7.2 and 7.5 as the correct form for 3D translations and scaling,

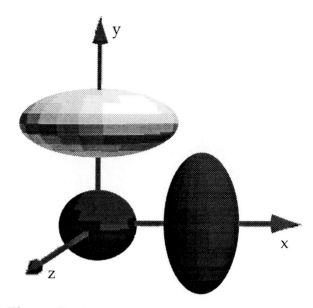

Figure 7.13
Differential scaling of a sphere. Starting with the centered sphere, the oblate ellipsoid (top) was generated by $(S_x, S_y, S_z) = (2,1,2)$. The prolate ellipsoid (right) was produced with $(S_x, S_y, S_z) = (1,2,1)$.

respectively. However, in extending rotations to 3D we run into some unforeseen complexity. There are three aspects to this complexity.

- There are now three axes about which rotation can take place. Rotations of θ_x, θ_y, and θ_z are now possible about the three independent axes. Interestingly, a single matrix is not capable of simultaneously representing these three independent rotations.

- The first problem is related to a second interesting aspect of rotations—they do not commute. That is, a rotation of 90° about the *x*-axis followed by a rotation of 90° about the *y*-axis gives a different configuration than a rotation of 90° about the *y*-axis followed by a rotation of 90° about the *x*-axis. *The order of rotations is important*.

- The rotation by θ degrees about an arbitrary axis is a valuable transformation but has no simple representation in terms of θ. It can, however, be expressed in terms of a single, composed matrix as a function of θ and the orientation parameters of the arbitrary axis.

The solution to the first problem is to define three rotation matrices, R_x, R_y, and R_z, corresponding to a rotation by θ about the x-, y-, and z-axes, as shown schematically in Figure 7.14. The last of these, R_z, is a simple extension of the 2D R matrix because the motion in both R and R_z occurs parallel to the x-y plane. The three matrices are expressed as:

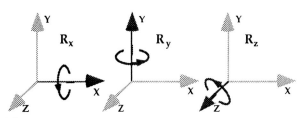

Figure 7.14
Rotation transformations about three Cartesian coordinate axes.

$$R_x = \begin{bmatrix} 1 & 0 & 0 & 0 \\ 0 & \cos\theta & \sin\theta & 0 \\ 0 & -\sin\theta & \cos\theta & 0 \\ 0 & 0 & 0 & 1 \end{bmatrix}, \qquad [7.7]$$

$$R_y = \begin{bmatrix} \cos\theta & 0 & -\sin\theta & 0 \\ 0 & 1 & 0 & 0 \\ \sin\theta & 0 & \cos\theta & 0 \\ 0 & 0 & 0 & 1 \end{bmatrix}, \qquad [7.8]$$

$$R_z = \begin{bmatrix} \cos\theta & \sin\theta & 0 & 0 \\ -\sin\theta & \cos\theta & 0 & 0 \\ 0 & 0 & 1 & 0 \\ 0 & 0 & 0 & 1 \end{bmatrix}. \qquad [7.9]$$

Substituting these rotation matrices for M in Equation 7.1 and multiplying gives the familiar equations for rotation about the x-axis:

$$x' = x \qquad [7.10]$$
$$y' = y\cos\theta - z\sin\theta$$
$$z' = y\sin\theta + z\cos\theta$$

and similar sets of equations for rotations about the y- and z-axes.

Secondary Transformations

The most important secondary transformations are *reflections* and *shearing*. The introduction of a new axis increases the number of such transformations.

Reflections

Reflections can be classified as occurring through one, two, or three planes. As examples of each of these classes, consider the following three reflection matrices:

$$M_x = \begin{bmatrix} -1 & 0 & 0 & 0 \\ 0 & 1 & 0 & 0 \\ 0 & 0 & 1 & 0 \\ 0 & 0 & 0 & 1 \end{bmatrix}, \qquad [7.11]$$

$$M_{xy} = \begin{bmatrix} -1 & 0 & 0 & 0 \\ 0 & -1 & 0 & 0 \\ 0 & 0 & 1 & 0 \\ 0 & 0 & 0 & 1 \end{bmatrix}, \qquad [7.12]$$

$$M_{xyz} = \begin{bmatrix} -1 & 0 & 0 & 0 \\ 0 & -1 & 0 & 0 \\ 0 & 0 & -1 & 0 \\ 0 & 0 & 0 & 1 \end{bmatrix}. \qquad [7.13]$$

Although this sequence of transformations appears to be simply a case of increasing negativism, it involves some interesting geometry. Equations 7.11–7.13 also each have two other forms corresponding to cycling the (−) sign through other possible scale factors. Comparison of Equations 7.11–7.13 to Equation 7.5 confirms that reflections are special instances of the more general class of scaling transformation.

M_x corresponds to simple mirroring through the y-z plane. M_{xy} corresponds to mirroring through both the y-z and x-z planes. M_{xyz} corresponds to mirroring the object through all three coordinate planes and is designated as the *parity operator*, written as $P(X)$. In vector notation it can be expressed as:

$$P(X) \rightarrow -X . \qquad [7.14]$$

That is, performing the parity operation on any vector simply inverts it.

A curious effect is that both the simple mirror operators (e.g., M_x) and the parity operator, $P = M_{xyz}$, change right-handed systems into left-handed systems and visa versa. These operators are very useful to designers in developing systems with a unique parity. In modeling a

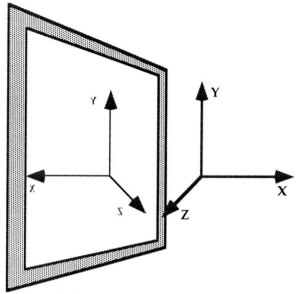

Figure 7.15
Mirror transformation. Note how a simple
reflection changes a right-hand coordinate
system into a left-hand coordinate system.

human form, for instance, only the right hand,
arm, and leg need to be designed. The corresponding left limbs are designed by copying the
right limbs and applying a simple mirror or
parity operation.

Shearing

As discussed in the 2D section, shearing may be
thought of as a coordinate-dependent translation in which the cross section in one dimension
is preserved while its position along that dimension depends on the other dimension. We can
define analogous 3D shearing as preserving the
cross section parallel to a given plane but
making the cross section's position a function of
the third coordinate. Thus, for instance, a y-de-
pendent shear could be written as:

$$x' = x + a\,y,\qquad\qquad [7.15]$$
$$y' = y,$$
$$z' = z + b\,y.$$

where
$a, b =$ shearing constants, one of
which may be zero.

This transformation may be written in matrix form as

$$Sh_y = \begin{bmatrix} 1 & 0 & 0 & 0 \\ a & 1 & b & 0 \\ 0 & 0 & 1 & 0 \\ 0 & 0 & 0 & 1 \end{bmatrix}. \qquad [7.16]$$
(shear along y-axis)

Figure 7.16 shows the results of applying
this transformation to a simple object.

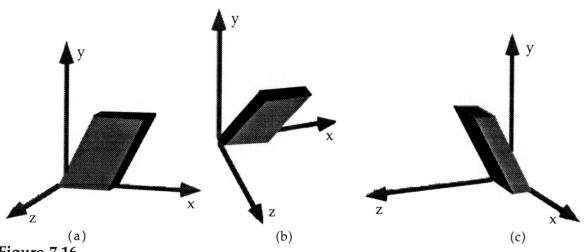

(a)   (b)   (c)

Figure 7.16
Shearing transformation in 3D – Shearing parameters in Equation 7.16 are:
    a) $a = 1/3$; $b = 0$
    b) $a = 1/3$; $b = 1/3$
    c) $a = 0$; $b = 1/3$

Inverse Transformations

All of the M transformations presented to this point have inverse transformations indicated as M^{-1}. The role of M^{-1} is to return the transformed object back to its original state. We can summarize the inverse transformations with the matrix element substitutions listed in Table 7.1.

As mentioned in the 2D discussion, one can readily verify that M^{-1} is correct by multiplying it by M. If M^{-1} correct, the result will yield the identity matrix, I.

Rotation about an Arbitrary Axis – Matrix Composition

As with lower dimensional transformations, complex operations may be composed by concatenating a series of more primitive transformations. Such transformations include shearing in directions other than the coordinate axes and reflections through planes displaced from the origin and not parallel to planes containing the axes. One of the most useful operations is rotation about an arbitrary axis (see Figure 7.17).

The general algorithm for the rotation of an object about an arbitrary axis requires the following sequence of five steps: shift the axis to the origin, align it with one of the coordinate axes, perform the desired rotation, undo the initial alignment, and shift back to the original position. Note that any of the three coordinate axes may be used for the alignment. We have chosen the y-axis to assist in visualizing the process. Note also that the alignment process requires two rotation steps in general.

To get more specific, consider what is required to rotate an object by an angle θ about an axis, A, which contains point P a distance D from the origin. Seven primary transformations which accomplish the five-step algorithm are summarized here and illustrated in Figure 7.18.

1. Translation, T, of the object/axis system a vector distance $-D$ so that some point, P, on the axis lies on the origin.

2. Rotation R_x about the x-axis by θ_x in order to bring axis A into the x-y plane.

3. Rotation R_z about the z-axis by the angle θ_z to align axis A with the y-axis.

4. Rotation R_y by the desired angle, θ.

Table 7.1
Inverse Transformation Matrix Elements

Transformation	M Parameters	M⁻¹ Parameters
Translation	T_x, T_y, T_z	$-T_x, -T_y, -T_z$
Scaling	S_x, S_y, S_z	$1/S_x, 1/S_y, 1/S_z$
Rotation	θ	$-\theta$
Reflection	(-1)	(-1)
Shearing	a, b	$-a, -b$

5. Rotation R_z^{-1} about the z-axis by the angle $-\theta_z$ to undo step (3).

6. Rotation R_x^{-1} about the x-axis by the angle $-\theta x$ to undo step (2).

7. Translation, T^{-1}, of point P a distance D to undo step (1).

How might we express this sequence of primary transformations in terms of the familiar homogeneous matrix formalism? It is clear from the figures that we need more information than just θ in order to specify the four matrices, T, R_x, R_y, and R_z and their relevant inverse matrices. In particular, we need the location of P and the orientation of A.

Assume that coordinates of point P are the triad, (P_x, P_y, P_z). This information is sufficient for specifying the two translations, T and T^{-1}.

$$T = \begin{bmatrix} 1 & 0 & 0 & 0 \\ 0 & 1 & 0 & 0 \\ 0 & 0 & 1 & 0 \\ -P_x & -P_y & -P_z & 1 \end{bmatrix}, \quad [7.17]$$

and

$$T^{-1} = \begin{bmatrix} 1 & 0 & 0 & 0 \\ 0 & 1 & 0 & 0 \\ 0 & 0 & 1 & 0 \\ P_x & P_y & P_z & 1 \end{bmatrix}. \quad [7.18]$$

In order to define the rotation matrices we need to specify the orientation of the rotation axis, A. We can specify this orientation in terms of a triad of angles, (α, β, γ) which the vector A makes with x-, y-, and z-axes at the origin. We can then define a unit vector, L, parallel to A in terms of the unit vectors (i,j,k) and its x, y, and z components, (a,b,c):

$$L = a\,i + b\,j + c\,k \quad [7.19]$$

where
a = x-component of L,

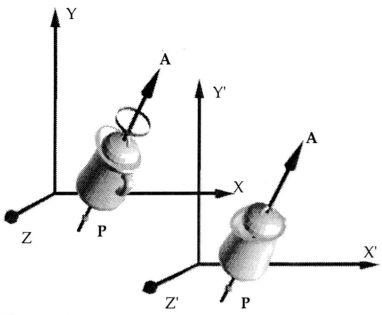

Figure 7.17
Rotation about an arbitrary axis. The object in the upper left system is to be rotated by $\theta = 90°$ to give the lower right configuration.

i = unit vector in x-direction, and so on.

The relationship between the angles, (α, β, γ), and the components, (a,b,c), is simply:

$$a = \cos \alpha, \qquad [7.20]$$
$$b = \cos \beta,$$
$$c = \cos \gamma.$$

As defined in Equation 7.20, a, b, and c are called the *direction cosines*. Figure 7.19 demonstrates these relationships and clarifies how the rotation parameters are derived from the orientation angles.

From Figure 7.19 and because L is a unit vector, the following expressions may be written:

$$a^2 + b^2 + c^2 = 1 \qquad [7.21]$$
$$(\textbf{\textit{L}} \text{ is a unit vector}),$$
$$d^2 = b^2 + c^2 \qquad [7.22]$$
$$(\text{by construction}).$$

The rotation, R_x, required to take A (and L) into the x-y plane, also swings d onto the y-axis. The angle involved in the rotation is θ_x, and, in

this case, it will have a negative value because of the right-hand rule. A positive angular rotation about the x-axis carries the y-axis into the z-axis. The rotation parameters for R_x may be written:

$$\cos \theta_x = \frac{b}{d}, \qquad [7.23]$$

$$\sin \theta_x = -\frac{c}{d}. \qquad [7.24]$$

Similarly, inspection of Figure 7.19 leads to the following expressions for θ_z, the angle required to rotate L onto the y-axis within the x-y plane.

$$\cos \theta_z = d \qquad [7.25]$$

$$\sin \theta_z = a \qquad [7.26]$$

Because the R_z rotation carries the x-axis into the y-axis in a right-handed system, the angle θ_z is positive. Equations 7.23-7.26 allow us to complete the specification of the rotation matrices, R_x and R_z. These are written:

$$R_x = \begin{bmatrix} 1 & 0 & 0 & 0 \\ 0 & \dfrac{b}{d} & -\dfrac{c}{d} & 0 \\ 0 & \dfrac{c}{d} & \dfrac{b}{d} & 0 \\ 0 & 0 & 0 & 1 \end{bmatrix}, \qquad [7.27]$$

and

$$R_z = \begin{bmatrix} d & a & 0 & 0 \\ -a & d & 0 & 0 \\ 0 & 0 & 1 & 0 \\ 0 & 0 & 0 & 1 \end{bmatrix}. \qquad [7.28]$$

The final rotation of the object by θ degrees occurs, in this case, about the y-axis, and the rotation matrix is the familiar

$$R_y = \begin{bmatrix} \cos \theta & 0 & -\sin \theta & 0 \\ 0 & 1 & 0 & 0 \\ \sin \theta & 0 & \cos \theta & 0 \\ 0 & 0 & 0 & 1 \end{bmatrix}. \qquad [7.29]$$

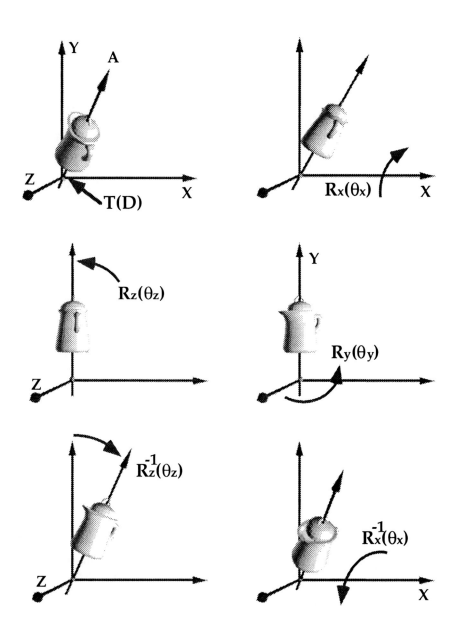

Figure 7.18
Primary transformations composed to generate a rotation about an arbitrary axis. Note that each figure shows the *result* of the transformation indicated. Also note that transformation (7), the final shift back to *P*, is not shown.

The inverse matrices for steps 5–7 are readily derived from Table 7.1. Now that we have the component primary transformations, the final concatenated matrix, *M*, for the rotation of an object about an arbitrary axis may be computed by the product matrix shown in the following box.

$$M = T(D) \cdot R_x(\theta_x) \cdot R_z(\theta_z) \cdot R_y(\theta) \cdot R_z^{-1}(\theta_z) \cdot R_x^{-1}(\theta_x) \cdot T^{-1}(D).$$ [7.30]

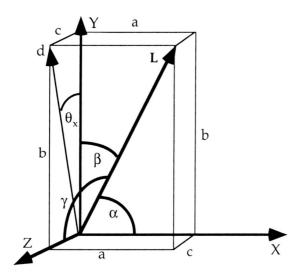

Figure 7.19
Rotation angle, θ_x, in terms of orientation angles and direction cosines.

Although this expression looks scary, every element in it is defined above. By substituting numerical values corresponding to an actual rotation, the matrix multiplication reduces M to a simple 4×4 numerical matrix.

Projections and Viewing in 3D

Now that we know how to represent objects with a polyhedral structure and to manipulate them with matrix operators, the next step is to explain the fundamentals for viewing our models on the screen. The addition of a third dimension in world coordinates adds complexity to the viewing task. Because scene models are represented in 3D but viewing occurs in 2D, an additional process called *projection* must be added to the viewing pipeline. Projection can be thought of as the process of collapsing a 3D representation into a 2D image. Burger and Gillies present a summary of the projection operation in concise vector notation.[4]

A helpful model for understanding projection is the analogy between projection of computer graphics images and projection of slide film shown in Figure 7.20. In a slide film projector, light starts at the bulb of the projector, passes through the slide, and focuses an image of the slide on the screen. In computer graphics projection, the eye is analogous to the projector bulb, the display screen is analogous to the slide, the world scene is analogous to the slide screen image, and the direction of the light is reversed. Figure 7.20 illustrates several important concepts concerning projection.

- The 2D graphics image results from projecting rays from the "real" 3D graphical object (model) onto the graphics screen, generally lying in the x-y plane. This configuration is helpful in deriving the mathematics for perspective projections.

- In order that the world coordinates of the scene objects have positive z values, a left-handed coordinate system has traditionally been used. This choice preserves the conventional configuration of the *x*- and *y*-axis on the graphics screen and aligns the viewing direction with the *z*-axis.

- The light rays shown in 7.19(b) are real only between the screen and eye. In the region between the screen and 3D object the rays are purely mathematical or *virtual*.

- The light ray structure in 7.20(a) is actually more complex than that shown. In actual practice, two additional lenses are used, one to concentrate light from the bulb on the slide (object), and a second to focus the image of the object on the screen. In the process the image is inverted.

- The white light from the bulb in 7.20(a) is filtered by the slide transparency and passes colored rays to produce the final colored image.

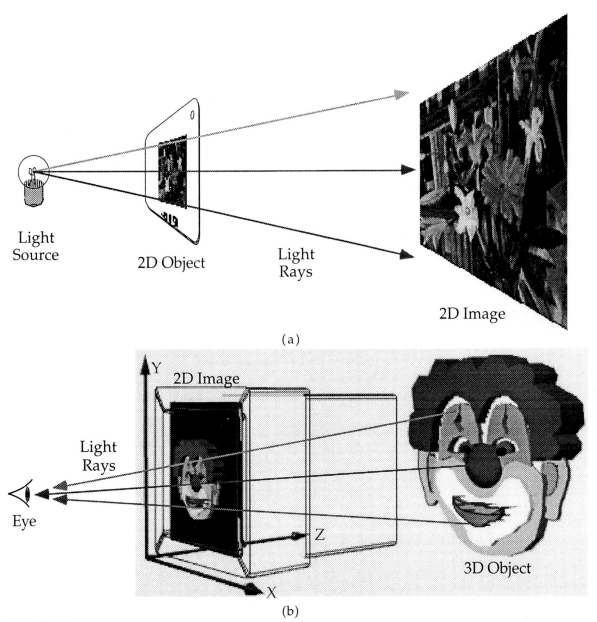

Figure 7.20
Analogy between slide projection and graphics projection. Note the reversal in light ray direction between (a) and (b).

Classes of Projections

Projections commonly used in computer graphics fall into three categories which can be summarized as:

- **Parallel Orthographic** – Parallel rays from the object travel in the (–z) direction and strike the *x-y* viewing plane along a normal to the plane. An example is the projection of your shadow on a N-S wall by the sun setting due west. This is the simplest projection and is useful in architectural and CAD applications.

- **Parallel Oblique** – Parallel rays from the object strike the x-y viewing plane and make a non-zero angle with respect to the

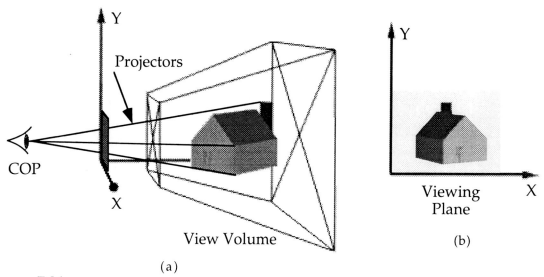

(a)

(b)

Figure 7.21
Definition of 3D viewing terms. The projectors map the 3D object from the view volume in (a) onto the 2D viewing plane in (b).

z-axis. This projection is more complex than the orthographic projection but encodes the z-depth of the projected point.

- **Perspective** – Converging rays from the object intersect the x-y viewing plane, creating the 2D image, and continue to the eye. The position of a point on the screen is a function of its depth, z, in world coordinates.

In order to specify these projections in more detail, we need to define several additional terms related to 3D viewing. These are illustrated in Figure 7.21.

- **View volume** – That region of world coordinate space to be projected onto the viewing plane. For perspective projection it is a truncated pyramid.

- **Center of projection** *(COP)* – The location of the eye (or camera) onto which the projected rays converge. For parallel projection, we use the direction of projection.

- **Projectors** – Those rays from the object scene used to create the image on the viewing plane. *Projector* is a mnemonic for *projection vector*.

- **Viewing plane** – The plane onto which the 2D image is projected. In practice, this corresponds to the VDT screen and is customarily chosen as the x-y plane.

With these definitions in mind, let us examine each of the three projection classes in more detail and present the matrix which performs the projection transformation.

Parallel Projection

When the projectors are all anti-parallel to the z-axis we have the case of *orthographic* parallel projection. The effect is to map all view volume triads, (x,y,z), onto view plane pairs, (x',y'), according to the equations:

$$x' = x, \qquad\qquad\qquad [7.31]$$
$$y' = y,$$
$$z' = 0$$

(since viewing plane is the x-y plane).

In matrix formalism, this can be considered a transformation of the form $X' = XM_1$, where M_1 is given by

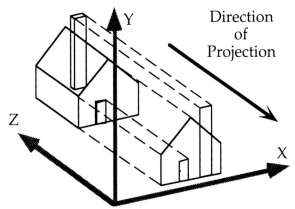

Figure 7.22
Parallel projection.This unique parallel projection, in which the direction of projection is in the (−z) direction, is called an *orthographic* projection. Note that the $(x´,y´)$ coordinates of an image point are independent of the z coordinate of the object point.

$$M_1 = \begin{bmatrix} 1 & 0 & 0 & 0 \\ 0 & 1 & 0 & 0 \\ 0 & 0 & 0 & 0 \\ 0 & 0 & 0 & 1 \end{bmatrix}. \qquad [7.32]$$

The relationship between projectors, object, and image is shown schematically in Figure 7.22.

Orthographic parallel projections are particularly useful for applications such as architectural CAD. Floor *plans* are generated by setting the direction of projection in the (−y) direction. The front view (shown here) and side views are called *elevations*. This projection mode has the advantage of mapping parallel lines of the object into parallel lines on the image. Lines lying in a plane parallel to the x-y plane preserve their orientation and length. All other lines are foreshortened. The primary disadvantage of an orthographic projection is the loss of visual cueing on the depth (z-coordinate) of points on the object.

Oblique Projections

Another class of parallel projections, called oblique projections, retains the parallelism preserving advantages of orthographic projections while overcoming the lack of depth cueing. The basic idea is to retain the parallelism of the projectors but introduce a non-zero angle, γ, be-

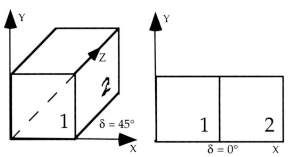

Figure 7.23
Two cavalier projections. Parallel projectors make an angle of γ = 45° with respect to the z-axis. Shown are two of an infinite set of projections as a function of the angle, δ, the angle between the x-axis and the projector projected on the x-y plane.

tween the projectors and the z-axis. The choice of γ determines the scale of the depth encoding of the z dimension. Two standard choices include:

- **Cavalier** – The choice of γ = 45° gives a depth encoding factor of one. That is, the edges of a unit cube normal to the x-y plane will project onto the viewing plane with a length of one unit. Figure 7.23 illustrates two possible cavalier projections of a unit cube located at the origin.

- **Cabinet** – Choosing γ = 26.56° yields a depth encoding factor of one-half. Lines of length L normal to the viewing plane now project with a length $L´ = 0.5\,L$. Two possible cabinet projections are shown in Figure 7.24.

Defining μ as the unit vector parallel to the oblique projectors, we have the following relationships.

$$\mu = a\,i + b\,j + c\,k \qquad [7.33]$$

where
  a,b,c = direction cosines
  i,j,k = unit vectors along (x,y,z) axes.

For cavalier projections, the γ = 45° constraint gives $c = \cos γ = 0.707$. The direction cosines a and b are each arbitrary but constrained by the relationship $a^2 + b^2 = 0.5$. Different cavalier projections are generated by

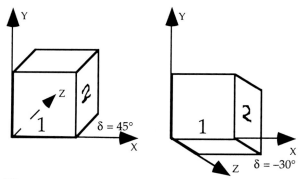

Figure 7.24
Cabinet projections for two different angles, δ.
Note how the z-depth is now encoded by a scale factor of 0.5. Note also how parallel lines project as parallel.

different choices of a and b. A useful angle for specifying these projections is the angle, δ, defined as:

$$\delta = \tan^{-1}\left(\frac{a}{b}\right).$$ [7.34]

This is the angle the vector, d, makes with respect to the x-axis, where d is the component of the unit projector which is perpendicular to the z-axis.

$$d = a\,i + b\,j\,.$$ [7.35]

The only change in this formalism for cabinet projections is to set

$$\frac{d}{c} = \frac{1}{2}\,.$$ [7.36]

This leads to

$$\gamma = \tan^{-1}\left(\frac{d}{c}\right) = 26.56°.$$ [7.37]

A whole family of cabinet projections are generated for various δ angles. Particularly useful choices are 30° and 45°. Figure 7.24 shows cabinet projections for $\delta = 45°$ and $-30°$.

The transformation equations mapping the 3D point, (x,y,z), onto the viewing plane at (x',y'), are:

$$x' = x - \frac{d}{c}\frac{a}{d}z\,,$$ [7.38]

$$y' = y - \frac{d}{c}\frac{b}{d}z\,.$$

These equations may be simplified and put in matrix form as M_2:

$$M_2 = \begin{bmatrix} 1 & 0 & 0 & 0 \\ 0 & 1 & 0 & 0 \\ \dfrac{-a}{c} & \dfrac{-b}{c} & 0 & 0 \\ 0 & 0 & 0 & 1 \end{bmatrix}.$$ [7.39]

Some interesting observations are apparent from comparing Figures 7.23 and 7.24. Both oblique projections correctly encode z-depth information, with cavalier projection having the edge since the encoding is one-to-one. However, all parallel projections distort the perspective image generated by our eyes. Of the two oblique projections, this nonperspective distortion is severe for cavalier projections but much less objectionable for cabinet projections. Cabinet projections provide a compromise between readily decoded depth information and visual realism.

Perspective Projection

Perspective projection provides the most visually realistic transformation of 3D scenes onto 2D viewing planes. Perspective projections mimic the process by which the eye maps world scenes into images on the retina and the process used by a camera in recording images on film. We therefore intuitively recognize images created by perspective projections as "real" or correct and detect those made by other projections as "unnatural" or distorted. The one exception to this general rule are photographs taken by telephoto lenses which closely approximate orthographic parallel projections. These photographs are intuitively interpreted as natural even though virtually no effects of perspective projection are perceptible.

The mathematics of mapping an object point at (x,y,z) into an image point at (x',y') with perspective projection is simply derived from similar triangles shown in Figure 7.25.

The coordinates of the five points indicated in Figure 7.25 are as follows:

$$a \rightarrow (0,y,z) \qquad d \rightarrow (0,0,0)$$
$$b \rightarrow (0,y',0) \qquad e \rightarrow (0,0,z)$$
$$c \rightarrow (0,0,-D)$$

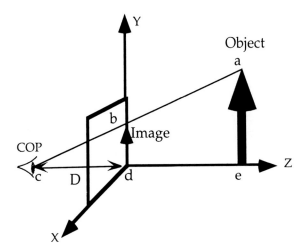

Figure 7.25
Perspective projection of object *ae* onto viewing plane image *bd*. Center of projection (COP) is located on the negative *z*-axis at coordinate $(0,0,-D)$. The viewing plane has the equation, $z = 0$.

Projector *a-b-c* forms the hypotenuse of two similar triangles, *ace* and *bcd*. Setting the tangents of the common angle equal gives:

$$\frac{y'}{D} = \frac{y}{(z+D)}, \qquad [7.40]$$

from which

$$y' = y\,\frac{D}{(z+D)} \qquad [7.41]$$

and

$$y' = y\left(\frac{1}{\frac{z}{D}+1}\right). \qquad [7.42]$$

Similar arguments can be used to show that the x′ coordinate is given as:

$$x' = x\left(\frac{1}{\frac{z}{D}+1}\right), \qquad [7.43]$$

and the trivial result

$$z' = 0. \qquad [7.44]$$

The three transformation equations, 7.42–7.44, can be summarized in homogeneous coordinate representation as $X' = XM_3$, where M_3 is given by

$$M_3 = \begin{bmatrix} S(z) & 0 & 0 & 0 \\ 0 & S(z) & 0 & 0 \\ 0 & 0 & 0 & 0 \\ 0 & 0 & 0 & 1 \end{bmatrix}, \qquad [7.45]$$

and

$$S(z) = \left(\frac{1}{\frac{z}{D}+1}\right) \qquad [7.46]$$

(z-dependent scale factor).

Equation 7.46 emphasizes the most important aspect of perspective projection—the scale factors transforming object coordinates to image coordinates are *depth-dependent*. The *z*-dependence of (x',y') points is the basis for perspective side effects such as the non-parallel projection of parallel lines. The emergence of *vanishing points* arises directly from this side effect. Figure 7.26 illustrates perspective projection and the vanishing point concept.

We conclude the section on projections by a short object lesson on the power of mathematical abstraction. A casual scan of the figures of this section may appear intimidating as new phenomena such as depth encoding and vanishing points are encountered. Without a careful reading of the mathematics it is natural to worry about such unnecessary questions as: How do I pick the vanishing points? How do I set the projection angle, δ? and so on.

The point of the object lesson is that all the subtle and mysterious projection effects presented in this chapter are contained in the three projection matrices, M_1, M_2, and M_3. Applying these matrices to the sets of points defining the world scene generates the various projections and all associated effects. Note in particular the simplicity of the matrices. M_1 (parallel projection) contains nothing except the numeric constants 0 and 1. M_2 (oblique projection) contains only the direction cosines, (a,b,c), specifying the angle of the parallel projectors. M_3 completely specifies perspective projection with two parameters: D, the distance from the origin to the eye, and the variable, z, the depth coordinate of the point being projected. Thus, with two numbers, four constants, and one variable we can compute the three matrices, M_1, M_2, and M_3, which completely specify parallel, oblique, and perspective projections. This is one of the most convincing examples of the power of the homogeneous coordinate representation.

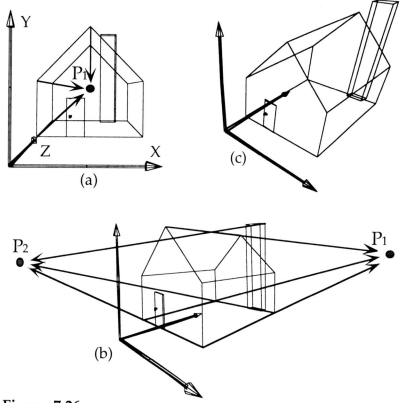

(a)

(c)

(b)

Figure 7.26
Perspective projections. Foreshortening of the z-axis in (a) produces one vanishing point, P_1. Foreshortening the x- and z-axis results in two vanishing points in (b). Adding a y-axis foreshortening in (c) adds an additional vanishing point along the negative y-axis.

Pascal Example –
3D Projections

To illustrate the simplicity of the concepts involved in 3D projections we develop an algorithm, Project, and implement it in Pascal. What criteria and features should we consider in designing a 3D projection algorithm?

- The algorithm should rely on *hierarchical data structures*, as illustrated in Figure 7.10, for representing 3D objects.

- The algorithm should provide options for the *three projection modes* (parallel, oblique, and perspective) described above.

- To observe the behavior of various projection modes it should be possible to view the graphical objects from various viewpoints. This capability is realized by providing *rotation options*.

- To encourage use and the intuition which comes with easy access to 3D object manipulation programs, the algorithm should be equipped with an easy-to-use *graphical user interface (GUI)*.

Figure 7.27 illustrates the implementation of these design specifications. The specific implementation of each feature is discussed in detail below.

Viewing in 3D

As indicated earlier in this chapter, there are two approaches to viewing in 3D. The first involves fixing the COP in a permanent (x,y,z) coordinate system and transforming the coordinates of the world objects to obtain the desired viewpoint and viewing direction. This we consider the fundamental viewing operation, and we have in place all the mathematical formalism necessary for this mode of 3D viewing.

The second, completely equivalent, mode of viewing is the synthetic camera model.

Hierarchical Data Structure

The world scene, consisting of a cube centered at the origin and a tetrahedron on down the z-axis was represented by the twelve points and ten polygons listed in Table 7.2.

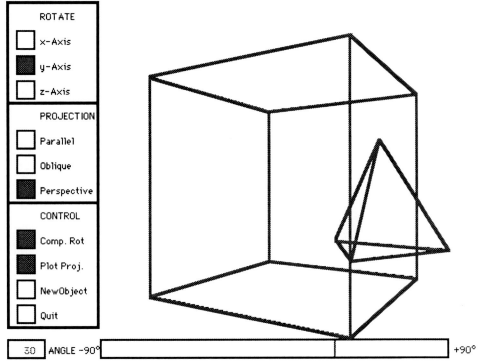

Figure 7.27
Output and graphical user interface of **Project** . Note the hierarchical menu structure with four major functional blocks: ROTATE, PROJECTION, CONTROL, and ANGLE selection. The first three operate as pick devices (selectable by clicking the mouse) and the last as a valuator device (dragging the pointer selects the angle read out in the lower left-hand box).

The first data item is the number of points in the file. Next comes twelve lines of data, each corresponding to a point in the format: Point i, x_i, y_i, z_i. The "10" in line 14 is the number of polygons for which the points form the basis. The last ten lines are the polygon vertex table in the format: polygon number, number of vertices in this polygon, and the vertex (point) numbers constituting that polygon. Note the efficiency that this two-level hierarchy permit—each point is specified only once but can contribute to three or more polygons. Any transformations (rotations, translations, or projections) *involve only the points*. The polygonal structure is preserved through the transformation and rides along through the viewing pipeline, including the final 2D plotting. The program **Project** makes use of a higher-level function to plot the polygons.

Note that no attempt was made to distinguish the two objects in the scene. For complex scenes made from many objects or scenes in which one wishes to manipulate objects individually, it is necessary to maintain an object table with pointers to individual objects. The present table considers the combination of cube + tetrahedron to be one object.

Table 7.2
Data Structure for Cube/Tetrahedron Scene

12	
1 -100 100 100	10
2 100 100 100	1 4 1 2 3 4
3 100 -100 100	2 4 2 8 7 3
4 -100 -100 100	3 4 1 5 8 2
5 -100 100 -100	4 4 1 4 6 5
6 -100 -100 -100	5 4 3 7 6 4
7 100 -100 -100	6 4 5 6 7 8
8 100 100 -100	7 3 9 10 11
9 -100 -100 323.2	8 3 11 10 12
10 0 73.2 273.2	9 3 10 9 12
11 100 -100 323.2	10 3 11 12 9
12 0 -100 150	

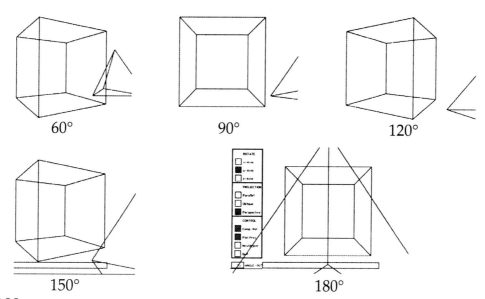

Figure 7.28
Project images of object rotated in 30° increments about the *y*-axis. Note that the tetrahedron, located about 300 units along the *z*-axis originally, swings around and "collides" with the COP (eye) located at z = −300.

ROTATE Module

When one of the *ROTATE* buttons is clicked, it lights up and assigns the appropriate axis of rotation. Clicking a second axis button re-assigns the rotation axis. No actual rotation computation is performed, however, until the *Comp.Rot* button is clicked. Each button remains lit until the *New Object* or *Quit* button is selected. This retains a partial graphical record of the operations performed to date on the object.

The coordinate system used for rotations is the standard graphics system centered in the display window, with *y*-axis pointing up, *x*-axis pointing to the right, and the *z*-axis pointing along the line of sight into the screen. After a few minutes of practice, the user develops an accurate intuition about the behavior of the system and can predict what the resulting image will be before performing the selected rotation. This, in fact, is the primary pedagogical value of programs like **Project**. Figure 7.28 shows a continuing series of 30° rotations about the *y*-axis following the configuration shown in Figure 7.27.

Note the problem of interference of the displayed image of the graphical object and the menu items. Careful clipping to a viewport would eliminate this problem. There are two attractive features of **Project** which Figure 7.28

illustrates. First, it demonstrates graphically the phenomena of an object swinging behind the COP located here at z = −300. The back plane of the tetrahedron extends to z = − 323 for the 180° rotation case.

Secondly, all images in Figure 7.28 were generated by a sequence of two button clicks—*Comp.Rot* and *Plot Proj*. The program remembers the indicated status of *axis = 'y'*, *projector = 'P'*, and *angle = 30* indicated in Figure 7.26 and uses them for all subsequent computations and displays, until the user overwrites them with another selection. All three parameters may be altered at will at any point during a user session.

PROJECTION Module

The purpose of the *PROJECTION* module of the menu is to select the mode of projection. This is accomplished by setting the parameter projector to a character value of ('L', 'O', 'P') for parallel, oblique, and perspective projections, respectively. Upon exiting the *CONTROL* option *Comp.Rot*, this parameter is used to set the projection matrix M equal to M_1, M_2, or M_3 defined in the projection section of this chapter.

The programming of this assignment operation raises an interesting issue of computational efficiency. The issue is this: M_1 and M_2 are completely determined once and for all by the selection of parallel and oblique projection. The optimal strategy for these projections is given by the algorithm:

1. Select *axis* and *angle*, and set $R = R_x$ or R_y or R_z.
2. Select projection and set a projection matrix $P = M_1$ or M_2.
3. Compose the rotation and projection matrix to generate a final matrix $M = RP$.
4. Apply M to all points (x_i, y_i, z_i) to generate (xp_i, yp_i).
5. Reconstruct the transformed polygons from (xp_i, yp_i) and plot.

However, the z-dependence of the perspective projection, M_3, requires a different strategy. We can call this strategy *delayed evaluation*, and it is the basis of the algorithm used in **Project**. We separate the steps of computing the rotation from that of computing the projection by assigning a separate *CONTROL* button to each operation. The actual projection routine assumes a parallel projection matrix, M_1, as default value and modifies it to an oblique projection matrix, M_2, or perspective projection matrix, M_3, as required. By adopting the delayed evaluation strategy, we can treat all three projection modes in an identical manner.

Implementing this strategy in **Project** we follow the algorithm:

1. Select *axis* and angle, and set $R = R_x$ or R_y or R_z.
2. Select projection and assign pointer *projector* to store latest selection.
3. Upon selection of *CONTROL* option, *Comp.Rot*, apply R to present object, (x_i, y_i, z_i), to generate rotated object which is stored back into (x_i, y_i, z_i). This option may be repeated to effect multiple rotations.
4. Upon selection of *Plot Proj. CONTROL* option, use the latest value of *projector* to set $M = M_1, M_2,$ or M_3, and apply it individually to each point (x_i, y_i, z_i) to generate projected points, (xp_i, yp_i).
5. Shift these points to the center of the screen, restructure them as polygons, and plot the polygons.

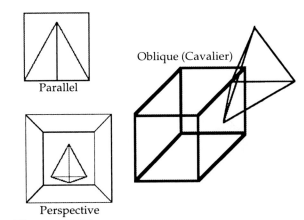

Figure 7.29
Output of **Project** for three different projection modes.

Figure 7.29 shows the output of **Project** for selection of each of the three projection modes with no rotations applied.

The reader can readily verify most of the features of the three projections from this figure. For example, parallel projections give no depth cuing, oblique projections correctly encode the z-depth for lines parallel to the z-axis, and perspective projections involve one or more vanishing points. However, **Project** also provides a useful tool for investigating the properties of projections for "non-textbook" cases, e.g. when planes are not parallel to the viewing plane and edges are not parallel to the z-axis. Figure 7.30 demonstrates non-intuitive difficulties arising from an oblique projection of the scene after a y-axis rotation of $-45°$.

CONTROL Module and GUI

The behavior of the *CONTROL* module is fairly apparent from the listed menu options. *Quit* exits the program and *New Object* opens a query window from which the user can select the hierarchical file specifying a new scene. *Plot Proj.* and *Comp.Rot* have been discussed. However, *Project* contains several helpful graphical user interface features that are not apparent from the figures. These include:

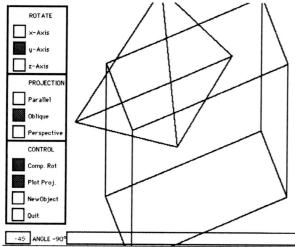

Figure 7.30
Oblique projection of scene following a –45°
rotation. Note how z-depth cuing is confused
because no edges satisfy the criterion of z-axis
parallelism. In fact, it takes considerable
concentra-tion to interpret the flattened parallelepiped as a cube, but it can be done.

- As the user moves the cursor over each
  control button (except the left *ANGLE*
  box), the box border switches from blue to
  magenta to indicate a tentative selection.

- Pressing the mouse button while a control
  button is tentatively selected switches
  the button state to active, causing the
  button to turn solid magenta and selecting
  the desired control option.

- The angle valuator box becomes active
  whenever the cursor is within the box.
  When it is active, a magenta indicator
  bar appears and follows the cursor.

- The *ANGLE* readout box become active
  whenever the angle valuator box is active, and the presently selected angle is
  presented and continuously updated. Any
  desired integer degree reading is easily
  selected. When the cursor leaves the

valuator box, the current angle is locked
in the angle output box and used for subsequent calculations.

- Both the angle valuator and *ANGLE*
  readout box blink while the angle valuator box is selected. This is a helpful side
  effect of the algorithm used to update
  the numerical value and angle indicator
  bar information.

- After a plot has been generated the program pauses (loops) until the mouse button is pressed, after which control is returned to the menu options.

Although these features are not exhaustive,
they do provide a flexible and capable system
for viewing 3D objects in wire frame mode from
any angle with any of the standard projections.
Additional options which would improve performance might include:

- A valuator for selecting D, the COP
  position along the z-axis.

- Capabilities for additional
  transformations, including scaling and
  translation.

- The data structures for decoupling objects
  and manipulating them individually.

- The capability of restoring the initial
  configuration to start a new sequence.

The problem with implementing such extended features lies not only with the additional complexity of the programming involved.
It also involves the steeper learning curve for
potential users. Mastering a 3D object manipulation package easily requires that it be modular and conceptually simple. Each additional
feature extends the range of transformations
possible and increases the difficulty of mastery.
As it stands, Project represents a reasonable
compromise between capability and simplicity.

Pascal Program Project

```
program Project;
{Program to read the X, Y, Z coordinates of      }
{an object and the polygon connectivity information }
{for the object,rotate it repeatedly upon demand  }
{about any axis by N degrees and display the      }
{projected image with a user-selectable projection. }
{All interaction is menu-driven.                  }
  const
    Nctrl = 15;
    nd = 4;
    D = 400;
    a = 0.5;              {Direction Cosines }
    b = 0.5;              {of Oblique Projector}
    c = -0.707;           {for Cavalier projection.}
    rotate = [2, 3, 4];
    projection = [6, 7, 8];
    control = [10, 11, 12, 13];
    draw = [2, 3, 4, 6, 7, 8, 10, 11, 12, 13, 14];
  type
    mat = array[1..4, 1..4] of real;
    vect = array[1..3] of real;
    BoxArray = array[1..Nctrl] of Rect;
  var
    x, y, z: array[1..500] of real;
    xp, yp, zp: array[1..500] of real;
    key: array[1..500] of integer;
    ind: array[1..500, 1..5] of integer;
    npp, shade: array[1..500] of integer;
    box: BoxArray;
    vectIn, vectOut, P, R, M: mat;
    i, j, k, npts, rank, nplanes: integer;
    active, xm, ym, angle: integer;
    done: Boolean;
    axis, projector: char;
    th, dt, Lmag: real;
    window: rect;
    Pt: Point;

{****************** diagmat *********************}
  procedure diagmat (var xmat: mat; nd: integer);
{procedure to generates identity matrix}
    var
      i, j: integer;
    begin
    for i := 1 to nd do
      begin
        for j := 1 to nd do
          xmat[i, j] := 0.0;
        xmat[i, i] := 1.0;
      end;
    end;

{****************** matmlt *********************}
  procedure matmlt (var d, a, b: mat; r, nd: integer);
{Calculates matrix product: D=A*B }
    var
      n, i, j, k: integer;
      sum: real;
```

```
    temp: mat;
    begin
    n := nd;
    for i := 1 to r do
      begin
        for j := 1 to n do
          begin
            sum := 0.0;
            for k := 1 to n do
              sum := sum +
                a[i, k] * b[k, j];
            temp[i, j] := sum;
          end;
      end;
    for i := 1 to r do
      for j := 1 to n do
        d[i, j] := temp[i, j];
    end;

{****************** GetObject ******************}
  procedure getObject;
{Procedure to read hierarchical data structure.}
    var
      filename: string;
      j, i, n, nppp: integer;
      infile: text;
    begin
    reset(infile, OldFileName
        ('File of Input Object?'));
    readln(infile, npts);
    for i := 1 to npts do
      begin
        readln(infile, n, x[i], y[i], z[i]);
      end;
    read(infile, nplanes);
    for i := 1 to nplanes do
      begin
        read(infile, n, nppp);
        for j := 1 to nppp do
          read(infile, ind[n, j]);
        npp[i] := nppp;
      end;
    end;

{************* Set Rotation Matrix *************}
  procedure SetRot (axis: char; degrees: real;
                    nd: integer; var R: mat);
    var
      s, c: real;
      i: integer;
    begin
    th := degrees * 2 * 3.141592654 / 360.0;
    diagMat(R, nd);
    c := cos(th);
    s := sin(th);
    vectIn[1, 4] := 1.0;
    if axis = 'x' then
      begin
        R[2, 2] := c;
        R[3, 3] := c;
        R[2, 3] := s;
```

```
            R[3, 2] := -s;
         end;
      if axis = 'y' then
         begin
            R[1, 1] := c;
            R[3, 3] := c;
            R[1, 3] := -s;
            R[3, 1] := s;
         end;
      if axis = 'z' then
         begin
            R[1, 1] := c;
            R[2, 2] := c;
            R[1, 2] := s;
            R[2, 1] := -s;
         end;
   end;

{******************* Menu  *********************}
  procedure Menu (var box: BoxArray);
{Procedure to draw interactive menu for selecting}
{   • Rotation axis                               }
{   • Rotation angle                              }
{   • Projection Mode                             }
   const
      Nctrl = 15;
      T = 10;
      B = 400;
      L = 1;
      R = 550;
   type
      BoxArray = array[1..Nctrl] of Rect;
   var
      SBox: Rect;
      Top, Bot, Left, Right: Integer;
      CLabel: array[1..Nctrl] of string;
      color: array[1..Nctrl] of LongInt;
      i: integer;
   begin
   for i := 1 to Nctrl do
      color[i] := blueColor;
   color[1] := whiteColor;
   color[5] := whiteColor;
   color[9] := whiteColor;
   color[15] := redColor;
   CLabel[1] := 'ROTATE';
   CLabel[2] := 'x-Axis';
   CLabel[3] := 'y-Axis';
   CLabel[4] := 'z-Axis';
   CLabel[5] := 'PROJECTION';
   CLabel[6] := 'Parallel';
   CLabel[7] := 'Oblique';
   CLabel[8] := 'Perspective';
   CLabel[9] := 'CONTROL';
   CLabel[10] := 'Comp. Rot';
   CLabel[11] := 'Plot Proj.';
   CLabel[12] := 'NewObject';
   CLabel[13] := 'Quit';
   CLabel[15] := 'ANGLE';
                            {Open Drawing Screen}
   SetRect(SBox, L, T, R, B);
```

```
      SetDrawingRect(SBox);
      ShowDrawing;
{Outline Main Menu Sections}
      PenSize(3, 3);
      Top := -15;
      Bot := Top + 104;
      Left := 5;
      Right := 100;
      SetRect(SBox, Left, Top, Right, Bot);
      FrameRect(SBox);
      Top := Bot - 3;
      Bot := Bot + 100;
      SetRect(SBox, Left, Top, Right, Bot);
      FrameRect(SBox);
      Top := Bot - 3;
      Bot := Bot + 125;
      SetRect(SBox, Left, Top, Right, Bot);
      FrameRect(SBox);
{Iterate to produce control buttons}
{ and name boxes.}
      PenSize(2, 2);
      for i := 1 to Nctrl - 2 do
         begin
            Left := 15;
            Right := Left + 20;
            Top := 25 * i - 45;
            Bot := Top + 20;
            SetRect(Box[i], Left, Top,
                  Right, Bot);
            ForeColor(color[i]);
            FrameRect(Box[i]);
            MoveTo(Right + 5, Top + 15);
            ForeColor(blackColor);
            WriteDraw(CLabel[i]);
         end;
      Left := 5;
      Right := Left + 40;
      Top := Bot + 15;
      Bot := Top + 20;
      SetRect(Box[15], Left, Top, Right, Bot);
      ForeColor(color[15]);
      FrameRect(Box[15]);
      MoveTo(Right + 5, Top + 15);
      ForeColor(blackColor);
      WriteDraw(CLabel[15]);
      Move(5, 0);
      WriteDraw('-90°');
      Left := 100;
      Right := 460;
      ForeColor(color[14]);
      SetRect(Box[14], Left, Top, Right, Bot);
      FrameRect(Box[14]);
      MoveTo(Right + 5, Top + 15);
      WriteDraw('180°');
   end;


{************* Apply Rotation  ******************}
  procedure transformRot (R: mat);
{Procedure to apply rotation matrix to all points.}
      var
```

```pascal
      i: integer;
   begin
      for i := 1 to npts do
         begin
            vectIn[1, 1] := x[i];
            vectIn[1, 2] := y[i];
            vectIn[1, 3] := z[i];
            vectIn[1, 4] := 1.0;
            matmlt(vectOut, vectIn, R, 1, nd);
            x[i] := vectOut[1, 1];
            y[i] := vectOut[1, 2];
            z[i] := vectOut[1, 3];
         end;
   end;

{************ Projection transform ************}
   procedure transformView (projector: char);
{Procedrue to apply viewing projection}
{ to all points.}
      var
         i: integer;
   begin
      DiagMat(M, nd);   {Use parallel projection}
      M[3, 3] := 0.0;    {as default.}
      for i := 1 to npts do
         begin
            vectIn[1, 1] := x[i];
            vectIn[1, 2] := y[i];
            vectIn[1, 3] := z[i];
            vectIn[1, 4] := 1.0;

            case projector of
               'O':    {Adjust projection }
                  begin  {matrix for oblique.}
                     M[3, 1] := -a / c;
                     M[3, 2] := -b / c;
                  end;
               'P':    {Compute z-dependent }
                  begin  {scale factor.}
                     M[1, 1] := 1 / (z[i] / D + 1);
                     M[2, 2] := M[1, 1];
                  end;
            end;
            matmlt(vectOut, vectIn, M, 1, nd);
            xp[i] := vectOut[1, 1];
            yp[i] := vectOut[1, 2];
            zp[i] := vectOut[1, 3];
         end;
   end;

{****************** Plot Proj ******************}
   procedure plotProj;
{Procedure to shift points to (xc,yc) of screen, }
{reconstruct polygons from vertex table, and     }
{plot out resulting projected polygons.          }
      const
         xc = 300;
         yc = 200;
      var
         xx, yy: array[1..6] of integer;
         i, j, np, np1: integer;
         zz: array[1..6] of real;
         window: rect;
         triPoly: PolyHandle;
         pat: pattern;
   begin
      penPat(black);
      penSize(2, 2);
      for i := 1 to nplanes do
         begin
            np := i;
            for j := 1 to npp[np] do
               begin
                  zz[j] := zp[ind[np, j]];
                  xx[j] := round(xp[ind[np, j]]) + xc;
                  yy[j] := -round(yp[ind[np, j]]) + yc;
               end;
            np1 := npp[np] + 1;   {Close polygon.}
            xx[np1] := xx[1];
            yy[np1] := yy[1];
            tripoly := OpenPoly; {Open polygon}
            moveto(xx[1], yy[1]);     { structure.}
            for j := 2 to np1 do
               lineto(xx[j], yy[j]);
            closePoly;
            framePoly(tripoly);
         end;
   end;

{* * * * * * * * MAINPROGRAM * * * * * * * * * * * *}
{Program to decode menu selections and jump     }
{to the appropriate worker routines.            }
begin
   done := false;
   DiagMat(M, nd);
   getObject;
   menu(Box);
   repeat     {until done}
      repeat     {Loop until control button pushed.}
         repeat{Loop to highlight}
            GetMouse(Pt);    { active button-box}
            for i := 1 to Nctrl - 1 do
               if i in draw then
                  begin
                     ForeColor(BlueColor);
                     if PtInRect(Pt, Box[i]) then
                        begin
                           active := i;
                           ForeColor(magentaColor)
                        end;
                     FrameRect(Box[i]);
                  end;
            while PtInRect(Pt, Box[14]) do
               begin          {Read angle}
                  GetMouse(Pt);   {box valuator}
                  xm := Pt.h;
                  ym := Pt.v;
                  moveto(xm, box[14].top + 2);
                  forecolor(magentaColor);
                  eraseRect(box[14]);
                  lineto(xm, box[14].bottom - 2);
                  angle := (xm - 100) div 2;
```

```
            moveto(box[15].left,
                box[15].bottom - 5);
            eraseRect(box[15]);
            writeDraw(angle);
            forecolor(blueColor);
            frameRect(box[14]);
            frameRect(box[15]);
          end;
      until Button;
      foreColor(magentaColor);     {Color active}
      paintRect(box[active]);  {button}
      ForeColor(BlueColor);        {Reframe it.}
      FrameRect(Box[active]);
      if active in rotate then        {Assign}
        case active of   { selected axis.}
            2:
              axis := 'x';
            3:
              axis := 'y';
            4:
              axis := 'z';
        end;
      if active in projection then  {Assign }
        case active of   {selected projector.}
            6:
              projector := 'L';   {Parallel case}
            7:
              projector := 'O';   {Oblique case}
            8:
              projector := 'P';   {Perspective}
        end;
    until active in control;
    case active of
        10:       {Concatenate rotations.}
          begin
            setRot(axis, angle, nd, R);
            transformRot(R); {Perform rotation}
          end;
        11:
          begin         {Perform projection}
            transformView(projector);
            PlotProj;
            repeat        {Loop while marveling}
            until button;  {at output.}
            SetRect(Window, 100, 0, 550, 400);
            EraseRect(Window);
          end;
        12:
          begin
            GetObject;
            menu(Box);
          end;
        13:
          done := true;
    end;
  until done;
end.
```

Conclusions

The chapter begins by highlighting new transformations possible in 3D which were undefined in 2D. These include rotation about an arbitrary axis and the parity operations. In addition, the viewing pipeline now requires an additional operation, *projection*, for transforming 3D scenes onto 2D viewing planes. Two modes for viewing 3D scenes from any desired viewpoint includes the fixed world/movable camera and the fixed camera/movable world paradigms. Since the world is easily moved by the homogeneous coordinate formalism, the latter mode was selected for the viewing transformations presented in this chapter.

Before objects can be transformed, however, they must be represented. A range of representations was summarized, and the polyhedral representation high-lighted as a compromise offering simplicity of data structure with reasonable visual realism. The advantage of using hierarchical data structures in scene representations was discussed. Transformations in 3D are provided naturally through extensions of the homogeneous coordinate matrix representation. The only additional complexity arises from the need for three independent rotation matrices for rotations about the three coordinate axes and a seven-matrix composition for rotation about a general axis. Projection was illustrated by describing the three principle classes—parallel, oblique, and perspective—graphically and mathematically. The projection operations are readily formulated as transformation matrices within the homogeneous coordinate representation. The algorithm **Project** was developed to demonstrate the three classes of projections within a user-friendly GUI environment providing three axes of rotation.

Exercises

7.1   Visual realism is the goal for many, but not all, computer graphics images. List and discuss briefly three applications in which the computer origin of the image is unmistakable and a desired attribute of the image.

7.2   Certain objects have a unique parity, that is, a clearly identified right- or left-handedness. List five objects which have unique parity and five others which do not.

7.3   An interesting aspect of projection from 3D world coordinates to 2D viewing coordinates is that it is not a symmetric one-for-one mapping. That is, a given 3D object will always project to a unique image, but a given image may originate from numerous objects. Sketch three different objects which will all project to the same image.

7.4   Two viewing modes were labeled *fixed world/movable camera* and *fixed camera/-movable world*. Which of these two modes seems most intuitive to you? Which would you expect to be computationally simpler? Give reasons for your answers.

7.5   The text suggested that a linear file of (x,y,z) points specifying all points on the surface of an object would be the most concrete possible representation. How might such a file be modified to encode attributes such as color and texture? Can you suggest an even more fundamental representation? (*Hint: How does physics describe objects?*) What are the problems with such concrete models?

7.6   *Wire frame* models represent a compromise between simplicity and visual realism. What are the advantages and disadvantages of wire frame images? How many line segments are required to represent the globe and the camera in Figure 7.6?

7.7   Polyhedral representations are another compromise between visual realism and tractable data structures. A close analogy can be made between the polyhedral representation technique of graphics and the summation approximation to integration in calculus. Discuss this analogy, identifying specifically the analogous quantities and terms in each approach.

7.8   The hierarchical data structures usually associated with polyhedral representations provide a number of computational and efficiency advantages. Discuss some of these and give some numerical comparisons with a non-hierarchical structure.

7.9   The polyhedral approach provides the basis for several of the algorithms for solving the *hidden surface* problem. Speculate on how the polygon structure might be useful for solving this problem.

7.10   The more visually realistic camera shown in Figure 7.11 is based on the polygon representation whose wire frame rendering is shown in Figure 7.6. What additional techniques for enhancing visual realism are apparent in Figure 7.11?

7.11   The translated object in Figure 7.12 appears larger than the original object even though no scaling is involved. Why is that?

7.12   Figure 7.13 illustrates how useful new shapes may be generated by differential scaling of simple original objects. Sketch two other simple original shapes and several useful objects which may be generated from them by differential scaling.

7.13   Rotations, in general, do not commute. That is, $R_x R_y \neq R_y R_x$. Prove this by a sketch comparing the results of $R_x R_y$ applied to some nonsymmetric object to the results of applying $R_y R_x$ to the same object, using $\theta = 90°$.

7.14   Show mathematically that $R_x R_y \neq R_y R_x$ by letting $R_x(\theta)$ and $R_y(\phi)$ operate on vector $(x,y,z,1)$ in each order.

7.15   The text claims that both the simple mirror transformation, S_x, and the parity transformation, S_{xyz}, convert right- to lefthanded systems. Prove this with a sketch of a right hand to which you apply both S_x and S_{xyz} and comparing the results. What rotation was necessary to produce identical left hand images?

7.16   Write down the matrix, Sh_x, for an x-shear with $a = b = 0.5$. Sketch the result of applying this shear to a cylinder whose base is at the origin and lies in the y-z plane.

7.17   Verify through matrix multiplication that the Table 7.1 parameters of the M^{-1} matrices do indeed yield matrices which are the inverses of the M matrices.

7.18   Two variations to the algorithm for rotation about an arbitrary axis illustrated in Figure 7.17 involves step 4 rotations of $R_x(\theta)$ and $R_z(\theta)$. Write down the seven-matrix concatenated Ms which will produce the desired rotations (see Equation 7.30). Are these concatenations unique or are they equivalent variations?

7.19   Figure 7.20 illustrating the analogy between slide projection and graphical image projection is only a mnemonic—an aid to memory. The configuration of light rays in an actual slide projector differ significantly from Figure 7.20(a). Sketch the actual configuration of rays (a physics textbook is a good reference for this problem).

7.20   Most science and engineering texts use right-handed coordinate systems. Most computer graphics texts, however, use a left-handed system in discussing projection. Why?

7.21   Parallel and oblique images are both distorted compared to the perspective images produced by cameras and our eyes. Why, then, are they useful?

7.22   What z-encoding factor would the choice of an oblique projection angle $\gamma = 30°$ produce?

7.23   What is the main difference between perspective projections on the one hand and the two parallel projections on the other? How does this difference effect the projection process computationally?

7.24   Assuming that the wall and floor planes of the house in Figure 7.26(b) are parallel with the corresponding xy-, xz-, and yz-planes, prove that the vanishing points

P_1 and P_2 lie along the z- and x-axis, respectively.

7.25   How would you extend the hierarchical data structure of Table 7.2 to include each object as a distinct item? Will your proposed data structure accommodate scenes with an arbitrary number of objects?

7.26   List five additional features your would propose for the **Project** program and rank them in order of: a) value for a friendly and useful GUI, and b) programming complexity.

Endnotes

1.   Tufte, Edward R., *Envisioning Information*, p. 12, Graphics Press, Cheshire, CN (1990).
2.   Fiume, Eugene L., *The Mathematical Structure of Raster Graphics*, Academic Press, Inc., Harcourt Brace Jovanovich, Publishers, Boston, MA (1989).
3.   Rogers, David F. and Adams, J. Alan, "Three Dimensional Transformations and Projections," from *Mathematical Elements for Computer Graphics*, McGraw-Hill Book Company (1976), reprinted in *Tutorial: Computer Graphics*, John C. Beatty and Kellogg S. Booth (eds), IEEE Computer Society Press, pp. 256–269, Piscataway, NJ (1982).
4.   Burger, Peter and Gillies, Duncan, *Interactive Computer Graphics*, Addison-Wesley Publishing Company, Wokingham, UK (1990).

Chapter 8

Three-Dimensional Graphics –
Geometric Modeling and Visibility

...the single application in our industry that continues to hold the most
fascination for advanced computer users not to mention the most potential
benefit for mankind, is scientific visualization.
Phil LoPiccolo, Editor, Computer Graphicx World

We introduced three-dimensional graphics with very concrete examples of how 3D objects may be represented, manipulated, and displayed by projecting 3D world coordinates onto a 2D viewing surface. As in all areas of computer science, 3D graphics is subject to trade-offs along the concrete/abstract spectrum. The concrete examples illustrated in the last chapter have the virtue of simplicity and clarity but suffer from limitations intrinsic in the choice of polyhedral representations. Many of these limitations are overcome by moving to more abstract representations. Several of the more abstract representations for geometric modeling are presented in this chapter.

The second main emphasis of the chapter considers implementation issues of 3D clipping and hidden surface removal. These operations greatly improve the visual realism of the image and may be considered refinements inserted in the viewing pipeline.

Geometric Modeling

The polyhedral representation is capable of displaying a 3D object to any degree of accuracy. While this is true theoretically, in practice polyhedral representation may require such a vast database of polygons that it overwhelms available computing capability. This computational limitation is one factor suggesting alter-native representations for modeling geometric objects.

A second factor encouraging us to seek a less restrictive representation arises from the "natural" shape of objects. Most manufactured objects and many natural objects are better modeled by combinations of curved surfaces than by combinations of polygons. Many other natural objects are better modeled by fractal curves and surfaces than by combinations of polygons. In this section we outline techniques for representing curved surfaces and manipulating the objects constructed by these curved surfaces. In a later chapter we consider fractal geometry.

All alternative techniques in geometric modeling represent of a higher level of abstraction than that of the polyhedral technique. More abstraction means simply that "we are saying more with less." That is, the goal of abstraction in geometric modeling is to define the shape of objects with the smallest possible set of numbers. This is possible by having a "theory" about the objects, that is, an assumed relationship between the coordinates on the surface of the object. The information defining the shape of the object then resides in some combination of the functional form of this relationship and the parameters controlling the functions.

The first technique for more accurately modeling 3D objects is a straightforward extension of the parametric curve approach introduced in the 2D discussion. For an excellent survey of a variety of geometric modeling techniques, see Mortensen.[1]

Parametric Surfaces

In the chapter on 2D representation we saw that parametric curves provided an enormous gain in *expressiveness* at a very low cost in the number of required parameters. That is, with a relatively few control points we could design curves of any shape we desired.

Since a surface is a 2D structure occupying a 3D space, we need to extend our parametric representation as follows:

- Increase the number of parameters from one, (*t*), to two, (*s,t*), in order to address each point in the 2D surface.

- Express the 3D structure of the curved 2D surface by introducing a parametric z coordinate, $z(s,t)$.

These extensions are summarized by the equations,

$$x = f_x(s,t) , \qquad\qquad [8.1]$$
$$y = f_y(s,t) ,$$
$$z = f_z(s,t) .$$

That part of the surface generated from $0 \le s \le 1$ and $0 \le t \le 1$ is called a *patch*. The vector form of this point on the parametric surface is given by

$$P(s,t) = i\,x + j\,y + k\,z , \qquad [8.2]$$

where
    (x, y, z) = given by Equation 8.1
and
    (i, j, k) = unit vectors.

As an example of how 3D objects may be uniquely specified parametrically, consider the following definition of a sphere:

$$x = x_c + R \sin \pi s \cos 2\pi t, \qquad [8.3]$$
$$y = y_c + R \sin \pi s \sin 2\pi t,$$
$$z = z_c + R \cos \pi s,$$

where
    R = radius of sphere,
    (x_c, y_c, z_c) = coordinates of center of sphere,
    $(t,s) \to (\theta, \phi)$ of spherical coordinates.

Similarly, a circular cylinder is defined parametrically as:

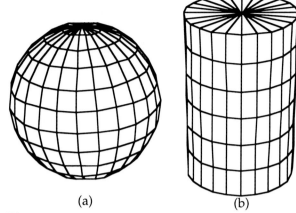

(a)   (b)

Figure 8.1
Parametric 3D objects with isoparametric curves.
    a)   Sphere with 24 *t* and 12 *s* intervals
    b)   Cylinder with 24 *t* and 6 *s* intervals.

$$x = x_c + R \cos 2\pi t, \qquad\qquad [8.4]$$
$$y = y_c + R \sin 2\pi t,$$
$$z = z_c + s,$$

where
    R = radius of circle,
    (x_c, y_c, z_c) = coordinates of center of circle
                       generating the cylinder,
    $(t, s) \to (\theta, z)$ of cylindrical coordinates.

These objects with several isoparametric curves are shown in Figure 8.1.

The simplicity and symmetry of the regular geometric objects of Figure 8.1 permit a parametric representation of the complete object in terms of simple linear and trigonometric functions. The complexity of many objects of interest in computer graphics, however, forces us to consider more complex parametric representations.

Bicubic Surface Patches

In our discussion of 2D curve representation we observed that cubic polynomials provided an effective compromise offering power and flexibility at a relatively small cost in mathematical complexity. This approach is readily extended to 3D with similar cost/benefit advantages. The general polynomial form for points in the surface of the bicubic patch is given as:

$$x(s,t) = \begin{aligned} & c_{11}\,s^3\,t^3 && + c_{12}\,s^3\,t^2 && + c_{13}\,s^3\,t && + c_{14}\,s^3 \\ & + c_{21}\,s^2\,t^3 && + c_{22}\,s^2\,t^2 && + c_{23}\,s^2\,t && + c_{24}\,s^2 \\ & + c_{31}\,s\,t^3 && + c_{32}\,s\,t^2 && + c_{33}\,s\,t && + c_{34}\,s \\ & + c_{41}\,t^3 && + c_{42}\,t^2 && + c_{43}\,t && + c_{44}\,, \end{aligned}$$

and
$$y(s,t) = d_{11}\,s^3\,t^3 + \ldots + d_{44},$$
$$z(s,t) = e_{11}\,s^3\,t^3 + \ldots + e_{44},$$
[8.5]

where

c_{ij}, d_{ij}, e_{ij} = coefficients of polynomials fixed by control points.

Just as with 2D curves, 3D patches may use a variety of control strategies, including Bézier, Hermite, and B-Spline bases. Recall that Bézier curves required four control points with the end points controlling the curve position and the two inner points controlling the tangent vector at the end points. Bézier patches extend this control strategy in a logical fashion using sixteen control points. The four corner points control the position of the patch and lie on its surface. The intermediate twelve points control the tangents to the patch along the edges and at each corner and may be used by the designer to "pull" the surface of the patch into the shape desired.

The sixteen control points form a polyhedral surface which serves as the convex hull that will always completely contain the resulting smoothly curved patch. One example of a Bézier control point polyhedral surface is shown in Figure 8.2.

The Bézier form of the bicubic parametric patch has a very concise matrix formulation specifying a vector point, $P(s,t)$, on the surface in terms of the sixteen control points, $P_{00}, \ldots P_{33}$. This relationship is expressed as:

$$P(s,t) = S\,B\,P\,B^T\,T^T,$$ [8.6]

where
$$S = [s^3\ s^2\ s\ 1],$$
(s parameter row vector)

$$B = \begin{bmatrix} -1 & 3 & -3 & 1 \\ 3 & -6 & 3 & 0 \\ -3 & 3 & 0 & 0 \\ 1 & 0 & 0 & 1 \end{bmatrix},$$ [8.7]

(Bézier coefficient matrix)

$$P = \begin{bmatrix} P_{00} & P_{01} & P_{02} & P_{03} \\ P_{10} & P_{11} & P_{12} & P_{13} \\ P_{20} & P_{21} & P_{22} & P_{23} \\ P_{30} & P_{31} & P_{32} & P_{33} \end{bmatrix},$$ [8.8]

(Control point matrix)

$$B^T = \text{Transposed } B \text{ matrix} \quad [8.9]$$
(Switch rows and columns)

$$T^T = \begin{bmatrix} t^3 \\ t^2 \\ t \\ 1 \end{bmatrix}.$$ [8.10]

(Transposed t parameter vector)

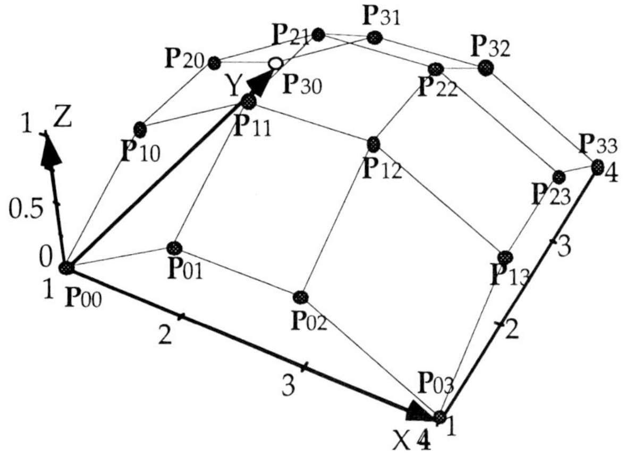

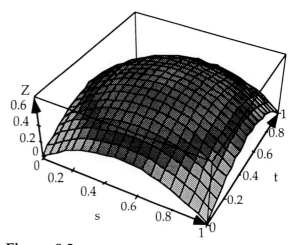

Figure 8.2
Control points for bicubic, Bézier patch. The four corner points anchor the patch and will lie in its surface. The inner twelve points "pull" on the surface and control its shape in exactly the same way the inner two points control 2D Bézier curves.

Figure 8.3
Bicubic Bezier patch corresponding to control points shown in Figure 8.2. Note the change in z-scale due to the curve being pulled, but not reaching the top four control points at z = 1.0.

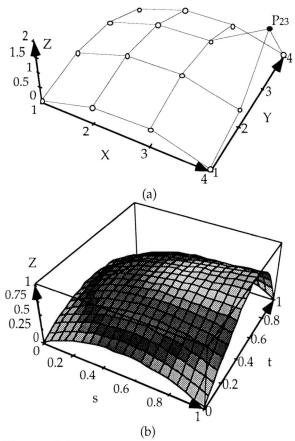

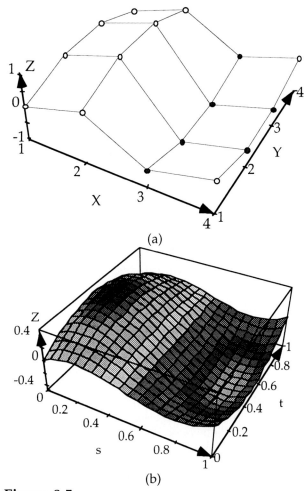

Figure 8.4
Effects of variation of single control point.
a) Control points with P_{23} moved from $z = 0.5$ to $z = 2.0$.
b Resulting bicubic Bézier patch. Color coding of z elevation, shown as shading, helps visualize the range of influence of the control point modification.

The control points of the P matrix shown in Figure 8.2 lie on a square x-y grid, four units on a side. The z values of the corners is zero, the eight middle edge points have z = 0.5, and the four center points have z = 1.0. Substituting these values into Equation 8.6 and multiplying out gives a simple set of parameters for the bicubic Bézier patch:

$$c_{34} = d_{43} = 3.0 \qquad c_{44} = d_{44} = 1.0$$
$$e_{34} = 1.5 \qquad e_{24} = -1.5 \qquad [8.11]$$
$$e_{43} = 1.5 \qquad e_{42} = -1.5$$

and all other c_{ij}, d_{ij}, and e_{ij}s = 0.

Figure 8.5
More complex bicubic Bézier patch. The last two rows of the P point matrix have been given negative values for non-zero elements.
a) Control points. Negative z points are solid; positive are circles.
b) Resulting bicubic patch. Note sinusoid-like shape which results from non-zero third-order coefficients for the s parameter.

Plotting the resulting parametric equation produces the smooth, parametric surface shown in Figure 8.3.
Now, to demonstrate that surface patches do respond to changes in the control points, let's vary one of the edge points, changing its z-value from $0.5 \rightarrow 2.0$. Figure 8.4 illustrates the effect of modifying a single point.
The example above illustrates how the moving of a single control point can significantly modify the shape of the parametric surface. Since there are sixteen points to manipulate, the user has a tool of

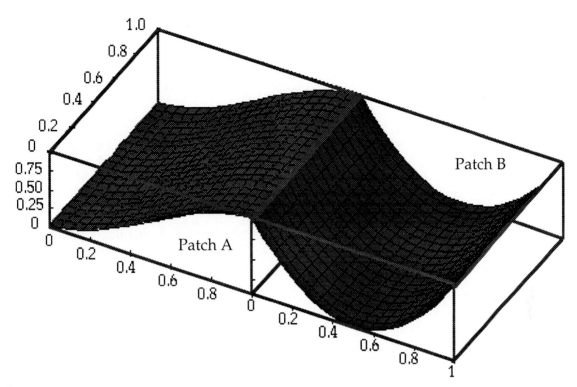

Figure 8.6
Splicing two patches together with C^0 continuity but not C^1 continuity. That is, the surfaces are seamless but not smooth across the transition.

considerable power for sculpting the 3D surface shape desired. By changing the sign of the control points in the last two rows of the point control matrix, for instance, we can generate the surface shown in Figure 8.5.

The parametric representation of the bicubic patch of Figure 8.5 (b) can be obtained by multiplying out the matrices in equation 8.6 and is represented as:

$$
\begin{aligned}
x(s,t) &= 1.0 + 3.0\,s, & \text{[8.12]} \\
y(s,t) &= 1.0 + 3.0\,t, \\
z(s,t) &= 0. + 1.5\,s - 4.5\,s^2 + 3.s^3 \\
&\quad + 1.5\,t - 9\,s^2\,t + 6\,s^3\,t \\
&\quad - 1.5\,t^2 + 9\,s^2\,t^2 - 6\,s^3\,t^2.
\end{aligned}
$$

As one might expect, the more complex patch now requires cubic terms in the s parameter. Quadratic terms (order 2) are still adequate in the t parameter.

Modeling complex surfaces

As indicated by the figures above, bicubic Bézier patches provide an excellent interactive tool for modeling smooth curved surfaces. However, in many applications it is necessary to model more detail than can be provided by a single patch. Two options available to the user needing to model more complexity include a) using a set of connected Bézier patches or b) turning to a more complex repre-sentation. Let's consider option a) first.

Two critical aspects of connecting Bézier patches, the seamlessness and smoothness of the connection, may be specified as C^0 and C^1, indicating continuity of the surface itself and continuity in the first derivatives. Continuity of the surface joins of patch A and patch B is achieved by setting the first row of the P matrix of B equal to the last row of the P matrix of A. In Figure 8.6 we show the results of joining surface A, defined by P_A to surface B, defined by surface P_B, where:

$$P_{zA} = \begin{bmatrix} 0 & 0 & 0 & 0 \\ 0 & 0 & 0 & 0 \\ 1 & 1 & 1 & 1 \\ 1 & 1 & 1 & 1 \end{bmatrix} \qquad [8.13]$$

(Patch A control point matrix),

$$P_{zB} = \begin{bmatrix} 1 & 1 & 1 & 1 \\ 0 & 0 & 0 & 0 \\ 0 & 0 & 0 & 0 \\ 1 & 1 & 1 & 1 \end{bmatrix} \qquad [8.14]$$

(Patch B control point matrix).

Clearly the patches in Figure 8.6 are continuous, but the transition from patch A to patch B is not smooth along their adjoining edge. In order to obtain a smooth transition, the slope of the patches must be continuous along the joining curve. This is achieved by adjusting the third row of P_A and the second row of P_B to assure that each set of four points (three, actually) $[P_{20A}, P_{30A}, P_{10B}, P_{20B}]$ are colinear. By adjusting P_B in Equation 8.15, a smooth connection results between patch A and patch B as illustrated in Figure 8.7.

$$P_{zB} = \begin{bmatrix} 1 & 1 & 1 & 1 \\ 1 & 1 & 1 & 1 \\ 1 & 1 & 1 & 1 \\ 0 & 0 & 0 & 0 \end{bmatrix} \qquad [8.15]$$

(Modified patch B matrix).

For even more complex modeling involving multiple Bézier patches, it has been shown that both C^0 and C^1 continuity are achieved by making the eight control points surrounding the common corner point coplanar. This constraint makes good sense intuitively and is relatively easy to implement computationally.

Figures 8.5–8.7 illustrate why bicubic Bézier patches have become such a popular tool for surface modeling. The obvious advantages include:

- *Ease of interactivity* – The control point effects are readily observed and understood, and the control points themselves are easily modified, either numerically or via interactive devices such as mice and data tablets.

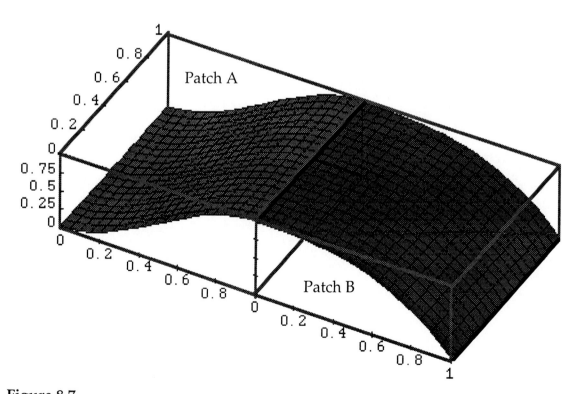

Figure 8.7
Splicing Bézier patches to achieve both C^0 and C^1 continuity. Note the fortuitous similarity of the surface to an automobile body design, the task for which Bézier patches were invented.

- *Representational efficiency* – Complex surfaces are represented by a very small set of numbers. Figure 8.5, for instance, requires only fourteen coefficients, and the double patch surfaces of Figures 8.6 and 8.7 require only eleven and ten coefficients, respectively.

We conclude the discussion of bicubic Bézier patches (sometimes called the tensor product approach) with the following observation on the power of abstraction. The matrix representation of parametric surfaces given by equation 8.6 is much more abstract than the simple polygonal surfaces described in the last chapter. The benefits of flexibility and expressiveness achieved by this abstraction, however, far outweigh the increased mathematical complexity.

Other Bicubic Parametric Bases

The sixteen control point basis proposed by automotive engineer Bézier is just one of a number of different representations of parametric surfaces. Among the most popular of these are B-splines, beta-splines,[2] and the Hermite form of the bicubic surface.

Hermite Form

The Hermite formulation is a generalization of *Coons' patches*, a modeling approach developed by Steven Coons for the Ford Motor Company.[3] The Hermite form can be expressed in a tensor product similar to the Bézier form given in Equation 8.6.

$$P(s,t) = S\,H\,P\,H^T\,T^T, \qquad [8.16]$$

where
S and T = parameter vectors defined in Equation 8.6

$$H = \begin{bmatrix} 2 & -2 & 1 & 1 \\ -3 & 3 & -2 & -1 \\ 0 & 0 & 1 & 0 \\ 1 & 0 & 0 & 0 \end{bmatrix}, \qquad [8.17]$$

(Hermite coefficient matrix)

$$P = \begin{bmatrix} P_{00} & P_{01} & P_{00}^{t} & P_{01}^{t} \\ P_{10} & P_{11} & P_{10}^{t} & P_{11}^{t} \\ P_{00}^{s} & P_{01}^{s} & P_{00}^{st} & P_{01}^{st} \\ P_{10}^{s} & P_{11}^{s} & P_{10}^{st} & P_{11}^{st} \end{bmatrix}, \qquad [8.18]$$

(Geometric matrix)

where

$P_{00} = P(s{=}0,t{=}0)$,   First anchor point
$P_{01} = P(s{=}0,t{=}1)$,   Second anchor point
$P_{10} = P(s{=}1,t{=}0)$,   Third anchor point
$P_{11} = P(s{=}1,t{=}1)$,   Fourth anchor point

$$P_{00}^{t} = \frac{\partial P(s{=}0,t{=}0)}{\partial t},$$
$\quad$ = Tangent vector along t at point 1
$\dots$
$$P_{11}^{t} = \frac{\partial P(s{=}1,t{=}1)}{\partial t},$$
$\quad$ = Tangent vector along t at point 4

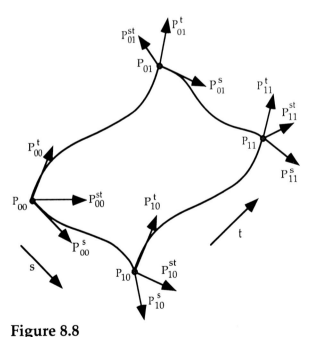

Figure 8.8
Control vectors of bicubic Hermite parametric patch. Functions of vectors include:
Control points (solid circles)
Tangent vectors along t (Pt00, ..., Pt11)
Tangent vectors along s (Ps00, ..., Ps11)
Twist vectors (Pst00, ..., Pst11)

$$P_{00}^s = \frac{\partial P(s=0,t=0)}{\partial s},$$

$$= \text{Tangent vector along } s \text{ at point 1}$$

...

$$P_{11}^s = \frac{\partial P(s=1,t=1)}{\partial s},$$

$$= \text{Tangent vector along } s \text{ at point 4}$$

$$P_{00}^{st} = \frac{\partial^2 P(s=0,t=0)}{\partial s \partial t},$$

$$= \text{Twist vector at point 1}$$

...

$$P_{11}^{st} = \frac{\partial^2 P(s=1,t=1)}{\partial s \partial t}.$$

$$= \text{Twist vector at point 4}$$

The geometrical interpretation of these sixteen control vectors is shown in Figure 8.8. The vectors of the geometry matrix, P, can be divided into four classes of vectors with four vectors per class.

- **Anchor points**: P_{00} ... P_{11} – These four points specify the corners of the bicubic Hermite patch and will lie on the curved surface.

- **Tangent vectors along** t: P_{00}^t ... P_{11}^t – These four vectors specify the partial derivative with respect to parameter t of the surface patch at points P_{00} ... P_{11}. The geometric meaning of P_{00}^t is the following: Move to P_{00} and define this as point 1; then increment t by a very small amount while keeping s constant and move to that point on the surface specified by the new parameter setting. Call this point 2. P_{00}^t is the vector from point 1 to point 2.

- **Tangent vectors along** t: P_{00}^s ... P_{11}^s – These four vectors specify the partial derivative of the surface patch at points P_{00} ... P_{11} with respect to parameter s.

- **Twist vectors** P_{00}^{st} ... P_{11}^{st} – These four vectors specify how far one moves along the parametric surface at each of the four corner points as both s and t are incremented. They are a measure of the corkscrew-like behavior of the surface in the vicinity of the corner points.

Some of the interesting characteristics of bicubic Hermite patches and the control strategies for molding them include the following.

- The four bounding curves are standard Hermite cubic curves and are determined completely by the two end points and two tangent vectors at each end point.

- With the four corner points and bounding curves fixed, the interior shape of the patch may be manipulated by varying the twist vectors. The special case of a bicubic Hermite patch with twist vectors equal to zero is called a *Ferguson patch*.[4]

- An optimal control strategy for molding Hermite patches is to view the control points and vectors from two or more views and drag the control points and ends of the tangent and twist vectors to achieve the desired patch shape.

- Continuity of a multipatch surface is easily achieved by specifying the tangent and twist vectors to be colinear.

Superquadrics

The critical reader will appreciate the increase in representational power that bicubic paramatric patches provide in comparison to more concrete representations such as polyhedrons described previously. The gain in flexibility and expressiveness is paid for by an increase in the level of abstraction and the complexity of the mathematical machinery required to build a model from control points. The nearly universal adoption of Bézier surface representation by automobile body designers indicates that the costs in complexity are well worth the benefits bicubic patches provide.

This exercise suggests that extending the level of abstraction even further may lead to even more powerful modeling tools. *Superquadrics* provide an exceedingly simple yet elegant step in this direction.[5] Superquadrics are easily understood as a minor reformulation of the parametric representation of a sphere given in Equations 8.2–8.3 with the addition of two exponential *shape parameters*, e_1 and e_2. A superquadric is a closed surface traced out by the vector, $P(s,t) = [x\ y\ z]$, as s and t vary in the range $-\pi/2 \leq t \leq \pi/2$ and $0 \leq s \leq 2\pi$.

$$P(s,t) = [(C_t^{e_1} C_s^{e_2})\ (C_t^{e_1} S_s^{e_2})\ (S_t^{e_1})] \qquad [8.19]$$

where

$C_t = \cos t$ (t = angle of latitude)
$S_s = \sin s$ (s = angle of longitude)
e_1, e_2 = shape parameters

The (s,t) parameters are closely related to the conventional polar coordinates, (ϕ, θ), which may be obtained by:

$$\theta = 90° - t \qquad\qquad [8.20]$$
$$\phi = s$$

Computationally, Equation 8.19 must be further refined before it will generate real numbers for plotting routines. In particular, when the user selects noninteger shape parameters e_1, e_2, a straightforward calculation with Equation 8.19 will generate imaginary components for negative values of the sin and cos functions. To suppress

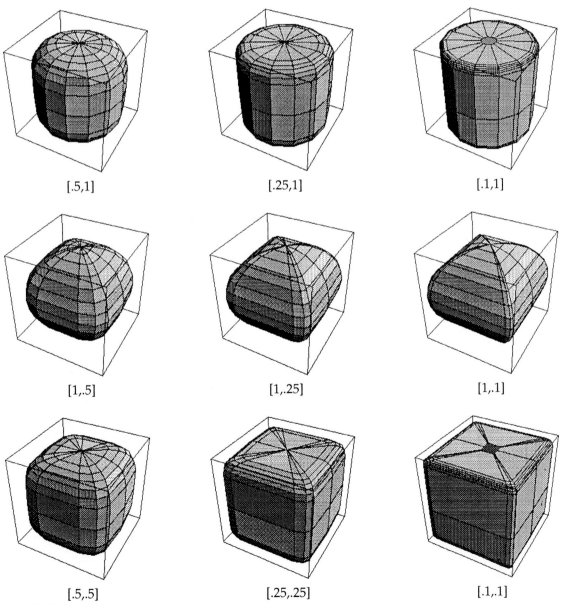

[.5,1]   [.25,1]   [.1,1]

[1,.5]   [1,.25]   [1,.1]

[.5,.5]   [.25,.25]   [.1,.1]

Figure 8.9
Three families of superquadrics and associated shape parameters.

this problem, we have made the following replacements:

$$(\cos t)^{e1} \rightarrow Sign(\cos t)\,(Abs(\cos t))^{e1} \quad [8.21]$$

and so on.

For $(e_1,e_2) = (1,1)$, the parametric equation for the superquadric [8.19] reduces to an equivalent of Equation 8.3 with a resulting parametric spherical object identical to that shown in Figure 8.1. However, most interesting and useful things happen as we begin to vary the shape parameters, e_1,e_2. If we hold e_1 equal to 1 while turning e_2 down from 1 to zero, the superquadric gradually transforms itself from a sphere into a closed cylindrical can. If we hold e_2 equal to 1 while turning e_1 down from 1 to zero, the superquadric transfigures from a sphere into a curved "pin cushion." Finally, if we simultaneously turn both

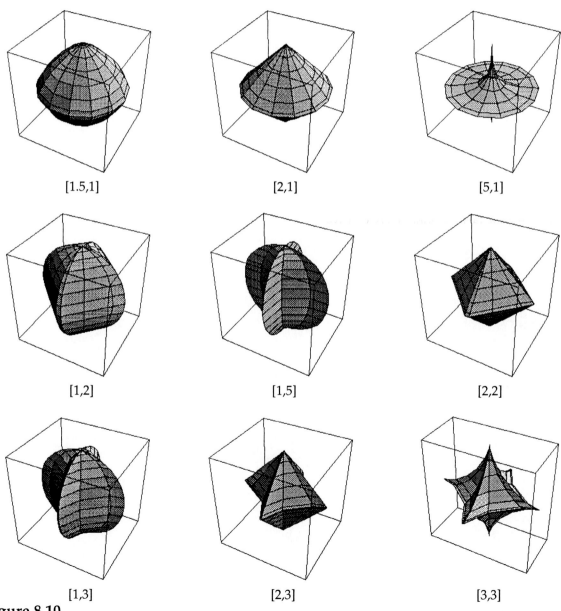

[1.5,1]   [2,1]   [5,1]

[1,2]   [1,5]   [2,2]

[1,3]   [2,3]   [3,3]

Figure 8.10
Examples of superquadrics with $[e_1,e_2] \geq 1$.

e_1 and e_2 down towards zero, the superquadric evolves into a cube. These three families of solids are illustrated in Figure 8.9.

Although the metamorphosis illustrated for shape parameters $(e_1, e_2) \leq 1$ are fascinating, superquadric families associated with $(e_1, e_2) > 1$ are even more intriguing. Figure 8.10 shows examples from these families.

It is quite remarkable that a single representation with only two free parameters is capable of such a range of solid shape descriptions. These families of superquadrics provide an efficient basis of primitive solid shapes for modeling more complex scenes.

Extensions of Superquadrics

The first natural extension of the superquadric representation is to introduce three independent scale factors for the x, y, and z directions. This leads to the parametric equation for the point vector,

$$P(s,t) = [(a_x C_t^{e_1} C_s^{e_2}) \ (a_y C_t^{e_1} S_s^{e_2}) \ (a_z S_t^{e_1})] ,$$

$$[8.22]$$

where

a_x, a_y, a_z = scale factors along the (x,y,z) axes.

Another function that is valuable for computing properties such as the visibility and shading of the superquadric surface at parametric point (s,t) is the vector normal to the surface at that point. This vector, $N(s,t)$, is given in terms of the parameter of [8.20] as:

$$N(s,t) = [(\frac{1}{a_x} C_t^{2-e_1} C_s^{2-e_2})$$
$$(\frac{1}{a_y} C_t^{2-e_1} S_s^{2-e_2})$$
$$(\frac{1}{a_z} S_t^{2-e_1})].$$

$$[8.23]$$

The second extension to superquadrics is to add the ability to mold and distort the primitive through an interactive 3D display. Barr[6] and Pentland[7] have each described such systems. Pentland's program, *SuperSketch,* can stretch, bend, taper, and twist any of the superquadric primitives or composite objects built from primitives. This is a powerful and efficient technique for modeling natural forms, and Pentland shows a reasonably accurate model of a human head composed of only thirteen primitives specified by less than one

hundred bytes of information. A complete human body can be modeled by approximately three hundred bytes of information.

The third extension of superquadrics is the ability to construct composite objects using Boolean operations such as AND and NOT on more primitive component objects. This capability generally goes under the title of *constructive solid geometry* in the CAD field and is the topic to which we turn next.

Constructive Solid Geometry

Constructive solid geometry (CSG) was invented by Requicha, Voelcker, and their coworkers at the University of Rochester in the late 1970s.[8] The basic concept of CSG is to use regularized Boolean operators such as union (OR), intersect (AND), and difference (AND + NOT) acting on primitive solids to construct more complex solids.

CSG Primitives

This "building-block geometry" approach begins with a set of primitive solid objects such as the block, sphere, cylinder, cone, torus, and wedge shown in Figure 8.11. Each of these primitives is easily described by a small set of user-defined parameters specifying the primitive's geometry, location, and orientation.

In CAD of manufactured products, great care is spent on the details of rounding sharp corners to produce objects of greater beauty and eliminate safety hazards. This rounding usually involves slicing off corners with a plane—chamfer—or smoothing corners with an arc—fillets. These processes are easily carried out with CSG techniques applied to some of the sharp-cornered primitive solids of Figure 8.11. However, this two-stage process can be simplified by substituting primitives with parametrically-smoothed edges and corners—namely, superquadrics. Since superquadrics are well-defined mathematical objects, it is a straightforward task to determine their geometry (extent), location, and orientation and use them to augment the library of primitive solids shown in Figure 8.11.

Figure 8.11
Standard primitive solids used in constructive solid geometry.

CSG Boolean Operations

The three Boolean functions most useful in CSG are *union, intersect,* and *difference.* These Boolean functions operate on solids in much the same fashion that the Boolean operators OR (+), AND (*), and AND NOT operate on ordinary Boolean variables. Let's examine each of these operations to understand how they can be used to build complex models from primitive solids.

Union

The *union* of object A and object B is the object obtained by the spatial OR of the two input objects. That is, we can define X to be the union of A and B with the regularized Boolean operator, $\cup$, as:

$$X = A \cup B . \qquad [8.24]$$

The "spatial OR" interpretation of union follows from the functional definition: if a point in space is contained in either object A OR object B, then it is contained in object X. Since X represents the "sum" of its two constituent objects, either constituent could have been picked first. This leads to the conclusion that the union operation is commutative.

$$A \cup B = B \cup A . \qquad [8.25]$$

The operation of union is the most easily visualized and understood of the three regularized Boolean operations on solids and is illustrated in Figure 8.12

Intersection

The *intersection* of object A and object B is the object obtained by the spatial AND of the two constituent objects. That is, we say that a point is contained in the intersection of A and B if the point is contained in object A AND in object B. The mathematical form stating that X is the intersection of A with B is:

$$X = A \cap B . \qquad [8.26]$$

Again, by symmetry arguments, it is clear that the intersection operation is commutative.

$$A \cap B = B \cap A . \qquad [8.27]$$

The intersection operation is useful in designing simple objects not available in the library of primitive solids. For instance, if the library contained "box" but not "wedge," we could easily design a wedge by the intersection of two boxes as indicated in Figure 8.13. Similarly, a spherical lens is generated by the intersection of two spheres with centers offset by something less than a radius.

Difference

The regularized Boolean difference operation is analogous to the operation of AND NOT in Boolean set theory. We say that an object X is the difference between A and B if every point in X is contained in A AND NOT contained in B. The mathematical symbol used to introduce the concept of regularized Boolean difference was the "–*" which we shall simplify to a standard minus sign.

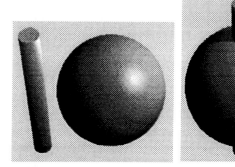

Figure 8.12
The *union* of primitive solids in constructive solid geometry.

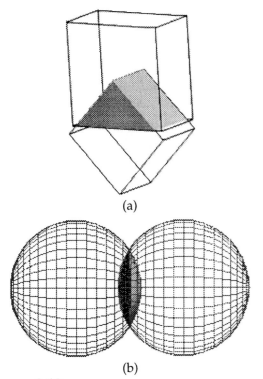

(a)

(b)

Figure 8.13
Examples of intersection in constructive solid geometry.
  a) Intersection of two boxes generates wedge.
  b) Intersection of two spheres generates lens.

$$X = A - B \qquad [8.28]$$
(regularized Boolean difference).

Because subtracting object B from object A yields a different object from that obtained by subtracting object A from object B, the difference operation is noncommutative.

$$A - B \neq B - A \qquad [8.29]$$
(difference is noncommutative).

It is particularly valuable for the design of parts which involve drilling or milling away material at the manufacturing stage. Examples of the difference operation are shown in Figure 8.14.

Tree Structure in CSG

The final object constructed by CSG may be represented by the root of an ordered, binary tree. The leaves (terminal nodes) of the tree are either primitive solids or transformation operations. Non-terminal nodes represent either Boolean operations ($\cup$, $\cap$, or $-$) applied to the two incoming branches or transformations to be applied to rigid solids. Each subtree at a node represents the solid resulting from the Boolean operations and geometric transformations occurring below it. This tree structure is illustrated in Figure 8.15. This figure defines the CSG language program required to create the two-holed plate of Figure 8.14(b).

This ordered, binary tree structure may be considered the language for representing constructive solid geometry. It is concise, well-defined, and capable of expressing any object which can be constructed by CSG. One interesting property of the language, however, is that it is not unique. That is, there are often many ways of constructing the same final object. For instance, a hole may be drilled in a plate by the difference operation between the plate and a cylinder the diameter of the hole. The cylinder, however, can be of any length longer than the thickness of the plate and must completely penetrate the plate.

Extensions of CSG

As indicated earlier, the synthesis of super-quadrics with CSG techniques provides a particularly powerful tool for modeling solid objects, especially those with rounded and life-like forms. Two other useful techniques for generating more general primitive solids for input into CSG trees are *lathing* and *extrusion*. Lathing is the CAD equivalent of turning a part on a lathe—any object whose outline is constant as it spins about one axis is allowed. Extrusion is the CAD equivalent of a cookie cutter—any object formed by the linear translation of a closed 2D figure is allowed.

Early mainframe systems *GMSolid* (by General Motors Corporation) and *ROMULUS* (by Evans and Sutherland) were among the first CAD programs to make full use of CSG and included lathing and extrusion.[9] Modern personal workstation CAD programs.include CSG.[10]

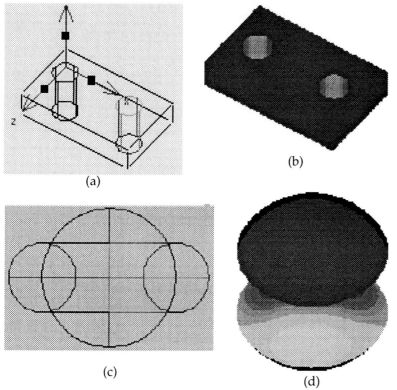

(a)

(b)

(c)

(d)

Figure 8.14
The regularized difference operation in constructive solid geometry.
    a) Subtracting the two cylinders from the plate
    generates the drilled holes, (b).
    c) Subtracting the torus from the sphere
    generates the "apple core," (d).

Defining a Viewing Volume

The basic function of 3D clipping within the viewing pipeline is to specify a window in 3D space which is to be mapped onto a 2D viewport. However, a "window in 3D space" is most directly interpreted as a 3D viewing volume. That portion of the 3D world scene within the viewing volume gets projected onto a viewport on the screen. That portion lying outside of the viewing volume is clipped away and does not appear. Computationally it is advantageous to clip in 3D rather than after the whole scene has been projected onto 2D because of the reduction in the amount of projection required.

Clipping in 3D is quite analogous to clipping in 2D with the following two extensions:

- In addition to the top, right, bottom, and left clipping planes, we must introduce two additional planes, the *front clipping plane* and *back clipping plane* (both parallel to the x-y view plane).

- The "natural" viewing volumes depend on the type of projection. For parallel orthographic projection, the viewing volume is a rectangular parallelepiped (box). For perspective projection it is a truncated pyramid.

Clipping in 3D

So far in this chapter we have considered representation issues and have introduced several advanced techniques for building models in the world coordinate system. These techniques extend the tools for representation well beyond the simple, but functional, polyhedral representation presented in the last chapter.

The next step is to return to implementation issues and extend the tools available for viewing the models we have learned to create. The two geometric concepts we consider next are 3D clipping and problem of removing those surfaces which are invisible because of facing away from the camera or being hidden by intervening objects.

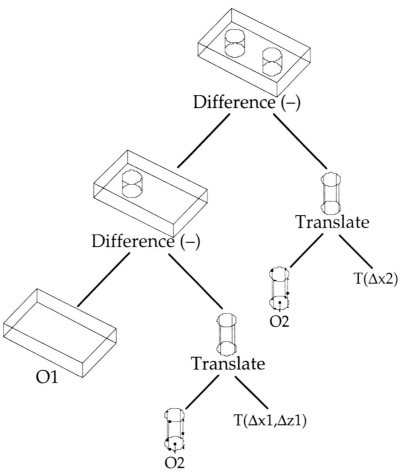

Figure 8.15
Ordered, binary tree structure defining the CSG language. Terminal nodes are either primitive objects (O1 or O2) or transformations. Intermediate nodes are regularized Boolean operators or transformations. The root node is the final product of the constructive solid geometry process.

These 3D extensions are illustrated in Figure 8.16.

As can be seen in Figure 8.16, 3D clipping involves discarding objects and portions of objects lying outside a box for the parallel projection case and those lying outside a truncated pyramid for the perspective projection case. As one might expect, clipping against the regular parallelopiped (box) is the more easily solved problem. Let us consider both cases in more detail.

3D Clipping in Orthographic Projection

The first question to resolve in developing a clipping algorithm is: What shall we clip? For the sake of simplicity we shall restrict our discussion to the clipping of lines and polygons. One might suspect that the process of clipping a 3D line with a box resembles clipping a 2D line with a rectangle so closely that the Cohen-Sutherland approach would apply. This, fortunately, is the case. The second happy surprise is that the Sutherland-Hodgeman polygon clipping algorithm may also be generalized to 3D.

To simplify the mathematics of the Cohen-Sutherland algorithm tests, the first step is to transform the clipping volume from the arbitrary parallelepiped defined as $[X_R,X_L,Y_T,Y_B,Z_B,Z_F]$ into the unit cube at the origin defined as $[1,0,1,0,1,0]$. This transformation and the resulting *normalized view volume* are shown in Figure 8.17.

The transformation applied to the view volume and all associated objects in the scene can be expressed as the 4×4 matrix, M.

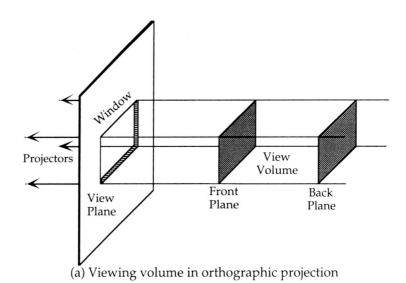

(a) Viewing volume in orthographic projection

$$M = \begin{bmatrix} S_x & 0 & 0 & 0 \\ 0 & S_y & 0 & 0 \\ 0 & 0 & S_z & 0 \\ T_x & T_y & T_z & 1 \end{bmatrix}, \quad [8.30]$$

(Normalized view volume matrix)

where

$$S_x = \frac{1}{(X_R - X_L)},$$
(x axis scale factor)

$$S_y = \frac{1}{(Y_T - Y_B)},$$
(y axis scale factor)

$$S_z = \frac{1}{(Z_B - Z_F)},$$
(z axis scale factor)

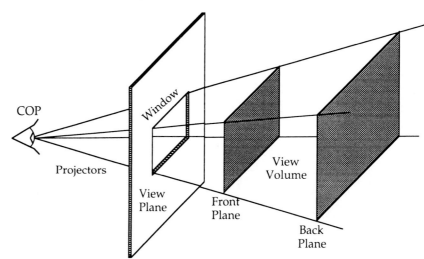

(b) Viewing volume in perspective projection

Figure 8.16
Viewing volumes for 3D clipping.

$T_x = -S_x X_L,$
(x translation to move window to origin)

$T_y = -S_y Y_B,$ (y translation to move window to origin)

$T_z = -S_z Z_F.$ (z translation to move window to origin)

The next step is to extend the four-bit classification code, *TBRL*, for each end point to a six-bit code to account for front plane clipping (hither) and back plane clipping (yon). This code can be written:

$$TBRLHY, \quad [8.31]$$
where
   $T = 1$ if point is above top plane (y>1); 0 otherwise

The result of this transformation is to take an arbitrary window view volume and transform it into a normalized cubic view volume which can be considered a 3D viewport.

   $B = 1$ if point is below bottom plane (y<0); 0 otherwise

$R = 1$ if point is to the right of the R.H.S. plane (x>1); 0 otherwise

$L = 1$ if point is to the left of the L.H.S. plane (x<0); 0 otherwise

$H = 1$ if point is in front of the hither (front) plane (z<0); 0 otherwise

$Y = 1$ if point is behind the yon (back) plane (z>1); 0 otherwise.

The two end points of each line are then encoded as

$$C_1 = T_1 B_1 R_1 L_1 H_1 Y_1 \qquad [8.32]$$
and
$$C_2 = T_2 B_2 R_2 L_2 H_2 Y_2$$

and the line classified as *trivially in* or *trivially out* by the tests:

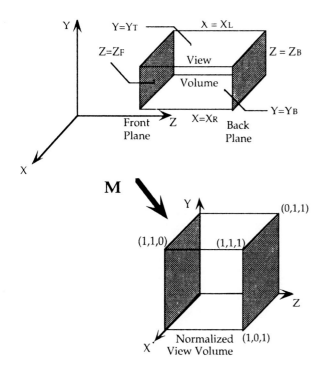

Figure 8.17
Transformation of view volume into normalized view volume.

Trivially in: $(C_1 = 000000)$ AND $(C_2 = 000000)$
Trivially out: $(C_1$ AND $C_2) \neq (000000)$.   [8.33]

The trivially out AND test produces a six-bit answer in which a "1" at any bit location indicates that the corresponding binary digits of both C_1 AND C_2 were "1."

Next, we enter the Cohen-Sutherland iterative or recursive loop that classifies all lines as trivially in, trivially out, or neither. Trivially in lines are plotted; trivially out lines are discarded; and lines classified as neither are intersected with the plane(s) which prevented their classification in one of the trivial categories. A convenient way to calculate the intersection of lines with the normalized clipping planes is to express each line in its two-point parametric form and substitute the equation of the plane as the value of the variable. For a line between points $P_1 = (x_1, y_1, z_1)$ and $P_2 = (x_2, y_2, z_2)$ this becomes:

$$x = x_1 + t(x_2 - x_1), \qquad [8.34]$$
$$y = y_1 + t(y_2 - y_1),$$
$$z = z_1 + t(z_2 - z_1), \text{ with}$$
$$0 \leq t \leq 1. \qquad \text{(parameter range)}$$

Assume, for example, that the line crossed the back plane ($z = 1$). To locate the 3D point of intersection between the line and clipping plane, we substitute the value of $z = 1$ from the plane equation into Equation 8.34 for the line and compute the corresponding value of the parameter, t_i.

$$1 = z_1 + t_i(z_2 - z_1) \qquad [8.35]$$

$$t_i = \frac{1 - z_1}{z_2 - z_1} \qquad [8.36]$$

This value of t_i is then used in Equation 8.34 to compute a new end point, $P_i = (x_i, y_i, 1)$. Assuming for the moment that the point P_2 lay behind the $z = 1$ clipping plane, the line segment $(P_2–P_i)$ is discarded, and the surviving line segment, $(P_i–P_1)$, re-enters the clipping stream. The process is continued for all lines and all clipped segments until they classify as trivially in or trivially out.

Note that the value for t_i computed in Equation 8.36 is itself a valuable test for intersection of the line segment $(P_2 – P_1)$. If t_i lies in the range, $0 \leq t_i \leq 1$, the line segment intersects the back plane; if not, it doesn't.

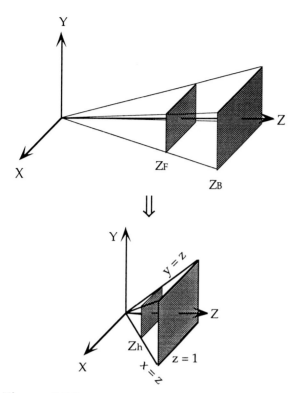

Figure 8.18
Transformation of perspective view volume into canonical view volume.

3D Clipping in Perspective Projection

As we expected, the symmetry of orthographic projections allowed an easy extension of clipping algorithms from 2D to 3D. At first glance, the non-parallelism of the clipping planes in perspective projections seems to add serious complications. However, there are two alternative approaches, each involving a simple transformation, for converting the truncated pyramid viewing volume into a shape that simplifies computation.

Canonical view volume

The result of the canonical view volume transformation is to convert the arbitrary truncated pyramid of Figure 8.16 (b) into the equivalent of a normalized view volume which we call the canonical view volume. The back plane of the canonical view volume has $z = 1$, the front plane has $z = Z_h$, and all sides of the truncated pyramid make angles of 45° with respect to the base. The

top plane of the pyramid has the equation $y = z$, the bottom plane has $y = -z$, the right-hand plane has $x = z$, and the left-hand plane has $x = -z$. This geometry is illustrated in Figure 8.18.

Assuming a center of projection (COP) at the origin, the canonical view volume transformation can be performed by the matrix of equation 8.28 with the following modifications:

$$T_x = T_y = T_z = 0 , \qquad [8.37]$$

$$S_z = \frac{1}{Z_B} , \qquad \text{(z axis scale factor)} \quad [8.38]$$

X_R, X_L, Y_T, Y_B = coordinates of view volume window at back plane.

This transformation generates a new front plane, $Z_h = S_z Z_F$, and scales the viewing volume to a 45° pyramid.

The *TBRLHY* Cohen-Sutherland code is then generated by the tests:

$T = 1$ if point is above top plane ($y > z$); 0 otherwise,
$B = 1$ if point is below bottom plane ($y < z$); 0 otherwise,
$R = 1$ if point is to the right of plane ($x > z$); 0 otherwise,
$L = 1$ if point is to the left of plane ($x < z$); 0 otherwise,
$H = 1$ if point is in front of hither plane (front) ($z < Z_h$); 0 otherwise,
$Y = 1$ if point is behind the yon plane (back)($z > 1$); 0 otherwise.

Note the similarity with the parallel projection code of Equation 8.31.

Again, the test for intersection of the line with various clipping planes is obtained by substituting the equation of the plane into the parametric form of the line, Equation 8.34. If, for instance, a line intersects the right-hand side ($x = z$ plane), we can solve for the value of the parameter, t_i, at the point of intersection.

$$x = z \qquad [8.39]$$
$$x_1 + t_i (x_2 - x_1) = z_1 + t_i (z_2 - z_1)$$
$$t_i = \frac{z_1 - x_1}{(x_2 - x_1) - (z_2 - z_1)} \qquad [8.40]$$

With this value of t_i we can compute the intersection point, $P_i = (x_i, y_i, z_i,)$, using Equations 8.34 and proceed with the line clipping algorithm.

Perspective → parallel view volume

The second approach is a bit less intuitive, but conceptually more elegant. The idea is to transform the canonical view volume of the approach just discussed into a parallel-sided view volume for which all of the arguments of parallel projection 3D clipping would apply. Recall from our discussion of perspective projection that the projection operator acted like a depth-dependent scale factor. If we apply a similar depth-dependent scale factor to the truncated pyramid clipping volume, we can pull it into the shape of a parallel-epiped similar to the normalized view volume of Figure 8.17.

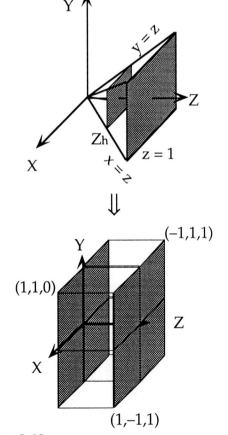

Figure 8.19
Transformation of canonical view volume into bi-normalized viewing volume. This parallel viewing volume simplifies both clipping and perspective projection.

The M matrix that performs this operation is given as:

$$M = \begin{bmatrix} S_x & 0 & 0 & 0 \\ 0 & S_y & 0 & 0 \\ 0 & 0 & S_z & 0 \\ 0 & 0 & T_z & 1 \end{bmatrix}, \qquad [8.41]$$

(Perspective → parallel matrix)

where

$$z \neq 0 ,$$
$$S_x = \frac{1}{z},$$
$$S_y = \frac{1}{z},$$
$$S_z = \frac{1}{1 - Z_h},$$

and

$$T_z = \frac{Z_h}{Z_h - 1}.$$

This transformation maps the canonical view volume into the "binormalized" viewing volume, shown in Figure 8.19, whose clipping planes are given below.

$$\begin{aligned} \text{top} &\to y = 1 \\ \text{bottom} &\to y = -1 \\ \text{right} &\to x = 1 \\ \text{left} &\to x = -1 \\ \text{front} &\to z = 0 \\ \text{back} &\to z = 1. \end{aligned}$$

From this point on, the previous discussion of the normalized parallel view volume applies, and one can easily implement the extended Cohen-Sutherland algorithm. There are some interesting "side effects" of the perspective → parallel projection. One of the most appealing is that this transformation has automatically accomplished the perspective transformation. After clipping, the only remaining task is to map the already projected objects onto the desired viewport.

This concludes our discussion of 3D clipping. The message that emerges from this discussion is the importance of the correct representation for the solution of difficult problems. By selecting the appropriate representation for the clipping volume, much of the complexity introduced by the third dimension is eliminated, and the clipping techniques introduced in the 2D environment apply with only minor modifications.

Hidden Surface Algorithms

The final topic of this chapter is hidden surface removal. The route to the summit of a realistic graphical display of world scenes involves establishing a base camp and then building higher camps according to a systematic plan. The base camp of visual realism corresponds to the selection of the fundamental polyhedral representation for solids. Higher camps, each closer to the goal, include perspective projection and 3D clipping. However, the end product of these three processes is still only a wire frame model that may be sufficient for certain engineering applications but is far removed from a realistic rendering of the objects in the scene being rendered.

The next step towards our goal of visual realism is to recognize that the back side of a solid objects is invisible and that objects situated behind nearer objects are either totally or partially obscured by these closer objects. Techniques for implementing these two properties of images of real scenes are classified as *hidden surface removal* algorithms. To emphasize that the objective is to identify the visible portion of the scene being projected, some authors refer to these techniques as *visible surface* algorithms. The invention and refinement of hidden surface removal algorithms was the dominant topic in the early years of computer graphics research and continues as an area of active investigation. Sutherland, Sproull, and Schumacker summarize the results of this early research in their comparative study of ten hidden surface algorithms.[11]

Several considerations are important in the design of hidden surface algorithms.

- **Sorting is central** – At the most abstract level, all polygons are sorted into two classes: visible and invisible. At the most concrete level, each pixel is colored according to the results of sorting the objects in line at that pixel location. The order and types of sorting are the principal features distinguishing various hidden surface algorithms.

- **Coherence is critical for efficiency** – The recognition that objects are solid, surfaces are closed, and edges are connected improves the efficiency of hidden surface algorithms. These coherence properties of solid objects provide useful tools for restricting the search space in which sorting must occur.

- **Machines make a difference** – As academics we prefer the discussion of graphics concepts to be maintained at a high level of abstraction in order to keep it "clean" and machine independent. However, the practical fact is that several of the most successful and efficient hidden surface algorithms are based primarily on the pixel or scan-line structure of real graphics display devices. A hidden surface algorithm optimized for a raster-scan device will almost certainly not be appropriate for a vector display device.

Sorting Considerations

Many hidden surface algorithms rely on sorting objects according to their x and y extents (view plane coordinates) and most involve sorting on z depth. Therefore, the efficiency of sorting algorithms plays a central role in the efficiency of hidden surface removal algorithms. However, the efficiency of sorting depends on whether the items to be sorted are randomly distributed or nearly in order. This dependency of efficiency on the number of items, N, for several standard sorting techniques is shown in Table 8.1.

Since complex scenes involve sorting tens or hundreds of thousands of polygons, conventional wisdom would indicate using the more efficient but complex sorts like quick sort, tree sort, or radix sort. However, the coherence of objects leads to databases of nearly sorted polygons or with large blocks of nearly sorted polygons. In these cases, the simpler sorts like selection, insertion, and even bubble sort may be just as efficient. In such cases, the simplicity and clarity of the simpler sorts make them the preferred choice. For additional information on sorting considerations, see Sedgewick[12] or Knuth.[13]

Table 8.1
Sorting Algorithm Dependency on N

Sort Type	Random distribution	Nearly in order
Bubble sort	N^2	N
Shell sort	$N^{3/2}$	N
Quick sort	N log N	N^2
Tree sort	N log N	N
Radix sort	N	N

Coherence Considerations

Coherence describes the extent to which the scene or the image of the scene is locally constant. As one moves from one polygon on a given object into another, it is very likely that color and shading will remain largely unchanged. Similarly, because of the physical coherence of solid objects, it is impossible for the z-depth of the polygon surface to change significantly as one moves from one polygon into an adjacent polygon. Such coherence properties are frequently exploited in hidden surface algorithms. Several kinds of coherence have been used in hidden surface algorithms. These can be classified as:

- **Edge coherence** – The visibility of an edge changes only when it crosses another contour edge.

- **Face coherence** – Faces (polygons) are generally small compared to the size of the image and may therefore not conflict.

- **Area coherence** – A particular element of the output image and its neighbors on all sides are likely to be influenced by the same face.

- **Object coherence** – Individual bodies are confined to local volumes which may not conflict. This coherence extends to hierarchical objects composed of more primitive objects.

- **Depth coherence** – Different polygons at a given image location are generally well separated in depth relative to the depth variation of each.

- **Scan line coherence** – The set of segments imaged on one scan line and their x-intercepts are closely related to those of the previous scan line.

- **Frame coherence** – In processing animated images, the image does not change very much from frame to frame.

Machine Dependence of Algorithms

Sutherland, *et al*, developed a taxonomy for classifying hidden surface algorithms along a spectrum ranging from pure object-space analysis to pure image-space analysis.

| Object-space analysis | Image-space analysis |
| No machine dependence | Use pixels, scan lines |

Object-space algorithms work with the geometry of objects to compute exactly the portions of each object and face that are visible. The accuracy of the results depends only on the precision of real numbers on the computing system used but not on any characteristics of the display system (e.g., pixel, scan line, or screen resolution). Object-space algorithms have the advantage of being "exact" although the computational load increases as the complexity of the scene increases.

Image-space algorithms rely on features such as the pixel or scan line structure of the display device to limit the computation required for distinguishing visible from invisible surfaces. As a result the computational load depends on the resolution of the screen and less strongly on the number of polygons. By limiting the computational accuracy to pixel or scan line integers, image-space algorithms produce "good enough" resolution rather than exact results.

Hidden Surface Algorithms

In the following discussion we will make several simplifying assumptions, all of which are based on sound physical arguments and none of which reduce the generality of the algorithms in any significant way. These assumptions include:

- Objects are closed polyhedra.

- Polygons are obtuse (i.e., no interior angles $\geq 180°$).

- No intersecting planes are allowed.

Let us consider in some detail the following major hidden surface algorithms that represent the most commonly used approaches for eliminating those surfaces which are invisible:

- Back-Face Removal,
- Z-Buffer (depth-buffer),

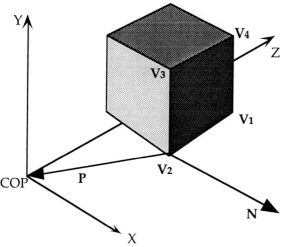

Figure 8.20
Geometry for back face test. The normal, *N*, to the (V_1, V_2, V_3, V_4) polygon is computed by taking the cross product of any two successive edge vectors. When *N* is dotted with *P*, a projector from any vertex of the polygon, the sign of the dot product indicates the visibility of the polygon.

• Scan Line,
• Painter's Algorithm (depth sort),
• Warnock's Area Subdivision.

Back-Face Removal

The basic concept in back-face removal involves plotting only surfaces "facing the camera" since the back side of objects are invisible. Note that this technique will automatically remove approximately fifty percent of the polygons in a scene viewed in parallel projection and somewhat greater than fifty percent of polygons in perspective projections. The closer the objects are to the COP in perspective projection, the higher percentage of polygons that the back-face algorithm removes. A little reflection on the appearance of a cube in various parallel and perspective projections will convince the reader of the truth of these statements.

The back-face removal algorithm, however, applies only to objects considered individually—it does not take into consideration the "interaction" between objects. That is, many polygons surviving the back-face removal algorithm (i.e., "front-faces") will still be obscured by front-faces even closer to the viewer. So, while back-face removal

is *necessary* for eliminating fifty percent or more of the invisible surfaces in a scene, it is not *sufficient* for eliminating all hidden surfaces.

Note that the back-face removal algorithm is built on the spatial coherence of objects. That is, the component surfaces of an object "hang together," defining a closed volume occupied by the object. Any projector ray from the COP through the viewing screen to the object pierces the object at two points, a visible front surface and an invisible back surface. The back-face removal algorithm is a technique for identifying which is which.

In Figure 8.20 we show the geometric interpretation of this algorithm. Each polygon is assumed to have vertices numbered in a clockwise fashion (as seen from outside the polyhedron). The normal, *N*, is easily generated as the cross product between any two successive edge vectors. Using a left-handed coordinate system convention, *N* represents the vector perpendicular to the face and points *outward* from the polyhedron. Edge vectors are defined as $V_{i+1} - V_i$. Therefore,

$$N = (V_2 - V_1) \times (V_3 - V_2) . \qquad [8.42]$$
$$\text{[left-handed system]}$$

The sign of the dot product of *N* and *P* (a projector from any polygon vertex) indicates the visibility of the polygon.

$$N \cdot P \geq 0 \quad \rightarrow \text{Visible} \qquad [8.43]$$
$$N \cdot P < 0 \quad \rightarrow \text{Invisible}.$$

This algorithm can be summarized in the following steps:

Back-Face Removal Algorithm

Repeat for all polygons in the scene:
1. Number all polygon vertices, $V_1, V_2, \ldots V_n$, in clockwise fashion.
2. Compute the normal vector, $N = (V_2 - V_1) \times (V_3 - V_2)$.
3. Using a projector, *P*, from any polygon vertex, compute the dot product,
   $Vis = N \cdot P$.
4. Test and plot if visible
   IF $Vis \geq 0$ then
         PLOT
   else
         SKIP

To summarize the back-face removal algorithm, visible faces are those pointing towards the viewer at the COP. Since the normal to the face indicates which direction the polygon is facing, we can see a face when there is some component of the normal, N, along the direction of the projector ray, P. The projection of N along P is measured by the dot product, $N \cdot P$. An identical argument says that invisible faces are those pointing away from the viewer. The dot product is negative for the back face case because N and P lie in opposite hemispheres. The indeterminate case in which $N \cdot P = 0$ is interpreted as visible since the edge of the face can be seen although the projected area is zero. The results of applying this algorithm to two primitive objects are shown in Figure 8.21.

In conclusion, the back-face removal algorithm uses object coherence that applies to all solid objects modeled as convex polyhedra. It provides a simple, straight-forward method of eliminating all *self-hidden* faces and reduces the size of the polygon database requiring additional hidden surface processing by fifty percent or more. Therefore, it should always be the first hidden surface algorithm to be applied.

Z-Buffer Algorithm

We turn now to the problem of how to recognize and correctly eliminate the invisible front faces surviving the back-face removal algorithm which are obscured by some object closer to the camera. The first method described is a pure image-space algorithm known as the *z-buffer* or *depth-buffer* algorithm.

The concept of the z-buffer algorithm is to create two parallel arrays, $I(x,y)$ and $Z(x,y)$, in which (x,y) are pixel coordinates, $I(x,y)$ is the intensity (or color) at that screen location, and $Z(x,y)$ is the dynamic z-buffer in which the smallest z coordinate of any polygon examined to date is stored. $I(x,y)$ corresponds to the intensity (or color) of that closest polygon.

The $Z(x,y)$ array is initialized to 1.0 corresponding to the back plane of the normalized coordinated system, and the corresponding $I(x,y)$ array is initialized to some background color. The first polygon is then projected onto the viewing screen and the $Z(x,y)$ and $I(x,y)$ arrays loaded with the depth corresponding to each (x,y) pixel and the color of the polygon. Then the next polygon is projected and the z_2 depth computed for each (x,y) pixel in its projection. As each z_2 is computed, it is compared to the existing $Z(x,y)$ buffer, and, if $z_2 < Z(x,y)$, the element $Z(x,y)$ is replaced by z_2 and the corresponding $I(x,y)$ is replaced by I_2, the color of the second polygon. This process is repeated for all polygons. The resulting $I(x,y)$ is the correct image, accurate to the nearest pixel, with hidden surfaces removed.

Another way to understand the depth-buffer algorithm is to consider it as a pixel-wise bubble sort of the z-depth of all polygons pierced by the projector ray to the pixel. As each smaller value of z is found for pixel (x,y), it is used to overwrite $Z(x,y)$ and to update $I(x,y)$ to the intensity or color of the corresponding polygon. This interpretation is illustrated in Figure 8.22.

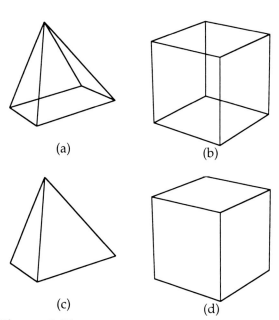

(a) (b)

(c) (d)

Figure 8.21
Application of back-face removal algorithm to two primitive objects, (a) and (b). Objects (c) and (d) in which only front faces are shown help remove the "Necker illusion"[14] apparent in the top two wire frame representations.

The algorithm can be summarized as:

Z-Buffer Algorithm

1. For each pixel, (x,y), of the viewport, establish a Z-buffer array and an   intensity/color array and initialize.
   1.1 For all x and y
      1.1.1 $Z(x,y) = 1.0$ [Back plane of clipping volume]
      1.1.2 $I(x,y) = Bkg$ [Background color, e. g., black]

2. For all polygons of the scene projected onto the viewport
   2.1 For each (x,y) of projected polygon i, compute $z_i(x,y)$
   2.2 IF $z_i(x,y) < Z(x,y)$ THEN
      $Z(x,y) = z_i(x,y)$
      $I(x,y) = I_i$ [I_i = intensity of polygon i]

3. Plot $I(x,y)$ [Image with hidden surfaces removed]

The calculation of depth z as a function of x and y is performed by using the equation of the plane in which the polygon lies and solving for z:

$$z = \frac{-Ax - By - D}{C} \qquad [8.44]$$

Note that the z-buffer algorithm is strictly an image-space algorithm, using the computed z-depth as the key for a bubble sort. It has the advantage of computing every thing necessary for displaying correct visible surfaces but only to the pixel resolution of the display screen. Since the screen has a finite pixel resolution, more complexity in the scene (i.e., more polygons) can occur only through a decrease in the average polygon size. Thus, the efficiency of the z-buffer algorithm is relatively insensitive to image complexity.

The algorithm does require, however, two arrays of numbers, at least one of which must be real. If this requirement taxes the computing resources available, the algorithm may be decomposed into individual scan line arrays and performed one scan-line at a time.

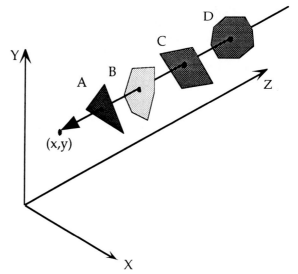

Figure 8.22
Z-buffer algorithm for hidden surface removal. Two arrays, $Z(x,y)$ and $I(x,y)$ store the depth and color of the polygon closest to the x-y viewing screen. These dynamic arrays are updated by scanning all polygons of the screen. The final image is contained in $I(x,y)$.

Scan-Line Algorithm

The scan-line algorithm is another image-space algorithm. It processes the image one scan-line at a time rather than one pixel at a time. By using area coherence of the polygon, the processing efficiency is improved over the pixel oriented method.

Using an active edge table, the scan-line algorithm keeps track of where the projection beam is at any given time during the scan-line sweep. When it enters the projection of a polygon, an *IN* flag goes on, and the beam switches from the background color to the color of the polygon. After the beam leaves the polygon's edge, the color switches back to background color. To this point, no depth information need be calculated at all. However, when the scan-line beam finds itself in two or more polygons, it becomes necessary to perform a z-depth sort and select the color of the nearest polygon as the painting color. This concept is shown in Figure 8.23.

Accurate bookkeeping is very important for the scan-line algorithm. We assume the scene is defined by at least a polygon table containing the (A, B, C, D) coefficients of the plane of each polygon, intensity/color information, and pointers to an edge table specifying the bounding lines of the polygon. The edge table contains the coordinates of the two end points, pointers to the polygon table to indicate which polygons the edge bounds, and the inverse slope of the x-y projection of the line for use with scan-line algorithms. In addition to these two standard data structures, the scan-line algorithm requires an *active edge list* that keeps track of which edges a given scan line intersects during its sweep. The active edge list should be sorted in order of increasing x at the point of intersection with the scan line. The active edge list is dynamic, growing and shrinking as the scan line progresses down the screen.

In Figure 8.23, the active edge list for scan line SL_1 contains edges E_1 and E_2. From the left edge of the viewport to edge E_1, the beam paints the background color. At edge E_1, the *IN* flag goes up for the left-hand polygon, and the beam switches to its color until it crosses edge E_2, at which point the *IN* flag goes down and the color returns to background.

For scan-line SL_2, the active edge list contains E_1, E_3, E_5, and E_6. The *IN* flag goes up and down twice in sequence during this scan. Each time it goes up pointers identify the appropriate polygon and look up the color to use in painting the polygon.

For scan line SL_3, the active edge list contains the same edges as for SL_2, but the order is altered, namely E_1, E_5, E_3, E_6. Now the question of relative z-depth first appears. The *IN* flag goes up once when we cross E_1 and again when we cross E_5, indicating that the projector is piercing two polygons. Now the coefficients of each plane and the (x,y) of the E_5 edge are used to compute the depth of both planes. In the example shown the z-depth of the right-hand plane was smaller, indicating it is closer to the screen. Therefore the painting color switches to the right-hand polygon color which it keeps until edge E_6.

Note that the technique is readily extended to three or more overlapping polygons and that the relative depths of overlapping polygons must be calculated only when the *IN* flag goes up for a new polygon. Since this occurrence is far less frequent than the number of pixels per scan line, the scan-line algorithm is more computationally efficient than the z-buffer algorithm.

The scan-line hidden surface removal algorithm can be summarized as:

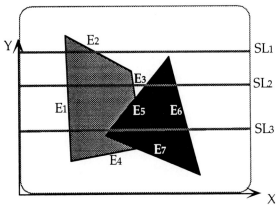

Figure 8.23
Scan-line hidden surface algorithm. Scan-line SL_1 must deal only with the left-hand object. SL_2 must plot both objects, but there is no depth conflict. SL_3 must resolve the relative z-depth of both objects in the region between edge E_5 and E_3. The right-hand object appears closer.

Scan-Line Algorithm

1. Establish the necessary data structures.
    1.1 Polygon table with coefficients, color, and edge pointers.
    1.2 Edge table with line end points, inverse slope, and polygon pointers.
    1.3 Active edge list, sorted in order of increasing x.
    1.4 An *IN* flag for each polygon. Value = on or off.

2. Repeat for all scan lines:
    2.1 Update active edge list by sorting edge table against scan line y value.
    2.2 Scan across, using *BKG* color, until an *IN* flag goes on.
    2.3 When 1 polygon flag is on for surface S_1, enter intensity (color) I_1 into refresh buffer.
    2.4 When 2 or more surface flags are on, do depth sort and use intensity S_n for surface n with minimum z-depth.
    2.5 Use coherence of planes to repeat for next scan line.

The scan-line algorithm for hidden surface removal is well designed to take advantage of the area coherence of polygons. As long as the active edge list remains constant from one scan to the next, the relative structure and orientation of the polygons painted during that scan does not change. This means that we can "remember" the relative position of overlapping polygons and need not recompute the z-depth when two or more *IN* flags go on. By taking advantage of this coherence we save a great deal of computation.

Painter's Algorithm

The two previous algorithms have used image-space processing which relies on the finite pixel and scan-line display resolution. The painter's algorithm is based purely on object-space sorting. This method, sometimes referred to as the *depth-sorting* algorithm, is conceptually quite intuitive but a bit difficult to implement in practice.

The concept is to map the objects of our scene from the world model to the screen somewhat like an artist creating an oil painting. First she paints the entire canvas with a background color. Next, she adds the more distant objects such as mountains, fields, and trees. Finally, she creates the foreground with "near" objects to complete the painting. Our approach will be identical. First we sort the polygons according to their z-depth and then paint them to the screen, starting with the far faces and finishing with the near faces.

A first approximation to the painter's algorithm is the following:

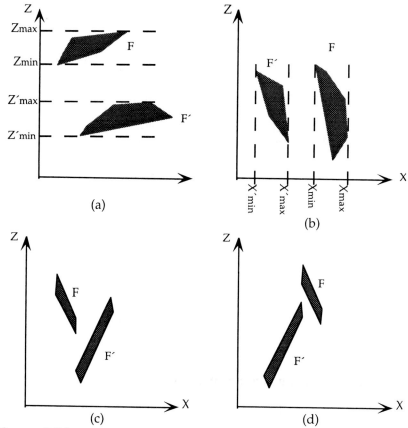

(a)

(b)

(c)

(d)

Figure 8.24
Tests applied by painter's algorithm:
  a) Is *F* behind and non-overlapping *F'* in the *z* dimension?
  b) Is *F* behind *F'* in *z* and non-overlapping in *x* or in *y*?
  c) Is *F* behind *F'* in *z* and totally outside of *F'* with respect to the view plane?
  d) Is *F* behind *F'* in *z* and is *F'* totally inside *F* with respect to the view plane?
Successful passing of any test with a single overlapping polygon permits *F* to be painted.

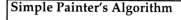

Simple Painter's Algorithm
1. Sort all polygons by z-depth, largest z first.
2. Scan-convert (paint) polygons in this order.

Problems immediately become apparent with this algorithm. First, we must define what is meant by the "z-depth" of a polygon which has a number of vertices. A reasonable convention is to sort the z

coordinates of the vertices of the polygon and pick the maximum z value as the key for polygon sorting. With this convention, the simple painter's algorithm would be adequate for solving the hidden surface problem for faces *F* and *F'* well separated in *z* as shown in Figure 8.24 (a). However, most scenes involve objects that overlap in their *z* dimensions. These may or may not be rendered correctly by the simple painter's algorithm. To handle such overlaps, we have to refine the algorithm with several additional tests.

The refined painter's algorithm may then be expressed as a type of bubble sort of the *z*-depth list of faces produced by the simple algorithm. The deepest face, F, is compared to the second deepest face, F', to see if there is any z overlap. If there is none and if F' is the only overlapping face, F is painted to the screen. If there is overlap, F and F' are subject to a series of tests to see if their order should be interchanged. If F passes any of these tests (described below), it qualifies as behind F' and is painted to the screen. If it fails all the additional tests, F and F' are interchanged and the sorting resumes with the new F. The overlap tests must be carried out between F and all overlapping faces. Once F passes any of these tests with all overlapping faces, it is guaranteed to be behind all overlapping surfaces and is plotted.

The additional tests are spelled out in the following algorithm summary, and three of the tests are illustrated in Figure 8.24 (b), (c), and (d).

Refined Painter's Algorithm

1. Sort polygon faces by largest z-value of each, largest first.

2. Repeat for all surfaces:
   2.1 Test surface of greatest depth, F, with all others.
   > 2.1.1 If no overlap in z, PLOT (paint).
   > 2.1.2 If overlap with surface F', then make 5 tests.
   >> Plot F if it passes any of the tests.
   >> 1) X-extents of F, F' do not overlap.
   >> 2) Y-extents of F, F' do not overlap.
   >> 3) If F is wholly on that side of the plane of F' facing away from the viewpoint, then F will not obscure any part of F' and F' will overwrite F. (i.e., F is "outside" of F')
   >> 4) If F' is wholly on that side of plane F facing the viewpoint, again, F will plot and be correctly overwritten when F' plots. (i.e., F' is "inside" of F)
   >>> N. B.: Tests (3) and (4) are not the same.
   >> 5) The projections of polygons F and F' do not overlap. [Must do an edge compare test.]
   > 2.1.3 If F fails all five tests, assume F obscures F'.
   >> $\therefore$ Switch $F \leftrightarrow F'$
   >> Then F' is plotted first and F later, properly overwriting F'.
   >>> 2.1.3.1 If switch does occur, F' must then be checked against all "lower" polygons.

---

3. To handle cyclic and intersecting planes, (∞ loops):
   3.1 Flag polygons that are switched to last place.
   3.2 They may not be moved again.
   3.3 Clip intersecting or cyclic planes apart.
   >> 3.3.1 Treat one plane as clip plane.
   >> 3.3.2 Snip second plane into two new planes, A,B.
   >> 3.3.3 Add A & B to polygon list.
   >> 3.3.4 Continue.

Warnock's Area Subdivision Algorithm

John Warnock, inventor of *PostScript*, proposed an elegant divide-and-conquer hidden surface algorithm.[15] The algorithm relies on the area coherence of polygons to resolve the visibility of many polygons in image space. Depth sorting is simplified and performed only in those cases involving image-space overlap.

Warnock's algorithm classifies polygons with respect to the current viewing window into trivial or non-trivial cases. Trivial cases are easily handled. For nontrivial cases, the current viewing window is recursively divided into four equal subwindows, each of which is then used for reclassifying remaining polygons. This recursive procedure is continued until all polygons are trivially classified or until the current window reaches the pixel resolution of the screen. At that point the algorithm reverts to a simple z-depth sort of the intersected polygons, and the pixel color becomes that of the polygon closest to the viewing screen.

Classification Scheme

All polygons are readily classified with respect to the current window into the four categories illustrated in Figure 8.25.

The classification scheme is used to identify certain trivial cases that are easily handled. These "easy choice tests" and the resulting actions include:

1. For polygons **outside** (disjoint) from the window, set the color/intensity, $I(w)$, of the window equal to the background color, *BKG*.

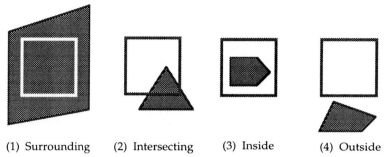

(1) Surrounding   (2) Intersecting   (3) Inside   (4) Outside

Figure 8.25
Classification scheme for Warnock hidden surface algorithm. The square is the current window used to classify polygons into the categories shown.

2. There is only one **inside** or **intersecting** polygon. Fill the window area with BKG, then scan-convert (paint) the polygon with *I(poly)*, the polygon color.

3. There is only one **surrounding** polygon. Fill the window with *I(poly)*.

4. If more than one polygon intersects, is inside, or surrounds, and at least one is a **surrounding** polygon.

   4.1 Is one surrounding polygon, P_S, in front of all others? If so, paint window with $I(P_S)$. The test is: Calculate the z-depths for each polygon plane at the corners of the current window. If all four z-depths of the P_S plane are all smaller than any z-depths of other polygons in the window, then P_S is in front.

If the easy choice tests do not classify the polygon configuration into one of these four trivial action cases, the algorithm recurs by dividing the current window into four equal subwindows. Note that test 4.1 is a very easy and clean test for identifying a surrounding up-front polygon. That is, since the polygon's plane, not just the polygon itself, must be cleanly separated in z, some P_S polygons fail the test because they overlap in z with other polygon planes. In this instance, cases will frequently be missed in which the back polygons themselves should be obscured by P_S but fail the plane separation test. However, rather than revert to the complex geometrical tests of the painter's algorithm, Warnock's algorithm

simply makes the easy choices and invokes recursion for non-trivial cases. Figure 8.26 shows the application of the algorithm with four levels of recursion applied to the complete image and eight levels along a selected boundary.

A noteworthy feature of Warnock's algorithm concerns how the divide-and-conquer area subdivision preserves area coherence. That is, all polygons classified as *surrounding* and *outside* retain this classification with respect to all sub-windows generated by recursion. This aspect of the algorithm is the basis for its efficiency. The algorithm may be classified as a radix four quick sort. Windows of 1024 × 1024 pixels may be re-solved to the single pixel level with only ten recursive calls of the algorithm.

While the original Warnock algorithm had the advantages of elegance and simplicity, the perfor-mance of the area subdivision technique can be improved with alternative subdivision strategies. Some of these include:

- Divide the area using an enclosed polygon vertex to set the dividing boundary.

- Sort polygons by minimum z and use the front polygon as the window boundary. This greatly reduces the number of levels of recursion required.

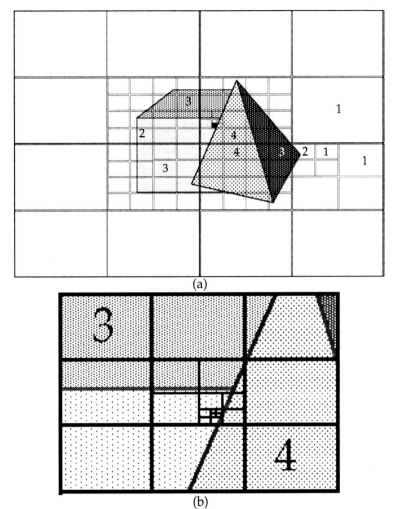

Figure 8.26
Warnock's area subdivision algorithm. (a) The whole image at four levels of recursion. (b) A selected portion with one eight-level refinement shown.

Conclusions

This chapter explores the *expressive power* achieved by moving from simple polyhedral representations to more abstract mathematical formulations. Bézier's parametric cubic surfaces were shown to be a particularly flexible and powerful tool for modeling smooth curved surfaces. The recently introduced superquadric representation provides an even more elegant tool for modeling primitive solids in an infinite variety of shapes. Once such primitive solids are available, the techniques of constructive solid geometry (CSG) offer methods of constructing complex objects by the Boolean operations of union, intersection, and difference applied to the geometric primitives.

After introducing these new representations, we returned to the task of implementation. The next two implementation issues (following projection, introduced in the last chapter) are those of 3D clipping and hidden surface removal. The Cohen-Sutherland clipping algorithm is shown to be easily extended from 2D to 3D using the techniques of homogeneous coordinate transformations, normalized and canonical view volumes, and the perspective → parallel volume transformation. Finally, techniques for hidden surface removal were introduced, starting with the algorithm for back-face removal and proceeding through four standard hidden surface algorithms. Implementation of an effective visible surface algorithm is a large and essential step towards the goal of visual realism of synthetic images.

Exercises

8.1 The ability of abstract representations to model complex geometric shapes with a minimal set of numbers lies with the underlying "theory" relating coordinates on the model surface. Compare the *concrete* (set of polygons) and *abstract* (superquadric) *representations* of a cube, cylinder, and sphere in terms of the required database and/or theory definition for a reasonable good model of these primitives. Which is more efficient for each of the cases?

8.2 From your solid geometry textbook, locate and write down the parametric form for spheroids. Clearly identify the variable parameters, and indicate the range of shape parameters for the two cases: oblate spheroid and prolate spheroid. Sketch these two cases.

8.3 Write a procedure to interactively enter the sixteen control points for a Bézier patch. A useful technique might be to specify each location in the *x-y* plane by mouse pointer and then use four *x-z* or *y-z* profiles (corresponding to the rows or columns of *P*) to specify the *z* elevation of each point.

8.4 Write a procedure to carry out the matrix multiplications indicated in equation 8.6 to compute the parametric surface of a Bézier patch. Step through the *s* and *t* parameters in twenty increments each to generate a table of (x,y,z) triplets corresponding to nodes on the isoparametric curves in the surface.

8.5 Integrate the procedures of problems 8.3 and 8.4 into a Bézier patch program which plots out user-designed parametric surfaces in orthographic projection. A useful data structure for this surface is to consider it a set of 19×19 polygons whose vertices are all possible 2×2 adjacent coordinate triplets of the table from problem 8.4.

8.6 Use the Bézier patch program from problem 8.5 to reproduce the parametric curves shown in Figures 8.3, 8.4, 8.5, 8.6, and 8.7.

8.7 Use the Bézier patch program from problem 8.5 to illustrate and answer the following

questions: How many relative maxima and minima can Bézier patches exhibit? How many inflection points (change of curvature from + to –) can a Bézier patch contain?

8.8 When Bézier patches are spliced together to model an object, continuity at the seams is maintained by making the edge points identical and the slope control points co-linear. Discuss the problem this introduces when one of the slope control points is moved to alter the model. How many additional points need be adjusted? Propose an algorithm for handling this problem.

8.9 For what applications might a Hermite parametric surface have an advantage over the Bézier form?

8.10 Write a program to compute the isoparametric curves for twenty equal increments in *s* and *t* for the superquadric representation and plot the results as an orthographic, wire frame projection. Use the program to plot four of the cases shown in Figures 8.9 and 8.10.

8.11 Describe three design applications in which the superquadric representation would be particularly useful. What advantages do superquadrics have over parametric cubic representations?

8.12 Discuss and sketch the design of three objects by the *union* operation of CSG.

8.13 Discuss and sketch the design of three objects by the *intersection* operation of CSG.

8.14 Discuss and sketch the design of three objects by the *difference* operation of CSG.

8.15 To implement CSG in an application program, a whole new set of problems arises. Describe three such problems and suggest possible algorithms for their solution.

8.16 Discuss and expand on the statement "CSG is an object-oriented language which may be represented as an ordered, binary tree."

8.17 The text claims that CSG "is not unique." Sketch a single object designed by three distinct CSG programs.

8.18 The six-bit Cohen-Sutherland classification code used in 3D line clipping can specify the location of the end point of the line in any one of 27 distinct regions. Yet, in digital logic you learned that 6 bits are capable of addressing 64 distinct objects. Why are these two numbers different?

8.19 Write down the clipping test for single point clipping in terms of the following three parameters:
    1) View volume parameters,
$[X_R, X_L, Y_T, Y_B, Z_B, Z_F]$
    2) Normalized view volume parameters,
$[1,0,1,0,1,0]$
    3) The Cohen-Sutherland code, $C = TBRLHY$.

8.20 List five kinds of geometric coherence which have proven useful in visible surface algorithms. Give a concrete example of each and indicate how the coherence improves the efficiency of the algorithm.

8.21 Classify the back-face and four hidden surface removal algorithms presented in this chapter along the object space/image space continuum. Why do most practical visible surface algorithms use image-space techniques?

8.22 Consider the efficiency of back-face removal in parallel and perspective projections. With the help of a sketch, prove that this algorithm removes approximately fifty percent of the polygons in parallel projection.

8.23 Consider the efficiency of back-face removal in perspective projections. Show, through sketches of a cube, how the efficiency rises from ≥ fifty percent to 83.3% as the cube and COP become closer to each other.

8.24 Consider the efficiency of back-face removal in perspective projections. Using a sketch of a sphere, derive an analytical expression for the efficiency of back-face removal as a function of the distance between the center of the object and the COP.

8.25 The back-face removal algorithm was discussed only for convex polyhedrons. Discuss and sketch the problems encountered when the polyhedron is concave (i.e. contains some exterior angles between faces of ≤ 180°.) What simplification or reduction of the data would you suggest to eliminate these problems?

8.26 Write a back-face removal program and apply it to a scene containing a cube and a regular tetrahedron.

8.27 Write a simple painter's algorithm hidden surface removal program. Apply it to a scene containing a cube and regular tetrahedron. Can you make it fail? Can you suggest scenes for which it will fail?

Endnotes

1. Mortenson, Michael E., *Geometric Modeling*, John Wiley & Sons, New York, NY (1985).
2. Barsky, Brian A., *Computer Graphics and Geometric Modeling Using Beta-splines*, Springer-Verlag, Heidelberg (1988).
3. Coons, Steven, "Surface Patches and B-Spline Curves," in *Computer Aided Geometric Design*, R. Barnhill and R. Riesenfeld (eds), Academic Press, (1974).
4. Ferguson, D., "Multivariate curve interpolation," *JACM* **II/2**, pp. 221–228, (1964).
5. Barr, A., "Superquadrics and Angle Preserving Transformations," *IEEE Computer Graphics Appl.* **1**, pp. 1–20 (1981).
6. Barr, A., "Global and Local Deformation of Solid Primitives," *Computer Graphics* **18** (3), pp. 21–30 (1984).
7. Pentland, Alex P., "Perceptual Organization and the Representation of Natural Form," *Artificial Intelligence - An International Journal* **28** (3), pp. 293–331 (1986).
8. Requicha, A. A. G., "Mathematical Models of Rigid Solid Objects," Technical Memo No. 28, Production Automation Project, University of Rochester, Rochester NY (1977). See also: Requicha, A. A. G. and H. B. Voelcker, "Solid Modeling: A Historical Summary and Contemporary Assessment," *IEEE Computer Graphics and Applications* **2** (2), pp. 9–24, March (1982).
9. Mortenson, Michael E., *Geometric Modeling*, John Wiley & Sons, New York, NY (1985).
10. Figures 8.11 – 8.15 were all generated on IN-CAD, a Macintosh CAD system with full CSG, extrusion, and lathing ca.pability. Available

from Infinite Graphics, Inc., 4611 East Lake Street, Minneapolis, MN 55406

11. Sutherland, Ivan E., Sproull, Robert F., and Schumacker, Robert A., "A Characterization of Ten Hidden-Surface Algorithms," *Computing Surveys* **6**, (#1), Association of Computing Machinery, March (1974). See reprint in Beatty and Booth, *Tutorial: Computer Graphics*, Second Edition, , IEEE, Computer Society Press, Los Angeles, CA (1982).

12. Sedgewick, Robert, *Algorithms*, Addison Wesley Publishing Company, Reading, MA (1983).

13. Knuth, Donald E., *The Art of Computer Programming*, Vol 3, Addison Wesley Publishing Company, Reading, MA (1973).

14. Firebaugh, Morris W., *Artificial Intelligence – A Knowledge-Based Approach*, p. 508, PWS-Kent Publishing Company, Boston, MA (1988).

15. Warnock, J. E., *A Hidden Surface Algorithm for Computer Generated Halftone Pictures*, University of Utah Computer Science Report TR$-15 (NTIS AD-753 671) (1969).

Chapter 9

Three-Dimensional Graphics –
Visual Realism and Color

**If the goal in shading a computer-synthesized image is to simulate a
real physical object, then the shading model should in some way
imitate real physical shading situations.**
Bui-Tuong Phong

The goal of visual realism in computer graphics is attained most directly by a systematic refinement of our techniques for representing scenes in computer memory and displaying them on some output device. So far, we have studied the polyhedral representation of objects and various alternatives based on parametric representations. Our first step toward visually realistic rendering was achieved through the application of visible surface techniques to the polyhedral representation. Visible surface techniques correctly take into account the effects of an object's geometry and the geometrical relationships of multiple objects on the visibility of all objects in a scene. They say nothing about the shading or color with which an object is rendered. These subjects are central to realistic rendering and are the topics of this chapter.

The correct rendering of a scene requires not only an accurate representation of the objects composing the scene but also an accurate representation of the visual environment in which the objects exist. The visual environment includes such factors as the distribution and spectral intensities of all light sources, the optical properties of all objects in the environment (opacity, color, reflectance, and surface texture), and the optical properties of the medium carrying light from the sources to the objects and eventually to the observer. The extent to which rendering programs take all these effects into account determines the quality of visual realism achieved.

As in several previous case studies, models for shading and color range from concrete, overly sim-plistic techniques to physically correct but mathematically complex approaches. We introduce a simple shading model in this chapter and consider the more complex but physically correct models in the next. The simple model is incomplete because it lumps many secondary effects into simple categories such as *ambient light intensity*. The simple model is a combination of physics and heuristic approximations of physical effects. It represents a compromise between visual realism and computational cost.

As a final note, the compromise between visual realism and computational costs involves interactions between representation schemes, hidden surface algorithms, and shading models. Polyhedral representations simplify the hidden surface removal task but complicate the task of computing the shading of curved surfaces. Parametric representations simplify the task of computing surface shading but complicate the task of hidden surface removal. The interesting result demonstrated in this chapter is that, through the use of clever shading algorithms, the relatively primitive polyhedral representation can achieve a visual realism approaching that of the parametric representation.

A Simple Reflection Model

In 1975, Bui-Tuong Phong proposed a simple reflection model to improve upon the shading models in use at that time.[1] In addition to the simple shading model, Phong proposed a new

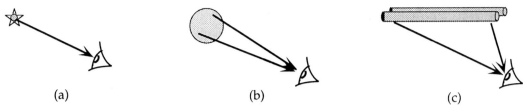

(a)   (b)   (c)

Figure 9.1
Range of sources from point to extended.
    a) Star → as close to a point source as nature provides
    b) Sun → really an extended but often considered as a point source
    c) Fluorescent light → typical extended source

algorithm to average the shading on polygonal representations of smooth surfaces that recovered the smooth appearance of the original surface. The Phong algorithm provided a significant improvement over Gouraud shading, an averaging algorithm which greatly enhanced the smooth appearance of polygonal surfaces.[2] The success of the Phong shading model rests on what we might call the principle of *model authenticity*. This principle can be summarized as:

> *In order to successfully simulate some process of nature, any model must recognize and successfully simulate the natural laws by which the process occurs.*

This principle is suggested in Phong's quotation introducing the chapter and serves as the basis for David Marr's successful theory of human vision.[3] It is the guiding principle behind the approaches to visual realism of both this and the next two chapters.

Sources and Surfaces

Before we investigate the Gouraud and Phong models in detail, it is helpful to define some of the characteristics of sources and surfaces.

Sources

The sources of illumination for a scene are broadly classified as either *point sources* or *extended sources*. In fact, there are no ideal point sources in nature —the concept logically involves an infinite energy density. In practice, we consider stars and objects such as fireflies and auto headlights viewed from a distance as good approximations of point sources. A good heuristic test for distinguishing between point and extended sources is to answer the question: Can I distinguish the *size* of the source by looking at it? If the answer is "no," then it is a point source; if "yes," then it is an extended source.

Note, when this definition is applied rigidly to the sun, it classifies the sun as an extended source. This is the correct classification as you can verify by noting the fuzzy shadows cast by sharply defined objects in sunlight. Since the disk of the sun subtends a solid angle of approximately 0.5 degree diameter, rays from different parts of the sun can diverge by up to one half degree. However, in practice, this divergence of the sun's rays from parallelism is not detectable in most renderings of computer graphics scenes. So the sun is usually classified by graphics texts as a point source.

Extended sources are much more common in practice than point sources. Examples include fluorescent lights and windows. Extended sources all exhibit a common property which identifies them as extended (or distributed). That is that rays striking the observer from different parts of the source are measurably divergent. Rays from point sources, which strike a point on the image, are by definition all parallel. The equivalence of the "size" and "parallelism" tests for point/extended sources is illustrated in Figure 9.1.

Point sources can be located anywhere, of course, even in the midst of a scene being rendered. In circumstances in which the distance from the source to the scene is comparable with the dimensions of the scene itself, rays from the source will have considerable divergence. In fact, rays from a source near a polygon will diverge over the surface of the polygon. That is, the angle of incident rays and their distance from source to surface will vary significantly as one scans across a single polygon. This greatly complicates the computation of the amount of light striking the polygon at a given point.

Since much of human history was spent outdoors with the sun and moon as the primary source of illumination, we have a deeply rooted instinct for interpreting lighting from an approximate point source approximately at infinity as the most natural. This fact, combined with the computational simplification achieved, leads us to the first heuristic of our simple model.

> Heuristic 1: *All point sources are located at infinity.*

This compromise achieves considerable simplification at a relatively small cost in loss of visual realism.

Ambient Lighting

The observant reader may already feel uneasy over the difficulties involved in computing the illumination of a given polygon surface from extended sources. Problems such as these provided the motivation for inventing calculus. To calculate the intensity of light striking any point on the polygon from a distributed source involves integrating the intensity distribution over the surface of the source and correctly taking into account the dependence of the intensity upon distance from source to polygon surface. This is a difficult and computationally intensive task.

Upon further consideration the curious reader may be overwhelmed to discover that such source-to-object integrations are only the tip of the iceberg. The core of this discovery is the recognition that *each surface* illuminated by all point and extended sources becomes, itself, a source of light for illumination of all other line-of-sight surfaces of the scene. Each of these surfaces, in turn, re-reflects light to other surfaces, including the original one, thus achieving an "infinite regression" of reflections and illumination. The partial history of the scattering of one ray is shown in Figure 9.2. Both ray tracing and radiosity algorithms are attempts to recognize and solve this real, physical, and enormously complex problem.

In the simple illumination model, this complexity is "swept under the rug" by defining all such secondary reflection effects as *ambient illumination*. This heuristic states that all secondary scattering and background illumination effects can be represented by a uniform, isotropic ambient lighting (i.e., the same in all directions).

> Heuristic 2: *All illumination other than that from point sources comes from isotropic ambient lighting.*

The ambient lighting heuristic simplifies the task of accounting for diffuse lighting and secondary scattering effects at a relatively low cost in loss of visual realism. It can be thought of as a gross averaging or integration of these effects for a scene with a random distribution and orientation of objects. As we shall see shortly, it reduces computation of illumination due to scattered light to a trivial additive factor.

Surfaces

Light striking a surface can undergo a variety of processes depending on the optical properties of the material. In the most general case these processes include:

- **Diffuse reflection** – light scattered isotropically by a matte surface,

- **Spectral reflection** – light scattered by mirror-like, shiny surfaces,

- **Transmission** – light penetrates surface according to Snell's law.

Transparent objects can be further classified as translucent or clear. For translucent objects, the light is scattered internally and gives the object a cloudy or "milky" appearance. Clear objects transmit the ray in a straight line through the object with the angular relationship at each surface being determined by Snell's law. This variety of processes is illustrated graphically in Figure 9.3.

Figure 9.3 illustrates a number of important relationships. Three of these are based on the conservation of energy:

$$I_i = I_R + I_t \qquad\qquad [9.1]$$
(Law of energy conservation),

$$I_R = I_r + I_d$$
(reflected light may be spectral or diffuse),

$$I_t = I_s + I_{t'} + I_c \, ,$$
(transmitted light may be scattered, refracted, or absorbed)

where
I_i = Integrated intensity (power density) of the incident beam,
I_R = Integrated intensity of all reflected rays, both spectral and diffuse,

I_t = Integrated intensity for all rays transmitted through the surface,

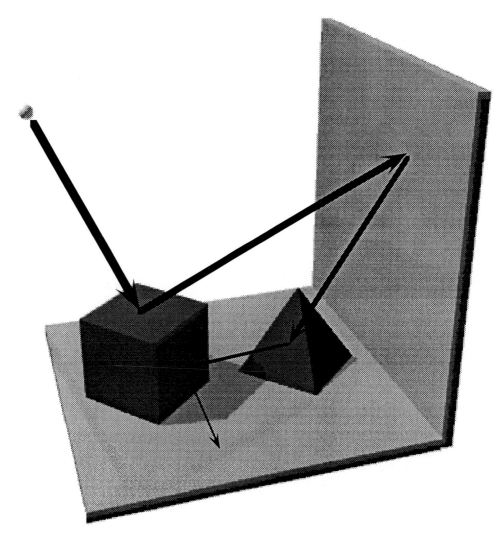

Figure 9.2
Successive scattering of a single ray from a point source. As light from the point source illuminates the top surface of the cube, it becomes a secondary source illuminating all other line-of-sight surfaces. At each scattering a portion of the ray's energy is absorbed, leaving a reduced-intensity reflected ray.

I_s = Integrated intensity of spectrally reflected rays (mirror reflection)

I_d = Integrated intensity of diffusely reflected rays

I_s = Integrated intensity of all primary scattered rays

I_c = Integrated power density of all absorbed light energy (converted to heat), both internally and on the surface.

The three laws of energy conservation given in [9.1] state simply that energy never simply disappears. The light energy striking the surface of an object shows up either as transformed light energy (reflected, transmitted, or scattered) or as heat energy (absorbed).

Snell's law of refraction gives us an additional equation governing the relationship of the angles that the incident and refracted rays make with the normal to the surface, N. For a ray incident in media 1 and refracted in media 2, Snell's law may be stated:

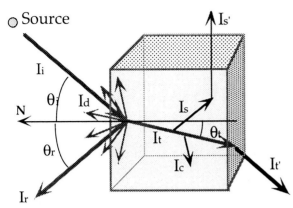

Figure 9.3
Processes which may occur when a light ray strikes a surface.

I_i = Incident ray (Spectral reflection)
I_r = Reflected ray
I_c = Converted ray
I_d = Reflected rays (Diffuse reflection)
I_t = Transmitted ray (Media 2)
I_s, $I_{s'}$ = Internally scattered rays
$I_{t'}$ = Transmitted ray (Media 1)

$$n_1 \sin \theta_1 = n_2 \sin \theta_2 \qquad [9.2]$$
(Snell's law of refraction),

where

n_1 = Index of refraction of media 1
($\sim$1.0 for air),
n_2 = Index of refraction of media 2
($\sim$1.5 for most glass),
θ_1 = Angle of incident ray with respect to surface normal,
θ_2 = Angle of refracted ray with respect to surface normal.

Finally, the law of spectral reflection for mirror-like surfaces yields the equation:

$$\theta_i = \theta_r \qquad [9.3]$$
(Perfect spectral reflection).

Any physically correct illumination model must take all of these effects into account. In actual practice, computation of all these effects in accordance with the physical laws 9.1–9.3 is an extremely time consuming task. Various illumination models attempt to simplify these calculations with heuristic approximations.

The simple illumination model makes several key assumptions which limits the range of applicability of the model but also greatly simplifies the computations. First, it assumes that all objects are opaque. That is, it ignores transparent objects and assumes that $I_t = I_c$ and that all absorption takes place on the surface. Therefore, we can state heuristic 3 as:

> **Heuristic 3:** *All objects of the scene are opaque.*

You might run your own *in situ* experiment to determine how much generality is lost by this assumption. Look about you, and note how many objects can be classified as *transparent* and how many *opaque*. Only objects constructed from glass, clear plastics, or liquids can qualify as transparent. Again, since the trigonometric functions of Snell's law are computationally expensive, this heuristic costs us little and buys us much.

A final heuristic in the simple illumination model deals with the unrealistic mathematical abstractions of "point source" and "perfect spectral reflection" given in Equation 9.3. The heuristic, first proposed by Warnock,[4] replaces the equality of [9.3] with the approximation, $\theta_i \approx \theta_r$. The two problems which Warnock's heuristic effectively solve include:

- **The real extended nature of most mathematical point sources** – Spectral reflections are responsible for the "highlights" seen in actual physical scenes. An ideal point source would produce an ideal "point" reflected highlight according to Equation 9.3. Since we have noted that even the sun is not an ideal point source, real highlights are extended rather than point like in appearance. That is, we should be able to observe the spectral highlight by viewing at angles *near*, but not just precisely *at* θ_r.

- **Deviations from perfect mirror reflections** – Most surfaces are neither perfectly reflecting (glossy) nor perfectly "flat" (matte). Due to imperfections of real surfaces, they produce a spectral reflection centered along angle θ_r but with a finite angular distribution about this angle. Different surfaces will generate distributions with different angular distributions. The distribution of highly glossy, specular surfaces is sharply peaked at $\theta = \theta_r$—more matte surfaces generate broader distributions.

The theoretical mathematical description of the angular dependence of specular reflection of a point source by a perfect mirror is given by:

$$I_{th}(\theta) = k_s\, I_i\, \delta(\theta - \theta_r)\,, \qquad [9.4]$$

where
k_s = the fraction of the incident beam which is reflected,
$\delta(\theta - \theta_r) = 1$ when $\theta = \theta_r$; 0 otherwise.

Warnock's heuristic broadens the distribution function by using a function of $\cos(\theta - \theta_r)$ raised to the power n. That is,

$$I_w(\theta) = k_s\, I_i\, \cos^n(\theta - \theta_r)\,, \qquad [9.5]$$

where
$n = 1 \rightarrow 100$ depending on how shiny the surface is.
($n = 1$ for matte surface;
$n = 100$ for highly reflective surface)

We summarize this heuristic as:

> **Heuristic 4:** *The spectral reflection intensity is proportional to the $\cos(\theta - \theta_r)$ raised to some power n which depends on the glossiness of the surface.*

One interesting property of specular reflection is that it is independent of the color of the surface. The color of the reflected beam, I_s, is the same as that of the incident beam. If this seems difficult to believe, you can verify it with a simple experiment. Simply hold up a book with a glossy cover at the correct orientation so that you can observe some quasi point source with $\theta_i = \theta_s$. Using different colored objects as the specular reflecting surface, you will always get the same color for the highlight—namely, the color of the source light.

Color

One of the most important characteristics of a surface is its color. The difference in color exhibited by different objects illuminated by the same light source is due to a difference in the absorption coefficient, k_a, for different wavelengths, λ_i, of incident light. Since in our simple

illumination model all light is either absorbed or reflected, the reflection coefficient, k_r, is also λ dependent because of energy conservation.

$$k_a(\lambda) + k_r(\lambda) = 1\,, \qquad [9.6]$$

where
$k_a(\lambda)$ = fraction of incident light of wavelength λ which is absorbed,
$k_r(\lambda)$ = fraction of incident light of wavelength λ which is reflected.

So, for instance, when sunlight (approximately white light) strikes a green object the reddish portion of the spectrum is absorbed and green wavelengths are reflected.

The approximation used in the simple illumination model is to consider the color of an object as fully described by the reflectivity coefficient, $k_r(\lambda)$. Further, it is assumed that the color of spectrally reflected light is the color of the light source rather than that of the surface. Finally, it is assumed that the spectral distribution of ambient light is that of white light. These approximations can be summarized by the following heuristic:

> **Heuristic 5:** *The color response of a surface element is given by*
> - *The reflection coefficient $k_r(\lambda)$ applied to incident point source and ambient light,*
> - *Specularly reflected light which retains the color of the point source,*
> - *Ambient light which is white.*

Note that this heuristic describes fairly accurately the behavior of specularly reflected light but grossly over simplifies several other important aspects of real optics. First, by using only $k_r(\lambda)$ to describe the reflection behavior of a surface, we ignore the difference in color of point sources in computing the diffuse reflection. Secondly, by assuming that the ambient background light is white, it ignores the interaction of proximate color surfaces on each other—the "bleeding" of color from one surface onto nearby surfaces. These faults of the simple illumination model are corrected by the more realistic radiosity model.

The Simple Illumination Model

Now that we have defined some of the terms used in describing illumination and some useful heuristics to reduce the complexity of modeling the behavior of real light precisely, we can begin to build up the simple shading model. Let's define a term, *SHADE*, which will represent the color with which we shade a given polygon of our polyhedral scene and incrementally build the model by adding successive terms corresponding to each physical process.

Combining the ambient lighting heuristic with the simple color model heuristic, we can describe the *ambient light* contribution to the shading term as:

$$SHADE = k_r(\lambda)\, I_a \qquad [9.7]$$
$$\text{(ambient term)},$$

where

$k_r(\lambda)$ = color-dependent reflection coefficient of the surface,
I_a = intensity of ambient light striking the surface.

The second term in the simple illumination model is the *diffuse reflection* of light from *point sources*. In Figure 9.4 we show the important parameters for this process. Simple geometric considerations lead to Lambert's law of cosines which states that the intensity of light reflected from a perfect diffusing surface is proportional to the cosine of the angle, θ, between the light source direction, L, and the normal to the surface, N. Since $\cos \theta = L \cdot N$, this can be expressed mathematically as the second term in the shading equation:

$$SHADE = k_r(\lambda)\, I_a + k_r(\lambda)\, I_i\, L \cdot N \qquad [9.8]$$
$$\text{(adding diffuse term)}$$

where

I_i = intensity of incident light source i measured at the surface.

Note that both the ambient term and the diffuse reflection term are independent of the viewing angle. At first this may seem a bit surprising since one might expect intuitively that an illuminated surface viewed along the direction anti-parallel to the normal would appear brighter than one viewed along a glancing angle. However, since truly diffuse surfaces emit an equal intensity in all directions, this is not the case.

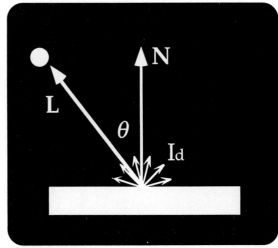

Figure 9.4
Diffuse reflection from a point source. Lambert's law says that the intensity, I_d, of diffusely reflected light is proportional to $\cos \theta = L \cdot N$, the cosine of the angle between the surface normal and vector, L, pointing towards the light source. Note that the intensity I_d is isotropic—the same in all directions.

An interesting geometric cancellation takes place when a surface is viewed at a glancing angle. Although each unit surface area appears reduced in size (and hence emits less light toward the viewer), a given solid angle of viewing area includes more surface area units as the glancing angle ϕ increases towards 90° from the normal. The shrinkage in surface area is proportional to $\cos \phi$ of the glancing angle. The growth of the number of units of surface in the same viewing solid angle grows as $(1/\cos \phi)$, so the two effects precisely cancel. Thus, the apparent intensity of a diffusely reflecting surface appears constant from any viewing angle.

The dependence of light intensity on distance, r, from a point source is proportional to r^{-2}. Since we are assuming that $r = \infty$ for all point sources, the intensity of illumination of all point sources would be zero for a physically correct dependence on distance. However, since objects in a real scene become dimmer with increasing distance, we can provide some depth cueing by introducing another heuristic. This heuristic states that the intensity of an object illuminated by a point source falls off inversely with the distance from the *observer* to the object. Thus, the distance correction to the simple shading model may be added by rewriting the shading equation as:

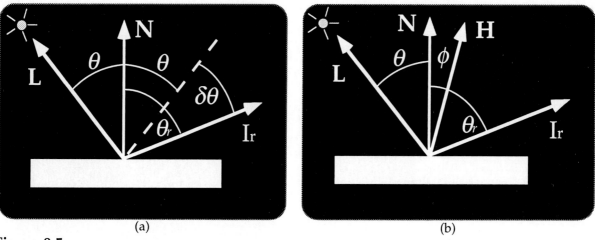

(a)   (b)

Figure 9.5

Angular relationships for specular reflection. The error angle $\delta\theta$ is the deviation of the viewing direction angle, θ_r, from the ideal angle, θ. The half-angle direction, H, splits the angle between the source direction, L, and viewing direction, I_r.

$$SHADE = k_r(\lambda)\, I_a + \frac{k_r(\lambda)\, I_i\, L\cdot N}{d+K} \qquad [9.9]$$

(adding distance effect)

where
$d = D + z$ = distance of polygon
    from observer,
D = distance of observer
    from view plane,
K = arbitrary constant to be adjusted
    to optimize realism.

Note that the distance term in Equation 9.7 is not intended to accurately simulate the inverse square law of intensity vs. distance from a point source. Rather, it provides a simple heuristic for depth cueing based on our experience of closer objects appearing brighter.

The final term in the simple illumination model involves a mathematical representation for specular reflection. As heuristic 4 indicated, specular reflection can be effectively modeled by using a term in $\cos^n(\delta\theta)$ where $\delta\theta = \theta - \theta_r$ is a measure of the deviation from ideal specular reflection and n is some number in the range of $1 \leq n \leq 100$, depending on the glossiness of the surface. A dull, matte surface would have n values in the range of one while a highly polished, glossy surface would have a large value of n. Figure 9.5 illustrates the angles involved in this model and an alternative form of expressing the relationship in terms of the *half-angle* vector, H.

A careful comparison of Figure 9.5(a) and 9.5(b) allows us to derive a relationship between

the error angle, $\delta\theta$, and the angle ϕ between the half-angle vector H and the normal, N.

$$H = \frac{L + I_r}{|L + I_r|}, \qquad [9.10]$$

$$\theta + \phi = \theta_r - \phi, \qquad [9.11]$$

$$2\,\phi = \theta_r - \theta, \qquad [9.12]$$

$$\phi = \frac{\theta_r - \theta}{2} = \frac{\delta\theta}{2}. \qquad [9.13]$$

We can use the trigonometric and geometric identities

$$\cos\delta\theta = \cos 2\phi = 2\cos^2\phi - 1, \qquad [9.14]$$

$$\cos\phi = H\cdot N, \qquad [9.15]$$

to write

$$\cos^n\delta\theta = [2\,(H\cdot N)^2 - 1]^n. \qquad [9.16]$$

The important point is that $\cos^n\delta\theta \propto (H\cdot N)^{2n}$, and the vector formulation is easily computed in terms of the light direction, L, and the viewing direction, I_r. With this formulation of the specular reflection angular dependence, we can add in the fourth term to the shading equation as:

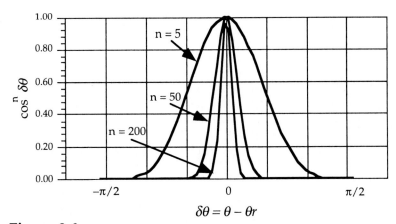

Figure 9.6
Dependence of specular peaking term, $\cos^n \delta\theta$, on coefficient n. Note how the distribution approaches ideal reflection (a spike at $\delta\theta = 0$) as $n \to \infty$.

The addition of specular reflection introduces a dependence upon viewing angle into the shading equation. This is illustrated in Figure 9.7 in which the vector, V, points towards the viewer. For this particular case the total diffuse reflection intensity I_d is approximately equal to the spectral intensity, I_s. For the particular viewing angle shown, the spectral intensity is at the maximum value since the angle of incidence is equal to the angle of reflection. As the viewing angle changes, the spectral reflection intensity will fall off, but the diffuse intensity will remain constant as indicated by the spherical distribution of I_d.

$$SHADE = k_r(\lambda)\, I_a + \frac{I_i\, (k_r(\lambda)\; L\cdot N + k_s\, (H\cdot N)^n)}{d + K},$$

[9.17]

where
k_s = reflection coefficient,
$2 \le n \le 200$ to accommodate the change from $\delta\theta$ to ϕ.

The reflection coefficient, k_s, is a measure of the fraction of incident light which is specularly reflected. In general, it is a function of incident angle, θ, increasing as θ increases and reaching approximately 1 as $\theta \to 90°$. Since there are no simple heuristic for describing this behavior, we shall assume k_s is a constant for each surface. The effect of varying the glossiness coefficient, n, is illustrated in Figure 9.6.

The final refinement of the simple illumination model is to take into account multiple point sources. Since the light from each source adds independently to the brightness of a given polygon's illumination, the appropriate method for modeling their influence is to add the diffuse and specular reflection terms that depend on the incident point sources. This may be expressed as:

$$SHADE = k_r(\lambda)\, I_a + \sum_{i=1}^{m} \frac{I_i\, [k_r(\lambda)\; L_i\cdot N + k_s\, (H_i\cdot N)^n]}{d + K}$$

[9.18]

where
m = total number of point sources.

Limitations of the Simple Shading Model

The strength of Phong's simple shading model is that it incorporates enough physics to simulate the major lighting effects in a polygon scene at a relatively modest computational cost. However, the heuristics—sometimes called "hacks"—used in the simple model to approximate the physics of illumination are both overly simplistic and incomplete. Some lighting effects not accounted for in the simple shading model include:

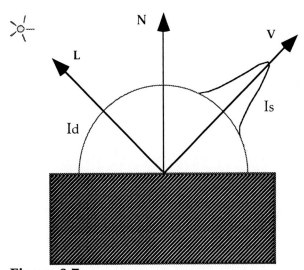

Figure 9.7
Angular distribution of diffuse and specular reflection. A viewer along vector V would observe a maximum reflected highlight of the source. For the case shown, $I_s \approx I_d$.

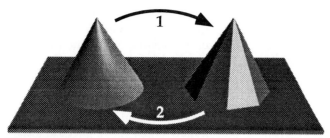

Figure 9.8
Closing the representation loop. For purposes of simplicity in data storage and hidden surface removal, arc 1 was used to transform the original object on the left into the polyhedron on the right. Interpolative shading techniques, shown as arc 2, attempt to recover the original shape from the polygon representation.

- By placing all point sources at infinity, the model fails to properly consider the real r^{-2} dependence of illumination as a function of distance between source and object.

- By limiting spectral reflections to point sources only, the model ignores the reflection of other objects and multiple reflections of point sources by specular surfaces.

- By considering all objects opaque the model ignores the large class of translucent and transparent objects.

- By approximating the effects of surface-to-surface reflections by an ambient light term, the model ignores observable effects such as "color bleeding."

Much of the research in computer graphics has been directed toward refining the simple illumination model in order to overcome these limitations. The physical laws of diffuse and specular reflection first captured in the simple illumination model provide the basic structure for more sophisticated illumination models such as ray tracing.

Interpolative Shading Techniques

The simple shading model of Equation 9.16 is designed to give each polygon in a scene the appropriate, constant shade according to the simplifying assumptions outlined above. As we have noted in earlier chapters, there are advantages to using a simple polyhedral representation, including simplicity of the data base and relative ease of solving the hidden surface problem. The price we pay is that every scene is composed of only polygons, and each of these has a constant shading value. The result is that all objects have a "faceted" appearance, including smoothly curved surfaces. Facets broadcast the polyhedral nature of the scene and destroy any semblance of visual realism.

The goal of interpolative shading techniques is to recover the appearance of the curved surfaces which the polyhedral representation is designed to approximate. This objective is illustrated in Figure 9.8 as arc 2 transforming the polygon representation back to the original curved surface. The two leading interpolative techniques are *Gouraud interpolation* and *Phong interpolation*.

Assumptions of Interpolative Techniques

As the basis of their interpolation algorithms, both Gouraud and Phong made several simplifying assumptions. These include:

- Those polygons contributing to the smooth surface are identified and can be distinguished from polygons across sharp edges.

- An approximate normal to the original smooth surface can be computed at each vertex by averaging the normals to the polygons common to the vertex. This process is illustrated in Figure 9.9.

- The shading of a particular pixel can be obtained by a bilinear interpolation of the appropriate quantities from adjacent vertices.

The basic distinction between Gouraud and Phong interpolation is the choice of quantity to be interpolated. Gouraud interpolates the *shading*; Phong interpolates the *normal vector*. Let's consider each of these in more detail.

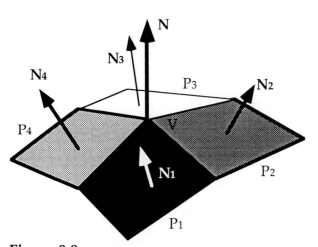

Figure 9.9
Computing the normal to the surface at vertex V. Vertex V is the vertex common to polygons P_1, P_2, P_3, and P_4 whose normals are N_1, N_2, N_3, and N_4, respectively. The surface normal, N, may be computed by averaging the surrounding polygon normals.

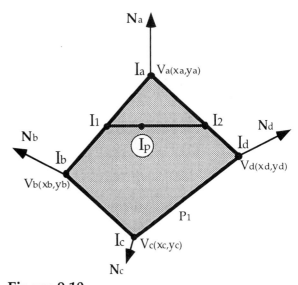

Figure 9.10
Intensity interpolation of Gouraud shading. The surface normals, $N_a...N_d$, are used to compute the intensities, $I_a...I_d$, at the bounding vertices. These, in turn, are interpolated to compute the intensities, I_1 and I_2, at the ends of the scan line. These end point intensities are interpolated to compute the intensity I_p at an arbitrary internal point.

Gouraud Interpolation Shading

The interpolated quantity for Gouraud shading is the *vertex shading value*. First, the surface normals at each vertex bounding the polygon are computed by averaging the normals of each polygon surrounding the vertex as shown in Figure 9.9. Once the surface normal for vertex i, called N_i, is known, the simple shading model given in [9.16] (or any other shading model) can be used to compute the intensity of illumination at each of the bounding vertices. These intensities, in turn, can be used to compute the intensity at any point along the polygon boundary lines. Finally, the edge intensities are used to compute the intensity at any point along the internal scan line across the polygon. Figure 9.10 demonstrates the relevant variables for this bilinear interpolation.

We summarize these steps in the Gouraud shading algorithm listed below.

The Gouraud interpolation algorithm greatly improves the appearance of smooth objects that have been modeled as polyhedrons. However, several anomalies of Gouraud shading cause it to fail the test of visual realism. These flaws include:

- **Mach banding** – While the shading produced by Gouraud interpolation is continuous across polygon boundaries, the first spatial derivative is discontinuous in general. Interestingly, the human retina func-

tions as a differentiator of intensity levels and can readily detect such discontinuities which are interpreted as bright "Mach" bands. For an object to appear smoothly shaded, both the illumination intensity and its first derivative must be continuous.

- **Highlight anomalies** – As a side effect of how surface normals are computed and intensities interpolated, highlights may be completely invisible or move erratically as light sources or objects move. The highlights which do appear will erroneously tend to cluster at vertex locations. Small highlights which would naturally occur near the center of a polygon will be missed completely.

- **Geometric anomalies** – Certain geometric configurations of polygons will lead to computed normal vectors which result in erroneous shading. Figure 9.11 illustrates one simple case in which the averaging of polygon normals, N_p, leads to parallel surface normals, N_s, and hence a uniform shading intensity which completely masks the surface shape.

- **Polygonal profile** – Both Gouraud and Phong interpolation produce smooth shading across polygon boundaries, but neither alter the basic polyhedral structure of objects modeled in a scene. Thus, while interpolation techniques recover the smooth surfaces of original objects, the polygonal profile remains as an artifact identifying the representation as polyhedral.

Gouraud Shading Algorithm

1. For each vertex bounding polygons in the area to be smoothed, compute the surface normals by averaging the polygon normal vectors for those polygons surrounding the vertex. Use only those polygons which are part of the smoothed surface. For instance, in Figures 9.9 and 9.10, we would compute:

$$N_a = \frac{1}{4} \sum_{i=1}^{4} N_i \,. \qquad [9.19]$$

2. Repeat for each polygon of the surface:
   2.1 Repeat for each vertex of the polygon: Use the normal values in a shading model to compute the shading value at each vertex. For example, the shading at vertex V_b can be computed using the normal N_b in [9.15] for single source illumination as:

$$I_b = k_r(\lambda)\, I_{amb} + \frac{I_i\,(k_r(\lambda)\, \mathbf{L \cdot N}_b + k_s\,(\mathbf{H \cdot N}_b)^n)}{d + K} \qquad [9.20]$$

   2.2 Repeat for each scan line of the polygon:
   2.2.1 Interpolate the appropriate vertex values to compute the intensity values at teach end of the scan line. To compute the intensity I_1 at a position (x_1,y_1) along the edge connecting V_a and V_b, use:

$$I_1 = I_a \frac{y_b - y_1}{y_b - y_a} + I_b \frac{y_1 - y_a}{y_b - y_a} \,. \qquad [9.21]$$

   2.2.2 Interpolate the scan line end-value intensities to compute the intensity value at each intermediate pixel along the scan line. To compute I_p at point (x_p,y_p) along a scan line with end point intensities I_1 and I_2, the interpolation equation is:

$$I_p = I_1 \frac{x_2 - x_p}{x_2 - x_1} + I_2 \frac{x_p - x_1}{x_2 - x_1} \,. \qquad [9.22]$$

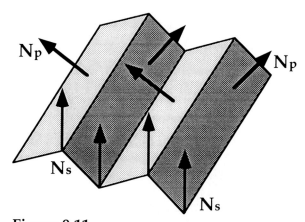

Figure 9.11
Geometric anomaly stemming from polygon normal averaging algorithm. The resulting surface normals, N_s, will produce a completely uniform Gouraud shading of this surface.

Phong Interpolation Shading

Two of the most serious problems of Gouraud shading, Mach bands and highlight anomalies, are resolved by Phong interpolation. In contrast to Gouraud shading which interpolates *intensities*, Phong shading involves a bilinear interpolation of the *surface normals*. By using a vector, N_p, Phong shading provides three times as much information at each pixel as does Gouraud shading. This allows the full shading model to be applied at each pixel and results in a much more realistic treatment of geometry-dependent features such as highlights.

The important interpolation vectors used in Phong shading are shown in Figure 9.12.

In Figure 9.13 we illustrate graphically the progress to this point in the quest for realistic rendering of a polyhedra-based world scene.

Both the success of Phong shading in solving the specular reflection problem and one of the remaining unsolved problems of this algorithm are illustrated in Figure 9.14. As we indicated in the discussion of Gouraud shading, the correct and consistent treatment of highlights (specular reflection) is a difficult problem. In Figure 9.14(a) the light source is positioned so that the angle of incidence lies along the light vector and the angle of reflection lies along the vector pointing to the camera for light striking the brightly lit polygon. The Phong-shaded Figure 9.14(b) correctly renders this highlight. In Figure 9.14(c), the light source has been moved so that the deviation from the maximum in specular reflection is about the same for the four upper central polygons. The result for the simple polygonal model (and for a Gouraud-shaded rendering) is that the specular highlight is almost completely lost. However, Phong shading correctly renders the shifted highlight in Figure 9.14(d). As the light source moves from situation (b) to situation (d), the Phong-shaded highlight moves from image (b) to image (d) in a smooth and consistent fashion.

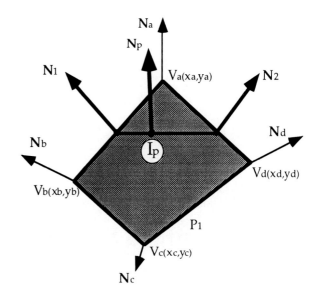

Figure 9.12
Phong interpolation shading vector diagram. Note that vector N_1 interpolates N_a and N_b; vector N_2 interpolates N_a and N_d; and, finally, vector N_p interpolates N_1 and N_2 and is used to compute the final shading value I_p.

Phong Shading Algorithm

1.   For each vertex bounding polygons in the area to be smoothed, compute the surface normals by averaging the polygon normal vectors for those polygons surrounding the vertex. Use only those polygons which are part of the smoothed surface. Use [9.17].

2.   Repeat for each polygon of the surface:

2.1 Repeat for each scan line of the polygon:

2.1.1 Interpolate the appropriate surface normal vectors to compute intermediate normal vectors at each end of the scan line. To compute the normal N_1 at a position (x_1, y_1) along the edge connecting V_a and V_b, use:

$$N_1 = N_a \frac{y_b - y_1}{y_b - y_a} + N_b \frac{y_1 - y_a}{y_b - y_a}. \qquad [9.23]$$

2.1.2. Interpolate the scan line end-value normals to compute the normal vector, N_p, at each intermediate pixel. To compute N_p at point (x_p, y_p) along a scan line with end point normals, N_1 and N_2, use:

$$N_p = N_1 \frac{x_2 - x_p}{x_2 - x_1} + N_2 \frac{x_p - x_1}{x_2 - x_1}. \qquad [9.24]$$

2.1.3 Use the normal value, N_p, with the simple shading model to compute the final shading value for the pixel at (x_p, y_p). For example, the shading I_p can be computed using the normal N_p in [9.17] for single source illumination as:

$$I_p = k_r(\lambda)\, I_{amb} + \frac{I_i\,(k_r(\lambda)\, L \cdot N_p + k_s\,(H \cdot N_p)^n)}{d + \mathbf{K}}$$

$$[9.25]$$

The remaining problem with both Gouraud and Phong shading is very apparent in Figure 9.14 and detectable in Figure 9.13. That problem is the "straight-edge" profile of any object constructed from polygons. Phong shading can correctly recover the smooth internal surface from its polygonal representation, but since the basic structure remains unmodified, the polygon profile remains as an artifact of the representation.

A final observation on the relative computational efficiency of Gouraud and Phong shading is in order. Note that, as bilinear interpolations, both require $2N + N \times M$ interpolation calculations per polygon, where N is the number of scan lines and M the average number of pixels per scan line. However, the Gouraud algorithm is much more efficient than the Phong algorithm for two reasons. Gouraud interpolation involves only scalars (intensities), whereas Phong interpolation operates on vectors (surface normals). This provides an automatic factor of three advantage of Gouraud over Phong. In addition, the fairly complex calculation of the simple shading model must be performed only at the vertices of Gouraud-shaded polygons (typically three or four times). In Phong interpolation, the shading function must be applied at each of the $N \times M$ pixels of the polygon. This gives a considerable efficiency advantage to Gouraud shading over Phong shading.

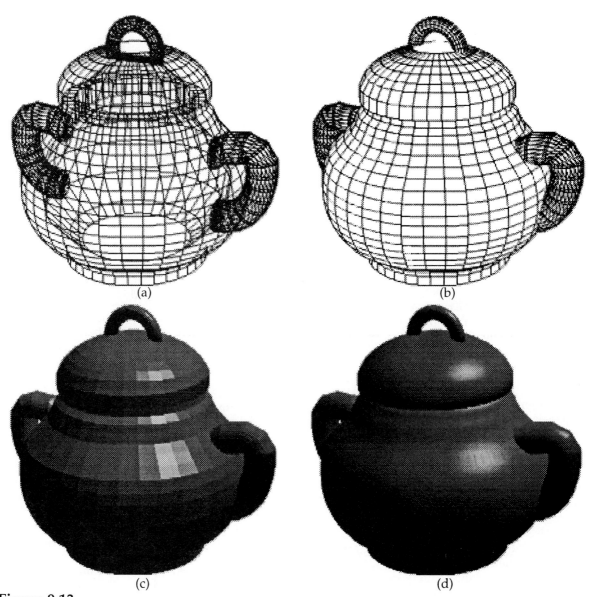

(a)   (b)

(c)   (d)

Figure 9.13
Steps toward visual realism. (a) Simple wire frame model; (b) application of hidden surface removal; (c) application of simple shading model with specular reflection; (d) result of Phong interpolative shading.

Color Models

Color provides one of the most powerful computer graphics tools for visualization. Its availability, resolution, and ease of implementation have become one of the best measures of sophistication in graphics systems. Color has long been recognized as essential for building and manipulating complex CAD graphics. It is now widely used for a variety of tasks from encoding data in medical imaging to highlighting—in red—the negative bottom line on spreadsheets.

The apparent advantages of four, eight, and sixteen colors offered by early two-, three-, and four-bit color systems led to the demand for increased color resolution. The desktop publishing industry pioneered the introduction of *true color* capability in its quest for photographic-quality electronic images from scanners and video sources. Near photograph-quality is possible with the 256 colors available on 8-bit color systems, and the industry is rapidly moving towards 24–32-bit true color capability. Many excellent monitors are available for the display of true color images, and color hard copy is now available on ink jet, thermal transfer (wax), and laser printers.

To better master the techniques involved in the effective use of color, it helps to understand the models which explain the production and reflection of various colors. The integration of color image generation hardware and software, color image processing programs, and color image output devices is a nontrivial task requiring familiarity with color models, color device protocols, and color image standard formats.

Properties of Light

The two disciplines most directly concerned with color perception are physics and physiology. In physics, colored light is described by a relatively few simple concepts. The physiology of color is much more complex and less well understood.

Physics of Color

The visible spectrum consists of electromagnetic waves with wavelengths in air between 400 and 700 nanometers (nm). One nanometer is equal to 10^{-9} meters. The color of a given photon of light is completely defined by its frequency, f. Associated with this frequency is a wavelength, λ, and the

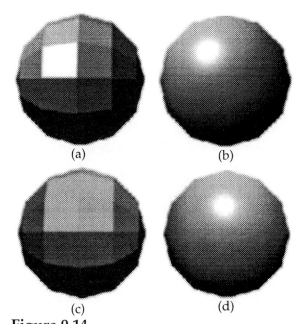

(a)   (b)

(c)   (d)

Figure 9.14
Highlight behavior under simple polygonal shading and Phong shading. The polyhedral model of a sphere shows a "flashing" effect as various facets pick up specular reflections from a moving light source (a,c). With Phong shading, the highlight moves smoothly to reflect the moving source (b,d).

relationship between f and λ is governed by the speed of light, c, according to the equation:

$$c = f \lambda \quad \text{(speed of light)}, \qquad [9.26]$$

where
  $c = 2.9979458 \times 10^8$ meters/second
    for transmission in vacuum,
   $= 2.25 \times 10^8$ meters/second
    for transmission in water,
   $= 1.97 \times 10^8$ meters/second
    for transmission in crown glass.

Note that the speed of light is strongly dependent upon the medium through which it is transmitted. Since the frequency of light is unchanged as it moves from one medium into another, the wavelength must change. In air, the speed of light is very close to that in vacuum. As light enters water, however, its speed (and wavelength) drop sharply to about 3/4 that in air. Figure 9.15 illustrates the relationship between frequency, wavelength, and color.

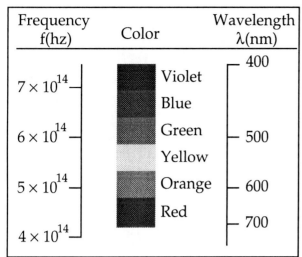

Figure 9.15
Relationship between frequency, color, and wavelength in air for the visible spectrum. The principle hues labeled as color patches represent samples of the underlying continuous spectrum.

Some sources, such as monochromatic lasers, emit light of a single frequency. However, most sources, such as the sun and incandescent lights, emit light of many frequencies. Light from such sources is defined by its *spectrum*, $I(\lambda)$. The $I(\lambda)$ spectrum is a measure of the energy of a given wavelength which passes through a unit area in a certain time. This is sometimes called a *power spectrum* and its units are watts/m^2. The power spectrum may be used to measure the *emission intensity* of a source, the *transmission intensity* of

light flowing through space, and the *illumination intensity* of light striking a surface.

Isaac Newton discovered that a beam of white light could be refracted into a rainbow spectrum of colors by a glass prism. Newton interpreted this effect as the resolution of white light into its component colors. He confirmed this interpretation by using a second prism to recombine the dispersed spectrum into a beam of white light. Figure 9.16 illustrates dispersion of a white beam into a color spectrum and the associated power spectrum, $I(\lambda)$.

Another important physical concept states that colored light behaves in either an additive or subtractive mode, depending on the physical process under consideration. This concept applies directly to computer graphics color output devices.

- **Additive mode** – The color of light observed in the processes of *emission* and *transmission* is the result of the addition of individual hues being emitted or transmitted. This is the basic principle of RGB monitors.

- **Subtractive mode** – The color of light observed in the *diffuse reflection* of light from colored objects is the result of the subtraction of absorbed hues from the incident beam. Thus, an object appears green in sunlight because most of the red and blue portions of the spectrum are absorbed. This is the basic principle of graphics hardcopy devices.

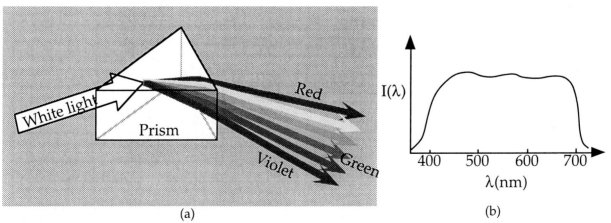

(a)   (b)

Figure 9.16
The spectral composition of white light. (a) White light is dispersed by a glass prism into its component color spectrum. (b) The intensity distribution of a typical beam of white light.

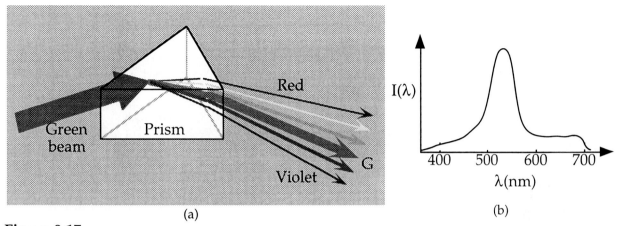

(a)   (b)

Figure 9.17
Resolution of green light into its color spectrum.

Most beams of colored light are not, in fact, monochromatic but rather an intensity spectrum with a peak at the wavelength corresponding to the observed color. This point is emphasized in Figure 9.17 in which a beam of green light is resolved by the same prism used in Figure 9.16 into the intensity spectrum which has a peak between 500 and 550 nanometers.

Physiology of Color

The physiology of color perception is a far more complex and less understood area than the physics of color. Human response to color varies greatly from the total inability of color blind individuals to distinguish different hues of the same intensity to the capability of the trained eye to distinguish an estimated 350,000 shades of color. Most people can detect a change in wavelength of about 2 nm over a considerable portion of the spectrum. Not surprisingly, the spectral sensitivity of the human eye peaks at about 555 nm and closely matches the intensity distribution of sunlight.

Two of the most successful computer graphics color models are based on the tristimulus (or trivariance) principle which states that any color may be approximated by the appropriate mixture of three primary colors. This concept has a distinguished historical tradition. Painters have been aware for centuries that most any desired color can be obtained by the appropriate mixture of three primary pigments. Nearly two hundred years ago Thomas Young proposed that the retina contained red, green, and blue light sensitive "particles" that responded independently to these three colors. Modern physiology interprets these particles as red, green, and blue sensitive cones, and the spectral response of each has been measured. The tristimulus principle is the basis for the RGB (red, green, blue) and CMY (cyan, magenta, yellow) color models.

Although tristimulus models have been highly successful in providing the theoretical basis for such technologies as RGB monitors and CMY printers, they remain incomplete as representations of all aspects of color perception. Several effects unaccounted for by the tristimulus theory include:

- **Context dependency** – The colors we perceive are very dependent on the color context in which they appear. This is shown graphically in Figure 9.18.

- **Color constancy** – Colors may be perceived and correctly identified under radically differing colors of illumination. For instance, our eyes quickly "renormalize" after putting on a pair of heavily tinted ski goggles. Three observers, one with green, one with yellow, and one with rose-colored goggles, will all correctly identify a variety of colors even though the light received by each is radically different in hue.

- **Spectral degeneracy** – Consider the perceived color yellow. Yellow light can be generated by a sodium source with an extremely "pure" spectrum, that is, $I(\lambda)$ will consist of a narrow spike at 589 nm. A broad spectral peak centered about this wavelength will result in an identical perceived color. A mixture of red and green

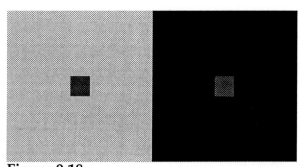

Figure 9.18
Context dependency of color perception. The color perceived for the identical inner squares depends on the color environment in which they appear.

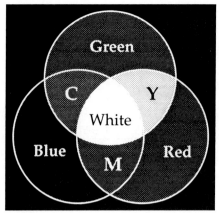

Figure 9.19
Projection of three primary colors of the RGB model. In this additive process, an equal mixture of red, green, and blue light produces white light, while mixtures of two of the three primaries produce cyan, magenta, and yellow (C,M,Y).

light containing no trace of yellow wavelengths will also be perceived as yellow. In fact, there is an infinite number of $I(\lambda)$ spectra which produce the identical perceived color. This spectral degeneracy is difficult to explain in tristimulus theory.

- **Effects of shading** – Edwin Land, the inventor of the Polaroid camera, made some fortuitous and remarkable discoveries on the nature of human color perception. After taking black-and-white slides of color scenes through red, green, and blue color filters, he was attempting to recover the original scene by projecting white light back through the B/W slides using color filters to reconstitute the original color scene in accord with RGB color theory. In the process, the green filter was accidentally dropped and broken. However, to the amazement of the researchers, the full color image was generated by projecting the shaded slides using the only red and blue filters and pure white light.

   In additional experiments, a colorful scene was photographed with black-and-white transparency film through red-and-green filters and re-projected using only the red filter and white light. A full color image was produced! When the black-and-white shaded slides were removed, the screen was filled with pink light from the two projectors. That is, using only red light, white light and shading, it is possible to generate full color images. Land concluded that the eye is able to see color independently of wavelength, a result totally at odds with conventional tristimulus theory.

Trivariate Color Models

Conventional color models based on the tristimulus theory all contain three variables and so are called trivariate models. Let us now consider three of the most useful models, the conversion relationships between them, and the most widely accepted color standard.

RGB Model

The RGB model is based on the assumption that any desired shade of color can be obtained by mixing the correct amounts of red, green, and blue light. As Land has shown, the exact hues chosen are not important as long as they include a long wavelength hue (red), a medium wavelength hue (green), and a short wavelength hue (blue). If, for instance, circular red, green, and blue beams are projected onto a white screen in a darkened room, we get the color pattern shown in Figure 9.19.

The additive nature of the RGB model is very apparent in Figure 9.19. Adding red, green, and blue light produces white light, while adding red and blue light produces magenta light, and so on. This linear superposition is expressed mathematically as:

$$C = rR + gG + bB , \qquad [9.27]$$

where

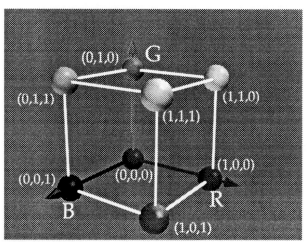

Figure 9.20
RGB color cube. Note how the primary colors define unit vectors along the axes. The three corners opposite R, G, and B are cyan (C), magenta (M), and yellow (Y), the basis of the CMY model. The line connecting black (0,0,0) and white (1,1,1) is the gray scale line.

C = color or resulting light,
(r,g,b) = color coordinates in range $0 \rightarrow 1$,
(R,G,B) = red, green, blue primary colors.

It is very helpful to visualize the range of colors, or *gamut*, specified by Equation 9.25 as a 3D RGB *color cube* shown in Figure 9.20.

Figure 9.20 illustrates the coordinates and colors of the corners of the RGB color cube. Most light, however, can be represented by a 3D color vector which terminates at some arbitrary point in the interior of the cube. To understand the additional shadings possible with the color cube representation, consider the shadings possible on the surface of the cube. In Figure 9.21 a transformed view of the color cube is presented in which subcubes interpolate the color between the four corners of the cube.

The RGB color model is particularly important because it is the basis for control of most color monitors. For this reason it is also the preferred color model for graphics languages and image processing programs. A typical interactive RGB color picker for selecting the three color coordinates is shown in Figure 9.23.

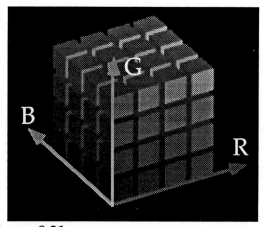

Figure 9.21
Transformed RGB color cube with interpolated hues.

CMY Model

The *cyan, magenta, yellow* (CMY) color model is a subtractive model based on the color absorption properties of paints and inks. As such it has become the standard for many graphics output devices like ink jet and thermal transfer printers. The principle of the CMY model is illustrated in Figure 9.22 in which white light beamed toward the viewer is intercepted by partially overlapping cyan, magenta, and yellow filters. The cyan filter

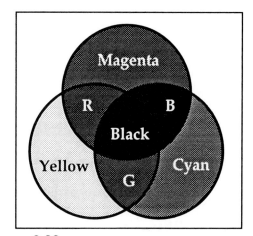

Figure 9.22
Filtering of white light by cyan, magenta, and yellow filters. In this subtractive process, the magenta filter subtracts green light out of the white beam, leaving only its complement, magenta. Subtracting all three colors leaves no light at all,—black.

removes red light from the beam and passes only cyan, the complementary color to red.

In the printing trade this model is frequently called the CMYK model in which the K stands for *black*. The reason for black is that, although theoretically the correct mixture of cyan, magenta, and yellow ink should absorb all the primary colors and print as black, the best that can be achieved in practice is a muddy brown. Therefore, printers like the Hewlett-Packard *PaintJet* have a separate cartridge for black ink in addition to the cyan, magenta, and yellow ink cartridge(s).

The CMY model can also be represented as a color cube as shown in Figure 9.24.

One can understand the subtractive nature of the CMY model in the following sense. When white light falls on a white page, virtually all the light is reflected and so the page appears white. If white light strikes a region of the page which has been printed with cyan ink, however, the ink absorbs the red portion of the spectrum and only the green and blue portions are reflected. This mixture of reflected light appears as the cyan hue.

In terms of the CMY color cube coordinates, one can think of the origin, (0,0,0), as three color filters with a tint so faint that they appear as clear glass. In terms of absorbing inks, the origin corresponds to pastel shades of cyan, magenta, and yellow so faint as to appear white. As one moves up along the **M** axes from (0,0,0) towards (0,1,0), it corresponds to turning the density of a tinted filter up towards the maximum possible. In terms of inks, this motion up the **M** axis corresponds to moving from a pale pastel towards a pure magenta. If one uses all three filters in sequence (or a mixture of C, M, and Y inks), eventually all light is absorbed as one gets to pure colors of filters or inks. This is point (1,1,1).

The RGB and CMY color cubes are useful in expressing the transformations between the two color models. Suppose, for instance, that we know a certain ink may be specified by the CMY coordinates, (C,M,Y) and we would like to know what mixture of light, specified as (R,G,B) in the RGB cube, is reflected. Looking at Figure 9.24 we note the following 3D vector relationships:

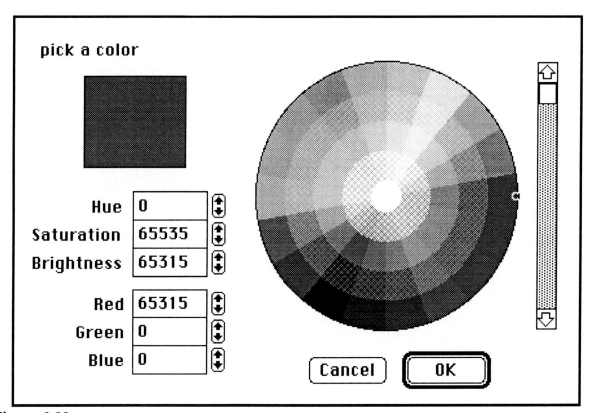

Figure 9.23

Interactive color picker supporting both the RGB color model and the HSV (hue, saturation, value) color model. The user can select any hue from the color wheel by either pointing and clicking or by numerical control of the RGB arrows. The brightness is controlled by the slide control along the right-hand side.

$$Red + Cyan = Black$$
$$Green + Magenta = Black \}$$
$$Blue + Yellow = Black$$

$$[9.28]$$

Expressing each set of coordinates as a column vector we note that we can write:

$$Black = \begin{bmatrix} 1 \\ 1 \\ 1 \end{bmatrix}.$$

$$[9.29]$$

In this column vector notation, Equations 9.26 may be summarized:

$$\begin{bmatrix} R \\ G \\ B \end{bmatrix} = \begin{bmatrix} 1 \\ 1 \\ 1 \end{bmatrix} - \begin{bmatrix} C \\ M \\ Y \end{bmatrix}.$$

$$[9.30]$$

The inverse transformation can be thought of as solving the following problem: Given light of a certain color, (R,G,B), reflected from a page illuminated with white light, what mixture of ink, (C,M,Y), is required? Using Figure 9.20, we can write a set of equations resembling [9.26] with **White** substituted for **Black**. Since, on the RGB color cube, white has coordinates (1,1,1), the transformation equation becomes:

$$\begin{bmatrix} C \\ M \\ Y \end{bmatrix} = \begin{bmatrix} 1 \\ 1 \\ 1 \end{bmatrix} - \begin{bmatrix} R \\ G \\ B \end{bmatrix}.$$

$$[9.31]$$

The CMYK colors are the *Process Colors* of offset printing. Several image processing, drawing, and desktop publishing programs now have the capability of the *color separation* of colored images. The process of color separation involves producing four black-and-white images (or negative images) corresponding to the four colors, cyan, magenta, yellow, and black. These separations are then used photographically to produce the four plates for each of the four inks of the offset press. To produce the final color image, each sheet is printed separately with each of the four color plates. Since alignment is critical, accurate crosshairs are printed on each of the four color negatives to assist the printers in achieving good color registry. In Figure 9.25 we show the results of color separating Figure 9.24

HSV Model

The three variables of hue, saturation, and brightness (value) were chosen as the basis for the intuitive color model proposed by Alva Ray Smith.[5] By

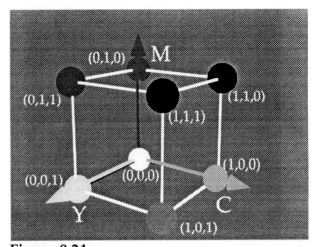

Figure 9.24
The CMY color cube. Each corner is labeled with its (*c,m,y*) coordinates. Note that the RGB color cube is transformed into a CMY color cube by interchanging colors across the major diagonals.

allowing specification of concepts such as hue, tints, shades, and tones, the HSV model is easier to use from the standpoint of artists and designers than the more theoretical RGB and CMY model. For instance, it is difficult to visualize what combinations of red, green, and blue pigments are necessary to produce pink or brown paint.

Hue is defined as that quality which distinguishes one color family from another, for instance, red from blue. It is best associated with the physical property of wavelength, and the range of possible hues is obtained by marching around the perimeter of the color wheel shown in Figure 9.23. *Saturation* is defined as the purity of the color, that is, the ratio of light of the color of the dominant hue to all light present in the color. On the color circle of 9.23, the saturation is 1.0 along the perimeter and 0 at the center. *Brightness* (value) is hard to define, but "you'll know it when you see it." It is the opposite of darkness and corresponds to what you see when you turn the intensity up on your CRT or the voltage up on the dimmer control of a floor lamp. Technically, it is proportional to how many photons of the given hue and saturation are emitted by a source or reflected from a colored object per second. One can think of it as the average of the power spectrum, $\langle I(\lambda) \rangle$.

Just as the RGB and CMY models have a 3D geometric representation, so does the HSV model. The representation is called the HSV single hexcone model and is shown in Figure 9.26. The cylindrical coordinate system uses saturation as the radial axis, value as the axial axis, and hue as an angle measured from red as $\phi = 0°$. The primary colors of the RGB and CMY systems are appear alternatively about the perimeter at multiples of 60°.

The top plane (value = 1) of the HSV hex-cone closely resembles the color circle of Figure 9.23 and can be generated by projecting the colors seen by looking along the diagonal ray connecting white, (1,1,1), to black, (0,0,0), of the RGB color cube. One of the primary advantages of the HSV representation is the direct geometric interpretation it provides of artists' concepts of tints, tones,

and shades. By slicing the hex-cone by any half plane containing the value axis, we get a triangle, shown in Figure 9.27, which directly displays all three terms.

The conversion between the HSV and RGB representations can be accomplished by a linear mapping from one color space to the other. The algorithm proposed by Smith for converting a set of hex-cone coordinates, (H,S,V), to a set of color cube coordinates, (R,G,B), is given as follows.

Figure 9.27 can be interpreted in terms of a painter mixing pure pigments with white-and-black pigments to obtain her final color. First she

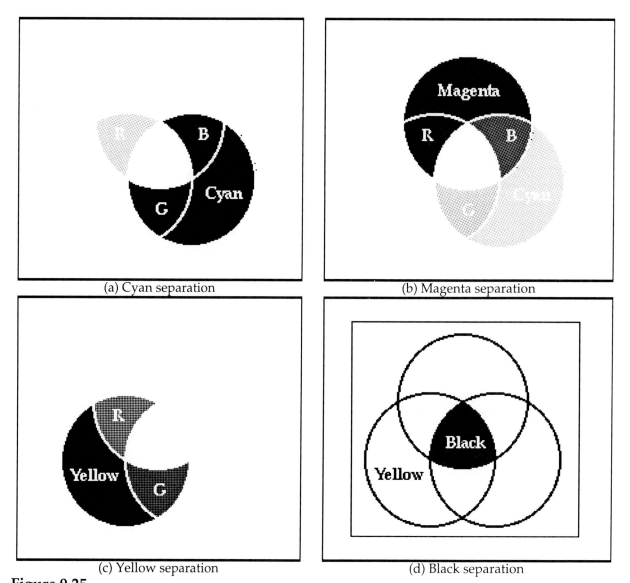

(a) Cyan separation	(b) Magenta separation
(c) Yellow separation	(d) Black separation

Figure 9.25
Color separations of Figure 9.22. These are positives; the program has an option for printing negatives as well. (Separations by *Canvas 3.0.*)

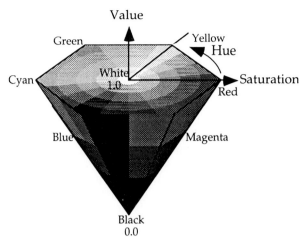

Figure 9.26
HSV color hex-cone. The color space of the hue, saturation, brightness (value) system is a hexagonal-sided cone using a cylindrical coordinate in which *hue* is measured by the angle, ϕ. *Value* ranges from 0 (black) to 1 (white), and *saturation* ranges from 0 on the axis to 1 along the perimeter.

selects the hue, for example, red. By mixing red and white pigments, the various tints are obtained. Adding more white pigment moves the color from the pure red, $(H,S,V) = (0°, 1,1)$ through various pinks, to white, $(0°,0,1)$. Mixing pure red with black pigment forms various shades, moving the color from pure red, $(0°,1,1)$, down the boundary of the hex-cone to pure black, $(?,0,0)$. Note that along the V axis, hue is undefined. Finally, mixing pure red with varying amounts of both white and black pigments forms the possible tones within the interior of the hex-cone.

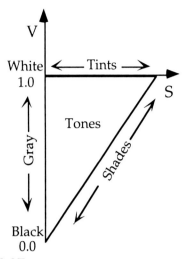

Figure 9.27
Half-plane slice through the HSV hex-cone showing the locations of tints, tones, shades and grays.

Algorithm for Converting (H,S,V) to (R,G,B)

Given: Hue on the range $0° \le H \le 360°$
    Saturation on the range $0 \le S \le 1$
    Value on the range $0 \le V \le 1$
if S = 0 **then**   {Achromatic case-gray scale only}
    if H = Undefined **then**
        R = V
        G = V
        B = V
    else
        if H has a value, raise error flag
        end if
else   {Chromatic case - hue has a value}
    if H = 360 **then**
        H = 0
    else

        H = H/60   {Reduce hue range
                    to $0 \le H < 6.0$}
    end if
    I = trunc(H)   {Compute largest integer
                    below H}
                    {I points to one of hex-cone
                    primaries}
    F = H – I   {Fraction of distance between
                    HSB primaries}
    M = V*(1 – S)   {Develop first linear
                    interpolant}
    N = V*(1 – S*F) {Develop second linear
                    interpolant}
    K = V*(1 – S*(1–F)) {Develop third linear
                    interpolant}
    case I **of**   {Assign set of RGB values to
                    interpolants}
        0:   (R,G,B) = (V,K,M)
           {Red → yellow range}
        1:   (R,G,B) = (N,V,M)
           {Yellow → green range}
        2:   (R,G,B) = (M,V,K)
           {Green → cyan range}
        3:   (R,G,B) = (M,N,V)
           {Cyan → blue range}
        4:   (R,G,B) = (K,M,V)
           {Blue → magenta range}
        5:   (R,G,B) = (V,M,N)
           {Magenta → red range}
    end case
end if
end.

CIE Chromaticity Diagram

Early experiments with the tristimulus model of color revealed a puzzling problem. An observer was asked to match a test light projected on a screen by independently varying the intensity controls on projectors of monochromatic red, green, and blue lights to generate an adjacent response light. Experimental results indicated that many of the sample test lights were impossible to match by any combination of intensities of the RGB response lights.

The reason for this inability lies in the spectral response of the retinal cortex. Thus, for instance, a relatively pure cyan test light could nearly be matched by a roughly equal addition of blue and green response lights. However, these intensities of green and blue excite a red response within the eye which prevented a good color match. The only way in which a color match could be achieved was by redirecting the red response projector to add some red light to the original test light. By gradually turning up the intensity until the red component of the (test + red) response light matched the red excitation of the (blue + green) response light, a perfect color match could be achieved. This can be expressed mathematically by rewriting Equation 9.27 as:

$$C + rR = gG + bB , \qquad [9.32]$$

which may be rewritten as

$$C = gG + bB - rR , \qquad [9.33]$$

where
(r,g,b) are color coordinates on range 0– 1.

Note the presence of a negative quantity of red in Equation 9.31. This negative term can be seen in the negative portion of the I(red) spectrum of Figure 9.28. This figure shows the set of color matching functions, r, g, and b capable of matching all wavelengths of the visible spectrum using red light of wavelength 700 nm, green light of wavelength 546 nm, and blue light of wavelength 436 nm.

A final problem with tristimulus models like the RGB color cube is the difficulty of using them for routine color analysis and manipulation. That is, to use a 3D model effectively, one must visualize and move a vector in 3D color space—a fairly difficult task.

In 1931, the Commission Internationale de L'Eclairage (CIE) established an international color definition in terms of a 2D chromaticity diagram and associated standard observer functions shown in Figure 9.29.

To work around the problem of requiring negative quantities of a primary color, the CIE standard specified three *hypothetical colors*, X, Y, and Z to use as the basis for an additive, tristimulus model. The great advantage of these three new hypothetical primary colors is that all visible hues may be generated by the addition of *positive* amounts of each primary. Hence, we have solved the problem of negative coordinates in

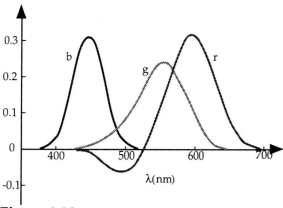

Figure 9.28
Color matching functions. With these proportions of monochromatic red, green, and blue light, the color of the wavelength shown will be matched.

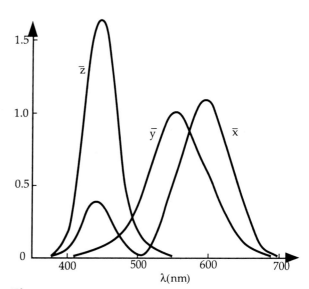

Figure 9.29
CIE standard observer functions. These three functions give the relative amounts of the three CIE colors, X, Y, and Z required to specify the entire spectrum of visible light. This basis uses:
$\lambda_x = 700$ nm; $\quad \lambda_y = 543.1$ nm; $\quad \lambda_z = 435.8$ nm.

color space.

Comparing Figures 9.28 and 9.29, one notes that the color matching functions of [9.28] closely resemble the standard observer functions of [9.29] with some shifts and scaling of the intensity axis. One can think of the new XYZ colors as RGB colors which have been shifted in some *perception space* in such a way as to stimulate the perception of all visible hues by positive amounts of the hypothetical primaries.

The transformation from 3D color space coordinates (X,Y,Z) to 2D space defined by the coordinates, (x,y), is accomplished as follows. We can define the fractions of each of the three primaries as

$$x = \frac{X}{X+Y+Z}, \, y = \frac{Y}{X+Y+Z} \quad , \, z = \frac{Z}{X+Y+Z}.$$

[9.34]

Note also that

$$x + y + z = 1.$$ [9.35]

From [9.33] it is clear that, upon selection of any two fractional coordinates, the third is determined. The CIE committee selected x and y as the basis of the 2D chromaticity diagram shown in Figure 9.30. The chromaticity diagram with points labeled (x,y) consists of a projection of the points generated by intersecting the (X,Y,Z) vector with the $x + y + z = 1$ plane onto the xy plane. The variable lost in this projection is the brightness or luminance of the original (X,Y,Z) color. This luminance may be incorporated by use of the Y variable. The chromaticity diagram coordinate can then be considered as the triplet, (x,y,Y), projected onto the xy plane. The transformation between the two systems is given as:

$$X = x\frac{Y}{y}, \; Y = Y, \; Z = (1 - x - y)\frac{Y}{y}.$$ [9.36]

The CIE chromaticity diagram provides a color standard of great utility and explanatory power. Useful applications include:

- It provides a numerical standard for translating hue and saturation information between various color models.

- It provides an intuitive definition of complementary colors and offers a simple, graphical algorithm for calculating them.

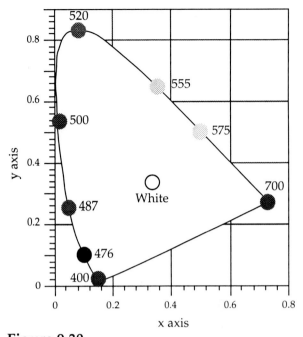

Figure 9.30
CIE Chromaticity Diagram. The points along the perimeter counter clockwise from $\lambda = 700$ nm to $\lambda = 400$ nm correspond to the saturated hues of the visible spectrum. The straight line from violet (400 nm) to red (700 nm) is called the purple line and cannot be produced by light of a single wavelength. As one moves from the perimeter to the white point, tints are generated.

- It provides a natural definition of tint and facilitates a quantitative measure of this property.

- It provides a basis for defining the color gamut (space) for display and output devices. The gamut of RGB monitors is readily represented on a CIE chromaticity diagram.

- The color changes of objects may be mapped as trajectories on a CIE diagram. For instance, the maximum of the blackbody spectrum of heated objects is readily represented on a chromaticity diagram.

Figure 9.31 illustrates several of these concepts.

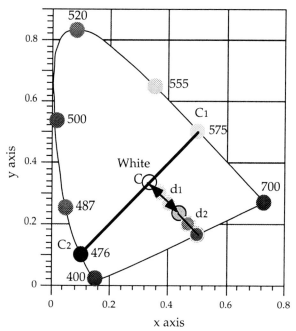

Figure 9.31
Use of CIE chromaticity diagram for locating complementary colors and computing saturation.

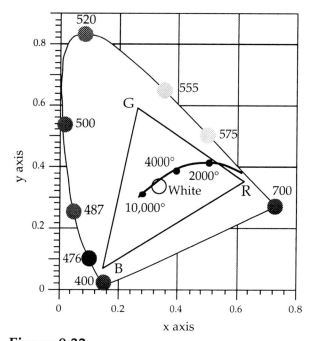

Figure 9.32
Plot of RGB color monitor gamut and the trajectory of a heated blackbody. Note how color monitors are capable of displaying only part of the visible spectrum. Heating an object transforms its color from "red hot" to "white hot" and beyond.

The complementary color of any hue, C_1, is readily obtained by drawing a straight line from that color through the white point, C. The intersection of this line with the pure hue perimeter defines the complementary color, C_2. The correct mixture of C_1 and C_2 light will produce white light. The CIE diagram also makes it clear that some colors, such as green, do not have a complementary color. That is, there is no single, pure wavelength which, when added to the original color, will produce white light. The colors along the purple line are mixtures of red and violet light rather than hues of a single wavelength.

The saturation at any given point on the CIE diagram is defined as the fraction of a point's distance from the white point, C, to the saturated color at the perimeter. So, for instance, the pinkish magenta point shown in Figure 9.31 has a saturation given as:

$$S = \frac{d_1}{d_1 + d_2}.$$ [9.37]

Figure 9.32 shows how color gamuts of color output devices and color trajectory for variable objects are represented on a chromaticity diagram.

Figures 9.31 and 9.32 graphically illustrate some of the most useful applications of the CIE chromaticity diagram. Comparing the color gamut of an RGB monitor with that of typical printing inks, one finds that the ink gamut is smaller and almost totally surrounded by the RGB monitor gamut. The conclusion is that RGB monitors can show colors which are unprintable by the ink in question. The gamut of color film, on the other hand, encompasses that of both RGB monitors and printer's ink. Hence, one can photograph colors that cannot be displayed on a color monitor.

Conclusions

We began the chapter in the context of model authenticity, the principle that states that realistic rendering requires a realistic simulation of the physics of light. Heuristics were introduced for approximating physical processes which are too computationally expensive for exact solution. Terms for ambient lighting and specular reflections were shown to achieve considerable realism at little computational cost. Phong's simple shading algorithm was assembled term by term to provide an effective illumination model and to serve as the basis for more advanced rendering techniques.

The faceted appearance of polyhedral surfaces remained the major drawback of this convenient representation. However, Gouraud demonstrated that the shape of curved surfaces could be recovered from their polyhedral representation through interpolative shading. Phong extended this work by interpolating normal vectors, a process that achieves excellent realism at the cost of an increased computational load. Neither Gouraud nor Phong interpolation can hide the polygonal profile associated with the polyhedral representation of curved surfaces, however.

Finally, we examined color in great detail as one of the most valuable tools available for achieving realism in computer graphics. To use color effectively in applications programs, the programmer should understand both the elementary physics of light and the color models which relate the physics, physiology, and technology of color perception. This is a non-trivial task, and we spent the rest of the chapter in surveying the leading color models, plotting the geometric basis for the model, and giving algorithms for conversion between the various models.

Exercises

9.1 In the introductory material, illumination models and vision models were cited as cases in which recognition of the physical laws underlying a process was essential to improving computer simulation of the process. Discuss two other areas in which this *model authenticity* principle applies.

9.2 Point sources are a convenient mathematical concept for computer graphics rendering algorithms but are physically impossible. Why?

9.3 To verify that the sun is indeed an extended source, run the following experiment to measure the divergence of rays from the sun. Make a "pin-hole camera" (punch a hole in a piece of cardboard with a sharp pencil), tape it to a window facing the sun, and move an observing screen (any piece of paper will do) back from the camera until the image of the sun is about 1 inch across. Stop at this point and measure accurately the diameter of the sun's image, d, and the distance from the camera to the screen, D. The maximum divergence of the sun's rays (in radians) is d/D. What do you measure in degrees?

9.4 In developing the simple illumination model we claimed that as the viewing angle, ϕ, increased, the apparent size of each incremental emitting surface shrank by $\cos \phi$, but that the number of emitting increments per solid angle grew by $(1/\cos \phi)$. Draw a sketch illustrating these geometrical effects and prove that the apparent intensity of a diffuse surface remains constant.

9.5 Equations 9.1 summarize the conservation of energy for interactions of light with matter. Rewrite these equations for the following two situations: a) a perfectly opaque object, and b) a perfectly transparent sheet of glass.

9.6 Warnock's algorithm for specular reflection provides an effective solution to two problems in achieving visual realism. What are these two problems? Include a clipping with a photograph (e.g., from a news magazine) illustrating the "highlight" phenomena which Warnock's algorithm addresses.

9.7 Compute and plot the Warnock distribution function, equation 9.5, for the following values of n: 2, 20, 200, 2000.

9.8 The color behavior of diffuse and specular reflection differ considerably. Run some simple experiments using objects such as matte and glossy book covers to identify these differences and clearly describe them.

9.9 Discuss the *distance effect* given in Equation 9.9. What is the purpose of the distance effect and what variables are used to achieve it? If the intensity of light from a point source falls off as r^{-2} power, why don't we use a squared term in [9.9]?

9.10   The heuristics used in the simple shading model oversimplify or neglect certain important physical processes essential for visual realism. Identify three such failings of the model, describe the nature of the failure, and rank them in the order you suspect they contribute to poorer quality images.

9.11   The text claims that the purpose of Gouraud and Phong interpolative shading is to recover the smooth surfaces lost by going to a polyhedral representation. Why do we have to go through this "circular argument;" that is, why didn't we just stick with a smooth representation in the first place?

9.12   A key concept for both Gouraud and Phong shading is that it is possible to distinguish and label those polygons which are to be interpolated from those which aren't. What will happen if this distinction is not made?

9.13   The basic difference between Gouraud and Phong interpolative shading is the quantity which is interpolated. Identify this quantity for each of the two shading types and list the relative advantages of selecting one quantity over the other.

9.14   Write a routine to read a database containing vertices of four quadrilateral polygons (like those shown in Figure 9.9), compute the normals to each, and compute the resulting average normal, **N**, at the common vertex.

9.15   Pick an ambient light background intensity and a single light source direction and apply Gouraud shading to the four-polygon object of problem 9.14.

9.16   Pick an ambient light background intensity and a single light source direction and apply Phong shading to the four-polygon object of problem 9.14.

9.17   Re-orient the light source direction in problem 9.16 to achieve a specular highlight near the center of one of the polygons.

9.18   What is *Mach banding* and for which interpolative algorithm is it the most serious problem?

9.19   Neither Gouraud nor Phong solved the problem of the "polygon profile" of smooth objects. What would you suggest as an algorithm for solving the problem?

9.20   Is frequency or wavelength the determining factor in the hue of light?

9.21   An interesting result in the physiology of color perception is that many different spectral distributions, $I(\lambda)$, can produce the identical perceived color. Sketch three $I(\lambda)$s, one monochromatic, one using a yellow filter on white light, and one using a mixture of red and green filters on white light, which would produce a perception of yellow light.

9.22   The two important modes of color production are the additive and the subtractive mode. Explain each mode and give an example.

9.23   Most color models are trivariate, that is, they specify the value of three variables such as R,G,B or X,Y,Z. Edwin Land was able to produce full color images using just *two* light sources, for instance, red and white. What additional factor was the key to success of the Land color system? What property of white light may have contributed to the success of this system?

9.24   Assuming that various shades of red are produced by moving from dark red (0.1,0,0) to bright red (1,0,0) and various tints of pink achieved by moving from pure red (1,0,0) towards white (1,1,1), sketch the location on an RGB color cube and identify the colors associated with the following RGB coordinates: (0,0,0); (0,0,0.5); (0,0.5,1); (0,0.2,0); (0.8,0,0.8); and (0.5,0.5,0.5).

9.25   Write a program to draw, color, and project an RGB color cube similar to that shown in Figure 9.19.

9.26   What basic difference distinguish the RGB color model from the CMY color model? What are the main applications of the CMY model? How does the CMYK model differ from the CMY model, and why is the K needed?

9.27 Develop an algorithm for transforming RGB coordinates into HSV coordinates. (*Hint: see Smith reference.*)

9.28 What problems did the CIE chromaticity diagram solve? From the discussion in the text, sketch one possible gamut for printing inks and one possible gamut for color film.

Endnotes

1. Bui-Tuong Phong, "Illumination for Computer Generated Pictures," *Communications of the ACM* **18**, No. 6, pp. 311–317, June (1975).
2. Gouraud, H., "Computer Display of Curved Surfaces," *Department of Computer Science, Univ. of Utah* UTEC-CSc-**71-113**, June (1971). See also: *IEEE Trans.* **C-20**, pp. 623–629, June (1971).
3. Marr, David, *Vision*, W. H. Freeman and Company, New York, NY (1982).
4. Warnock, John, "A Hidden-Surface Algorithm for Computer Generated Half-Tone Pictures," *Technical Report* **TR 4-15**, NTIS AD-753 671, Computer Science Department, University of Utah, June (1969).
5. Smith, A. R., "Color gamut transformation pairs," *Computer Graphics* **12**, pp. 12–19 (1978).

Chapter 10

Three-Dimensional Graphics – Realistic Rendering

Part of the beauty of ray tracing is its extreme simplicity — once you know the necessary background, the whole thing can be summed up in a paragraph.
Andrew Glassner

The radiosity method offers a fundamentally new approach to image synthesis by beginning from basic principles of conservation of energy.
Michael Cohen and Donald Greenberg

The simple shading model of Phong achieves considerable success with realism in rendered scenes by incorporating several principles of optics into a heuristic shading algorithm. This success suggests that the closer we can approximate the physics of light, the better results we can expect from our illumination algorithms. The present chapter outlines three significant approaches for achieving visual realism. The first two are based on optics and energy conservation and overcome many of the problems of the simple shading model to produce images of striking realism. The third approach emphasizes the importance of shading and texture in visual realism. These three approaches define the state of the art in realistic rendering.

The approach based on physical optics is called *ray tracing*. Ray tracing appears intuitively to be the natural approach to rendering a physical scene. This technique solves many of the problems encountered or overlooked in the simple shading model, the most obvious being the correct handling of refraction by transparent objects. At its most basic level, ray tracing can be considered as the Phong shading model incremented by the possibility of multiple specular reflections and Snell's law of refraction. By the nature of the approach, ray tracing is the ultimate image space hidden surface removal algorithm. Yet, by introducing multiple specular reflections, we lose one of the simplifying assumptions of earlier chapters—that back face removal should be the first step of any rendering program. Since back faces can indeed be visible through reflection, they cannot be eliminated automatically.

The second approach, one that effectively complements ray tracing, is the *radiosity* algorithm. With a basis in thermodynamics, radiosity algorithms are founded on the solid principle of energy conservation. Radiosity is the ultimate object space illumination model. It can be considered as a macroscopic model in contrast to the microscopic ray tracing model. Each surface of a scene is considered—correctly—as the source of light illuminating every other surface. As such, the radiosity algorithm is a global illumination model and is independent of the particular viewpoint. Using the physical basis of energy conservation, the radiosity approach has solved difficult effects such as *color bleeding*, which have defeated previous algorithms.

The third approach extends the simple shading model with sophisticated generalized shaders and mapping techniques. By efficient simulation of the optical effects of reflections and shadows, the *RenderMan™* approach[1] achieves remarkable visual realism and is becoming a de facto standard interface for describing and rendering 3D images. The design criteria, algorithms, interface standard, and output of *RenderMan* are presented in detail.

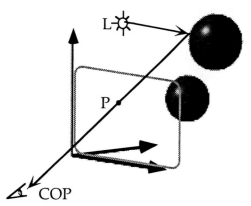

Figure 10.1
Forward ray tracing. Millions of rays are emitted by the light source L, and one particular ray is shown as reflecting off the larger sphere and striking the center of projection (eye point) through pixel P.

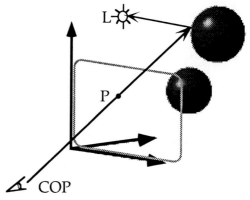

Figure 10.2
Backward ray tracing. Rays originating at the COP pass through each pixel, P, of the image and continue until they strike the nearest surface or exit the view volume. Upon striking the surface the ray's shading is determined by a combination of a shading model applied to the surface plus possible spectral reflection and refraction effects.

Ray Tracing

The first recursive formulation of the ray tracing algorithm was proposed by Whitted in 1980.[2] A detailed discussion of the subject, including many refinements and extensions, is given by Glassner.[3]

Forward Ray Tracing

The concept of ray tracing is based on our understanding of the physics of light emission, transmission, refraction, reflection, and absorption. The basic idea is illustrated in Figure 10.1.

Light is emitted by the source, L, and travels in all directions, illuminating the world coordinate scene. The scene can be composed of transparent, translucent, and opaque objects of varying degree of reflectivity. One particular ray can strike the larger sphere, illuminating it, and be reflected toward the eye along a ray which intersects the screen at pixel P. The color and shading of pixel P is determined by the light emanating from the intersection point of the ray with the closest surface to P in the scene being viewed— in this case, the larger sphere.

While such a model can correctly simulate the behavior of real light rays, a moment's reflection quickly indicates the fatal flaw in any forward ray tracing algorithm. In order to correctly determine the intensity of every pixel on the screen, such an enormous number of rays would have to be generated at L and propagated through the world scene that the largest supercomputer would bog down. Thus, forward ray tracing is completely impractical from a computational point of view.

We are rescued from this computational morass by the optics *principle of reciprocity*. Reciprocity states that all ray diagrams in optics are equally valid if all ray directions are reversed. This leads us to the more tractable algorithm of *backward ray tracing*.

Backward Ray Tracing

Backward ray tracing is the same as forward ray tracing, but with all ray directions reversed. This is illustrated in Figure 10.2.

Note the tremendous computational advantage of backward ray tracing over forward ray tracing. To correctly shade an n × m pixel screen using backward ray tracing requires only n × m primary rays rather than the untold billions of rays which would be necessary to generate a well-resolved image using forward ray tracing.

Surface Interactions

It is clear that the first step in any backward ray tracing algorithm is to project rays from the eye through each pixel and compute the intersection point of the ray with the nearest surface. This involves testing the ray equation against all objects in the scene in order to determine which interaction point is closest. This, the reader can recognize, is a form of the z-buffer algorithm and is sometimes given the name "ray casting." If the ray tracing algorithm stopped at this point, we would, in fact, have only a z-buffer hidden surface removal algorithm. Ray tracing algorithms generally include more physics than this. Figure 10.3 shows some of the processes that occur when a ray strikes an optical surface. These processes include successive reflection and refraction.

Figure 10.3 illustrates a number of important concepts involved in backward ray tracing (henceforth called just ray tracing). First, back face removal is not allowed for ray tracing algorithms since the back face of object A may both refract a ray transmitted through A and may itself be reflected by object B. Secondly, the reciprocity principle helps us interpret the ray diagram in the following manner. Ray 1 can be considered as the shading model color of the front surface summed with a possible incident ray 2 which reflects along 1 plus a possible refracted ray 3 which bends at the surface along 1. Ray 3, in turn, can be considered as the sum of a reflected ray 4 plus an incident refracted ray 7, and so on.

This process can be continued for all secondary rays until any of several trivial conditions apply. These conditions include:

- The ray strikes a light source (or comes close).

- The ray's intensity becomes diminished below a certain threshold.

- The ray becomes trapped by internal reflection (in transparent objects).

- The ray exits the world scene.

In practice, most algorithms "age" the secondary rays by the number of surfaces with which they have interacted. Then the ray is "retired" after N interactions, where N depends on the scene but typically does not exceed five or so. This retirement corresponds to the fact that any ray (except in unusual circumstances) has such a reduced intensity through scattering and absorption that its contribution is insignificant after a few reflections.

The reader can sense that we are setting ourselves up for a recursive solution to the ray tracing problem. This is indeed the case, and we turn next to an elegant recursive algorithm for ray tracing.

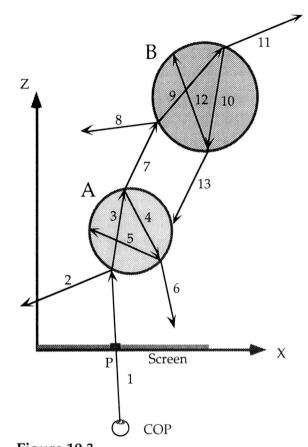

Figure 10.3
Secondary reflection and refraction processes. Incident ray 1 can be partially reflected (2) and partially refracted (3) at the first surface intersection. A partial set of subsequent reflected and refracted rays is shown. Since each ray leaving a surface is capable, in general, of generating a reflected and refracted ray upon intersecting the next surface, the process becomes a natural candidate for a recursive algorithm.

Recursive Ray Tracing

The computation of the color intensity at a given pixel due to the processes indicated in Figure 10.3 can be represented as a recursive traversal of the binary tree diagrammed in Figure 10.4.

Note that the nodes of the binary tree correspond to interactions at a surface and result in both a geometric process (spawning of two new rays) and the summation of information returned by these rays with the results of a shading model applied to that point on the surface. These two essential components of the recursive ray tracing algorithm are illustrated in Figure 10.5.

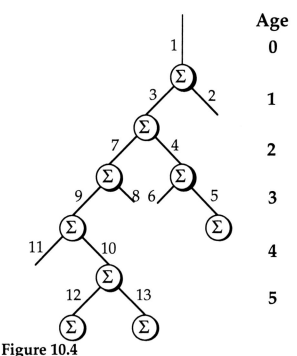

Age
0
1
2
3
4
5

Figure 10.4
Recursive traversal of binary ray tree. Computing the ray-tracing diagram of Figure 10.3 corresponds to the five-level recursive traversal of the binary tree shown here. The branches correspond to rays shot out and information flowing back to the node. The ⊕ symbol at each node indicates that the shading model color of that surface is added to the information carried back by the transmitted and reflected rays. The depth (or ply) of the traversal is indicated by the *Age* column.

Rays leaving the scene without intersecting a surface return $I(\lambda)$ = black and terminate the traversal down that branch. A retired ray stops spawning new rays and returns either black or the shading model color of the next surface it intersects, depending on the algorithm chosen. These concepts form the basis for the recursive ray tracing algorithm.

Recursive Ray Tracing Algorithm

The following outline of a simple recursive algorithm is due to Watt.[4]

procedure RayTrace(start,direction:vectors;
    depth:integer; **var** color:colors);
var

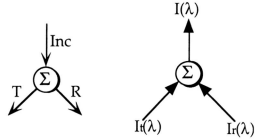

Figure 10.5
Two phases of binary tree traversal. On the left, a ray incident on the surface spawns two new rays, transmitted ray, T, and reflected ray, R. On the right, information carried back by these rays is summed with the local color and passed back up the tree.

```
    intersection-point,reflected-
    direction,transmitted-direction:vectors;
    local-color,reflected-color,transmitted-
    color:colors;

begin
    if depth > maxdepth
    then color:=black;
    else
    begin
    {Intersect ray with all objects and find
    intersection point if any) that is
    closest to start of ray}
    if {no intersection}
        then color:=background-color
        else
        begin
            local-color:={contribution of local
            color model at intersection-point}
            {calculate direction of reflected ray}
            RayTrace(intersection-
    point,reflected-direction, depth+1,
    reflected color);
            {Calculate direction of transmitted
    ray}
            RayTrace(intersection- point,
            transmitted- direction,depth+1,
            transmitted-color);
            Combine(color,local-color,local
            weight, reflected-color, reflected-
    weight,transmitted color,
    transmitted-weight);
        end
    end
end     {RayTrace}
```

Thus, as Glassner suggests in the introductory quotation, the concept of ray tracing is simple, and the recursive formulation provides an elegant implementation algorithm. However, as with many great ideas, ray tracing is easier said than done. Consider first the problems of geometry.

Geometrical Considerations

Two practical problems which must be solved by ray tracing algorithms are computationally efficient models for reflection and refraction, and efficient algorithms for computing the ray intersection of the nearest face. Consider the first problem.

Reflection and Refraction

Recall from Chapter 9 that the law of mirror reflection and Snell's law of refraction can be written:

$$\theta_i = \theta_r \quad \text{(Mirror reflection)} \qquad [10.1]$$

$$n_1 \sin \theta_1 = n_2 \sin \theta_2 \qquad [10.2]$$
$$\text{(Snell's law of refraction)}$$

Given an incident ray, I, making an angle, θ_i, with the normal to the surface, N, Equation 10.1 tells us how to compute the angle, θ_r, that the reflected ray, R, makes with the normal. However, rather than work with a reflected angle, it is much more convenient to compute the R vector directly.

Using a vector diagram like Figure 9.7, one observes that the two light vectors in mirror reflection have components parallel to the surface which are continuous and components perpendicular to the surface which are reversed. Thus, we can write:

$$I = I_{||} + I_\perp, \qquad R = R_{||} + R_\perp, \qquad [10.3]$$

but

$$I_{||} = R_{||}, \qquad I_\perp = -R_\perp, \qquad [10.4]$$

so

$$R = I - 2\,I_\perp$$

and, since

$$I_\perp = (I \cdot N)\,N \qquad [10.5]$$

we get
$$R = I - 2\,(I \cdot N)N \qquad [10.6]$$

This is readily computed by a dot product and vector addition.

The task in refraction is to express the refracted (transmitted) ray, T, in terms of the two vectors, I and N, while incorporating Snell's law. A ray, I, in medium 1 with index of refraction, n_1, making an angle θ_1 with the normal, N, will be bent along T at an angle θ_2 in medium 2 with index of refraction n_2. First, we define the relative index of refraction, n, as:

$$I = \frac{n_2}{n_1} = \frac{\sin \theta_1}{\sin \theta_2} \qquad [10.7]$$

Next, we can express both the incident and refracted rays in terms of unit vectors parallel and perpendicular to the surface:

$$I = u_{||} \sin \theta_1 + u_\perp \cos \theta_1 \qquad [10.8]$$

and
$$R = u_{||} \sin \theta_2 + u_\perp \cos \theta_2 \qquad [10.9]$$

Assuming N is a normalized (unit) vector, we can express $u_{||}$ and $u_\perp$ as:

$$u_\perp = N$$
$$u_{||} = \frac{1}{\sin \theta_1}(I - N \cos \theta_1) \qquad [10.10]$$

Substituting 10.7 and 10.10 into 10.9 gives:

$$R = \frac{1}{n} I + (\cos \theta_1 - \frac{1}{n} \cos \theta_2)\,N \qquad [10.11]$$

The cosine functions can be expressed in vector terms:

$$\cos \theta_1 = I \cdot N \qquad [10.12]$$

$$\cos \theta_2 = \sqrt{1 - \sin^2 \theta_2} \qquad [10.13]$$

$$= \sqrt{1 - \frac{1}{n^2}(1 - (I \cdot N)^2)} \qquad [10.14]$$

Substituting 10.12 and 10.14 into 10.11 gives a vector expression for R:

$$R = \frac{1}{n} I + \left(I \cdot N - \frac{1}{n}\sqrt{1 - \frac{1}{n^2}(1 - (I \cdot N)^2)}\right)N \qquad [10.15]$$

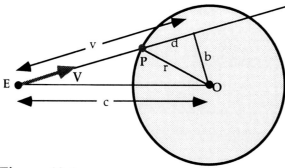

Figure 10.6
Intersection point, *P*, in terms of points *E*, *O*, and ray unit vector, *V*.

Algorithm for ray-sphere intersection

$v = EO \cdot V$ [10.19]

$dsq = r^2 - \sqrt{EO \cdot EO - v^2}$ [10.20]

if (dsq < 0)
    then
        no intersection
    else
        begin
            $d = \sqrt{dsq}$ [10.21]
            $P = E + (v - d)V;$ [10.22]
        end;

Ray Intersections

For reasons we shall return to shortly, the intersection of a ray with a sphere is of great importance in ray tracing. Consider the following simple algorithm by Hultquist[5] for computing the intersection of a ray and a sphere. For the plane containing the ray unit vector, *V*, the ray origin, *E*, and the center of the sphere, *O*, as shown in Figure 10.6, we can write the algorithm for the intersection point, *P*.

From Figure 10.6, we get the following algebraic relationships:

$$v^2 + b^2 = c^2, \qquad [10.16]$$

$$d^2 + b^2 = r^2, \qquad [10.17]$$

$$d = \sqrt{r^2 - (c^2 - v^2)}. \qquad [10.18]$$

In terms of the ray origin, *E*, and two vectors, *V* and *EO*, the algorithm for intersection point, *P*, can be written:

The simplicity of the above algorithm explains, in part, why the featured objects in so many ray-traced scenes are spheres. Since the polyhedral representation is so widespread in computer graphics, however, we should also present an algorithm for the intersection point of a ray with a polygon. At the most abstract level, this algorithm can be stated as a two step process:

1. Compute the intersection point, P_i, of the ray with the plane containing the polygon.

2. Test to see if P_i is contained within the polygon.

We assume that the polygon is defined as a triangle with vertices V_1, V_2, and V_3 as shown in Figure 10.7. Planar polygons with *n* vertices in which *n* > 3 can readily be reduced to n – 2 triangles to which the algorithm is applied. A quadrilateral, for instance, can readily be split along either diagonal into two triangles.

A more refined version of the algorithm follows.

Algorithm for ray-polygon intersection

1. To compute intersection of ray $R(t)$ with plane containing V_1, V_2, V_3:

    1.1 Compute normal to plane

$$N = \frac{(V_2 - V_3) \times (V_1 - V_2)}{|(V_2 - V_3) \times (V_1 - V_2)|}. \qquad [10.23]$$

    1.2 Compute equation of plane

$$N \cdot P + d = 0 \qquad [10.24]$$
        (General equation of plane).
    where

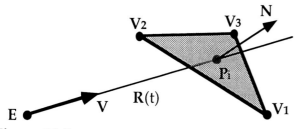

Figure 10.7
Geometry for ray-polygon intersection computation.

P = any point in plane,
d = Constant (offset of plane from origin),
  $= - V_1 \cdot N$. [10.25]

1.3 Express ray, $\mathbf{R}$, as parametric vector

  $R(t) = E + t\,V$. [10.26]

1.4 Compute value of parameter, t_i, for intersection

  $R(t_i) = P_i$ [10.27]
    (Intersection condition).

Solving for t_i after substituting 10.26 and 10.27 into 10.24

  $$t_i = - \frac{d + N \cdot E}{N \cdot V}.$$ [10.28]

1.5 Test to weed out unwanted cases.

  if $N \cdot V = 0$ **then**(Ray R is parallel to plane)
      discard
  else if $t_i \le 0$ **then**
      (Intersection is behind ray origin)
      discard
  else if $t_i > t_{min}$
      (A closer intersection already exists)
  else
    $$P_i = E - \frac{d + N \cdot E}{N \cdot V} V$$ [10.29]
  endif;

2. Test to determine if P_i lies within polygon:
  2.1 Use V_1 as origin and edges to V_2 and V_3 as basis vectors

  2.2 Express relative vector to P_i parametrically

  $(P_i - V_1) = \alpha (V_2 - V_1) + \beta (V_3 - V_1)$. [10.30]

  2.3 Solve any 2 of the 3 equations in 10.30 for 2 unknowns, α and β

  2.4 Make test

  if $(\alpha \ge 0)$ **and** $(\beta \ge 0)$ **and** $(\alpha + \beta \le 1)$ **then**
      P_i is inside polygon
  else
      P_i is outside polygon
  endif.

Limitations of Ray Tracing Algorithms

Ray tracing algorithms based on the algorithms described above have achieved remarkable realism in rendering synthetic scenes. However, they suffer from various shortcomings which limit the visual realism possible with this technique. Among these are:

- Ray tracing algorithms still rely on simplifications of the Phong shading model for such terms as ambient lighting. Real illumination involves every incremental area of a scene serving as a source of illumination for every other incremental area in the scene. This produces effects such as "color bleeding" in which a given colored surface affects the color of nearby surfaces.

- Ray tracing is built on the abstraction of light as mathematical rays and ignores the wave-like properties of light such as diffraction and dispersion. Thus, ray-traced images show reflected, refracted, and shadow outlines as infinitely sharp. Since diffraction limits the sharpness of real images, ray tracing still fails the test of model authenticity.

- Ray tracing algorithms work in image space and as such are local illumination models. By this, we mean that changing the viewpoint requires recomputing the ray-traced image from scratch. The ray-traced image is completely dependent on the position of observer and screen in relation to the world scene and thus does not qualify as a global illumination model.

Extensions of Ray Tracing

In an ideal ray tracing program, the rendering time should depend only on the desired image resolution and be independent of the complexity of the scene. In practice, each ray must be tested for intersection with each object of the scene and the list of resulting intersections sorted to identify the surface nearest the ray's origin. The problem of intersection calculation is made even more complex because of the fact that secondary and older rays can originate *anywhere* in the viewing volume. It is estimated that up to ninety-five percent of the time to render a ray-traced image is spent in computing the intersections of rays with objects. It is not surprising that much of the research on ray tracing involves techniques for speeding up this process.

Various extensions have been introduced to improve the performance of ray tracing algorithms and minimize the limitations listed above. These include:

- **Using bounding boxes or bounding spheres to enclose objects in the scene.** If the primary test ray does not intersect the bounding surface, then it clearly will not intersect any enclosed object, and the surfaces of the object can be ignored for intersection checking. This significantly improves the program efficiency.

- **Using *divide and conquer* algorithms for reducing intersection calculations.** The concept is to partition the viewing volume into boxes and classify all the objects in the scene into these boxes. Rays then need be tested only for intersection with those objects which exist in the boxes the ray penetrates. The use of this spatial coherence greatly improves the efficiency of ray-tracing algorithms.[6]

- **Sending test *shadow rays* from each intersection point towards each light source, L_j.** If an intervening surface is encountered, then the present point under test is in the shadow of that source, and the illumination model should reduce the shading value accordingly by switching off L_j.

- **Extending the shading model to account for point source illumination through transparent objects.** A "spreading function" can be used to distribute the refracted beam in a manner analogous to Warnock's distribution function for specularly reflected light.

- **Substituting a real camera lens model for the simple pin-hole camera model assumed above.** This provides foreground-background blurring that simulates the depth-of-field effects of real camera and visual images.

- **Using distributed ray tracing to simulate gloss, translucency, penumbras, and motion blur.**[7] By using stochastic (random) sampling techniques with sixteen rays per

pixel, Cook[8] was able to solve a number of the "signature" problems of ray tracing. He was able to simulate translucency, depth of field, blurred reflections, shadow penumbras, and to alleviate the aliasing problem.

Radiosity

As we have noted in the discussion of ray tracing, incorporating the physics of reflection and refraction into illumination models greatly enhances the visual realism of rendered images. However, the heuristics of shading models employed by ray tracing algorithms prevents them from successfully rendering all optical effects.

Several of the failings of ray tracing algorithms are overcome by taking an even more fundamental approach based on the thermodynamic principle of the conservation of energy. Thermal engineers use this principle to develop methods for predicting the flux of radiant (heat) energy within enclosures.[9] This approach, called the *radiosity* method, yields rendered images which are so realistic that it is difficult to distinguish them from photographs of real scenes. This success can be interpreted as the natural result of an accurate simulation of the global illumination environment.

The radiosity solution of the global illumination problem was invented at Cornell University by Michael Cohen, Donald Greenberg, and their colleagues.[10] While its algorithmic complexity and computational costs have slowed widespread acceptance, the radiosity algorithms are now available commercially, most notably on Hewlett-Packard graphics systems.

Physics of Radiosity

The radiosity illumination model is based on the following two underlying physical principles:

- Energy is conserved at each point on a surface. That is, the light energy incident upon a surface and generated in the surface must be balanced by the light energy emitted from the surface or absorbed by the surface in the form of heat.

- Each point on a surface serves as a source of light for illuminating every other surface element in the scene within its line of sight (and even possibly hidden elements through reflection).

A quick inspection of indoor environments indicates that a major portion of light "doing the illumination" is diffuse rather than spectral in origin. Based on this fact and to simplify the algorithm, the original formulation of the radiosity approach ignores spectral reflections and assumes perfect Lambertian diffuse reflection only.

We can capture the two principles of energy balance by the radiosity relationship:

Radiosity(i) = Emission(i) +

Reflectivity(i) $\int_{env}$ *Radiosity(j) × Formfactor(i,j)*

where

Radiosity(i) = B_i = Total rate of energy leaving surface i. This is the sum of the emitted and reflected energy. The units on radiosity are those of a *power density* [energy/unit time/unit area] = [Power/unit area]

Emission(i) = E_i = The rate of light energy emitted from a surface. The source of this light energy is the conversion of other forms of energy, e.g. electricity. The units are the same as those of radiosity.

Reflectivity(i) = ρ_i = The fraction of incident light which is reflected back into the environment. It is a dimensionless ratio.

Formfactor(i,j) = F_{ij} = The fraction of light energy leaving surface j which strikes surface i.

Integral(env) = Integral over the environment in which element i exists.

Written symbolically in terms of a finite number of elements, N, this becomes:

$$B_i = E_i + \rho_i \sum_{j=1}^{N} B_j F_{ij}. \qquad [10.31]$$

Since there are N patches in the scene, all illuminating each other, this is equivalent to N equations in N unknowns, and can be written:

$$E = F B, \qquad [10.32]$$

where

$$E = \begin{bmatrix} E_1 \\ E_2 \\ \dots \\ E_N \end{bmatrix}, \qquad [10.33]$$

$$F = \begin{bmatrix} f_{11} & f_{12} & \cdots & f_{1N} \\ f_{21} & f_{22} & \cdots & f_{2N} \\ \cdots & \cdots & \cdots & \cdots \\ f_{N1} & f_{N2} & \cdots & f_{NN} \end{bmatrix}, \qquad [10.34]$$

with

$f_{ij} = (1 - \rho_i F_{ij})$ *for i = j ,*

$f_{ij} = -\rho_i F_{ij}$ *for i ≠ j ,*

and

$$B = \begin{bmatrix} B_1 \\ B_2 \\ \dots \\ B_N \end{bmatrix}. \qquad [10.35]$$

This appears to be a simple problem in the solution of N equations in N unknowns. The unknowns are the B_i radiosity values for each patch element in the scene. The source emission values, E_i, are assumed to be known, and the formfactors, F_{ij}, can be calculated by techniques we discuss shortly. Since a planar element cannot illuminate itself, all $F_{ii} = 0$, and the F matrix has all diagonal elements equal to one and all off-diagonal elements less than one. This well-conditioned matrix is readily solved by iterative techniques such as the Gauss-Seidel method. As the radiosity technique has been refined, the problem size has risen steadily from a few thousand-patch scenes to scenes involving the order of one hundred thousand patches.

The mathematical formulation of the radiosity technique expressed in Equation 10.32 is elegant but deceptively simple. Consider some of the "details" which must be addressed in any practical radiosity algorithm.

- **Color values** – Since realistic scenes involve color, any realistic radiosity algorithm must deal with variously colored sources and reflective patches. In practice, the solution is to assign each source and reflective color an RGB triplet value and determine the patch intensity in terms of three radiosities, B_{Ri}, B_{Gi} and B_{Bi}. Since trivariate color models are additive, the solution of Equation 10.32 then involves solving *three* sets of N equations in N unknowns and summing the solutions, $B_i = B_{Ri} + B_{Gi} + B_{Bi}$.

- **Form factor calculations** – Between eighty and ninety percent of the computational

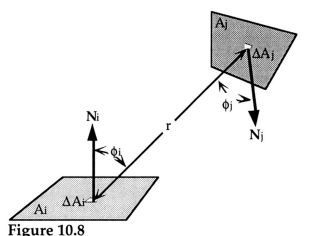

Figure 10.8
Geometric basis for formfactor calculation in a non-occluded environment. The geometric parameters shown describe differential area, ΔA_i, on patch A_i, in relation to differential area, ΔA_j, on patch A_j.

task of radiosity algorithms involves calculating the geometric formfactors. Formfactors are strictly geometric in nature and involve the distance between interacting elements and the relative orientation of the two elements illuminating each other. Once a form factor is computed, it can be stored and used repeatedly, as long as the relative geometry of the two elements remains constant. It is independent of the source intensities, reflectivities, or color values of any part of the system, including the two elements generating the formfactor.

- **Hidden surface removal** – The most difficult part of the radiosity algorithm is solving the hidden surface problem. A form factor, F_{ij}, giving the effect of element j in illuminating element i is meaningless if some third element, k, comes between element i and j, blocking the view of each from the other. Even more troublesome is the case when element k *partially* obscures either element. Effective solution to this problem, generally through refinement of the formfactor calculation, remains the focus of radiosity researchers.

Let's consider some of these problems in more detail.

Form factor calculations

To compute the interaction, F_{ij}, of element j with a line-of-sight element i, the important parameters are the distance and relative orientations of the two elements. Figure 10.8 indicates how these parameters can be specified.

Assuming planar patches A_i and A_j with dimensions within an order of magnitude of the distances separating them, it is necessary to integrate the effects of differential areas, ΔA_i and ΔA_j on each other. Cohen and Greenberg write the differential formfactor as:[11]

$$F_{\Delta Ai\, \Delta Aj} = \frac{\cos\phi_i\,\cos\phi_j}{\pi\,r^2}. \qquad [10.36]$$

This formfactor is normalized to give a value of one for the limiting case where patch A_j becomes a hemisphere of radius r centered at ΔA_i.

In order to compute the effect of the whole patch A_j on the differential element, ΔA_i, we integrate over A_j.

$$F_{\Delta Ai\, Aj} = \int_{A_j} \frac{\cos\phi_i\,\cos\phi_j}{\pi\,r^2}\,dA_j. \qquad [10.37]$$

The final non-obscured formfactor is defined as the area average of the differential formfactor given by [10.37]. Thus,

$$F_{Ai\, Aj} = \langle F_{\Delta Ai\, Aj}\rangle \qquad [10.38]$$

$$= \frac{1}{A_i}\int_{A_i} F_{\Delta Ai\, Aj}\,dA_i$$

$$= \frac{1}{A_i}\int_{A_i}\int_{A_j} \frac{\cos\phi_i\,\cos\phi_j}{\pi\,r^2}\,dA_j\,dA_i$$

This is the formal, mathematical expression for the formfactor. It does not, however, solve the hidden surface problem. We can resolve this problem by inserting a switching function, *HID*, into [10.38] to give:

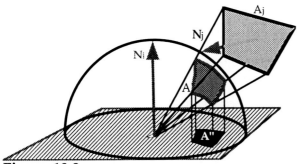

Figure 10.9
Formfactor calculation by successive projection. The formfactor is A''/π.

$$F_{Ai\,Aj} = \frac{1}{A_i} \int_{A_i} \int_{A_j} \frac{\cos\phi_i \cos\phi_j}{\pi r^2} HID \, dA_j \, dA_i$$

[10.39]

where
    HID = 1 if element dA_i can "see"
              element dA_j

          = 0 if not.

While this expression for the formfactor formally includes a hidden surface function, it does not specify how HID is to be computed. This is the subject we consider next.

Projective techniques – The Hemi-Cube

It has been shown that the formfactor calculation [10.38] is equivalent to a series of projections. Nusselt[12] used a hemisphere of unit radius with center at dA_i to compute the formfactor for patch A_j as shown in Figure 10.9. Note that the projection of the patch onto the hemisphere, A', correctly accounts for the $\cos\phi_j$ and r^{-2} term, and the projection of A' onto the A_i surface, called A'', corrects for the $\cos\phi_i$ term.

$$A' \propto \frac{\cos\phi_j}{r^{-2}}$$

[10.40]

and
$$A'' \propto A' \cos\phi_i .$$

Since the area of the hemisphere projected onto A_i is π, the formfactor is given by the ratio of A'' to π:

$$F_{Ai\,Aj} = \frac{A''}{\pi} .$$

[10.41]

The interesting result of the projective technique is that the result is *independent of the shape* of the projective surface. Cohen and Greenberg used this property to propose a *hemi-cube* scheme for computing the formfactor and extend the technique to solve the hidden surface problem. This technique is illustrated in Figure 10.10.

In the hemi-cube approach, a cube is centered about dA_i with the top plane of the cube parallel with the surface element, dA_i. The patch A_j, whose formfactor is to be computed, is projected onto the hemi-cube in a fashion identical to the projection used in Figure 10.9. The surface of the hemi-cube is subdivided into $N \times N$ square "pixels," where N is typically in the range 50 – 100 (N is shown as 8 in Figure 10.10). The hemi-cube has a unit height and a coordinate system with the origin at dA_i, z-axis coincident with N_i and x- and y-axes parallel to the edges of the cube. The incremental contribution of each shaded pixel of area ΔA and coordinates (x,y,z) to the formfactor can be shown to be:

$$\Delta F_{AiAj} = \frac{1}{\pi (x^2 + y^2 + 1)^2} \Delta A,$$

[10.42]

(for top pixels)

$$\Delta F_{AiAj} = \frac{z}{\pi (x^2 + y^2 + 1)^2} \Delta A.$$

[10.43]

(for side pixels)

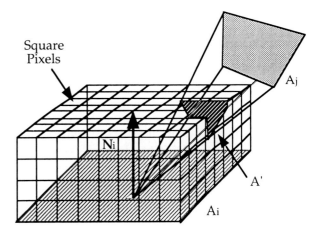

Figure 10.10
The hemi-cube, invented by Cohen and Greenberg for computing radiosity formfactors. By shooting rays through the square pixels surrounding dA_i, they solved the hidden surface problem.

If, in Figure 10.10, the projected patch, A', encloses R pixels, the final formfactor for patch A_j illuminating A_i is given by the sum of all pixel contributions:

$$F_{AiAj} = \sum_{q=1}^{R} \Delta F_{AiAj} . \qquad [10.44]$$

The advantage of the hemi-cube approach is that it is fairly straightforward to incorporate a hidden surface algorithm to eliminate the contribution of those patches which are shielded by other objects. Note that the i_{th} row of the formfactor matrix, **F**, is generated by constructing a hemi-cube about dA_i and computing Equation 10.44 for all other patches, A_j. When more than one A_j patch shades a given pixel, a depth sort determines which is the closest. The incremental formfactor contribution from the closest patch is summed into [10.44] and the rest are discarded. This technique is completely analogous to the z-buffer algorithm for hidden surface removal described previously.

Thus, the hemi-cube approach is useful for solving both the formfactor computation and the hidden surface problem.

Upon solution of the radiosity equation, the radiosity, B_i, of each patch is known. Because of the finite size and different geometries of each patch, each B_i will be different in general, even for adjacent patches. In order to achieve continuous shading across patch boundaries, the patch intensity is assigned to each vertex and the Gouraud interpolation algorithm applied during projection.

Advantages of the Radiosity Approach

The primary advantages of the radiosity approach stem from the principle of model authenticity. Radiosity provides a global solution to the illumination computation task that is based on the established physical principle of the conservation of energy. The Cornell group has built physical models and performed radiometric measurements which validate the radiosity model. That is, the radiosity model accurately simulates reality.

As an authentic model, radiosity solves several previously unsolved problems including shadows with proper penumbrae and color bleeding. But perhaps the most attractive feature of the radiosity model is its global nature in object space. That is, as an accurate solution for surface illumination, the radiosity method is completely *viewpoint independent*. Once the radiosity solution is obtained, images from a given viewpoint are readily rendered by the projective techniques already discussed. The image projection task is far less computationally intensive than the task of obtaining the radiosity solution. Although the radiosity solution can take minutes (or even hours), images of the scene can be rendered in fractions of a second. The computing power of most workstations is adequate for real time image computation as the observer "walks through" the scene described by the radiosity solution.

Problems of the Radiosity Approach

The basic radiosity approach described above has a number of remaining problems which limit the visual realism of rendered images or make the approach awkward to use. Among these are

- **Absence of highlights** – Since the radiosity model described above assumes only diffuse surfaces and ignores specular reflections, images rendered by simply projecting a radiosity solution will lack the highlights and reflected images which characterize ray-traced images.

- **Aliasing due to hemi-cube sampling** – The regular structure of the hemi-cube pixels introduce aliasing effects in sampling patches, particularly polygon patches. The projection of a given source patch past the straight edge of an occluding surface can generate alternating over- and under-estimation of the incremental formfactor on a sequence of hemi-cube pixels. The visual artifact of aliasing can appear as a plaid pattern in the image.

- **$O(N^2)$ problem size** – Since a scene with N patches generates a radiosity matrix of size $N \times N$, the problem size is of the order of N^2 in both time and memory requirements. If one refines the accuracy of solution by doubling the number of patches, the number of formfactors which must be calculated grows by a factor of four.

- **Global nature of the solution** – Solving the radiosity equation, $E = F\ B$, involves solving 50,000 simultaneous equations for the 50,000 unknown B_i radiosities. After the B_i surface intensities are determined, the resulting image is quickly rendered, but, in the meanwhile, the user can only stare at a blank screen. That is, since the solution is global, no information is known about the solution until it is all known. This is in contrast to ray tracing which generally uses a scan line algorithm to grind out and display the image pixel by pixel.

Much of the research in radiosity involves extensions to the technique in order to solve these problems.

Extensions to the Radiosity Approach

Active research in radiosity continues on problems of reflection, diffraction, and refraction and how to eliminate the artifacts associated with hemi-cube algorithm. Some of the major successful extensions include the following.

Progressive refinement

The progressive refinement extension successfully attacks the last two problems (N^2 problem size and wait for global solution) by recognizing two basic principles, one from physics and one from physiology.

- The brightest patches cast the most light and hence have the most effect on illuminating the scene.

- When an image *looks* good enough, it *is* good enough.

The basic concept of progressive radiosity is to modify the radiosity algorithm to incorporate these two principles.[13]

It does this by starting with the brightest source or emitting patch, bounding it with a hemi-cube, and *shooting* light through the pixels of the hemi-cube to illuminate all of the $N-1$ other patches. The brightest source is the patch with the largest $B_i A_i$ product corresponding to the greatest total light energy emission. The resulting radiosities of the newly illuminated $N-1$ patches are then scanned for the brightest source and the process repeated. Light from this patch is projected through its hemi-cube to illuminate all other patches, including the original brightest patch. After the first two brightest patches have been fired, the third brightest patch is shot, and the process continues until the image converges to a stable illumination balance. Convergence is easily

detected visually by noting subsequent iterations of the cycle produces no detectable change in the appearance of the scene.

Note that progressive radiosity fundamentally reverses the direction we visualize light moving as it achieves an equilibrium distribution. This direction reversal is analogous to the distinction between forward and backward ray tracing. In the full radiosity matrix formalism we compute the radiosity of patch i by *gathering* the light emitted by all the other j patches. The contribution to patch i's radiosity from patch j's light is (see [10.31]):

$$B_i = \rho_i\, B_j\, F_{ij}. \qquad [10.45]$$

By inverting the process, progressive radiosity assumes i becomes a source, *shooting* light towards other j patches. The question then is: What is the radiosity, B_j, of each patch due to the present brightest patch, B_i? That is, we need to express B_j in terms of B_i.

$$B_j = \rho_j\, B_i\, F_{ji}. \qquad [10.46]$$

We know both ρ_j and B_i but not F_{ji}. Rather than marching out to each of the j patches and building a hemi-cube about them to compute F_{ji}, it would save effort to use our existing hemi-cube designed to compute F_{ij} and relate the two terms using symmetry principles. From the symmetry of the integrand in [10.37] it is clear that we can write:

$$F_{ij}\, A_i = F_{ji}\, A_j. \qquad [10.47]$$

The radiosity B_j due to B_i can then be written:

$$B_j = \rho_j\, B_i\, F_{ij} \frac{A_i}{A_j}. \qquad [10.48]$$

As a final note before presenting the progressive radiosity algorithm, it is possible (and in fact, likely) that a given patch i, which was one of the early patches shot, will receive enough additional radiosity, ΔB_i, from subsequent shots that the stored energy, $A_i \Delta B_i$, will exceed the unshot energy of any other patch. In that case, ΔB_i is shot again and set to zero. The following algorithm uses ΔB to refer to un-shot radiosity.

Progressive radiosity algorithm

repeat
    {*select patch i with greatest stored energy*}
    for j = 1 **to** N **do**
        begin
            {*compute F_{ij} relating i to each j patch*}
            $DB_{ij} = \rho_j \, DB_i \, F_{ij} \, A_i / A_j$.
            $DB_j = DB_j + DB_{ij}$
            $B_j = B_j + DB_{ij}$
        end
    $DB_i = 0$
until image is good enough

There are several significant features of the progressive radiosity extension. Most important is the property that a complete image can be rendered after the first cycle of refinement. That is, the illumination balance, after the brightest patch is shot, corresponds to that achieved with the simple shading model using a single, distributed source. By displaying the image after each cycle, the user can monitor the computation and interactively control the level of refinement according to the task requirements.

The visual effect of observing progressive refinement is both instructive and intuitively satisfying. One first sees a somewhat dimly lit scene with harsh shadows. With the second cycle, the illumination level rises significantly, and the shadows begin filling in as an additional source clicks on and an effective *ambient* component appears. With each successive cycle, the illumination level grows by successively smaller increments until the change is undetectable. At that point, the user declares the image "good enough" and halts the process. Greenberg has demonstrated scenes in which visual convergence occurs in 25–30 shots, and he states that 98 percent of the energy is accounted for after one hundred shots.[14]

To accelerate the process, an artificial ambient term can be introduced for the first few cycles to "excite" patches occluded from the brightest patches. As the process converges, the artificial ambient term is gradually turned down and eliminated altogether for the final cycles.

Ray-traced Form Factors

As previously mentioned, the hemi-cube used in full radiosity matrix (gathering) mode can cause aliasing problems. In progressive refinement algorithms, the hemi-cube continues to cause problems, primarily due to uneven sampling of surrounding patches. The heart of the problem is the

blind nature of the algorithm which shoots rays through the pixels of the source hemi-cube. This problem is analyzed in detail, and an alternate formfactor algorithm based on ray tracing is proposed by Wallace *et al.*[15]

The heart of the ray tracing formfactor (RTFF) algorithm consists of two clever tricks. First, the RTFF algorithm's primary task is to determine the radiosity at the vertices of each of the illuminated *j* patches. Since Gouraud interpolation requires the patch shading intensity at each of its vertices in any case, this is a useful shortcut. The second concept of the RTFF algorithm is to compute the formfactor itself by summing the differential formfactors of individual sampling rays from the vertex of *j* back to the source at i. Since ϕ_1, ϕ_2, and *r* are known exactly for each of the sampling rays, Equation 10.36 specifies the incremental formfactor contribution of each ray.

The only remaining issue in the RTFF algorithm is how to specify the rays from vertex *j* to the source patch, *i*. Here the algorithm exhibits another of its advantages—its flexibility. A fast, approximate radiosity solution can be obtained using a minimal number of sampling rays from vertex to source, e.g. one. More accuracy is achieved by increasing the number of sampling rays. Rays can be distributed over the source patch with either a regular pattern or distributed randomly. Stochastic processes serve as an effective antialiasing technique since the eye interprets random distributions of pixels as noise rather than structure in the image.

Wallace shows that formfactors computed with the RTFF algorithm converge rapidly to the analytic values as the number of rays increases from one to sixteen, at which point they are nearly identical. Using the RTFF algorithm Wallace was able to calculate a splendid view of the nave of Chartres cathedral in just under an hour on a Hewlett-Packard 9000 workstation. The scene model consisted of 9,916 polygons with 74,806 vertices and thirty stained-glass window light sources. The solution required 60 steps of progressive refinement and used 1.1 million rays.

Integrating Radiosity and Ray Tracing

It must be quite apparent to the reader by now that ray tracing and radiosity are complementary techniques. That is, the strengths of ray tracing (excellent rendering of specular reflections and refractions) are completely lacking in the basic radiosity algorithm, while the strengths of radiosity (view independence, extended sources, accurate

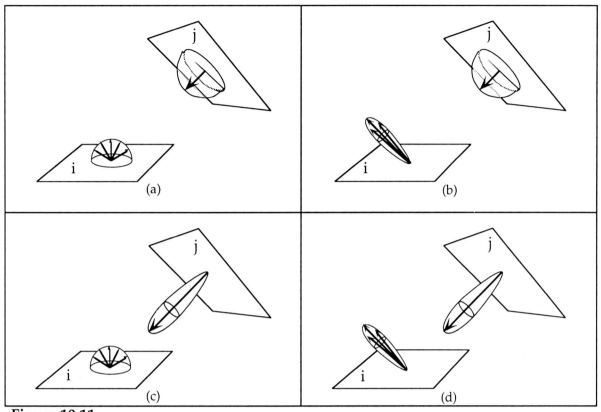

Figure 10.11
Illumination mechanisms. (a) Light diffusely scattered from j scatters diffusely from i; (b) Light diffusely scattered from j scatters specularly from i; (c) Light specularly scattered from j scatters diffusely from i; (d) Light specularly scattered from j scatters specularly from i.

penumbra, and color bleeding) are totally lacking in basic ray tracing algorithms. The logical next step is to integrate the two techniques with an attempt to preserve the strengths of each in the final product.

The most obvious way to proceed in merging these two techniques is to note that radiosity provides an accurate solution to the diffuse light equilibrium (ambient light background) while totally ignoring specular effects of reflection and refraction. Ray tracing provides an accurate solution for specular reflection and refraction effects while approximating diffuse shading with a simple model based on an nonphysical ambient lighting term. This suggests a two-pass process in which, first, the energy conservation principle of radiosity is used to establish the global balance of diffuse illumination, followed by a view-dependent ray-tracing process to determine specular reflection and refraction effects. After the first pass radiosity solution, the algorithm would shift to a recursive ray tracing mode and substitute the radiosity solu-

tion in place of the simple shading model when computing the diffuse shade at each intersection point.

This algorithm will improve the visual realism of rendered images over that possible by either technique used independently. However, this "linear superposition" of the radiosity and ray-traced solution is still not complete. To understand the missing term, consider the four mechanisms in Figure 10.11 by which light from patch *j* reaches and is re-emitted from patch *i*.

Note that radiosity algorithms assume only mechanism (a), and ray tracing algorithms account for both (b) and (d) involving specular reflections. However, neither algorithm takes process (c), diffuse scattering of spectrally reflected light, into account. So the linear superposition of these two algorithms would also neglect this effect.

Two of the earliest efforts to integrate elements of ray tracing and radiosity were the independent approaches of Immel[16] and Kajiya.[17] Immel *et al* have extended the basic radiosity

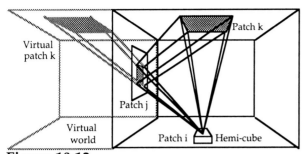

Figure 10.12
Extension of radiosity algorithm to mirror reflections. Extra formfactors are added for *virtual patches* corresponding to mirror reflections of light from real patches.

method to include specular reflections. They accomplished this by computing the intensity distribution for every surface in the environment in terms of directional intensities for a number of discrete directions. The rendering process then consists of looking up the intensities pointing back to the eye and displaying them as the image. This approach preserves the advantages of a view-independent solution while adding specular highlights to rendered images.

Kajiya has proposed a rendering equation that resembles the radiosity equation but which uses geometric optics rather than only diffuse assumptions for transforming light from sources to observer. To integrate the integral rendering equation he uses Monte Carlo (stochastic) ray tracing to sample the environment. He computes the diffuse component of surface intensity by randomly sending sampling rays from the intersection point throughout the environment. Thus, Kajiya showed that the ray tracing approach can be extended through stochastic processes to achieve a diffuse lighting component consistent with geometric optics.

Wallace *et al* have proposed an integration of ray tracing and radiosity that takes into account all four of the transfer mechanisms outlined in Figure 10.11.[18] Basically, the Wallace algorithm introduces extra formfactors to the conventional radiosity algorithm that correspond to mirror reflections of patch *k* through reflective patch *j* to patch *i* as indicated in Figure 10.12.

Through the use of *virtual patches* the algorithm correctly takes into account all four of the transfer mechanisms of Figure 10.11.

As suggested earlier, the algorithm uses a two-pass approach to calculate illumination. In the first pass (preprocess), all four transfer mechanisms are employed to compute the correct diffuse compo-

nent. In the second pass (post-process), the view-dependent specular-to-specular and diffuse-to-specular mechanisms generate a specular component which is added to the diffuse component to produce the final image.

Using Kajiya's rendering equation, Sillion and Puech[19] have proposed an extension of the Wallace two-pass algorithm which removes the restriction limiting specular reflections to single plane mirrors. Their extended form factor, F_{ij}, measures the energy leaving surface *i* and reaching surface element *j* after any number of specular reflections or refractions. This extends the radiosity solution to include multiple specular reflections (Wallace's algorithm computed only one) as well as refraction (transparent and translucent objects).

Sillion and Puech's algorithm closely follows the intuitive two-pass algorithm introduced at the beginning of this section. In pass one, the extended radiosity solution (including all four mechanisms from Figure 10.11) provides a view-independent illumination value for each patch in the scene. The second pass computes the directional distribution of light reaching the observer by a classical ray-tracing algorithm, simplified as follows:

- Since the extended radiosity solution has already solved the problem, no shadow rays are needed. This makes the computation more efficient and independent of the number of light sources.

- The shading model value of intensity is simply the radiosity solution.

The integration of raytracing and radiosity approaches has effectively solved the realistic rendering problem. Images produced by the integrated algorithms discussed above are difficult to distinguish from photographic images. As each research group added refinements to these rendering techniques, their stunning images were presented at SIGGRAPH conferences and received with cheers and applause. The images themselves have become identified with a given algorithmic approach and research institution. Such recognition is certainly well deserved and an appropriate reward for the tremendous effort and ingenuity involved in producing realistic images.

This discussion, however, also indicates the limitations of the advanced realistic rendering techniques as tools for visualization available to the average designer/engineer/scientist. Among these limitations are:

- **Slow rendering speeds** – A typical scene involving several thousand patches typically requires an hour or more to render on a powerful workstation. While this is an amazing performance compared to the hours or days of mainframe time required by earlier techniques, it is too slow to provide a useful tool for designers.

- **Hand crafting of scene databases** – The research papers generally do not describe the database structures used to represent scenes. No standard has emerged from academic research which would enable the free exchange of models and encourage the comparison of refinements on standard data sets.

- **Unavailability** – With some significant exceptions discussed next, the advanced rendering algorithms are not generally available to users outside of the graphics research community. The reasons for this are the heavy computational requirements, program fragility, and lack of modeling standards naturally associated with research projects.

We turn next to those "significant exceptions" which represent some of the first examples of advanced rendering techniques emerging from the laboratory into the market place.

Available Rendering Tools

The genius of a market economy is the speed with which techniques developed in the laboratory appear in commercial products. Within a year or two of the publication of a significant new technique, it appears either in software or in hardware in the form of application-specific integrated circuits (ASICs). Realistic rendering algorithms provide textbook examples of this technology transfer. We consider two examples, the first a hardware solution and the second a software solution for realistic rendering.

Hardware Implementation

Authors must balance the risks of appearing "promotional" against the readers' "need to know." Since the product we describe incorporates essentially all of the advanced rendering

techniques discussed up to this point, we will tilt in favor of the readers need to know. We discuss this product only as a case study of rendering features commercially available, and not as the promotion of the ultimate graphics machine. The only constant of the computer industry is that a description of the "state of the art" is obsolete the day it is written. With these qualifications, consider the features of the Hewlett-Packard Personal VRX graphics work station.

Hardware features

A summary of the HP Personal VRX system includes:

- A Motorola 68040 processor with i860 Accelerator

- A separate ASIC-based graphics processor box

- An HP 19-inch monitor with 1280 × 1024 display resolution and 8-bit color

- Two 200 MB internal hard drives
- 16 MB of RAM

- Peak graphics performance of 66 MFLOPS

- A $33,000 price tag.[20]

Figure 10.13 shows the HP Personal VRX workstation.

Graphics functions

The graphical features of the HP Personal VRX read like a graphics maven's wish list. The ASIC graphics processor has "committed to silicon" the following graphics functions:

- Radiosity algorithm with progressive refinement and specular highlights
- Ray tracing
- Texture mapping
- Color anti-aliasing
- Support for stereoscopic image generation
- Advanced lighting models
- NURBS to sixth order for surface representation.

In addition to these graphics functions built into the hardware of the system, the HP Personal VRX supports GKS, PHIGS, X Windows, and Motif industry graphics standards. It also supports CAD features such as sectioning, capping, interference checking, contour mapping, and deformation animation.

By building many of the rendering algorithms in firmware, Hewlett-Packard achieves high graphics processing speed. For instance, the HP Personal VRX can render 20,000 quadrilaterals, 50,000 triangles, or 270,000 vectors per second. This speed allows real-time "walk through" of scenes previously solved by the radiosity method.

The HP Personal VRX graphics workstation and similar workstations available from other vendors are capable of solving the most sophisticated rendering tasks facing large design, engineering, and image processing organizations. However, the price puts them out of reach for smaller firms and educational institutions on limited budgets. Does this mean that realistic rendering is impossible for "the rest of us?"

Software Implementation

Fortunately, the answer to that question is an emphatic "no." Before introducing a leading software solution to the problem of fast, realistic rendering, consider what features one might wish for in a software implementation.

- **Separation of model building and rendering functions** – This feature would allow the user to build models with her favorite CAD system and submit the model file to the renderer. The renderer would then operate in the background mode, returning control of the system back to the user.

- **A standard, platform-independent interface** – This feature would permit models built on one system to be rendered on another and would allow graphical images to flow smoothly between platforms and throughout a network.

- **A flexible rendering language** – The rendering language should be flexible enough to accommodate new rendering and

Figure 10.13
The HP Personal VRX workstation. This platform provides all of the ray tracing and radiosity rendering techniques described above.

shading techniques as they appear and should take advantage of a growing library of texture and surface maps.

- **High quality images** – The renderer should be free of aliasing and faceting artifacts which have plagued most previous algorithms.

- **Fast rendering** – It would be highly desirable to achieve the image realism of a hybrid ray-tracing/radiosity algorithm without paying the heavy computational price required by the algorithms outlined here.

- **Availability in software on standard personal computers and workstations** – It would be highly desirable to simply purchase a commercial rendering package and use it as a postprocessor to existing image synthesis systems. No additional RISC or ASIC graphics processing cards should be required in order to produce high-quality rendered images.

Surprisingly, such a system is now available and is becoming a *de facto* standard for rendering high-quality images. That system is called *RenderMan*™.[21] Figure 10.14 shows the famous "Utah teapot" produced with *RenderMan*.

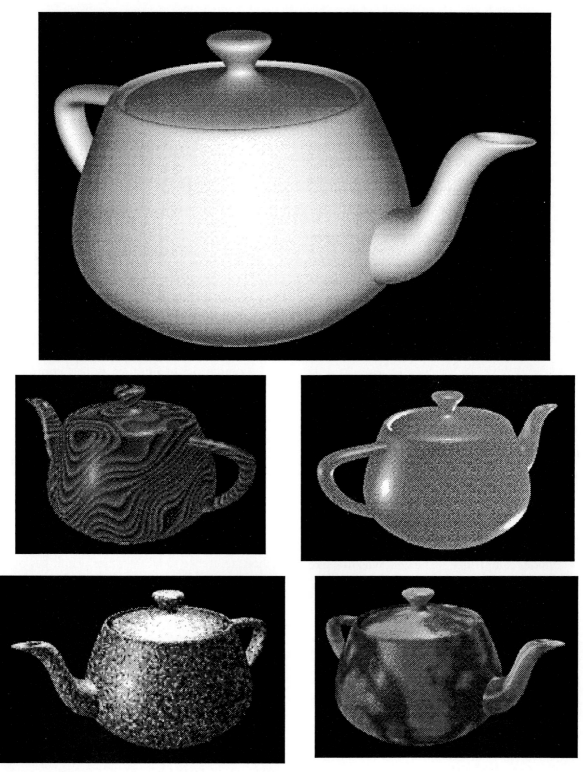

Figure 10.14
Images of the Utah teapot generated with *RenderMan*.

Background of **RenderMan**

RenderMan is the product of a talented team of computer scientists from the Computer Division of Lucasfilm, Ltd. which later became Pixar. The group includes Pat Hanrahan, Ed Catmull, Loren Carpenter, Rob Cook, and Alvy Ray Smith. In 1981 Loren Carpenter wrote REYES whose acronym stands for *Renders Everything You Ever Saw*.[22] The goal of the designers of REYES was to build an architecture optimized for fast, high-quality rendering of complex, animated scenes. *Fast* was defined as the capability of rendering a feature-length film in approximately a year; *high-quality* meant indistinguishable from live-action motion picture photography; and *complex* meant as visually rich as real scenes, as opposed to the table/lamp/glass sphere scenes typical of previous rendering experiments. REYES was used successfully to produce the Genesis effect in *Star Trek II – The Wrath of Khan* and served as the foundation for *RenderMan*. Pixar's *RenderMan* has subsequently been used to produce the Academy Award winning film, *Tin Toy* and the water creature in the film, *The Abyss*.

REYES Architecture

Rather than simply extending or refining ray tracing and radiosity algorithms (some of which had not yet been invented), the REYES designers decided to start with a clean slate and include only optimized techniques which they had developed. These include stochastic sampling, distributed ray tracing, and shade trees.[23] The goals and assumptions of the design group included:

- **Model complexity** – The goal was to make visually rich images, far more complex than any pictures previously rendered. Scenes consisting of hundreds of thousands of geometric primitives were contemplated.

- **Model diversity** – The goal was to support a variety of geometric primitives, including "data amplification" primitives such as procedural models, fractals, graftals, and particle systems.

- **Shading complexity** – Because surface reflection characteristics are complex, a programmable shader was considered necessary for producing surface color, reflections, bump maps, shadows, and refraction effects.

- **Minimal ray tracing** – The team observed that few objects in natural scenes seem to require ray tracing. Accordingly, they considered it more important to optimize the architecture for complex geometries and large models than for the non-local lighting effects produced by ray tracing and radiosity.

- **Speed** – Since the goal of the design team was to produce animated image sequences for movies, speed was critical. Assuming 24 frames per second, rendering a 2 hour movie in a year would require a rendering speed of about 3 minutes per frame.

- **Image quality** – The renderer should be free of aliasing and faceting artifacts such as jagged edges, Moiré patterns in textures, temporal strobing, and highlight aliasing.

- **Flexibility** – The architecture should be capable of incorporating new image rendering techniques which continue to emerge. That is, it should be an "open architecture" accessible through the generality of a programming language.

Some of the key concepts incorporated in the REYES architecture include *geometric locality*, *point sampling*, and the use of *micropolygons* as the basic geometric unit. Geometric locality involves the use of texture mapping and environment mapping whenever possible to substitute for the more expensive process of ray tracing. This allows the calculation of a shading value for a given primitive without reference to all the other primitives of the scene and thereby eliminates much bookkeeping and "data thrashing" required in ray tracing and radiosity. Point sampling involves a Monte Carlo technique (stochastic sampling), called *jittering*, to replace aliasing with less objectionable noise artifacts. Jittering causes sharp edges of a scene to appear as slightly blurry rather than jagged. Micropolygons are planar quadrilaterals approximately 1/2 pixel on a side. Surface shading is then represented by a single color per micropolygon. Every geometric primitive of the scene is resolved into micropolygons by a process called *dicing*, and all visibility and shading calculations are performed exclusively on micropolygons.

The basic rendering technique of REYES combines the *z*-buffer algorithm operating on micropolygons with shading models that have capabilities of texture mapping. Each object is turned into micropolygons as it is read in. A small primitive object can be diced directly into micropolygons, while a larger object may be split into smaller primitive objects or patches which are subsequently diced into micropolygons. The resulting micropolygons are shaded, sampled, and compared to values currently in the z-buffer. Since only one object is processed at a time, the amount of data necessary at any time is minimized, and the scene can contain arbitrarily many objects.

With this background the reader can better understand the overview of the REYES algorithm offered by Cook *et al.*

The advantages of the REYES algorithm include very effective antialiasing through stochastic sampling, high speed achieved through locality and the simplicity of micropolygons, and a rendering time linearly proportional to the scene complexity (model size). In addition, because of the flexibility of the REYES architecture, the authors were able to extend it easily to include the following features:

- Motion blur
- Depth of field

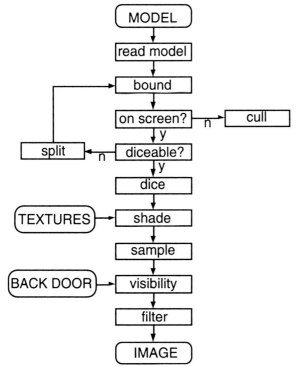

Figure 10.15
Overview of REYES rendering algorithm.

- Constructive solid geometry (CSG)
- Shadows
- Transparency

The extended REYES architecture became the foundation for *RenderMan*. In the words of Pixar's founder, Ed Catmull,

*"… we now understood what it meant to **describe** an image. This opened the door to the definition of an interface that could be independent of algorithms, hardware, and speed of execution. Pat Hanrahan put all that we knew about geometry, lighting models, ray tracing, antialiasing, motion blur, and shade trees into a compact interface which he named RenderMan."*

The RenderMan Interface

Rather than the tens of thousands to hundreds of thousands of patches typical of radiosity scenes, the Pixar team estimated that typical natural scenes would require 80,000,000 polygons. To process such huge models, they designed a "REYES Machine" using highly parallel, special-purpose hardware. In the process, they recognized the need for a standard interface between the modeling system and the rendering system. *RenderMan* defines such an interface standard.

Features provided by *RenderMan* are summarized below:

- **It provides a scene description methodology.** This consists of a complete, C-like graphical programming language. It includes a great variety of shape representations including polyhedra, quadrics, parametric curves and surfaces (Bézier, Hermite, Catmull-Rom, B-splines, and NURBs), all of the standard geometric transformations, and a digital camera viewing model.

- **It provides an elegant, highly realistic rendering engine.** Built on REYES, it offers all of the features and advantages of this algorithm as well as the extensibility of a general programming language. This makes incorporating procedural models such as fractal and graftal generators a simple procedure.

- **It generalizes the concept of shader.** In addition to the surface shader presented in the REYES discussion, it offers *light source* *shaders* to calculate the color and intensity of light reaching the surface, *displacement shaders* for moving groups of micro-polygons in the surface to simulate bumps and pits, and *atmosphere shaders* to render effects such as fog, haze, and smoke.

- **It provides a library of useful textures.** The Pixar team has emphasized that *shading* is at least as important as *shape* in determining the visual realism of images. To simulate the complex textures of natural objects, *RenderMan* provides a library of standard textures including wood, marble, stone, carpet, and plastic. Each texture has user-defined parameters such as grain, swirl, roughness, transparency, and so on to provide variety. Texture mapping buys a great deal of realism at a small computational price.

- **It offers a platform-independent model/-renderer interface standard.** This standard, called the *RenderMan Interface Byte-stream* protocol (RIB), describes the format for output files produced by CAD modelers which serve as input to the *RenderMan* rendering engine. At the time of this writing, *RenderMan* and RIB file modelers were available on the Macintosh, PCs using 386 or 486 processors, Silicon Graphics SCI-4D, Sun 3, Sun 4, and Sparc workstations. It is likely that *RenderMan* will become the *de facto* 3D scene description standard in the same way that PostScript has become the *de facto* page description standard.

Using *RenderMan*

There are two distinct modes for using *RenderMan*. The distinction arises from the manner in which the user constructs the model of the scene. In the first mode the user writes code in the *RenderMan* language to describe the scene and calls the shaders to render the image. This is best described as the *programming mode*.

The second mode involves coupling an independent modeling program with *RenderMan*. In this *CAD modeling mode*, the user creates the model using the design tools available on 3D CAD systems and exports the model in a RIB format file. *RenderMan* is then called to render the RIB file.

Programming Mode

RenderMan provides a complete programming language with which the user can define the scene, light sources, shaders, atmospheric conditions, camera position, and projection to be used in creating the image. Among other features, this language includes:

- **Data types** – The scalar, vector, and opaque classes of data types include special graphics types such as *RTPoint*, *RtMatrix*, *RtBound*, *RtVoid*, and *RtLightHandle*.

- **Surface primitives** – The three categories of surface primitives include polygon, parametric, and quadric surfaces. The polygon class includes planar, convex polygons, general polygons which can be concave and contain holes, and polyhedral structures using vertex tables for increased efficiency. Parametric surfaces include Bézier, Hermite, Catmull-Rom, NURBs, and B-splines. The six quadric primitives supported are spheres, cones, cylinders, hyperboloids, paraboloids, and toruses. All surfaces are generated by the appropriate procedure calls.

- **Hierarchical modeling** – *RenderMan* supports hierarchical structures of graphical objects with the "world object" as the root of the hierarchy. Attributes may be applied selectively to sections of the parent/-children tree with the *RiAttributeBegin* and *RiAttributeEnd* functions. After a call to the later functions the original graphics environment is restored and inherited by subsequent children.

- **Standard transformations** – All of the standard graphics transformations are supported by simple procedure calls. In addition, constructive solid geometry (CSG) operations are available for modeling complex objects.

- **Virtual Camera projection model** – *RenderMan* supports an intuitive synthetic camera model for selecting the COP, viewing direction, and field of view.

- **Shading pipeline** – The shading pipeline contains procedures for specifying the illumination, reflection/transmission of surfaces, and atmospheric effects. Light sources include an ambient term, distant sources (parallel rays), point sources, and spotlight. Surface shaders contain parameters for ambient, diffuse, and specular reflections and transparency. Special shaders are available for plastic, wood, matte, metal, marble, and stone surfaces. Atmospheric effects are rendered by volume shaders with special functions for depth cueing and fog.

The structure of a general *RenderMan* program is shown in the boilerplate example from *The RenderMan™ Companion.*

```
#include <ri.h>
render(nframes)          /*Basic program using the
                            RenderMan Interface*/
int nframes;
{
    int frame;

    RiBegin();           /*Options may now be set */
                         /* IMAGE OPTION SECTION*/
        RiDisplay(...);
        RiFormat(...);
        ...
        /* CAMERA OPTION SECTION*/
        RiClipping(...);
        RiDepthOfField(...);
        RiProjection("perspective", RI_NULL);
                         /* The current trans-*/
                         /* formation is cleared so the
                            camera can be specified.*/
        RiRotate(...); /* These transformations address
        RiTranslate(...); /* the world-to-camera */
        ...              /*transformation controlling
                           placement and orientation of the
                           camera.*/
    for(frame = 1; frame <= nframes; frame++) {
        RiFrameBegin( frame );
        /* FRAME-DEPENDENT OPTION
        SECTION*/
            /* Can still set frame-dependent
            options, camera xforms*/
            RiWorldBegin().
        /* SCENE DESCRIPTION SECTION*/
            /* The camera xform is now set;
            options are frozen*/
            /* and rendering may begin. We
            are in world space.*/
            RiAttributeBegin();    /* Begin a
            distinct object*/
                RiColor(...);
                /* Attributes fit in here.*/
                RiSurface(...);
                RiTransformBegin();
                    RiTranslate(...);
```

```
                    /* Object-positioning*/
                    /* commands        */
                    RiRotate(...);
                    ...
                    RiSphere(...);
                    RiPolygon(...);
                    RiPatch(...);
                RiTransformEnd();
            RiAttributeEnd();
            /* Restore the parent's attributes.*/
            /* Otherobjects, otherspaces*/
        RiWorldEnd();
        /* The scene is complete. The image is ren-*/
        /* dered and all scene data is discarded. Other
        /*scenes may now be declared with other world
        blocks.   */
        RiFrameEnd();   /* Options are restored.*/
    }
    RiEnd();
}
```

Next, we show a working *RenderMan* program with the image it generates in Figure 10.16.

```
##RenderMan RIB-Structure 1.1
##Scene "Table_Cube"
##Frames 1
version 3.03
projection "perspective" "fov" [30.800]
clipping 5.750 113.764
worldbegin
light "distantlight" 1 "intensity" [1.000]"from" [0 0 0]"to" [-
    0.346 -0.621 0.703]
light "distantlight" 2 "intensity" [0.250]"from" [0 0 0]"to"
    [0.400 0.750 -0.530]
attributebegin
attribute "identifier" "name" "World"
scale 1.000 1.000 -1.000
translate -0.163 0.290 -8.575
rotate 0.000 0 1 0
rotate 0.000 1 0 0
rotate 0.000 0 0 1
scale 0.729 0.729 0.729
attributebegin
attribute "identifier" "name" "Object1"
translate 0.262 -1.027 1.155
rotate 319.200 0 1 0
rotate 22.100 1 0 0
rotate -19.000 0 0 1
scale 1.138 1.138 1.138
attributebegin
attribute "identifier" "shadinggroup" "Object1shade"
color [0.539 0.312 0.186]
opacity [1.000 1.000 1.000]
surface "wood" "Ks" [0.937] "Kd" [1.000] "Ka" [1.000]
    "roughness" [0.250] "grain" [10.000] "swirl" [0.000]
sides 1
polygon "P"[0.000 0.000 -1.000 -0.694 0.056 -1.000
    0.694 0.056 -1.000 0.002 0.000 -1.000 ]
```

```
polygon "P"[0.002 0.000 -1.000 0.694 0.056 -1.000
    0.694 -0.056 -1.000 0.002 0.000 -1.000 ]
polygon "P"[0.002 0.000 -1.000 0.694 -0.056 -1.000
    -0.694 -0.056 -1.000 0.000 0.000 -1.000 ]
polygon "P"[0.000 0.000 -1.000 -0.694 -0.056 -1.000
    -0.694 0.056 -1.000 0.000 0.000 -1.000 ]
polygon "P"[-0.694 0.056 -1.000 -0.694 0.056 1.028
    0.694 0.056 1.028 0.694 0.056 -1.000 ]
polygon "P"[0.694 0.056 -1.000 0.694 0.056 1.028 0.694
    -0.056 1.028 0.694 -0.056 -1.000 ]
polygon "P"[0.694 -0.056 -1.000 0.694 -0.056 1.028
    -0.694 -0.056 1.028 -0.694 -0.056 -1.000 ]
polygon "P"[-0.694 -0.056 -1.000 -0.694 -0.056 1.028
    -0.694 0.056 1.028 -0.694 0.056 -1.000 ]
gpolygon [4] "P"[-0.694 0.056 1.028 -0.694 -0.056 1.028
    0.694 -0.056 1.028 0.694 0.056 1.028]
attributeend
attributebegin
attribute "identifier" "name" "Object4"
translate 0.021 0.458 0.012
rotate 180.000 0 1 0
rotate 0.400 1 0 0
rotate -89.700 0 0 1
scale 0.669 0.669 0.669
attributebegin
attribute "identifier" "shadinggroup" "Object4shade"
color [0.871 0.020 0.800]
opacity [1.000 1.000 1.000]
surface "metal" "Ks" [1.000] "Ka" [0.809] "roughness"
    [1.000]
sides 1
gpolygon [4] "P"[-0.599 0.599 -0.599 0.599 0.599 -0.599
    0.599 -0.599 -0.599 -0.599 -0.599 -0.599]
polygon "P"[-0.599 0.599 -0.599 -0.599 0.599 0.599
    0.599 0.599 0.599 0.599 0.599 -0.599 ]
polygon "P"[0.599 0.599 -0.599 0.599 0.599 0.599 0.599
    -0.599 0.599 0.599 -0.599 -0.599 ]
polygon "P"[0.599 -0.599 -0.599 0.599 -0.599 0.599
    -0.599 -0.599 0.599 -0.599 -0.599 -0.599 ]
polygon "P"[-0.599 -0.599 -0.599 -0.599 -0.599 0.599
    -0.599 0.599 0.599 -0.599 0.599 -0.599 ]
gpolygon [4] "P"[-0.599 0.599 0.599 -0.599 -0.599 0.599
    0.599 -0.599 0.599 0.599 0.599 0.599]
attributeend
attributeend
attributeend
attributeend
worldend
```

Note that the programming mode gives the user the maximum flexibility and control over the quality of the rendered image. It is a relatively simple matter to add two more cubes to the scene and change the shaders and opacity as follows:

Figure 10.16
Image of scene Table_Cube rendered with *Render-Man* program. The metallic finish of the cube and the wood grain are produced by the metal and wood shaders (Object 1 and Object 4 of the program, respectively).

```
/* TABLE*/
surface "wood" "Ks" [0.937] "Kd" [1.000] "Ka" [1.000]
    "roughness" [0.250] "grain" [10.000] "swirl" [2.530]

/* LEFT CUBE */
color [0.581 0.720 1.000]
surface "metal" "Ks" [1.000] "Ka" [1.000] "roughness"
    [0.500]

/* CENTERCUBE */
opacity [0.500 0.500 0.500]
surface "plastic" "Ks" [0.875] "Kd" [0.869] "Ka" [0.802]
    "roughness" [0.250]

/* RIGHT CUBE */
color [0.809 0.089 0.112]
surface "stippled" "Ks" [1.000] "Kd" [1.000] "Ka" [0.809]
    "roughness" [0.250] "grainsize" [0.031] "stippling"
    [1.000]
```

These programming changes produce the changes in appearance of objects in the scene shown in Figure 10.17.

Figure 10.17
Effects of changes in *RenderMan* shaders.

Finally, keeping the model's geometry identical with that of Figure 10.17, the following changes in shaders produce the image of Figure 10.18.

```
/* TABLE*/
color [0.934 0.748 0.694]
surface "carpet" "Kd" [0.600] "Ka" [0.848] "nap" [2.000]
    "scuff" [2.000]

/* LEFT CUBE */
surface "rmarble" "Ks" [1.000] "Kd" [0.950] "Ka" [0.875]
    "roughness" [0.000] "veining" [8.000] "specularcolor"
    [1.000]

/* CENTERCUBE */
opacity [1.000 1.000 1.000]
surface "spatter" "Ks" [0.875] "Kd" [0.869] "Ka" [0.822]
    "roughness" [0.250] "specksize" [0.480] "sizes"
    [5.000]

/* RIGHT CUBE */
color [0.697 0.363 0.108]
surface "wood" "Ks" [0.950] "Kd" [0.882] "Ka" [0.776]
    "roughness" [0.250] "grain" [10.000] "swirl" [0.625]
```

The price the user pays for this programming flexibility is the effort involved in tediously "hand crafting" each scene and image.

CAD Modeling Mode

In practical design environments, the preferred mode is to create the model with a CAD package and submit the model to *RenderMan* as a RIB file. Many CAD systems support the rapid, intuitive design of 3D objects. Therefore, they provide the natural user interface for designing models for realistic rendering. From the designer's point of view, *RenderMan* can be considered the final pass for processing the user's design.

In Figure 10.19, the scene generated using CAD modeler, *Swivel 3D Professional*, is shown. The process of building the model is discussed in the chapter on design. The model itself required about one-half hour to construct by a reasonably skilled designer. *Swivel 3D Professional is* one of a growing number of design and modeling programs that support the *RenderMan* RIB format. So, for instance, to select the shader to use for a particular object, the object is selected and the *Select Color* menu opens a shader sub-menu. Selecting a particular shader opens additional sub-menus from which the particular shader parameter values are selected. The windows providing parameter selection are shown in Figure 10.21.

Figure 10.18
Additional texture mapping changes by *RenderMan*.

Figure 10.19
CAD model designed with *Swivel 3D*. Note that the polygonal basis for the model is quite apparent. To add interest and realism, we have invoked the shadow and antialiasing rendering features of the modeler.

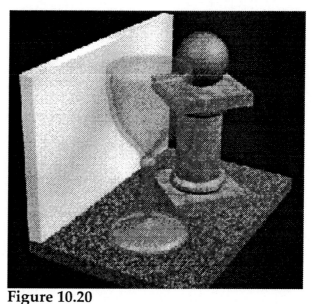

Figure 10.20
RenderMan image of model shown in Figure 10.19. In the model, the pedestal has been set to marble and the glass has been set to plastic with the top half given a transparency of 0.5 and the bottom part a transparency of 0.75. The floor surface is generated by the carpet shader.

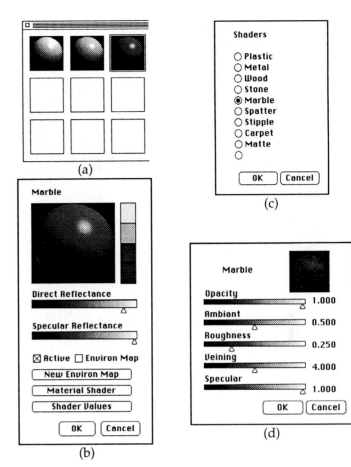

Figure 10.21
Material shader windows for setting *RenderMan* parameters. Clicking on the palette icon and the object to be shaded causes the shader icon palette summary to open (a). Double clicking the right icon opens the menu, (b). Clicking the *Material Shader* button opens the *Shaders* menu, (c). After selecting a shader, the *Shader Values* button is clicked and its attributes set with the valuators, (d). *Swivel 3D* automatically incorporates these attributes into the RIB file it exports for *RenderMan*.

After the surface attributes were set by the interactive menu selection outlined in Figure 10.21, the RIB file corresponding to this model was generated and submitted to *RenderMan* for image generation. The results are shown in Figure 10.20.

The increase in visual realism achievable by surface mapping is obvious in Figure 10.20. In particular, the marble pedestal and carpeted floor surface improve the realism of the scene, and the transparency of the glass conveys a convincing (if non-physical) image. The shaders and their attributes were set very simply using the series of hierarchical windows presented in Figure 10.21.

Object Libraries for Scene Generation

One of the most useful features of CAD systems is the library of parts and objects available to the designer. To design the more complex scene of Figure 10.22, we built the room (two walls and floor) and picture by modifying the basic cube primitive of *Swivel 3D*. Then the filing cabinet, table, chair, and serving tray were imported from

an object library and positioned, using orthographic projections. Next, the colors and textures were selected with the menu windows shown in Figure 10.21. Finally, the export file type was set to *RIB* and the output file generated for input to *RenderMan*.

The process of designing a world model like that shown in Figure 10.22 takes less than an hour for a moderately skilled designer. It is important to note that the design occurs completely in 3D space, maintaining complete flexibility of object position, camera position, and projection type until the desired projected image is achieved. The complete 3D representation of the model, including camera position, directions of light sources, and surface shaders and parameters, is encoded in the RIB file exported to *RenderMan*. The RIB file is a standard text file of *RenderMan* language commands which can be edited with any standard word processor. The model shown in Figure 10.22 is represented by a 900 Kb RIB file.

There are several interesting features distinguishing the model image of Figure 10.22

Figure 10.22
Office scene produced with 3D CAD modeler, *Swivel 3D*. Surface attributes such as transparency of the glass table top and carpet texture have been tagged to the surfaces but not rendered by the modeler.

and the rendered image of Figure 10.23. First is the obvious aliasing of straight edges of the model image. These may be suppressed by invoking an antialiasing option of the modeler as was done in Figure 10.17. Second is that surface shaders are merely attached to the surfaces in the RIB files generated by the modeler but are not used in generating the image produced by the modeler. The final feature of note is that shadowing of the model image is a rendering option of the modeler (invoked in Figure 10.17 but not in 10.22), but the results of shadowing are not transmitted through the RIB file.

The RIB file is then rendered by *Renderman*, and several hours later the image shown in Figure 10.23 is complete. Rendering takes place in background mode, however, and the machine is available for other tasks during the process.

Several features of the *RenderMan* image enhance its visual realism as compared to the modeler image. First is the antialiasing which eliminates the prominent aliasing observable in Figure 10.22. Second is the improved realism of several of the surfaces produced by texture mapping shaders. The only shading controls available on the modeler are the relative values of ambient and specular light intensity. These values are passed through the RIB file to *RenderMan* which has, in addition, a rich repertoire of built-in shaders and the capability of user-defined shaders.

While the *RenderMan* image is more realistic than the plastic-like scene of the modeler, it still fails the test of photorealism. An examination of Figure 10.23 reveals these failings.

Figure 10.23
RenderMan image of Figure 10.22 office scene model.

- The specular surfaces of the tea set fail to reflect objects in their environment which an accurate ray-traced solution would have generated.

- The chair, table, and file cabinet appear to be floating a few inches above the floor. This is a common artifact associated with the absence of a global solution such as that provided by radiosity. A global solution produces local shadows in regions where the objects contact the floor.

- The rendered solution shown does not include shadows of any kind. The resulting flat and featureless image is a signature of the local shading model used by *RenderMan*.

But surely, you must be thinking, *RenderMan* should be able to do better than this or it wouldn't be capable of producing the realistic visual effects in films like *The Abyss*. The solutions to these problems in realistic rendering are provided by two additional generalized texture maps. These are called *environment maps* and *shadow maps*.

Environment Maps

Environment maps address the problem of inter-object reflections—an image of the filing cabinet which should be visible in the tea set. An environment map assumes a viewpoint near the middle of the reflective object and precomputes an image from that viewpoint. This image is then mapped onto the surface and added to the specular and ambient light emitted from the reflective surface.

Environment mapping is a relatively inexpensive technique for rendering highly reflective objects. It works well when the surfaces are fairly small compared to the distance to the objects being reflected and is less well suited to rendering highly convoluted surfaces that reflect themselves. It also suffers from the "hand crafting syndrome," that is, the user must select which objects will use environment maps and then call the appropriate routines for each object. This *ad hoc* approach contrasts sharply with the automatic and complete rendering which ray-tracing algorithms carry out on well-specified scenes.

Shadow Maps

A shadow map begins as a depth image, rendered from the viewpoint of a light source. By encoding the depth image at each pixel with the distance from the light source, rather than the color of the surface, the result can be used to determine whether any point in the scene is in shadow.

To create a shadow map the user takes the following steps. First, in a copy of the RIB file, any objects that need not cast shadows are removed. Next, the scene is moved to position the camera at the light source, and the file rendered to a *zfile*. Then, the *MakeShadow* routine is called to convert the zfile to a shadow map. Finally, the light source shader in the original RIB file takes the shadow map name as an argument, and the file is rendered.

Shadow mapping provides a relatively inexpensive and geometrically accurate technique for producing shadows. However, it is open to the same criticisms as environment mapping due to the hand crafting requirements and its *ad hoc* nature.

RenderMan provides a very effective and efficient solution to the problem of achieving visual realism. It overcomes the intrinsic limitations of a local shading model by generalizing the shader concept to include bump, texture, shadow, and environment mapping. The combination of these techniques offers a system capable of producing images rivaling in visual realism the best results of the more physically-based ray tracing and radiosity solutions. The primary message in this discussion, however, is that *RenderMan* provides the high-end personal computer and graphics workstation user with an economical, software solution for achieving visual realism.

Conclusions

This chapter has presented three of the most successful approaches for achieving visual realism in rendering images of world scenes. The first two approaches, ray tracing and radiosity, are firmly rooted in the physics of light and its interaction with the environment. As such, they have both proven very effective in achieving aspects of visual realism, but neither approach, in its raw form, produces totally realistic images. Rather, they behave as complementary approaches, each contributing features missing from the other. Current research involves integration of the two approaches in a system which preserves the advantages of each. Considerable progress has been made towards this goal.

The *RenderMan* approach relaxes the emphasis on the *physical authenticity* of the image rendering process and focuses instead on *psychological* and *perceptual authenticity*. By switching the approach from the simulation of *reality* to the simulation of the *appearance of reality*, the Pixar team has achieved a system for rendering photo-realistic images at minimal computational cost. By defining the RIB file interface format and making *RenderMan* available on a variety of platforms, they are well on their way to establishing a *de facto* scene description language and rendering standard.

Exercises

10.1   In the introductory material, illumination models and vision models were cited as cases in which recognition of the physical laws underlying a process was essential to improving computer simulation of the process. Discuss two other areas in which this principle of *model authenticity* applies.

10.2   Is the direction of light rays we see illuminating a scene better explained by *forward* or *backward* ray tracing? Explain.

10.3   Why is backward ray tracing preferred over forward ray tracing for computer image rendering algorithms? Is the less preferred approach possible even with a supercomputer? Estimate how many rays might be necessary to generate an image with the less preferred method. Compare that number with the number of rays which must be considered for the more preferred method.

10.4   Consider a scene similar to Figure 10.3 containing only opaque, reflective spheres. If the coefficient of specular reflection is 0.5, how many levels of recursion are required before the contribution of reflected light falls below 10% of its intrinsic brightness? How many for 1%?

10.5   How many rays must be computed to produce a 640 × 480 pixel image by ray tracing if recursion proceeds to three levels and 10% of the rays spawned strike transparent objects? How many for a 1024 × 768 pixel image carried to five levels of recursion with 30% transparent hits?

10.6   For a mirror surface, the relationship between the reflected ray, *R*, the incident ray, *I*, and the normal to the surface, *N*, is given by Equation 10.6:

$$R = I - 2\,(I{\cdot}N\,)N.$$

Verify this equation by sketching vector diagrams corresponding to each step in the proof, [10.3] – [10.5].

10.7   Study a number of images generated by ray tracing in computer graphics journals or computer trade magazines. What features do all these images seem to share?

10.8   The ray tracing technique in its original formulation is not a *complete* rendering model—certain optical effects are ignored. List three such omissions in the order of their detrimental effects on visual realism, with the most glaring omissions first.

10.9   Why do improved ray tracing algorithms use bounding boxes or bounding spheres?

10.10   Write an algorithm for generating shadows by using *shadow rays* within the ray tracing framework.

10.11   What is meant by *color bleeding*? Clip three images, real or computer generated, which illustrate color bleeding.

10.12   Discuss a problem of engineering design (possibly in the area of electrical motor design) in which the thermodynamic radiosity approach could provide a useful solution.

10.13   What is the physical principle on which radiosity is based? Is this principle just a useful approximation or a basic law of physics? How does it apply to light?

10.14   A symmetric matrix is one in which the matrix is unchanged upon row-column interchange. That is, $M_{ij} = M_{ji}$. Determine whether the radiosity formfactor matrix, *F*, is symmetric and interpret your conclusion. What condition is necessary for $F_{ij} = F_{ji}$? (*Hint: consider Equation 10.37.*)

10.15   The radiosity discussion claimed that the projection of the Nusselt hemisphere (see Figure 10.9) onto the A_i patch had an area of π. Using a sketch of the geometry, prove this.

10.16   Estimate the number of computations required for a radiosity solution in three colors for a 50,000 patch scene using a 50 × 50 pixel resolution hemi-cube. Assume a scene complexity in which, on average, each pixel of each hemi-cube is shaded by three patches.

10.17   Discuss the advantages of the hemi-cube algorithm in computing radiosity formfactors.

10.18   Discuss in the order of their importance (most important first) three effects which radiosity computes correctly that are missing from the simple ray tracing algorithm.

10.19   Discuss in the order of their importance (most important first) three effects which ray tracing computes correctly that are missing from the simple radiosity algorithm.

10.20   The progressive refinement radiosity algorithm begins by selecting the brightest patch to use as a source of illumination for all other patches. If *brightness* is defined as total energy emission, show how this is calculated in terms of the parameters of the problem. Verify your result using dimensional analysis.

10.21   What do we mean when we say that the standard radiosity algorithm uses a *gathering* approach, whereas progressive radiosity uses a *shooting* approach?

10.22   Explain how progressive radiosity provides immediate feedback to the user while the standard radiosity algorithm does not. Why is this important?

10.23   Many of the best features of ray tracing and radiosity can be merged by using radiosity to compute the shading of surfaces in a ray tracing algorithm. What significant process is overlooked in this simple merger?

10.24   What advanced rendering techniques are available on the Hewlett-Packard Personal VRX graphics work station?

10.25   What are the advantages of separating the *model building* and *rendering* functions?

10.26   Are the goals and assumptions of the REYES design group consistent with the *model authenticity* principle proposed in the text? If so, in what ways? If not, how can REYES generate realistic images while violating or ignoring the physical principles required by model authenticity?

10.27   The key concept of *geometric locality* is both a strength and a weakness of the REYES architecture. Discuss this strength and weakness and how each is manifested in the image generation process.

10.28   What part do micropolygons play in the REYES architecture and what are their advantages?

10.29   Discuss five of the most attractive features of *RenderMan*.

10.30   What leading feature of ray tracing is missing in *RenderMan*, and how does *RenderMan* try to compensate for this omission?

10.31   What features provided by radiosity algorithms are missing from *RenderMan*? Can *RenderMan* compensate for these omissions?

Endnotes

1. *RenderMan* is a registered trademark of Pixar.
2. Whitted, Turner, "An Improved Illumination Model for Shaded Display," *Communications of ACM* **23**, No. 6, pp. 343–349, June (1980).
3. Glassner, Andrew S. (Ed), *An Introduction to Ray Tracing*, Academic Press, San Diego, CA (1989).
4. Watt, Alan, "Fundamentals of Three-Dimensional Computer Graphics," Addison-Wesley Publishing Company, Wokingham, England (1989).
5. Hultquist, Jeff, "Intersection of a Ray with a Sphere," *Graphics Gems*, Andrew S. Glassner (ed),Academic Press, Inc., San Diego, CA, pp. 388–389, (1990).
6. Kaplan, Michael R., "The Use of Spatial Coherence in Ray Tracing," in *Techniques for Computer Graphics*, David R. Rogers and Rae A. Earnshaw (eds), Springer-Verlag, New York, NY, pp. 173–193, (1987).
7. Cook, Robert L., Porter, Thomas and Carpenter, Loren, "Distributed Ray Tracing," *Computer Graphics* **18**, No. 3 (*SIGGRAPH '84 Proceedings*), pp. 137–145, July (1984).
8. Cook, Robert L., "Stochastic Sampling in Computer Graphics," *ACS Trans. on Computer Graphics* **5**, No.1, pp. 51–72 (1986).
9. Siegel, Robert and Howell, John R., *Thermal Radiation Heat Transfer*, Hemisphere Publishing Corp. (1978).
10. Goral, Cindy M., Torrance, Kenneth E., Greenberg, Donald P, and Battaile, Bennett, "Modeling the Interaction of Light Between Diffuse Surfaces," *Computer Graphics* **18**, No. 3 (*SIGGRAPH '84 Proceedings*), pp. 213–222, July (1984).
11. Cohen, Michael F. and Greenberg, Donald P., "The Hemi-Cube – A Radiosity Solution for Complex Environments," *Computer Graphics* **19**, No. 3, (*SIGGRAPH '85 Proceedings*), pp. 31–40, July (1985).
12. Siegel, Robert and Howell, John R., *Op cit.*
13. Cohen, Michael F., Chen, Shenchang Eric, Wallace, John R., and Greenberg, Donald P., "A Progressive Refinement Approach to Fast Radiosity Image Generation," *Computer Graphics* **22**, No. 4, (*SIGGRAPH '88 Proceedings*) pp. 75-84, August (1988).
14. Greenberg, Donald P., Panel Session, "Distributed Graphics: Where to Draw the Lines?," *Computer Graphics* **23**, No. 5,

(*SIGGRAPH '89 Panel Proceedings*) pp. 271-276, December (1989).

15. Wallace, John R., Elmquist, Kells A., and Haines, Eric A., "A Ray Tracing Algorithm for Progressive Radiosity," *Computer Graphics* **23**, No. 3, (*SIGGRAPH '89 Proceedings*) pp. 315-324, August (1989).

16. Immel, David S., Cohen, Michael F, and Greenberg, Donald P., "A Radiosity Method for Non-Diffuse Environments," *Computer Graphics* **20**, No. 4,(*SIGGRAPH '86 Proceedings*) pp. 133-142, August (1986).

17. Kajiya, James T., "The Rendering Equation," *Computer Graphics* **20**, No. 4, (*SIGGRAPH '86 Proceedings*) pp. 143-150, August (1986).

18. Wallace, John R., Cohen, Michael F, and Greenberg, Donald P., "A Two-Pass Solution to the Rendering Equation: A Synthesis of Ray Tracing and Radiosity Methods," *Computer Graphics* **21**, No. 4,(*SIGGRAPH '87 Proceedings*) pp. 311-320, August (1987).

19. Sillion, François and Puech, Claude, "A General Two-Pass Method Integrating Specular and Diffuse Reflection," *Computer Graphics* **23**, No. 3,(*SIGGRAPH '89 Proceedings*) pp. 335-344, July (1989).

20. Hewlett-Packard price quotation by phone, February, 1991.

21. Upstill, Steve, *The Renderman™ Companion: A Programmer's Guide to Realistic Computer Graphics*, Addison-Wesley Publishing Company, Reading, MA (1990).

22. Cook, Robert L, Carpenter, Loren, and Catmull, Edwin, "The Reyes Image Rendering Architecture," *Computer Graphics* **21**, No. 4,(*SIGGRAPH '87 Proceedings*) pp. 95-102, July (1987).

23. Cook, Robert L, "Shade Trees," *Computer Graphics* **18**, No. 3 (*SIGGRAPH '84 Proceedings*), pp. 223–231, July (1984).

Chapter 11

Fractals –
Objects of Fractional Dimension

Philosophy is written in this grand book - I mean universe - which stands
continuously open to our gaze, but it cannot be understood unless one first learns to
comprehend the language in which it is written. It is written in the language of
mathematics, and its characters are triangles, circles, and other geometrical figures,
without which it is humanly impossible to understand a single word of it; without
these, one is wandering about in a dark labyrinth.
Galileo

Clouds are not spheres, mountains are not cones, coastlines are not circles, and bark is
not smooth, nor does lightning travel in a straight line. ... Mathematicians have
disdained this challenge, however, and have increasingly chosen to flee from nature
by devising theories unrelated to anything we can see or feel.
Responding to this challenge, I conceived and developed a new geometry of
nature and implemented its use in a number of diverse fields
Benoit Mandelbrot

What is new is the ability to start with an actual image and find the fractals that will
imitate it to any desired degree of accuracy. Since our method includes a compact way
of representing these fractals, we end up with a highly compressed data set for
reconstructing the original image.
Michael Barnsley and Alan Sloan

Fractals play a very special role in computer graphics. They form the basis for some of the most beautiful and exquisite images ever generated by humans or machines. Computer graphics provided the most significant tool used in the discovery of fractal geometry. Because many natural objects are fractal in nature, fractal geometry gives us new tools for modeling natural scenes. With the solution of the *inverse problem,* fractal representations provide an image compression technique for solving one of the most troublesome problems of computer graphics—the huge size of graphics image files.

We have seen that one of the best measures of visual realism in computer graphics is the extent to which shading models and rendering algorithms incorporate the physics of light and its in-teractions with objects. Yet, in spite of the successes of ray tracing and radiosity techniques, experts in computer graphics can consistently detect the artificial nature of synthetic images (i.e., computer-generated images). Even novices in computer graphics often sense something artificial about synthetic images, with the objects themselves providing clues on the rendering technique. Glass balls, teapots, and checkerboards suggest ray tracing while walls, tables, and lamp shades hint at radiosity. It is rare, indeed, to find a synthetic image of natural objects that is at all convincing in its visual realism. That is, the representation and rendering techniques we have discussed to date are extremely effective in displaying objects that are human-made, symmetrical, or geometric primitives, but they fail miserably in generating realistic images of such common objects as trees, clouds, and mountains. Why is that?

The answer is both simple and profound, and it is deeply rooted in the concept of dimensionality itself. The simple answer is given by Yale mathematician Benoit Mandelbrot in the introductory quotation who observes that most natural objects do not conform to simple geometric shapes. The more profound answer is that the geometry best describing most natural objects is not traditional 3D Euclidean geometry, but rather what Mandelbrot describes as the *fractal geometry of nature*.[1] Mandelbrot coined the term *fractal* to describe both natural and mathematical objects that share the property of having *fractional dimensionality*, a term we define shortly. The concept of dimensionality plays a key role in distinguishing fractal objects from those 1D, 2D, and 3D objects we have studied so far. For this reason, the study of fractals as fractional-dimension objects is the natural concluding chapter of our N-Dimensional approach to computer graphics.

Fractal geometry is another confirmation of the principle of *model authenticity* introduced in

previous chapters. This principle holds that realistic simulation of physical systems requires recognition and accurate simulation of the physics governing the behavior of those systems. The computer graphics task of rendering realistic images of natural scenes requires, according to this principle, that we model such scenes using the appropriate geometry—fractal geometry. Fractal geometry is one aspect of the emerging field of chaos and nonlinear dynamics, a revolutionary new area of physics and mathematics research.[2] The remarkably realistic renderings of scenes based on fractal geometry confirm the principle of model authenticity.

The Fractal Geometry of Nature

Perhaps the most noteworthy aspect of fractal geometry is the enormous range of objects and systems it is capable of describing. A partial list includes: mountain landscapes, clouds, rainfall patterns, snowflakes, frost patterns, island formations, sea coasts, river basin patterns, tree branching, arteries, veins, bronchioles, high-energy physics particle jets, percolation patterns, moon craters, galaxy structure, Brownian motion of molecules, structure of magnetic domains, radio noise, stock market fluctuations, and the mountain landscape in the movie *Star Trek II: Wrath of Khan*.

The science of chaos and fractal geometry is a classical example of an interdisciplinary field. The following areas have both contributed to—and profited greatly from—the study of fractal geometry:

- Physics
- Mathematics
- Computer graphics
- Art and music
- Data Compression and Communications.

Chaos theory and fractal geometry have also contributed significantly to the following fields:

- Medicine
- Engineering
- Economics
- Cinema.

The unifying and central role of fractal geometry is illustrated in Figure 11.1.

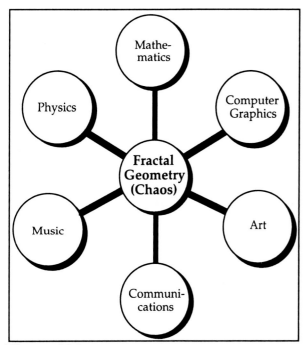

Figure 11.1
Fractal geometry and chaos theory play a central and unifying role in many disciplines.

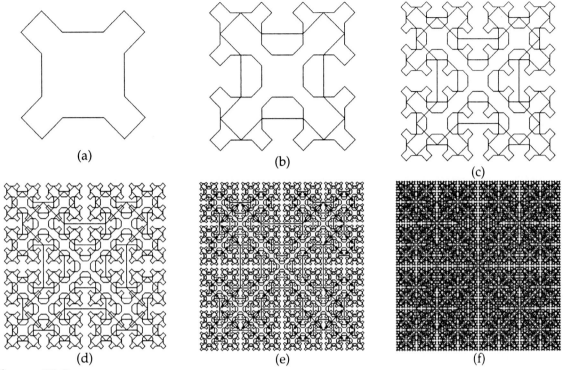

(a) (b) (c)

(d) (e) (f)

Figure 11.2
Sierpinski Gasket . What starts as a simple set of sixteen 1D lines becomes more complex and "space filling" with each iteration. By the sixth iteration, the 1D figure has evolved into a 2D figure.

Properties of Fractals

Fractal objects share certain characteristics which distinguish them from more traditional objects defined by Euclidean geometry. These include:

- Fractals have the property of *self-similarity* or *statistical self-similarity*. That is, upon magnification of the structure of a fractal, new structure emerges that appears identical or statistically similar to that of the original structure.

- The generating functions or algorithms for fractals are generally *simple*, but usually lead to structure that is amazingly *complex*.

- The natural language for generating fractals is *iteration* or *recursion.*

- The dimensionality of fractals is *noninteger* (i.e., fractional).

Let's examine some of these properties in more detail.

Fractional Dimensions

Our indoctrination with traditional Euclidean geometry makes the *integer* classification of *n*-dimensional systems seem like the only natural and logical one. We all know intuitively what 1D, 2D, and 3D objects are. A line or smooth curve is a 1D object; a plane, polygon, or Bézier patch is a 2D object ; and a sphere, cylinder, or superquadric is a 3D object. However, Figure 11.2 suggests that life may not always be so simple.

It is clear that what starts out as a 1D outline tends toward a 2D figure as each level of recursion is carried out.

Another experiment illustrating the ambiguity of our traditional concept of dimension is the following. Start with a flat sheet of white paper. It is clearly a 2D object. Now crumple it up somewhat. What is it now? Well, it is a sort of random set of somewhat curved 2D patches. Now crumple it tighter and tighter until it is about the size of a golf ball. Hold it between your thumb and forefinger and call across the room to your friend, "Let's go play golf!" She'll reply, "Fine, I see

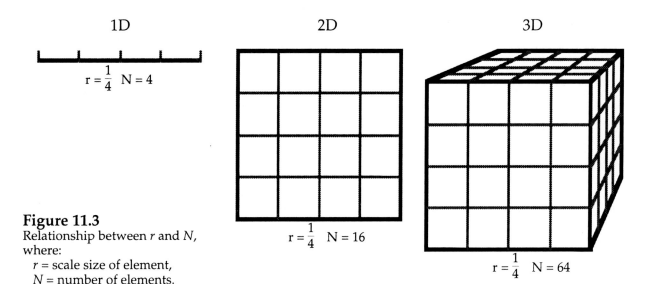

Figure 11.3
Relationship between *r* and *N*,
where:
  r = scale size of element,
  N = number of elements.

you've got a ball." But a golf ball is 3D and this is only a sheet of paper. Is it 2D or 3D?

So the concept of dimensionality must be considered in a more systematic and analytic way. The following definition of dimension D was proposed by Hausdorff early in the twentieth century.[3] Consider the problem of measuring the coast line of England. Using a satellite photograph and a ruler with appropriate divisions, say 1 km, we would measure a length we can designate L_1. To get a more accurate answer, we could use a series of high-altitude aircraft photographs and a ruler with finer divisions of say one hundred or ten m to determine a new length, L_2. If this were still not adequate, we could send out teams of surveyors with meter sticks who would report back a length, L_3.

Note that L_1 represents the length of coast line of the major land masses, bays, and other geologic features with a scale of a few kilometers or more. However, big bays have little bays and big peninsulas have smaller peninsulas, and L_2 is a better representation of such smaller-scale features. The L_3 answer generated by the surveyors' meter sticks represents an even finer-grained measurement. In principle, this refinement could continue indefinitely down through the centimeter and millimeter scales appropriate for rocks and pebbles until we reached the millimicron scale of atoms.

How are the measurements, L_1, L_2, and L_3 related? Obviously, $L_1 < L_2 < L_3$. That is, the result obtained is determined by the scale of the ruler used to make the measurement. In other words,

the size of irregular objects depends upon the number of increments used to determine the size. This is not the case for regular Euclidean objects. This scale dependence of fractal objects provides the basis for the definition of dimensionality.

Consider the relationship between the number of incremental elements, N, and the element size, r, for the following 1D, 2D, and 3D objects.

Note that the relationship between the scale *r* and number of elements, *N*, may be written:

$$1D: \ N\,r^1 = 1,$$
$$2D: \ N\,r^2 = 1,$$
$$3D: \ N\,r^3 = 1.$$

This may be generalized for dimension, *D*, as:

$$N\,r^D = 1. \qquad [11.1]$$

The quantity *D* is defined as the Hausdorff dimension and may be extracted from Equation 11.1 and expressed in terms of the number of elements and their size as:

$$D = \ln(N) \, / \, \ln(1/r). \qquad [11.2]$$

Note that nothing in the defining Equation 11.2 requires that D assumes only integer values. For fractal objects D takes on noninteger values. Consider D for the following fractal objects.

The von Koch triangular snowflake has some very interesting properties. The geometric generator applied iteratively to each section of the figure is shown in 11.4(a), and the results of the

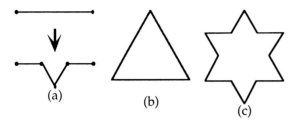

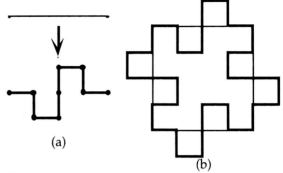

(a)

Figure 11.4
von Koch fractal triangle generator. Applying the geometric substitution shown in (a) to each segment of the triangle (b) produces first iteration of the von Koch snowflake, shown in (c). Since N = 4 and r = 1/3, the Hausdorff dimension of the Koch triangle is D ≅ 1.26.

Figure 11.5
von Koch fractal square generator. Applying the substitution indicated in (a) to each segment converts the square into the fractal curve shown after the first iteration in (b). Since N = 8 and r = 1/4, the dimensionality of this fractal is D = 1.5.

first iteration given in 11.4(c). Note that the length of the "shoreline" (perimeter) of the original triangle is $L_1 = 3$; after one iteration, the perimeter is $L_2 = (4/3)L_1$; after two iterations, $L_3 = (4/3)^2 L_1$; and so on. Thus the perimeter of the von Koch *snowflake* goes to infinity as the number of iterations goes to infinity, even though the curve itself is bounded by the square subtending 11.4(c). Substituting the number of elements used to measure a side (N = 4) and the length of each (r = 1/3), Equation 11.2 yields the dimensionality D = 1.2618... for the von Koch snowflake.

In light of the previous discussion of the length of coastline, one might expect that the dimensionality of an object would increase as the complexity of sub-structure increases. The von Koch square, shown with its generator and the results of the first iteration in Figure 11.5, exhibits a complexity greater than that of the triangular snowflake. Now, to characterize the increase in length of shoreline after each iteration, we need N = 8 elements each of length r = 1/4 unit. Substituting these values into Equation 11.2 does, in fact, yield an increased dimensionality of D = 1.5.

An intuitive interpretation of the dimensionality of fractals has been given by Richard Voss, one of Mandelbrot's colleagues at IBM, who stated, "Fractal dimension measures how the length of a coast line changes as we change the size of the ruler." We will discuss shortly algorithms for generating fractal landscapes which accurately simulate mountain scenes. An interesting result of the research on the dimensionality of natural fractal objects is the *X.2 Rule*. This rule states that very realistic fractal coast lines, mountains, and clouds

are generated by objects with dimensionality D_i, where:

Coastlines	$D_i = 1.2$,
Mountains	$D_i = 2.2$,
Clouds	$D_i = 3.2$–3.3.

A natural interpretation of the fractional dimension of coastlines involves their "area filling" character. That is, as we move from the simple triadic Koch curve through the more complex quadric Koch curve to the highly irregular Sierpinski curve the dimension ranges from 1.26 through 1.5 to nearly 2. Mountain landscapes involve distorting a smooth, 2D surface by stochastic processes acting on the third dimension. If the disturbance is small, "rolling hills" with D ≈ 2.1 result; increasing the dimension to D ≥ 2.5 causes a rugged landscape with jagged peaks and steep-walled canyons. Modeling of clouds requires specifying at each 3D point a fourth dimension such as the temperature or translucency of the condensation at that point.

Classification of Fractals

From the preceding discussion, several properties of fractals provide the basis for a classification system, including dimensionality, self-similarity, and generation technique. One property which cleanly distinguishes two distinct classes of fractals is the role of chance in their generation and resulting structure. Figure 11.6 summarizes this classification scheme.

Deterministic Fractals

Deterministic fractals have structures which are fixed uniquely by the algorithm employed in their creation. That is, for a given set of parameters, a deterministic fractal generator will produce identical structures each time it is run. Chance plays no role in the final structure of the deterministic fractal.

Interestingly, identical fractals may be produced by distinct algorithms. The Sierpinski gasket, for instance, can be generated by the "Chaos Game" algorithm or by an iterated function system algorithm discussed presently. Some of these algorithms do employ random number generators within the deterministic program. The final structure of the fractal, however, shows no indication of random processes and is a function of the control parameters only.

Stochastic Fractals

The distinctive characteristic of stochastic fractals is that random processes play a central role in determining the structure of the fractal object. Phenomena such as turbulence, seacoast, and mountain formation are deterministic at a physical level but are extremely sensitive to the initial conditions, a property common to all chaotic systems. The complex interaction of the system with the initial conditions and subsequent environment results in apparently random turbulent behavior and fractal mountain landscapes.

It is virtually impossible to accurately represent the initial condition and successfully simulate the subsequent system development of such natural systems. A far more tractable approach has been to simulate the fractal geometry of such objects by introducing random processes in creating the scenes. The approach has proven successful in simulating Brownian motion, percolation behavior, and mountain geography.

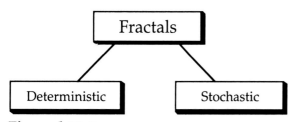

Figured 11.6
Classification scheme for fractals based on the role of chance.

Generating Fractals

The best way to understand fractals is to study algorithms for generating the major types of fractals, build programs to implement these algorithms, and observe the graphical results. The broad categories of fractals defined in the last section can be further refined according to the general algorithmic approach used in generating the fractal.

Categories of Fractal Algorithms

The fractals of interest in this chapter can all be generated by the following classes of algorithms:

- **Linear replacement mapping** – Fractal curves such as the Koch and Sierpinski curves are generated by successive refinement of a given line by some generator function.

- **Iterated function systems** – Many natural objects such as ferns and trees can be generated by the successive application of a series of contractive affine transformations.

- **Complex plane mapping** – Mathematical objects such as the Julia and Mandelbrot sets are generated by successive mapping on the complex plane.

- **Stochastic processes** – Mountain landscapes and other irregular objects are generated by applying random processes within a recursive algorithm.

Linear Replacement Mapping

The basic idea of replacement mapping is that a generator function maps a given, parent structure into a new, more complex child structure. An original object is defined, and, in the first iteration, the replacement mapping is applied to each element of the original object, producing a refined child object. In the second iteration, each element of the child object is transformed into an even more refined grandchild object, and so on. Theoretically, a fractal generated by replacement mapping would require an infinite number of iterations. In practice, for graphical applications, the iteration or recursion need continue only until the structures being mapped fall to subpixel dimensions. The simplest form of replacement mapping is *linear* replacement mapping, the conversion of a single line into a more complex object.

The basic algorithm for linear replacement mapping is summarized below.

Linear Replacement Mapping Algorithm

1. Define initial structure in terms of lines defined by end points.
2. Define replacement mapping replacing each line with refined set of lines.
3. Iterate refinement until desired level is achieved.

To implement this algorithm we add two additional conditions:

1. The algorithm should be generalized enough to map any arbitrary configuration of lines by a conversion of each line into another arbitrary set of lines.

2. The algorithm should be capable of iteration to an arbitrary level of refinement.

In order to implement the first condition, the first two steps of the algorithm can be isolated to individual subroutines. To satisfy the second condition we can use a file swapping technique to avoid limiting the problem size by the dimensions of internal data structures. The following Pascal program implements the Linear Replacement Mapping Algorithm, subject to the generality conditions.

Pascal Program **Koch**

```
program Koch;
{Program to draw and iteratively refine  }
{ von Koch curves by the method of       }
{ linear replacement mapping.            }

   type
      RealFile = file of real;

   var
      x1, y1, x2, y2, dx, dy: real;
      x, y: integer;
      i, j, Nit: integer;
      infile, outfile: RealFile;
      Name: string;
      done: Char;

{********** Define Object ***********}
   procedure DefineObject (var Name: string);
      {Procedure to generate and write original database.}
```

```
      const
         xmax = 512;
         ymax = 342;

      var
         xc, yc: real;
         dx, dy: real;
      begin
         Name := 'Triadic Koch Curve';
         rewrite(outfile, 'Ch11:Koch.datA');
         xc := xmax / 2;
         dy := ymax / 4;
         dx := 1.1547 * dy;
         write(outfile, (xc - dx), 2.5 * dy);
         write(outfile, xc, 0.5 * dy);
         write(outfile, (xc + dx), 2.5 * dy);
         write(outfile, (xc - dx), 2.5 * dy);
         close(outfile);
      end;

{************* SetIO ***************}
   procedure setIO (Nit: integer; var infile, outfile:
                    RealFile);
      {Procedure to set input & output files as a function of
       Nit.}

      var
         even: boolean;

      begin                    {Father/Son data files .}
         even := ((Nit mod 2) = 0);
         if even then
            begin
               reset(infile, 'Ch11:Koch.datA');
               rewrite(outfile, 'Ch11:Koch.datB');
            end
         else
            begin
               reset(infile, 'Ch11:Koch.datB');
               rewrite(outfile, 'Ch11:Koch.datA');
            end;
      end;

{************* Refine ***************}
   procedure Refine (var outfile: RealFile; x1, y1, x2,
                     y2: real);
      {Procedure to successively refine the input line into
       new output.}

      const
         Nout = 5;

      var
         i: integer;
         xp, yp: array[1..Nout] of real;

      begin
         dx := (x2 - x1) / 3;
         dy := (y2 - y1) / 3;
         xp[1] := x1;
```

```
        yp[1] := y1;
        xp[2] := x1 + dx;
        yp[2] := y1 + dy;
        xp[3] := xp[2] + 0.5 * dx + 0.866 * dy;
        yp[3] := yp[2] - 0.866 * dx + 0.5 * dy;
        xp[4] := xp[2] + dx;
        yp[4] := yp[2] + dy;
        xp[5] := x2;
        yp[5] := y2;
        for i := 1 to 5 do
            write(outfile, xp[i], yp[i]);
    end;

begin                    {Main program}
    Nit := 0;
    DefineObject(name);

    repeat
        hideall;
        showdrawing;
        setIO(Nit, infile, outfile);
                    {Read first point to get started.}
        read(infile, x1, y1);         x := round(x1);
        y := round(y1);
        moveto(x, y);
                    {Now iterate until eof(infile).}
        repeat
            read(infile, x2, y2);
            x := round(x2);
            y := round(y2);
            lineto(x, y);
            Refine(outfile, x1, y1, x2, y2);  {Refine line.}
            x1 := x2;                {Substitute last into first.}
            y1 := y2;
        until eof(infile);

        close(infile);
        close(outfile);
        Nit := Nit + 1;
        moveto(20, 20);
        writedraw(name);
        moveto(20, 30);
        writedraw(' Nit = ', Nit : 1);
        readln(done);
    until (done = 'd');
end.
```

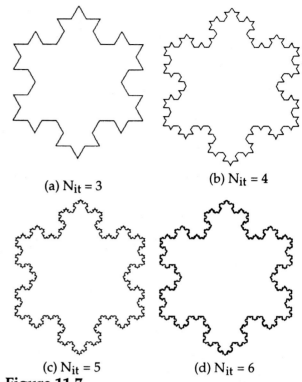

(a) $N_{it} = 3$ (b) $N_{it} = 4$

(c) $N_{it} = 5$ (d) $N_{it} = 6$

Figure 11.7
Triadic von Koch curves ("snowflake") for iterations 3 – 6.

produces the figures shown in 11.4(b) and 11.4(c) for the first two iterations. Output for the next four iterations is shown in Figure 11.7.

The structure of the Koch program makes its modification for producing other linear replacement mapped fractals a relatively simple affair. For instance, to generate the quadric von Koch fractals of Figure 11.5, the subroutines *Define-Object* and *MapLine* which implement steps 1 and 2 of the algorithm, respectively, are replaced by:

Note that the original object is defined by procedure **DefineObject** by writing out a set of points to a file. These points effectively define the vertices of an initial polygon. The second feature of this program is that, by "ping-ponging" input and output files, the complexity of the resulting fractal is limited only by the size of the storage medium and/or the compute time for a given iteration, and not by some arbitrary upper limit imposed by an internal data array.

Procedure **Refine** generates the replacement shown in Figure 11.4(a). Running the program

```
procedure DefineObject (var name: string);
{Procedure to generate and write original database.}

    const
        xmax = 512;
        ymax = 342;

    var
        xc, yc: real;
        d, min: real;
begin
    name := 'Quadric Koch Curve';
    if ymax < xmax then
        min := ymax
```

```
      else
         min := xmax;
         rewrite(outfile, 'Ch11:Koch.datA');
         xc := xmax / 2;
         yc := ymax / 2;
         d := min / 5;
         write(outfile, (xc - d), (yc - d));
         write(outfile, (xc + d), (yc - d));
         write(outfile, (xc + d), (yc + d));
         write(outfile, (xc - d), (yc + d));
         write(outfile, (xc - d), (yc - d));
         close(outfile);
      end;
```

and

```
procedure MapLine (var outfile: RealFile; x1, y1, x2,
                     y2: real);
{Procedure to successively refine the input line into
new output.}
      const
         Nout = 9;
      var
         i, j: integer;
         xp, yp: array[1..Nout] of real;
begin
      dx := (x2 - x1) / 4;
      dy := (y2 - y1) / 4;
      xp[1] := x1;
      yp[1] := y1;
      xp[2] := xp[1] + dx;
      yp[2] := yp[1] + dy;
      xp[3] := xp[2] + dy;
      yp[3] := yp[2] - dx;
      xp[4] := xp[3] + dx;
      yp[4] := yp[3] + dy;
      xp[5] := xp[4] - dy;
      yp[5] := yp[4] + dx;
      xp[6] := xp[5] - dy;
      yp[6] := yp[5] + dx;
      xp[7] := xp[6] + dx;
      yp[7] := yp[6] + dy;
      xp[8] := xp[7] + dy;
      yp[8] := yp[7] - dx;
      xp[9] := x2;
      yp[9] := y2;
      for i := 1 to Nout do
         write(outfile, xp[i], yp[i]);
end;
```

Substituting these two procedures and rerunning the program produces the first two iterations shown in Figure 11.5 and the next two iterations shown in Figure 11.8.

One of the difficulties in designing the mapping algorithm is to identify the symmetries of the problem in order to build a transformation which is independent of orientation of the original line. The LOGO turtle graphics language is the natural

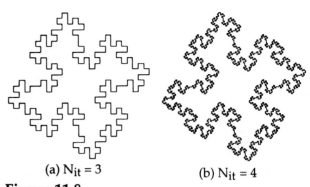

(a) $N_{it} = 3$ (b) $N_{it} = 4$

Figure 11.8
Quadric von Koch fractal with further refinement.

language for implementing such mappings. Turtle graphics commands such as FORWARD N, RIGHT θ, and LEFT θ, all with respect to the present turtle pointer direction, avoid the *ad hoc* tricks used in the MapLine procedure.

More complex space filling transformations, such as the Sierpinski gasket, are most naturally implemented by mapping a *set of lines* into a new, more complex set. This can be considered as a pattern replacement mapping instead of a linear (line) replacement mapping.

Note that the deterministic fractals produced by replacement mappings display all of the advertised properties of fractals: *self-similarity*, *complex structures* arising from simple rules, a *non-integer* dimensionality, and production by *iteration*.

Iterated Function Systems

Iterated function systems (IFSs) have a number of fascinating properties which make them particularly valuable tools in fractal geometry. These properties include:

- IFSs generate fractals through a repeated application of a set of contractive affine transformations.

- IFSs can generate both rigid, geometric shapes and realistic, life-like forms. We illustrate these two extremes with the Sierpinski triangle and the Black Spleenwort fern.

- IFSs can generate fractals using either deterministic procedures or random (chaotic) processes. Remarkably, these two different algorithms generate the same fractal!

- IFSs demonstrate the concept of *strange attractors*. This concept has emerged from the new science of dynamic systems and chaos.

- IFSs provide the basis for a highly efficient image compression system developed by Michael Barnsley.[4]

Recall from earlier chapters that an affine transformation in 1D is defined as:

$$x' = S x + T .$$ [11.3]

In 2D, the set of affine transformations may be written in Barnsley's notation as

$$w_i(x) = w_i \begin{bmatrix} x_1 \\ x_2 \end{bmatrix} = \begin{bmatrix} a_i & b_i \\ c_i & d_i \end{bmatrix} \begin{bmatrix} x_1 \\ x_2 \end{bmatrix} + \begin{bmatrix} e_i \\ f_i \end{bmatrix}$$ [11.4]

where $1 \le i \le n$ = the number of sequential transformations.

This may be reformulated in terms of the familiar homogeneous coordinates as

$$X' = X W_i ,$$ [11.5]

where
$$X' = [x' \ y' \ 1]$$

= transformed 2D coordinate vector,

$$X = [x \ y \ 1]$$

= original 2D coordinate vector,

$$W_i = \begin{bmatrix} a_i & c_i & 0 \\ b_i & d_i & 0 \\ e_i & f_i & 1 \end{bmatrix}$$

= contractive affine transformation.

The term *contractive* simply means that the effect of applying the transformation to an object is to produce a compressed image, that is, one in which any two points are closer together than they were in the original object. From the homogeneous representation of Equation 11.5, the coefficients a_i, b_i, c_i, and d_i are recognized as the product of scale and rotation factors, and e_i and f_i as translations. The index i indicates that the first iteration of an iterated function system generally involves the simultaneous application of n distinct transformations to the present object to produce a new image. This image becomes the object of the next iteration. Each distinct sequence, W_n, generates a distinct fractal, and Barnsley tabulates the W_n for a number of different fractal objects.[5]

Iterated Function System Algorithm

1. Define an initial graphical object in pixel array, t(i,j).
2. Define set of contractive, affine transformation coefficients, $(a...f)_n$.
3. Repeat until screen resolution reached
    3.1 Repeat for all pixels of object
        3.1.1 If pixel ON, repeat for all n transformations
            Apply X´= X Wi
            Set image, s(X´) = ON
        3.2 Replace t(i,j) by s(i,j)
    3.3 Plot t(i,j).

Sierpinski Triangle

Now let's investigate the behavior of this deterministic algorithm by applying it to several initial objects. An intuitively "natural" object on which to iterate is the upper-right triangle. Below we list a Pascal program for implementing the IFS algorithm.

Pascal Program IFS

```
program IFS;
{Program to compute fractals using IFSs.}
{Ref.: Barnsley, "Fractals Everywhere , p. 88}
    const
        pixdim = 120;
    type
        pic = array[1..pixdim, 1..pixdim] of Boolean;
        vec = array[1..4] of real;
        dimvec = array[1..4] of integer;
    var
        s, t: pic;
        a, b, c, d, e, f, p: vec;
        x, y: dimvec;
        i, j, k, dpix: integer;
        box: rect;

{********** Pset **************}
    procedure pset (x, y: integer);
    {Procedure to plot point at pixel (x,y).}
    begin
        moveto(x, y);
        lineto(x, y);
```

```
        end;
{********* Define Object **********}
    procedure DefineObject (var t: pic);
    {Procedure to define initial graphical object}
        var
            i, j: integer;
    begin
    {Initialize object to an upper half-diagonal square.}
        for i := 1 to pixdim do
            for j := 1 to pixdim do
                if j < i then
                    begin
                        t[i, j] := true;
                        pset(i, j);
                    end;
        SetRect(box, 1, 1, pixdim, pixdim);
    end;


{************* SetCoef **********}
    procedure SetCoef (var a, b, c, d, e, f: vec);
    {Procedure to set up coefficient of affine transform.}
        var
            i: integer;
    begin    {Set problem parameters for Sierpinski
                triangle.}
        for i := 1 to 3 do
            begin
                a[i] := 0.5;
                b[i] := 0;
                c[i] := 0;
                d[i] := 0.5;
                e[i] := pixdim / 2;
                f[i] := 1;
            end;
        e[1] := 1;
        f[3] := pixdim / 2;
    end;


{***************Main Program***************}
begin
    DefineObject(t);
    SetCoef(a, b, c, d, e, f);
    dpix := pixdim div 2;
    {Map next generation of image A(n+1) = W(A(n))}
    repeat
        for i := 1 to pixdim do
            for j := 1 to pixdim do
                if t[i, j] then
                    begin
                        for k := 1 to 3 do
                            begin
                                x[k] := trunc(a[k] * i +
                                         b[k] * j + e[k]);
                                y[k] := trunc(c[k] * i +
                                         d[k] * j + f[k]);
                                s[x[k], y[k]] := true;
                            end;
                    end;
        {Now plot.}
        EraseRect(box);
        for i := 1 to pixdim do
```

```
        for j := 1 to pixdim do
            begin
                t[i, j] := s[i, j];
                s[i, j] := false;
                if t[i, j] then
                    pset(i, j);
            end;
        dpix := dpix div 2;
        WriteLn('dpix = ', dpix);
    until button or (dpix < 1)
end.
```

Note that the first two steps of the IFS algorithm have been isolated in the procedures *DefineObject* and *SetCoef*, respectively. This permits easy extension to alternative initial objects and sets of affine transformations. The set of three affine transformation coefficients for producing a Sierpinski triangle are listed in Table 11.1.

Table 11.1
Coefficients of IFS map for Sierpinski Triangle Fractal

W_i	a	b	c	d	e	f
1	0.5	0	0	0.5	1	1
2	0.5	0	0	0.5	1	*pixdim*/2
3	0.5	0	0	0.5	*pixdim*/2	*pixdim*/2

where *pixdim* = size of original object in pixels.

Figure 11.9 demonstrates the iterative refinement produced by the IFS algorithm applied to the object triangle.

The behavior of the Sierpinski IFS can be described as "eating away" the original solid triangle parent to produce three solid, half-size sons and an identically sized blank space. This process is iteratively applied to each solid son at each level.

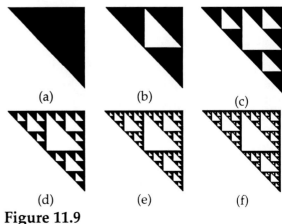

(a)   (b)   (c)

(d)   (e)   (f)

Figure 11.9
Sierpinski triangle IFS applied to triangular object.

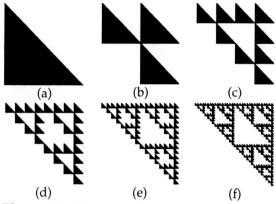

(a) (b) (c)

(d) (e) (f)

Figure 11.10
Iterations of the Sierpinski IFS applied to an original object which is the negative of that in Figure 11.9. Note similarity between 11.9(f) and 11.10(f).

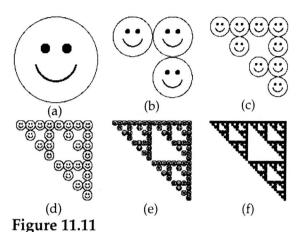

(a) (b) (c)

(d) (e) (f)

Figure 11.11
Iterations of the Sierpinski IFS on an arbitrary initial object. Again, note the similarity of Figures 11.10(f) and 11.11(f).

What happens if the Sierpinski triangle IFS is applied to some initial object other than the "natural" initial triangle? To explore the behavior of this IFS, let's select an object as "different" from the original initial triangle as possible. One such object is the photographic negative of the original square image which can be produced by changing all 0s to 1s and all 1s to 0s in the original list-map. This is readily accomplished in **DefineObject** by changing the IF test from "j < i" to "j > i." Making this single change in the IFS program results in the iteration sequence shown in Figure 11.10.

The surprising result apparent from comparison of the final iterations in Figures 11.9 and 11.10 is that, starting from radically different initial states, the Sierpinski IFS converged to the same fractal shape. If one considers each iteration as progressive moments in time, both initial objects have moved, under the influence of the IFS, to the same fractal structure. It appears that the Sierpinski fractal triangle has some "strange attraction" for both of these initial shapes.

If these two very different objects are both attracted to the same final state, the natural question arises: Will the Sierpinski IFS attract *any* initial shape to the same fractal structure? To explore this possibility, let's start with some whimsical initial object of a kind entirely different from the two previous triangles. Figure 11.11 indicates what happens to a smiley face under the influence of the Sierpinski IFS.

This result confirms our speculation that the fractal Sierpinski triangle does indeed act as a strange attractor of initial objects under the influence of this particular IFS. This concept of strange attractor emerged from the study of chaos and is central to the dynamic behavior of non-linear systems.

Strange attractors exist not only for mathematical objects such as the Sierpinski triangle but also for natural objects such as trees and ferns. We turn next to an outstanding example of one such natural fractal.

Black Spleenwort Fern

Barnsley has shown that the IFS specified in Table 11.2 is capable of generating a fractal pattern closely resembling the Black Spleenwort fern leaf. The algorithm for iterating the function system differs from that used above in the following ways:

- Rather than mapping the whole object window to a new image window with each iteration, only a single point is mapped by each transformation.

- The particular transformation used to map the point is selected randomly according to an *a priori* probability specified for each affine transformation of the set. This probability is indicated as "*p*" in Table 11.2.

Table 11.2

Coefficients of IFS map for Fern Fractal

W_i	a	b	c	d	e	f	p
1	0	0	0	0.16	0	0	0.01
2	0.85	0.04	−0.04	0.85	0	1.6	0.85
3	0.2	−0.26	0.23	0.22	0	1.6	0.07
4	−0.15	0.28	0.26	0.24	0	0.44	0.07

The random iteration algorithm proposed by Barnsley for generating the fern is summarized below.

Random Iteration IFS Algorithm

1. Define set of contractive, affine transformation coefficients, $(a...f,p)_i$
2. Repeat for n iterations
   2.1 Pick transformation i randomly with probability p_i
   2.2 Apply $X' = X W_i$
   2.3 Plot point (x_i', y_i')
   2.4 Set $X = X'$.

The main program of the Pascal implementation is given below. The output of program Fern is shown in Figure 11.12 for varying numbers of iterations. The early iterations of the program seem to sprinkle points at random across the page, but soon the hazy outline of the fern leaf appears. With an increased number of iterations the interior points gradually fill in, and after a few hundred thousand iterations, the leaf is essentially solid at the resolution shown.

Pascal Program Fern

```
program Fern;
{Program to generate fractal fern.}
{Ref.: Barnsley, "Fractals Everywhere"}
    type
        vec = array[1..4] of real;
    var
        a, b, c, d, e, f, p: vec;
        x, y, newx, newy, r: real;
        k, xp, yp: integer;
        n:LongInt;
begin         {Main Program}
    {Select fractal model and read parameters.}
    GetCoef(a, b, c, d, e, f, p);
    {Initialize coordinates and counter.}
    x := 0;
    y := 0;
    n := 1;
```

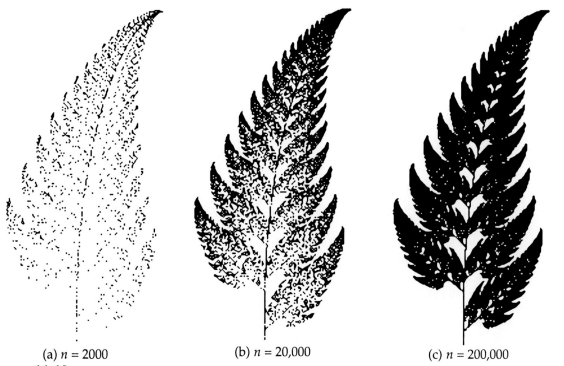

(a) $n = 2000$ (b) $n = 20,000$ (c) $n = 200,000$

Figure 11.12

Black Spleenwort Fern after varying numbers of iterations, n.

Figure 11.13
The Black Spleenwort fern generated by the IFS
algorithm.

Note that in program **Fern**, the user must
supply routines **SetCoef** and a random number
generator, **Rand**. Figure 11.13 shows the output of
the IFS fern program after some 8 million
iterations at a more detailed resolution. This
figure demonstrates convincingly several of the
distinguishing features of fractal objects. First, the
Black Spleenwort fern exhibits an approximate
self-similarity. That is, the main frond has numerous subfronds, each of which have numerous
sub-subfronds, and so on, with the daughter
object closely resembling (but not duplicating) the
parent object.

Secondly, the fractal fern is a strong strange
attractor. All of the leaves shown in Figures 11.12
and 11.13 start with point(0,0). However, it is easy
to verify that the final shape of the fractal generated with the fern IFS is *independent* of the starting
point. That is, the dynamics of the fern IFS attracts
any starting point onto the identical final fractal
fern. Finally, the similarity of the IFS fern fractal
to natural fern leaf structures is so striking that it
strongly suggests that natural ferns must exhibit
fractal geometry.

Note that, although the sequence of points
leading to the fractal fern (trajectory) is stochastic,
the fractal itself is deterministic with a structure
determined by the strange attractor specified by
the IFS affine transformations of Table 11.2. The
final class of deterministic fractals we study in this
chapter also involve iterative mapping, but in a
new environment—the complex plane.

Complex Plane Mapping

Some of the earliest work in what Mandelbrot
later named as fractal geometry was done by the
French mathematicians, Gaston Julia (1883–1978)
and Pierre Fatou (1878–1929). They studied the
effects of iterative mapping of points on the complex plane. The work of these researchers (and
others like Cantor, Peano, and Hausdorff) was described by their more conventional colleagues as
"pathological," "psychotic," and a "gallery of
monsters." It was not until Mandelbrot recognized the unifying principles and delineated the
field of fractal geometry that research resumed
and the beauty of fractals was recognized. The
Julia and Mandelbrot sets are two of the most
beautiful and interesting complex mathematical
objects yet discovered.

```
    ForeColor(greenColor);
    repeat
        n := n + 1;
        r := Rand;     {Pick random r; 0≤r<1.}
        if (r > p[1]) and (r < (p[1] + p[2])) then
            k := 2
        else if (r > (p[1] + p[2])) and (r < (p[1] +
            p[2] + p[3])) then
            k := 3
        else if (r > (p[1] + p[2] + p[3])) then
            k := 4
        else
            k := 1;
        newx := a[k] * x + b[k] * y + e[k];
        newy := c[k] * x + d[k] * y + f[k];
        x := newx;
        y := newy;
        xp := 200 + round(75 * x);
        yp := 550 - round(50 * y);
        pset(xp, yp);
    until n=200000
end.
```

Mathematical Preliminaries

Both the Mandelbrot and Julia sets were originally investigated using iterations of the complex mapping

$$z_{n+1} = z_n^2 + c \,, \qquad [11.6]$$

where

z_{n+1}, z_n, and c are all complex numbers.

Recall the properties of complex numbers like z. The complex number $z = a + bi$, where a = the real part (a scalar), b = the imaginary part (a scalar), and $i = \sqrt{-1}$.

An equivalent expression for z is the coordinate pair, (a,b), identifying a point on the complex plane, $\mathbb{C}$. These concepts are illustrated by Figure 11.14.

For two complex numbers, $z = a + b\,i$ and $w = c + d\,i$, the important algebraic operations of addition, subtraction, and multiplication are given as:

$$z + w = (a + c) + i\,(b + d) \,. \qquad [11.7]$$

$$z - w = (a - c) + i\,(b - d) \,. \qquad [11.8]$$

$$z\,w = (ac - bd) + i\,(ad + bc) \,. \qquad [11.9]$$

The *polar representation* provides an alternate useful form for complex numbers. In the polar representation, the complex number, $z = a + b\,i$, is expressed as:

$$z = r\exp(i\theta) = r\,(\cos\theta + i\sin\theta) \,, \qquad [11.10]$$

where

$r = |r| = \sqrt{a^2 + b^2}$
= the *magnitude* or *modulus* of z,

$\theta = \tan^{-1}(b/a)$
= the *phase* of z.

The polar representation simplifies the calculation of functions such as the square root of complex numbers. If, for instance, $z = r\exp(i\theta)$, the square root of z is a new complex number, w, given as:

$$w = \sqrt{z} = s\exp(i\,\phi) \,, \qquad [11.11]$$

where

$s = \sqrt{r}$,

and

$\phi = \theta/2$.

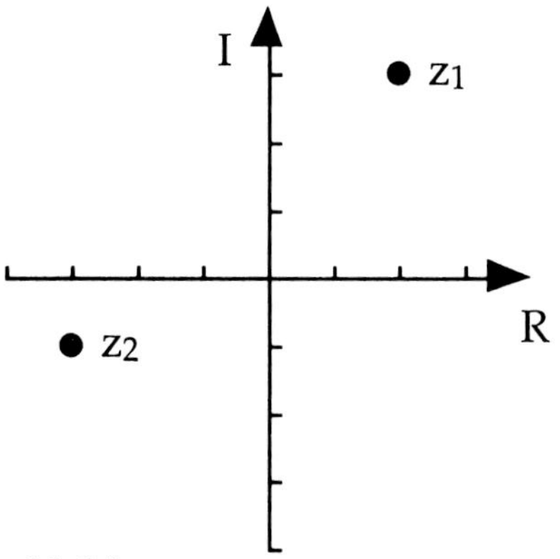

Figure 11.14
The complex plane, with two points:
- $z_1 = 2 + 3\,i$
- $z_2 = -3 - i$

Julia Sets

Julia sets arise from combining the concept of strange attractors with iterative mapping on the complex plane. The Julia set of the polynomial mapping function, $F(z)$, is the boundary between the basin of attraction of the strange attractor at $z = 0$ and a strange attractor at $z = \infty$. To illustrate what this means, first consider a case of the simple quadratic function:

$$F(z) = z^2 \,. \qquad [11.12]$$

Note that this is a special case of Equation 11.6 for which $c = 0$. Under this mapping, all points in the complex z plane fall into one of the following three categories:

- Points with modulus > 1 which flee to the attractor at ∞,
- Points with modulus < 1 which spiral into the attractor at (0,0),
- Points with modulus = 1, the chaotic Julia set on the unit circle.

We can illustrate these three cases with the algorithm Complex_Map.

Complex_Map Algorithm

1. Draw unit circle on complex plane.
2. Request initial point, z_1, from the user.
3. Repeat until done
    3.1 Compute $z_{n+1} = z_n^2$
    3.2 Draw and label line from z_n to z_{n+1}.

Pascal Program **Complex_Map**

```
program Complex_Map;
{Program to compute and plot}
{Complex mappings.}
   const
      scale = 100.0;
      size = 400;
   type
      complex = record
                   r: real;
                   i: real
                end;
   var
      Nit, xp, yp: integer;
      sd4, sd2: integer;
      z, znew: complex;
      circle: rect;
      out: text;
{**********Prod ***********}
   procedure prod (a, b: complex; var c: complex);
   {Does complex multiplication: c = a • b}
   begin
      c.r := a.r * b.r - a.i * b.i;
      c.i := a.r * b.i + a.i * b.r;
   end;

begin
   rewrite(out, 'Ch11:Complex.dat');
   showtext;
   writeln('Initial Value of z: (Zr,Zi)?');
   ReadLn(z.r, z.i);
   showdrawing;
   Nit := 1;
   ForeColor(cyanColor);
   sd4 := size div 4;
   sd2 := size div 2;
   SetRect(circle, sd4, sd4, 3 * sd4, 3 * sd4);
   FrameOval(circle);
   ForeColor(blueColor);
   drawline(0, sd2, size, sd2);
   drawline(sd2, 0, sd2, size);
   PenSize(2, 2);
   xp := round(z.r * scale + size div 2);
   yp := round(-z.i * scale + size div 2);
   ForeColor(redColor);
   WriteLn(' Nit  Re(z)  Imag(z)');
   WriteLn(out, ' Nit  Re(z)  Imag(z)');
   writeln(Nit : 3, ' ', z.r, z.i);
```

```
   writeln(out, Nit : 3, ' ', z.r, z.i);
   moveto(xp, yp);
   WriteDraw(Nit : 3);
   moveto(xp, yp);
   repeat                  {Iterative loop}
      prod(z, z, znew);
      z.r := znew.r;
      z.i := znew.i;
      xp := round(z.r * scale + size div 2);
      yp := round(-z.i * scale + size div 2);
      lineto(xp, yp);
      Nit := Nit + 1;
      write(Nit : 3, ' ', z.r, z.i);
      write(out, Nit : 3, ' ', z.r, z.i);
      WriteDraw(Nit : 3);
      MoveTo(xp, yp);
      readln;
   until button;
end.
```

Output of Complex_Map demonstrates graphically the dynamics of the complex mapping and the effects of strange attractors on the trajectories of the points under this transformation. First, let's examine the motion of a point with modulus < 1. After ten mappings, the initial point is pulled into the strange attractor at (0,0).

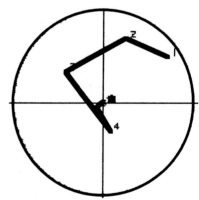

Figure 11.15
Mapping of initial point with modulus < 1.0. Note effect of strange attractor at $z = (0,0)$.

```
Nit   Re(z)     Imag(z)
 1   7.0e-1    5.0e-1
 2   2.4e-1    7.0e-1
 3  -4.3e-1    3.4e-1
 4   7.4e-2   -2.9e-1
 5  -7.9e-2   -4.3e-2
 6   4.4e-3    6.8e-3
 7  -2.7e-5    6.0e-5
 8  -2.8e-9   -3.2e-9
 9  -2.4e-18   1.8e-17
10  -3.2e-34  -8.8e-35
11   0.0e+0    0.0e+0
```

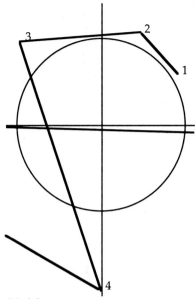

Figure 11.16
Trajectory of mapping for initial point of modulus
> 1.0. Note effect of strange attractor at ∞.

```
Nit   Re(z)    Imag(z)
 1   9.0e-1    6.0e-1
 2   4.5e-1    1.1e+0
 3  -9.6e-1    9.7e-1
 4  -1.6e-2   -1.9e+0
 5  -3.5e+0    5.9e-2
 6   1.2e+1   -4.1e-1
 7   1.5e+2   -1.0e+1
 8   2.3e+4   -3.1e+3
 9   5.2e+8   -1.4e+8
10   2.5e+17  -1.5e+17
11   3.9e+34  -7.2e+34
12   -INF      -INF
```

Figure 11.16 indicates the trajectory of a point with modulus > 1. Now the point flees toward ∞ and reaches it after eleven transformations, according to Complex_Map.

Finally, let's examine the chaotic behavior of points in the Julia set itself. These are points lying on the circle of radius one which is the boundary between the basin of attraction of the (0,0) attractor and that of the attractor at ∞ .

Figure 11.17 illustrates a very important feature of chaotic systems—*the extreme sensitivity of such systems to initial conditions*. In principle, the trajectory of the point should wander through the Julia set circle indefinitely. In practice, the limited precision of real numbers prevents this ideal behavior, and the trajectory falls off the Julia set into the strange attractor. Many natural systems, such as the three-body gravitational problem, turbulent flow, and the weather, are chaotic systems subject to extreme sensitivity to initial conditions. This sensitivity is captured in the parable of the *butterfly effect*—the disturbance caused by a butterfly fluttering its wings in China can, in principle, propagate into a hurricane in the Caribbean Sea!

Interesting Julia Sets

In the above discussion, the unit circle is shown to be the Julia set for the complex transformation, $F(z) = z^2$. While the example nicely illustrates the concepts of iterative mapping and domains of attraction, the Julia set for this transformation is less than sensational. However, the addition of a single, complex constant to the transformation produces a family of Julia sets, most of which are interesting and some of which are quite dazzling.

The interesting quadratic Julia sets arise for various choices of c in the transformation:

$$F(z) = z^2 + c . \qquad [11.13]$$

There are three algorithms for plotting the Julia sets corresponding to the boundaries of the strange attractor basins at 0 and ∞. We can identify these as:

• Backward mapping
• Forward mapping
• Boundary scanning.

First we discuss each algorithm, then list a Pascal implementation for the forward mapping algorithm, and finally show output generated by this program.

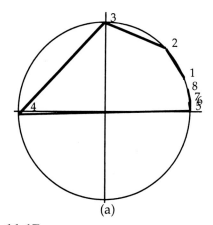

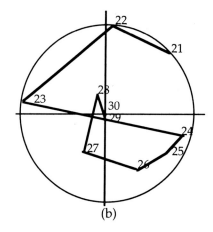

(a)   (b)

Figure 11.17

Initial trajectory of point located on the Julia set (modulus = 1). The initial point is (0.9230769, 0.3846153).

N_{it}	Re(z)	Imag(z)
1	9.2e-1	3.8e-1
2	7.0e-1	7.1e-1
3	-8.4e-3	1.0e+0
4	-1.0e+0	-1.7e-2
5	1.0e+0	3.3e-2
6	1.0e+0	6.7e-2
7	9.9e-1	1.3e-1
8	9.6e-1	2.6e-1

However, after about twenty iterations, the trajectory begins to fall off the chaotic Julia set and spiral into the strange attractor at (0,0). By point 30 it has visibly disappeared, and the following computed points document its "last gasp."

30	-1.3e-3	3.3e-3
31	-9.2e-6	-8.4e-6
32	1.3e-11	1.5e-10
33	-2.4e-20	3.9e-21
34	5.5e-40	-1.8e-40
35	0.0e+0	-0.0e+0

Backward mapping

The backward mapping algorithm is suggested by an examination of Figures 11.15–11.17. Note that all points z_{n+1} on a given trajectory are farther from the unit circle boundary (Julia set) than the corresponding z_n point. This suggests that, if we reverse the mapping direction, the Julia set itself will act as an attractor for the trajectory. This, in fact, is the case. That is, by selecting any initial point on the z plane and mapping it backwards, it will be pulled onto the Julia set within the first 10–30 iterations and spend the rest of its iteration life hopping from point to point on the set.

Since forward iteration is defined as $z_{n+1} = z_n^2 + c$, to reverse the direction of motion along the trajectory, we must write:

$$z_{n+1} = \pm\sqrt{z_n - c}. \qquad [11.14]$$

Note that there are two roots for each iteration of the backward mapping algorithm. That is, there are two possible precursor points which can map

to any given point under the inverse transformation. The backward mapping algorithm may be summarized as:

Backward mapping algorithm

1. Start with an arbitrary point, z_1, on the complex plane.
2. Repeat for i = 1 to 30   {This gets trajectory onto Julia set.}

   2.1 Compute $z_{i+1} = \pm\sqrt{z_i - c}$
   2.2 Select (+) or (–) root randomly with equal probability
   2.3 Set $z_i = z_{i+1}$.
3. Repeat until set is outlined distinctly {Julia set will "grow in" point by point.}

   3.1 Compute $z_{i+1} = \pm\sqrt{z_i - c}$
   3.2 Select (+) or (–) root randomly with equal probability
   3.3 Plot point z_{i+1}
   3.4 Set $z_i = z_{i+1}$.

Forward mapping

The forward mapping algorithm iterates on each point in the vicinity of the Julia set to see if it flees to ∞ (set pixel white) or lies on the Julia set or basin of the zero attractor (set pixel to color). This results in what Devaney calls the *filled-in Julia set*.[6] The algorithm for forward mapping is a relatively simple extension of the *Complex_Map* algorithm.

Forward Mapping Algorithm

1. Request starting parameters
   1.1 Input N_{it}, the number of iterations at each point
   1.2 Input (C_r, C_i), the complex constant, c.
2. For each pixel in the 2×2 complex plane
   2.1 Repeat for N_{it}
       2.1.1 Compute $z_{n+1} = z_n^2 + c$
       2.1.2 IF $(z_{n+1})^2 > 10$, exit 2.1 loop (pixel = white)
       2.1.3 Set $z_n = z_{n+1}$.
   2.2 IF $(z_{Nit})^2 < 10$, plot pixel in Color.

Boundary Scanning

The boundary scanning algorithm combines the forward mapping algorithm with the formal definition of Julia sets as the boundary between the two basins of attraction. The basic idea is to color a pixel as part of the Julia set if it does not flee to ∞ but an adjacent pixel does. This algorithm can be summarized as:

Boundary Scanning Algorithm

1. Select an $M \times N$ pixel grid to scan a 2×2 complex plane.
2. For each (m,n) pixel on this grid
   2.1 Repeat for 20 iterations
       2.1.1 Compute $z_{n+1} = z_n^2 + c$
       2.1.2 IF $|z_{n+1}| > 2$, color pixel white and exit 2.1 loop.
   2.2 If pixel (m,n) does not flee towards ∞
       2.2.1 Compute the first 20 points on the trajectories of he four pixels, $(m+1,n)$, $(m-1,n)$, $(m,n+1)$, $(m,n-1)$
       2.2.2 IF at least one of these four escapes, color (m,n) black
       2.2.3 IF all four do not escape, color (m,n) white.

Of the three algorithms, the first and last display the true Julia set, that is, the boundary between two basins of attraction. The second algorithm for filled-in Julia sets produces more visually appealing images and is implemented below.

Pascal Program Julia

```
program Julia;
{Program to compute and plot Julia set.}
   const
       scale = 0.01;
       R = 10;
   type
       complex = record
               r: real;
               i: real
            end;
   var
       i, j, k, n, row, col, Nit: integer;
       x, y: real;
       z, znew, c: complex;
       done, gone: Boolean;

   procedure prod (a, b: complex; var c:complex);
   {Does complex multiplication: c = a • b}
   begin
       c.r := a.r * b.r - a.i * b.i;
       c.i := a.r * b.i + a.i * b.r;
   end;

   procedure add (a, b: complex; var c:complex);
   {Does complex addition: c = a + b}
   begin
       c.r := a.r + b.r;
       c.i := a.i + b.i;
   end;

   procedure plot (c, r: integer);
   {Procedure to pixel (c.r).}
   begin
       moveto(c, r);
       lineto(c, r);
   end;

begin
   showtext;
   writeLn('How many iterations at each point?');
   readLn(Nit);
   writeLn('Value of C: (Cr,Ci)?');
   ReadLn(c.r, c.i);
   showdrawing;
   ForeColor(blackColor);
   n := 0;
   for col := 1 to 400 do
       for row := 1 to 400 do
           begin
               z.r := (col - 200) * scale;
```

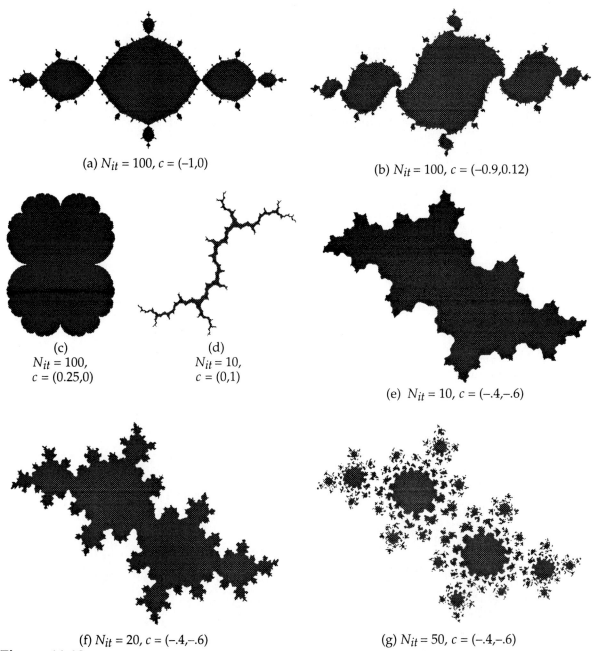

(a) $N_{it} = 100$, $c = (-1,0)$

(b) $N_{it} = 100$, $c = (-0.9,0.12)$

(c)
$N_{it} = 100$,
$c = (0.25,0)$

(d)
$N_{it} = 10$,
$c = (0,1)$

(e) $N_{it} = 10$, $c = (-.4,-.6)$

(f) $N_{it} = 20$, $c = (-.4,-.6)$

(g) $N_{it} = 50$, $c = (-.4,-.6)$

Figure 11.18
Julia sets (filled-in) by forward mapping algorithm.

```
          z.i := (row - 200) * scale;                     done := (n > Nit);
          repeat                                        until done or gone or button;
              prod(z, z, znew);                         if done then
              add(znew, c, z);                              plot(col, row);
              gone := (z.r * z.r + z.i * z.i >         n := 0;
                  R);                                   end;
              n := n + 1;                          end.
```

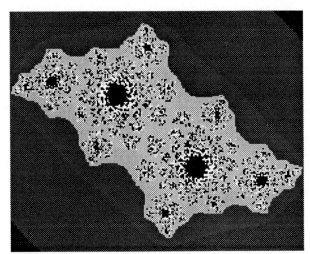

Figure 11.19
Julia set for c = (–0.4,0.6) using color-coding, shown as shading, of flight times.

Program Julia produces the output for the *c* values shown in Figure 11.18. A number of interesting features are apparent in this figure. Perhaps the most striking is the rich variety of fractal objects "hidden" in the simple quadratic function, $F(z) = z^2 + c$. The approximate self-similarity appears in each figure—lobes have sub-lobes which have sub-sublobes, branches have sub-branches which have sub-sub-branches, and

so on. Finally, Julia sets range from formal mathematical patterns, (a) and (b), through suggestive natural shapes, (c) and (d), to the "monsters," (e) – (g), that distressed early mathematicians.

A curious side effect of program Julia is the apparent dependence of the final fractal shape upon the number of iterations, N_{it}, as indicated in (e) – (g). Conversion of the complex type to double precision yields identical results, thus eliminating round-off error as the source of the side effect. This suggests that perhaps the effect is real, that is, that the true Julia set is a disconnected set of points rather than the connected set shown in (e). To verify this assumption, we color encoded the "flight time," that is, the number of iterations required for the point to flee to infinity. The results of this run are shown in Figure 11.19.

Another method of understanding flight times is through 3D encoding of the iterative map. Figure 11.20 shows the Julia set after 100 iterations as black islands surrounded by an ocean whose depth is inversely proportional to the number of iterations required to flee to infinity.

Figures 11.18(e) – (g) correspond to slicing Figure 11.20 at N_{it} = 10, 20, and 50 respectively, and it is quite obvious that the filled-in Julia set is strongly dependent on the number of iterations.

Note that parameters used to represent Julia sets are the complex *z numbers* themselves. As we

Figure 11.20
Julia set with flight times encoded as 3D inverse depths.

move on to the Mandelbrot set, the parameters used to represent the set are the complex *c numbers*.

The Mandelbrot Set

The Mandelbrot set has been described as the most complex mathematical object ever discovered. It is generated on the complex plane as the set of points (μ_r, μ_i) which, when successively mapped with the function,

$$z_{n+1} = z_n^2 - \mu,$$ [11.15]

do not cause the complex number z_n to fly off to infinity. Equation 11.14 is the form in which Benoit Mandelbrot originally defined this set, but it is clear from comparison of this equation to Equation 11.6 that $\mu = -c$ of our previous formulation.

The algorithm for generating the Mandelbrot set is a minor modification of the forward mapping algorithm for Julia sets. The main difference is that the key parameter used to represent the set is the parameter μ (equivalent to $-c$ in the Julia set algorithm). We can summarize this algorithm as:

Mandelbrot Set Algorithm

1. Select a window in complex μ space and a viewport in screen pixel space and the appropriate scale and offset parameters for mapping window to viewport.
2. For all pixels in the viewport
    2.1 Compute the corresponding (μ_r, μ_i) point
    2.2 Set $z_1 = (0,0)$
    2.3 Repeat

    Compute $z_{n+1} = z_n^2 - \mu$

    IF $z_{n+1}^2 > 10$ then *gone* = true
    $n = n+1$
    until *gone* or $n > 100$.
    2.4 IF not *gone* then plot pixel corresponding to (μ_r, μ_i)
    2.5 Set n = 0.

Implementing this algorithm produces the stark, beetle-like Mandelbrot set representing those complex μ values for which the attractor at ∞ in complex z-space does not pull the point to infinity under iterated mapping by the function

$F(z) = z^2 - \mu$. A relatively simple modification to the algorithm encodes the "flight time" that it takes those pixels not in the Mandelbrot set to flee to ∞. This code can be used to color-code points surrounding the Mandelbrot set. Such color coding provides additional insight into the dynamics of iterative mapping trajectories and adds greatly to the visual interest of the graphics. Below we present a Pascal implementation of a color-coded Mandelbrot set generator.

Pascal Program **Mandelbrot**

```
program Mandelbrot;
{Program to compute and plot the Mandelbrot set.
  const
     Nit = 100;
     scale = 0.005;
     R = 10;
  type
     complex = record
            r: real;
            i: real
         end;
  var
     i, j, k, n, row, col: integer;
     x, y: real;
     z, znew, c: complex;
     done, gone: Boolean;
  procedure prod (a, b: complex; var c: complex);
  {Does complex multiplication: c = a • b}
  begin
     c.r := a.r * b.r - a.i * b.i;
     c.i := a.r * b.i + a.i * b.r;
  end;
  procedure sub (a, b: complex; var c: complex);
  {Does complex subtraction: c = a - b}
  begin
     c.r := a.r - b.r;
     c.i := a.i - b.i;
  end;
  procedure plot (c, r, n: integer);
  {Procedure to pixel (c.r) in color code n.}
  begin
     case n of
        0..4:
           ForeColor(blueColor);
        5:
           ForeColor(cyanColor);
        6:
           ForeColor(greenColor);
        7:
           ForeColor(magentaColor);
        8..11:
           ForeColor(redColor);
        12..20:
           ForeColor(yellowColor);
        21..99:
           ForeColor(whiteColor);
```

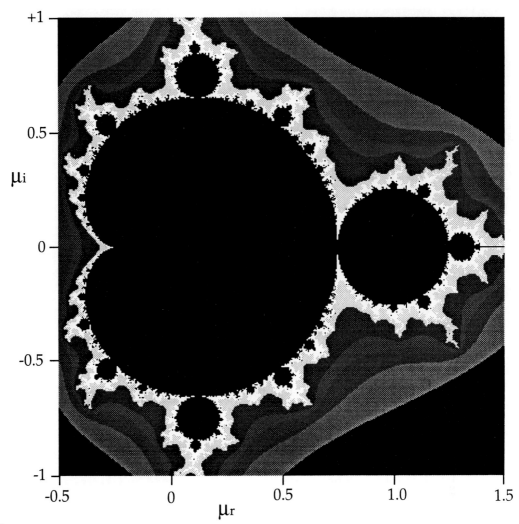

Figure 11.21
The Mandelbrot Set (black) with color-coded flight times.

```
        100:
            ForeColor(blackColor);
        otherwise
            ForeColor(blackColor);
    end;
    moveto(c, r);
    lineto(c, r);
    r := 400 - r;
    moveto(c, r);
    lineto(c, r);
  end;
begin
  for col := 1 to 400 do
    for row := 1 to 200 do
      begin
```

```
        z.r := 0.0;
        z.i := 0.0;
        c.r := (col - 100) * scale;
        c.i := (200 - row) * scale;
        repeat
            n := n + 1;
            prod(z, z, znew);
            sub(znew, c, z);
            done := (n > Nit);
            gone := (z.r * z.r + z.i * z.i > R);
        until done or gone or button;
        plot(col, row, n);
        n := 0;
      end;
end.
```

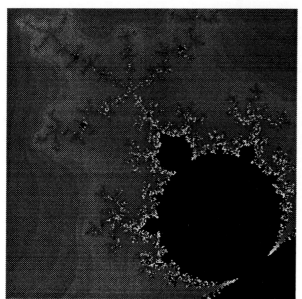

Figure 11.22
Segment of the Mandelbrot set with corners at
$c_1 = (-0.64167, 0.6930)$ and $c_2 = (-0.453, 0.511)$.

Figure 11.23
Segment of the Mandelbrot set with corners at
$c_1 = (-0..5963, 0.5821)$ and $c_2 = (-0.5550, 0.5390)$.

The output of program **Mandelbrot** is shown in Figure 11.21. The labeling was added to the figure by an image processing program.

The fascination inspired by the Mandelbrot set stems from several sources. This set exhibits all of the previously discussed features distinguishing fractals, including an infinite complexity which emerges as the researcher explores selected regions in finer and finer detail. With a program no more complex than program **Mandelbrot**, anyone can soon be discovering new regions of the set which no human has ever seen before. Such a voyage of discovery is documented in the captivating video animation, *Nothing but Zooms*, produced by the Cornell University Supercomputer Center.[7]

Let's explore the Mandelbrot set by successively magnifying regions near the boundary that look interesting. Using the more conventional mapping notation, $F(z) = z^2 + c$, we can examine a smaller region of the complex c plane defined by diagonally opposite corners, c_1 and c_2, as shown in the following figures. (Note that the convention using c positive along the real axis effectively mirrors Figure 11.21 about the imaginary axis.)

In just three successive magnifications we are already examining, in Figure 11.24, a region $\sim 7\times 10^{-6}$ the size of the original Figure 11.21. This exploration may be continued indefinitely and

Figure 11.24
Segment of the Mandelbrot set with corners at
$c_1 = (-0.5624, 0.5623)$ and $c_2 = (-0.5572, 0.5570)$.

soon reveals elegant fractal patterns never observed before.

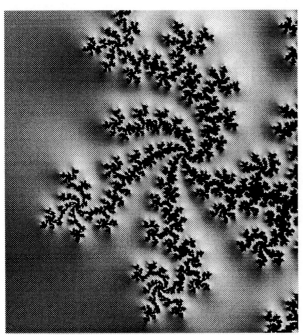

Figure 11.25
Segment of the Mandelbrot set with corners at
$c_1 = (-0.5624, 0.5623)$ and $c_2 = (-0.5572, 0.5570)$
displayed as a shaded relief map.

Figure 11.26
Mandelbrot set rendered as a 3D "island" of
stability. The greater the depth off shore, the faster
the iterated z point flees towards infinity.

Visualizing the Mandelbrot set in 3D provides additional insight into the fractal structure of this object. Figure 11.25 shows the same region of Figure 11.23 as a shaded relief map illuminated from the upper right. The complete Mandelbrot set is shown as a 3D object in Figure 11.26. This representation is helpful in visualizing the set itself as a region of stable trajectories and all points off the set as "sliding off to infinity."

To conclude the discussion of complex plane mapping, we demonstrate the relationship of the Mandelbrot set to Julia sets with Figure 11.27. Recall that Julia sets are represented on the z plane while the Mandelbrot set uses the complex number, c, as its basis. Different Julia sets are distinguished by different values of c. This implies that a Mandelbrot set displayed as an $m \times n$ pixel image is really an index or catalog of $m \times n$ Julia sets for which the complex c serves as the key.

To examine elements of this catalog, we can select various c values on the Mandelbrot set and compute the corresponding Julia sets. Figure 11.27 illustrates this procedure, indicating a number of points on the Mandelbrot set and their corresponding Julia sets (compressed to twenty-five percent of their full linear scale). An interesting aspect of this figure is that some regions show a

rather intuitive similarity in structures (e.g., filamentary regions of the Mandelbrot set giving filamentary Julia sets) while other regions show surprising differences in structure.

This concludes our discussion of fractals generated by iterative mapping on the complex plane. We have concentrated on the Mandelbrot set and Julia sets of the mapping $F(z) = z^2 + c$ for two reasons. First is the key role they played in the historical development of fractal geometry. Second is their intrinsic beauty, mathematical simplicity, and awesome complexity.

The reader should not, however, get the impression that this introduction to complex plane mapping exhausts the topic. The most obvious extension is to study the Julia sets of other complex analytic functions. Two classes of functions which have been studied extensively include:

- Transcendental functions – $\sin(z)$, $\sinh(z)$, $\exp(z)$ and various combinations,

- Rational maps (quotients of two polynomials) – $R(z) = p(z)/q(z)$.

Study of the dynamic behavior of iterated complex mappings (i.e., *trajectories*) continues to yield information on the location of strange attractors, their basins of attraction, and splendid fractal images. Research results emerging from these studies have been extended to understanding the stability of dynamical physical systems such as the solar system.

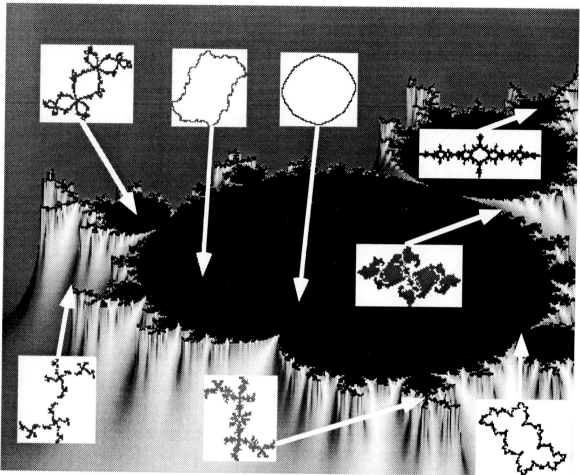

Figure 11.27
The Mandelbrot set as catalog of Julia sets. The Julia set in the lower, right-hand corner of the figure, for example, corresponds to $(c_r, c_i) = (-0.13, 0.64)$.

Stochastic Fractals

The single characteristic shared by all of the fractals discussed to this point is that they are deterministic. That is, running the fractal generating algorithm again will result in a structure identical with that generated in the first run. However, one of the distinguishing features of many natural objects (e.g., coastlines, clouds, and mountains) is that they are *statistically* self-similar but unique. In order to examine this vary large class of fractal objects we must introduce the concept of *stochastic* (or random) *fractals*.

The distinguishing feature of stochastic fractals is that the dominant behavior of the fractal structure depends on random processes. Thus, no two coastlines, river basins, or mountain skylines will ever be identical, although certain small segments may closely resemble each other.

Stochastic fractals are particularly significant for the following reasons. First, landscapes generated as stochastic fractal images are so convincing in their depiction of natural scenes as to leave no doubt in the mind of the observer that they accurately represent nature. The logical implication of this observation is that natural objects such as mountains, river basins, and the cratered surface of the moon must obey fractal geometry. A wealth of recent research in physics, chemistry, meteorology, and related scientific disciplines has confirmed the fractal nature of a great variety of natural objects.

This is particularly important for computer graphics because of the principle of model authenticity. Model authenticity requires that realistic images of computer-generated (i.e., artificial) objects must be based on models which are consistent with "the real thing." This means that the most realistic renderings of natural scenes can be achieved using stochastic fractal models.

The second significant aspect of stochastic fractals is that they have provided the first real commercial application of fractals. As we have already indicated, several science fiction movies have already used fractal landscapes and firestorms as the natural background for their imaginary worlds. As fractal algorithms improve and fractal ASIC hardware appears, this trend will most certainly accelerate.

The two examples of stochastic fractals we consider are Brownian motion and fractal landscapes. The first example represents one of the earliest random processes observed in physics, and the second illustrates the basic algorithms used in generating the imaginary worlds of the movie industry.

Brownian Motion

In 1828, Robert Brown, a botanist, noted an irregular zigzag motion of pollen grains floating on the surface of liquids. This effect, now known as *Brownian motion*, was fully explained in one of Einstein's famous 1905 papers. Einstein's theory and Jean Perrin's exhaustive set of measurements of the motion of particles of various sizes in different fluids firmly established the kinetic theory of matter.

Brownian motion is an important example of the general class of problems called the *random-walk problem*. The random-walk problem, in its simplest 1D form, involves the motion resulting from the flip of a coin. If it's heads, the coin-flipper takes one step ahead; if it's tails, s/he steps back one step. The resulting motion is called a random-walk. In the case of the Brownian motion of floating particles (2D) or particles suspended in fluids (3D), the motion is caused by forces exerted on the particles by collisions with molecules of the fluid. The statistical fluctuations in the rate of collisions from various directions result in unbalanced forces causing the particles to skitter across the surface of the liquid.

To illustrate Brownian motion in 1D we present two algorithms, the first a random-walk algorithm and the second a midpoint displacement algorithm. Both algorithms are expressed in terms of a displacement along one axis, d(t), as a function of time, t.

Random-walk Algorithm

1. Set d(0) = 0 for time t = 0.
2. For t = 1 to 256
    2.1 Flip a coin with a balanced random number generator, *ran*
        If heads (i.e., *ran* > 0)
            d(t) = d(t-1) + step
        else
            d(t) = d(t-1) – step
    2.2 Plot (t, d(t)).

The Pascal implementation of this algorithm is virtually verbatim, with the only extensions being the balanced random number generator, ran, and the pen size of 2×2 pixels to mask the intrinsic jitter built into the algorithm. This implementation produces a *trace* of the 1D Brownian motion in which the displacement is plotted along the *y*-axis and time along the *x*-axis. A selected example of the output of Random_Walk is shown in Figure 11.28.

Pascal Program Random_Walk

```
program Random_Walk;
{Program to generate Brownian trace}
{by Random-Walk algorithm.}

    const
        xmax = 256;
        ymax = 200;
        step = 2;

    var
        x, d, t: integer;
        i, xp, yp: integer;
        flip: real;
        time: DateTimeRec;

{********* ran *********}
function ran: real;
{Function to return a random real number}
{on range –1 < ran < +1.}
begin
    ran := random / 32768
end;

begin                    {Main program}
    pensize(2, 2);
    d := 0;
    {Get "Random" randomized.}
    gettime(time);
    randSeed := time.Minute * 60 + time.Second;
    for i := 1 to xmax do
        begin
            flip := ran;
```

```
        if flip > 0 then
            x := step
        else
            x := -step;
        d := d + x;
        xp := i;
        yp := ymax div 2 - d;
        drawline(xp, yp, xp, yp);
    end;
end.
```

Figure 11.28
Brownian trace generated by Random_Walk.

Mandelbrot has observed that the displacement trace in 1D Brownian motion is reminiscent of the skyline of a mountainous scene. An interesting feature of Random_Walk is that to get an "interesting" profile, like that shown in Figure 11.28, the user must filter out a number of "dull" runs showing much less relief. This sorting for appealing output may appear to be cheating yet is similar to what sightseers do on vacations. Millions of visitors each year all travel thousands of miles through relatively dull countryside to marvel at the prominent relief of the Teton mountains of Wyoming. Both Nature and Random_Walk produce more dull than interesting scenes.

The second algorithm, random midpoint displacement (RMD), grew out of Norbert Wiener's studies of Brownian motion in the 1920s. The basic concept is similar to the *linear replacement mapping* algorithm we used to generate von Koch fractals, with a random displacement of the center point of the line substituted for the deterministic replacement pattern of the von Koch fractal. This algorithm can be summarized as follows.

Random Midpoint Displacement Algorithm

1. Initialize parameters
    1.1 Set trace(0) = trace(T_{max}) = 0 for times t = 0 and $t = T_{max}$
    1.2 Set number of iterations, $N_{it} = \log_2(T_{max})$
    1.3 Set variance sigma = $T_{max}/2$ {arbitrary choice of scale factor.}
2. Repeat for n = 1 to N_{it} {i.e., subdivide line until we hit pixel level}
    2.1 *Sigma = sigma*/2 {reduce variance in half}
    2.2 Repeat for all line segments at this level
        2.2.1 Divide line segment in half, creating two new line segments
        2.2.2 Displace midpoint by *ran×sigma*, where –1 < *ran* ≤ +1.
        2.2.3 Plot displaced point.

The Pascal program, MidPoint, is a straightforward implementation of this algorithm in which the main program handles the bookkeeping and the procedure RMD subdivides each line sent to it and applies the random midpoint displacement. To conserve space we have also deleted the function *ran* and its initialization.

Pascal Program **MidPoint**

```
program MidPoint;
{Program to generate Brownian trace by}
{method of Random Midpoint Displacement.}
    const
        xmax = 256;
        ymax = 200;
    type
        image = array[0..xmax] of real;
    var
        trace: image;
        n, m, Nit, d, Mmax: integer;
        sigma: real;
        time: DateTimeRec;

{*********** RMD ********}
procedure RMD (var trace: image;
                    i, j: integer; sigma: real);
{Function to apply random displacement}
    var
        k: integer;
        dy, ave: real;
    begin
        k := (j - i) div 2;
        dy := sigma * ran;
        ave := (trace[i] + trace[j]) / 2;
        trace[i + k] := ave + dy;
        moveto(i + k, ymax div 2 - round(trace[i + k]));
        lineto(i + k, ymax div 2 - round(trace[i + k]));
    end;

begin         {Main Program}
    pensize(1, 2);
    sigma := xmax div 2;
    Nit := round(ln(xmax) / ln(2));
    d := xmax;
    trace[1] := 0;
    trace[xmax] := 0;
```

Figure 11.29
Brownian trace generated by Random Midpoint Displacement program, MidPoint.

```
for n := 1 to Nit do
    begin
        sigma := sigma / 2;
        Mmax := round(exp((n - 1) * ln(2)));
        for m := 1 to Mmax do
            RMD(trace, (m - 1) * d, m * d, sigma);
        d := d div 2
    end;
end.
```

While MidPoint effectively implements the algorithm shown, it efficiently bypasses the problem associated with bisecting and storing lines by taking advantage of the fact that, at each level, lines are defined by the end points which have been plotted at that level. These end points are fixed, and successive midpoint bisections operate only on the intervals between the fixed end points. By successively bisecting the trace down to the pixel level and plotting each midpoint as it is generated, MidPoint generates the Brownian trace without resorting to any line plotting.

Mandelbrot has generalized the technique of random midpoint displacement to what he calls *fractional Brownian motion* (fBm) and applied fBm techniques to the study of river discharges, coastlines, distribution of natural resources, and mountain terrain. One of the leading advantages of the random midpoint displacement algorithm over simpler techniques like the random-walk method is that it is more easily extensible to generating fractal landscapes. For this reason it was the first and has remained the favorite algorithm for creating artificial scenes.[8]

The simple random midpoint displacement algorithm presented here suffers from flaws which prevent precise simulation of Brownian motion. The most obvious of these is the fixed nature of each midpoint displacement after it is generated. While this flaw is not apparent in 1D Brownian traces, it causes "creases" in 3D Brownian landscapes. Richard Voss has indicated a refinement, successive random additions, which treats all points equivalently and eliminates the crease problem.[9]

Fractal Mountain Landscapes

The random midpoint displacement algorithm is readily extended to generate fractal mountain landscapes. The basic idea is to start with a planar 2D figure such as a quadrilateral or triangle and successively subdivide each side, randomly displacing its midpoint as shown in Figure 11.30.

The RMD algorithm suggested by Figure 11.30 is a 3D extension of the 1D RMD algorithm for Brownian motion. It can be summarized as follows.

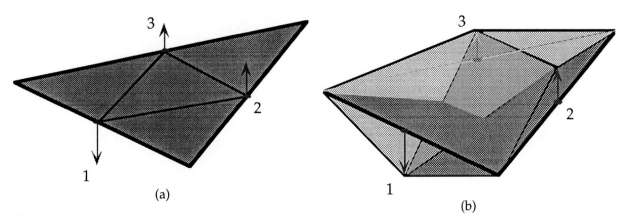

(a)

(b)

Figure 11.30
Random midpoint displacement algorithm for generating fractal landscapes. Midpoints are displaced randomly in sign and magnitude in the vertical direction—here 2 and 3 upwards and 1 downwards. The process is repeated on each of the four resulting triangles.

Fractal Mountain Landscape RMD Algorithm

1. Initialize starting parameters
   1.1 Define initial triangle as three (x,y) pairs in the $z = 0$ plane
   1.2 Define initial variance as $\sigma = <L>/2$, where $<L>$ = average side length
   1.3 Define light source direction
   1.4 Define camera position
2. Repeat until desired resolution is obtained
   2.1 Reduce $\sigma = \sigma/2$
   2.2 For all triangles at this level of refinement
      2.2.1 Compute midpoints of each side
      2.2.2 Displace each midpoint by $\Delta z = ran \times \sigma$
3. Project resulting 3D model onto a 2D image
   3.1 Use back face removal to eliminate invisible surfaces
   3.2 Sort visible triangles by distance from camera
   3.3 Project triangles onto image with Painter's algorithm
   3.4 Shade each triangle with simple shading model

As might be expected, the generation of the 3D model of the fractal landscape requires less computation than rendering the model. One additional problem introduced by the 3D extension of the 1D RMD algorithm is the increased complexity of bookkeeping. The complexity is not apparent in the first iteration transforming the planar triangle (a) into the four-triangle profile of (b). The problem arises at the next level of bisection, however, when step two of the algorithm is applied to each of the four resulting triangles in (b). If the algorithm is first applied to the left-most of the four triangles of (b) and then, independently, to the center triangle, in general a tear or "cave" in the surface will develop. This results due to the fact that the midpoint of the boundary edge has undergone two independent displacements. This unwanted side-effect violates the physical constraint that the surface must be continuous.

Two possible solutions to this problem include:

- Careful record keeping to note that the midpoint of the common edge has already

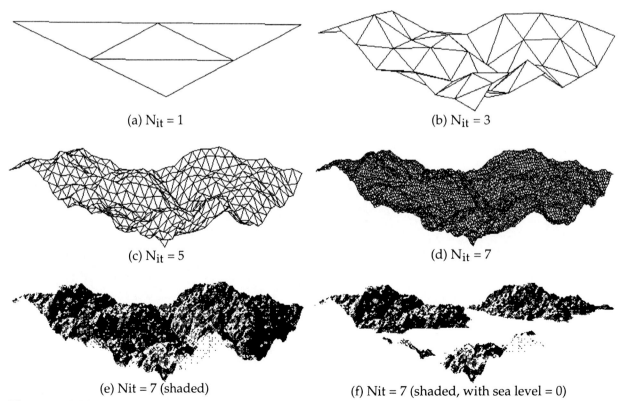

(a) $N_{it} = 1$ (b) $N_{it} = 3$

(c) $N_{it} = 5$ (d) $N_{it} = 7$

(e) Nit = 7 (shaded)   (f) Nit = 7 (shaded, with sea level = 0)

Figure 11.31
Generation of fractal mountain landscape by RMD algorithm.

been displaced by the left-most triangle. When the center triangle is processed, it will use this value for the midpoint displacement rather than calculating a new one.

- Independent calculation of the midpoint displacement for each triangle sharing a common edge, followed by an averaging of the two results to produce a single value.

To achieve visual realism of fractal mountain landscapes, this simple RMD algorithm is usually augmented with a color scheme typically encoded by the *z*-value of displacement. Triangles with the highest elevations may be colored white to simulate snow; the next lower elevation band is given some mix of gray/brown/yellow to simulate rock structure; the band beneath that may be shaded various colors of green to indicate forest foliage; and the lowest levels may be colored a uniform blue to simulate a lake at the bottom of the valley. Such a height-encoded color scheme achieves an impressive degree of visual realism.

In Figure 11.31 we present the output of one simple RMD program.[10]

Figures (a) – (d) represent wire frame output for the odd levels of refinement from level 1 through level 7 which is approaching the pixel resolution of the screen. The camera viewing angle was selected to be 30° with respect to the z = 0 plane. Figure (e) also used 7 levels of iteration, but was rendered as a shaded model. An interesting feature of this particular program is a "seal level" control which was set at z = 0 in Figure (f). This mode allows the generation and study of fractal coastlines and islands.

Fractal Applications

We have already indicated that the first major application of fractal geometry was the generation of artificial landscapes for the imaginary worlds of the movie industry. There are two additional applications which should prove to be of even more immediate interest and value to computer graphics users.

- Fractal Design Tools
- Fractal Image Compression Techniques

Fractal design tools open up new opportunities for designers and artists to produce complex and random patterns with more appeal than output from conventional geometry programs. Fractal image compression techniques promise to resolve many of the problems associated with the enormous storage demands imposed by graphical images. Products in both of these applications areas are commercially available.

Fractal Design Tools

Many programs have been written to generate and explore particular types of fractals. The public domain *MacFractal* generates Sierpinski triangles, Brownian traces, and fractal mountain landscapes. The *Beauty of Fractals Laboratory* provides elegant tools for investigating the Julia and Mandelbrot sets. To the best of our knowledge, however, no

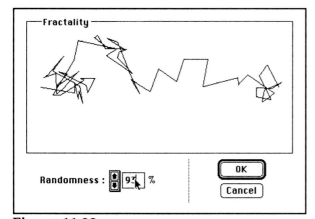

Figure 11.32
Control window for fractal line option of *PixelPaint Professional.*

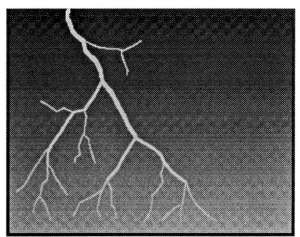

Figure 11.33
Lightning scene generated with fractal line option of *PixelPaint Professional.* Randomness was set at 82%, and the line width was manually reduced as the "tree" was traversed.

single program has appeared which generates all of the standard fractal types.

Several commercially available painting programs now incorporate generators for certain fractal shapes. We illustrate here three examples — a Brownian trace generator and two fractal tree generators.

Brownian Trace Generator

The program *PixelPaint Professional* contains a fractal line option with a user controlled "randomness" parameter shown in Figure 11.32. With the randomness set in the range 90%–95%, the line tool generates a good approximation to a 2D random walk of a Brownian particle (shown in the sample window).

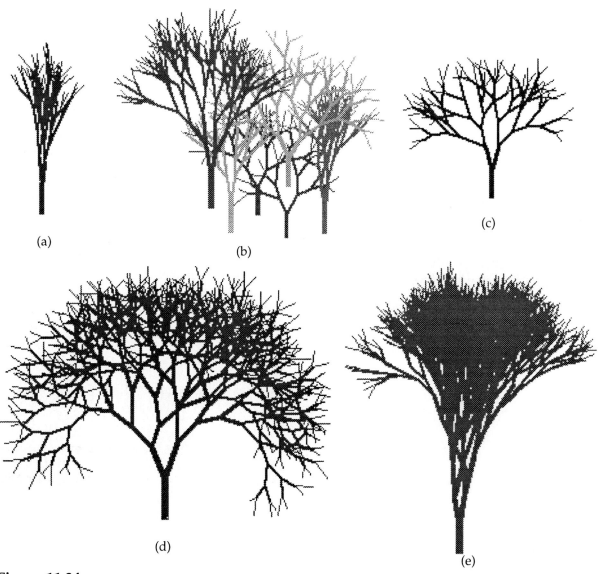

(a)

(b)

(c)

(d)

(e)

Figure 11.34
Fractal trees generated using *Kid Pix*[11].

(a)

(b)

(c)

(d)

(e)

Figure 11.35
Fractal trees generated using *PixelPaint* program.

Turning the randomness down produces a less jagged line more closely resembling a 1D Brownian displacement trace. Although the design process rarely calls for a single fractal line, this tool is useful in designing irregular natural phenomena such as surfaces cracks and lightning. In Figure 11.33 we show a lightning stroke scene constructed with the fractal line generator.

Fractal Tree Generators

Fractal plant generation is the subject of intense research which is yielding interesting results on plant morphology and realistic images.[12] The charming children's program, *Kid Pix*, contains a stochastic fractal tree generator capable of producing interesting effects. Upon selection of the tree icon, each click of the mouse produces a random tree of varying sizes and shapes at the cursor position as shown in the top row of Figure 11.34. The user has two control options: the color and tree size category. The *option* key switches the generator from standard to large size trees shown in the bottom row.

As Figure 11.34 indicates, even simple fractal tree algorithms can produce trees of great variability suggestive of natural objects. The primary limitation of the fractal trees of *Kid Pix* is the lack of leaves. The following program simulates leaves by terminating each terminal branch with a branch cluster.

An undocumented feature of the regular *PixelPaint* program includes an elegant fractal tree generator. Upon selecting *Special Effects + pencil* icon + *option* key, each click of the mouse button produces a fractal tree such as the ones shown in Figure 11.35.

Note the interesting 3D effect generated by the combination of outlining the left side of each branch with black and the sequential generations of the branches. In addition, this algorithm varies the length of branches randomly, enhancing the

realism of the resulting tree images. This algorithm fails the model authenticity test primarily through the uniform color of trunk, branches, and leaves. In Figures 11.35(d) we attempted to overcome this problem by dragging the trunk portions of a brown fractal tree onto a green fractal tree.

Figure 11.36 shows how fairly realistic scenes can be designed by generating fractal trees on a smoothly shaded background. The illusion of a 3D scene is created through use of the Painter's Algorithm to creating a background and add trees sequentially from the background to the foreground. This technique, in combination with the intrinsic 3D appearance of individual trees, creates an impression of 3D structure in the scene.

These examples illustrate the design potential of simple stochastic fractal tools. The obvious extension of these techniques is to combine in a single paint/drawing program the following stochastic fractal forms:

- Fractal landscapes with user-controlled dimension (roughness),

Figure 11.36
Fall scene designed using *PixelPaint* fractal trees.

- Fractal trees with user control on trunk/branch/leaf branching and size,

- Fractal grasses and flowers with user control of seed and bloom,

- Fractal craters and projection onto spherical geometry (moonscapes),

- Fractal clouds, fog, and smoke.

Such a program would provide the designer of natural scenes the same power and flexibility that sophisticated CAD systems provide for the design of conventional geometric objects.

Fractal Image Compression Techniques

As the integration of the graphics areas of animation, video, and multimedia progresses, effective image compression techniques are assuming increasing importance. The fractal image compression technique invented by Michael Barnsley is probably the most significant application of fractals in computer graphics. The history of the evolution of this technique is a fascinating example of harnessing abstract mathematical concepts to solve difficult technological problems.[13]

To illustrate the potential for image compression using fractal techniques, consider the fractal fern shown in Figure 11.13 and the set of twenty-eight iterated function system (IFS) coefficients shown in Table 11.2 used to generate the fern image. Assume your assignment is to transmit the image of the fern to a colleague overseas. To keep your colleague's options for further image processing or electronic publishing open, you decide on magnetic media (disk) or, if both sites support it, e-mail. Then the question arises: What format provides for most efficient transmission?

One option is to send the image in PICT or TIFF image file format. Depending on the desired resolution, this option would require between 32 Kb (for the image shown) to several Mb. A second option, suggested by Table 11.2, is to send the 28 real coefficients from which the fractal image was generated. This corresponds to 112 bytes of information. Particularly if you are using e-mail and a slow modem, the choice is obvious. That is, the IFS fractal encoding of this image achieves an image compression ratio of between 285 and 10,000 or more.

But, you protest, those twenty-eight numbers by themselves are not sufficient for generating the image. This is a proper objection, and the complete solution is to send along the rules for interpreting the coefficients. This means sending along the Pascal program, Fern.p, at a cost of some 1,919 bytes. Even sending along this more general program (capable of interpreting other IFS fractal images as well), you are achieving an image compression ratio of over 1,500 at the higher resolution.

Even more impressive results emerge as we examine how the image compression ratio depends on resolution. For PICT and TIFF files, doubling the resolution corresponds to quadrupling the image file size. However, the IFS coefficients are capable, in principle, of infinite resolution. So as the trend towards higher and higher resolution graphics images continues, the advantage of fractal image compression techniques increases.

So the advantages of sending the fractal fern image in compressed IFS format is beyond question. However, the image you wish to transmit to your colleague may not be a fern, tree, or Sierpinski triangle, all of whose coefficients are tabulated in Barnsley's book, *Fractals Everywhere*. Suppose the image you wish to transmit is a captured video frame, a scanned image of your grandmother, or an elegant design that you created with a paint program. What IFS coefficients do you e-mail to your colleague? The answer to this question involves solving what Barnsley defines as the *inverse problem*.

The Inverse Problem and the Collage Theorem

When Barnsley began his research into fractals, the predominant research approach was to postulate a new linear replacement map, IFS, complex map, or stochastic process and then investigate the nature of the resulting fractal image. This research approach is represented as the top row of Figure 11.37.

Barnsley formulated (and later solved) what he called the *inverse problem*:

Given an arbitrary image, what set of IFS transformations will encode it?

The inverse problem can be conceptualized as the bottom row of Figure 11.37.

Given: **Find**:

IFS Coefficients

a	b	c	d	e	f	p
0	0	0	0.5	0	0	0.05
0.42	-0.42	0.42	0.42	0	0.2	0.4
0.42	0.42	-0.42	0.42	0	0.2	0.4
0.1	0	0	0.1	0	0.2	0.15

$\Rightarrow$

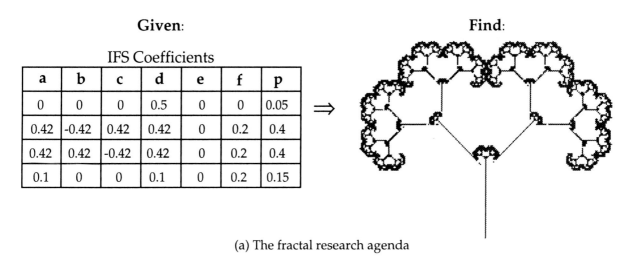

(a) The fractal research agenda

Given: **Find:**

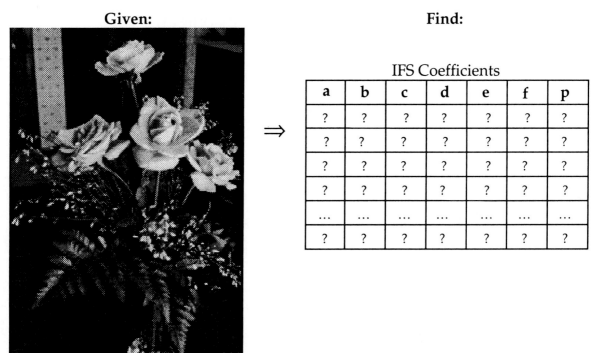

$\Rightarrow$

IFS Coefficients

a	b	c	d	e	f	p
?	?	?	?	?	?	?
?	?	?	?	?	?	?
?	?	?	?	?	?	?
?	?	?	?	?	?	?
...	...	...	...	...	...	...
?	?	?	?	?	?	?

(b) The inverse problem

Figure 11.37
Traditional fractal research *vs.* the inverse problem.

As Figure 11.37 indicates, the traditional fractal research agenda can be stated: *Given an algorithm, what is the image?* The inverse problem can be stated: *Given an image, what is the algorithm?*

The *Collage Theorem* of Barnsley is the key to solving the inverse problem.[14] The Collage Theorem says, in effect, that an image may be represented to any desired degree of accuracy by a union of contractive affine transformations of itself. This is quite a mouthful, so let's review what some of the terms mean and then illustrate it with examples.

Affine transformations include the scaling, rotations, and shears we studied as homogeneous, 2D transformations. Contractive means that any two points on the transformed image are closer together than they are on the original image. As the first example of the Collage Theorem, assume

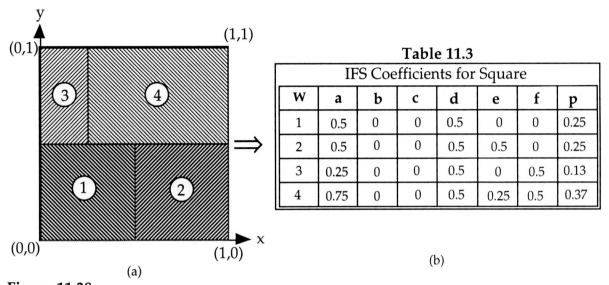

Figure 11.38
Collage Theorem used to encode a square as a 4-transformation IFS.

Table 11.3

IFS Coefficients for Square							
W	a	b	c	d	e	f	p
1	0.5	0	0	0.5	0	0	0.25
2	0.5	0	0	0.5	0.5	0	0.25
3	0.25	0	0	0.5	0	0.5	0.13
4	0.75	0	0	0.5	0.25	0.5	0.37

we wish to generate the IFS code for a unit square as shown in Figure 11.38. The four affine transformations, W_1, W_2, W_3, and W_4 shown in Table 11.3 map the original unit square into the four labeled rectangles which serve as the collage for representing the original square.

The coefficients in Table 11.3 can be written down from a careful examination of Figure 11.38(a), interpreted using equation 11.4. For example, transformation W_3, corresponding to rectangle 3, requires scaling the unit square by 0.25 in x and 0.5 in y and shifting it 0.5 units in y (coefficients a, d, and f). Since its area is one eighth of a unit, we assign its probability 0.13. The coefficients for the other three contractive affine transformations may be similarly read off by examination of the collage (a).

Running program *IFS* with the coefficients of Table 11.3 will, indeed, generate the unit square, our original image. Thus we see how the Collage Theorem provides the critical tool for mapping an image into the coefficients of the IFS algorithm.

The collage of a square from the four rectangles of Figure 11.38 provides a "perfect fit," with no overlap nor uncovered areas of the target image. In comparison with natural objects like clouds, mountains, and trees, this example appears a bit contrived. How could the Collage Theorem be applied to generate the fractal algorithm for an irregular natural object like a tree or leaf?

Barnsley proposes the *Collage algorithm* as an interactive geometric modeling tool for using the Collage Theorem to find the IFS code for an image. The algorithm defines the steps necessary to transform a target image, T, into a set of contractive affine transformations, $\{W_n, p_n: n = 1,2,...,N\}$, which specify the attractor image, A, which closely represents T.

Collage Algorithm

1. Process the target image, T, to generate a closed polygon approximation.
2. Repeat for $n = 1$ to N until the collage, T', adequately represents the target T
   2.1 Duplicate image T to produce image D_n
   2.2 Contract and transform D_n until it fits an unfilled niche in T
       2.2.1 Drag D_n into the niche in T
       2.2.2 Record the transformation, $W_n = \{a_n, b_n, c_n, d_n, e_n, f_n\}$
       2.2.3 Compute and record $p_n = area(D_n)/area(T)$

The collage, T', is formally defined as the union of the W_n transformations:

$$T' = \bigcup_{n=1}^{N} W_n(T) \qquad [11.16]$$

where

$W_n = n^{th}$ *tile* of the collage.

Barnsley provides a measure, $h(T,T')$ of the "goodness of fit" between the collage, T', and the original image, T. If $h(T,T')$ is small, the collage is a good fit to the target, and the Collage Theorem guarantees that the attractor, A, defined by the set W_n will also give a good fit to T. The goal of the Collage algorithm is the achieve the maximum goodness of fit with the minimum number of collage tiles. This corresponds to simultaneously minimizing both $h(T,T')$ and N.

Let's use an image of a real natural object to illustrate the Collage algorithm. Figure 11.39(a) is the scanned image of a maple leaf from the author's own backyard. Figure 11.39(b) represents the output of three image manipulation processes:

1. Convert (a) to a 2-color level image (i.e., all black interior),

2. Apply an image outline tracer,

3. Convert the bit-mapped outline to a series of polygon sections and group them.

The output of step (3) is a polygonal object that is easily manipulated by any drawing program. Steps 2.2 and 2.2.1 of the Collage Algorithm were performed using the mouse and various image manipulation options of a drawing program to produce the collage of Figure 11.39(c). Steps 2.2.2–2.2.3 were omitted for the purpose of this illustration but could be accomplished by careful, quantitative use of standard drawing programs.

An undocumented feature of the drawing program displayed a visual "goodness of fit" indicator shown in Figure 11.39(d). First, the five tiles representing T' were grouped, removed from the target, and colored black. Next, the target leaf, T, was colored green. Finally, the black collage was dragged over the green target, and, unexpectedly, the area in common between the two images turned pink. Thus, with N fixed at five, we visually maximized the goodness of fit by maximizing the pink area. This corresponds to minimizing $h(T,T')$ by minimizing the sum of black and green areas.

A little reflection reveals that the Collage Theorem is both mysterious and powerful. Note that in neither the procedure outlined for building the square collage of Figure 11.38 nor that for the leaf collage of Figure 11.39 is there any specification of the shape parameters of the original image. That is, the strange attractor, A, defined by the IFS coefficients of Table 11.3 "knows" that it is a square, and W_n recorded for the leaf transformation leading to Figure 11.39(c) "know" that they should regenerate not just *any* leaf, but *this particular* leaf. Both of these IFS codes have encoded the shape of the original object without recording a single absolute coordinate.

The power of the Collage Theorem is exploited in the commercial image compression system we turn to next.

The two illustrations shown for solving the inverse problem using the Collage Algorithm range from a perfect solution for the square to a messy first approximation for the leaf. Using more care, a drawing program user could undoubtedly achieve a better collage for the leaf than the one shown. In addition, using a few more tiles to fill the vacant niches in T would significantly improve the goodness of fit.

However, the reader must sense that applying the Collage Algorithm manually as we did in these two examples is not an efficient image compression technique. The question then becomes: Can the process be automated? That is, is it possible to build a system which takes raw images as input and produces a set of IFS codes from which the raw image can be reconstituted? The answer, happily, is yes!

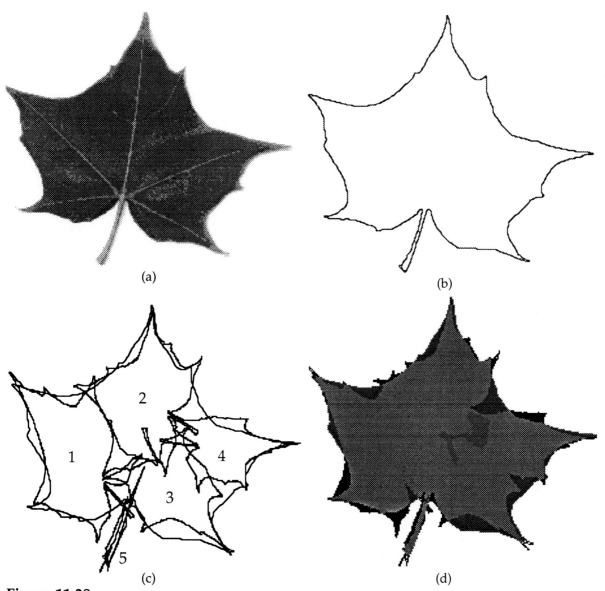

(a)

(b)

(c)

(d)

Figure 11.39
The Collage Algorithm. Generating IFS code for a leaf.

Automating Fractal Image Encoding

Barnsley conceived a system for automatically encoding images as IFS coefficients, and he and Alan Sloan, a mathematics colleague at the Georgia Institute of Technology, have established *Iterated Systems, Inc.* for developing and marketing image compression products using this technology. While the details are proprietary, the outline of the process are given in the Barnsley references above.

The fractal encoding image compression process is summarized in the following steps.

- **Image Segmentation** – Standard image processing techniques are used to break up the digitized image into segments. These techniques grew out of the field of computer vision and include edge detection, color separation, texture variation, and spectrum analysis. Segments correspond to the computer's identification of individual objects in the image scene. These image processing techniques have been highly developed for applications in such areas as the colorization process of old black and white movies.

- **Indexing the IFS Code Library** – The image compression system uses a library of IFS codes corresponding to a large number of objects. Objects are cataloged according to their IFS codes, with objects which appear similar having adjacent IFS code. The Collage Algorithm is applied automatically to each segment and the resulting transformation coefficients used to search the IFS code library for the best fractal approximation. By indexing the IFS code library according to similarity of appearance, this search process is relatively efficient. The Collage Theorem guarantees that a suitable IFS code can be found. The final compressed image corresponds to the set of IFS codes for each segment of the original image.

- **Reconstruction from IFS Code** – Once the IFS codes for each segment are identified, the fractal encoding process is complete. To reconstruct the original image, the IFS code is fed to a random iteration algorithm such as that implemented in the program *IFS* earlier in this chapter. Since the total image is the sum of its composite segments and each segment is represented by an approximate IFS code, the program *IFS* serves as the decoder for reconstructing the original image. This playback stage corresponds to image decompression.

In addition to the tremendous compression ratios, the fractal image compression technique has other advantages. First is its *stability*. As the collage becomes more accurate, the resulting IFS code better represents the original image, but the code does not need to be exact in order to get acceptable image encoding. Second, the IFS code is *robust*. That is, small perturbations in the code will not seriously damage the image.

What problems remain with the fractal image compression technique? The principle problems are associated with the computationally intensive nature of the encoding and decoding phases. Barnsley and Sloan's early results indicated that complex color images require about 100 hours to

encode and 30 minutes to decode using software on a dual-68020 system. This would appear to rule our fractal image compression as a feasible technique, at least for personal workstations.

Iterated System's P.OEM™

A highly successful approach to solving the bottlenecks for specific applications in computer science is to work out the solution in software and, after the algorithm is tested and proven, convert the algorithm to firmware. This firmware takes the form of Application Specific Integrated Circuits (ASICs). ASICs can be considered as special processors dedicated to solving specific tasks at high speeds. The fractal image encoding task is a natural candidate for conversion to ASICs.

Iterated Systems has developed a fractal image compression board which they market under the name P.OEM™ ("Pictures for OEMs"). The P.OEM™ board consists of eight fractal-transform ASICs and an Intel i960 RISC processor. Image playback (decoding) is performed by improved decompression software modules. Both the P.OEM™ board and image decompression software is compatible with 80286 and higher PCs.

The features and performance specifications of the P.OEM™ system are summarized below.

- Input consists of any scanned or frame grabber image in Targa format.
- Can achieve 500–1 image compression ratios.
- Can store 2 minutes of color video on a 1.44 Mb floppy disk
- Can store 1 hour of color video on a 45 Mb hard disk
- Can store over 12 hours of color video on a CD-ROM
- Can store over 30,000 high definition images on a CD-ROM
- Can store over 100,0000 high compression mode images on a CD-ROM
- Requires 0.5 seconds to compress 160×100 gray-scale video images.
- Requires 4 seconds to compress draft quality images.
- Requires 120 seconds to compress high definition images.

Iterated Systems offers *Fractal Factory™ Video Player* for decompressing video tape sequences and playing them back on 286/386/486 VGA systems. It also offers *Fractal Factory™ Slide Projector* for displaying up to sixty high definition slides

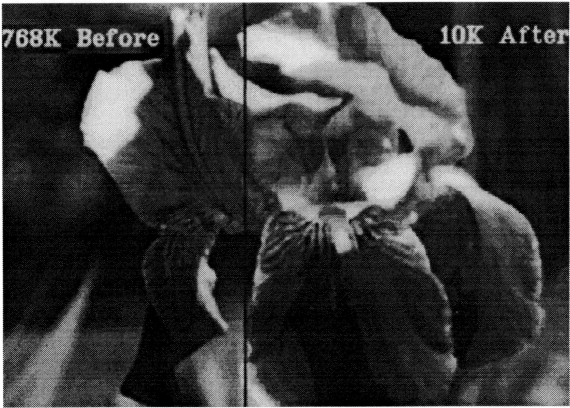

Figure 11.40
Scanned image of Iterated Systems photograph indicating the compression ratio possible with fractal image compression. The original photograph indicates no image degradation due to the compression/decompression cycle.

stored on a single 1.2 Mb disk. For users wishing to use the *Fractal Factory*™ playback modules but not willing to buy the P.OEM™ image compression board, Iterated Systems provides image compression services. To give some indication of the quality of the fractal image compression/decompression process, we show as scanned image of a promotional photograph from Iterated Systems, Inc. in Figure 11.40. This image was scanned at 150 dots/inch as a TIFF file and cropped slightly to reduce the file size.

From these specifications it is apparent that fractal image compression is an established tech

nology with great commercial potential. It has the promise of reducing image storage and retrieval tasks to a time and space scale similar to that required for text documents. This technological advance has serious implications for all aspects of multimedia, with particular relevance to the integration of video information on personal workstations. Perhaps the most important lesson to be learned from this discussion is that even the most esoteric mathematical formalism such as IFSs and the Collage Theorem can yield practical technological products in a very short time span.

Conclusions

As objects of fractional dimension, fractals provide a fascinating conclusion to our discussion of N-dimensional graphics. Computer graphics played a key role in the discovery of fractal geometry, and fractal geometry has returned the favor by providing important tools for the design of natural objects and the compression of graphics images. Fractal geometry illustrates again the importance of the principle of model authenticity to computer graphics. Since the structure of most natural objects is fractal, synthetic images of such objects must incorporate fractal geometry models in order to achieve visual realism. The movie industry has recognized this principle and now routinely uses fractal geometry as the basis for its imaginary landscapes.

Fractal geometry is a manifestation of the dynamic behavior of chaotic systems, a huge class of natural systems ranging from the neural network activity of the brain to motion of galaxies. Iterated function systems (IFSs) were shown to be capable of representing objects of arbitrary shape, and examples were presented for geometric shapes such as squares and natural shapes such as leaves. Finally, the solution of the IFS *inverse problem* was demonstrated as an effective technique for fractal image compression. Additional readings on fractal geometry are listed in this reference.[15]

Exercises

11.1   Solve Equation 11.1 for the Hausdorff dimension, D, given in 11.2.

11.2   Plot the perimeter of the von Koch triangle snowflake as a function of the number of iterations, n. Is the perimeter an arithmetic or geometric function of n? Show that the perimeter $L \to \infty$ as $n \to \infty$.

11.3   The discussion in this chapter claims that realistic coastlines are obtained by curves with dimensionality $D = 1.2$. Find duplicate maps of some geologic feature (island, bay, or seashore) with significantly different scales (levels of detail), and measure a given segment of shoreline with two rulers which differ by at least a factor of four in scale (r). (Hint: Normalize the length measured with the crude ruler to $N_1 = 1$ and r_1

$= 1$. Express N_2 and r_2 as multiples of N_1 and r_1.)

11.4   The discussion claims that realistic coastlines are obtained by curves with dimensionality $D = 1.2$. Sketch examples of what you would expect shorelines of $D = 1.05$ and $D = 1.75$ to look like. Using a map of the United States, locate sections of the Great Lakes or ocean coastline which resemble your sketches.

11.5   The discussion claims that realistic mountain landscapes are obtained by surfaces with dimensionality $D = 2.2$. Locate and photocopy examples of landscapes you would expect to represent surfaces of $D = 2.1$ and $D = 2.6$.

11.6   The discussion claims that realistic clouds are obtained by objects with dimensionality $D = 3.2–3.3$. We can interpret three of these dimensions as the position triplet (x,y,z) of each point in the cloud. The fractional dimension may be interpreted as temperature or density of the cloud at point (x,y,z). Locate and photocopy two images of clouds, one in the range of $r = 3.2$ and one in the range of 3.7.

11.7   Reprogram the *Linear Replacement Mapping* algorithms for Triadic and Quadric Koch fractal by converting the MapLine subroutine to the turtle graphics language. The three routines you need to implement, in terms of the turtle motion and the direction it is pointing, are:

   FORWARD(N_{pixels});   {Draw an N pixel
        line in turtle direction.}
   RIGHT($\theta_{degrees}$);   {Turn turtle
        direction right by θ degrees.}
   LEFT($\theta_{degrees}$)   {Turn turtle
        direction left by θ degrees.}
   What advantages does the turtle graphics language offer?

11.8   Reprogram the *Linear Replacement Mapping* algorithm to provide the capability of mapping a *set of lines* into a new, refined set of lines.

11.9   Revise the DefineObject procedure of the IFS algorithm to generate a smiley face similar to that of Figure 11.11, and verify the algorithm's behavior under repeated iteration.

11.10 Revise the DefineObject procedure of the *IFS* algorithm to generate an open square, and verify the algorithm's behavior under repeated iteration.

11.11 Revise the DefineObject procedure of the *IFS* algorithm to generate three different starting objects of your own design, and verify the algorithm's behavior under repeated iteration. Interpret your results in terms of the Sierpinski triangle acting as a *strange attractor* under *IFS* dynamics.

11.12 Revise the Fern *IFS* program to begin the iteration at several (5–10) different starting points, and verify that they all converge to the same fern-shaped strange attractor. Do any of your runs exhibit anomalous behavior (i.e., points outside the dominant fractal shape)?

11.13 Revise the Fern *IFS* program to explore the role of each of the four affine transformations by color-coding each random selection. Interpreting the coefficients of the affine transformations in Table 11.2 may help you predict which elements of the fern leaf will turn green (k = 1), red (k=2), blue (k=3), and magenta (k=4). Were you right?

11.14 Run Fern five times with the number of iterations set at 200 and compare the output patterns. Are they identical? (If so, your random number generator must be putting out identical random sequences each run. Modify it to produce a different random sequence each run.) Once your program produces distinct random sequences, answer the following questions:
a) Is the output stochastic?
b) Is the output deterministic?
c) How do you explain the apparent contradiction in (a) and (b)?

11.15 To gain experience working with complex numbers like $z = 2 + 3i$ and $w = -3 - i$, compute value of the following complex numbers:
a) $z + w$
b) $z - w$
c) $z w$

d) $\sqrt{z w}$
e) the value of the polar coordinates $(r\ \theta)$ which represent $z w$.

11.16 Use the program Complex_Map to trace the trajectories of the points (0.4,0.5), (–0.8,0.2), (0.6,–0.8), and (0.7,0.8) under the iterative transformation $F(z) = z^2$. Interpret your results in terms of "basins of attraction."

11.17 Use the program Julia to compute the filled-in Julia sets for the complex constants, c = (–0.01,1), (–0.745,–0.113), (–1.3,0), and (0.3,–0.04).

11.18 Use the program Julia to investigate the dependence of the filled-in Julia sets on the number of iterations, N_{it}. For two of the points, c = (–1,0) and (–0.9,0.12), plot the sets for N_{it} = 10, 20, 50, and 100. Interpret your results.

11.19 Plot the Julia set for $F(z) = \sin(z)$.

11.20 Modify the program Mandelbrot to explore some interesting region of the Mandelbrot set. A suggested approach: Use the mouse button event to select the lower left-hand coordinate (in complex space) of a square box with a scale factor S = 0.1 of the present value. Then each zoom will show you an area of 0.01 that of the previous complex region. Repeat the zoom operation five times, and make a probabilistic argument as to why your final view of the Mandelbrot set has never before been seen by human eyes.

11.21 The text claims that the Mandelbrot set acts as a catalog of Julia sets. What does this mean? (*Hint: distinguish between the z-plane and the c-plane.*)

11.22 In both the Mandelbrot and Julia sets, enormous complexity results from the application of very simple *production rules*. Such behavior is not unique to these mathematical objects. Discuss two other examples of such complexity. Some suggestions: Cell behavior in the Game of LIFE and the track of an ant programmed to "go home" in a complex environment.

11.23 Run program **Random_Walk** several times. How many time did you have to run it until it produced what you would consider an "interesting" profile? What aspect of the algorithm is responsible for this boring behavior? Suggest and implement a modification of the algorithm to produce more interesting profiles.

11.24 In the theory of Brownian motion, mean square correlation of a given displacement at a given time, *d(t)*, with its subsequent displacement a time δt later, $d(t+\delta t)$, is proportional to the time interval, δt, with a variation of σ according to the equation:

$$<\,|\,d(t) - d(t+\delta t)\,|^2> = \sigma^2\,\delta t \qquad [11.15]$$

Check to see if the program **Random_Walk** exhibits this behavior by computing and plotting the LHS of 11.15 vs. *dt* for a range of δt. What is σ for this model?

11.25 Repeat the analysis of problem 11.24 for the program **Midpoint**. What is σ for this model of Brownian motion?

11.26 Another property of Brownian motion is that the distribution of the quantity $\Delta = d(t) - d(t+1)$ is Gaussian, that is, of the form:

$$f(t) = c\,exp(-\Delta^2/2\sigma^2) \qquad [11.16]$$

For both **Random_Walk** and **Midpoint** plot histograms of the quantity Δ^2 and compare them with the theoretical distribution given in 11.16. What is the best value for σ in each case?

11.27 Why is the random midpoint displacement algorithm easier to extend to fractal mountain landscapes than is the random walk algorithm?

11.28 Write a program to implement the fractal mountain landscape RMD algorithm, and use it to project a wire frame view of the landscape for the first five levels of refinement.

11.29 Explain how a fractal mountain landscape program can be used to study coastline and island formations.

11.30 Locate a commercial painting/drawing program with fractal options and use it to generate or simulate several different natural scenes.

11.31 Define the *Collage Theorem* in your own words. Write down a step-by-step procedure (algorithm) on how it should be applied to generate the IFS code for some arbitrary object.

11.32 Sketch, by hand, how you would apply the Collage Algorithm to generate a 4-transform IFS code for an upright, equilateral triangle. Verify the set of W_n you generate by submitting them to the program *IFS*.

Endnotes

1. Mandelbrodt, Benoit B., *The Fractal Geometry of Nature*, W. H. Freeman and Company, New York, NY (1977, 1982, 1983).
2. Gleick, James, *CHAOS – Making a New Science*, Viking Penguin, Inc., New York, NY (1987) For a more rigorous, mathematical treatment, see: Barnsley, Michael and Demko, Stephen, (eds) *Chaotic Dynamics and Fractals*, Academic Press, Orlando, FL (1986).
3. Hausdorff, F., "Dimension und äusseres Mass," *Mathematische Annalen* **79**, pp. 157–179 (1919).
4. Barnsley, Michael F. and Sloan, Alan D., "A Better Way to Compress Images," *BYTE Magazine*, pp. 215–223, January (1988).
5. Barnsley, Michael, *Fractals Everywhere*, Academic Press, Inc., Boston, MA (1988).
6. Peitgen, Heinz-Otto and Saupe, Dietmar (eds), *The Science of Fractal Images*, pp.137–167, Springer-Verlag, New York (1988).
7. *Nothing but Zooms*, Video animations of the Mandelbrodt set available from ART MATRIX, P.O. Box 880, Ithaca, NY 14851-0880 (607)277-0959.
8. Fournier, A., Fussell, D., and Carpenter, L. "Computer Rendering of Stochastic Models," *Comm. of the ACM* **25**, pp. 371–384 (1982).
9. Voss, R., "Random Fractal Forgeries," in Earnshaw, R. A.., (ed), *Fundamental Algorithms for Computer Graphics*, Springer-Verlag, Berlin (1985); also in SIGGRAPH Short Course notes on Fractals, San Francisco, CA (July 23, 1985).
10. *MacFractal*, a program in the public domain written by Mark Alan Zimmer (1984).
11. *Kid Pix* was written by Craig Hickman and is available from Brøderbund Software, P. O. Box 12947, San Rafael, CA 94913-2949.
12. Prusinkiewicz, Przemyslaw, Lindenmayer, Aristid, and Hanan, James, "Developmental Models of Herbaceous Plants for Computer Imagery Purposes," *Computer Graphics* **22**, No. 4, pp. 141–150, August (1988).
13. "Fractal research: Payoff at last,", *EDN News* **35**, No. 19A, p. 1 (Sept. 20, 1990).
14. Barnsley, Michael F., Jacquin, Arnaud, Malassenet, Francois, Reuter, Laurie, and Sloan, Alan D., "Harnessing Chaos for Image Synthesis," *Computer Graphics* **22**, No. 4, pp. 131–140, August (1988).

15. Additional readings:
Peitgen, H. O. and Richter, P. H., *The Beauty of Fractals—Images of Complex Dynamical Systems*, Springer-Verlag, Berlin (1986).
Devaney, Robert L. and Keen, Linda (eds), *Chaos and Fractals—The Mathematics Behind the Computer Graphics*, Proceedings of Symposia in Applied Mathematics **39**, American Mathematical Society, Providence, RI (1989).
Becker, Carl-Heinz and Dörfler, Michael, *Dynamical Systems and Fractals*, Cambridge University Press, Cambridge, UK (1986).
Devaney, Robert L., *Chaos, Fractals, and Dynamics*, Addison–Wesley, Menlo Park, CA (1990).
Pickover, Clifford A., *Computers, Pattern, Chaos, and Beauty—Graphics from an Unseen World*, St. Marten's Press, New York, NY (1990).
Morrison, Foster, *The Art of Modeling Dynamic Systems*, John Wiley & Sons, Inc., New York, NY (1991).
Casti, John L., *Alternate Realities—Mathematical Models of Nature and Man*, John Wiley & Sons, Inc., New York, NY (1989).
Prusinkiewicz, Przemyslaw and Sandness, Glen, "Fractals—Koch Curves as Attractors and Repellers," *Computer Graphics and Applications* **8**, IEEE, pp. 26–40, November (1988).
Dewdney, A. K., "Computer Recreations —A computer microscope zooms in for a look at the most complex object in mathematics," *Scientific American* **235**, pp. 16 – 20, August (1985).
Dewdney, A. K., "Computer Recreations—Beauty and profundity: the Mandelbrodt set and a flock of its cousins called Julia," *Scientific American*, pp. 140 – 145, August (1987).
Sorensen, Peter R., "Fractals," *BYTE Magazine*, pp. 157–172, September (1984).
Schroeder, Peter B., "Plotting the Mandelbrot Set," *BYTE Magazine*, pp. 207–210, December (1986).
Turk, Greg, "Fractal Program," *BYTE Magazine*, p. 172, September, (1984).
Field, Michael and Golubitsky, Martin, *Symmetry in Chaos*, Oxford University Press, Oxford, (1992).

Section 3

Applications of Visualization

The goals of this section are:

Chapter 12
Survey the visualization tools provided by graphics-based operating systems and high-level graphics languages and to illustrate their use in the design of GUIs for applications programs.

Chapter 13
Examine some of the visualization tools available for graphics designers and engineers and to demonstrate the use of CAD and finite element methods for product design and analysis.

Chapter 14
Summarize some of the capabilities of tools available to mathematicians and scientists for visualizing theories, data, and system simulations.

Chapter 15
Illustrate tools and techniques for the analysis, processing, and compression of graphical images and to introduce techniques for volume visualization.

Chapter 16
Demonstrate the techniques of virtual reality for visualizing imaginary worlds and to investigate animation and video tools available for building metarealities.

Chapter 12

The Visual Interface – Designing GUIs

The metaphor is perhaps one of man's most fruitful potentialities. Its efficacy verges
on magic, and it seems a tool for creation which God forgot
inside one of His creatures when He made him.
Ortega y Gasset

The problem ... is that slavish adherence to a metaphor prevents the
emergence of *things that are genuinely new.*
Ted Nelson

...applying the Macintosh style to poorly designed applications and
machines is like trying to put Béarnaise sauce on a hot-dog.
Alan Kay

Fenestracryptophobia: The fear of Windows programming. Symptoms range from
mild headaches to outright disorientation and confusion. In worst cases, suffering
programmers find it difficult to manage even
simple events such as opening a window.
Michael Floyd

New developments in any particular field only becomes part of the general culture
when they enter the experience of people who are not
specialists in that area..
Waddington

T o this point in the text we have presented the background and motivation for the study of computer graphics and examined the major techniques and algorithms for creating graphical models and rendering them realistically. This is the subject matter of traditional computer graphics courses and the primary focus of the computer graphics *research* community.

However, for the far larger computer graphics *user* community, the primary concern is what computer graphics can do for them. The central thesis of this book is that the best measure of the value of computer graphics tools is the extent to which they assist the user in visualizing the task at hand. For computer programmers, the task is to build the most natural and intuitive user interface for the application under construction. For designers, the task is to create unique and compelling images in a fluid environment free of limitations on color, texture, patterns, shape, and form. For engineers, the task is to build a precise design of component parts and composite systems and test their behavior under a variety of conditions. For mathematicians, the task is to understand the behavior of functions and the relationships and ramifications of postulates. For scientists, the task is to understand the correlation of data and to predict the behavior of systems under various hypotheses.

The common thread in all these applications is that well-designed graphics greatly aids the user in carrying out the task at hand. We define the Graphical User Interface, or GUI, as the set of graphical input and graphical output routines through which the user interacts with the application program. Graphical input may be produced by any cursor-controlling input device (e. g., keyboard arrows, data tablet, and light pen). The graphical input device of choice of the vast majority of the personal workstations is the mouse. The mouse provides both position (via cursor) and event (via button) information, and, as we have seen, can be readily transformed into any of the logical input devices. The combination of graphical output in the form of menus, windows, and controls with graphical input from the mouse forms the basis for interactive dialog with the computer. The purpose of an efficient GUI is to optimize the information content of this interactive dialog.

Classes of GUI Tools

It is helpful to distinguish between several classes of graphical user interface tools in order to clarify the subject of this chapter. One helpful categorization is given as follows:

- **GUI Operating Systems (Environments)** – GUI operating systems function predominantly within a Window-Icon-Menu-Pointer (WIMP) environment. The two leading WIMP systems for personal workstations are Microsoft's *Windows* for Intel 80X86-based machines and Apple's Macintosh operating system with its *Toolbox* of GUI routines. Windows is a software-based "shell" running under the DOS operating system. The Macintosh Toolbox is a set of 1200 ROM and disk-based routines which provide access to QuickDraw graphics, the Window Manager, the Event Manager, the Menu Manager, the Dialog Manager, and so on. For UNIX workstations, *X Windows* is the leading GUI system.

    Some confusion may arise from the relationship of GUI operating systems to the base operating systems. IBM's Presentation Manager GUI is based on the OS/2 operating system, Windows is based on MS-DOS, and most X Windows systems run under UNIX. To avoid confusion between the base operating system and the GUI, it is useful to describe the *combination* of the two as the *operating environment*.

- **Symbolic Programming Languages** – The next level up in abstraction includes the symbolic programming languages through which the programmer can call the routines provided by the GUI operating system. Borland's *Turbo Pascal* and *Turbo C* and Symantec's *Think Pascal* and *Think C* are examples of high level languages with links to GUI operating system routines. Note that both GUI operating environments and the programming languages linking them are machine dependent.

- **Graphical Programming Languages** – More abstract yet are the graphical programming languages such as Apple's *HyperCard* for the Macintosh and Microsoft's *Visual Basic* for the PC. Graphical programming languages are distinctly object-oriented with a library of graphical objects capable of hierarchical relationships and a symbolic language or hypertext capable of specifying messages to control the behavior of graphical objects.

- **Standard Graphics Languages** – Graphics languages such as GKS, PHIGS, and FIGS are designed as a library of machine-independent routines, callable from symbolic programming languages. In addition to providing higher-level graphics functionality (e.g., 3D, hidden surface, and shading routines), graphics languages such as PHIGS address two other serious issues— the *representation* of graphical objects (data and file structures) and *networking* of graphical workstations. Both of these issues will assume increasing importance as the trend towards integration of heterogeneous workstations sharing common graphical information continues.

When we speak of designing a GUI, we mean using some combination of the GUI tools listed above to build an *application program* in which the human/computer communication is optimized using interactive graphics techniques. We are explicitly **not** concerned with *building* GUI environments such as Windows, the Mac Toolbox, or X Windows themselves, but rather with *using* the tools they provide for building more mundane applications with elegant graphical interfaces. Powerful, readily available, and inexpensive GUI tools have established a new paradigm for communicating with computers. Applications programs without good GUIs most likely indicate "living fossils," generally with mainframe lineage, or products of companies headed for Chapter 11 (in the courts, not this book).

Principles of GUI Design

Several principles should inform and guide the designer of effective GUIs for applications programs.[1] Several of the principles of good GUI design evolved from systematic studies of strategies for effective human-computer interaction.[2]

1. **Sensitivity** – Perhaps the first principle of good GUI design is the sensitivity to good design in general. Good design involves building smooth, effective, and unobtrusive interfaces between humans and the objects with which they interact. Good design is often most evident when it is missing. Two examples from the author's personal experience illustrate this. In the first case, a soda dispenser on campus has a small lip, presumably for catching overflow foam, which serves instead to trip and spill the soda cup as it is removed. In the second case, the seat belt fixture in the bucket seat of the author's car seems better designed to stab drivers where they interface the seat than to perform any useful function. Examples of bad design from the computer world include the DOS "Abort, Retry, Fail?" trap and the ambiguity of the Macintosh trash can ("trash this *file*" but "eject that *disk*"). By cultivating an awareness of good design in the world at large, systems designers can become more sensitive to good design in GUIs.

2. **Task Understanding** – The first step in effective GUI/application program design is to achieve a thorough understanding of the task for which the program is being designed. This involves not only an analysis of the task mechanics, but a study of users, their background and skills, the environment in which the task is accomplished, the institutional setting, and communications requirements. The task analysis should be user-centered, with user interviews and interaction at every level of the development. Complete task understanding evolves through successive refinement as feedback is obtained from users interacting with prototype systems.

3. **Transparency** – The goal of an effective GUI/application program is to make the *computer* "invisible" and to focus the user's complete attention on the *task* to be accomplished. In a perfectly designed GUI/appli-

cation program, the user should be aware only of the work in progress and totally unaware of the tools s/he is using to perform the work. To the extent that the user must withdraw attention from the task at hand and ask, "Now let's see, how do I perform the next step?", the GUI/application program has failed the transparency principle.

4. **Integration** – The goal of good GUI design for application programs is the seamless integration of the GUI with the application program. There is nothing quite as obvious or awkward as a command-line program onto which a GUI has been pasted. The integration of a GUI with an application program does *not* involve simply replacing the command interpreter with a menu window, but rather requires a complete restructuring of the application program. This restructuring should be guided by the intuitive approach used by practitioners in the field, and should involve good psychological, artistic, and engineering design.

5. **Consistency** – In the design of GUI/application programs for general users who are likely to be users of other programs, consistency of metaphor is of great value. The genius of the desktop metaphor is that, once the user has mastered a single program, it is relatively easy to master subsequent programs. The closer the designer sticks to a consistent metaphor, the greater is the transference of skills for novice users.

6. **Feedback** – Effective feedback is an important principle in the design of any interface and particularly important in the rich environment possible with GUIs. Graphical feedback should indicate the status of the system at all times ("Wait, I'm busy computing" or "Alright, what should we do next?"), the action options available to the user, an indication of what objects are active or selected, and an indication of the progress in time-consuming tasks like file copying. By simply switching the active cursor to a moving watch or hour-glass, the GUI informs the user, "Stand by while I complete the task you just assigned me." Well-designed feedback should give the user a feeling of control of all aspects of the application.

7. **Balance** – A well-designed GUI/application program must balance *simplicity* against *features*. There is tremendous pressure in the market place to match and surpass the feature list of the competitors' products in each new release of a product. Soon, even a well-designed GUI becomes overloaded and cumbersome. Each menu item has submenus which, in turn, may have items with submenus and so on, with a decrease in transparency at each level. While such feature-rich programs may appeal to "power users," the loss of simplicity may leave the average user confused and overwhelmed.

The commercial failure of most integrated packages (with notable exceptions like *MS-Works*) containing word processor, spreadsheet, database, drawing program, and communications package indicates the risk of violating the balance principle. An interesting attempt to solve the problem of simplicity/features balance is the *Short Menus/Full Menus* option of *Microsoft Word*. *Short Menus* keeps it simple for new users while *Full Menus* provides access to all features for power users.

Incorporation of these principles in the design of GUIs will result in intuitive, efficient applications programs which are enjoyable to operate. Most failures of existing applications programs may be traced to a violation of one or more of these principles.

Application Programmer Interface (API)

As has been noted frequently throughout this text, abstraction plays the same important role in computer graphics as it does in computer science generally. Nowhere is this capability of "saying more with less" more apparent than in application programmer interface services (API) available for GUI design. Rather than struggling with nitty-gritty tasks like drawing rectangles and writing strings to the screen, the interface designer working in a GUI environment has a host of powerful GUI objects and event management tools readily available. A single procedure call within the GUI environment often produces the same effect as dozens of lines of code in a more primitive graphics language.

Good programming practice entails use of the most powerful tools within the most productive environment available for program development. The nearly unanimous consensus within the commercial program development community is that the object-oriented tools of the WIMP environment maximize the productivity of programmers writing applications. Therefore, our subsequent discussion assumes the availability of a GUI environment equivalent to that provided by the Macintosh Toolbox, Microsoft Windows, or X Windows System.

Objects for APIs

Object-oriented programming is the dominant programming paradigm for building GUIs. In fact, both the development of GUIs and object-oriented programming emerged simultaneously from the research at Xerox PARC. Rather than consider GUIs as the outgrowth of object-oriented programming concepts, it is probably more accurate to consider object-oriented programming as an attempt to formalize and provide a theoretical basis for the success of GUIs. In any case, GUIs are the exemplars of object-oriented programming.

What are the basic objects available to GUI programmers? A list common to most WIMP systems will include:

- **Windows** – These may be overlapping or tiled and may include controls for positioning, resizing, and scrolling. Desktop metaphors generally include an *active* window in the foreground through which the interactive dialog occurs.

- **Icons** – Icons are the graphical symbols for *objects* such as files, folders, and disks and *actions* such as erasing pixels (eraser icon), spraying colored pixels on a bitmap (spray-can icon), and deleting a file (trash-can icon). Icons should be designed for maximum mnemonic value.

- **Menus** – If windows and icons represent the nouns of an object-oriented language, menus represent the verbs. They typically consist of a row of object categories located at the top of a screen or window. When a given category is selected, a column of possible actions or attributes is displayed. These are the messages of OOP. Menus may also be presented as an array of icons indicating messages the user can send to objects.

- **Pointer** – The pointer is the primary method through which the user controls and interacts with the application program. A variety of pointers have been developed, but the dominant one is the mouse providing a position-controlled cursor and messages via button events.

- **Controls** – Controls may be considered as *intelligent* icons or specialized windows that respond to mouse messages and provide instant feedback and program control. They include such forms as command buttons, check boxes, dials, and scroll bars.

- **Clipboard** – The clipboard serves as a temporary, internal storage bin into which any data object can be cut or copied and from which the object can be transferred (pasted) into any compatible destination. It facilitates seamless communication of numerical, textual, graphical, and dynamic data from any program into any other compatible program.

Let's examine these GUI objects in more detail and show some examples of each.

Windows

To illustrate some of the features common to most windows, a typical window associated with a word processing file is shown in Figure 12.1 along with some of the feature options.

As indicated by the feature arrows, windows available in a GUI environment are not simply static rectangles, but rather intelligent objects capable of responding to messages. To send the message, "Close this file," the user clicks the cursor in the "Close box." To send the message, "Expand this window to fill the screen," the user clicks in the "Auto Resize box." To send the message, "Scroll forward or backward through the document," the user has three methods available. First, s/he can drag the scroll box downward or upward to the desired location. Secondly, s/he can position the cursor on the down or up arrows in the vertical scroll bar and press the button to smoothly scroll in the desired direction. Thirdly, clicking in the scroll bar above or below the scroll box pages up or down.

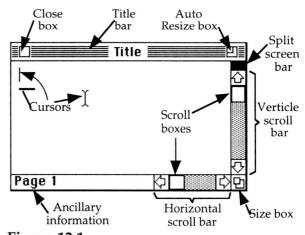

Figure 12.1
Features of a typical document window (from Microsoft Word for the Macintosh).

The relationship between windows within the desktop metaphor is examined in Figure 12.2. In Figure 12.2(a), the order of the windows, from top down, is A-B-C. Window A, the active window, is on top and not overlapped by any other window. Its active status is indicated by the shaded title bar and displayed control features. The inactive windows, B and C, are overlapped by window A and do not have active title bars or operative controls.

In order to activate Window C, the user simply positions the cursor within its visible boundary and clicks. It immediately becomes the active window with operative controls and moves to the top of the desktop as shown in Figure 12.2(b).

Two of the most common messages sent to windows are: "Move yourself to here" and "Resize yourself to this shape." Both are done by dragging. To reposition a window, the cursor is placed in the title bar, the button pressed, and the window dragged into its new position. To resize a window, the cursor is placed in the Size box and the corner dragged to the desired size.

The high-level routines for creating and manipulating windows on the Macintosh are provided by the Window Manager. The Window Manager specifies both the attributes of this OOP object as well as the messages which may be sent to it. The attributes of a window are specified by a WindowRecord data structure.

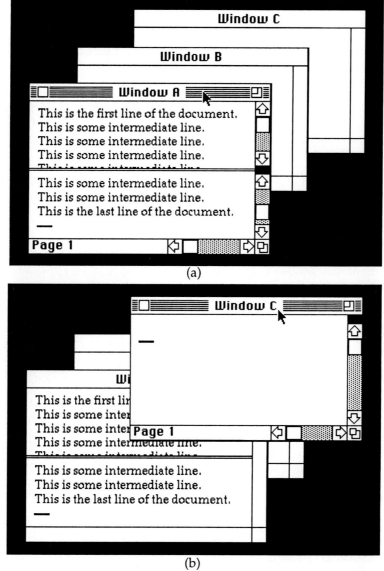

(a)

(b)

Figure 12.2
Relationship between windows in the desktop metaphor. Clicking Window C brings it to the front and activates its controls.

Window Messages

The following are examples of the more than forty procedures and functions which Window Manager provides for the creation and manipulation of windows.

FUNCTION NewWindow;
PROCEDURE CloseWindow;
PROCEDURE SetWTitle;
PROCEDURE HiliteWindow;
PROCEDURE BringToFront;

PROCEDURE SendBehind;
FUNCTION FindWindow;
PROCEDURE MoveWindow;
PROCEDURE DragWindow;
FUNCTION GrowWindow;
PROCEDURE SizeWindow:;
FUNCTION PinRect;
PROCEDURE SetWindowPic;
FUNCTION GetWindowPic;

This list illustrates the range and variety of actions of which window objects are capable.

Window Attributes

```
TYPE WindowRecord =
        RECORD
            port:              GrafPort:           {window's grafport}
            windowKind:        INTEGER;            {window class]
            visible:           BOOLEAN;            {TRUE if visible}
            hilited:           BOOLEAN;            {TRUE if highlighted}
            goAwayFlag:        BOOLEAN;            {TRUE if has go-away region}
            spareFlag:         BOOLEAN;            {reserved for future use}
            strucRgn:          RgnHandle;          {structure region}
            contRgn:           RgnHandle;          {content region}
            updateRgn:         RgnHandle;          {update region}
            windowDefProc:     Handle              {window definition function}
            dataHandle:        Handle              {data used by windowDefProc}
            titleHandle:       StringHandle;       {window's title}
            titleWidth:        INTEGER;            {width of title in pixels}
            controlList:       ControlHandle;      {window's control list}
            nextWindow:        WindowPeek;         {next window in window list}
            windowPic:         PicHandle;          {picture for drawing window}
            refCon:            LONGINT;            {window's reference value}
        END;
```

Icons

Icons are the atoms—the most fundamental objects—of the GUI environment. Iconology is the study of icons or artistic symbolism. It is interesting to compare the power and expressiveness of icons with that of conventional alphabetic symbols. The natural language alphabet provides the richest of all languages in terms of its expressive power—all of Shakespeare was written as combinations of just twenty six characters. Since we can express *any* fact or concept with natural language, its expressiveness must be unlimited. What are the expressive limits of iconic representations?

There is a profound difference between symbolic (alphabetic) representations and iconic representations.[3] Alphabetic letters are totally meaningless as individual symbols and assume their semantic value (meaning) only when combined into words and sentences. Icons, on the other hand, must convey their total meaning as individual objects. As of yet, there has been no syntax developed for relating a string of icons or giving an icon string an emergent meaning which transcends that of the individual icons. Since there is only a finite number of icons but an infinite number of combinations of alphabetic symbols, we must conclude that symbolic language is more expressive than iconic language.

However, this does not mean that iconic language is inferior to symbolic language for certain applications. As we saw in the first chapter, icons can convey meaning much more rapidly and robustly than symbolic language in many instances. In addition, icons have the advantage of being relatively language- and culture-independent, making iconic systems much easier to port to international markets. For all of these reasons, the Macintosh User Interface Guidelines recommends:[4]

Whenever an explanation or label is needed, consider using an icon instead of text.

The expressive capability of a number of types of icons is illustrated in Figure 12.3. Each of these icons is a *resource* of type ICON and stored in 128 bytes.

Icons are stored as relocatable, editable bitmaps called *resources*. This allows editing of the icon corresponding with a given program without completely recompiling the program. Icons may be created or edited with the utility program called *ResEdit*. Two Toolbox routines are available for manipulating icons:

```
FUNCTION GetIcon(iconID: INTEGER) : Handle;
PROCEDURE  PlotIcon(theRect: Rect; the
Icon:Handle);
```

Given the resource ID, iconID, GetIcon returns its *handle* which is a pointer to the master pointer to its location in the heap. Given this handle, PlotIcon plots the icon in the rectangle specified by theRect.

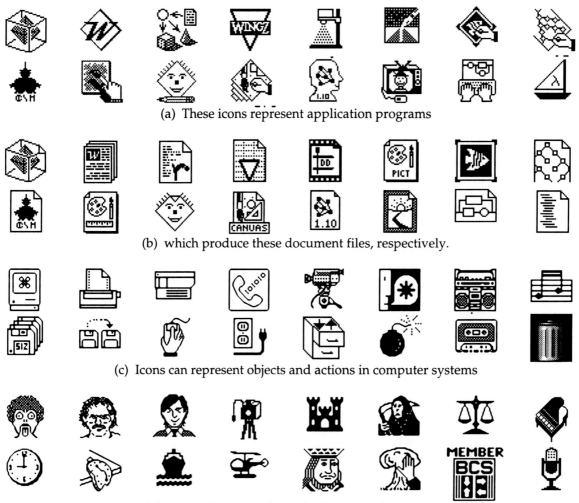

(a) These icons represent application programs

(b) which produce these document files, respectively.

(c) Icons can represent objects and actions in computer systems

(d) or a wide range of people, things, and activities.

Figure 12.3
Examples of icons representing, (a) application programs, (b) corresponding files, (c) computer system elements, and (d) various objects.

To edit the generic icon for an application,

into a more interesting icon equipped with quill pen,

we simply use *ResEdit* to open the resources for the program whose icon we wish to edit. Opening an arbitrary program, *SetFile*, with *ResEdit* generates a menu of icons, Figure 12.4(a), representing all of the resources associated with *SetFile*. Selecting "ICN#" opens an editing window, Figure 12.4(b), in which we can edit the icon into the shape desired and automatically generate a mask for displaying the selected icon.

The *ResEdit* icon editor allows the programmer to alter the pixels of the icon by clicking on them. Clicking on a white pixel changes it to black and vise versa. After the icon is designed, a single command creates the mask shown on the right side of Figure 12.4(b) used to invert the original icon to indicate selection. The icons at the bottom of the editing window indicate the actual icon as it would be displayed as well as half-scale icons available for use in menu applications.

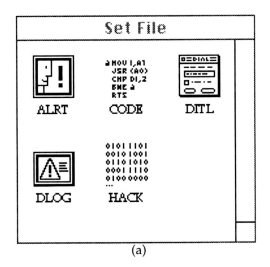

(a)

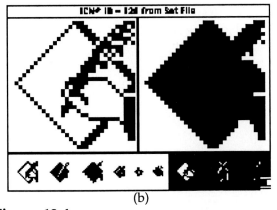

(b)

Figure 12.4
Use of resource editor program, *ResEdit*, to edit
program icon.
　a)　Menu of resources associated with *SetFile*
　　　as displayed by *ResEdit*.
　b)　Editing window for modifying the icon
　　　associated with *SetFile* and generating a
　　　mask image to use for icon selection.

Menus

A standard programming technique for providing
the user with options for controlling the operation
of an interactive program is to list available
alternatives and request a selection indicated by a
number or letter. This mode both informs the user
of allowed options and constrains the response
with a syntax of limited actions. The widespread
acceptance of pre-WIMP application programs like
Lotus 123™ is due in large part to the helpful task
environment possible with menus. Lotus 123™ also
extended the menu concept to include submenus
for action classes which included multiple options.

The principle contribution of WIMP environments to the menu mode of interaction was the
standardization of menu formats and provision of
a set of standard menu manipulation routines. A
typical menu (from Microsoft Word™) is shown in
Figure 12.5.

De facto standards are emerging for the "look
and feel" of menu structures. The Macintosh *de
facto* standard for application programs specifies
the **File** menu in the left-most position, followed
by the **Edit** menu, and then various formatting and
utilities menus. Not only does this menu pattern
persist across Macintosh applications, but it has
also spread to other GUI systems and platforms.
Figure 12.6 shows the comparable menu from MS-
Word for Windows. The striking similarity permits the rapid transference of skills learned on one
platform to the totally different platform.

The Toolbox provides a Menu Manager which
performs the save specification of attributes and
actions for menus as the Windows Manager does
for windows. The attributes of menus are defined
by a *MenuInfo* data type as follows.

Menu Attributes

The following record structure indicates the menu
attributes which the programmer can set.

```
TYPE MenuInfo =
     RECORD
          menuID:        INTEGER;        {menu ID}
          menuWidth:     INTEGER;        {menu width  in pixels}
          menuHeight:    INTEGER;        {menu height  in pixels}
          menuProc:      Handle;         {menu definition procedure}
          enableFlags:   LONGINT;        {tells if menu or items are enabled}
          menuData:      Str255;         {menu title (and other data)}
     END;
```

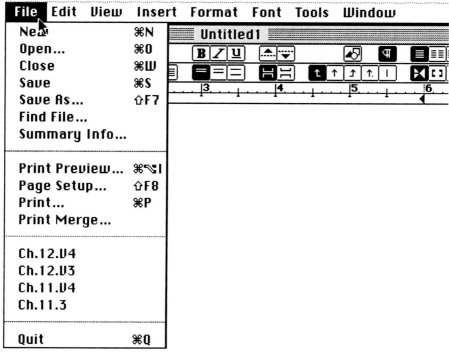

Figure 12.5
Typical menu bar and action options for handling files in Microsoft Word for the Macintosh.

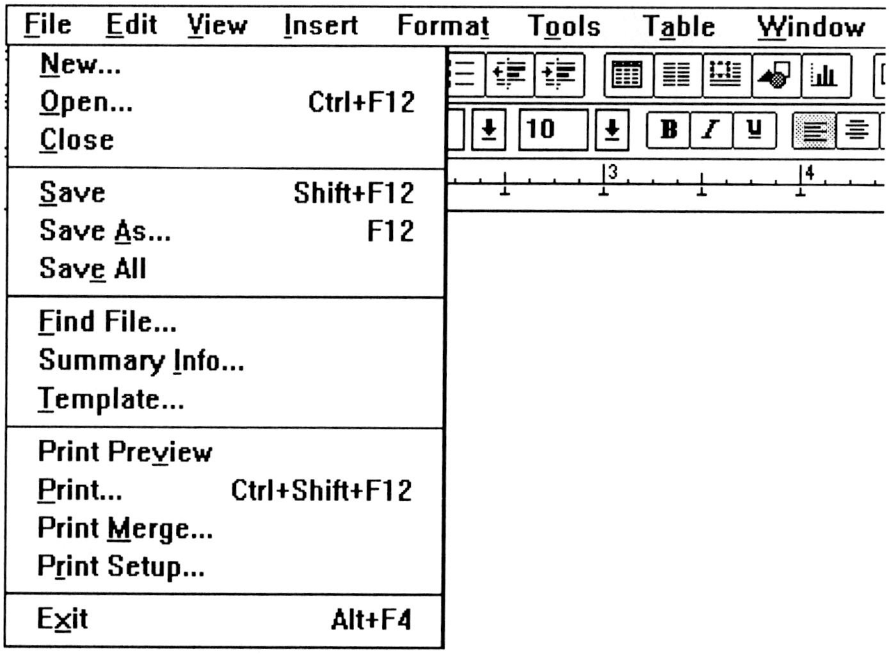

Figure 12.6
Typical menu bar and action options for handling files in MS-Word™ for Windows. Note the similarity between the Windows system and Macintosh menu structures.

Menu Messages

The following are examples of the more than thirty procedures and functions which Menu Manager provides for creating and manipulation of menus.

```
FUNCTION NewMenu;
PROCEDURE DisposeMenu;
PROCEDURE AppendMenu;
PROCEDURE HiliteMenu;
PROCEDURE InsertMenu;
PROCEDURE DeleteMenu;
FUNCTION MenuSelect;
PROCEDURE DisableItem;
PROCEDURE SetItem;
FUNCTION MenuKey;
PROCEDURE CalcMenuSize:;
FUNCTION CountMItems;
PROCEDURE SetMenuFlash;
PROCEDURE FlashMenuBar;
```

This list illustrates that a similar range and variety of actions are available for menus as for windows. The GUI application designer can access all of these attributes and menu manipulation routines through any high-level programming language.

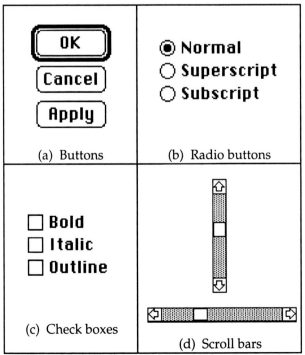

Figure 12.7
Predefined control types from the Toolbox Control Manager.

Pointer

The Toolbox provides an Event Manager to interpret messages sent by the mouse pointing device and the keyboard. The Event Manager provides four routines for reading the mouse:

```
FUNCTION Button;
PROCEDURE GetMouse;
FUNCTION StillDown;
FUNCTION WaitMouseUp;
```

In addition, Event Manager provides PROCEDURE GetKeys for reading the current state of the keyboard and FUNCTION TickCount to return the number of ticks (sixtieths of a second) since the system last started up.

It should be noted that these pointer routines are *stand-alone* routines, not associated with any particular window, menu, or control. The Window Manager, Menu Manager, and Control Manager each provide specialized routines which interpret the interaction of the mouse with their special graphical objects.

Controls

The Toolbox provides a Control Manager to create controls and interpret messages sent them by the mouse. The Control Manager provides four predefined control types shown in Figure 12.7.

Control Messages

The Control Manager provides nearly thirty high-level routines for creating controls and interpreting messages sent to the controls. The list includes the following:

```
FUNCTION NewControl;
PROCEDURE DisposeControl;
PROCEDURE SetCTitle;
PROCEDURE HiliteControl;
FUNCTION FindControl;
PROCEDURE DrawControl;
PROCEDURE DragControl;
FUNCTION TrackControl;
PROCEDURE MoveControl;
FUNCTION TestControl;
PROCEDURE MyAction;
FUNCTION GetControlMin;
PROCEDURE SetCtlValue;
FUNCTION GetControlMax;
```

This list illustrates the range and variety of actions of which Control objects are capable. In

```
TYPE ControlRecord =
      PACKED RECORD
            nextControl:        ControlHandle:     {next control}
            contrlOwner:        WindowPtr;         {control's window}
            contrlRect:         Rect;              {enclosing rectangle}
            contrlVis:          Byte;              {255 if visible}
            contrlHiLite:       Byte;              {highlight state}
            contrlValue:        INTEGER;           {control's current setting}
            contrlMin:          INTEGER;           {control's minimum setting}
            contrlMax:          INTEGER;           {control's maximum setting}
            contrlDefProc:      Handle;            {control's definition function}
            contrlData:         Handle             {data used by controlDefProc}
            contrlAction:       ProcPtr            {default action procedure}
            contrlRfCon:        LONGINT;           {control's reference value}
            contrlTitle:        Str255;            {control's title}
      END;
```

addition to these predefined controls, the Control Manager allows the GUI application designer to define *custom* control types declared by FUNCTION MyControl.

Control Attributes

As complex OOP objects, controls have a number of attributes. The *ControlRecord* data type shown above specifies the attributes associated with each control.

Examples of GUI Interfaces

To illustrate the tools available for building graphical user interfaces, we next present several applications programs built with various GUI environments. The applications are arranged in order of decreasing abstraction and increasing complexity. The first two examples demonstrate that abstract graphical objects such as "intelligent" controls, icons, and windows provide powerful object-oriented tools for GUI programming. By giving such objects names and attaching the methods for handling events, OOP graphical programming allows the programmer to "say a lot" with very little code. Thus, for instance, a GUI front-end to customize an operating system can be built with only a line or two of code for each control option.

Some abstraction in GUI design is sacrificed but more programmer control is achieved by use of a high-level language program with embedded calls to the graphical tools of the MacIntosh Toolkit GUI environment. Considerable abstraction is still available through access to the high-level window and event functions of the operating system. The third application makes use of these functions to

build an application program for simulating laboratory experiments with digital filters.

The final example illustrates the abstraction available through generalization (platform-independent FIGS routines) and increased functionality (extension from 2D to 3D with rendering) within the framework of a procedural language. This application illustrates the ease with which 3D objects may be transformed using high level routines based on homogeneous coordinates.

Graphical Programming in *Visual Basic*

Graphical programming languages like *Visual Basic* closely approximate the ideal of object-oriented programming. This is accomplished by a radical revision of conventional program design. Rather than writing code which defines and displays graphical objects, graphical programming starts with graphical objects and embeds code that defines their behavior. This new paradigm represents a profound change in emphasis in program design and is best understood in object-oriented language.[5]

A generalized, three-step algorithm for graphical programming is stated as follows:

1. Construct the graphical objects that make up the user interface.

2. Define attributes for the objects to customize their appearance and behavior.

3. Embed code in each object to define methods for implementing its messages.

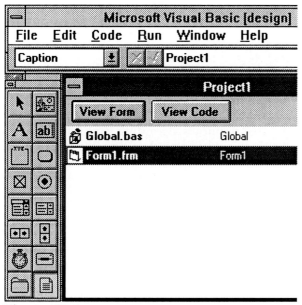

Figure 12.8
The *Visual Basic* project design environment.

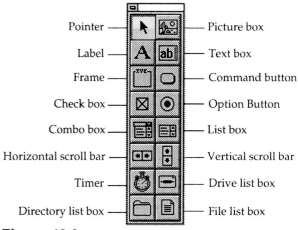

Figure 12.9
The *Visual Basic* Toolbox.

The purpose of the GUI environment is to provide standard tools for carrying out this three-step algorithm.

Features of *Visual Basic* Language

Visual Basic is essentially a hybrid of *Microsoft QuickBasic* and Microsoft's *Basic Professional Development System*. Among its useful features are the following:

- It provides an object-oriented, project-based environment for creating Windows applications. Three elements of this environment shown in Figure 12.8 include the *master control menu* for designing the application, a *Project Window* containing the GUI window (Form1.frm) and global Basic code, and a *Toolbox* of graphical objects.

- The Toolbox objects are controls such as command buttons, option buttons, scroll bars, and menu bars which can be embedded in the form to create the GUI window. The various tools of the Toolbox are labeled in Figure 12.9.

- Each graphical object inherits a set of *properties* (attributes), depending on its class. *Forms* are objects which inherit a certain class of properties, *text boxes* inherit a

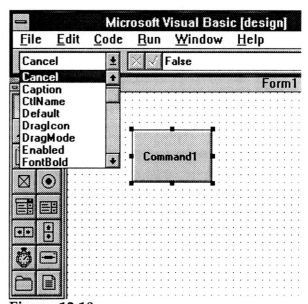

Figure 12.10
Partial list of attributes of Command1 button.

different set, and *command buttons* still another. A few of the attributes of the Command1 button on Form1 are shown in Figure 12.10.

- A variety of *messages* can be sent to these objects. The menu of actions supported for event-driven programming include clicks, double clicks, dragging, key presses, and the clock. Some of the messages available to the Form1 object are shown in the Proc menu of Figure 12.11.

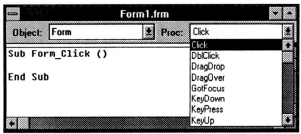

Figure 12.11
Partial list of messages which can be assigned to Form1.

- Each graphical object has an associated code window in which more complex *methods* associated with the object are embedded. Figure 12.11 shows the skeletal program associated with Form1 which opens when Form1 is double-clicked.

- Applications can display multiple windows and communicate with other applications through dynamic data exchange (DDE).

- *Visual Basic* provides a *Shell* function for executing operating system commands and running other programs. This is useful for improving the graphical user interface for existing programs and in building applications which integrate other applications.

- The language supports several data types including *integer*, *long* (integer), *single* (floating), *double* (floating), *currency* (fixed decimal), and *string*.

- It supports a hierarchy of variable scoping, from the local *procedure* level, through the *form* and *module* level, to the *global module* level.

- It supports several standard control structures, including *If...Then...Else*, *Select Case*, *Do* loops, and *For* loops.

To summarize the *Visual Basic* graphical programming metaphor, a GUI application program is a set of one or more forms and associated controls, all of which may contain embedded code segments that can be activated by user-supplied events. Rather than dwell on the details, let's illustrate graphical programming by building two application programs.

GUI Application 1: *MiniOp* – Simple Operating System Shell

Assume you are a consultant to a small, start-up enterprise with limited data processing experience and capability. Prior to hiring you as a consultant, the company switched from a 640K, 8088-based machine to a 386SX machine with 4Mb of memory and the Windows operating environment. The hardware supplier advised the company's CEO that a software package containing a good word processor, spreadsheet, and relational data base was really all that the company required. They subsequently purchased MS-Word, MS-Excel, and dBASE. Since many of the company records are in 5.25 inch floppy disk format, and they want to migrate towards 3.5 inch floppy disk format, the new machine has both a 5.25 inch and 3.5 inch floppy drive.

The company must rely on several relatively inexperienced, part-time clerical staff and data input personnel to handle data processing. The CEO has asked you to develop a user-friendly, specialized operating system shell which will perform a limited number of disk operations and allow personnel access to the three applications programs. Working closely with the CEO, you determine that the specialized shell should have the following functional specifications.

MiniOp System Specifications:

1. Button-selectable disk operations to
    1.1 Format either drive A: or drive B:,
    1.2 List the directories of either disk A: or disk B: in a scrollable window,
    1.3 Copy either A: → B: or B: → A:.

2. Button-selectable options to run the programs
    2.1 MS-Word,
    2.2 MS-Excel,
    2.3 dBASE.

3. Upon turning the machine on, a MiniOp menu providing functions 1 and 2 appears.

4. After executing any of the functions in 1 and 2, the system returns to the MiniOp menu.

MiniOp Design and Implementation

The design of *MiniOp's* GUI directly reflects the system specifications. These are readily imple-

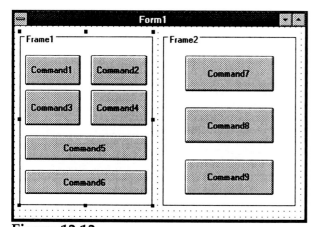

Figure 12.12
Results of Step 1. Constructing the graphical objects used by MiniOp.

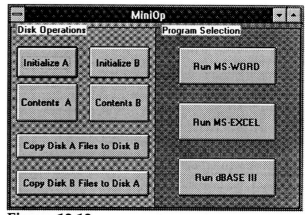

Figure 12.13
Results of Step 2. Resetting attributes to customize the MiniOp controls. This is the GUI presented to the user.

mented within the general framework of the three-step graphical program design algorithm:

Step 1 – Construct the graphical objects

1.1 *Visual Basic* is opened and two frames dragged onto the Form1 window. Frame1 will contain the disk operation controls and Frame2 will contain the program run options. Frames correspond to both a logical and physical grouping of functions.

1.2 Control buttons Command1...Command6 corresponding to the six disk operations specified in (1) are dragged onto Frame1.

1.3 Control buttons Command7...Command9 corresponding to the three applications programs specified in (2) are dragged into Frame2. The status of the GUI design at this point is shown in Figure 12.12.

Note that, throughout the design, the appearance (i.e., graphical layout) of the GUI interface is completely fluid. That is, at any point in the design, buttons, boxes, frames, and forms may be moved and resized. Thus, the *Visual Basic* graphical design editor serves for graphical objects much as a word processor does for text.

The next step in the design of the MiniOp GUI serves to customize it to our particular applications and name the graphical objects for use in subsequent embedded code.

Step 2 – Redefine attributes to customize controls

2.1 The most obvious attribute we need to redefine in order to enhance the mnemonic value of the controls is the Caption. We successively select Command1 and change its caption from Command1 → Initialize A, Command2 → Initialize B, and so on up to Command9 → Run dBASE III. In addition, Form1 is changed to MiniOp, F r a m e 1 to Disk Operations, and Frame2 to Program Selection.

2.2 The second attribute requiring redefinition is the CtrlName. This is the name used to address the object in subsequent code segments. It is helpful to redefine the CtrlName of Format A to FormatA, Contents A to DirA, Run dBASE III to dBASE, and so on.

2.3 A final attribute of the frames which is useful for visual cueing is BackColor. We select a pale red for the set of disk operations as a warning that damage can be done if the wrong button is pushed. A relaxing, pale blue is chosen as the workspace background for the *Word*, *Excel*, or *dBASE* options.

2.4 Finally, the form and frames are resized and positioned to present a pleasing, unified GUI menu window shown in Figure 12.13.

Step 3 – Embed code to build methods

At this point the "look and feel" of the GUI is pretty much determined. If the application is executed, the buttons will appear to depress nicely when pushed, but, of course, nothing will happen because we have not yet added the methods to the graphical objects.

Methods are attached to *Visual Basic* objects by double clicking the object in design mode and inserting Basic code into the skeletal program which appears. Since MiniOp is essentially a translation program to convert GUI commands into the equivalent DOS/Windows commands, our main task is to insert these lower-level commands into the *Visual Basic* subroutines attached to each control.

Using the Shell function of *Visual Basic*, the translation of the GUI "Run" commands are accomplished by a single line of code. After double-clicking the *Run* MS-WORD button, we edit the skeletal WORD_Click() subroutine to read:

```
Sub WORD_Click ()
    z1 = Shell("C:\winword\winword.exe", 1)
End Sub
```

Equivalent messages are embedded in subroutines EXCEL_Click() and dBASE_Click(). Now each of the *Run* buttons contains the appropriate method for carrying out the message the user sends it by clicking the *Run* button at run time.

We follow a similar strategy to embed methods in the *Initialize* buttons. Double clicking the *Initialize A* button opens the code window for subroutine *FormatA_Click()* into which we insert the Shell command to give:

```
Sub FormatA_Click ()
    x = Shell("Command.COM /C Format A:", 1)
End Sub
```

Parallel code is generated for *Initialize B*. Similar Shell commands are embedded in the Copy buttons. Subroutine CopyAtoB is edited to read:

```
Sub CopyAtoB_Click ()
    x = Shell("Command.COM /C Copy A:*.* B:", 1)
End Sub
```

When the *Copy Disk A Files to Disk B* button is clicked at run time, the appropriate DOS window is opened and commands issued.

The Shell command was proving so useful that we attempted to implement the Contents buttons by issuing the DIR command through the Shell function. The system did function as directed, but the results were unsatisfactory because the directory flashed on the screen and immediately disappeared as control returned to the MiniO*p* GUI window. So some other strategy was required.

The *File list box* tool from the Toolbox is the ideal solution to the problem. The *file list box* displays the files contained in the current directory in a scrollable window. So we return to step 1 of the GUI design algorithm and drag two file list boxes,

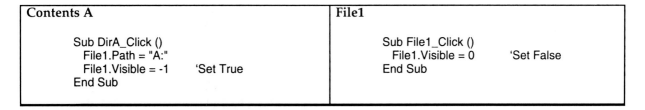

Contents A	File1
Sub DirA_Click () 　　File1.Path = "A:" 　　File1.Visible = -1 　　'Set True End Sub	Sub File1_Click () 　　File1.Visible = 0 　　'Set False End Sub

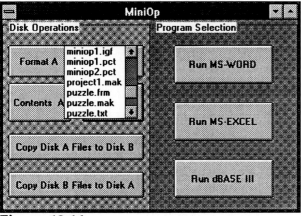

Figure 12.14

Run time operation of **MiniOp** after clicking *Contents B* button. Clicking the file list window causes it to disappear and redisplay the **MiniOp** GUI window.

File1 and *File2*, into the vicinity of the [*Initialize + Contents*] buttons. In step 2 we set their **Visible** attribute to False so that they will not appear, initially, at run time.

The control strategy we would like to implement for displaying the contents of disks A and B is the following:

- Upon clicking the *Contents A* button, the scrollable *File1* window will appear superimposed on the [*Initialize A + Contents A*] buttons.

- Upon clicking the *File1* window, it will disappear.

Embedding the following code in the *Contents A* and *File1* objects implements these messages.

Parallel methods are attached to the *Contents B* and *File2* objects. The results of clicking *Contents B* at run time are shown in Figure 12.14.

In concluding the discussion of **MiniOp**, several observations are in order. First is that specification 3 is implemented by selecting the *Make EXE File* option under *File* in *Visual Basic* and issuing the **MiniOp** command in the *AUTOEXEC.BAT* file. Second, the reader should note that the average method in this GUI application requires only one line of Basic code. A skillful *Visual Basic* programmer could create this practical GUI application in about 15–20 minutes.

Finally, this example illustrates the power of abstraction and its incarnation in object-oriented programming. The programming environment provides a toolkit of standard graphical objects, default values for their attributes, and integrated event processing for standard messages such as clicking. By handling all the bookkeeping for subroutine naming, control array generation, and so on, *Visual Basic* frees the application programmer to concentrate on the logic and control of the algorithm rather than the nitty-gritty details associated with attractive design.

MiniOp illustrates how useful applications can emerge from a graphical programming environment with a minimum of programming effort. Next, we turn to an interesting graphics application that requires substantially more programming.

GUI Application 2: 15-Puzzle Design

Suppose your AI instructor has assigned a project in heuristic search concepts based on the 15-Puzzle desk accessory supplied with the Macintosh operating system. Rather than use the University's Macintoshes, you would prefer to study the 15-Puzzle on your own new Windows-based 486 machine. Since the 15-Puzzle did not come with the Windows desk accessories, you decide to build your own 15-Puzzle with *Visual Basic*.

To learn how the puzzle operates, you spend a few minutes getting acquainted with it and solving it on one of the University's Macs (see Figures 12.15-16).

Figure 12.15
Original state of
Macintosh 15-Puzzle
desk accessory.

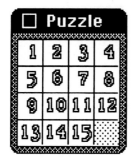

Figure 12.16
Final state of 15-Puzzle
(puzzle solved).

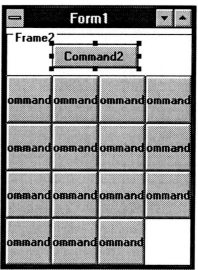

Figure 12.17
The completed geometric design of the GUI for the
15-puzzle. This represents the design at the end of
step 1. The *form* of the GUI now exists, but the
content is still missing.

Design Specifications for Puzzle

You decide that the *Visual Basic Puzzle* should
perform identically to the Macintosh *Puzzle* with
the following three exceptions:

1. It should allow reinitialization at any point
    during play.

2. It should include both even and odd
    permutation groups.[6]

3. It should signal successful solution through
    audio feedback.

Again, we follow the generalized, three-step
graphical programming algorithm.

Step 1 - Construct the graphical objects

1.1 *Visual Basic* is opened and we drag a single
     frame (Frame2 in Figure 12.17) which will
     serve as the outline of our puzzle and
     contain all the tiles and controls.

1.2 A square command button is dragged to
     the upper left corner of what will become
     the tile array of the puzzle. This button
     automatically assumes the name
     Command1 but shows only as "ommand"
     in Figure 12.17.

1.3 Command1 button is copied and pasted
     fourteen times to complete the array of
     fifteen tiles. This process instructs *Visual
     Basic* to create a control array in which each
     button has the same name, Command1,
     but unique indices ranging from one to
     fifteen.

1.4 A second control button, Command2, is
     dragged to the top of the puzzle as shown
     in Figure 12.17. This control will eventually
     send the message to randomize the puzzle.

Step 2 - Redefine attributes to customize the controls

2.1 The *Caption* of Form1 is changed to
     "Puzzle".

2.2 The *Caption* of Frame2 is changed to the
     null string.

2.3 The *BackColor* of Frame2 is changed to
     maroon by a color chart menu.

2.4 The following changes are made to the
     attributes of Command1 tiles. Changes are
     necessary for one tile only—the other tiles
     of the array inherit the changes.
     Caption: Command1 changed
      individually to 1,2,3,…,15.
     CtlName: Command1 → Tile.
     FontSize: 8.25 → 18.

2.5 The following changes are made to the
     attributes of the Command2 button.
     Caption: Command2 → Initialize
     CtlName: Command2 → Start

Figure 12.18
The 15-puzzle visual interface after Step 2. This completes the graphical design and labeling of the GUI. Note that at this stage the puzzle "looks correct" but still knows nothing of the rules of play or state representation.

The visual interface of the 15-puzzle GUI is now complete and is shown in Figure 12.18.

Step 3 - Embed code to build methods

Determining the "look and feel" of the GUI by performing Steps 1 and 2 is the easy part of designing the 15-puzzle. Building the methods to implement constraints and actions of the game is considerably more difficult. What specific problems must we solve?

- A state function which specifies the board state must be developed.

- A method for randomizing the tiles at any point during play must be provided.

- A legal move generator must recognize legal moves of 1, 2, or 3 tiles and implement them.

- A final state detector must continuously monitor for both legal puzzle solution states (1 → 15 and 15 → 1) and respond with audible and visual feedback.

Solution Algorithm

An appropriate choice of representation is essential for an efficient solution to the puzzle. The natural data structure to represent the puzzle state is a 4 × 4 matrix which we will call State(I,J). If row 3, column 2 contains Tile 10, then State(3,2) = 10. This variable array, the designator of the blank tile location, (Rblank, Cblank), and several other global variables are defined in the Global.BAS window shown below.

Global.BAS Specifications

```
Global State(4, 4) As Integer
                'Identifies tile state
Global GoalState1(4, 4) As Integer
                'Specifies Goal State 1
Global GoalState2(4, 4) As Integer
                'Specifies Goal State 2
Global Const D = 720
                'Geometric size of tile
Global Const Yoff = 720
                'Y offset value for row 1
Global Rblank, Cblank As Integer
                'Row, Column of blank tile
Global TileRow(1 To 15), TileCol(1 To 15) As
 Integer
                'Row, Column index for tile
```

Randomization Algorithm

The algorithm for initializing the tiles in random fashion may be summarized:

```
For row I = 1 to 4 do
For column J = 1 to 4 do
    Repeat
        Pick random number R on range 1 – 15
        If R has not yet been assigned
            State(I,J) = R
            Mark R as assigned
    Until State(I,J) is assigned.
```

This algorithm is implemented by double clicking the Initialize button and embedding the following code:

Initialize

```
Sub Start_Click ()
  Static TileV(16) As Integer
  Dim I, J, k As Integer
  ' Set up goal states
```

```
k = 0
For I = 1 To 4
For J = 1 To 4
  k = k + 1
  GoalState1(I, J) = k
  GoalState2(I, J) = 16 - k
Next J
Next I
Randomize
'Clear arrays and move tiles off board
For I = 1 To 15
  Tile(I).Move 0, 0
  TileV(I) = 0
Next I
For I = 1 To 4
For J = 1 To 4
  State(I, J) = 0
Next J: Next I
Frame1.BackColor = &H80&
' Now set each tile to a different random number
For I = 1 To 4
For J = 1 To 4
If (I * J > 1) Then
Do While State(I, J) = 0
  k = Rnd * 16
  If (k > 0) And (k < 16) Then
  If TileV(k) = 0 Then
    TileV(k) = 1
    TileRow(k) = I
    TileCol(k) = J
     'This shoudn't be necessary - but is.
    Tile(I).Visible = 0
    Tile(k).Move D * (J - 1), D * I
     'This shoudn't be necessary - but is.
    Tile(I).Visible = -1
    State(I, J) = k
  End If
  End If
Loop
End If
Next J
Next I
' Set row and column of blank tile.
Rblank = 1
Cblank = 1
End Sub
```

Several items of interest in the Start_Click() subroutine embedded in the Initialize button object include:

- The two possible goal states are defined as global, 4×4 arrays.

- When randomizing the State(I,J) array, element (I,J) = (1,1) is left blank. This initial condition is recorded as Rblank = 1 and Cblank = 1.

- The vector, TileV(K), is used to keep track of which tiles have been assigned.

Legal Move Generator and Final State Detector

The legal move rules of the 15-puzzle can be summarized as:

1. If a tile, Index, on the same row as Rblank is clicked, shift all tiles between Index and Rblank one space towards Rblank.

2. If a tile, Index, on the same column as Cblank is clicked, shift all tiles between Index and Cblank one space towards Cblank.

3. If a tile, Index, is clicked such that TileRow(Index) ≠ Rblank and TileCol(Index) ≠ Cblank, do nothing.

The logical object in which to embed both the legal move generator and the final state generator is the tile button being clicked. We therefore double click Tile button "1" and embed the following code in subroutine Tile_Click.

```
Sub Tile_Click (Index As Integer)
'SHIFT TILES WITHIN ROW
  If TileRow(Index) = Rblank Then
    dX = TileCol(Index) - Cblank
    dXm = Abs(dX)
    Select Case dXm
      Case 1        'Move one tile horizontally
        Tile(Index).Move Tile(Index).Left - dX * D,
          Tile(Index).Top
        State(Rblank, Cblank) = Index
        Temp = Cblank
        Cblank = TileCol(Index)
        TileCol(Index) = Temp

      Case 2        'Move two tiles horizontally
        Neighbor = State(Rblank, (Cblank + Sgn(dX)))
        Tile(Neighbor).Left = Tile(Neighbor).Left - Sgn(dX)
          * D
        Tile(Index).Visible = 0
        Tile(Index).Left = Tile(Index).Left - Sgn(dX) * D
        Tile(Index).Visible = -1
```

```
        State(Rblank, Cblank) = Neighbor
        State(Rblank, (Cblank + Sgn(dX))) = Index
        Temp = Cblank
        Cblank = TileCol(Index)
        TileCol(Index) = TileCol(Neighbor)
        TileCol(Neighbor) = Temp
      Case 3          'Move three tiles horizontally
        Neighbor1 = State(Rblank, (Cblank + Sgn(dX)))
        Neighbor2 = State(Rblank, (Cblank + 2 *
          Sgn(dX)))
        Tile(Neighbor1).Left = Tile(Neighbor1).Left -
          Sgn(dX) * D
        Tile(Neighbor2).Left = Tile(Neighbor2).Left -
          Sgn(dX) * D
        Tile(Index).Visible = 0
        Tile(Index).Left = Tile(Index).Left - Sgn(dX) * D
        Tile(Index).Visible = -1
        State(Rblank, Cblank) = Neighbor1
        State(Rblank, (Cblank + Sgn(dX))) = Neighbor2
        State(Rblank, (Cblank + 2 * Sgn(dX))) = Index
        Temp = Cblank
        Cblank = TileCol(Index)
        TileCol(Index) = TileCol(Neighbor2)
        TileCol(Neighbor2) = TileCol(Neighbor1)
        TileCol(Neighbor1) = Temp
    End Select
  End If
'SHIFT TILES WITHIN COLUMN
  If TileCol(Index) = Cblank Then
    dY = TileRow(Index) - Rblank
    dYm = Abs(dY)
    Select Case dYm
      Case 1              'Move one tile vertically
        Tile(Index).Move Tile(Index).Left, Tile(Index).Top
          - dY * D
        State(Rblank, Cblank) = Index
        Temp = Rblank
        Rblank = TileRow(Index)
        TileRow(Index) = Temp

      Case 2              'Move two tiles vertically
        Neighbor = State((Rblank + Sgn(dY)), Cblank)
        Tile(Neighbor).Top = Tile(Neighbor).Top -
          Sgn(dY) * D
        Tile(Index).Visible = 0
        Tile(Index).Top = Tile(Index).Top - Sgn(dY) * D
        Tile(Index).Visible = -1
        State(Rblank, Cblank) = Neighbor
        State((Rblank + Sgn(dY)), Cblank) = Index
        Temp = Rblank
        Rblank = TileRow(Index)
        TileRow(Index) = TileRow(Neighbor)
        TileRow(Neighbor) = Temp
      Case 3              'Move three tiles vertically
        Neighbor1 = State((Rblank + Sgn(dY)), Cblank)
        Neighbor2 = State((Rblank + 2 * Sgn(dY)),
          Cblank)
        Tile(Neighbor1).Top = Tile(Neighbor1).Top -
          Sgn(dY) * D
        Tile(Neighbor2).Top = Tile(Neighbor2).Top -
          Sgn(dY) * D
```

```
        Tile(Index).Visible = 0
        Tile(Index).Top = Tile(Index).Top - Sgn(dY) * D
        Tile(Index).Visible = -1
        State(Rblank, Cblank) = Neighbor1
        State((Rblank + Sgn(dY)), Cblank) = Neighbor2
        State((Rblank + 2 * Sgn(dY)), Cblank) = Index
        Temp = Rblank
        Rblank = TileRow(Index)
        TileRow(Index) = TileRow(Neighbor2)
        TileRow(Neighbor2) = TileRow(Neighbor1)
        TileRow(Neighbor1) = Temp
    End Select
  End If
'Test to see if puzzle is solved
  Str1$ = ""
  Str2$ = ""
  Str3$ = ""
  For I = 1 To 3
    For J = 1 To 4
      Str1$ = Str1$ + Str$(State(I, J)) + " "
      Str2$ = Str2$ + Str$(GoalState1(I, J)) + " "
      Str3$ = Str3$ + Str$(GoalState2(I, J)) + " "
    Next J
  Next I
  I = 4
  For J = 1 To 3
    Str1$ = Str1$ + Str$(State(I, J)) + " "
    Str2$ = Str2$ + Str$(GoalState1(I, J)) + " "
    Str3$ = Str3$ + Str$(GoalState2(I, J)) + " "
  Next J
  ' If puzzle solved, beep and blink.
  If (Str1$ = Str2$) Or (Str1$ = Str3$) Then
    For k = 1 To 5
      For I = 1 To 5
        Tile(I).Visible = 0
      Next I
      For J = 1 To 10
        Frame1.BackColor = &HC0&
      Next J
      Beep
      For I = 1 To 5
        Tile(I).Visible = -1
      Next I
      For J = 1 To 10
        Frame1.BackColor = &HC00000
      Next J
    Next k
  End If
End Sub
```

Several details of Tile_Click deserve mention.

- Clicking the tile with Caption = n sets Index = n. This allows easy and automatic identification of its location through Tile-Row(Index) and TileCol(Index) and subsequent calculation of the distance dX or dY between the selected tile and the blank location.

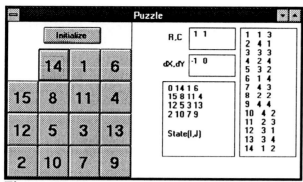

Figure 12.19
Puzzle form with Text windows used in debugging program.

- The magnitude of these distances, dXm and dYm, make natural pointers to Select Case statements for carrying out the allowed one, two-, and three-tile moves.

- The blocks of the Select Case statements carry out the tile moves and associated bookkeeping and reassignment of Rblank and Cblank.

- To test for problem solution, the string representing the present board state is tested for equality with the goal state strings, "1 2 3 4 ...15" and "15 14 13 ... 1."

- Upon detection of a goal state, the game board flashes between red and blue and beeps repeatedly.

- The symbolic assignment of background colors is done automatically by the designer selecting BackColor attribute for the frame and then selecting the desired color from a color menu window.

- Since each tile button is an element of the Tile array, the code in subroutine Tile_Click(1) automatically copies itself into Tile_Click(2) ... Tile_Click(15). All objects of the array inherit the changes made in any object of the array.

Graphical Debugging in GUI Design

Visual Basic supports all standard debugging tools, including setting breakpoints and stops, single stepping, and procedure stepping (stepping around procedure calls). Variables may be monitored throughout the design phase by use of the Immediate Window and through customized, designer text windows.

The Immediate Window provides access to the value of variables through two modes. The first mode involves embedding Debug.Print *[variables]* commands in the code. This prints the values of the designated variables into the Immediate Window at run time. The second mode involves using a Stop command at the point of interest in the code. At run time, execution halts at the Stop command and the designer can query the value of all variables with the "?*variable*" command within the Immediate Window.

Designer-customized text boxes provide an alternate mode for monitoring the value of variables at run time. In this mode, the designer drags text windows onto the form, attaches helpful captions if desired, and assigns the value of text strings associated with each window to a concatenated string containing the variables of interest. Figure 12.19 shows four text boxes which proved valuable in debugging the 15-puzzle application program. The text boxes dynamically displayed the variables

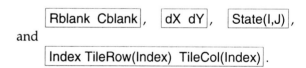

and

The output in the first two text boxes is generated by the commands (eliminated in the above version of Tile_Click):

```
Text1.Text = Str$(Rblank) + " " + Str$(Cblank)
Text2.Text = Str$(dX) + " " + Str$(dY)
```

The *Puzzle* form during an intermediate stage of program design and debugging is shown in Figure 12.19. Graphical debugging by the simultaneous monitoring of relevant variables and the GUI under design is a powerful development tool.

GUI Application 3: Digital Electronics Laboratory *Simulator*[7]

Four key concepts in digital electronics include:

- Signal to noise ratio (S/N),
- Analog to digital conversion (ADC),
- Digital to analog conversion (DAC),
- Filtering.

These concepts are usually investigated in an electronics laboratory environment consisting of the instruments illustrated in Figure 12.20.

There is great pedagogic value in actually hard-wiring the experiment outlined in Figure 12.20 and exploring digital electronics concepts by verifying the behavior of the system. However, time and equipment constraints generally limit the range of investigations possible in a real laboratory environment. Function generators have finite impedances and limited voltage ranges, laboratory ADCs and DACs have fixed bit resolutions (word length), and so on.

Laboratory experiments such as the one outlined in Figure 12.20 are ideal candidates for *simulation*. Simulation experiments are valuable investigation tools for two important reasons. First, they require an explicit model of the process under investigation. Experimental confirmation of the model predictions strengthens the credibility of the model's correctness. Deviation between experimental results and model predictions signals an error in experimental technique, model correctness, or both. The second advantage of simulation is that it extends the range of experimental investigation. ADCs and DACs are no longer limited to 12-bit precision, signal generators are no longer limited to ±15 volts, and instruments may have infinite bandwidths.

Simulator *System Specifications*

Next we list the specifications for both the system

capabilities and the graphical user interface for controlling the system. A conscious effort was made to exploit the high-level routines of the Macintosh toolkit to build a GUI for Simulator consistent with the look and feel of a well-designed WIMP application program.

1. Function generator controls
   1.1 Amplitude: user selectable
   1.2 Frequency: user selectable
   1.3 Phase angle between Generator #1 and Generator #2: default to 0°
2. ADC and DAC parameters
   2.1 Sampling frequency: user selectable
   2.2 Bit resolution: independently selectable
   2.3 Voltage range: independently selectable
3. Filter design
   3.1 Analog filter coefficients: user defined
   3.2 Cutoff and sampling frequencies: user defined
   3.3 Digital filter coefficients: derived from 3.1 and 3.2 + user modifiable
   3.4 Digital filter switch: user selectable – ON or OFF
4. GUI design
   4.1 Graphical windows for the display of signals
      4.1.1 Output of Generator #1
      4.1.2 Output of Generator #2
      4.1.3 Result of summing signals (i.e., input to ADC)
      4.1.4 Result of signal processing (i.e., output of DAC)
   4.2 Master control window with options
      4.2.1 GO to run simulation
      4.2.2 Filters to open filter coefficient window
      4.2.3 ADC & DAC to open parameter setting window
      4.2.4 Input Params to open generator parameters window
   4.3 Status window to report current status of system parameters

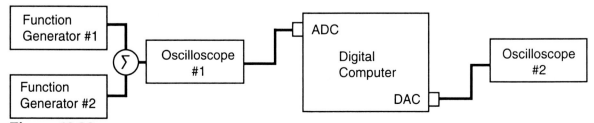

Figure 12.20
Laboratory setup for demonstrating S/N, ADC, filtering, and DAC.

4.4 Consistent WIMP desktop metaphor used throughout
  4.4.1 Application control completely event driven through mouse
  4.4.2 Alert box used to guide user
  4.4.3 Application written in THINK Pascal
  4.4.4 Compiled application executed by clicking application icon

Simulator *GUI Features*

Simulator

Simulator was written and compiled in Think Pascal to create an executable object file. Double clicking the Simulator icon displays the six windows shown in Figure 12.21.

The graphical information presented in Figure 12.21 illustrates an important concept of noise in signal processing. This figure also demonstrates the power of a well-designed GUI for visualizing system behavior. Note that it was generated by just three clicks of the mouse button.

S/N Example

An effective GUI provides the simulation application user with an intuitive mechanism for varying system parameters and exploring the resulting

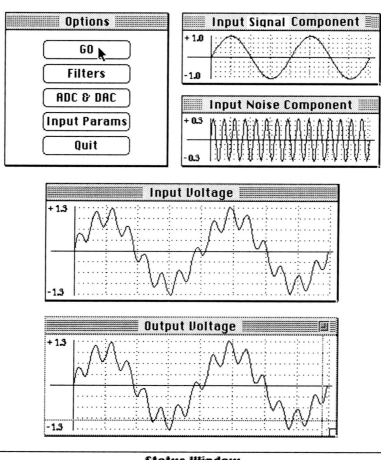

Figure 12.21
Simulator windows for program control, signal plotting, and status reporting. Shown are default values resulting from the first GO command.

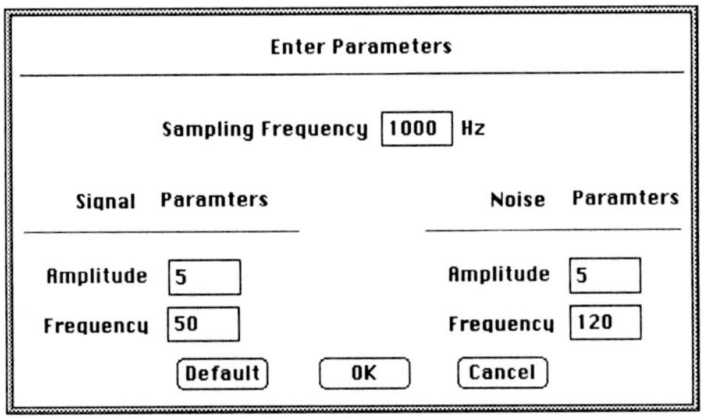

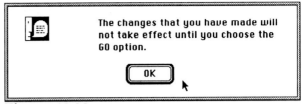

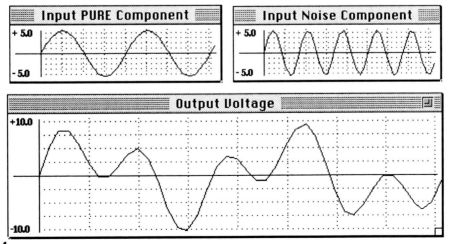

Figure 12.22
The Enter Parameters window opens upon clicking Input Params control button. New parameters are entered by clicking in the parameter box and editing the values. When all values are entered, the OK button is clicked.

Figure 12.23
Alert dialog box available to GUI designers for assisting users..

system behavior. Let's see how Simulator does this.

Suppose, for instance, that we want to know what a five volt, 50 hz signal combined with five volt, 120 hz noise looks like when sampled at 1000 hz. The logical selection in the Options control window for changing these parameters is Input Params. Clicking on this button opens the Enter Parameters window shown in Figure 12.22. Clicking in the appropriate parameter boxes allows us to edit the input parameters to the desired values shown.

Upon clicking the OK button of the Enter Parameters window, another useful feature char-

acterizing well designed GUIs is exhibited. In order to display the simulation results based on the new set of parameters, it is necessary to issue the GO command. To remind the user of this additional step required by the simulation, Simulator recognizes a change in parameters and issues the reminder to the user shown in the Alert window, Figure 12.23.

Following the advice in this window, we observe the changes shown in Figure 12.24.

DAC Resolution and Sampling Frequency

Subtle interactions between the word lengths of the ADC and DAC, the sampling rate, and signal frequencies are readily investigated with Simulator. To modify the resolution of the ADC and/or the DAC, we push the ADC & DAC button in the Options window. The window shown in Figure 12.25 opens, and we can edit in the desired number of bits in the ADC and DAC words.

Figure 12.24
New simulation experiment resulting from parameters shown in Figure 12.22. Note that the Output Voltage window is resizable which allows manual zooming by dragging the corner box. The x-axis has been expanded ~ 2 times.

We begin the next series of simulations by setting the word lengths $N_{ADC} = N_{DAC} = 12$ and the sampling frequency F_S =10,000 hz.

Figure 12.26 shows the effect of reducing the word length, N_{DAC}, of the DAC from the industrial standard of 12 bits down to 3 bits. Distortion becomes apparent (at this magnification) at 5–6 bits. The slight signal distortion apparent in Figure 12.24 is eliminated in the first three frames of Figure 12.26 by increasing the sampling frequency from 1,000 hz to 10,000 hz. The importance of sufficiently high sampling frequency is demonstrated dramatically in frame (d) which shows the distortion resulting from too low frequency (F_S = 500 hz).

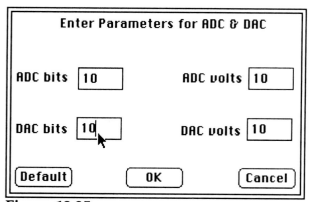

Figure 12.25
GUI window for modifying ADC and DAC parameters.

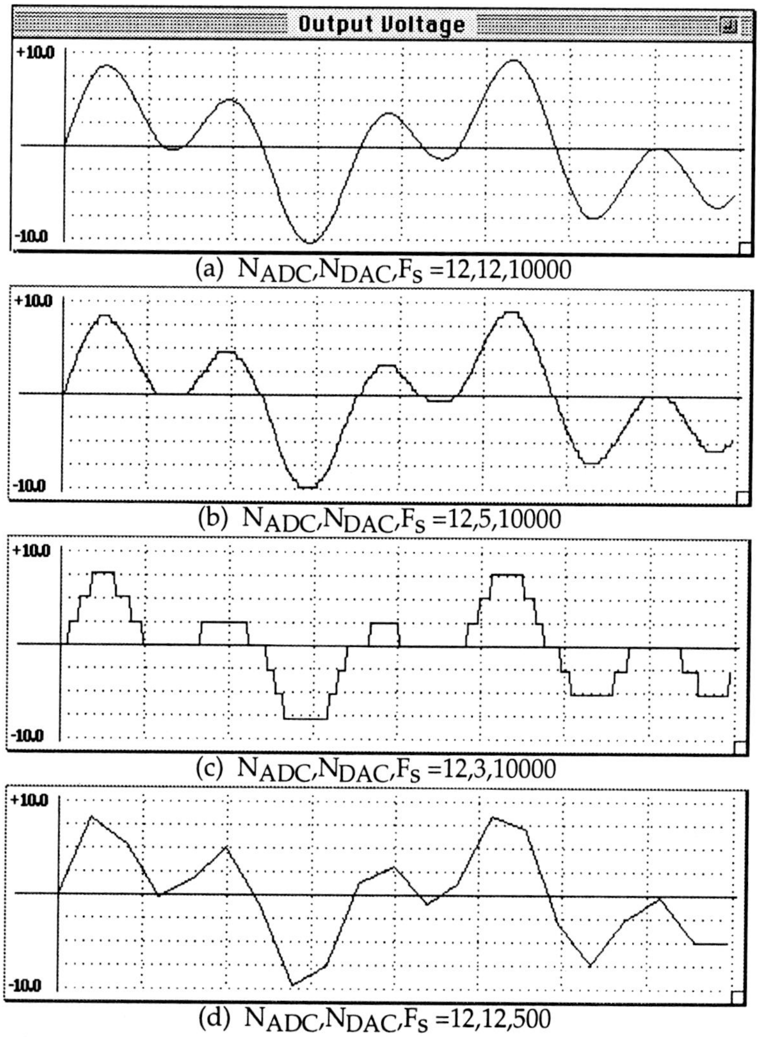

Output Voltage

(a) N_{ADC},N_{DAC},F_S =12,12,10000

(b) N_{ADC},N_{DAC},F_S =12,5,10000

(c) N_{ADC},N_{DAC},F_S =12,3,10000

(d) N_{ADC},N_{DAC},F_S =12,12,500

Figure 12.26
Sensitivity study of **Simulator** output to the digital to analog converter word length, N_{DAC}, and sampling frequency, F_S.

Note the ease with which such sensitivity studies are performed with a well designed GUI. Each **Output Voltage** graph in Figure 12:26 required one click of an **Options** window button, editing of one or two numeric values, and clicking the **OK** and **GO** buttons.

Filtering Example

A particularly strong feature of **Simulator** is its ability to apply a variety of digital filters to the incoming, digitized signals by specifying their analog filter coefficients. The subject of analog and digital filters is non-trivial and discussed in depth in Perdikaris.[8] While we do not have space to go into detail, some feeling for filter theory may be gained from the following relationships.

Expressed in Laplace transform notation, the behavior of a filter is defined by the transfer function, *G(s)*, relating the filter's output, *Y(s)*, to its input, *X(s)*, through:

$$Y(s) = G(s) X(s), \qquad [12.1]$$

where s is the complex frequency, $i\omega$.

A general, parametric form for the transfer function may be written as a partial fraction expansion,

$$G(s) = \frac{P_n s^n + P_{n-1} s^{n-1} + \ldots + P_1 s + P_0}{Q_n s^n + Q_{n-1} s^{n-1} + \ldots + Q_1 s + Q_0}. \quad [12.2]$$

Various filter characteristics (e.g., low-pass, high-pass, and band-pass) are specified by selecting the appropriate set of (P_n, Q_n) coefficients. To build an nth order, low-pass Butterworth filter, for example, one sets $P_0 = 1$ and Q_i according to Table 12.1.

Let's see if we can recover our 50 hz signal from the mixture of signal and 120 hz noise. To set the analog filter coefficients, we click the **Filters** button in the **Options** control window. A **Digital Filter Coefficients** window opens, and we click the **Analog** button. This opens an **Analog Filter Coefficients** window in which we enter the coefficients from Table 12.1. Then we enter the cutoff frequency and the sampling frequency. From these parameters, **Simulator** computes the digital filter coefficients. Upon clicking **GO**, **Simulator** then applies the digital transfer function to the input signal to produce the filtered output shown in Figure 12.27. Note the reemergence of the 50 hz signal as the filter order increases.

Table 12.1
Q Coefficients for nth Order Butterworth Filter

n	Q_0	Q_1	Q_2	Q_3	Q_4	Q_5
1	1	1	–	–	–	–
2	1	1.414	1	–	–	–
3	1	2	2	1	–	–
4	1	2.613	3.414	2.613	1	–
5	1	3.24	5.24	5.24	3.24	1

Concepts of filtering become much more intuitive after observing a series of simulation experiments like those in Figure 12.27. The key to effective simulation applications is a well-designed GUI exemplified in **Simulator**.

Simulator *Implementation*

Simulator is implemented in approximately 1,200 lines of Pascal code.[9] The Macintosh toolkit routines were used extensively in an attempt to maximize program abstraction.

The Environment

To establish the WIMP environment for **Simulator**,

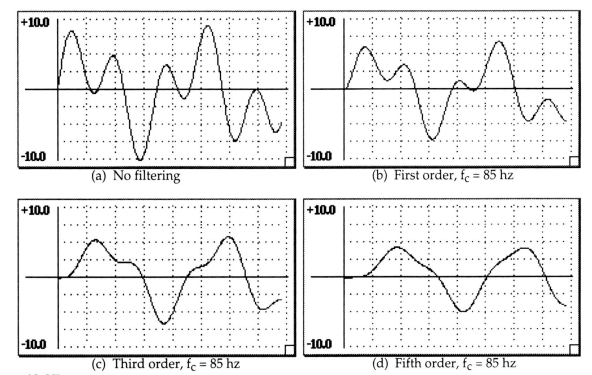

(a) No filtering

(b) First order, $f_c = 85$ hz

(c) Third order, $f_c = 85$ hz

(d) Fifth order, $f_c = 85$ hz

Figure 12.27
Effects of Butterworth low-pass filtering in **Simulator**.

the following sequence of operations is implemented.

```
procedure setup;
    WindowInit;
    MenuInit;
    ControlInit;
    MainLoop;
end;
```

WindowInit defines the windows that the program will use. In the Macintosh environment, for instance, this involves establishing pointers to the window definitions stored in the resource file. MenuInit defines the menus that the program will use. In the Macintosh environment, this involves obtaining pointers to the menu definitions stored in the resource file and displaying the menu bar. ControlInit follows a similar pattern as it relates to controls (or buttons or gadgets). MainLoop establishes the primary controll loop which monitors user input and interprets it as messages to the component objects of the program. Let's examine MainLoop in more detail.

MainLoop

The basic event-driven mode used in Simulator's GUI is illustrated in the following code segment.

```
procedure MainLoop;
begin
    Done := FALSE;
    while gDone = FALSE do
        HandleEvent;
end;
```

The HandleEvent procedure interprets an event that the user has initiated, such as a mouse click, and executes the appropriate action. This is usually done by examining the information that the operating system has returned about the event. This information may include such specifics as what window or control the user selected.

HandleEvent

In HandleEvent the richness and power of program abstraction become apparent. Consider the following Simulator routine.

Procedure **HandleEvent**

```
procedure HandleEvent;
{Handle an event that occurs - all actions take place
because of an event.}
  var
   gotOne: BOOLEAN;
   theChar: CHAR;
   dummy: BOOLEAN;
 begin

  if gWNEImplemented then
{Different versions of the MAC OS need a cerrtain}
{version of how to pass time to the system.}
   gotOne := WaitNextEvent(everyEvent, gTheEvent,
SLEEP, nil)
  else
   begin
    SystemTask;
    gotOne := GetNextEvent(everyEvent, gTheEvent);
   end;

 if gotOne then          {Did something happen???}

  case gTheEvent.what of

   mouseDown:            {Mouse button clicked...}
   HandleMouseDown;
   keyDown, autoKey:     {Key pressed, handle
                          APPLE-key combinations..}
    begin
    theChar := CHR(BitAnd(gTheEvent.message,
     charCodeMask));
    if (BitAnd(gTheEvent.modifiers, cmdKey) <> 0) then
     HandleMenuChoice(MenuKey(theChar));
    end;
   updateEvt:            {A window has been uncovered
                          and needs updating.}
    begin
    BeginUpdate(WindowPtr(gTheEvent.message));
                         { ALWAYS begin the update..}
    DrawControls(WindowPtr(gTheEvent.message));
                         {Redraw ALL controls..}
    CleanUpWins;      {Redraw all axes.and label}
    if READY_YET then   {Only do this if the user has
                          pressed GO at least one time}
    {This check is needed because all the windows
    generates update events when first created, and
    this would have caused flickering of the windows.}
    begin
        if WindowPtr(gTheEvent.message) = InWin
        then
            DoGraphs(1);
         if WindowPtr(gTheEvent.message) = OutWin
        then
            DoGraphs(2);
        if WindowPtr(gTheEvent.message) = NoiseWin
        then
            DoGraphs(3);
        if WindowPtr(gTheEvent.message) = PureWin
        then
```

```
        DoGraphs(4);
        if WindowPtr(gTheEvent.message) =
        ControlWin
        then
            ShowSettings;
    end;
    EndUpdate(WindowPtr(gTheEvent.message));
      { Don't forget to finish the update..}
    end;
  end;
end;
```

Note the range and variety of toolkit routines for carrying out complex tasks such as detecting program windows which have been uncovered and updating the graphical information which has been overwritten. Without abstract routines like Get-NextEvent, BeginUpdate, and DrawControls, Simulator would have required several times as much code to provide the same functionality.

GUI Application 4:
FIGSView—3D Object Manipulator

The final example of GUI applications design is a special purpose, 3D object viewing and manipulating program called FIGSView. FIGSView allows the user to select and manipulate an object in 3D space using an intuitive menu with mouse-controlled 2D input.

FIGSView is written in *Turbo Pascal for Windows* and exploits the high-level 3D routines from FIGS, a subset of the modeling/graphics language, PHIGS.[10] The design criteria for FIGSView are summarized as follows.

FIGSView *Specifications*

1. The program should provide an easy-to-use GUI to allow the user to select the following viewing options:
    1.1 Object choice (toggles between torus and cube)
    1.2 Rendering mode (toggles between wireframe and solid rendering)
    1.3 Projection mode (toggles between perspective and orthographic)
    1.4 Eyepoint location (jogs along z-axis)
    1.5 Scaling along all 3D axes
    1.6 Translation along all 3D axes
    1.7 Rotation about all 3D axes

2. Implementation should be in a machine-independent, high-level language.
    2.1 Pascal was selected to remain consistent with the main text language.

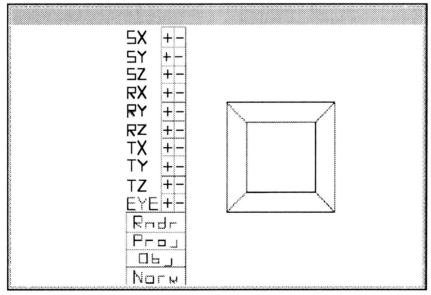

Figure 12.28
Graphical User Interface for *FIGSView.* Clicking on the "+" and "–" buttons causes action in the plus and minus direction. "Rndr" toggles the rendering mode between wireframe and solid; "Proj" toggles the projection mode between perspective and orthographic; "Obj" toggles object type between cube and torus; and "Norm" normalizes objects to their initial state.

2.2 All system and machine dependent code was isolated to interface units.

2.3 The user interface should appear as a resizable, relocatable window.

2.4 All actions should occur as event-driven (mouse) commands.

FIGSView *GUI Features and Performance*

Upon double clicking the *FIGSView.exe* application in a MS-Windows environment, the window shown in Figure 12.28 opens and displays a small cube in the work area. Several clicks on the "+" option of each of the scaling commands, SX, SY, and SZ produce the head-on, perspective view shown.

The minimalist menu structure reflects the fact that FIGS does not support string handling or the standard controls and *gadgets* available in many GUI toolkits. All symbols were drawn by defining points and connecting them with the FIGS *fPolyline* function. Messages are sent to the system by clicking on the appropriate "+" or "–" buttons, causing jogging in the direction indicated. Clicking on the "Rndr," "Proj," and "Obj" buttons toggles the rendering mode, projection option, and object selection, respectively. The "Norm" command normalizes the object to its initial state.

Although the simple menu structure limits the generality of this application, the event-driven GUI allows the user to demonstrate the effects of the three most common 3D graphical transformations. FIGSView also provides a useful tool for exploring some of the more difficult concepts of computer graphics. For instance, the Necker illusion (Which face is closest?) illustrated in the wireframe rendering of Figure 12.29(a) is resolved by the solid rendering of Figure 12.29(b). The effect of clipping on the front surface of the viewing volume is apparent in Figure 12.29(c).

FIGSView *Implementation*

The general control structure for event-driven FIGS programming is shown in the following *generic* program.

Program **Generic**

```
program Generic;

uses WinTypes, WinProcs, FIGS;

pprocedure WinMain;
var
vd:        fVIEWDATA;
done:      fBOOL;
event:     fEVENT;
menuitm:   MENUITEM;
winhandle: fWINDOWHANDLE;
begin
fOpenFigs (FIGSONLY);
winhandle := fCreateWindow;
SetUpViews (winhandle);
SetUpSegments;
fEraseWindow (winhandle);
fDrawView (OBJECT_VIEW, FALSE);
fDrawView (MENU_VIEW, FALSE);
fSetEventMode (GETEVENTS);
done := FALSE;
while done <> TRUE do
begin
  fGetEvent (@event);
  case event.eventType of
   BUTTON2DOWN:
       done := TRUE;
   BUTTON1DOWN:
       if event.view = MENU_VIEW then
          begin
            menuitm := GetMenuitem
              (event.mousePos.x,event.mousePos.y);
            DoAction (menuitm);
            fDrawView (OBJECT_VIEW, TRUE);
          end;
  end;
end;
fSetEventMode (IGNOREEVENTS);
fDestroyWindow (winhandle);
fCloseFigs;
end;

begin
  WinMain;
end.
```

The power of a modeling/graphics language such as PHIGS is achieved through abstraction. Thus, through its implementation of fifty of the most powerful PHIGS routines, FIGS is able to accomplish sophisticated 3D transformation tasks with very compact code. Consider, for instance the **FIGSView** routine, *DoAction*, which performs the essential work of the application.

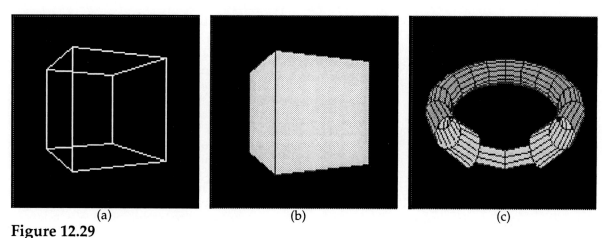

(a)   (b)   (c)

Figure 12.29
Three objects rendered by FIGSView. Scaling, translation, rotation, and rendering modes are all
controlled by clicking the mouse.

Procedure **DoAction**

```
procedure DoAction (action: MENUITEM);           XLATE_Y_PLUS:
var                                                  begin fTranslate (0, 5, 0, @m2); goto skip1; end;
 vd:  fVIEWDATA;                                  XLATE_Y_MINUS:
 m2:  f4x4MATRIX;                                    begin fTranslate (0, -5, 0, @m2); goto skip1; end;
 i, j: fINT;                                      XLATE_Z_PLUS:
label                                                begin fTranslate (0, 0, 5, @m2); goto skip1; end;
 skip1, skip2, skip3, skip4;                      XLATE_Z_MINUS:
begin                                                begin fTranslate (0, 0, -5, @m2); goto skip1; end;
 case action of
  SCALE_X_PLUS:                                   NORMALIZE:
    begin fScale (1.1, 1, 1, @m2);   goto skip1; end;   begin for i := 0 to 3 do
  SCALE_X_MINUS:                                           for j := 0 to 3 do
    begin fScale (0.90, 1, 1, @m2);  goto skip1; end;      begin
  SCALE_Y_PLUS :                                             m[i][j] :=  0.0;
    begin fScale (1, 1.1, 1, @m2);   goto skip1; end;        if i = j then
  SCALE_Y_MINUS:                                               m[i][j] :=  1.0;
    begin fScale (1, 0.90, 1, @m2);  goto skip1; end;         end;
  SCALE_Z_PLUS:                                            goto skip2; end;
    begin fScale (1, 1, 1.1, @m2);   goto skip1; end;
  SCALE_Z_MINUS:                                  EYEPOINT_PLUS:
    begin fScale (1, 1, 0.90, @m2);  goto skip1; end;   begin fQueryView (OBJECT_VIEW, @vd);
  ROTATE_X_PLUS:                                           vd.prp.z := vd.prp.z + 5.0;
    begin fRotateX (10, @m2);        goto skip1; end;      goto skip3; end;
  ROTATE_X_MINUS:
    begin fRotateX (-10, @m2);       goto skip1; end;  EYEPOINT_MINUS:
  ROTATE_Y_PLUS:                                         begin fQueryView (OBJECT_VIEW, @vd);
    begin fRotateY (10, @m2);        goto skip1; end;      if (vd.prp.z - 10.0) > 0.0 then
  ROTATE_Y_MINUS:                                             vd.prp.z := vd.prp.z - 5.0;
    begin fRotateY (-10, @m2);       goto skip1; end;      goto skip3; end;
  ROTATE_Z_PLUS:
    begin fRotateZ (10, @m2);        goto skip1; end;  RENDER_MODE:
  ROTATE_Z_MINUS:                                        begin fQueryView (OBJECT_VIEW, @vd);
    begin fRotateZ (-10, @m2);       goto skip1; end;      if vd.renderMode = WIREFRAME then
  XLATE_X_PLUS:                                               vd.renderMode := SOLID
    begin fTranslate (5, 0, 0, @m2); goto skip1; end;      else
  XLATE_X_MINUS:                                              vd.renderMode := WIREFRAME;
    begin fTranslate (-5, 0, 0, @m2); goto skip1; end;     goto skip3; end;
```

```
PROJECTION_STYLE:
      begin fQueryView (OBJECT_VIEW, @vd);
            if vd.projType = PARALLEL then
               vd.projType := PERSPECTIVE
            else
               vd.projType := PARALLEL;
            goto skip3; end;

OBJECT_TYPE:
      begin
            if currObj = CUBE_ID then
            begin
               fPostSegment (CUBE_ID,
                  OBJECT_VIEW, FALSE);
               fPostSegment (TORUS_ID,
                  OBJECT_VIEW, TRUE);
               currObj := TORUS_ID;
            end
            else
            begin
               fPostSegment (TORUS_ID,
                  OBJECT_VIEW, FALSE);
               fPostSegment (CUBE_ID,
                  OBJECT_VIEW, TRUE);
               currObj := CUBE_ID;
            end;
            goto skip4; end;

   else goto skip4; end; { case }

skip1:
fComposeMatrix (@m2, @m, @m);

skip2:
 if currObj = CUBE_ID then
 begin
  fOpenSegment (CUBE_ID);
   fOffsetElmntPtr (-1);
   fDeleteElmnt;
   fSetElmntPtr (0);
   fSetTransformation (@m, REPLACE);
  fCloseSegment;
 end
 else
 begin
  fOpenSegment (TORUS_ID);
   fOffsetElmntPtr (-1);
   fDeleteElmnt;
   fSetElmntPtr (0);
   fSetTransformation (@m, REPLACE);
  fCloseSegment;
 end;
 goto skip4;

skip3:
fComposeView (OBJECT_VIEW, @vd);

skip4:
end;
```

The key control algorithm and FIGS routine calls are shown in procedures **WinMain** and **DoAction**. The remainder of the approximately five hundred lines of FIGSView code is devoted primarily to defining the geometric objects and text used in the GUI window.[11]

FIGSView illustrates both the advantages and disadvantages of building GUIs with a machine-independent, standard graphics language. The programmer gains the advantage of access to powerful, abstract routines for easily performing complex tasks. The price paid for machine-independence is the loss of machine-dependent WIMP toolkits for easily constructing the windows, icons, menus, and controls which characterize modern GUIs.

Conclusions

Perhaps the most important contribution of computer graphics to computer science and software engineering is the concept of a supportive GUI development environment with full access to the toolkit of GUI design tools. The GUI development environment speeds the production of software applications by providing helpful debugging and diagnostic tools. The GUI toolkit provides graphical objects such as icons, menus, controls, windows, and the event handling routines for manipulating and interacting with these objects. This high level of abstraction enables the programmer to accomplish the same task with a few lines of code that would have required pages of code using more primitive graphical functions.

The high-level graphical objects available from GUI toolkits are best understood in object-oriented programming terms. Several GUI applications are developed from scratch using a variety of high-level and graphical programming languages. The abstraction provided by these programming environments makes it possible to develop sophisticated GUIs with a minimum of programming effort. Well-designed GUIs have proven to be the most important visualization tools in computer science.

Exercises

12.1 The discussion above states that alphabetic letters are meaningless as individual symbols. Is this true of all ASCII characters? What are the exceptions, and how do they get their meaning?

12.2 A typical icon is stored as 128 bytes. How many bits does an icon require? If the icon is square and there is one bit per pixel, what are the pixel dimensions of an icon? How many unique icons of this size are possible?

12.3 The discussion in this chapter indicates that we have not yet developed a syntax for expressing meaning from a string or configuration of icons. There are exceptions to this rule, particularly in nautical communications. Describe two such exceptions, and explain what can be said and how.

12.4 The icons of Figure 12.3(a) represent some of the most popular and powerful applications on the Macintosh. Identify as many of these applications as you can by scanning the hard disk of your campus computers, scanning trade journals, or asking your computer colleagues.

12.5 What is the difference between an *operating system* and an *operating environment*?

12.6 Scan the application programs available on your university's computer system or network for two examples: the best and worst cases of GUIs. Document the GUIs (or lack thereof) by screen dumps and comment on the features which make one a good interface and the other a poor interface.

12.7 In the discussion of sensitivity to good design, the text presented two personal experiences of poor industrial product design. From your own observation, describe two additional examples of poor design.

12.8 From your experience in working with computer systems, describe two examples of poor program design.

12.9 From your experience in working with application programs, describe one which best satisfies the transparency criteria for good GUI design and a second one which badly violates this principle.

12.10 Effective feedback at every stage of an application program's processing cycle is listed as an important principle of GUI design. Examine several programs that can be bogged down with a computationally intensive task, and describe the program and feedback mechanism that was most effective. Did any of the programs violate the feedback principle?

12.11 Many recent releases of popular application programs have shifted the balance between *simplicity* and *features* heavily toward the features side. Identify and discuss one such program and indicate the difficulties imposed by excessive menu selection and excessive nesting of menu options.

12.12 There are several significant differences between the Macintosh and Microsoft Windows approach to "doing windows." Identify these differences and discuss the pros and cons of each approach.

12.13 Open a document window on your favorite WIMP system and identify all of the messages which the window seems to understand with short, English phrases such as "Open yourself" and so on.

12.14 While remaining basically a command-line operating system, MS-DOS has added certain WIMP features in versions 4.0 and 5.0. Identify these features and document them with screen dumps.

12.15 Many of the OOP features of Microsoft's *Visual Basic* first appeared in Apple's *HyperCard*. List five of the features these two languages share which distinguishes them from standard procedural languages.

12.16 The text attempted to introduce *Visual Basic* using the OOP paradigm. List the distinguishing features of the language which justify this approach. Describe why it would be difficult to introduce *Visual Basic* as a standard procedural language.

12.17   Describe two additional applications programs that would be good candidates for programming in *Visual Basic*. Discuss what features of the application make them good candidates, and give a brief program specification for each.

12.18   Write a critical evaluation of the MiniOp application program, and suggest improvements and refinements.

12.19   Discuss the following statement in terms of *program abstraction:* MiniOp is a specialized operating system written in a graphical language (*Visual Basic*) which utilizes the graphical routines of a WIMP system (*Windows*) that is built on a command-line operating system (*DOS*).

12.20   Use *Visual Basic* or *HyperCard* to implement Conway's game of Life.

12.21   Write an application program of your choice in *Visual Basic* or *HyperCard*.

12.22   A curious characteristic of the 15-puzzle is that initial states are members of either an even or odd permutation group, and it is impossible, by legal moves alone, to convert from one to the other. Explore the implications of this statement by attempting to solve the Macintosh 15-puzzle in reverse order, 15-14-…-2-1.

12.23   Critique the algorithm for randomizing the puzzle tiles in subroutine Start_Click. Suggest an alternative algorithm based on a random shuffle.

12.24   What extensions would you suggest to *Simulator* to expand the range of simulation experiments?

12.25   Another valuable digital simulation program allows the user to drag AND, OR, and NOT gates to a design window, connect them, and observe the output for various combinations of digital input. The GUI of such a system is critical for its success. Sketch the overall design of such a digital designer, specify its properties, and indicate the GUI which would optimize its usefulness.

Endnotes

1. Laurel, Brenda, (ed),*The Art of Human-Computer Interface Design*, Addison-Wesley Publishing Company, Inc., Reading, MA (1990).
2. Shneiderman, Ben, *Designing the User Interface: Strategies for Effective Human-Computer Interaction*, Addison-Wesley Publishing Company, Inc., Reading, MA (1987).
3. Flanagan, Dennis, "Words and Pictures," *Pixel* **1**, No. 2, pp. 42–44, May/June (1990).
4. Apple Computer, Inc., *Inside Macintosh* I, p. I-32, Addison-Wesley Publishing Company, Inc., Reading, MA (1985).
5. Stevens, Al, "Visible Results with Visual Basic," *Dr. Dobb's Journal* **16**, No. 12, pp. 78–87, December (1991).
6. Tile puzzles such as the 8-Puzzle and the 15-Puzzle contain two disjoint permutation groups: even and odd. The even permutation group allows the solution $1 \rightarrow 15$ as shown in the Macintosh 15-Puzzle solution. The odd permutation group allows the reverse solution, $15 \rightarrow 1$. There is no allowed transformation which carries one group into the other. Random initialization will sample each class with equal frequency. We thank our student, John Marter, and mathematics colleague, Tom Fournelle, for calling this point to our attention.
7. This application was developed by Scott Singer, UW~Parkside student, as an independent project in *Real-time Computer Applications 450*.
8. Perdikaris, George A., *Computer Controlled Systems – Theory and Applications*, Kluwer Academic Publishers, Dordrecht, The Netherlands (1991).
9. *Simulator* source code is available upon request from the author:
      Morris Firebaugh
      Box 2000, UW-Parkside
      Kenosha, WI 53141
      morris@cs.uwp.edu
      (414)-595-2128   FAX: (414)-595-2056
10. FIGS was written by Dan Knudson. See Appendix B for the general structure of a FIGS program, a list of implemented routines, and their calling sequences.
11. A complete listing of *FIGSView* source code is available in DOS or Macintosh disk formats upon request from the author.

Chapter 13

Tools for Design and Engineering

Being trained in CAD is a relatively trivial aspect of engineering education. It is the overall integration of the computer into the engineering process that's important.
Joel Orr, President of Orr Associates[1]

If a computer system requires a student to spend 40 hours to get to the point where he can use it, then it is not effective in my opinion.
Woodie Flowers, MIT Professor of Engineering Design[2]

Finite element analysis is a computational technique for the solution of a variety of problems in such diverse fields as aircraft design, dam construction, modeling the motion of the inner ear, analysis of the stress in building components, and tectonic plate motion. In fact, finite element analysis is the foundation of the solution phase of modern computer-aided design (CAD).
McCormick, DeFanti, and Brown[3]

W e began the discussion of visualization tools with an introduction to the GUI tool kits available to programmers in building applications programs with modern interfaces. Next we turn to visualization tools of particular interest to designers and engineers. These application areas were the first to employ computer graphics extensively, and they continue to lead in the development of sophisticated visualization tools.

Due in part to their venerable history, Computer-Aided Design (CAD) software systems exhibit some of the best and worst features of software engineering, frequently in the same program. Among the best features are the range and sophistication of capabilities for the creation, grouping, dimensioning, organizing, transforming, and display of complex graphical objects. The development of many of the graphical algorithms and interactive techniques we have studied were motivated by their role in CAD systems.[4] However, because of their complexity and early origins, many CAD systems inherited command-line interfaces and the associated slow learning curves. One of the major challenges to both established CAD and Computer-Aided Engineering (CAE) systems has

been their complete redesign to incorporate modern OOP and GUI concepts.

Four reasons motivate this introduction to visualization tools for design and engineering.

- The features available on CAD tools illustrate many of the graphical algorithms presented in the text.

- The CAD interfaces presented to potential users make useful case studies in GUI design.

- CAE tools such as finite element analysis (FEA) provide methods for developing more authentic models for computer graphics applications.

- Readers may find the capabilities of the systems described appropriate for tasks they are considering.

The language of OOP provides the best context for introducing and understanding CAD tools. The graphical objects built by CAD tools generally

CADC Tools	CADD Tools	CAE Tools
3D Modeling programs	Drafting programs	Finite Element Analysis
Swivel 3D	*VersaCAD*	*COSMOS/M*
Easy to use	More complex	Very complex
Abstract and conceptual	Concrete and numerical	Concrete and physical
No dimensions required	Dimensions critical	Dimensions critical
No physics	Limited physics	Complete physics
Output:	Output:	Output:
Conceptual Design	Engineering Drawings	Deformations, strains

Figure 13.1
Spectrum of design and engineering tools.

correspond directly to real physical objects with properties such as color, density, and mass. Since complex manufactured objects are typically assembled from component parts, concepts such as hierarchy and class inheritance can be visualized in concrete terms. Techniques of layering and grouping become obvious strategies for dealing with the structure of complex objects.

Two other concepts stressed throughout the book reappear in this chapter. First is the power of abstraction. By giving names to graphical objects, it is possible to represent them as menu selections and construct libraries of the commonly used components of more complex objects. So, for instance, to draw a cube at some point on the screen, it is necessary only to select the cube object from a menu and click at the desired point.

The second concept is the importance of the physical validity of models. In order to perform accurate engineering analysis on the behavior of real objects under conditions of applied force, it is essential to include physical properties of mass and coefficients of elasticity. Finite element analysis is a tool of considerable precision for prototyping industrial components and building authentic models for computer graphics applications such as animation.

Classification of Design and Engineering Tools

Engineering design tools may be arrayed on the abstract ↔ concrete continuum shown in Figure 13.1. At one end of the spectrum lay the abstract *conceptual design* tools represented by the 3D modeling programs which help the designer to quickly

sketch the model s/he is visualizing. For purposes of classification in this text we designate these as CADC tools ("C" for *conceptual*). Next come the standard 2D and 3D drafting packages which enable the designer to quantify the abstract sketches generated by the modeler. These we classify as CADD for *computer-aided design and drafting* tools. Finally, by adding the properties of materials and forces, finite element analysis allows the engineer to study the behavior of the quantitative model generated at the CADD stage. FEA programs represent the most important example of the broader class of CAE—Computer-Aided Engineering—tools. An fine overview of CAD tools is given by Besant and Lui.[5]

Classes of Tools

Let's consider these three classes of design and engineering tools in a little more detail. An useful graphical survey of these topics is given by Kerlow and Rosebush.[6]

- **CADC: Conceptual Modeling Programs** – The first task of the design process usually involves sketching out the general system structure, often as a simple pencil sketch. Frequently this process is as informal as a "back-of-an-envelop" drawing, and the purpose is to help designers and their clients visualize the overall system design and geometric relationships between the major components of the design. This *free-hand sketch* stage of the design is very qualitative in nature and may use numerical values only for a rough estimate of the scale of the model. Skillful designers can create initial sketches in a few minutes for simple models and in a few hours for more complex systems. Modeling programs allow the designer to automate the initial design phase and then refine it with the added capabilities of realistic rendering of shading, shadows, and textures. For the same investment in time, the designer using CADC tools can generate much more realistic sketches and explore the effects of lighting and shadows on the appearance of the model.

- **CADD: Drafting Programs** – The next phase of design converts the qualitative sketch of the initial design into quantitative *detail drawings* required for the manufacturing process. The key concepts are precision, detail, and dimensioning. Every element and aspect of the model must be shown in the detail drawing with numerical dimensions sufficient for specifying the manufacture of the object. The relationships between the objects defined in the detail drawings are specified in *assembly drawings*. In addition to this geometric information, CADD programs should specify the tolerances, materials, surface finishes, and the bill of materials for complex structures. CADD programs have evolved from simple 2D drafting tools capable of producing correctly dimensioned blueprints to complex 3D systems capable of rendering models as shaded solids. Higher-end CADD programs include tools for constructive solid geometry, cutaway viewing, and specialized component libraries. In integrated manufacturing environments, the output of CADD programs may be routed directly to numerically controlled machinery (NCM) which implements the design with minimal human intervention. This integration is called CAD/CAM (CAD and computer-aided manufacturing).

- **CAE: Computer-Aided Engineering and Finite Element Analysis** – Engineers have traditionally used rules-of-thumb and canonical equations to guide the design of critical components of a system. These are reasonably accurate for simple objects and geometries, but as the complexity of a part increases, confidence in the predicted performance is lost. The traditional recourse for critical and safety-related components was

to build scale models and subject them to forces expected for the real object. Verification of engineering design by prototype testing is a very expensive, time-consuming process. Finite element analysis allows the realistic simulation of prototype building and testing at a fraction of the cost in a greatly reduced time frame. In addition, multiple models may be examined in order to optimize performance and save on material and manufacturing costs. In finite element analysis, the model is *discretized* into many small elements which are related by the laws of physics. Finite element analysis techniques have been refined and repeatedly tested and verified. The finite element analyses of properly constructed models are as trustworthy as those from scale-model prototypes, particularly when the uncertainties in scaling the results from prototypes is considered.

Automating Engineering Design

The obvious advantages of automation have irreversibly transformed design and engineering processes from manual operations to computerized systems in most design shops. The increased productivity and precision of CAD systems and the savings generated by substituting finite element analysis for prototype testing have converted cost conscious managers. However, there are additional, less obvious advantages to automating the design process which are worth considering. Among these are the following.

- **More attractive designs** – The sophisticated graphics possible with computer systems makes it possible to present beautifully rendered conceptual designs in 3D with cutaway views, realistic shading, and textures. Since approval of the preliminary design is generally the first hurdle before detailed design and engineering can proceed, it is critical to prepare the most attractive possible design. Well-rendered graphics will catch and hold the potential client's eye much more effectively than traditional line drawings or sketches.

- **Dealing with complexity** – The irreversible trend in industrial design is towards increasing complexity, as a glance under the hood of a modern automobile—compared to those of ten, twenty, or thirty years ago—

will confirm. Consider the thousands of engineering drawings necessary to specify all parts of such an automobile. Then consider the vastly more complex systems required in the space and nuclear power programs. Hierarchical data structures, subassembly architecture, and parts libraries of modern CAD systems provide tools capable of dealing with this complexity.

- **Effective archive and retrieval** – Most engineering drawings are modifications or extensions of previous engineering drawings. The magnetic media used for storage of designs and engineering analyses serves as an effective archive with efficient retrieval of source documents. Effective archival techniques involve standardization of part and subassembly structure notation which improves the efficient operation of the organization and its engineering protocols.

- **Distributed processing and teamwork** – Large engineering projects involve the work of many individuals on the primary task and numerous sub-assemblies. The coordination and integration of these efforts is facilitated by a network environment providing controlled access to the design of each component of the project. A multiple-workstation LAN sharing access to the engineering drawing archive provides the ideal environment for the design of subassemblies and their integration into the final design.

With this background in the motivation for computerized design and engineering tools, let's examine each class of tools and demonstrate the use of a leading implementation from each class to carry out realistic design examples.

Conceptual Design Tools - CADC

Suppose, as the group leader in an industrial design department, you want to gradually shift your design team over from the traditional pencil-sketch concept design mode to a computer system. None of the designers is a computer expert and, from your limited experience with CADD systems ported down from minicomputers, you are well aware of the long learning curve associated with conventional CAD systems.

What should a conceptual design tool provide?

As you begin the search for the ideal conceptual design tool, you list the following features it should have in order to gain acceptance from your computer-shy designers.

- **Good WIMP/GUI** – The program should maximize the use of graphics for selecting and manipulating objects. All messages sent to objects should utilize intuitive graphical techniques.

- **Numeric Options** – Although the majority of designs will rely on qualitative graphical input, there should be an option for overriding the graphical default values with direct numeric input.

- **Direct 3D manipulation with 2D controls** – Although it is difficult to visualize how it might be implemented, the system should provide direct manipulation of 3D objects in 3D space by some clever 2D sleight-of-hand.

- **Object design by sculpting** – The system should provide a minimal set of primitive objects which can be transformed into the desired shape in much the same way a sculptor chisels art objects from stone or a potter molds pottery from clay.

- **Object hierarchy** – In order that complex designs can be assembled from simpler objects or sub-assemblies, the system should support a parent-child hierarchy, hopefully with inheritance of characteristics like position and color.

- **Intuitive viewing options** – The program should provide options for orthographic and perspective projections from multiple viewpoints, minimally top/bottom, right/-left, and back/front.

- **Choice of rendering options** – The system should allow a choice of rendering modes, including wire frame, wire frame with hidden line removal, shaded, and Phong shading with user-specified, multiple light sources.

- **Minimal CAD features** – The program should provide a minimum set of the most useful CAD features, including multiple simultaneous views, rulers, snap grids, mirroring, lathing, extrusion, and zooming.

- **Library of 3D objects** – To avoid wasting time designing standard objects such as desks and chairs, there should be access to a library of *3D clip art* which can be cut and pasted into the 3D world scene.

As daunting as this list appears, commercial products for personal workstations now exist which provide all of these features and more. One such program is *Swivel 3D* by Paracomp, Inc.[7]

Additional concept design features

In addition to the essential features previously listed, *Swivel 3D* provides several advanced features which augment the quality of images possible and introduce new options for the presentation of conceptual designs. Among these are the following:

- **Skin objects** – Objects too complex to construct easily by lathing or extruding can be created by constructing linked objects defining the "skeleton" of the desired object and then stretching an elastic "skin" over the skeleton.

- **Special effects rendering** – Among the special effects which can be rendered are antialiasing, shadow calculation, projection of PICT images on 3D objects, and object edge enhancement.

- **Object attribute list** – Each object has an associated attribute list with user-defined fields such as type, weight, height, length, width, color, price, and so on.

- **Multiple file formats** – In addition to the RIB file format, *Swivel 3D* exports images to various paint and draw-type formats, including 24-bit PICT, 8-bit PICT, EPS, and DXF format for *AutoCAD*.

- **Animation** – Animation is readily accomplished by dragging an object through a series of positions and orientations which are recorded as key frames. A *tween* button then allows the user to specify how many frames should be computed in between the key frames.

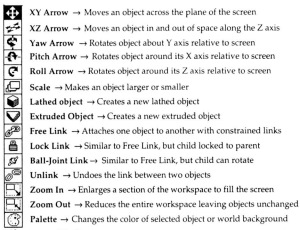

Figure 13.2
Tool menu available on *Swivel 3D* conceptual design package.

- *RenderMan*™ **interface** – *Swivel 3D* generates output files in RIB format which can be read and rendered photorealistically by *RenderMan*. As described previously, *RenderMan* offers advanced features such as texture mapping, transparency, and advanced shaders for wood, metal, plastic, stone, marble, and so on.

Swivel 3D tools

Before we demonstrate the use of this conceptual design program, let's examine the main objects constituting its GUI. Along the left-hand side of the work space, the menu of tools shown in Figure 13.2 is arrayed.

Numeric options for overriding the graphical default values are presented in four pull-down menu windows: World/Position, World/-Attitude, Object Position, and Object/Attitude. Figure 13.3 shows the World/Position window with various fields which can be edited and their default values. An identical window is associated with each object in the scene, allowing the user precise control of object position in 3D.

Numerical control of the orientation of the World scene and each individual object is provided by the Attitude window shown for a vase object in Figure 13.4.

Several other features discussed above are shown in the menu listings of Figure 13.5. The remaining features will be illustrated in the example of building a conceptual design.

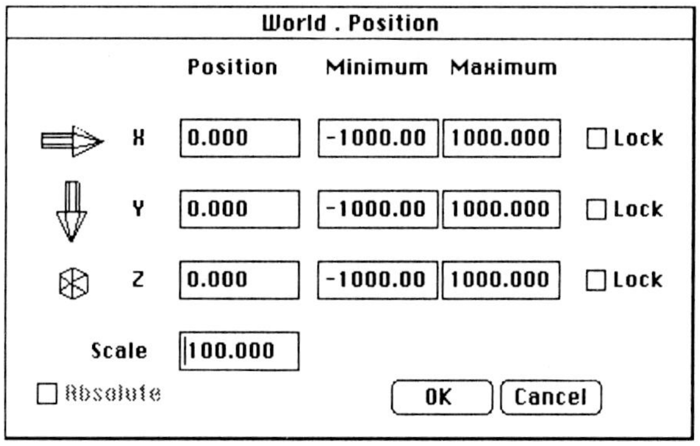

Figure 13.3
World Position window with default values
which can be edited by the user. Changing
X = 0 → 3 moves the scene 3 inches to the right.

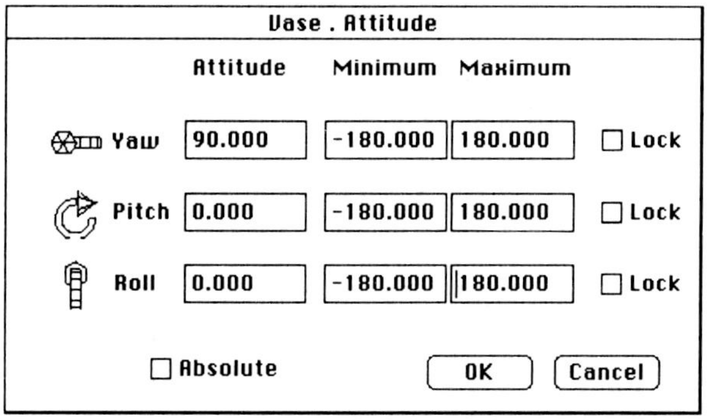

Figure 13.4
Attitude window specifying orientation of the object, *Vase*. The Minimum and Maximum parameters in both Position and Attitude windows permit user-defined constraints relative to the World (independent object) or parent (linked object).

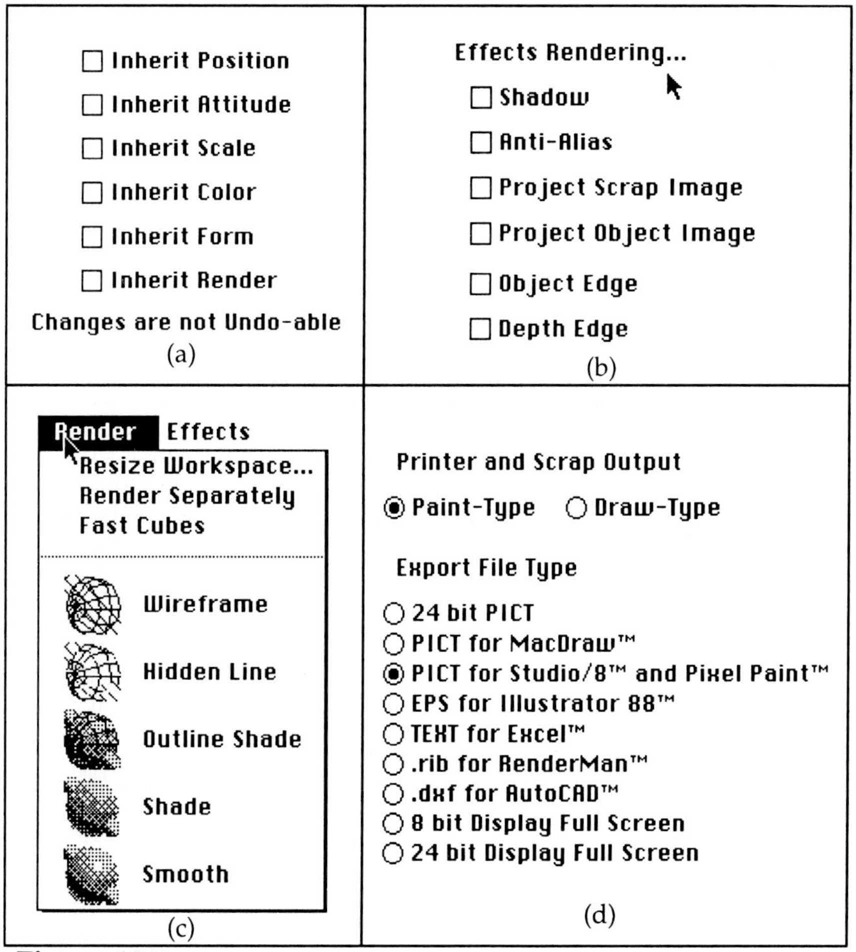

Figure 13.5
Additional features of *Swivel 3D* – (a) Object inheritance, (b) Special rendering effects, (c) Rendering options, and (d) Export file types.

Attributes of objects designed in *Swivel 3D* may be tabulated in a static *Info* record associated with each event. This record includes user-defined fields with values such as those shown in Figure 13.6.

With this sketch of the tools available in *Swivel 3D*, let's outline the steps required to create a design concept of a vase sitting on a table.

Conceptual Design Example

Suppose, as curator of an art museum exhibit on pottery, you wish to check out the visual design of the exhibit hall. Each art object will appear centered on individual tables, and you would like to design a prototype *table* and *vase* which then can be duplicated, modified, and positioned to simulate the appearance of the exhibit hall.

Vase	
Height	18 inches
Max Diam	8 inches
Material	Glass
Weight	6.3 lb
Surface	Marble
Color	Purple
Date Manu	11/1/91
$$ Price	$750

OK   Cancel

Figure 13.6
Object attributes record in *Swivel 3D*. The user
may define fields and assign values for each object
of the scene.

The two primitives supplied by *Swivel 3D*,
lathed and extruded objects, are easily transformed into the prototype exhibit objects. As the
simpler of the two, let's first consider the vase.

Vase Design

The following steps are required to design the
prototype vase.

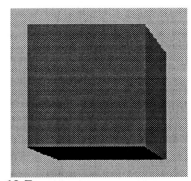

Figure 13.7
Lathed object created by selecting *Lathed object*
icon and clicking the work space screen. The
object's color was chosen using the *Select Color*
menu option.

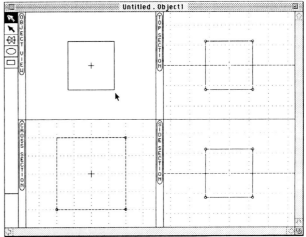

Figure 13.8
Object redesign window with object view and
three sections. The tool palette includes *Double
Arrow, Single Arrow, Free Poly, Oval,* and *Rectangle*
tools.

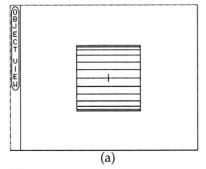
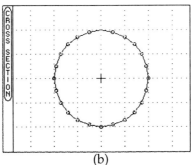
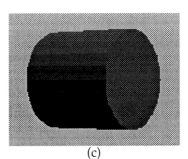
(a)   (b)   (c)

Figure 13.9
Effects of selecting *Oval* tool and clicking on *Cross Section,* (b). Returning to the World view indicates that
the cubic lathed object has been transformed into the lathed cylinder shown in (c).

1. Select the *lathed object* icon, 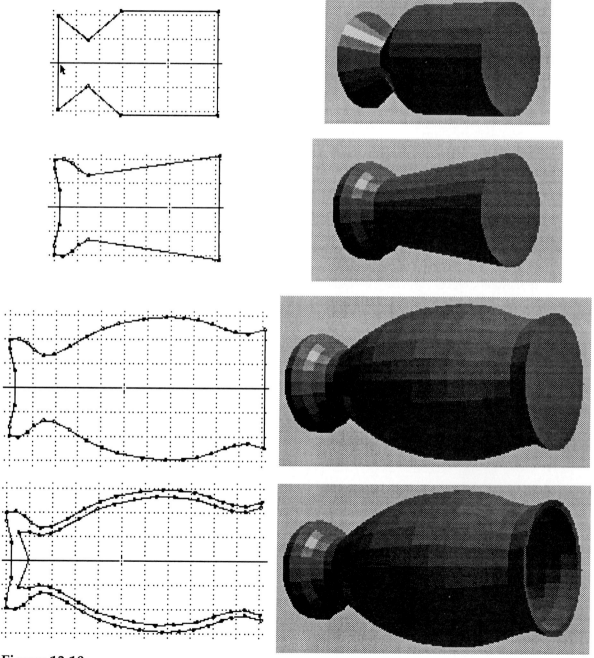, and click anywhere on the work space screen. The shaded cube shown in Figure 13.7 appears at the cursor position.

2. With this cube selected, select *Redesign object* option under the *Object* menu. The four-view design window shown in Figure 13.8 immediately opens.

Figure 13.10
Successive stages in transforming lathed cube into lathed vase. Each stage is generated by clicking in additional control points and dragging them to the shape desired.

(a)   (b)   (c)

Figure 13.11
Shading and rendering options in *Swivel 3D*. (a) Outline shader, (b) Phong shader, (c) Phong shader with anti-aliasing and shadows.

3. The *Oval* design tool is selected next and the *Cross Section* object clicked. The *Object View* and *Cross section* are immediately transformed into those shown in Figure 13.9.

4. Next, the *Double Arrow* tool is selected, the *Top Section* button clicked, and the detailed shape of the vase sculpted by adding points (<CTRL> + click) and dragging them to the desired position. Several stages in this process are illustrated in Figure 13.10.

5. The final step involves rotating the vase into an upright position and selecting one of several rendering options. Figure 13.11 demonstrates three such options.

Perhaps the most important lesson in this design example is the power inherent in good GUI design. For example, the output from step 1 (Figure 13.7) is generated by just 2 clicks of the mouse button. Step 2 is performed with a single mouse click and the output of step 3 (Figure 13.9) is produced by two additional clicks. The first frame of step 4 is accomplished with four mouse clicks and three dragging operations, and each

additional frame in this figure with one click and drag for each additional control point. The rotation of step 5 is performed by a select and drag on the *Roll Arrow*, and each rendering option of Figure 13.11 involves one to three additional menu selections. The complete design was accomplished without typing a single key.

Table Design

The next prototype object to design is a table on which to display the vase and similar pottery objects. Since tabletops generally display a translational symmetry rather than rotational symmetry, we use the *Extruded Object*, rather than a *Lathed Object*, as the basic primitive. The five steps in the table design are summarized as:

1. Design the tabletop by extrusion.
2. Design the table base by extrusion.
3. Design one table leg by lathing.
4. Copy and duplicate the leg three times.
5. Assemble the six parts to build the table and lock them together.

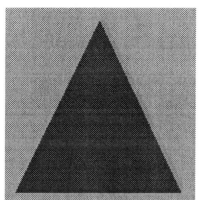

Figure 13.12
Extruded object created by selecting *Extruded object* icon and clicking the work space screen.

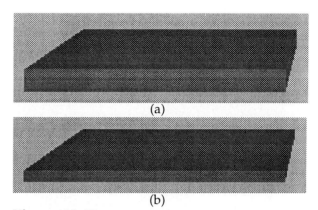

Figure 13.13
Redesign of extruded tabletop done by adding a point to the object in Figure 13.12, dragging the corners to make a rectangle, and rotating the object's attitude. Changing the thickness of (a) to yield (b) is done by dragging two points in *Top Section* view.

The following steps yield a reasonably realistic table design.

1.1 Select the *Extruded Object* icon, [icon], and click on the work space screen. Figure 13.12 shows the resulting extruded object after choosing a wood color by the *Select Color* option under *Effects*.

1.2 Next, the object is transformed by using the

Design New Object menu, adding an additional point (to make it rectangular), dragging the corner points to the desired shape, and rotating shown in Figure 13.13.

2. The base for the tabletop is also formed by ex-

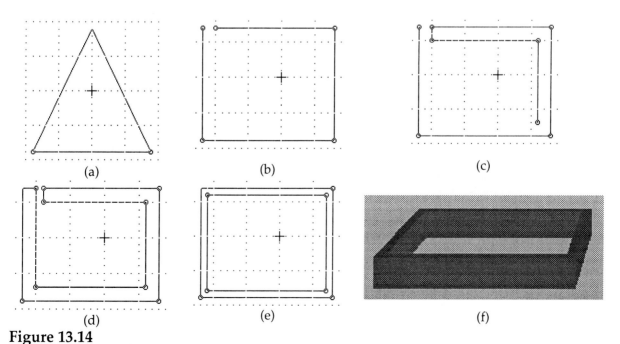

Figure 13.14
Steps in the design of the extruded base for the tabletop. (a) Cross section view of original object, (b) result of separating two points at peak of triangle and adding another, (c) adding three more points and dragging, (d) adding three more, (e) closing up figure (d) and thinning walls, (f) shaded rendering of (e).

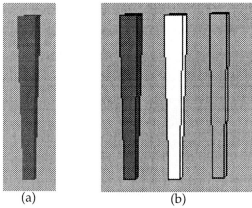

(a)   (b)

Figure 13.15
Building the legs for a table. The first leg, (a), is
designed by modifying four points on a lathed
object. The remaining three legs are generated by
copying (a) and duplicating. They are rendered as
Wire frame, *Hidden Line*, and *Outline Shade*.

of the table design. Figure 13.16 illustrates the
steps involved in this process. First, each
component is rendered as a wire frame without
back plane removal (i.e., show all edges). Next,
the world view angle is set to *Orthographic*. Then
the *World View* is set to *Bottom*, the base is centered on the tabletop and a leg is positioned in
each corner of the base, just as a carpenter would.
Then the *World View* is set to *Right* and each leg is
raised into the correct position.

5.2   Finally, the *Lock* icon is selected and each
component locked to the tabletop by dragging a
virtual line from the part to the tabletop. To create
a more attractive design, each leg is converted to a
circular cross section by a three-click series in
Redesign Object. Finally, the vase is resized and
dragged to the tabletop and centered in two views
to yield the orthographic image in Figure 13.17(a).

trusion, but now the process is a
bit more complex. First, the extruded object icon is selected and
another object clicked onto the
work space. Next, using the
Design New Object menu, seven
points are added in *Cross Section*
view and dragged to the desired
positions as indicated in Figure
13.14.

3. Next, the *Lathed Object* icon is
selected and the object clicked
into the work space. Dragging
four points in *Top Section* view results in the simple table leg design shown in Figure 13.15(a).

4. This table leg is copied and
duplicated three times, generating
the three legs shown in various
rendering options in Figure
13.15(b).

5.1   Graphically assembling the
six components into the completed product and locking them
in place completes the final phase

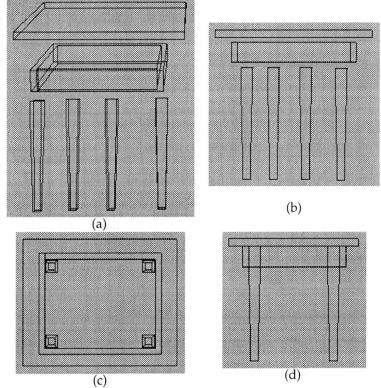

(a)   (b)

(c)   (d)

Figure 13.16
Constructing a table from component parts in *Swivel 3D*. The object (a) is a wire frame perspective view, (b) is an orthographic
front view, (c) is the bottom view after dragging base and legs into
correct position, and (d) is a right view after lifting the legs into
position.

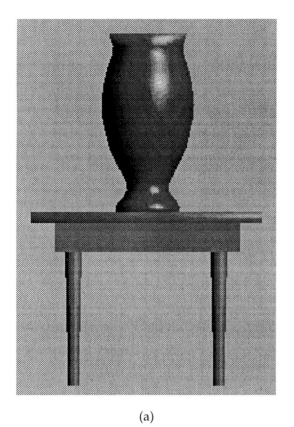

(a)

(b)

Figure 13.17
Final result of locking the vase to the table in orthographic view (a) and rendered in perspective with antialiasing and shadows in (b).

This example illustrates the power of abstraction for graphical design tools. By giving names to all of the commonly invoked graphical operations and providing access to them through standard GUI operations, *Swivel 3D* allows the rapid creation of conceptual designs with realistic rendering. Note that this image design was implemented entirely through mouse clicks and drag operations. The only keyboard operations involved entering "90" to specify reorienting the attitude of newly created objects. These keyboard entries could have been performed by dragging the objects with *Pitch* icon selected.

Three other features valuable for the process of conceptual design include the following:

- Ability to project images on either the 3D scene or any 3D object

- Physical constraints limiting the motion of objects in the scene

- Library of basic 3D objects, i.e. 3D clip art.

Figures 13.18–13.19 illustrate these features. In both cases, the basic objects are drawn from Paracomp's library of *Swivel Art*. In Figure 13.18, a portion of a scanned image has been projected on the computer screen.

In Figure 13.19, we demonstrate the use of constraints applied to the components of library objects to build "intelligent" objects. By keying in the appropriate limits on z motion (axis of drawers) in the *Object.Position* window (see Figure 13.3) and locking the x and y positions, the drawers are constrained to motions similar to those of real drawers moving on real tracks.

In addition to linear constraints, angular constraints may be applied to limit the pivoting motion of an object about a joint. This facilitates building conceptual models with physical validity.

CADD Tools

After the conceptual design has been completed and approved by management, the next phase of product development involves the production of *detail drawings* and *assembly drawings*. These must specify every feature of every component of the product, as well as the relationships among the components, in sufficient detail to control the production process performed by human workers or numerically controlled machines. Detail and assembly drawings define the basic manufacturing processes for integrated circuits, mechanical machinery, and architecture. Often, as in the case of architecture, such drawings must define the integration of multiple sub-systems like heating, plumbing, electrical, and communications into a master building design. Generation of detail and assembly drawings is the principal task of computer-aided design and drafting tools.

Computer-aided design was the first, and has remained the largest, direct application of computer graphics. As Figure 13.20 indicates, approximately 60% of the CAD market is devoted to mechanical design (MCAD), with the remaining 40% split roughly equally between electronic design (ECAD) and computer-aided engineering (CAE). In the early 1990s, the MCAD market alone produced over $8 billion worldwide and is projected to earn $12 billion annually by the mid-1990s.[8] For an interesting history of the evolution of graphical design from antiquity to electronic CAD, see Ryan.[9]

The evolution of the tools for CADD illustrates an interesting confluence of two streams of computer science. The first stream involved mainframe computers, usually running FORTRAN, with specialized graphics workstations, usually vector oriented, and data

![Next Machine drawn from a library of 3D clip art, shown on a desk with keyboard and mouse, with a scanned image projected on the screen]

Figure 13.18
Next Machine drawn from a library of 3D clip art. It was placed on the table and a scanned image was projected on the screen. The image of the resulting model was rendered by *Swivel 3D*.

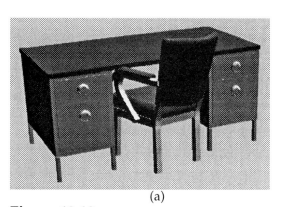
(a)

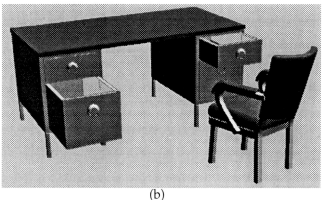
(b)

Figure 13.19
Intelligent furniture designed with *Swivel 3D*. (a) Original office scene, (b) sliding chair back and dragging two drawers partially open. The drawers are all constrained to move along their tracks, and stops limit their travel as with real ones.

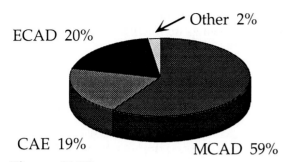

ECAD 20%

Other 2%

CAE 19%

MCAD 59%

Figure 13.20
Distribution of CAD market by area. The mechanical computer-aided design segment (MCAD) produces over $8 billion in software and hardware sales.

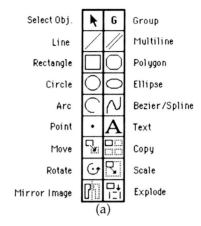

Figure 13.21
The *Tool Palette*, (a), defines primitive objects and some of their messages. The *Constraints Palette*, (b), lists additional messages.

tablets for interactive input. This is the environment in which CADD was born in the 1960s. The second stream emerged from "toy" programs such as *MacPaint* running on microcomputers using bit-mapped raster graphics and the mouse for interactive input. This technology evolved in the mid-1980s and produced the object-oriented drawing techniques discussed in our introduction to OOP. The implementation of highly sophisticated CADD techniques from the mainframe stream on raster graphics of the microcomputer stream resulted in the powerful systems presently available on personal workstations. Representative programs include AutoCAD™, VersaCAD™, MGM-Station™, MacBravo™, MiniCAD™, and CADD Level 1™.

The OOP metaphor offers an efficient device for introducing the features and capabilities of modern, personal workstation-based CADD tools. We will consider the objects available to the CADD designer, attributes of these objects, and what messages are available for manipulating and organizing objects into a finished drawing. We begin by examining *VersaCAD*™, one of many excellent CADD systems available on a range of workstations.[10]

Objects in CADD

Most CADD systems provide two classes of basic objects: graphical primitives and library objects.

Graphical Primitives

The graphical primitives available in *Versa CAD* are listed in Figure 13.21 and include:

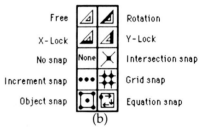

- Point
- Rectangle
- Ellipse
- Spline curve
- Line
- Polygon
- Arc
- Multiline
- Circle
- Bézier curve
- Text

Note the richer array of graphical primitives than were available on the conceptual design tool introduced earlier in the chapter. Most of these primitives have user-defined attributes, discussed shortly, which specify their appearance and creation options.

Library Objects

One feature distinguishing CADD systems from simpler drawing tools is the library of design symbols they provide. In Figure 13.22, one of several symbol libraries available for *VersaCAD* is shown.

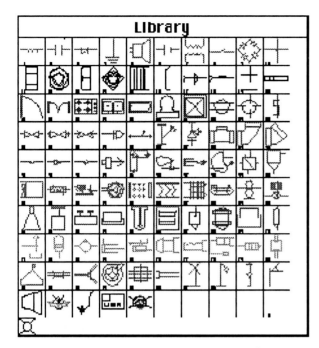

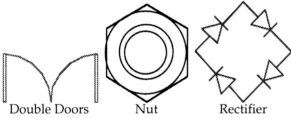

Double Doors   Nut   Rectifier

Figure 13.22
Library of standard design objects in electrical, mechanical, and architectural design. The designer selects the library symbol by clicking on its icon in the library below and dragging it to the drawing to produce labeled objects.

Attributes of CADD Objects

Most primitive CADD objects are more abstract than simple graphical primitives. That is, they have attributes which may define their structure and/or the message protocol to which they respond. Consider, for instance, the *VersaCAD Polygon* and *Bézier/Spline* objects. Figure 13.23 illustrates the options presented to the user when the graphical icons representing polygons and Bézier curves, respectively, are double-clicked.

Other *VersaCAD* objects (except for *Point* objects) offer similar user-selectable attributes with system-selected default values.

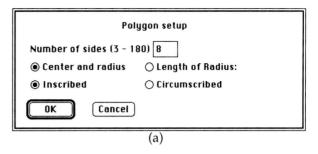

(a)

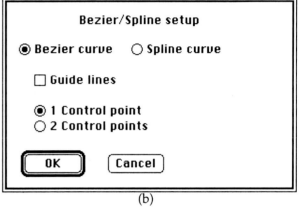

(b)

Figure 13.23
Attributes of primitive *VersaCAD* Objects. (a) For a polygon the user may select the number of sides and construction technique. (b) For curves, the user may choose Bézier or Spline curve and the construction technique for each.

Messages in CADD

Now that the basic CADD objects and their inherited attributes have been defined, the logical questions are: What OOP message can we send these objects and how do we send them? As standard, graphical objects, both the primitives and library symbols must understand the following messages:

- Create yourself
- Translate yourself
- Form a mirror image
- Duplicate yourself
- Delete yourself
- Rotate yourself
- Scale yourself
- Join a group.

In addition to these standard messages, objects in most CADD programs recognize the following special messages:

- Constrain yourself to start and end at the following grid points,

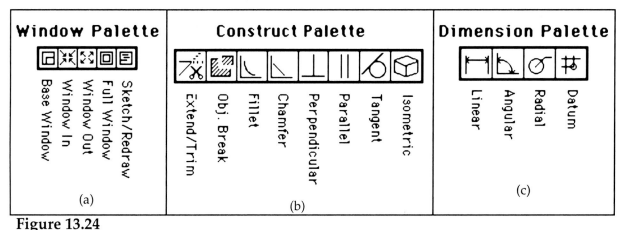

Figure 13.24
VersaCAD Palettes for sending messages to: (a) windows, (b) objects under construction, and (c) objects being dimensioned.

- Dimension yourself according to the following style,

- Crosshatch yourself according to the following pattern,

- Extend yourself to meet another object and trim excess construction,

- Break yourself into segments according to the following method,

- Make a fillet (round) between the following objects,

- Create a chamfer between the following two lines,

- Create a perpendicular line to the following object,

- Create a parallel line to the following line,

- Create a tangent line to the following circle, arc, or ellipse,

- Create an isometric view, given the following front, top, and right views.

In addition to these messages sent to individual objects or combinations of objects, a CADD program must provide messages to control the viewport on the drawing. These include establishing the drawing size (*Base Window*), zooming (*Window In* and *Window Out*), and reducing the viewport to fit the drawing (*Window Full*). These

options are shown in the Window Palette of Figure 13.24. Other construction and dimension messages are listed in the Construction Palette and Dimension Palette, respectively, of Figure 13.25 and the Constraint Palette of Figure 13.22 shows the options available for constraining objects during their construction.

CADD Example 1: Gear Design

To illustrate the design process and demonstrate several CADD techniques, consider the design of a gear. The craft of gear design is far from trivial. Optimized design requires precision in the gear

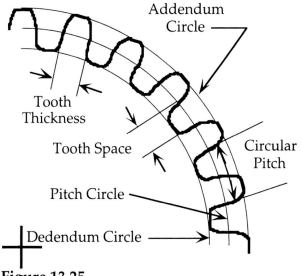

Figure 13.25
Nomenclature in spur-gear design.

tooth geometry in order to minimize wear and backlash.[11] As in other technical fields, gear design has developed its own nomenclature, some of whose terms are defined in Figure 13.25.

Assume the following specifications for the gear:

- Radius of pitch circle = 5.5"
- Addendum = 0.5"
- Dedendum = 0.5 "
- Number of teeth = 24

The CADD process to create the gear drawing can be summarized by the five steps:

1. Define the drafting environment.
2. Draw the front view.
3. Add the projected, side view section.
4. Dimension the drawing.
5. Add a border and title box.

Let's examine each of these steps in more detail.

1. Drafting Environment

1.1 The *Base Window* icon was double-clicked and the default drawing size accepted as approximately 27 inches wide by 19 inches high.

1.2 The *Settings/Units* menu was used to confirm *inches* as the default unit and one as the default line width.

1.3 The *Grid* icon was used to set the grid spacing to 1/4" in both x and y and turn on the grid visibility.

2. Front View

2.1 The first step was to design a single tooth.

2.1.1 First, a gear center was selected near the center of the drawing and its position marked with a 1" high "+" mark.

2.1.2 Next, the Addendum Circle and the Dedendum Circle were drawn with radii of 6" and 5", respectively, to serve as construction aids.

2.1.3 Seven inch long construction lines starting at the gear center were added as construction lines at angles of 82.5° and 97.5° to span.

2.1.4 Two Bézier curves, labeled 1 and 2 in Figure 13.26, were constructed to generate the *flank* (tooth surface inside the pitch circle) and *face* (tooth surface outside the pitch circle), respectively, of the gear tooth. The bottom of curve 1 and the top of curve 2 were constrained to lie parallel to the dedendum and addendum circles, respectively.

2.1.5 Curves 1 and 2 were grouped, duplicated, and reflected about the vertical axis to generate curves 4 and 5. The top of the tooth, curve 3, was drawn to connect curves 2 and 4 to complete the tooth design as shown in Figure 13.26 (b). The tooth in relation to the construction lines is shown in Figure 13.26 (c).

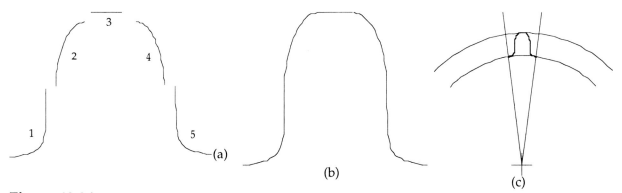

Figure 13.26
Construction of gear tooth by connecting four Bézier curve segments. The construction lines shown in (c) defined the angular and radial extent of the tooth and the tangents of the top and bottom of the curves. The use of snap grid option guaranteed continuity between the curve segments.

2.2 Next, the tooth was copied to complete the outline of the gear tooth structure.

    2.2.1 The *circular copy* option under the *copy* icon was selected and the following parameters set:
- Incremental rotation =   15.00
- Total number of copies = 24
- Object rotation =   15.00

    2.2.2 The center of rotation was then selected by clicking on the gear center. *VersaCAD* then generated the tooth outline shown in Figure 13.27.

    2.2.3 The gear shaft was then added by

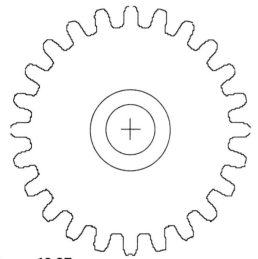

Figure 13.27
Gear design after circular copy of 24 teeth and the addition of concentric circles indicating the gear shaft.

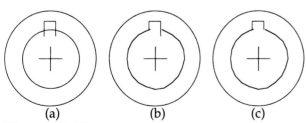

(a)   (b)   (c)

Figure 13.28
Use of *Extend/Trim* to build keyway. (a) A capped, double line is dragged upward, terminating at the correct depth of the keyway. (b) The *Extend/Trim* icon is clicked and the circle and left-hand side of the keyway trimmed. (c) The right-hand side and the remaining arc are then selected and trimmed to join.

dragging two concentric circles to produce Figure 13.27.

2.3 A keyway was added to the gear shaft.

    2.3.1 To add a 1/2″ wide by 1/4″ deep keyway to the shaft, the simplest method was to select the multi-line tool icon, set its width to 1/2″, and select the capped parameter.

    2.3.2 The keyway was then dragged into position as shown in Figure 13.28 (a).

    2.3.3 The *Extend/Trim* icon was then selected and applied to the inner circle and segments of the double line. This option cycles through all logical segments allowing the user to select the desired trimmed configuration. Three stages in the trim operation are shown in Figure 13.28.

2.4 Spokes were added by cutting away unnecessary metal to create holes.

    2.4.1 First, two construction lines were created at angles of 60° and 120° to assist in the design of six symmetric spokes.

    2.4.2 Next, two arcs centered in this angular region and concentric with the gear center were drawn and their endpoints connected with two rays as shown in Figure 13.29 (a).

2.4.3 Then the *Fillet* icon was selected, and

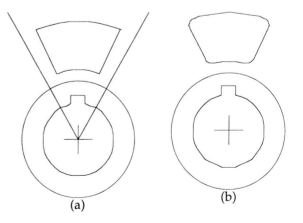

(a)   (b)

Figure 13.29
Construction of spokes by drawing cut-away holes. (a) Construction lines and initial cut-away hole built from two arcs and two lines. (b) Result of inserting fillets between arcs and lines of hole.

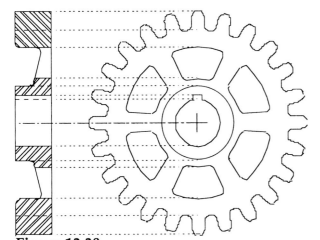

Figure 13.30
Cross section side view and front view of spur gear.

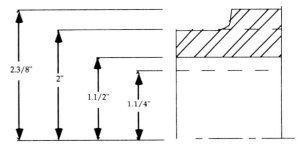

Figure 13.31
Details of dimension tool output of radii near keyway.

2.4.3 Then the *Fillet* icon was selected, and *VersaCAD* automatically inserted fillets between each user-selected pair of arcs and lines and trimmed off the overhang. The final hole design in relation to the gear shaft is shown in Figure 13.29 (b).

2.4.4 Finally, the two arcs, two lines, and four fillets were grouped and circularly copied to produce six holes, one every 60°. This completed the front view shown in Figure 13.30.

3. Projected Side-view Section

3.1 Dotted construction lines were drawn from each significant feature of the front view to assist in creating and understanding the side-view section.
3.2 The outline of the major components of the bottom half of the cross section were constructed using the line tool.
3.3 Fillets were inserted to round three selected corners.
3.4 The *Hatch* icon was selected, the material parameter set to "steel", and boundaries of the regions consisting of steel were selected to produce cross hatching.
3.5 The lower half of the gear cross section was mirror reflected about the axis to produce the top half.
3.6 The hatched region just above the axis was modified to account for the presence of the keyway. The final detail geometry for front

and cross section views is shown in Figure 13.30.

4. Dimensioning the Drawing

4.1 The *Dimension* palette was used to select either linear or angular dimensions as required.

4.2 Linear dimensioning, selected by the icon, was performed by the following four steps.
4.2.1 The first point was defined by clicking.
4.2.2 The second point was defined by clicking.
4.2.3 The depth (extension lines) was defined by dragging.
4.2.4 The numerical value was anchored by clicking.

4.3 Angular dimensioning, selected by the icon, was performed as follows.
4.3.1 The first line defining the angle was clicked.
4.3.2 The second line of the angle was clicked.
4.2.3 The depth (extension lines) was defined by dragging.
4.2.4 The numerical value was anchored by clicking.

A zoomed-in segment of the drawing illustrating the base-line dimensions is shown in Figure 13.31

5. Border and Title Box

5.1 A *border* was constructed using the *Box* icon and the width set to three pixels.

5.2 A *title box* was drawn with slots for important information such as the company name, part name, scale, drawing number, draftsperson, and so on.

The detail drawing shown in Figure 13.32 provides essentially all the information necessary for building the gear. In the exercises we investigate the few missing items and what other information might be useful.

Gear design appears to be a popular introductory example for many drawing and CADD systems. In Figure 13.33 we show a drawing which comes as an example with the *Canvas*™ *3.0* program.

Another feature which distinguishes more sophisticated CADD systems from simpler drawing programs is *associative dimensioning*. This means that the dimension object is "intelligent" and keeps track of the size of the object it is dimensioning. If the scale of the dimensioned object are modified, the dimension object will report the new dimensions. Dimension objects in associative dimensioning systems act as demons which monitor the dimensioned object's size. So, for instance, when the original drawing of Figure 13.33 was scaled down to 80 percent of its original size to fit on the page, all dimensions changed to 0.8 times their original values.

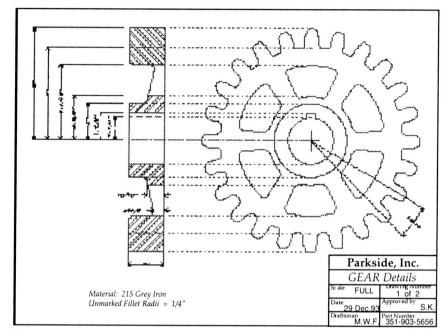

Material: 215 Grey Iron
Unmarked Fillet Radii = 1/4"

Parkside, Inc.		
GEAR Details		
Scale FULL	Drawing Number 1 of 2	
Date 29 Dec.93	Approved by S.K.	
Draftsman M.W.F.	Part Number 351-903-5656	

Figure 13.32
Gear details with dimensioning, cross section view, border and title box.

CADD Example 2 – Architecture

A second major area in which CADD plays a central role is in architectural design. Figure 13.34 shows the floor plan for the bedroom floor of a typical house. This figure illustrates several additional important features of CADD systems. These include:

- The use of color for classifying elements of the drawing.

- The use of a library of CADD design elements.

- The use of layers for classification of functionality.

The use of color clarifies the process of reading and understanding this reasonably complex drawing. All doors, for instance, may be colored magenta, all windows orange, and all bathroom fixtures yellow.

The apparent complexity and high degree of detail are easily achieved through the extensive use of *library objects*. Thus, the highly detailed small bathroom design shown in Figure 13.35 is accomplished by selecting and dragging in icons for the window, tub, sink, and so on.

Another feature distinguishing more advanced CADD systems from simpler drawing programs is the use of *layers*. Layers provide a mechanism for categorizing elements of a design according to function and for providing a hierarchical structure for the drawing. All of the doors of a floor plan, for instance, could be assigned to one layer, all of the windows to another, and all of the appliances to still another. The final drawing consists of the superposition of all the layers.

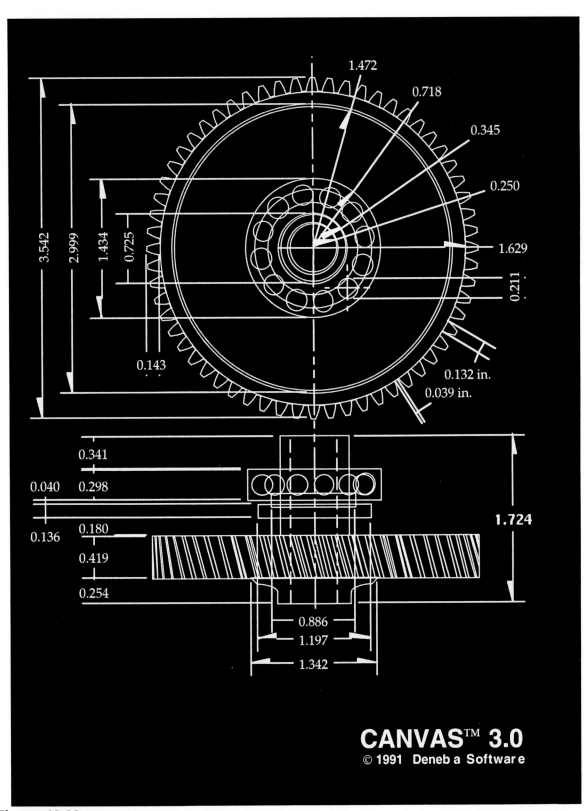

Figure 13.33
Gear design by Deneba Software using *Canvas™ 3.0.*

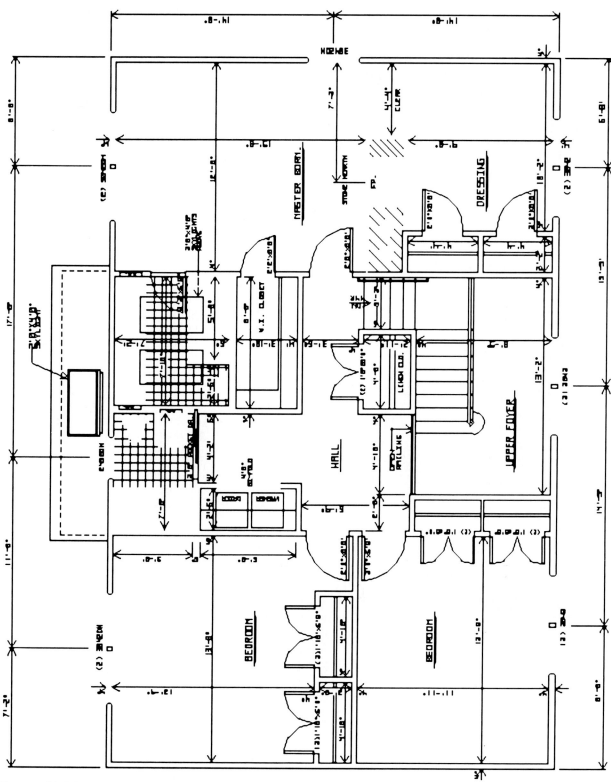

Figure 13.34
Architectural CADD drawing of a floor plan. (*Design by VersaCAD™.*)

Layering provides the advantages of classification by logical function and the class inheritance properties of hierarchical systems. So, for instance, to change the color of all doors from magenta to green or the hatching of all metal parts from iron to steel, one needs only to change the attributes for the layer as a whole after which each instance inherits the change.

The actual construction of a building involves integrating a number of radically different systems into a single design. Layering provides the key for this integration. So, for instance, the floor plan may be represented on layer #1, the plumbing on layer #2, the electrical distribution system on layer #3, and so on. A useful format for hard copy is to print each layer in a unique color on a single transparency. The relationships between various systems can then be readily visualized by superimposing the transparencies on the basic floor plan.

A final function of layering is to assist the designer of the original detail drawing. Layers can be assigned to various categories of the design process, including construction lines, format lines, title blocks, text, and dimensions. Judicious use of layers simplifies and organizes the process of design itself. A good summary of the topic is given by Gerlach.[12]

Figure 13.35 shows an enlarged view of the small bathroom from Figure 13.34 and illustrates the detail possible through the use of library objects.

As a final illustration of how the sophistication of CADD systems can speed the design process, consider the process of adding doors to the closet shown in Figure 13.36. The closet is rapidly drawn using the multiline tool set to *2-line, continuous* mode to give (a). Next, the library *Cut objects* option is selected, effectively adding intelligence to the library object about how it is to interact with its environment. Now, when the double-door object, (b), is selected from the library menu and dragged to the desired location as shown in (c), it automatically inserts itself into the wall by performing the *break* and *trim* operations. Thus, merging segments (a) and (b) to produce (c) requires a single click and drag using intelligent CADD objects. The conventional approach to this task would have required at least six operations— removal of the two top lines and the creation of four shorter lines.

Additional CADD Features

Most CADD packages provide many additional features which we do not have space to illustrate in detail. We can, however, summarize these features in the following three categories:

- Geometry Aids
- Database Extensions
- 3D Capabilities

Let's expand a bit on each of these.

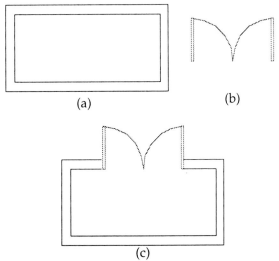

(a)   (b)

(c)

Figure 13.36
The use of intelligent CADD objects to speed design. Setting the library option to *Cut objects* allows the insertion of the double-doors, (b), into closet wall, (a), by a simple dragging operation to give (c).

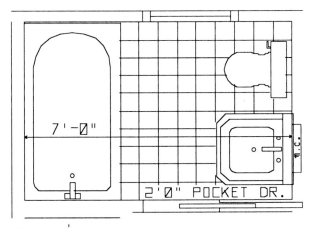

Figure 13.35
Enlarged segment from Figure 13.34. Note the detail possible through use of library objects.

Geometry Aids

Much of the effort in creating detail drawings involves a precise alignment of the components of the drawing. Several CADD tools to assist the designer in this task include:

- **Perpendicular** – Creates a line perpendicular to a target line or at some user-defined angle with respect to the perpendicular.

- **Parallel** – Creates a line parallel to a target line or at some user-defined angle with respect to the parallel line.

- **Tangent** – Creates a line tangent to a circle, arc, or ellipse.

- **Isometric** – Creates an isometric view of an object from the user-defined top, front, and end views (a.k.a. plan, elevation, and end views).

Database Extensions

Managing a large design project involves much more than the creation of several detail drawings and an assembly drawing or two. Among these tasks are the management of the drawings themselves, maintenance of up-to-date schedules of standard parts appearing in the drawings, and material requirements planning (MRP). Several of these tasks are described in detail in Besant and Lui.[13]

To assist the project manager and designers in managing such database information, *VersaCAD* provides the following tools in *HyperCard* format:

- **Drawing Manager** – Provides an easy, visual method of cataloging drawings and organizing them logically as icons.

- **Level Manager** – Provides for the naming of layers and the ability to turn layers on and off in saved 2D drawings.

- **Schedule** – Provides a database for storing and editing descriptive information such as the styles, dimensions, and manufacturers of parts like doors and windows.

- **Database** – Provides a way to attach data to symbols and text on the image of the detail drawing. Buttons are attached to the symbols and the attached information edited by clicking on the buttons.

- **Bill of Materials** – Automatically counts the number of times a particular part appears on a drawing and generates a spreadsheet-type report listing the total number of objects, total costs, associated labor costs, and so on. This tool helps automate the process of preparing purchase orders from the assembly drawings.

3D Capabilities

Most CADD systems provide at least some capability for design in 3D. *VersaCAD* allows the user to design objects in 2D and convert them to 3D objects by the processes of lathing and extrusion. A hierarchical 3D scene is created by merging the 2D drawings into a 3D work file. The 3D scene may be viewed in one, two, or four viewports simultaneously from any user-specified viewpoint. Rendering options include wireframe, hidden surface removal, and a simple shading model. Figure 13.37 shows the design of a simple 3D object and a more complex 3D scene.

Note the design power offered by the abstractions of *filleting* and *lathing*. The 2D outline of the bushing shown in Figure 13.37 was created in less than a minute from eight line segments. Adding three fillets to produce the smooth corners of (a) required another minute. Opening this 2D drawing as a lathed object in VersaCAD automatically produced the 3D object shown in perspective view in (b). The process of extrusion was used to produce objects shown in plan and isometric views in (c) and (d).

Finite Element Analysis

The first two applications discussed in this chapter have been purely geometric. Each includes some intelligence about the behavior of the models they are used to create. *Swivel 3D* supports constraints limiting the motion of one object relative to another. *VersaCAD* supports automatic trimming to merge two objects and the use of intelligent library icons. Such features greatly enhance the authentic appearance of the objects we are modeling but tell us nothing about how they behave in real world environments. If we wish to know how objects bend when subject to a force, or how they vibrate when struck, or how hot they get when one end is heated, or what magnetic fields they generate

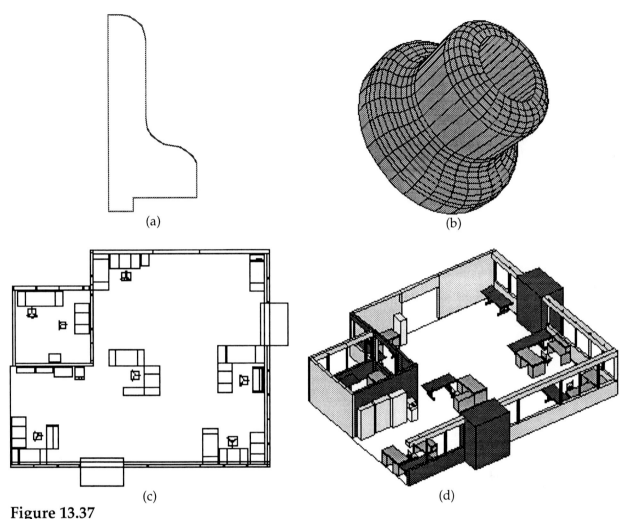

(a)

(b)

(c)

(d)

Figure 13.37
3D CADD designs. The 2D drawing of a bushing in (a) is transformed into the 3D object in (b) by the lathing operation. The plan and isometric views of a floor plan are shown in (c) and (d).

when current runs through them, we need more authentic models.

To build models with authentic *behavior* as well as *appearance*, we must greatly enrich the information content of the database. In short, we must add physics. That is, we need to attach physical attributes such as density and coefficient of elasticity to each object of the model, the constraints restricting motion, and the forcing function causing deflection for mechanical models. In addition, for computer modeling we must add algorithms for segmenting objects into small elements and solving the integral or differential equations governing the interactions between these elements. The method for implementing this more authentic model is called the *finite element method* (FEM).

Background

The finite element method is a general technique for numerical solution of the integral or differential equations governing the behavior of systems in science and engineering. Just as parametric splines emerged from the design of automobiles, the finite element method emerged from the aircraft industry. The fundamental ideas were contributed by engineers, applied mathematicians, and physicists. Courant wrote the seminal paper laying the foundation for the FEM.[14] Brauer has produced a gentle introduction to the subject,[15] and the standard reference work is by Zienkiewicz.[16]

One of the most distinctive features of the FEM is its generality. The original motivation for developing finite element analysis (FEA) was the study of components used in the aerospace industry. A mathematical model for studying the stress points and resonant frequencies of a Boeing 747 fuselage permits a much more rapid analysis at much lower cost than building and testing scale models. By pinpointing potential weaknesses, FEA facilitates successive refinement of engineering designs to optimize strength to weight ratios. After proving its value for structural analysis in the aerospace industry, the FEM has spread to those areas of science and engineering in which fields are described by differential or integral equations. These include:

- **Electromagnetic field analysis** – FEA is particularly valuable in optimizing the design of electromagnetic devices such as motors, generators, solenoids, and so on. It is used to study the field configurations in integrated circuits and electronic beam devices.

- **Thermal analysis** – The behavior of heat flow is of great interest to the automotive, electrical power, and nuclear industries. FEA provides the most accurate numerical method for predicting temperature distributions and heat fluxes in heating, cooling, and energy conversion devices.

- **Fluid dynamics** – The FEM provides a powerful tool for dealing with complex models of air flow past an auto body, coolant flow in a fission reactor, cloud formation in a weather pattern, and motion of the red spot on Jupiter. Because of the complexities and nonlinearities of such systems, FEA is essentially the only tool available.

Because of the generality of the FEM and great range of problems to which it may be applied, FEA constitutes the largest single class of supercomputer application. Using increasingly efficient solvers combined with convenient GUIs, most commercial FEA systems have been implemented on a range of workstations, including the PC and Macintosh.

Mathematical Basis

The FEM is particularly useful in analyzing physical phenomena that can be described in terms of a potential field, Φ, which obeys one of the following differential equations:

$$\frac{\partial^2 \Phi}{\partial x^2} + \frac{\partial^2 \Phi}{\partial y^2} = 0 \quad \text{(elliptic equation),} \qquad [13.1]$$

$$\frac{\partial^2 \Phi}{\partial x^2} - \frac{\partial \Phi}{\partial t} = 0 \quad \text{(parabolic equation),} \qquad [13.2]$$

$$\frac{\partial^2 \Phi}{\partial t^2} - \frac{\partial^2 \Phi}{\partial x^2} = 0 \quad \text{(hyperbolic equation).} \quad [13.3]$$

In many instances, the source of the potential exists in the region of space being modeled. In such cases, the elliptic equation (Laplace's equation) must be modified to include the source term, ρ, giving Poisson's equation:

$$\frac{\partial^2 \Phi}{\partial x^2} + \frac{\partial^2 \Phi}{\partial y^2} = \rho \quad \text{(Poisson's equation).} \quad [13.4]$$

In the case of mechanical structure analysis, the field Φ is the displacement, $u(x)$, resulting from applied forces. In the case of electrostatics, $\Phi = V(x)$, the electric potential, and for electromagnetic fields, $\Phi = A(x)$, the magnetic vector potential. For thermal problems, $\Phi = T(x)$, the temperature distribution.

Physical constraints, known as *boundary conditions*, provide additional tools for solving these differential equations. Boundary conditions generally fall in one of three classes:

Dirichlet → the *potential* is defined on the boundary, s. That is:

$$\Phi(s) = f(s) \qquad\qquad [13.5]$$

Neumann → the potential *gradient* is defined on the boundary, s. That is:

$$\frac{\partial \Phi}{\partial n} = f(s) \qquad\qquad [13.6]$$

Mixed → either the potential or its gradient is defined on the surface.

Physical Basis

The FEM has been represented in several formulations, all of which have been shown to be equivalent to Hamilton's energy minimization principle. This principle states that any perturbed system will respond by adjusting its free parameters so as to minimize the total energy of the system. Thus, when subject to forces, a physical object will flex and bend in such a way as to minimize the stored potential energy. When a source of heat is introduced into a system, heat will flow in such a way as to create a temperature distribution that minimizes the total thermal energy stored in the system. When current flows in conductors, magnetic fields are set up in the space surrounding the conductors in such a configuration as to minimize the total electromagnetic energy of the system.

Consider, for instance, an energy functional, $\mathcal{F}$, describing the total energy stored in the compressed spring system shown in Figure 13.38.

$$\mathcal{F} = \frac{1}{2} kx^2 + \int f \, dx \qquad [13.7]$$

where
  k = spring constant
  x = compression from relaxed state
  f = applied force

The energy minimization principle describing the equilibrium state may be written:

$$\frac{d\mathcal{F}}{dx} = 0 . \qquad [13.8]$$

Substituting Equation 13.7 into 13.8 gives:

$$0 = kx + f \qquad [13.9]$$

which is the well-known Hooke's Law relating force to displacement for a spring,

$$f = -kx. \qquad [13.10]$$

Thus, the energy minimization principle is equivalent to the basic force laws in its ability to describe the behavior of physical systems.

Discretization

Central to the implementation of the FEM is the fragmentation of every object in a finite element model (and, in some cases, the empty space between them) into small segments. The basic argument is that, as long as the dimensions of the finite elements (Δx, Δy) are chosen small enough, the quantities ($\partial \Phi$, ∂x, and ∂y) of Equations 13.1–13.4 may be replaced by ($\Delta \Phi$, Δx, and Δy) with little loss in accuracy of the model.

Sophisticated algorithms have been developed for fragmenting objects of arbitrary shape into triangular and rectangular finite elements (or their 3D equivalents).[17] For triangular discretization, each triangle is defined by three corner nodes at which the relevant potential will be calculated. The effect of 2D triangular discretization, then, is to convert the continuous field equations of 13.1–13.4 into a set of algebraic equations relating the $3N$ potential values of an N node system. What this accomplishes, in effect, is to replace the impossible task of solving differential equations in domains of arbitrary geometry with the completely practical task of solving $3N$ equations in $3N$ unknowns.

Consider the simplest possible problem in elasticity. If we are given the spring constant, k, and applied force, f, we can use Hooke's Law to solve for the unknown displacement from equilibrium, x. This represents a "1–node" finite element problem. For the more general finite element problem in elasticity, the spring constant, k, is replaced by the *stiffness matrix*, $\mathbf{K}$, whose elements are functions of the discrete geometry, Young's modulus of elasticity, and the shear modulus.[18] The scalar force is replaced by a force vector, $\mathbf{F}$, and the unknown displacement, x, is replaced by a vector, $\mathbf{U}$, of unknown displacements. In the general 3D case, each node i may be displaced along each axis giving the three unknowns, (u_{ix}, u_{iy}, u_{iz}). A problem with M *node*s then involves $3M$ unknown displacements and the solution of the stiffness matrix Equation 13.11 of order $3M$. This is the finite element analog of Hooke's Law, Equation 13.10.

$$F = K \cdot U \qquad [13.11]$$

Procedure

All finite element analysis problems involve a similar set of steps for their solution. At the most abstract level, these can be summarized as the following three steps.

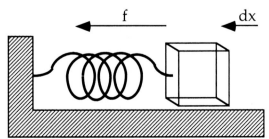

Figure 13.38
Storing energy in a spring system.

1. Preprocessing
2. Analysis
3. Postprocessing

Let's examine each of these steps in more detail.

Preprocessing – Model Building

The preprocessing step involves, by far, the greatest effort on the part of the FEA analyst. This step involves the following tasks:

- **CAD/Geometry** – The geometry of the model must be precisely specified. This involves building the outline of each object, using CAD features of the FEA system or importing a geometric model built with a standard CAD system.

- **Material Properties Specification** – Once the geometry of objects has been defined, the material properties of each must be specified. For mechanical systems this involves entering the Young's modulus of elasticity, the shear modulus, and density for problems involving gravity or vibration.

- **Mesh Generation** – Once an object is created it must be discretized. Most FEA systems provide a variety of mesh generation options, ranging from totally automatic to totally user-controlled. To help guarantee unique, singly defined nodes and continuous surfaces, a variety of merge and validation options are available.

- **Boundary Condition Application** – In mechanical problems, certain nodes or surfaces are constrained to have zero deflection or to move only in certain directions and not in others. FEA systems provide options for applying these BCs.

- **Forcing Function** – The purpose of the FEM is to study the response of a system to applied forces. FEA systems provide options for applying vector forces at each node of the system.

- **Model Validation** – Since building a complex FEA model requires considerable effort on the part of the analyst and since the solution of complex models requires signif-

icant computing resources, it is important to verify that the model is correct. While well-designed computer graphics is important for each of the steps above, it is particularly critical at this stage. By judicious use of color and options like shrinking the elements to visualize their structure, the user can readily detect flaws in the model. This prevents much grief at the later analysis and postprocessing stages.

The objective of the preprocessing phase is to build a complete and detailed model of the physical system. In addition to the CAD task of specifying the geometry of each object in the model, the user must assign the necessary physical attributes to each object and carefully direct the process of breaking up the model into a sufficiently refined mesh of finite elements. Finally, the forcing function which will excite the model must be defined, and the boundary conditions constraining its response must be specified. All of these tasks are most efficiently performed in a user-friendly, CAD-like environment in which a smooth graphical user interface plays a central role.

Analysis

Once the model has been completed, the analysis package is invoked. At this point the program takes over and automatically assembles the stiffness matrix, modifies it to include the boundary condition, and solves the system of N equations in the N unknown potential values. This is the compute-bound phase of the analysis. Simple models such as those shown below require less than a minute on a personal workstation. More complex models with thousands of elements may require an hour or more.

Computer graphics could play an informative role in helping the user visualize the analysis process, but in most commercial programs it does not. Since the analysis task is essentially numerical analysis, most packages merely list the progress of the analysis in a text report format. Graphical output in which the elements of the model would blink as they were being processed would contribute to the user's insight both on the dynamics of the solution process itself and potential problem areas in the case of unsuccessful analysis. Since such a graphical reporting mode would consume additional computing resources, an optimal system would offer it as a debugging option.

Postprocessing – Visualization

The purpose of the postprocessing phase is to provide the user with the clearest possible visualization of the solution and its implications. Here is where computer graphics plays a key role in FEA. Several visualization modes are offered on most analysis packages.

- **Deflection plots** – In mechanical systems, the "answer" provided by the analysis is the set of deflections of each node in the model as a result of the applied force. By proper scaling of these deflections and by redrawing the model based on the deflected points, the response of the system is readily understood. Displaying the original model in one color and the deflected model in a different color further enhances the visualization process.

- **Stress plots** – The primary purpose of mechanical FEA is generally to identify regions of intense stress since these indicate the points at which the part is likely to break when the force is exerted. A stress plot shows the outline of an object with the internal stresses color coded. Regions of high stress are instantly apparent.

- **Numerical values** – Stress plots generally include a color code key with which the user can interpret the stress values numerically. Additional numerical information on the numerical values of deflections is available in tabular form for each node in the system.

- **Animation** – Animation sequences may be generated by constructing a series of frames connecting the initial geometry to the final deflected geometry. Observations of such animation sequences helps the user develop an intuition concerning the dynamics of the processes under investigation.

Examples

To illustrate the techniques of FEA we will use COSMOS/M, one of the most capable FEA packages available. COSMOS/M runs on most platforms, including UNIX workstations, Macintoshes, and 286–486-based PCs.[19] It can analyze problems in linear and nonlinear structural mechanics, heat transfer, fluid flow, and electromagnetic fields. Models of up to 15,000 nodes and 60,000 degrees of freedom can be solved. The system consists of some 300 files consuming six megabytes of disk storage space. Designs may be imported in DXF and IGES format from other CAD systems, and completed models may be exported for analysis on mainframe and supercomputer FEA programs.

With this background in FEA we turn to some concrete examples.

Example 1: Hooke's Law –
Compare FEA results with theoretical results

In this example, we construct a simple beam of dimension 40"× 10"× 10", divide it into a simple mesh of 10 elements, anchor one end, and apply a stretching force to the other end. We then compare the elongation COSMOS/M computes with the theoretical result given by Hooke's Law (Equation 13.10).

1. Construct the model

Using mainly default values, the view, axes, and grid were specified as shown in Figure 13.39. Next, four points defining the corners of the beam were entered and the lines connecting them were specified. The resulting outline of the beam object is shown.

2. Mesh the model

Several options are available for the meshing process. We chose automatic meshing and specified approximately how large to make the elements. The results are shown in Figure 13.40.

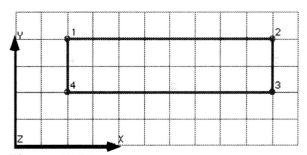

Figure 13.39
Outline of beam object created by COSMOS/M. The scale of the grid is 5" per square.

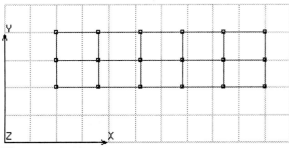

Figure 13.40
Results of automatically meshing the beam.

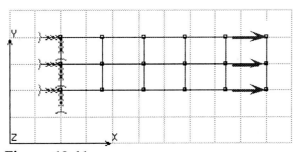

Figure 13.41
Application of boundary conditions. The left surface is clamped in both x and y. Forces of 100 lb are applied to each of the right hand nodes.

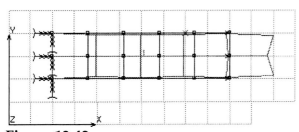

Figure 13.42
Magnified image of stretched beam. Note the "necking down" characteristic of extrusion.

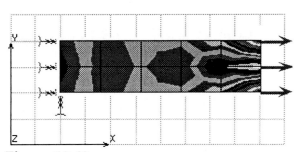

Figure 13.43
Stress distribution plot. The color code key indicates that the upper and lower right-hand corners experience the maximum stress.

3. Assign material properties

Under the MPROP menu, EX was specified to indicate Young's modulus in the x direction, and the value was set to 30×10^6 lb/in^2. Next, Poisson's ratio was selected and set to 0.3.

4. Specify boundary conditions

To specify a cantilevered beam, we must anchor one end with boundary conditions which prevent any motion in x, y, or z for the left end of the beam. This is readily accomplished by setting the displacement to zero under the BCond → Structural → Displacements menu. The **Forces** submenu of the BCond menu is used to set the forces equal to 100 lb at each node on the right-hand surface as shown in Figure 13.41.

5. Solve equations and display solution

After submitting the completed model to analysis, the postprocessor option is invoked to view the computed results. Of most immediate interest are the equilibrium displacements of each node of the excited model. These are displayed graphically in Figure 13.42 in which the computed deflections are superimposed on the original model.

6. Display the stress distribution

One of the most useful results of FEA is the distribution of stresses in the model being analyzed. High stress regions are the most likely to suffer cracking and failure. Activating the stress calculation in COSMOS/M produces the stress distribution shown in Figure 13.43.

7. Numerical verification of displacement

Using the tabulated values for the Δx displacements of the three right-end nodes, the average value for the beam elongation was computed and is shown in Table 13.1. The COSMOS/M result is seen to agree with the theoretical Hooke's Law result to within one percent.

Table 13.1
Comparison of FEA Results with Theory

COSMOS/M Results for Δx	Hooke's Law Results for Δx	% Difference
3.976×10^{-6} in.	4×10^{-6} in.	0.6

Example 2:   Modify model to compute bending deflection and compare with theory

Once the model is built and meshed, it is a relatively simple task to investigate its behavior under a variety of conditions. Suppose, for instance, that, instead of stretching the beam, we load it at the free end with a downward force of 300 lbs. This is readily accomplished by the two-step process of removing the horizontal force and applying a negative vertical force. The revised model indicating constraints and applied forces is shown in Figure 13.44.

The resulting deflection involves both bending and shearing. Figure 13.45 shows the resulting deflection plot superimposed on the original model.

Theory states that the resulting displacement in the y direction is given by a bending term involving Young's modulus, E, and a shear term involving the shear modulus, S:[20]

$$y = -\frac{L^3 F_y}{3Ek^2 A} - \frac{L F_y}{SA} \qquad [13.12]$$

where
   L = length of the beam = 40 in,
   F_y = magnitude of vertical force = 300 lbs,
   E = Young's modulus of elasticity for steel
       = 3×10^7 lb/in^2,
   A = cross section area of beam 100 in^2,
   S = shear modulus of steel
       = 1.26×10^7 lb/in^2, and
   k = radius of gyration of the cross section area about the neutral axis, given by:

$$k^2 = \frac{1}{A} \iint_A y^2 dA \ . \qquad [13.13]$$

In terms of the beam width, b, this integral evaluates to

$$k^2 = \frac{b^2}{12} = 8.33 \text{ in}^2.$$

Substitution of these values yields the theo-

Table 13.2
Comparison of FEA Results with Theory

COSMOS/M Results for Δy	Theoretical Results for Δy	% Difference
-2.61×10^{-4} in.	-2.65×10^{-4} in.	1.6

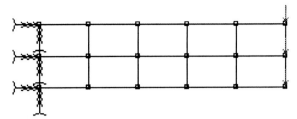

Figure 13.44
Revised FEA model of beam with $F_y = -300$ lbs applied at the nonconstrained end.

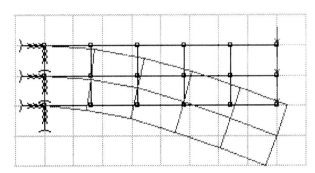

Figure 13.45
Deflection plot for end-loaded beam. This deflection results primarily from bending and, to a lesser degree, from shearing. The deflection has been magnified about 40,000 times to help the user visualize the effect.

retical displacement value given in Table 13.2.

Again, the agreement between the FEA results and theory is surprisingly good for a simple 10-element model. This gives us confidence to extrapolate FEA techniques to more complex models for which there are no standard analytical expressions.

Example 3: Distortion of plate due to forces acting on a circular hole

Suppose the top and bottom of a square plate were clamped and a lateral force exerted along the boundary of a circular hole in the center of the plate. What would be the resulting distortion in the shape of the plate?

Figure 13.46 represents the geometric design of an 8" × 8" plate with a hole of radius 1" at its center.

Next, boundary conditions are attached to the top and bottom surfaces to clamp them, and a force vector of 100 lbs is applied at each node defining the circular hole. The results are shown in Figure 13.47. After specifying the material

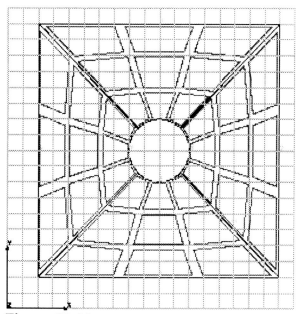

Figure 13.46
Plate design and segmentation into 36 finite elements. The shrink option helps isolate elements and detect connectivity problems.

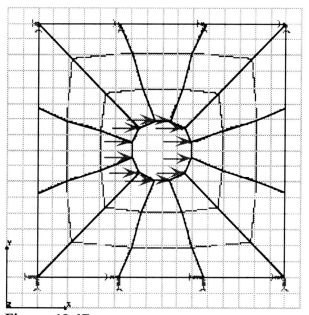

Figure 13.47
Boundary conditions limiting motion of top and bottom surface of the plate. Forces of 100 lbs are applied to each node of the circle.

properties to be those of steel, the model is ready to analyze.

This model is submitted for analysis, and 21 seconds later the user can examine the results of the FEA by plots like the deflection plot shown in Figure 13.48.

Additional insight into the behavior of the system may be obtained by studying the stress plot, viewing the model from a different perspective such as the isometric view shown in Figure 13.49, and animating the deflection sequence.

The examples above sample only a tiny fraction of the capabilities of COSMOS/M. For instance, BCond, one of ten menu options available, has five sub-menus: Structural, Thermal, Fluid Flow, Electro-Magnetic, and Load Options. The Thermal sub-menu has, in turn, the following sub-sub-menus: Temperature, Heat Flow, Nodal Heat, Element Heat, Heat Flux, Convection, and Radiation. Each of these sub-sub-menus has 10–14 sub-sub-sub-menu options, each of which requires 3–10 default or numerical specifications. So the user can send FEA objects 250 or more messages concerning boundary conditions alone.

We justify inclusion of FEA in a computer graphics book because of the central role graphics plays in the system/user interface and in the

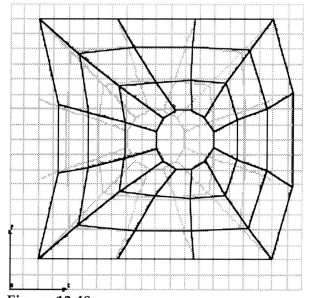

Figure 13.48
Deflection plot of plate under the influence of forces acting on the circumference of the circle.

visualization of both the model construction process and the postprocessing phase of the analysis. However, model authenticity may provide an even stronger argument for computer graphics professionals understanding the FEM. An important segment of the graphics industry deals with the design and production of computer animations, ranging from television advertisements featuring dancing bleach bottles to the realistic simulation of human motion. In the pursuit of realistic simulations, animators have been driven "back to the basics" of developing authentic models of human physiology and the forces associated with the skeletal and muscular structure. FEA has proven to be the optimal tool for achieving authenticity in applications such as modeling the response of the human body to muscular forces. There is no question but that the demand for increasingly realistic computer animations will expand the domain of application of the FEM.

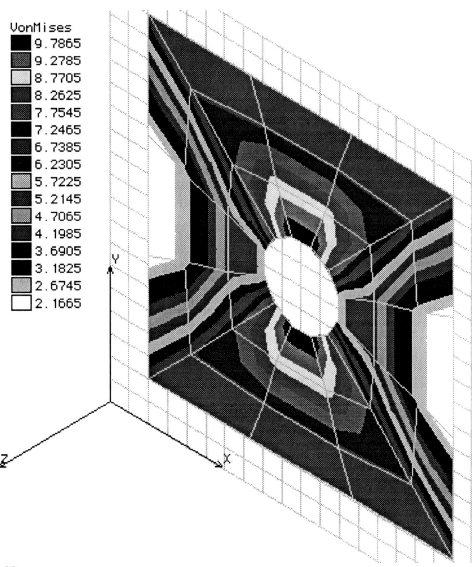

Figure 13.49
Stress plot with encoding key shown in isometric 3D view.

Conclusions

In this chapter we have demonstrated the central role of computer graphics in design and engineering tools. The product development process begins with a conceptual design, proceeds through a detailed engineering design phase, and, particularly for critical components, requires engineering analysis to detect potential failure modes to assure safe performance. We have identified these three phases of product development as CADC, CADD, and CAE and have illustrated each with several examples run on three of the leading application programs. These three programs incorporate most of the GUI features presented in the previous chapter as well as virtually all of the graphical transformation algorithms presented earlier in the book. All three use object-oriented programming as the paradigm through which the user creates and manipulates objects in a model.

Finally, this chapter has demonstrated that the development of more authentic computer models requires richer databases. To fully understand the behavior of the objects we design, it is necessary to augment our geometric models with information on the material properties of each object and the laws of physics governing their behavior. FEA tools combine CAD functionality with numerical analysis techniques and postprocessing visualization tools for efficiently performing accurate engineering analysis. Computer graphics provides the principle channel through which the FEA analyst builds and manipulates models. FEA, in turn, has become an essential technique for modeling the human body and other subjects of computer animation.

Exercises

13.1 On the abstract/concrete spectrum shown in Figure 13.1, *Swivel 3D* is positioned as abstract and COSMOS/M as concrete. From the features listed in the text, list as many arguments as you can for the validity of this characterization.

13.2 Skilled designers take great pride in their ability to create conceptual designs rapidly using only pencil and paper. Compare the advantages of this manual technique with the advantages of the CADC technique.

13.3 The integration of CADD with the manufacturing process (NCM controlled directly from engineering drawings) is called CAD/CAM. What function(s) would you suggest for computer graphics in the CAM aspect of this process?

13.4 In the discussion of Automating Engineering Design we discuss some less obvious advantages of CAD. From a scan of engineering and CAD journals in your library, find and photocopy product descriptions illustrating (or claiming) each of these advantages.

13.5 Nine features were listed as desirable for a concept design tool. Many of the painting/drawing programs available on personal workstations support several of these features. Select and use one such program, and rate it on each of the nine features on a scale of 0–10 (0 → totally missing, 10 → fully supported) and provide interpretative comments justifying your ratings.

13.6 Figure 13.11 exhibits certain artifacts related to the shading and rendering algorithms discussed in previous chapters. List at least three such artifacts and how they could be eliminated by more sophisticated rendering algorithms.

13.7 In summarizing the conceptual design of the vase we claimed that the process demonstrated good GUI design. How many click operations and click-and-drag operations were required to design the vase? Assume next that a pre-GUI interface with command line input (no mouse) was used for this task. Design a minimum set of command line instructions necessary for carrying out this design task, and estimate how many commands and numerical values would be required.

13.8 What features of the vase and table made the lathed cube and extruded triangle, respectively, the natural initial objects for their design?

13.9 Explain what we mean when we say that *Swivel 3D* is capable of the design of "intelligent objects." Discuss what constraints you would apply in the design of a human body from component torso, upper arm, lower arm, hand, fingers, and so on.

13.10 What features do high-level CADD systems like *VersaCAD* and *AutoCAD* offer that are missing in more elementary drawing programs like *WindowsDRAW* and *MacDRAW*?

13.11 What is meant by the statement, "Most primitive CADD objects are more abstract than simple graphical primitives"? Give examples illustrating your argument.

13.12 We achieved a reasonable shape for the single gear tooth (Figure 13.26) by a connected set of four Bézier curves and a straight line. More standard practice for gear design involves use of the *involute system* or the *cycloidal system*. Do some library research, and summarize one or the other of these two systems.

13.13 Describe the use and advantages of the *Extend/Trim* option of CADD systems.

13.14 Are the spokes of the gear illustrated in Figures 13.29–13.30 an optimum design? Why or why not? What suggestions would you have for improvement?

13.15 What is meant by *associative dimensioning*? In what situations would it be a particularly valuable feature of a CADD system?

13.16 Discuss the use and advantages of *layering* in CADD. How might layering be integrated with the use of color?

13.17 Library objects such as doors which automatically install themselves in walls were cited as examples of "intelligent objects." List three more candidates you would suggest being designed as intelligent objects, specify how they would behave intelligently, and describe the advantages they would offer the designer.

13.18 Describe some of the geometry aids which CADD systems provide and how they speed the design process.

13.19 What functionality would database extensions offer for CADD systems?

13.20 Both *Swivel 3D* and *VersaCAD* offer lathing and extrusion for converting 2D outlines into 3D objects. Many objects can be de-

signed by these two techniques. Describe five objects which cannot be. Could any of your five exceptions be approximated by constructive solid geometry operations on lathed and/or extruded objects?

13.21 One perspective holds that finite element analysis is a technique for adding intelligence to a model. What is the nature of this intelligence, and what does it provide beyond the geometrical models of CADD systems?

13.22 Much of the mathematical foundation of the FEM parallels that of the proofs in calculus. Discuss this parallelism using, as an example, the calculus concept of integration as the limiting case of the summation of rectangular areas.

13.23 Prove that Hooke's Law follows from applying the principle of energy minimization to the energy functional for a compressed spring.

13.24 Breaking a CADD model up into its finite elements is called the process of meshing. Elegant algorithms have been written for automatic meshing. What considerations do you think might be important for such an algorithm?

13.25 One of the most helpful features for model verification is the "shrink" option which shrinks the boundaries of each element by a user-specified factor while leaving the object outline unchanged. What type of errors will this option help detect?

13.26 The matrices involved in the stiffness equation of FEA are generally very sparse. To what do you attribute this? Does this characteristic help or hinder the solution process?

13.27 What are the six steps in the preprocessing phase of FEA? Rank them according to what you would expect to be the most time consuming.

13.28 Computer graphics is obviously very important in the preprocessing and postprocessing phases of FEA. How would you suggest computer graphics be used in the analysis phase?

13.29 The first two FEA examples presented in the text demonstrated the agreement of the "experimental" results of the FEM with theoretical predictions. What additional theoretical comparisons would you propose for verifying the performance of FEA systems?

13.30 Interpret the "necking down" observed in the FEA results of Figure 13.42 in terms of volume conservation of distorted objects.

13.31 Stress plots are particularly useful in identifying potential failure modes of objects under stress. Describe how you would use a FEA of the gear shown in Figure 13.30 to modify its design.

13.32 Discuss the complementary role of computer graphics and finite element analysis. In particular, consider the use of computer graphics in designing FEA models and visualizing the results of FEA, and the use of FEA for authentic simulation of complex mechanical systems used in computer animations.

Endnotes

1. Porter, Steven, "Educating our Engineers," *Computer Graphics World* **14**, No. 10, p. 47, October (1991).
2. Porter, Steven, *op cit*, p. 51.
3. McCormick, Bruce H., DeFanti, Thomas A., and Brown, Maxine D., *Computer Graphics* **21**, No. 6, Special Issue on "Visualization in Scientific Computing," November (1987) etc.
4. Machover, Carl and Blauth, Robert E. (eds), *The CAD/CAM Handbook*, Computervision Corporation, Bedford, MA (1980).
5. Besant, C. B. and Lui, C. W. K., *Computer-Aided Design and Manufacture*, Third Edition, Halsted Press Division of John Wiley & Sons, Chichester, UK (1986).
6. Kerlow, Isaac Victor and Rosebush, Judson, *Computer Graphics for Designers & Artists*, Van Nostrand Reinhold Company, New York, NY (1986).
7. Information on *Swivel 3D* may be obtained from:
     Paracomp, Inc.
     1725 Montgomery Street, 2nd Floor
     San Francisco, CA 94111-1030
8. Gantz, John, "A Healthy MCAD Market," *Computer Graphics World* **14**, No. 11, pp. 23–26, November (1991).
9. Ryan, Daniel L., *Modern Graphic Communications – A CAD Approach*, Prentice-Hall, Inc., Englewood Cliffs, NJ (1986).
10. Information on *VersaCAD*™ may be obtained from:
     VERSACAD Corporation
     2124 Main Street
     Huntington Beach, CA 92648
     (714) 960-7720
11. Luzadder, Warren J., *Fundamentals of Engineering Drawing*, Prentice-Hall, Inc. Englewood Cliffs, NJ (1977).
12. Gerlach, Gary M., *Transition to CADD – A Practical Guide for Architects, Engineers, and Designers*, McGraw-Hill Book Company, New York, NY (1987).
13. Besant, C. B. and Lui, C. W. K., *op cit*.
14. Courant, R., "Variational Methods for the Solution of Problems of Equilibrium and Vibrations," *Bull Am Math Soc* **49**, pp. 1–23 (1943).
15. Brauer, John R. (ed), *What Every Engineer Should Know about Finite Element Analysis*, Marcel Dekker, Inc., New York, NY (1988).
16. Zienkiewicz, O. C., *The Finite Element Method*, Third Edition, McGraw-Hill, London, UK (1977).
17. Burnett, David S., *Finite Element Analysis*, Addison-Wesley Publishing Co., Reading, MA (1987).
18. Yang, T. Y., *Finite Element Structural Analysis*, Prentice-Hall, Inc., Englewood Cliffs, NJ (1986).
19. Information on COSMOS/M is available from
     Structural Research and Analysis Corp.
     1661 Lincoln Blvd., Suite 200
     Santa Monica, CA 90404
     Phone: (213) 452-2158
20. Symon, Keith R., *Mechanics*, Third Edition, Addison-Wesley Publishing Company, p. 247, Reading, MA (1971).

Chapter 14

Visualizing Mathematics and Physics

Mathematica **is a model of consistency, most of the time.**
Theodore Gray

One will be struck by the complexity of this figure which I do not even attempt to draw. Nothing more properly gives us an idea of complication of the problem of three bodies and, in general, of all the problems in dynamics where there is no uniform integral.
Henri Poincaré

After a few checks against reality, you quickly learn to trust programs such as *Mathematica* **and** *Interactive Physics*. **In fact, if your simulated falling apple doesn't act just like your real falling apple, you tend to question your real-world experimental procedure before you question the program. And rightly so.**
Michael Swaine

T he principle of model authenticity was invoked to help explain the improvement in the realism of images rendered with ray tracing and radiosity algorithms. It provides the rationale for using fractal geometry for constructing images of natural objects and scenes. Model authenticity motivates the extensions of CADD programs to include "intelligent objects" such as doors and windows which insert themselves into walls, and the physical models of FEA in which all objects have attributes such as density, coefficient of elasticity, and knowledge of how they should respond to applied forces. This principle is essential for progress in achieving visual realism in computer graphics, and computer graphics, in turn, is essential for visualizing and interacting with the intelligent objects in authentic models.

Model authenticity is one aspect of the more general problem of the design of intelligent systems. Perhaps the single most important measure of progress in software engineering is the degree to which new systems are more intelligent than their predecessors. Intelligent systems assist the user in producing far better output far quicker and with much more fun than was possible with their

dim-witted ancestors. In this chapter we examine the capabilities and graphical output of two of the most useful tools in mathematics and physics.

In addition to outstanding examples of visualization tools, the two systems examined can be considered as *expert systems* or *simulation tools*.

Expert systems are an outgrowth of research in artificial intelligence, and one of the earliest examples is *MACSYMA*, a mathematical expert system originating at MIT. Stephen Wolfram has integrated the numeric and symbolic capabilities of an expert system with high-quality graphics in *Mathematica*.[1] This program provides a mathematics expert system comparable to *MACSYMA*, but with the tremendous advantage of an easy-to-use GUI and a powerful graphics system.

Simulation tools allow the user to create and study the behavior of physical, biological, or social systems by accurately representing them in software. Simulation models permit the student or researcher to develop an understanding and intuition for systems which may be too expensive or even impossible to build in the laboratory. *Interactive Physics*™, "the first physics laboratory on a computer," is an ideal example of simulation tools.[2] The program understands the fundamentals of Newtonian mechanics and applies them to any user-constructed system of springs, ropes, dampers, masses, and meters.

Several pedagogical purposes are served by introducing *Mathematica* and *Interactive Physics* in significant detail at this point. In addition to informing the reader of the capabilities of two of the leading analysis tools, the discussion illustrates the central role computer graphics plays in helping users visualize difficult concepts in physics and mathematics. *Mathematica*, in fact, contains a complete graphics language with capabilities for 3D rendering models with hidden surface removal and shading. *Interactive Physics* provides much more limited 2D graphics but offers an "intelligent" CADD environment for building and exploring the behavior of complex and chaotic systems.

Both *Mathematica* and *Interactive Physics* incorporate elegant computer graphics techniques which readers may wish to further explore and implement in their own application programs. With this motivation, let's consider each program in detail.

Mathematica – A System for Doing Mathematics by Computer

While it is correct to describe *Mathematica* as a comprehensive mathematics expert system augmented with powerful graphics, such a description overlooks many features which distinguish this package. A partial list of such features include the following.

- A library of over 850 numeric and symbolic functions for use in an interactive, calculator mode with arbitrary precision arithmetic. These functions are also extensible.

- A convenient representation of lists, vectors, and matrices and the standard operations of linear algebra for manipulating them.

- An extensive library of graphical functions for doing 2D and 3D graphics, including contour and density plots, with color, shading, and lighting attributes and parametric representations.

- A high-level programming language for combining all of the above functions and routines into more abstract units.

- A set of packages for specialized applications, including statistics, Laplace transforms, and the chemical elements.

- A notebook format for recording and executing *Mathematica* sessions. Notebooks behave like word processed documents with intelligent equations which produce symbolic, numerical, or graphical results when evaluated.

- Multimedia capabilities. *Mathematica* supports animation, the importing, generation, and exporting of sound, and terminal emulation tools.

- A hierarchical structure for efficient network programming. Separation of the program into a kernel (computation engine) and interface unit allows assigning computationally intensive tasks to the most efficient nodes of a network.

Syntax

The grammar of *Mathematica* consists of a set of expressions which the system evaluates upon demand by the user. These expressions may be mathematical functions or commands for performing operations such as **Plot3D** and **Do**. The syntax for expressing arguments, lists, and multiplication differs somewhat from the notation used by most high-level languages. The differences represent a conscious effort to remove the ambiguities of high-level languages and bring *Mathematica* expressions into a closer semblance of traditional mathematical expressions. Table 14.1 lists some major features of *Mathematica* syntax and indicates how they differ from other computer languages.

Novice *Mathematica* users sometimes trip over these syntax differences but soon learn to appreciate the logical distinctions on which they are based. The general philosophy of *Mathematica* is to make the semantics of the syntax as explicit and context independent as possible. Thus, the various semantics (meanings) of the mathematical expression c(a+b) are clarified by the *Mathematica* syntax:

c(a+b)   →   multiply variable *c* by the sum of
            variable *a* plus variable *b*,

Table 14.1

Comparison of Mathematica vs. High-Level Language Syntax

Feature	Mathematica	High-Level Language
Naming convention	Functions capitalized, e.g. `Sin[x]`	All functions case independent, e.g. `sin(x)`
Argument lists	Square bracket delimiters e.g. `Max[x,y,z]`	Parentheses delimiters, e.g. `max(x,y,z)`
List structure	Curly bracket delimiters, e.g. `{a,b,c,d,e}`	Parenthesis delimiters e.g. `(a,b,c,d,e)`
Multiplication	Unrestricted, e.g. `2a` or `2 a` or `2*a` (but not `ab` or `a2`)	Asterisk notation only, e.g. `2*a`
Variable naming	Lower case preferred, to avoid conflict with built-in objects, e.g. `a,x1,maximum`	No case restriction (except for Prolog) e.g. `A,x1,Maximum`
Parentheses	Used for logical grouping only	Used for: logical grouping, argument lists, sets, and lists
Reference to last result	`%` e.g. (User input **bold**) `Sqrt[25]` 5 `%+1` 6	Not supported
Argument order	Flexible through use of named arguments	Order is fixed
Program structure	Separable (hierarchical): platform independent computing engine (kernel) + platform dependent GUI	Integrated, single stand-alone programs

c[a+b] → user-defined function c has an argument whose value is the sum of variable *a* plus variable *b*,

c[[a+b]] → the (a+b)th element of list c.

The basic object in *Mathematica* is the expression. The architecture of evaluation closely resembles that of the LISP *Read–Eval–Print* loop. That is, the user types an expression, issues the evaluate message (with the *Enter* key), and *Mathematica* prints the results of evaluating the expression. LISP programmers will also recognize the functional representation used in expressions. That is, the *Mathematica* expression `x + y + z` is equivalent to the *Mathematica* full form `Plus[x,y,z]` and the LISP `(+ x y z)`, the

Mathematica expression `a = b` is equivalent to the *Mathematica* full form `Set[a,b]` and the LISP `(set a b)`, and so on.

With this background we can begin to use *Mathematica* to produce useful numeric, symbolic, and graphical results. A few examples illustrating the numeric and symbolic capabilities of *Mathematica* are presented next, followed by a more extensive set of graphics examples.

Numeric Examples

To illustrate some of the numeric calculations possible with *Mathematica*, consider the following examples. In each example the user enters the `boldface` expressions and the system responds with the `standard face` answer. Interpretive comments are on the right.

Example 1: Compute the value of (3×4)+(5×6).

| `3  4+5*6`
`42` | Note that either the space or "*" serves as the multiply symbol |

Example 2: Compute five raised to the 120th power.

| `5^120`
`7523163845262640050999913838222372338`
`03945956334136013765601092018187046051`
`1025390625` | This is standard exponential notation. Note the result in infinite precision arithmetic. |

Example 3: Convert the result of Example 2 to scientific notation.

| `N[%,20]`
`7.523163845262640051  10`^{83} | Issuing the numeric command converts the Example 2 results to scientific notation to an arbitrary precision of 20 places. |

Example 4: Calculate the one millionth prime number.

| `Prime[1000000]`
`15485863` | This is the 1,000,000th number in the series:
2,3,5,7,11,13,17,19,23,29 ... |

Example 5: Calculate the area under the sine curve from 0 to pi.

| `Integrate[Sin[x],{x,0,Pi}]`
`2` | Note the limits as a list structure and the built-in constant, Pi. The use of exact limits results in exact output. |

Example 6: Calculate the sum of three fractions.

| `1/3+1/4+1/5`
$\frac{47}{60}$ | Note the capability for rational arithmetic. |

Example 7: Find the root of the first-order Bessel function in the vicinity of 8.

| `FindRoot[BesselJ[1,x],{x,8}]`
`{x -> 7.01559}` | Note the natural syntax for this complex task.
`FindRoot` uses Newton's method. |

Example 8: Compute the square of the complex number z=3+5i.

| `(3+5I)^2`
`-16 + 30 I` | The system knows about complex numbers and uses $I = \sqrt{-1}$. |

Example 9: Compute the dot product, A·B, of two vectors, A=(3,6,2) and B=(5,3,7).

| `A={3,6,2};`
`B={5,3,7};`
`A.B`
`47` | First we define the two vectors as lists and then take the dot product with the period serving as the dot symbol. The semicolons suppress output of lists `A` and `B`. |

Example 10: Compute the cross product, A × B, of these two vectors.

| `<<Calculus`VectorAnalysis``
`CrossProduct[A,B]`
`{36, -11, -21}` | First we load the vector analysis package. Then we compute the cross product with the function of the same name. |

Example 11: Calculate the single matrix M which will rotate an object 20° about the arbitrary axis whose direction cosines are (0.3,0.4,0.886) and which contains the point P=(3,4,5). Recall, the solution is given by $M = T(-P) \cdot R_x \cdot R_z \cdot R_y(20°) \cdot R_z^{-1} \cdot R_x^{-1} \cdot T(P)$.

Input

`x=3`
`y=4`
`z=5`
`a=.3`
`b=.4`
`c=.866`
`th=N[20 Degree]`
`d=Sqrt[b^2+c^2]`
`T={{1,0,0,0},`
`   {0,1,0,0},`
`   {0,0,1,0},`
`   {-x,-y,-z,1}}`
`Rx={{1,0,0,0},`
`   {0,b/d,-c/d,0},`
`   {0,c/d,b/d,0},`
`   {0,0,0,1}}`
`Rz={{d,a,0,0},`
`   {-a,d,0,0},`
`   {0,0,1,0},`
`   {0,0,0,1}}`
`Ry={{Cos[th],0,-Sin[th],0},`
`   {0,1,0,0},`
`   {Sin[th],0,Cos[th],0},`
`   {0,0,0,1}}`
`M=T.Rx.Rz.Ry.Inverse[Rz].`
`Inverse[Rx].Inverse[T]`
	Here we define the point on the axis.
	
	Next we define the direction cosines.
	
	The radian value of theta is computed using built in function, **Degree**.
	Now set up the **T** matrix.
	
	Next, define the R_x matrix.
	
	This is the R_z matrix.
	
	This matrix does the actual rotation by θ.
	
	This matrix multiplication generates the answer, **M**.

Output

`3`
`4`
`5`
`0.3`
`0.4`
`0.866`
`0.349066`
`0.953916`
`{{1,  0,  0,  0},`
`{0,  1,  0,  0},`
`{0,  0,  1,  0},`
`{-3, -4, -5, 1}}`
	Upon evaluation, the system repeats the assignments.
	
	This is θ calculated in radians.
	This is the result calculated for d.
	
	This is the **T** matrix.

```{{1, 0, 0, 0},```
```{0, 0.419324, -0.907837, 0},```
```{0, 0.907837, 0.419324, 0},```
```{0, 0, 0, 1}}```
	This is the $\mathbf{R}_x$ matrix.

```{{0.953916, 0.3, 0, 0},```
```{-0.3, 0.953916, 0, 0},```
```{0, 0, 1, 0},```
```{0, 0, 0, 1}}```
	This is the $\mathbf{R}_z$ matrix.

```{{0.939693, 0, -0.34202, 0},```
```{0, 1, 0, 0},```
```{0.34202, 0, 0.939693, 0},```
```{0, 0, 0, 1}}```
	This is the $\mathbf{R}_y(\theta)$ matrix.

```{{0.945121, 0.303427, -0.12114, 0.},```
```{-0.288965, 0.949344, 0.123501, 0.},```
```{0.152483, -0.0817154, 0.984921, 0.},```
```{0.558086, -0.299079, -0.05519, 1.}}```
	This is the final answer, **M**, the matrix which will perform the desired 20° rotation about the arbitrary axis.

These examples represent only a random sampling of *Mathematica's* numerical capabilities. As the latter examples illustrate, *Mathematica* is fully capable of performing all of the numerical manipulations required in computer graphics.

Next, we examine examples illustrating *Mathematica's* symbolic processing capabilities.

Symbolic Examples

Any mathematics expert system must be able to manipulate symbols as well as numbers. Symbols represent a higher level of abstraction than numbers, and this abstraction permits them to stand for other symbols, combinations of symbols, or transformations on sets of symbols. In fact, the ability to define and manipulate symbols is at the core of the *Physical Symbol System Hypothesis*—the foundation of classical artificial intelligence.[3]

Mathematica supports all standard operations of algebra and calculus, including solving systems of equations, differential and integral calculus, and manipulations of lists, matrices, and sets. Transformation rules may be used to define symbols in terms of other algebraic expressions. Mapping operations allow applications of symbolic functions to elements of lists. Recursion is fully supported, making definition of recursive functions simply a matter of writing them down in standard mathematical syntax.

Consider the following examples of symbolic operations.

Example 1: Define symbols in terms of other symbols.

```a=b``` ```b```	Define *a* in terms of *b*.
```a``` ```b```	Evaluate *a*.
```b=c``` ```c```	Define *b* in terms of *c*.
```a+b+c``` ```3 c```	Now both *a* and *b* are defined in terms of *c*.

Example 2: Raise a symbolic expression to a power and expand its terms.

`(x+y+z)^4`
 	
$(x + y + z)^4$
 	
`Expand[%]`
 	
$x^4 + 4 x^3 y + 6 x^2 y^2 + 4 x y^3 + y^4 +$
$4 x^3 z + 12 x^2 y z + 12 x y^2 z + 4 y^3 z$
$+ 6 x^2 z^2 + 12 x y z^2 + 6 y^2 z^2 + 4 x$
$z^3 + 4 y z^3 + z^4$
	Define a symbolic object.
	
	This expands the previous result.

Example 3: Simplify and factor complex algebraic expressions. The polynomial, $-y(2x + y + 2z)(2x^2 + 2xy + y^2 + 4xz + 2yz + 2z^2)$ is expanded and added to the result of Example 2.

`%+Expand[-(y*(2*x + y + 2*z)* (2*x^2 +`
`2*x*y + y^2 + 4*x*z + 2*y*z +`
`2*z^2))]`
$x^4 + 4 x^3 z + 6 x^2 z^2 + 4 x z^3 + z^4$
`Factor[%]`
$(x + z)^4$
	Subtract a polynomial representing the y terms from the results of Example 2 (%). This polynomial can be generated using the `Collect[%,y]` function.
	The result is factored to yield a more compact result.

Example 4: Integrate a symbolic expression, $\int \dfrac{1}{(1-x^4)}\,dx$.

`Integrate[1/(1-x^4),x]` $\dfrac{ArcTan[x]}{2} - \dfrac{Log[-1 + x]}{4} - \dfrac{Log[1 + x]}{4}$	Integrating this simple function yields a surprisingly complex result.

Example 5: Differentiate a symbolic expression, the result of Example 4.

`D[%,x]` $\dfrac{-1}{4(-1+x)} + \dfrac{1}{4(1+x)} + \dfrac{1}{2(1+x^2)}$	Differentiating the result of Example 4 gives the following series.

Example 6: Simplify the result of Example 5 to recover the original expression.

`Simplify[%]` $\dfrac{1}{(1-x^4)}$	Calling the *Simplify* function does indeed recover the original expression.

Example 7: Solve a set of two equations in two unknowns.

`Solve[{a x + b y==c,d x + e y==f},{x,y}]` $\{\{x \rightarrow \dfrac{c\ e}{-(b\ d) + a\ e} - \dfrac{b\ f}{-(b\ d) + a\ e},$ $y \rightarrow -(\dfrac{c\ d}{-(b\ d) + a\ e}) + \dfrac{a\ f}{-(b\ d) + a\ e}\}\}$	This is the most general form for two, independent linear equations. Note that both equations and variables are given as lists.

Example 8: Solve the simple quadratic equation symbolically.

`a x^2+b x+c==0` $c + b x + a x^2 == 0$	Input the quadratic equation in standard form. Note the syntax for equality.
`Solve[%,x]`	Now solve this equation with respect to x.
$$\left\{\left\{x \to \frac{-\left(\frac{b}{a}\right) + \frac{\text{Sqrt}[b^2 - 4\ a\ c]}{a}}{2}\right\},\right.$$ $$\left.\left\{x \to \frac{-\left(\frac{b}{a}\right) - \frac{\text{Sqrt}[b^2 - 4\ a\ c]}{a}}{2}\right\}\right\}$$	Note that the answer is a list of lists of rules.

Example 9: Functions may be defined for handling both symbolic and numeric data.

`g=Function[{x,y},Sqrt[x*x+y*y]]`
$\text{Function}[\{x, y\}, \text{Sqrt}[x\ x + y\ y]]$
`g[e,f]`
$\text{Sqrt}[e^2 + f^2]$
`g[3,4]`
5
	This is one mode for defining a function.
	Here it is invoked with symbolic arguments, and then with numeric ones.

`h[a_,b_]:=Sqrt[a^2+b^2]`
`h[e,f]`
$\text{Sqrt}[e^2 + f^2]$
`h[3,4]`
5
	This is the more standard way to define a function if the function is to be used repeatedly.

Example 10: Mapping and pattern matching are readily accomplished. Note that "_" stands for "any expression."

`c[x_]:=x^3`
`Map[c,{1,2,3,4,5}]`
{1, 8, 27, 64, 125}
	This defines a cube function.
	Here it is mapped onto a list,
	giving a list of answers.

`l={1,2,3,a,x^3,b,x^5}` $\{1, 2, 3, a, x^3, b, x^5\}$	Define a list, *l*.
`Cases[l,x_Integer]` {1, 2, 3}	List the integers in list *l*.
`Count[l,x_Symbol]` 2	Count how many symbols are in *l*.
`Cases[l,x^_]` $\{x^3, x^5\}$	List cases fitting the pattern "x^_".

Again, these ten examples are but a brief, random sampling of the symbolic processing capability of *Mathematica*.

As useful and interesting as the numeric and symbolic processing features of this expert system are, the major advantage of *Mathematica* for visualizing mathematics lies in its extensive graphics capabilities. We turn to these next.

Graphics Examples

Most of the graphics examples presented to this point in the book could have been generated by *Mathematica*. This system provides one of the most striking examples of abstraction. That is, many of the examples requiring tens to hundreds of lines of Pascal code can be generated by two or three *Mathematica* commands. That is really what abstraction means—"saying more with less." Consider the following examples.

Example 1: Plot a set of (x,y) data pairs from Chapter 1.

```
t2={{10.00,  9.14},
    {8.00,   8.14},
    {13.00,  8.74},
    {9.00,   8.77},
    {11.00,  9.26},
    {14.00,  8.10},
    {6.00,   6.13},
    {4.00,   3.10},
    {12.00,  9.13},
    {7.00,   7.26},
    {5.00,   4.74}};
ListPlot[t2,Prolog->
AbsolutePointSize[10]]
```

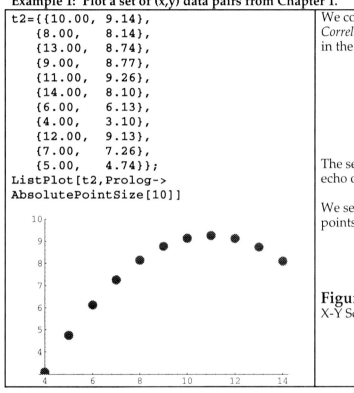

We copy in the second data set from the *Correlations in Data* example in Chapter 1 and edit in the proper list delimiters, { }.

The semicolon terminator suppresses a system echo of the data.

We send the message to plot this list of data in points ten pixels in diameter.

Figure 14.1
X-Y Scatter plot.

Example 2: Plot the first twelve prime numbers in bar chart format.

```
<<Graphics`Graphics`
p=Table[Prime[i],{i,12}]
{2, 3, 5, 7, 11, 13, 17,
19, 23, 29, 31, 37}
BarChart[p]
```

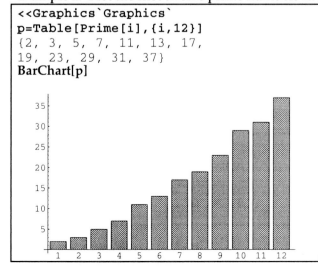

First, load the `Graphics` package. Then generate a data table using the *Prime* function in conjunction with the *Table* command. Then issue the *BarChart* message.

Figure 14.2
Bar Chart of first twelve primes.

Example 3: Make a pie chart of the first five primes.

```Take[p,5]```
```{2, 3, 5, 7, 11}```
```PieChart[%]```
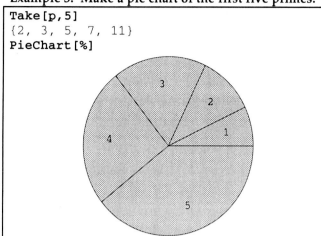
	Select the first five primes from the list, *p*.
	Send this sub-list to *PieChart*.
	
	Figure 14.3
	Pie Chart of first five primes.

Example 4: Plot a function showing how a square wave can be approximated by the Fourier synthesis of sine waves.

```f[x_]=Sum[Sin[(2n-1) x]/(2n-1),{n,1,4}]```
$\text{Sin}[x] + \dfrac{\text{Sin}[3\ x]}{3} + \dfrac{\text{Sin}[5\ x]}{5} + \dfrac{\text{Sin}[7\ x]}{7}$
```Plot[f[x],{x,0,2Pi}]```
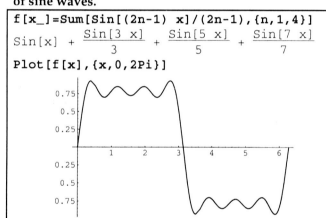
	Generate an approximation function from the first four Fourier terms.
	
	Now use the *Plot* command.
	
	Figure 14.4
	Fourier Series. Note the reasonable approximation to a square wave from the sum of only four components of the Fourier series.

Example 5:   Interesting functions may be superimposed with labels and grids.

```Plot[Evaluate[Table[BesselJ[n,x],{n,1,3}]],{x,0,10},```
```PlotStyle>{RGBColor[1,0,0],RGBColor[0,1,0],```
```RGBColor[0,0,1]},Frame->True,FrameLabel->{"X```
```value","Jn(X)"},GridLines-> Automatic]```
	This is the command to plot the Bessel functions of order 1,2, and 3 on the range of 0–10 with a frame, grid lines, and labels on the x and y axis.
	
	Figure 14.5
	Bessel functions of order 1, 2, and 3 with axes labeling and grid lines.

Example 6: Parametric plots are a natural mode for generating Lissajous figures.

| `ParametricPlot[{Sin[t],Sin[4t]},{t,0,2Pi}]`
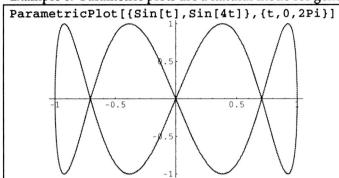 | This is the syntax for generating a 2D parametric plot.

Figure 14.6
The result is a Lissajous figure. |

Example 7: Three-dimensional function plot.

| `f1=Plot3D[Cos[x]*Cos[y],`
`{x,-Pi,Pi},{y,-Pi,Pi}]`
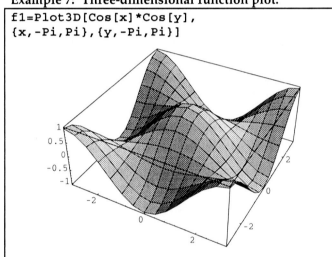 | Define an "egg carton" function and plot over one cycle in each coordinate.

Figure 14.7
Three-dimensional surface plot. |

Example 8: Contour plot of three-dimensional function.

| `ContourPlot[Cos[x]*Cos[y],{x,-Pi,Pi},{y,-Pi,Pi},`
`ColorFunction->Hue,ContourSmoothing->Automatic]`
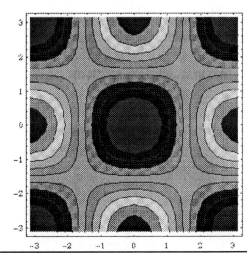 | Plot the contours (lines of equal elevation) of the 3D function used in Example 7.

Figure 14.8
Contour plot of the "egg carton" function. Note the color coding of elevation information, shown here as shading. |

Example 9: Three-dimensional parametric function.

| ```
ParametricPlot3D[
{t,Sin[2t] Sin[s],Sin[2t] Cos[s]},
{t,-Pi/2,Pi/2},{s,0,2Pi}, Ticks->None,
Boxed->False, Axes->False]
```<br><br> | Define a "bar-bell" parametric function.<br><br><br><br><br>**Figure 14.9**<br>Three-dimensional parametric surface plot. Note how this surface is equivalent to *lathing* a sine wave about the *x*-axis. |

Example 10: Composite three-dimensional parametric functions.

| ```
ParametricPlot3D[
{{t,Sin[2t] Sin[s],Sin[2t] Cos[s]},
{Sin[2t] Sin[s],t,Sin[2t] Cos[s]}},
{t,-Pi/2,Pi/2},{s,0,2Pi}, Ticks->None,
Boxed->False,Axes->False]
```<br><br>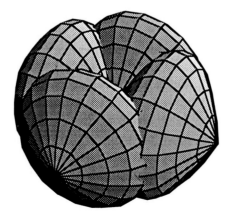 | Superimpose two bar-bells along the *x*- and *y*-axes.<br><br><br><br><br>**Figure 14.10**<br>Results of super-imposing two three-dimensional parametric surface plots. |

Example 11: Display three-dimensional object from one of many library units.

```<<Graphics`Polyhedra` Show[Polyhedron[Icosahedron]]``` 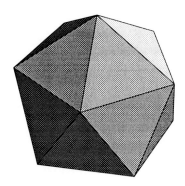	Load *Polyhedra* package. Display icosahedron. **Figure 14.11** Icosahedron (20-sided figure) from library of polyhedra.

Example 12: Apply transformation to 3D object to generate new 3D object.

```Show[Stellate[%]]``` 	Apply the *Stellate* function to the icosahedron shown in Figure 14.11. **Figure 14.12** A stellated icosahedron. Stellation is the replacement of each polygon by a pyramid with the original polygon as base.

Example 13: Generate an RGB color cube.

``` Show[Graphics3D[Table[{RGBColor[i/3,j/3,k/3], Cuboid[{1.25i,1.25j,1.25k}]}, {i,0,3},{j,0,3},{k,0,3}], Lighting->False]] ```	Set up a $4 \times 4 \times 4$ table of *cuboids* (unit cubes from the library), and color each according to its RGB coordinates.
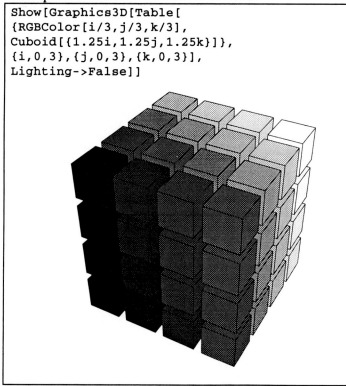	**Figure 14.13** Color cube illustrating the RGB color model, encoded as grayscale.

Example 14: Examine and label bottom layer of RGB color cube.

``` Show[Graphics3D[Table[{RGBColor[i/3,j/3,0], Cuboid[{1.25i,1.25j,0}]}, {i,0,3},{j,0,3}], Lighting->False,Axes->True, AxesLabel->{"Red","Green","Blue "},Boxed- >False, Ticks->{Automatic,Automatic,{0,1}}]] ```	Limit array to the bottom layer of the RGB cube, remove box, turn Axes on, and add RGB labels.
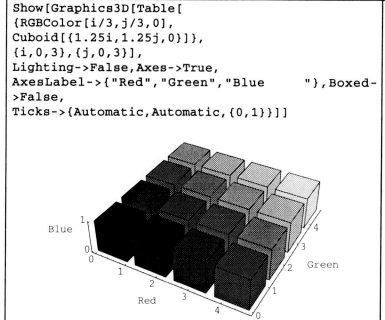	**Figure 14.14** Bottom layer of RGB color cube illustrating the mixing of red and green to produce yellow.

Example 15: Explore objects of intrinsic mathematical interest.

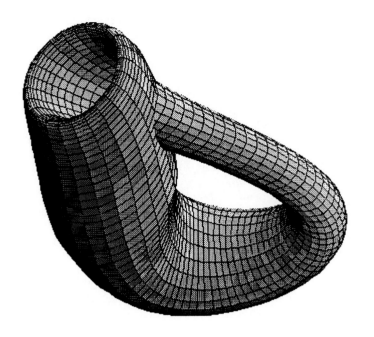

Figure 14.15
Mathematica provides the graphical tools for visualizing the topological structure of interesting mathematical objects such as this Klein bottle from Sample Notebook 1 by Wolfram Research.

Example 16: Investigate the dynamics of complex physical systems.

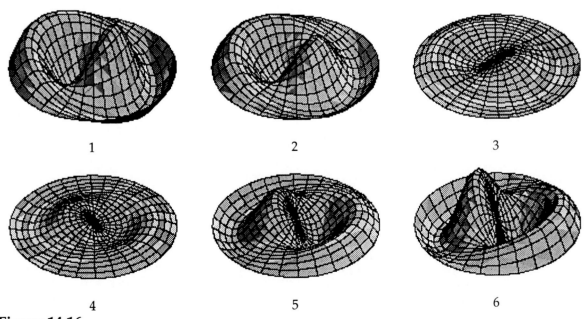

1   2   3

4   5   6

Figure 14.16
Frames from an animation sequence showing motion of drum membrane after excitation. By displaying animation at up to 60 frames per second, *Mathematica* helps the user visualize the complex motion described by differential equations.

The graphical examples presented above are an attempt to convey the potential of *Mathematica* as a tool for visualizing the world of mathematics and for modeling and understanding the behavior of complex systems in physics and engineering.

To conclude the discussion of *Mathematica*, three concepts should be emphasized.

- **Authenticity and accessibility** – Every example presented above was running live under *Mathematica* at the same time that Chapter 14 was open under *MS-Word*, the word processor used to write this text. As each *Mathematica* code segment and graphic was created, it was copied and pasted directly into the text document file. This exercise demonstrates the accessibility of a powerful, platform-independent, GUI-based mathematical expert system and its integration with other applications programs.

- **The power of abstraction** – Note that, in the first fourteen examples of this section, all code necessary to generate the graphics is presented immediately preceding the figures. In most cases, this requires one or two lines of *Mathematica* code. To create such figures with high-level languages, even those with access to graphics toolkits, would require ten to one hundred times as many lines of code.

- **A model of multimedia** – *Mathematica* epitomizes the trend in advanced, high-level, object-oriented programming. Graphical and text objects are easily imported and exported in a number of different formats. It supports animation, produces output in both PostScript and TEX, and runs on more than thirty platforms. It supports sophisticated sound generation routines. Complete books have been written in *Mathematica* notebook format.[4] Perhaps most interesting is the publication of *Mathematica Journal*, a journal dedicated to research carried out with *Mathematica*.[5] The important multimedia point is that *Mathematica Journal* is available in both conventional paper format and electronic format. Subscribers to the electronic format receive, along with their paper copy, a disk containing all of the essential *Mathematica* notebooks discussed in the paper format. This provides an easily accessible, machine-readable set of programs for verifying, exploring, and extending the research presented in the paper version of the journal.

Interactive Physics

Just as *Mathematica* is an expert system for mathematics, *Interactive Physics* is an expert system in the more restricted domain of classical Newtonian physics. It "knows" about massive objects and how they interact with each other, with gravity, and with external forces supplied by strings, springs, and dampers. It understands physical effects of air resistance, elasticity, and friction and more abstract concepts of force, acceleration, velocity, energy, and linear and angular momentum.

In addition to correctly simulating the response of a single object to some combination of forces and constraints, *Interactive Physics* correctly models the far more difficult problem of the interactions of multiple objects with each other. This involves the nontrivial concept of *objectness* based on the common sense (but hard to compute) principle that two objects cannot occupy the same space at the same time. To correctly simulate the behavior of real objects subjected to real world forces and constraints, any expert system must incorporate both the *laws of physics* and a representation of the *states* of objects—their shapes, positions, velocities, and angular velocities.

Finally, *Interactive Physics* provides a transparent GUI environment in which to design experiments and measure the resulting behavior of component objects in the system. The laboratory toolkit includes four basic object shapes, four classes of force constraints, representation of seven types of vectors, and meters for measuring seventeen different physical quantities. The meters can operate in both digital and analog mode and indicate both components and magnitude of vector quantities. Experimental measurements may be recorded by means of strip recorders or by *tracking*, the equivalent of strobe light photographs of an object's motion.

System Objects

Perhaps the most natural model for presenting and understanding *Interactive Physics* is that of OOP. The system supports a limited number of objects which have attributes and respond to messages sent by the user. The object-oriented approach is particularly appropriate since the objects of *Interactive Physics* more closely resemble real, physical objects than any of the OOP applications yet considered.

The physical objects available to the user in designing the physics workspace include two

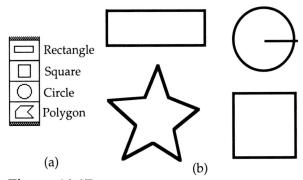

(a)

(b)

Figure 14.17
Mass objects available in *Interactive Physics*.
Selecting the toolbox icons in (a) allows the user to
design the objects shown in (b) by dragging the
cursor.

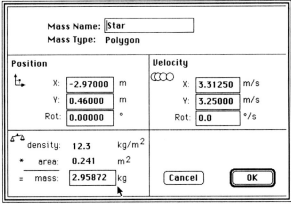

Figure 14.18
Physical attributes dialog box. Double clicking on
the star in Figure 14.17(b) opens this window in
which attributes may be modified by the user.

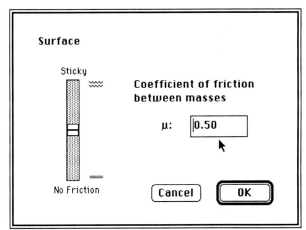

Figure 14.19
The coefficient of friction, μ, between two selected
objects can be modified by sliding the control or
typing in the next μ value.

classes of objects—*mass* objects and *no-mass*
objects.

Mass Objects

Four types of mass objects my be selected by
clicking the appropriate toolbox icon as indicated
in Figure 14.17.

Mass Object Attributes

The attributes of position, velocity, mass, and
density are displayed in a dialog box upon double-
clicking a mass object. The areal density defaults
to 10 kg/m² and is used in the equation

$$m = \rho A \qquad [14.1]$$

to compute the mass of the object from the fixed
area. Any of the attributes shown in boxes in
Figure 14.18, including the object's name, may be
reset by direct input from the user. The area is
determined by the design process. The object's
position may be modified graphically by selecting
it and dragging it to the desired position. Its
velocity may be set graphically by clicking on its
center point and dragging a v vector. It is this
value which is recorded in the dialog box and
which may be modified by direct user input.

Two other physical quantities, the *elasticity*
and the *coefficient of friction*, are important in
determining the behavior of interacting objects.
The elasticity determines how much energy is lost
upon collision and is an intrinsic property of the
object. Steel, for instance, has a high elasticity,
while putty has an elasticity nearly zero. The

coefficient of friction, μ, is a function of the
surfaces of the two objects sliding against each
other. The user can reset the default value of μ =
0.25 by selecting the two objects in question,
picking *Friction* from the *World* menu item, and
sliding the control to the desired value. This
process is illustrated in Figure 14.19. A similar
slider-control window is used to modify the
elasticity.

No-Mass Objects

The second important class of system objects are
the "no-mass objects" which serve to constrain
and exert forces on mass objects. To simplify the

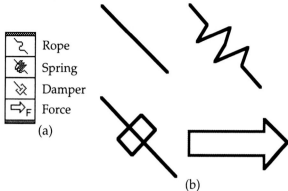

Rope
Spring
Damper
Force
(a)

(b)

Figure 14.20
No-mass objects used to apply forces to massive objects in *Interactive Physics*. Selection of icons from tool-box (a) produces objects in (b) upon dragging.

resulting calculations, *Interactive Physics* uses the approximations that no-mass objects have zero mass and do not collide with themselves or with massive objects. These approximations achieve a great reduction in complexity and are standard for presentation of physics concepts at the introductory level.

Figure 14.20 illustrates the toolbox icons representing no-mass objects and the results of selecting each icon and dragging the corresponding object into existence.

Because of the approximations mentioned above, no-mass objects have no purpose except for connecting massive objects together or applying external forces to massive objects. Since real-world objects respond only to net unbalanced forces or torques, the no-mass objects themselves can be considered from an OOP point of view as messages sent to massive objects telling them how to behave.

Sending OOP Messages to Interactive Physics Objects

All objects in *Interactive Physics* respond to the following messages:

- **Create yourself** → Select icon and drag object to desired size.

- **Destroy yourself** → Select object and issue cut command.

- **Duplicate yourself** → Select object, copy, and paste as desired.

- **Resize yourself** → Select and drag resize "hot" buttons.

- **Move to here** → Select and drag to desired location.

In addition, no-mass objects respond to messages specifying their connectivity and possible constraints. These include:

- **Relax** → Resizing a spring or rope with the Option key pressed "relaxes" it, i.e., resets it to a state neither compressed or extended.

- **Connect** → Dragging an end point of a no-mass object to any point on a massive object connects it to the massive object at that point.

Massive objects understand the following messages:

- **Reset your velocity to this** → Click at the center of mass and drag a velocity vector or drag the end of an existing velocity vector.
- **Anchor yourself** → Select the anchor tool, [anchor icon], and click within the object to anchor. Anchored objects can neither rotate nor translate.

The heart of the simulation itself can be summarized in a relatively abstract message:

- **Obey the laws of physics** → Clicking the *Run* icon.

To help understand how *Interactive Physics* implements this message to apply physical law to the user-defined physics workspace, we next examine the basic *method* which implements this abstract message.

Methods for Implementing the Laws of Motion

The basic force laws used by *Interactive Physics* may be summarized as:

Gravity:

$$F_g = m\,g\,, \qquad [14.2]$$

where

m = an object's mass, and
g = acceleration due to gravity
(default = –9.81 m/sec^2).

Spring and rope:

$$F_s = -k\,\Delta x\,, \qquad [14.3]$$

where

k = spring constant (default = 10 N/m), and
Δx = displacement from equilibrium (stretched length for rope).

Collision impulsive force:

$$F_p = \frac{\Delta p}{\Delta t}\,, \qquad [14.4]$$

where

Δp = change in momentum in the collision, and
Δt = average time during which collision occurred.

Friction sliding force:

$$F_{||} = \mu\,F_\perp u_{||}\,, \qquad [14.5]$$

where

$F_{||}$ = friction force parallel to sliding surface,
μ = coefficient of friction (default = 0.25),
$F_\perp$ = magnitude of normal force holding surfaces together, and
$u_{||}$ = unit vector anti-parallel to relative motion.

Force due to motion in viscous fluid ("damper"):

$$F_v = -b\,v\,, \qquad [14.6]$$

b = viscous damping coefficient
(default = 0.10 N·sec/m), and
v = velocity.

These forces may be summed vectorially to give the net force, F, the force term in Newton's second law of motion. This is the basic dynamic equation of *Interactive Physics*.

$$F = m\,a\,, \qquad [14.7]$$

where

$$a = \frac{dv}{dt} \cong \frac{\Delta v}{\Delta t}\,. \qquad [14.8]$$

Δv = change in velocity, and
Δt = small increment in time
(default value = 0.01 sec).

The fundamental method used in *Interactive Physics* to solve for the resulting motion is to integrate Equation 14.7 once to get the time dependent velocity, $v(t)$, and then to integrate the velocity to get the position vector, $x(t)$.

The velocity at time $t+\Delta t$ may be expressed in terms of the initial velocity, $v(t)$, and change in velocity Δv as:

$$v(t+\Delta t) = v(t) + \Delta v\,. \qquad [14.9]$$

Using Equation 14.8, this may be expressed in terms of known quantities as:

$$v(t+\Delta t) = v(t) + a\,\Delta t, \qquad [14.10]$$

where

$$a = \frac{F}{m} = \text{acceleration vector.}$$

To compute the change in position during time Δt, we can write:

$$x(t+\Delta t) = x(t) + \Delta x\,. \qquad [14.11]$$

Using the definition of velocity,

$$v(t) = \frac{dx}{dt}\,, \qquad [14.12]$$

we can write the displacement, Δx, as

$$\Delta x = <v>\,\Delta t \qquad [14.13]$$

where the average velocity, $<v>$, is given by

$$<v> = \frac{v(t+\Delta t) + v(t)}{2} \, . \qquad [14.14]$$

Combining Equations 14.10, 14.11, 14.13, and 14.14, we get

$$x(t+\Delta t) = x(t) + v(t)\,\Delta t + \frac{1}{2}\,a\,\Delta t^2 \, . \qquad [14.15]$$

Equations 14.10 and 14.15 provide the basic, iterative equations for tracing out the trajectory of massive objects. The acceleration, a, is determined by (F/m), both of which are known. The initial position, $x(t)$, and initial velocity, $v(t)$, are specified by the experimental design. After computing and plotting each position, $x(t+\Delta t)$, and velocity, $v(t+\Delta t)$, the substitution $x(t) \leftarrow x(t+\Delta t)$ and $v(t) \leftarrow v(t+\Delta t)$ is made and Equations 14.10 and 14.15 reapplied. The integration time increment, Δt, defaults to 0.01 second, but may be modified by the user to achieve better accuracy or more speed in the simulation.

Note that $x(t)$ is a vector, with components (x,y), which describes the trajectory as a function of time in 2D space. To simulate the rotation of objects, equations completely analogous to Equations 14.7–14.15 may be written in which torque, τ, replaces force, moment of inertia, I, replaces mass, angle θ replaces position, angular ve-

locity, ω, replaces velocity, and angular acceleration, α, replaces acceleration. The combination of $x(t)$ and $\theta(t)$ completely describes the resultant motion of each object.

The iterative algorithm described above constitutes the fundamental method for applying the laws of physics to simulate the behavior of massive objects. To observe and record this behavior, *Interactive Physics* provides an experimental environment to which we turn next.

Experimental Environment

The value of simulation tools for verification and learning is greatly enhanced by a well-designed environment in which experimental results are readily recorded and displayed. *Interactive Physics* provides several modes for visualizing the results of simulation experiments. These include meters, chart recorders, vector displays, and simulated strobe flash displays. Several of these are illustrated in Figure 14.21.

Physical quantities which may be displayed on meters or plotted on the chart recorder include: *time, position, velocity, acceleration, rotation, rotational velocity, rotational acceleration, translational kinetic energy, rotational kinetic energy, linear momentum, angular momentum, gravity force, air force, normal force, friction force, total force,* and *total torque*. For

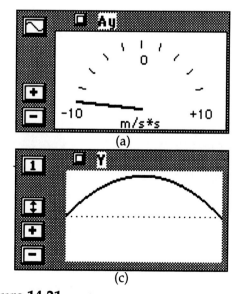

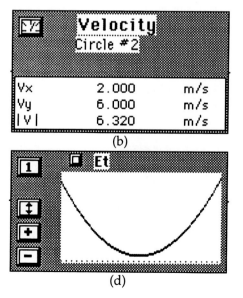

Figure 14.21
Meters and chart recorder output. (a) shows the acceleration due to gravity on an analog meter, (b) shows the initial velocity components on a digital meter, (c) is a chart recording of the y position in projectile motion, and (d) is a chart recording of the total kinetic energy as a function of time for projectile motion.

Table 14.2
Theoretical Validation for Projectile Motion

Quantity (units)	Number of Steps	Experimental value	Theoretical value	Percent error
h(m)	64	1.980	2.009	1.4
R/2(m)	64	2.000	2.000	0
T/2(s)	64	0.064	0.064	0
R(m)	127	3.970	4.000	0.75
T(s)	127	1.27	1.28	0.78

vector quantities, the user may select the x component, y component, or magnitude to record.

Two other methods are available for visualizing the behavior of *Interactive Physics* objects. The first is the *vector display* mode, and the second is called *tracking*. In the vector mode, the velocity, acceleration, and five different force vectors may be attached to massive objects and display the vector's magnitude and direction in real time as the simulation proceeds. In the tracking mode, the user can select to "freeze" the animation every 1, 2, 4, 8, 16, or 32 frames of the iteration. This mode resembles the strobe-light photographic method of recording air puck and air track collisions in the physics lab. A particularly effective visualization technique involves combining these two modes by tracking the motion of an object with attached acceleration and velocity vectors as illustrated in Figure 14.22.

Simulation Experiments

With this background in the objects, messages, methods, and experimental environment of *Interactive Physics*, we are ready to examine several specific simulation experiments.

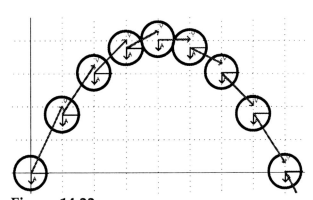

Figure 14.22
Tracking a projectile with attached acceleration and velocity vectors.

Experiment 1: Verify parameters T, h, and R for projectile motion.

The theoretical values for the flight time, T, maximum height, h, and range, R, for projectile motion are given in terms of the initial velocity, $v_o = (v_{ox}, v_{oy})$ as:

$$T = \frac{2\,v_{oy}}{g}\,, \qquad [14.16]$$

$$h = \frac{v_{oy}^2}{2g}\,, \qquad [14.17]$$

$$R = v_{ox}\,T\,. \qquad [14.18]$$

Initializing the system with $v_{ox} = 3.125$ m/s, $v_{oy} = 6.2784$ m/s and then running the simulation produced the trajectory shown in Figure 14.22. Single-stepping the simulation until the boundary condition $v_y = 0.000$ m/s was reached (top of flight path) produced the experimental results h, $R/2$, and $T/2$ given in Table 14.2. Continuing the simulation until ground level was reached, $y = 0.000$ m, produced the experimental values for R and T.

An interesting observation about Table 14.2 is that it suggests a "fence-post" type error in the simulation algorithm. That is, letting the simulation run to 128 steps gives precisely correct results for R and T but yields $y = -0.062$, violating the boundary condition.

Experiment 2: Verify energy and momentum conservation in elastic collisions.

One universal and extremely useful law of physics is the law of momentum conservation. This law states that the vector sum of $m_i v_i$ for all i particles before a collision is the same as that after the collision. Another valuable, but weaker, law states that, in elastic collisions, kinetic energy is conserved in the collision. That is, for collisions in which no energy is lost in deformation, the sum of $(1/2)m_i v_i^2$ before the collision is the same as that after the collision.

To verify the laws of conservation of energy and momentum, we turn *Snap Grid* to ON and construct two precisely defined masses, $M_1 = 5$ Kg and $M_2 = 10$ Kg, as shown in Figure 14.23. M_1 is given an initial velocity $v_1 = 10$ m/s by dragging the velocity vector.

Momentum before collision:

$$P = M_1 v_1$$

Momentum after collision:

$$P' = M_1 v'_1 + M_2 v'_2$$

Conservation of momentum:

$$\boxed{M_1 v_1 = M_1 v'_1 + M_2 v'_2}$$ [14.19]

Kinetic energy before collision:

$$KE = \frac{1}{2} M_1 v_1{}^2$$

Kinetic energy after collision:

$$KE' = \frac{1}{2} M_1 v'_1{}^2 + \frac{1}{2} M_2 v'_2{}^2$$

Conservation of energy:

$$\boxed{\frac{M_1 v_1{}^2}{2} = \frac{M_1 v'_1{}^2}{2} + \frac{M_2 v'_2{}^2}{2}}$$ 14.20]

Next, gravity is turned off using the slider control in the *Gravity* window under the *World* menu. Finally, to verify the conservation laws, an array of meters is assembled for each mass. This array is shown for the initial conditions of M_1 in Figure 14.24. An identical array of meters is assembled for M_2.

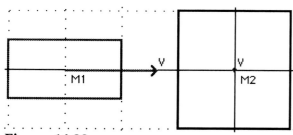

Figure 14.23
Initial state of elastic collision. M_1 has a mass of 5 Kg and M_2 =10 Kg. Both are assigned perfectly elastic surfaces.

Now the *Run* command is issued, and M_1 approaches, collides with, and rebounds off of M_2. One tenth of a second later, the animation frame shown in Figure 14.25 results.

It is a straightforward exercise to use the laws of energy and momentum conservation to predict the relationship between v'_1 and v'_2, the velocities of M_1 and M_2, respectively, after the collision.

Note that, by design, $M_2 = 2 M_1$. Using this equation with Equations 14.19 and 14.20 leads, after some algebraic simplification, to the relationship:

$$v'_2 = 2 v'_1$$ [14.21]

How can we check these three theoretical predictions of the conservation laws? With the meter arrays of *Interactive Physics* it is simply a matter of reading off the digital results shown in Figure 14.26 and comparing with the predictions of Equations 14.19, 14.20, and 14.21.

	Velocity M1			Momentum M1	
Vx	10.000	m/s	Px	50.000	kgm/s
Vy	0.0000	m/s	Py	0.0000	kgm/s
|V|	10.000	m/s	|P|	50.000	kgm/s

	Position M1			Kinetic Energy M1	
X	-1.5000	m	Ex	250.00	J
Y	0.0000	m	Ey	0.0000	J
			E	250.00	J

Figure 14.24
Experimental environment for monitoring the state of mass M_1. A similar array of meters reports the physical state of M_2.

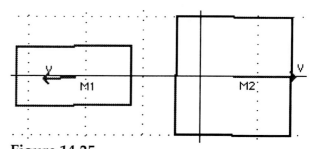

Figure 14.25
Relative motion of objects M_1 and M_2 after collision. These velocities of M_1 and M_2 are referred to as v'_1 and v'_2 below.

It is reassuring to note that momentum conservation [14.19] and the velocity relationship [14.21] are precisely verified. However, curiously, 0.08% of the kinetic energy seems to have been dissipated in the collision even though we initially specified both objects to be completely elastic. One clue as to where the missing energy has gone is apparent as the slight rotation Figure 14.25 indicates was introduced by the collision. Any rotation introduced into the final state objects contributes to rotational kinetic energy and thus reduces the energy available as translational kinetic energy.

To further explore this hypothesis it is a simple matter to add rotation meters to the simulated experiment. Adding *Rotation* and *Rotational Kinetic Energy* meters does, indeed, confirm that the collision algorithm has introduced rotations in both M_1 and M_2. However, the rotational kinetic energies computed are of the order of 10^{-5}J which is too small to balance the kinetic energy conservation equation.

Since considerable care was used to design the collision process to occur against flat surfaces and along the line containing the center of mass of the two objects, we conclude this rotation is an artifact of the collision algorithm.

Experiment 3: Explore the hypothesis: **The period of a pendulum clock depends on the size of the bob.**

Two approximations simplify the discussion of the simple pendulum clock at the introductory physics level.

- Treat the bob as a point mass at the end of an ideal string of length L.

- Constrain the oscillations to small angles so that $\sin \theta \cong \theta$.

With these approximations, the differential equation of motion of a simple pendulum reduces to that of a *simple harmonic oscillator* with a period, T, given as:

$$T = 2\pi \sqrt{\frac{L}{g}}, \qquad [14.22]$$

where

L = length of pendulum string, and
g = 9.81 m/s^2
= acceleration due to gravity.

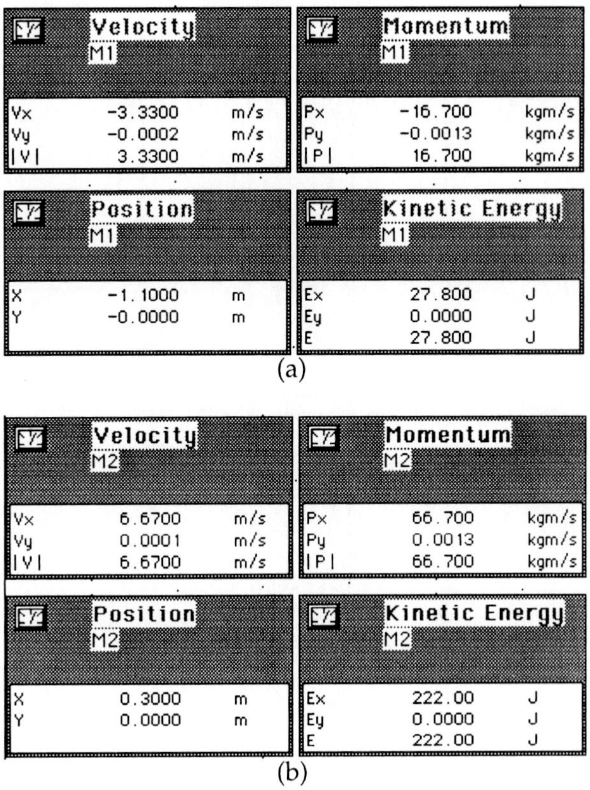

Figure 14.26
Postcollision dynamic variables for masses M_1 (a) and M_2 (b).

The effect of the small angle approximation is frequently investigated in the general physics laboratory because of the ease and accuracy with which angles and periods can be measured. However, except for the meter-stick-shaped *compound pendulum*, the dependence on shape or size of the pendulum bob is rarely explored.

Let's see what we can learn with *Interactive Physics*. Let's start with a string of length $L = 1.000$ m which will give a simple pendulum period of exactly 2.000 seconds by setting $g = 9.8696$ m/s^2. In the first series of experiments the bob was supported at its center of mass by the 1.000 m string anchored at the origin. In each case, the bob was assigned an initial x velocity of 0.5 m/s which produced a maximum angular deflection of about nine degrees as displayed in Figure 14.27.

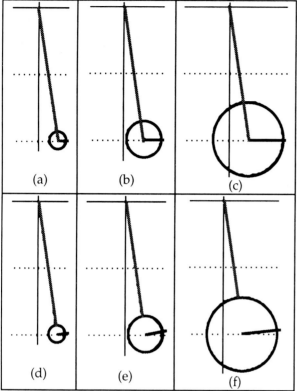

Figure 14.27
First three pendulum configurations for two series of experiments. The first series [(a), (b), and (c)] has the support string attached at the center of mass. The second series has the string attached at the top of the bob, inducing rotations as shown.

The period of oscillation was measured accurately as the radius of the bob was increased by factors of approximately two. The numeric results are recorded under T_{cm} in Table 14.3 and plotted as a function of bob radius in Figure 14.28. The results, surprising at first glance, are that *the period is completely independent of size of the pendulum bob.* On more reflection these results are consistent with Newton's proof that, in describing gravitational forces, the mass of a spherical object can be considered to be acting at its center of mass.

The string, being attached to the center of mass in Figure 14.27 (a), (b), and (c), is "unaware" of the size of the pendulum bob.

A real grandfather clock, on the other hand, has a pendulum bob rigidly attached to a pivoting arm. This causes the pendulum bob to rotate about its own center of mass as well as the arm pivot as it swings. Perhaps this will cause a size-dependent variation in period.

In the second set of experiments, the bob's center of mass was maintained precisely at 1.000 m below the origin (as in the first series), but the string was attached at the top of the bob. The effect of attachment is similar in inducing rotation of the bob as that forced by the rigid arm of the grandfather clock. This is apparent in frames (d), (e), and (f) of Figure 14.27. Again, the period was measured accurately by timing five complete cycles. The gratifying results are that the period does indeed increase as the radius of the bob increases. The numerical results are tabulated under T_{top} in Table 14.3 and plotted in Figure 14.28.

The shape of the T_{top} curve is consistent with a new *degree of freedom*—rotational kinetic energy—opening up. Now the string, in addition to lifting the bob up, must "crank" on it to get it rotating. Since its rotational inertia resists this, the whole process takes more time and hence the increase in period with bob radius. Note that the curve, smoothed in this figure, is quadratic in shape which is consistent with the quadratic increase in moment of inertia with radius.

This example has illustrated that *Interactive Physics* is well suited to investigate subtle properties of physical systems which are difficult to accomplish in a three-hour general physics lab.

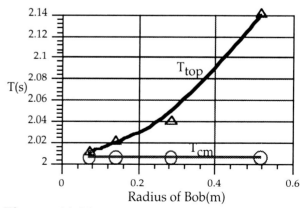

Figure 14.28
Dependence of pendulum period on size of pendulum bob. The T_{cm} series of measurements used bobs supported at the center of mass; the T_{top} series were supported at the top of the bob.

Table 14.3
Pendulum Period vs. Bob Radius

Radius(m)	T_{cm}	T_{top}
0.07	2.006	2.01
0.14	2.006	2.02
0.283	2.006	2.04
0.517	2.006	2.14

*Experiment 4: Study of Damped Harmonic
Oscillator*

Another experiment, which is discussed frequently in text books but rarely performed in the laboratory, is the mechanical damped harmonic oscillator. The main difficulty in doing lab experiments is in achieving an easily variable damping force. In this *Interactive Physics* simulation, variable damping is easily obtained by modifying the coefficient of friction between the block and the table on which it is sliding.

The initial condition of table, backstop, sliding block, and spring was designed in about two minutes and is shown with the spring stretched taut in Figure 14.29.

To explore the role of damping in this harmonic oscillator, we open a *Position* meter and set it to chart recorder mode. Next we select the block/table pair and set the coefficient of friction to zero for the first experiment. After turning on the velocity vector, we click *Run* and observe the motion in animation, two frames of which are shown in Figure 14.30.

With no damping ($\mu = 0$), the block will oscillate indefinitely with a sinusoidal motion indicated in the upper left recording of Figure 14.31. Objects obeying such motion are called simple harmonic oscillators.

To create a damped harmonic oscillator we introduce friction which serves to dissipate the energy stored in the system. *Interactive Physics* provides three mechanisms for introducing damping: air resistance, mechanical dampers with resistive force proportional to velocity, and two-body fric

tion. Since the block is already pressing against the table with a force equal to its weight, it is convenient to use this as a realistic and easily understood source of frictional damping. Incrementing the coefficient of friction, μ, allows us to visualize the effects of introducing damping. The five frames of Figure 14.31 with $\mu > 0$ demonstrate the effects of varying this parameter.

A rich mathematical formalism exists for describing harmonic motion. Much of it can be simulated and verified with *Interactive Physics*. That is not the point of this exercise, however. The main point to emphasize here is that the synthesis of an authentic physical model with simple graphics provides a powerful tool for visualizing and understanding scientific principles. The amusing experiment with $\mu = 0.5$ demonstrates this point.

In an attempt to illustrate strong overdamping, the coefficient of friction was turned up to $\mu = 0.5$. The chart recorder output of this experiment, shown in Figure 14.32(a), would do more to confuse than to clarify the resulting action if taken alone. However, the animation sequence (Figure 14.32(b) and (c)) describe precisely what happened in this simulation. By turning μ up to 0.5, the resisting friction force was so great that the block toppled forward and crashed ignominiously on its face. Imagine trying to interpret the physics of this process solely by examining numeric output based only on the mathematical formalism. Animation is indeed a powerful tool for visualization.

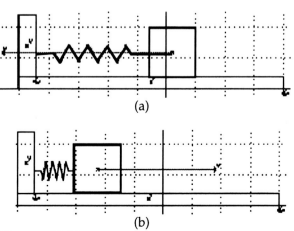

(a)

(b)

Figure 14.30
Two frames from the animated motion of the block sliding on a frictionless plane. Such a system is called a simple harmonic oscillator.

Figure 14.29
Initial configuration of damped harmonic oscillator experiment. The table and backstop are anchored, but the square block can slide. The equilibrium position of the block is near the center of the table.

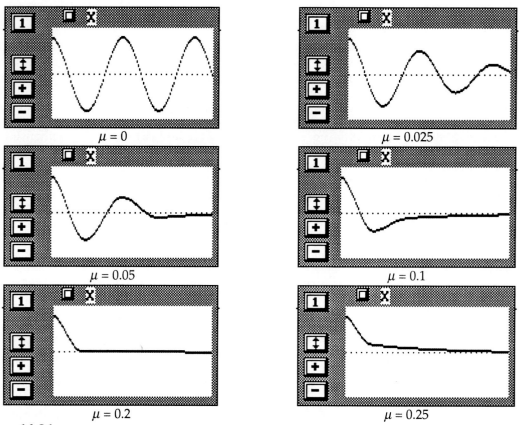

Figure 14.31
Chart recorder output of displacement versus time for a harmonic oscillator. Increasing the coefficients of friction introduces damping with critical damping occurring at approximately $\mu = 0.2$.

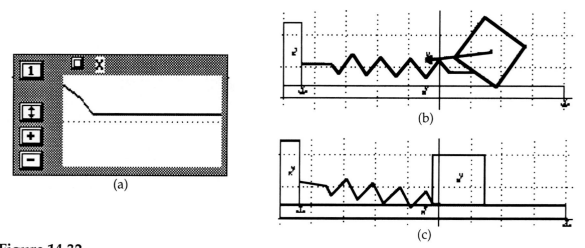

Figure 14.32
The strange case of super-overdamping. Turning up the coefficient of friction to $\mu = 0.5$ increased the friction force enough to cause the block to "trip" over friction and fall forward on its face. The chart recorder information in (a) would be difficult to interpret without the physical animation sequence of (b) and (c).

Experiment 5: Studies of Complex Systems

Physics is a reductionist science with the objective of explaining the behavior of the universe. Its program is to explain the behavior of complex systems in terms of the behavior of more elementary systems composing the complex system. By reducing the system to its most elementary particles and clearly specifying the behavior of these particles, one hopes to explain the behavior of the aggregate system. In its classical form, reductionism maintains that, in principle, if we know precisely the positions and velocities of all of its component particles, we should be able to predict the future of the universe. This reductionist philosophy explains why most diagrams in physics textbooks show one of two objects subject to, at most, three or four forces.

Henri Poincaré was the first to point out, however, that classical dynamics was incapable *in principle* of solving the three-body problem. This observation and the work of physicist Mitchell Feigenbaum and meteorologist Edward Lorenz are the cornerstones of the new science of chaos and the behavior of complex, dynamic systems.[6] Stephen Wolfram, the inventor of *Mathematica*, is founder of the journal *Complex Systems* and director of the Center for Complex Systems Research at the University of Illinois. This center is dedicated to research in this exciting new field.

The fatal flaw in the argument of reductionist determinism is the requirement for **precise** information. Poincaré's argument was that roundoff error in finite precision arithmetic prevented accurate integration of the equations of motion into the

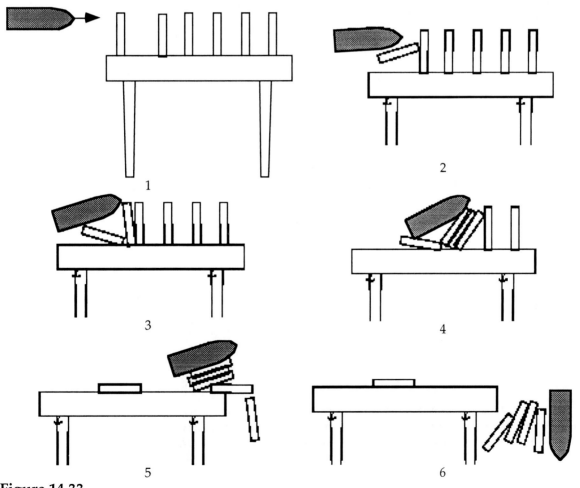

Figure 14.33
Animation sequence of projectile striking a row of dominoes. The initial collision of the projectile with the left-most domino causes a rotation in the projectile. In this orientation, the projectile effectively sweeps the remaining dominoes into a stack which spills off the end of the table.

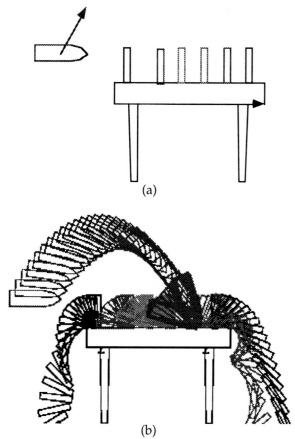

(a)

(b)

Figure 14.34
Changes in initial conditions produce different results. Firing the projectile upward as shown in (a) and giving it a rotation results in the trajectory and impact between the fourth and fifth dominoes as shown in (b). Tracking gives the illusion of motion on a single frame, and color-coding, shown as shading, helps clarify the process.

indefinite future. His argument, however, does not doom the ability to predict the motion of multiple-object systems on a shorter term.

The chief obstacle to the study of complex systems has been one of computational complexity. As the above examples illustrate, the study of single objects under the influence of simple forces or of two objects colliding already requires significant computation. As the number of objects, n, increases the number of potential interactions increases as n!. Not only must the equations of motion be integrated as described in the method section, but each object must also be continuously examined for a (forbidden) overlap with every other object. Such an overlap signals a collision for

which the conservation laws must be invoked with appropriate elasticities.

Interactive Physics is capable of simulating the behavior of multiple-object systems, and this feature is perhaps its greatest strength. Consider the following example (Figure 14.33) in which a projectile is fired at a row of dominoes.

Changes in the initial conditions lead to radically different outcomes. Figure 14.34 illustrates the effect of giving the projectile an upward component of velocity and an initial angular velocity.

Experiment 6: Studies of Chaotic Dynamics

One of the distinguishing features of chaotic systems is their extreme sensitivity to minute changes in initial conditions. This is beautifully illustrated in *Interactive Physics* by comparing the final states of a chaotic pendulum precisely ten seconds after it is released for a series of minutely differing initial states.

The initial state for each of the four experiments is a series of three pendula coupled by inextensible strings connected to their centers of mass and pivoting from point P as shown in Figure 14.35. The initial height, Y_1, of the left-most pendulum was set to the default value of 1.00000 m for run (a) and incremented by 0.00001 m in each successive run.

Figure 14.36 shows the state of motion of the system exactly 10.00 seconds after the system is released for the series of starting Y_1 values. Note that the only difference from one experiment to the next is a change of 0.001% in Y_1. This is far below the limit of detection visually and, in fact, corresponds to about 0.001 pixels on the screen image.

After several minutes of observing the violent whiplashes and collisions of the chaotic pendulum, the *Interactive Physics* experimenter gains a much clearer understanding of what chaos means. By carefully performing controlled experiments such as the one above, the user develops an

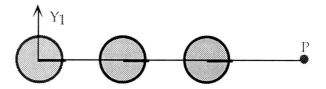

Figure 14.35
Initial condition for chaotic pendulum experiment. The three coupled pendula pivot about point P.

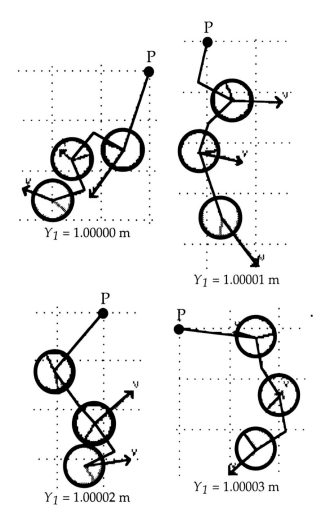

$Y_1 = 1.00000$ m

$Y_1 = 1.00001$ m

$Y_1 = 1.00002$ m

$Y_1 = 1.00003$ m

Figure 14.36
Final states 10.00 seconds after releasing chaotic pendulum. Note the extreme sensitivity to initial conditions displayed by this chaotic system.

intuition for difficult concepts, like sensitivity to initial conditions, which is almost impossible to obtain through any other medium. *Interactive Physics* has been judged to be such a valuable learning tool that one major publisher is now packaging the product with each copy of its introductory physics textbook.

Limitations of *Interactive Physics*

The reader has undoubtedly recognized several of the limitations of *Interactive Physics* from the above discussion. Such limitations are not atypical for expert systems which frequently provide great depth of knowledge in a very restricted domain. (*Mathematica* seems to have avoided most of these limitations.) Among them are:

- **Limited domain** – *Interactive Physics* deals only with the kinematics and dynamics of massive solid objects subject to gravity and mechanical forces. It ignores all strong (nuclear), electromagnetic, and weak forces and thus does not take into account the large and important domain of the motion of charged particles in electric and magnetic fields. Planned releases will expand its domain to include the interaction of charged particles.

- **Limited geometry** – To keep life simple and to optimize the animation speed, *Interactive Physics* deals only with 2D geometry and ignores the third dimension of the real world. Fortunately, most Newtonian problems are separable, with the laws applying independently in each Cartesian coordinate. For such problems, the 2D trajectories represent an accurate "slice" of the motion in 3D space.

- **Limited complexity** – In any given simulation the maximum number of massive objects is ten, the maximum number of constant forces is ten, and the number of ropes, springs, and dampers combined may not exceed five. While this limitation rules out the analysis of systems of arbitrary complexity, it permits the analysis of far more complex systems than those tractable with conventional techniques of analytical mechanics.

- **Limited graphics** – *Interactive Physics* provides only primitive 2D line drawings of vectors, objects, and their resulting motion. It lacks the elegant color, shading, and rendering models provided by *Mathematica* and other CAD systems discussed previously. This limitation is consistent with its design purpose as primarily an instructional tool, but it does limit its use in presentation graphics and related design applications.

Conclusions

We have examined two powerful expert systems in which computer graphics plays the central role in their usefulness and success as tools for visualization. *Mathematica* is changing the way in which mathematics is being taught and learned, and it provides a research tool of amazing power and produces graphical output of exceptional beauty. It is capable of producing essentially all of the graphics presented in this book with the exception of the ray tracing, radiosity, and Renderman renderings. *Interactive Physics* represents another giant step toward the goal of building intelligent models of the world. By incorporating the laws of Newtonian physics the system provides an accurate simulation of complex physical systems. The intuitive experimental environment of meters, dials, and chart recorders allows the user to run experiments which are totally impractical or impossible in the laboratory. The animation sequences, vector diagrams, and tracking capabilities enhance the visualization of unfamiliar concepts such as chaos. The performance of high-quality applications like *Interactive Physics* is helping to establish simulation programs as legitimate tools for teaching and research.

Exercises

14.1 Define the term expert system. Does *MACSYMA* qualify as an expert system? Does *Mathematica* qualify as an expert system? Compare *MACSYMA* and *Mathematica* on the basis of number of functions available to the user, number of lines of code, and the GUI provided by each.

14.2 Computer simulation models achieved national prominence through the work of MIT's Jay Forrester and the Club of Rome. Describe one of these early simulation models and the role that computer graphics plays in such models.

14.3 From your own studies in physics, chemistry, geology, or life science describe an example in which image processing helped illuminate or clarify some concept for you.

14.4 Give two examples from high-level languages such as BASIC, FORTRAN, or Pascal in which the use of parentheses, "( )," can lead to ambiguity and confusion. To what historical accident do you attribute this redundant use of parentheses?

14.5 What is the highest power to which five can be raised in standard, two-byte integer arithmetic? In long integer (four byte) arithmetic? In standard, four-byte real arithmetic?

14.6 From the *Mathematica* numerical Example 4, what do you estimate for the ratio of all numbers to prime numbers? Using a program like *Mathematica*, determine if this ratio is a constant as a function of number.

14.7 How does *Mathematica* know that numerical Example 6 is to be performed in rational arithmetic?

14.8 Verify that the results of numerical Example 7 are consistent with Figure 14.5. Which root is this? From the graphical results in Figure 14.5, estimate the values of the other roots for the first-order Bessel function in the range $0 \le x \le 10$ and verify your estimates with *Mathematica*.

14.9 Verify the results of numerical Examples 9 and 10 by hand. Keep track of the number of steps required and compute the *abstraction ratio* for *Mathematica* as the number of steps by hand divided by the number of *Mathematica* steps.

14.10 Verify the results of numerical Example 11 using a Pascal matrix multiply program. Compute the abstraction ratio for *Mathematica* /Pascal.

14.11 What high-level language is capable of the bindings illustrated in symbolic Example 1? Show the results of programming these assignments in that language.

14.12 What is the significance of the polynomial in symbolic Example 3? How do you think it was generated?

14.13 Show the plot for the sum of the Fourier series of graphical Example 4 with 2, 3, and

10 terms. Does the Gibbs *overshoot* persist as the number of terms increases?

14.14 The 1st, 2nd, and 3rd order J Bessel function is shown in graphics Example 5. Compute and plot the zeroth order J Bessel function over the same range.

14.15 The Lissajous figure shown in graphical Example 6 has four antinodes. Generate Lissajous figures with two, three, and ten antinodes.

14.16 Replace the cosine functions with sine functions and plot the corresponding figures in graphical Examples 7 and 8.

14.17 With graphical Example 9 as a model, use *ParametricPlot3D* to generate a spherical surface and an open cylindrical surface (pipe). Using Example 10 as a model, generate a globe with a cylindrical axis by superimposing these two figures.

14.18 From the discussion of *Interactive Physics* presented in the text (and possibly scanning a general physics textbook), what three major topics in Newtonian mechanics lie outside its domain?

14.19 The integration time interval, Δt, plays a central role in evaluating Equations 14.10 and 14.15 for the trajectories of objects. Describe an experiment, using numbers, for which the default value of 0.01 second is so large that serious error would occur. Describe a second experiment for which 0.01 is unnecessarily small and would waste simulation time.

14.20 The discussion in *Interactive Physics* Experiment 2 suggests that the law of kinetic energy conservation is weaker than that of momentum conservation. Why is this true?

14.21 From the meter readings in Figure 14.24 and Figure 14.26, what can you conclude about the laws of the conservation of momentum and conservation of kinetic energy? Give numerical values to bolster your conclusions.

14.22 Using Equations 14.19 and 14.20, derive Equation 14.21 relating the velocities of the two objects after collision. Could you use *Mathematica* to derive this symbolic result?

14.23 Figure 14.25 suggests that the collision between M_1 and M_2 has introduced rotations in both masses. Think about the problem and discuss what feature of the collision algorithm might be responsible. Discuss how you might verify your speculation experimentally. (Tools include different object shapes, control on integration interval Δt, and meters.)

14.24 Give one argument (or intuitive reason) why the period of a pendulum clock may depend on the size of its bob. Give one argument why it should not. Carefully define the mechanism for connecting the string to the bob.

14.25 In Figure 14.27, explain why the top row of bobs shows no rotation while the bottom row does.

14.26 Interpret the difference between the T_{top} and T_{cm} curves in Figure 14.28.

14.27 Explain the physical process which occurs for the case of $\mu = 0.5$ in Experiment 4. Describe a series of experiments you could use to determine the critical value of μ for which the block begins to lift off the table.

14.28 Describe two different scenarios for Experiment 5 (dominoes) in which a very minute change in initial conditions would lead to radically different outcomes.

14.29 James Gleick (see References) describes the sensitivity to initial conditions of chaotic systems by the allegory of the *Butterfly effect*. What is the Butterfly effect and how does it relate to the series of outcomes in Figure 14.36?

14.30 What mechanisms are most effective in introducing chaotic motion into the initially well-behaved pendulum swings of the system shown in Figure 14.35?

14.31 Some concepts and problems in physics are intrinsically 3D in nature and thus beyond the scope of analysis by *Interactive Physics*. Give three such examples.

14.32 Suppose your job assignment was to enhance the graphics and GUI of *Interactive Physics*. Based on the examples given in the book, what would be your first three priority improvements?

Endnotes

1 . Wolfram, Stephen, *Mathematica – A System of Doing Mathematics by Computer*, Second Edition, Addison-Wesley Publishing Company, Redwood City, CA (1991).

2. *Interactive Physics™ User's Guide*, Knowledge Revolution, 497 Vermont Street, SanFrancisco, CA 94107.

3. Firebaugh, Morris W., *Artificial Intelligence – A Knowledge-Based Approach*, p.27, 667, PWS-Kent Publishing Company, Boston, MA (1988).

4. Gray, Theodore W. and Glynn, Jerry, *Exploring Mathematics with Mathematica*, Addison-Wesley Publishing Company, Redwood City, CA (1990).

5. *The Mathematica Journal*, Addison-Wesely Publishing Company, 350 Bridge Parkway, Redwood City, CA 94065 Phone: 415-594-4423.

6. Schroeder, Manfred, *Fractals, Chaos, and Power Laws*, W. H. Freeman and Company, New York, NY (1991). For a more mathematical treatment, see: Hale, J. and Kocak, H., *Dynamics and Bifurcations*, Springer-Verlag, New York, NY (1991). For a less mathematical treatment, see: Gleick, James, *Chaos – Making a New Science*, Viking, New York, NY (1987).

Chapter 15

Image Processing and Analysis

New concepts are required that define human capabilities for analogical and metaphorical visualization, transformations of visually representable concepts, and generation of intuitive understandings that lead to conceptual scientific breakthroughs.
McCormick, DeFanti, and Brown[1]

Fluid dynamics is complicated and ugly – ugly in that if I were to try and show something at the blackboard I would probably write down two equations every minute for an hour, and they wouldn't give you a gut feeling for what is going on. But when you can isolate individual terms and image them using contour maps or graphs or color plots – the kind of thing that *Spyglass* **does – you can get that gut feeling.**
Doug MacAyeal[2]

I mage processing and analysis extend the domain of computer graphics and complement it with valuable techniques and tools. Confusion often arises concerning the distinctions between *computer graphics*, *image processing*, and *image analysis*. One useful classification scheme for distinguishing these three areas is based on the **purpose** for the processes involved. According to this scheme, the purpose of each of these subject areas may be summarized as follows.

- **Computer graphics** – The overall purpose of computer graphics is the *synthesis* of graphical images. That is, starting from some symbolic description which we represent as λ in Figure 15.1, we construct the corresponding pictorial or graphical representation. The symbolic description may consist of a series of command lines specifying primitive graphical objects and their attributes (as in traditional CAD) or a series of icon selections and cursor manipulations (as in GUI applications). Synthetic graphical images are generated by creating and merging more primitive graphical objects. Traditional computer graphics deals with the algorithms and tools available for generating synthetic images. It has been the focus of the book up to this point.

- **Image processing** – The purpose of image processing is the *transformation* of an existing image into a more desirable or useful image. The source of images can be computer graphics synthesis or one of many available image transducers, including video cameras, digital scanners, or libraries of digital images. Now the *object* (in the OOP sense) becomes the *image* itself, rather than the constituent objects which the image represents. The image may be stored as a bit map or a spreadsheet-like table in which the value of each cell represents pixel color values. Although there is no limit to the number of transformations available for mapping one image into another, they generally fall into one of two classes: (1) functional value mapping in which the value of the pixel is mapped against some function to produce a new value for the pixel, and (2) derivative mapping in which the value of a certain pixel is determined by the value of nearby pixels. The techniques of image processing are particularly valuable as visualization tools and in the preprocessing phases of image analysis.

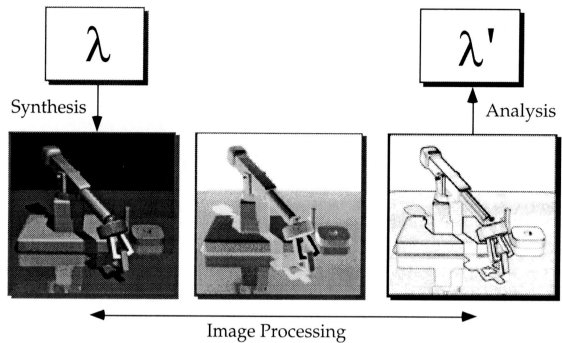

Figure 15.1
The computer graphics domain of graphics synthesis, image processing, and graphical analysis. Synthesis involves creating an image from an abstract, symbolic description, λ. Image processing involves transforming from one image to a new, more useful one. Analysis involves extracting a symbolic description, λ', of objects composing the image.

- **Image analysis** – The purpose of image analysis is to extract *symbolic information* from an image. *Computer vision* represents the ultimate and most demanding application of image analysis.[3] The goal of a computer vision system is to identify each person or object in the photograph that it has scanned. Less ambitious and more easily achieved tasks of image analysis involve *counting* (How many red blood cells are on this slide?) and *measurement* (What are the [x,y] locations of sample points along a bubble chamber track?). Many of the image processing techniques, which are valuable as visualization tools, are equally useful as preprocessing stages in the image analysis task. Note how image analysis is the inverse process to image synthesis. In its simplest terms, image synthesis involves mapping an abstract symbolic representation, λ, into a concrete image. In the simplest terms, image analysis involves mapping a concrete image into an abstract symbolic representation, λ'.

These three aspects of computer graphics are illustrated graphically in Figure 15.1. In terms of representing the domain of computer graphics, the vertical direction corresponds to abstraction. The abstract, symbolic command, λ = "Draw Robot Arm" maps into the concrete image in the lower left-hand corner. Sending "Invert yourself" and "Trace edges" messages to this image transforms it into the other two images. The edge outline shown in the lower right-hand corner is a particularly useful representation of the image for the purpose of template matching against projected image outlines from a library of known objects. A good match from this library allows an image analysis system to report, "λ' = Robot Arm with 3 objects."

It should be emphasized that image processing and image analysis deal with a much broader range of images than the artificial (synthetic) class described above. In fact, by far the largest class of input images for image processing systems can be classified as "natural" rather than artificial. That is, they are electronic photographs of the surface of one of the moons of Saturn, or a weather pattern as seen from a space satellite, or the image from a computer-aided tomography (CAT) scan. These are examples of images representing raw data objects produced by scientific research and medical diagnosis. The use of image processing for clarifying and interpreting such data is at the heart of the rapidly emerging field of scientific visualization.

Finally, the assumption throughout this chapter is that image processing and analysis apply to digital images such as those represented by PICT, TIFF, GIFF, and EPSF formats. Chemical processing of photographic images and electronic processing of television images have long and distinguished histories but differ fundamentally from digital image processing in two important aspects. First, photographic and video images are analog in nature, and the signals are inevitably degraded at each stage of processing. Digital images are immune to such noise and degradation. Second, it is much more difficult for photographic and video image processing to achieve the freedom and versatility of digital image processing. Digital image processing allows manipulation of selected portions of the image down to the pixel level. This is very difficult or impossible to achieve with any other medium.

Image Acquisition

As indicated above, image objects, which act as the "raw data" for image processing applications, arise from a number of sources. These may be conveniently categorized as:

- Artificial synthetic images,
- Theoretical synthetic images,
- Natural images.

Let's examine each of these categories in a little more detail and show examples of each category in Figure 15.2.

Artificial Synthetic Images

By artificial, we mean created as human artifacts. Someone sat down at a workstation and created the image with one of the application programs discussed in the previous chapters or some equivalent program. While these may be masterpieces of creative design and elegant rendering algorithms, they are in a fundamental sense the least interesting from an image processing and image analysis point of view. The reason for this is that such images are totally deterministic and completely

specified by a log of the drawing and rendering commands issued by the user.

If the intermediate image processing commands are used to augment the symbolic representation, λ, image analysis of any artificial synthetic image will yield the trivial result: $\lambda' \equiv \lambda$.

Theoretical Synthetic Images

The second category of synthetic images is classified as "theoretical." This class encompasses the whole range of simulation experiment results. They are artificial in the sense that they are the results of theoretical models constructed by humans. But they are indeterminate since the complexity of the theoretical model prevents the user from knowing what to expect, at least in detail, from the calculated results. Simulations in finite element analysis, *Mathematica*, and *Interactive Physics* all fall into this category, as do the complex supercomputer simulations in the fields of chemistry, astrophysics, fluid dynamics, and meteorology. The default image parameters may produce an acceptable graphical result, but often the image can be improved by applying one or more of the image processing transformations described in the following section.

Natural Images

Natural images constitute a large segment of the raw input data for image processing programs. In addition to a vast array of scientific, engineering, and medical image data, natural images include the whole range of video image processing as well as conventional photographs scanned into digital format. Specifically, natural image candidates for image processing emerge from the following sources.

- **Medical imaging** – This area includes diagnostic medicine (tomography, magnetic resonance imaging, and ultrasound), orthopedic prostheses (non-invasive 3D imaging, e.g., for hip replacements), and radiation treatment planning (effective treatment requires precision dosage to target tissue).

- **Brain structure and function** – A variety of imaging tools, such as proton emission tomography (PET), is shedding light on the function of various regions of the brain. The mapping of the neuroanatomy of the brain

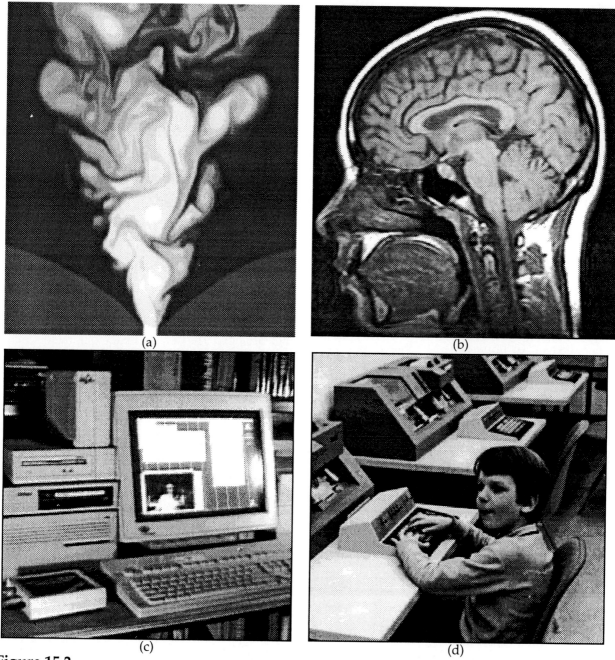

Figure 15.2
Images from various sources. (a) Supercomputer simulation of an extragalactic jet passing through an intergalactic shock wave;[4] (b) MRI scan of human brain; (c) video image of personal workstation; (d) scanned image of key punches.

is a task of enormous computational complexity but also of tremendous benefit through improved understanding of this vital organ.

• **Geoscience** – This area includes a host of application areas including cartography, meteorology, and geology. Cartographic compilation involves transforming raw photographic images into useful symbolic representations (maps). Meteorology involves the use of computational fluid dynamics for understanding and predicting the weather. Geology applications include the use of seismic data for locating mineral deposits.

- **Space exploration** – Images of a host of astronomical objects (including Earth) using wavelengths ranging from gamma rays to microwaves have provided such a wealth of data that our analytical facilities cannot keep up with the flow of incoming images. The visualization tools provided by image processing offer the only hope of coping with this flood of data.

- **Video imaging** – The video medium has become a consumer commodity and continues to offer the most penetrating and effective channel for news reporting and entertainment. The television industry is beginning to master image processing techniques for protecting the anonymity of vic-

tims in sensitive criminal proceedings and so on. In addition to the opportunities for creative uses, image processing offers temptations for serious abuses.

- **Photographic processing** – The advent of high-quality, digital scanners has opened the channel for capturing any hard copy image in digital form. This includes art work, photographs, and text through the use of optical character recognition. Scanners with spatial resolution of 300–600 dpi and color resolution of 16M are now available at prices in the range of $1–$2K. Libraries of high-quality, photographic clip art with no copyright restrictions are also available in CD-ROM format at well under $1 per photo.

Examples of images from these various sources are shown in Figure 15.2. Next, let us examine some of the image processing transformations available for these images.

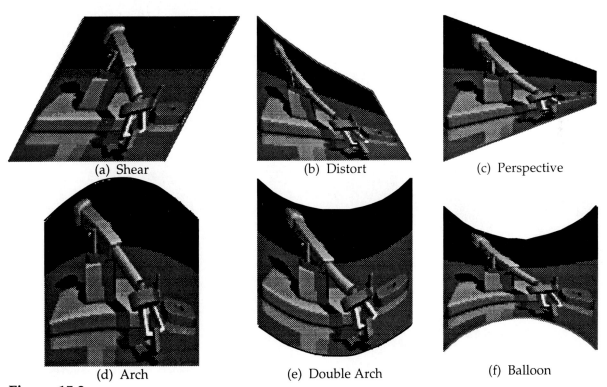

    (a) Shear   (b) Distort   (c) Perspective

    (d) Arch   (e) Double Arch   (f) Balloon

Figure 15.3
Geometric Image Processing. Images (a)–(c) were processed using *Canvas*™. Images (d)–(f) were processed using *Pixel Paint Professional*™.

Image Processing Transformations

What are the motivations for image processing? They range from the most serious applications in scientific visualization through commercial applications in advertising and art to pure creative exploration for personal satisfaction (i.e., play). A useful categorization of these purposes includes:

- **Image redesign** – A large class of applications of particular interest to commercial artists and advertisers involves geometric transformations of images and applications of visual effects. This class includes animations, dissolves, mosaics, and fractal transformations.

- **Noise removal** – The transmission of graphical images, particularly from low-power transmitters in space, can result in loss of information and the introduction of noise in various forms. Image processing techniques such as smoothing can help restore the quality of the original image.

- **Distortion removal** – Image acquisition techniques can introduce distortion into the original image. If the form of the distortion is known (e.g., by photographing a square grid), it is a relatively simple task to recover an undistorted image by mapping out the distortion.

- **Blur removal** – Photographs of moving objects often entail objectionable blurring which is readily removed by the appropriate image transformation process.

- **Image enhancement** – The quality of images can usually be improved by adjusting

(a)   (b)   (c)   (d)

Figure 15.4
Photographic Processes. (a) Setting brightness to 90%. (b) Setting brightness to 10%. (c) Setting contrast to 100%. (d) Using Invert Map to produce photographic negative. All images processed using *Digital Darkroom*™.

the brightness and contrast parameters. In addition to the intensity contrast, image processing techniques are available for improving the geometric contrast of objects by edge enhancements.

- **Computer vision** – The objective of computer vision is to *understand* the contents of an image. This involves complex pattern recognition processes that usually begin with edge detection and object segmentation. A number of image processing functions are available to carry out these tasks.

- **Visualization** – Numerous image processing functions are available for transforming images into alternate representations to assist the user in understanding and extracting meaning from the image. These include color mapping, contour mapping, 3D histogramming of 2D intensity data, and slicing of 3D images.

Image Redesign – Geometric Processing

A great variety of transformations are available for redesigning the geometry of images. Figure 15.3 illustrates several of these. Such geometric transformations provide valuable tools for artists and commercial designers.

(a)   (b)   (c)   (d)

Figure 15.5
Edge detection (spatial derivative) functions. (a) Original scanned image, (b) sharpened image, (c) blurred image, (d) edge detection.

Photographic Processing

Another useful class of image processing tools simulates processes available in the photographic darkroom. These include lightening, darkening, negative, and contrast adjustment. Figure 15.4 demonstrates some of the possibilities.

Image Enhancement – Edge Effects

A very useful category of image processing tools uses *changes in intensity* as the basis for the trans

formation function. These tools detect the spatial derivative of the intensity and map this derivative in various ways. By narrowing the spatial extent of the derivative, the image is *sharpened*. By broadening it, the image is *blurred*. By applying a threshold to the spatial derivative and mapping small values to white and large values to black, the transformation produces an *edge detector*. Figure 15.5 shows an initial scanned image and the effects of sharpening, blurring, and edge detection.

100:0   80:20   60:40

40:60   20:80   0:100

Figure 15.6
An experiment in morphing. The upper left image *morphs* into the lower right image with the percentages of each shown. Output is from *Morph*™ by Gryphon Software Corporation.

Image Morphing

The metamorphosis of one image into another is a particularly effective (and sometimes terrifying) image processing technique used increasingly in the movie industry. The original movie effects were created by a series of makeup changes and cross-dissolves from one image to another with the actors remaining motionless during the process. This metamorphosis or *morphing* is now readily accomplished electronically which accounts for its expanded role in advertising, science fiction movies, and horror films.

A variety of morphing techniques have been developed, ranging from geometric distortions similar to those in Figure 15.3 to actual polygon modeling of the object to be morphed and then application of spatial transformations to the model and filming the resulting changes.[5] A crude, but interesting, first approximation to morphing may be accomplished by the simple expedient of photographic double exposure. Commercial programs are now available for morphing on personal workstations. Gryphon Software Corporation markets an excellent example of such a program called *Morph*™.

Morph™ uses a 2D spatially-warped crossfade resembling the double exposure technique mentioned previously. Starting with two images of identical size, the user identifies key points on one image and selects corresponding key points on the second image. *Morph*™ can use any color or B/W images for input and produces output in the form of single morphs, *QuickTime* movies, or video output in PAL or NTSC format. An example of *Morph*™ output in single morph format is shown in Figure 15.6.

Special Effects

Commercial art designers and the video industry frequently need special effects for enhancing photographic images or modifying portions of their contents. One example familiar to television viewers is the use of the *mosaic* effect to camouflage the faces of participants in trials. Another popular special effect, called *posterizing*, involves reducing a normal gray scale image to a small number of shades, like one, two, three or four. Programs for art festivals and concerts often employ posterizing. The mosaic special effect is demonstrated in part (a) and posterizing to three shades of gray in part (b) of Figure 15.7.

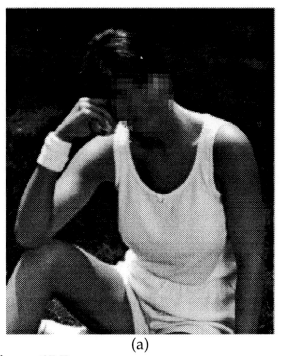

(a)

(b)

Figure 15.7
Special effects. (a) The *mosaic* effect has been applied to the model's face to conceal her identity, (b) the original photograph has been *posterized* to three shades.

Image Analysis Techniques

As indicated above, the ultimate goal of image analysis is the identification of a scene and all the objects in the image. This is an enormously complex and difficult task, usually classified as *computer vision* in the field of AI. The subject involves the integration of image processing techniques from computer graphics with pattern recognition techniques from AI and is covered in considerable detail by Schalkoff.[6]

Getting Into the Image

Many image processing programs provide functions such as sharpen, blur, invert, and mosaic as standard menu option for processing whole images or selected portions of images. However, for completely general image processing it is necessary to represent image in a convenient format which gives the analyst access to individual pixel values. With such access the analyst can easily duplicate all of the standard menu functions, tweak them to optimize the function for particular images, and investigate more complex transforma-

tions for difficult or novel cases. The mathematical formulations for several image processing transformations are presented in Rosenfeld and Kak.[7]

Some Mathematical Transformations

Several standard mathematical operations are useful in transforming graphical images. The image is defined as an intensity function, $f(x,y)$, at pixel location (x,y). For gray scale images, $f(x,y)$ may be represented by an 8-bit value in which 0 corresponds to black and 255 corresponds to white. For 8-bit color, $f(x,y)$ represents 256 addresses to a color look up table (CLUT) representing the color palette. For 24-bit ("true") color, $f(x,y)$ corresponds to a 24-bit code in which the red, blue, and green intensities are each encoded with 8-bit segments. Such encoding is equivalent to three overlapping 8-bit intensity functions, $f_R(x,y)$, $f_G(x,y)$, and $f_B(x,y)$.

The Laplacian

Edge detection is typically the first step in image segmentation, preprocessing phase of object identification. The most useful function for edge detection is the Laplacian operator defined as:

$$\nabla^2 f(x,y) \equiv \frac{\partial^2 f(x,y)}{\partial x^2} + \frac{\partial^2 f(x,y)}{\partial y^2} \qquad [15.1]$$

It is easy to show that the *five-point Laplacian* computed by taking differences from the four nearest neighbor pixels and assuming $Dx = Dy = 1$ reduces to:

$$\nabla^2 f(x,y) = f(x+1,y) + f(x-1,y) + \qquad [15.2]$$
$$f(x,y+1) + f(x,y-1) - 4 f(x,y)$$

That is, the five-point Laplacian is computed by taking (–4) times the value of the current pixel and adding to this value the value of the pixel immediately above, below, to the right, and to the left of it. This can be summarized as applying the following 3×3 window operator to each pixel:

$$\begin{bmatrix} 0 & 1 & 0 \\ 1 & -4 & 1 \\ 0 & 1 & 0 \end{bmatrix} \quad \text{Five-point Laplacian operator}$$

$$[15.3]$$

Image Sharpening

One source of image blurring in photography is the diffusion of dyes across sharp boundaries of the image. The time-dependent diffusion equation is given by:

$$\frac{\partial g}{\partial t} = k\nabla^2 g \qquad [15.4]$$

where
  $g(x,y,t)$ is the time dependent (degraded) image, and

  $g(x,y,0) = f(x,y)$
       $= $ original, unblurred image.

By expanding $g(x,y,t)$ around the latter time, $t = \tau$, and keeping only the first-order term, the original image, $f(x,y)$, can be restored by:

$$f(x,y) = g(x,y,\tau) - \tau k\nabla^2 g \qquad [15.5]$$
$$\text{(image restoration)}$$

This is another useful application of the Laplacian operator and may be represented in terms of discrete pixel coordinates by the five-point window operator:

$$\begin{bmatrix} 0 & -1 & 0 \\ -1 & 5 & -1 \\ 0 & -1 & 0 \end{bmatrix} \quad \text{Five-point restoration operator}$$

$$[15.6]$$

Zero Crossing Detector

Marr and Hildreth proposed a *zero crossing* edge detector based on smoothing the edges with a Gaussian function before applying the Laplacian operator.[8] The circularly symmetric Gaussian function is given by:

$$G(x,y) = \frac{1}{2ps^2} exp\left[-(x^2 + y^2)/2s^2\right] \qquad [15.7]$$

where
  σ = standard deviation or
       width of the Gaussian.

The transformed, *edge-detected* image, $f'(x,y)$, is then given in terms of the original image, $f(x,y)$, and $G(x,y)$ as:

$$f'(x,y) = (\nabla^2 G(x,y)) \times f(x,y) \qquad [15.8]$$

The $\nabla^2 G(x,y)$ function, also known as the *Laplacian of Gaussian* or LOG function, may be computed initially and stored for later convolution with various $f(x,y)$ images.

General Convolution Integrals

Note that all three of the above transformations involve specific instances of the general *convolution* defined as the 2D integral:

$$g(x,y) = \int\int h(x-x', y-y')f(x',y')dx'dy'. \qquad [15.9]$$

That is, the intensity of the transformed image, $g(x,y)$, at pixel (x,y) is a function of the intensities of other pixels at points (x',y'). In all three transformations, the convolution is *local*, that is, a given pixel intensity depends only on nearby pixel values. This means that the $h(\Delta x, \Delta y)$ *kernel* function dies off rapidly as Δx and Δy exceed a few pixels. In fact, the first two transformations involve only Δx and $\Delta y = \pm 1$.

Fourier Transformation

The 2D Fourier transform, *F(u,v)*, of image *f(x,y)* is given by:

$$F(u,v) = \int_{-\infty}^{\infty} \int_{-\infty}^{\infty} f(x,y)exp[-2pi(ux+vy)] \, dx \, dy$$

[15.10]

This function acts like a detector of spatial frequency components of the intensity variations along the *x*-axis (*u* component) and *y*-axis (*v* component). The Fourier transform contributes to image analysis in several areas.[9]

- It is a sensitive detector of textures. That is, plaid, striped, and solid regions of an image will have radically different Fourier spectra.

- It is translationally invariant. An object with a given texture will contribute the same Fourier frequency components independent of its position in an image.

- It is useful in building high-pass filters for edge enhancement and low-pass filters for noise reduction and smoothing.

Design of an Ideal Image Analysis Tool

Suppose you were designing an image analysis tool and wanted to optimize its flexibility and capability. What features would you want to incorporate?

As a starting point, you would probably specify the following.

- **Import file format flexibility** – The analysis system should be able to read all standard image formats (PICT, TIFF, EPS, and HDF) as well as spreadsheet data.

- **Direct access to pixel intensity values** – The numerical values of pixel intensities should be displayed, preferably in array format, with the option of selecting and modifying individual values.

- **Transparent data/image correlation** – The system should allow selection of a region of data and an indication of its mapping to the image as well as the inverse process.

- **An OOP representation of the image** – It should be possible to address the image as an object and send it messages concerning desired transformations.

- **A library of OOP transformation messages** – The system should provide a library of high-level messages instructing images to apply image transformations such as the Laplacian operator and fast Fourier transforms to themselves.

As the reader has probably guessed, image processing systems providing all these features and more already exist. We next discuss and show output from two outstanding examples: the NCSA *Image* and *DataScope* public domain programs and the commercial Spyglass, Inc. programs called *Transform*, *View*, and *Dicer*.

Implementations of Image Analysis Tools

Simulation studies constitute an area of intensive activity at the National Center for Supercomputer Applications (NCSA) at the University of Illinois. Scientists using NCSA facilities recognized early on the critical need for tools for visualizing the results of their supercomputer analyses. They developed a sophisticated network of Macintosh and Sun workstations to present the results of the supercomputer simulations and to share their analyses with each other. Of even more importance to the broader scientific community, they produced a sophisticated suite of programs, including *Image* and *DataScope*, for analysis of their scientific data. These programs are in the public domain and may be obtained without charge from the NCSA.[10]

To facilitate the sharing of data among people, projects, and machines on the network, NCSA created the *Hierarchical Data Format* (HDF). This TIFF-like file structure provides an object-oriented, tag-field format with the following features:

- Programs obtain information about the data in a file from the file itself. Through the use of tags, HDF files are self-describing.

- The tag-field structure provides generality. That is, different files can contain different mixtures of data and related information.

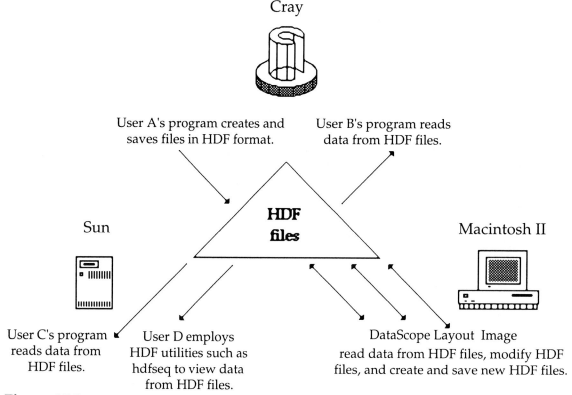

Cray

User A's program creates and saves files in HDF format.

User B's program reads data from HDF files.

HDF files

Sun

Macintosh II

User C's program reads data from HDF files.

User D employs HDF utilities such as hdfseq to view data from HDF files.

DataScope Layout Image read data from HDF files, modify HDF files, and create and save new HDF files.

Figure 15.8
The *Hierarchical Data Format* (HDF) communication function.

- HDF provides a standardized format for commonly used data sets, such as raster images, spreadsheets, and tables of scientific data.

- It provides a machine-independent format for communications between various platforms on a network.

- HDF is flexible enough to accommodate virtually any kind of data by defining new tags or combinations of tags.

The key communication role played by HDF files is illustrated in Figure 15.8.

Building on the base of the NCSA image processing tools, Brand Fortner has refined and extended them in the impressive *Spyglass* series.[11] These tools, *Transform* and *Dicer*, provide all of the features of our ideal image analysis system and allow the researcher to view her data through color enhancement, contour mapping, 3D representations, and slices through 3D data.

Transform *Examples*

The program *Transform*, from the Spyglass, Inc. series, approximates very closely the features specified for the ideal image analysis system. Figure 15.9 shows two images imported into transform. The first is an image scanned from a photograph, and the second is an image of a spreadsheet calculation of sine and cosine waves. Shown also in this figure is the mapping of a portion of the image with its HDF spreadsheet representation.

Transform provides a variety of display mode options for helping the user visualize the detailed structure of the data under investigation. Figure 15.10 illustrates several of the options available as menu selections for probing the structure of Figure 15.9(c) in more detail.

As useful as the display modes of Figure 15.10 are, the real strength of *Transform* lies in the generality of its image representation scheme and the ease with which this spreadsheet representation can be transformed.

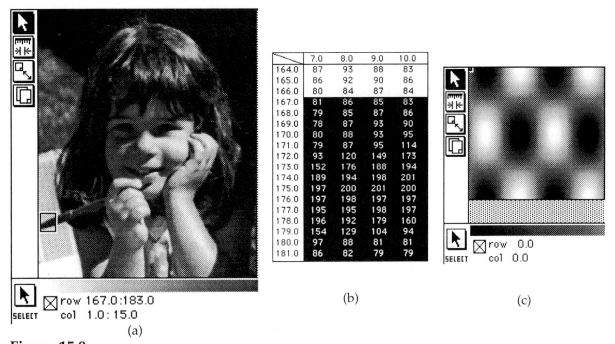

	7.0	8.0	9.0	10.0
164.0	87	93	88	83
165.0	86	92	90	86
166.0	80	84	87	84
167.0	81	86	85	83
168.0	79	85	87	86
169.0	78	87	93	90
170.0	80	88	93	95
171.0	79	87	95	114
172.0	93	120	149	173
173.0	152	176	188	194
174.0	189	194	198	201
175.0	197	200	201	200
176.0	197	198	197	197
177.0	195	195	198	197
178.0	196	192	179	160
179.0	154	129	104	94
180.0	97	88	81	81
181.0	86	82	79	79

row 167.0:183.0
col 1.0:15.0

(a)

(b)

row 0.0
col 0.0

(c)

Figure 15.9
Images imported into Spyglass *Transform*. (a) Image scanned from a photograph. (b) Small portion of HDF spreadsheet corresponding to highlighted rectangle at the left-hand side of (a). (c) Image of spreadsheet calculation of sine × cosine function.

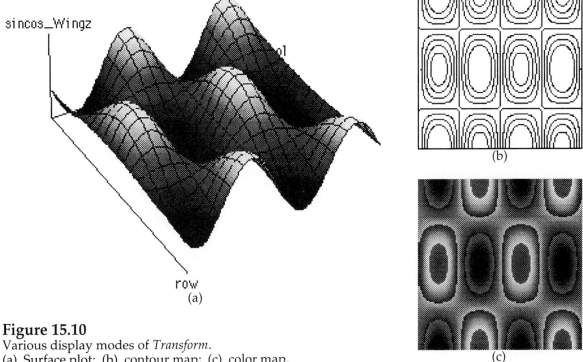

(b)

(a)

(c)

Figure 15.10
Various display modes of *Transform*.
(a) Surface plot; (b) contour map; (c) color map.

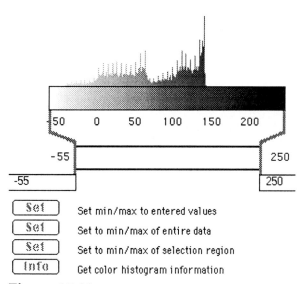

Set	Set min/max to entered values
Set	Set to min/max of entire data
Set	Set to min/max of selection region
Info	Get color histogram information

Figure 15.11
The *Color Bar* window after shifting the pixel intensity values downward by 100 units. The effect in this inverted palette is to lighten the image shown in Figure 15.12.

Example 1: Lightening

The transformation of lightening an image is very standard among image processing tools and readily accomplished with *Transform*.

1. An HDF file called Steve was opened by the *Paste New* command with the image in the clipboard. The scanned image had been opened, cropped, and copied to the clipboard by *Digital Darkroom*, an image processing program.

2. The *See Notebook* menu item was selected and the following transformation command typed in:

$$Steve2 = `Steve' - 100 \qquad [15.10]$$

This creates a new HDF file, Steve2, in which all of the intensities are shifted downward by 100 units (in this application, white = 0, black = 255).

Figure 15.12
The Lightening Transformation using *Transform*.

3. One of the dark pixels, now with a value of 143, was edited to a value of 250 to reestablish the intensity range from about –55 to 250, and the *Set* command of the *Color Bar* option clicked to redefine the intensity range as shown in Figure 15.11.

The very same lightening effect could have been achieved by simply opening the *Color Bar* window for the original image and resetting the maximum limit to 350, thereby mapping the 0–255 range of the original image to a lighter portion of the displayed palette. However, the above procedure indicates the ease with which each pixel of an image may be transformed. The original image and the lightened image are shown in Figure 15.12.

Example 2: Laplacian Operations – Sharpening and Edge Detection

The implementation of the Laplacian operation and other transformations based on the Laplacian are essentially trivial with the tools provided by *Transform*. Figure 15.13 illustrates the total extent of the programming required to compute the

Laplacian transformation using the five-point operator (Equation 15.3), the sharpening operation (Equation 15.6), and three edge detection strategies based on the Laplacian operation. The original image is indicated as *Robot*.

To create a new HDF file, Robot2, corresponding to application of the Laplacian operator on the Robot file, the command, "Robot2=lap('Robot')" was entered in the *Notebook* window of the Robot file and the *Calculate from Notes* menu option selected. The resulting image is shown as Robot2. Since the Laplacian operator produces large positive and negative numbers of approximately equal magnitudes at the intensity discontinuities, the resulting image is predominantly gray corresponding to an HDF pixel value of zero.

To implement the sharpening or image restoration transformation, the command, "Robot3=-Robot–lap('Robot')" was issued. The resulting image, Robot3, does, indeed, show sharpened outlines.

To eliminate the negative intensity values of the Robot2 file, the command, "Robot4=Abs(lap('Robot')) was entered in the Robot *Notebook*, and the image Robot4 was generated. This image suggests the outline of the edges, but its gray scale nature makes them indistinct.

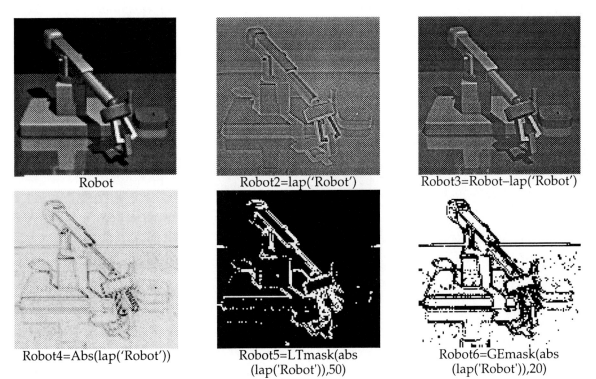

Robot   Robot2=lap('Robot')   Robot3=Robot–lap('Robot')

Robot4=Abs(lap('Robot'))   Robot5=LTmask(abs(lap('Robot')),50)   Robot6=GEmask(abs(lap('Robot')),20)

Figure 15.13
Laplacian Operations. Robot3 → Sharpening; Robot6 → Edge Detection.

To convert the "analog" Robot4 image to a binary image, the threshold command "Robot5=LTmask(abs(lap('Robot')),50)" was issued, and the image Robot5 appeared. This masking operation can be interpreted as: *If a pixel value is less than 50, color it black; else, color it white.*

Finally, a very effective edge detector is achieved using the "Greater Than" threshold command and setting the threshold to an intensity value of 20. Robot6 is generated by applying the "Robot6=GEmask(abs(lap('Robot')),20)" transformation to the original Robot image file.

This example illustrates a tiny sample of the functions and transformations available in *Transform*. Other functions available include ten trigonometric functions, ten mathematical functions, thirty-one functions for manipulating rows, columns, or an array as a whole, seven complex arithmetic functions including the FFT, seven specific kernel convolution functions, and a generic (user-defined) convolution function.

Transform also illustrates the power of abstraction. By considering images as named objects (in an OOP sense) and supplying a library of abstract, high-level messages that the user can send to the objects, this system provides tools for carrying out exceedingly complex image processing operations with a minimum of commands. This is really what abstraction is all about.

Tools for 3D Visualization

Assume your task is to design an optimum system for viewing 3D data arrays. Such data may involve a series of CAT scan images taken every two millimeters through the brain, or a set of neutron flux measurements at a lattice of (x,y,z) points in a fission reactor core, or a supercomputer simulation of the interaction of an extragalactic jet passing through an intergalactic shock wave. Much of the experimental data collected by seismologist and meteorologists is intrinsically 3D in nature, as are the theoretical calculations in astrophysics and fluid dynamics. What visualization techniques would help investigators in these areas interpret their 3D data?

Specifying a 3D Visualization System

An optimum 3D visualization system should provide, among others, the following features for viewing 3D data.

- Display an (x,y) intensity pattern at any user-defined z value. Such slices should also be available for all combinations of x, y, and z coordinates.

- Projection of the 2D intensity distribution on any user-defined parallelepiped within the measurement volume.

- Constructive solid geometry (CSG) capability for removing any user-defined parallelepiped within the measurement volume and projection of the measurements on the remaining surfaces.

- A user-friendly GUI for selecting and dragging any projection plane or volumetric object to any position within the viewing volume.

- An intuitive GUI for modifying the viewing position and perspective, including smooth interpolated zoom features.

- A smooth interpolation of projected data between the measured data values.

- Flexibility in selecting, modifying, and editing color display palettes.

- The ability to select and map individual colors.

- The ability to convert selected colors to a transparent mode.

- The ability to import data cube information from a variety of picture and spreadsheet formats.

An outstanding system supporting all of these features and many more is marketed by Spyglass, Inc., under the name *Dicer*.

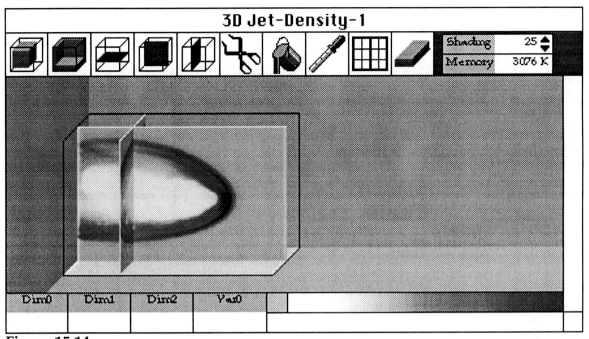

Figure 15.14
The *Dicer* Visualization Environment.

Implementation

The visualization environment that *Dicer* presents to the user is illustrated in Figure 15.14. The data set is a snapshot of a 3D, time-dependent simulation of a supersonic jet of material interacting with an ambient medium moving at right angles to the jet. The figure shows the tools menu along the top, the color palette along the bottom, and three perpendicular slices in the viewing workspace. The menu tools fall into two general classes:

- Projection objects and manipulations,

- Color tools and manipulations.

Projection Objects

The three classes of projection objects and manipulations include:

- Data slices →

Projection surfaces through the data volume, parallel to the three Cartesian planes.

- Data cubes →

Projection blocks and cutouts. Cutouts are invisible, except for their intersection with blocks.

- Tongs →

This tool is used to select and drag projection objects.

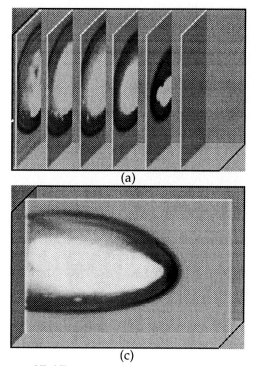
(a)

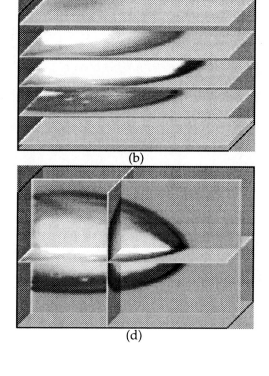
(b)

(c)

(d)

Figure 15.15
Configurations of data slices in *Dicer*.

Color Tools

Intelligent color manipulation offers a powerful technique for 3D visualization. Dicer provides four color tools for manipulation of the color palette and the active or *current* color. These are summarized as:

- Color table →

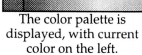

The color palette is displayed, with current color on the left.

- Paint tool →

Clicking on any color region converts that color to the current color.

- Eyedropper →

Changes the current color to the color sampled by clicking this icon.

- Transparency →

Causes selected colors to become invisible. Allows viewing through objects.

- Color eraser →

Inverse operation to the paint tool. Clicking on painted color returns it to palette color.

Example 1: Use of Data slices

Depending on the nature of the 3D data, various arrangements of slicing planes or combinations of planes may prove most effective for visualization purposes. Figure 15.15 shows some of the possible configurations.

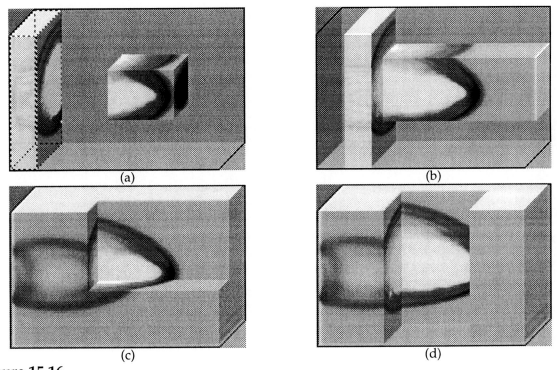

Figure 15.16
Data cubes for visualization. (a) and (b) are combinations of simple data cubes; (c) and (d) are single data cubes with cutouts.

Example 2: Use of Data Cubes

Data cubes support the union and subtraction operations of constructive solid geometry (CSG). Figure 15.16 shows four arrangements of data cubes and cutouts.

Example 3: Use of Color Tools

Judicious use of color can assist the researcher in highlighting certain features and discovering new patterns in the data under investigation. Two *Dicer* features offer particularly powerful tools for exploring the structure of the user's data. With the *Paint* option, the user can use a bright color to pour into the model to highlight contours of a given volume element (or *voxel*) intensity. The selected color replaces the color under the cursor and serves to trace the location of the original color contour throughout the model. The use of the *Paint* feature is shown in Figure 15.17(b).

The second feature involves a combination of the *Solid Fill* and *Transparency* options. First, the *Solid Fill* option is selected to compute the color at each 3D voxel (volume element) of the model. Then the *Transparency* tool is used to turn some range of the color palette invisible. Figure 15.17(c) shows the effect of the *Transparency* tool alone in dissolving away the invisible colors, leaving only the selected ones projected on the walls of the data cube. In Figure 15.17(d) the *Solid Fill* option has been used to dissolve away invisible colors and leave the 3D configuration of the remaining color contours. This tool offers an exceptionally useful technique for studying complex structures in 3D space.

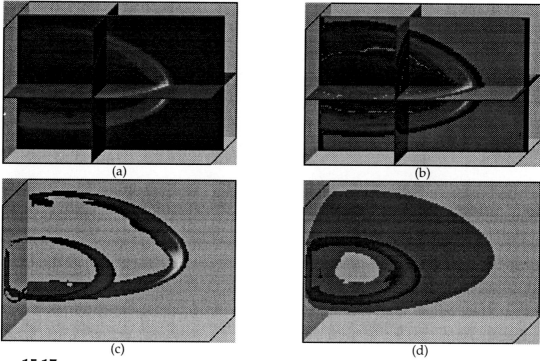

Figure 15.17
Color enhancements. (a) New color table; (b) effect of *painting* the dark shade with the current color; (c) effect of *transparency* in turning off darker shades; (d) *Solid Fill* effect showing 3D contour for this shade (darker shades are transparent).

Image Compression

One of the most valuable and practical areas of image processing is that of image compression. An excellent theoretical background and introduction to this topic is presented by Jain *et al.*[12] We have already introduced one promising image compression algorithm, based on the *Collage Theorem*, in the chapter on fractals. Two more techniques are discussed here.

Pattern Encoding

The first technique is based on redundancy reduction and pattern encoding. A prime example of this technique is the program, *Disk Doubler*.[13] By encoding repetitive character patterns numerically, *Disk Doubler* is able to reduce database files to nearly twenty five percent of their original size and image files to between thirty and fifty percent of their original size.

Disk Doubler requires just a few seconds to compress most files. Compressed files retain their names and are automatically decompressed as they are opened by application programs.

JPEG

Far more impressive compression ratios are achieved by the JPEG (Joint Photographic Experts Group) algorithm. The JPEG specification has been approved by the International Standards Organization (ISO) and emerged from experiments in communications services such as the French Minitel videotex system. Using averaging techniques, JPEG routinely achieves up to 20:1 compression ratios with very little image degradation, and even at 50:1, a quilting effect is barely discernible.

The JPEG procedure operates on image files represented by video signals. Standard PICT, TIFF, and EPS image files must, therefore, first be converted to the video signal values of chrominance and luminance. JPEG then divides the image into 8 × 8 pixel blocks on which a variation of Fourier transform called the discrete cosine transform (DCT) is applied. The DCT measures the variation

Figure 15.18
Image decompressed by *PicturePress* and reduced by a factor of two. The original 770K image was compressed to a 77K JPEG++ file.

in the chrominance and luminance within the block. Blocks with little variation can be represented compactly as average values.

Several commercial JPEG image compression systems, using both hardware and software techniques, are now available on personal workstations.[14] Apple Computer has adopted the JPEG standard as the image compression technique for its *QuickTime* multimedia protocol. Kodak offers a package called *Colorsqueeze* based on the JPEG standard. Adriann Ligtenberg, one of the authors of the JPEG specifications draft, is a founder of Storm Technology which has pioneered image compression techniques. This company offers a combination hardware/software package called *PicturePress* which uses an extension called JPEG++. *PicturePress* allows the user to apply different compression ratios to different regions of an image. Figure 15.18 shows a portion of an image compressed by a 10:1 ratio by *PicturePress*.

Conclusions

In this chapter we have attempted to integrate the areas of computer graphics, image processing and image analysis. Classical computer graphics is concerned with the synthesis of images based on

messages, often symbolic, from the designer. Image processing involves the transformation of images, generally at the pixel level, to produce new images of greater clarity or more value to the user. Image analysis is described as the set of techniques required to extract symbolic information from the image data. Many of the techniques of image processing, such as edge detection, are valuable at the early stages of image analysis. While many of the pattern recognition algorithms of image analysis fall more in the domain of artificial intelligence than computer graphics, image processing effectively links the two areas.

The first half of the chapter illustrated many of the image processing tools available in standard graphics packages. These tools are frequently more than adequate for standard applications such as sharpening, blurring, and tracing outlines. More complex applications require tools with more flexibility and generality. A scientific visualization program was demonstrated for importing images from various file formats and processing them with a wide range of mathematical transformations. Sophisticated techniques for visualizing and analyzing complex 3D data were presented next, and the chapter concluded with a discussion and demonstration of the JPEG image compression technique.

Exercises

15.1   Discuss the proposition: *Image processing is an essential component of computer graphics.*

15.2   An interesting analogy may be developed between computer graphics and chemistry. Discuss the analogy between image analysis and analytical chemistry (What elements compose a compound?). Discuss the analogy between image synthesis and organic chemistry (How are complex compounds built from more elementary materials?).

15.3   What graphical algorithms, transformations, and techniques are common to (synthetic) computer graphics, image processing, and image analysis?

15.4   Why are the synthetic images produced by CAD and rendering systems of little interest to image processing and image analysis people?

15.5   What properties of theoretical synthetic images make them more interesting than purely synthetic images? Interpret your answer in terms of the *complexity* of both the model and the resulting graphical images.

15.6   From a scan of professional magazines in the field of medicine, life science, chemistry, or physics, locate, duplicate, and discuss three examples in which image processing is important.

15.7   Discuss three examples from television, particularly commercials, of image redesign through geometric processing or *morphing*.

15.8   From direct observation of a science fiction or Walt Disney animation movie, identify three examples of image processing techniques and discuss them in terms of the categories of image processing presented in the chapter.

15.9   Although blurring is generally considered undesirable because of the loss of information, there are applications in which it is desired. Discuss three examples.

15.10 From a scan of newspapers, magazines, or fine arts programs, identify and duplicate three examples that appear to have been created by posterizing a photograph.

15.11 Assume a "slice" through an image parallel to the x-axis produced the following series of pixel intensities:

0, 0, 0, 1, 2, 3, 4, 5, 6, 6, 6, 6, 6, 4, 4, 4, 4, 2, 2, 2, 2, 2, 2, 2, 0, 0, 0, 0

Compute the series of pixel intensities resulting from applying the Laplacian operator numerically, as defined in Equation 15.2. Interpret your results.

15.12 To the series of pixel intensities resulting from exercise 15.11, apply the sharpening (image restoration) function defined by Equation 15.5. Do you observe an *overshoot* effect? Interpret your new results in terms of increased contrast at the edges of objects.

15.13 Compute and plot both the Gaussian and the LOG functions given in Equations 15.6 and 15.7 as a function of x, assuming $y = 0$.

15.14 Compute and plot the LOG function as a wire frame plot in 3D. Why is it sometimes called a *Mexican hat* function?

15.15 Discuss how the convolution integral, Equation 15.8, may be considered as "action at a distance" in terms of its influence on a pixel at (x,y). Look up the rules of the game of *Life* and interpret the game as a convolution.

15.16 Figure 15.9(c) is an image approximately 128 pixels on a side generated by the function, $sin(2\omega x)cos(\omega y)$. What is the numerical value of ω? If this function were substituted into Equation 15.9, what would the corresponding Fourier transform, $F(u,v)$, look like?

15.17 What features of an image will Fourier analysis reveal? Describe how Fourier analysis could be used for object classification.

15.18 What does the color map of Figure 15.10(c) reveal that is not apparent in the contour map of Figure 15.10(b)?

15.19 The brightness/darkness of an image may be changed by two techniques: multiplying each pixel intensity value by a constant or adding a constant to each value. Which do you think is preferable? Will either technique result in a change in contrast?

15.20 Why is the background color *gray* in Robot2 of Figure 15.13 and *white* in Robot4?

15.21 In the discussion of *Tools for 3D Visualization*, several desired specifications were listed. What additional ones would you suggest?

15.22 What additional rendering features would you suggest for improving the visual realism of the 3D contour of Figure 15.17(d)?

15.23 How large would the 24-bit TIFF file of an 8.5 × 11 inch 300 dpi scanned image be?

15.24 Why does the JPEG image compression algorithm lend itself naturally to parallel processing? What are the implications for ASICs?

Endnotes

1. McCormick, Bruce H., DeFanti, Thomas A., and Brown, Maxine D., "Visualization in Scientific Computing," *Computer Graphics* **21**, No. 6, p. C-5, November (1987).
2. Pfitzer, Gary, "Antarctic Insights,", *Computer Graphics World* **15**, No. 1, pp. 81–82, Jan. (1992).
3. Firebaugh, Morris W., *Artificial Intelligence – A Knowledge-Based Approach*, See Chapter 14, "Pattern Recognition" and Chapter 15, "Computer Vision," PWS-Kent, Boston, MA (1988).
4. Norman , Michael L., Burns, Jack O., Sulkanen, Martin E., and Cox, Donna J., *Nature* **335**, No. 6186, pp. 146–149, September 8, (1988) The simulation was carried out using the ZEUS code developed by M. Norman and D. Clarke using a grid of 400 x 400 zones. The color palette was created by Donna J. Cox using the ICARE software. For more information, contact:
   Michael L. Norman
   5600 Beckman Institute, Drawer 25
   405 North Mathews Street
   Urbana, IL 61801
   norman@merlin.ncsa.uiuc.edu

5. Sorensen, Peter, "Morphing Magic," *Computer Graphics World* **15**, No. 1, pp. 36–42, Jan. (1992).
6. Schalkoff, Robert J., *Digital Image Processing and Computer Vision*, John Wiley & Sons, Inc., New York, NY (1989).
7. Rosenfeld, Azriel and Kak, Avinash C., *Digital Picture Processing*, Academic Press, New York, NY (1976).
8. Marr, D. and Hildreth, E., "Theory of Edge Detection," *Proc. Royal Soc. London* **207**, pp. 187–217 (1980).
9. Niblack, Wayne, *An Introduction to Digital Image Processing*, Prentice Hall International, Englewood Cliffs, NJ (1986).
10. For information on *Image* and *DataScope*, contact:
    NCSA Software Development
    152 Computing Applications Bldg.
    605 E. Springfield Ave.
    Champaign, IL 61820
    (217) 244-0638
    softdev@ncsa.uiuc.edu
11. For information on the *Spyglass* series contact:
    Spyglass, Inc.
    701 Devonshire Drive, c-17
    Champaign, IL 61820
    (217) 355-1665
12. Jain, Anil K., Farrelle, Paul M., and Algazi, V. Ralph, "Image Data Compression," Ekstrom, Michael P. (ed), *Digital Image Processing Techniques*, Academic Press, Inc., Orlando, FL (1984).
13. Information on *Disk Doubler* is available from :
    Salient Software, Inc.
    124 University Avenue, Suite 103
    Palo Alto, CA 94301
    (415) 321-5375
14. Eight JPEG image compression systems are evaluated by Charles Seiter in "Image Compression Matures," *MacWorld*, pp. 146–151 March (1992).

Chapter 16

Visual Realities

All things are in flux.
Heraclitus, ~500 B.C.

...a model means an encapsulation of some slice of the real world within the confines of the relationships constituting a formal mathematical system.
John Casti

We graphicists choreograph colored dots on a glass bottle so as to fool the eye and mind into seeing desktops, spacecraft, molecules, and worlds that are not and never can be...
Frederick Brooks

The central concern of interactive system design is what I call a system's virtuality. This is intended as a quite general term, extending into all fields where mind, effects and illusions are proper issues.
Theodore Nelson

VR is the first medium that doesn't narrow the human spirit.
Jaron Lanier

Knowledge is power and permits the wise sovereign and the benevolent general to attack without risk, conquer without bloodshed, and accomplish deeds surpassing all others.
Sun Tzu

Computer graphics is destined to play a central role in what is emerging as one of the greatest technical enterprises ever undertaken. This enterprise is the culmination of one of the main themes of this text, the concept of *model authenticity*. The ultimate implementation of model authenticity involves the construction of detailed models (data bases) representing either imaginary or actual world systems. Various aspects of this enterprise have been identified as *alternate realities*,[1] *artificial reality*,[2] *virtual reality*,[3] and *mirror worlds*.[4] Computer graphics provides windows through which we can observe virtual worlds and the eyes by which we can visualize new realities.

How does a mirror world differ from virtual reality? The reader is probably well aware that almost all combinations of the adjectives *cyber-, tele-, alternate, artificial, virtual,* and *mirror* with the nouns *reality, space, presence, perception,* and *world* have been used to describe various aspects of this exciting, embryonic science. We will attempt here to distinguish between these various aspects and explore some of the implications of ultimate model authenticity. From a computer graphics perspective, however, many of the problems and objectives are common to any variation of the field. To simplify the discussion and capture the essence of the relationship of computer graphics to these new realities, we propose the term *metareality*.

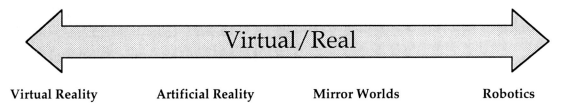

| Virtual Reality | Artificial Reality | Mirror Worlds | Robotics |

A *metalanguage* is a language used to talk about another language, and, in general, the term *meta* applied to a given discipline signifies a related and more comprehensive discipline designed to deal critically with the given discipline (e.g., metapsychology and metamathematics). Metareality, then, is a *reality used to represent or describe another reality*. It is a reality about another reality. The implementation consists of an integrated software and hardware system designed to maximize the sensory information flow to the user. The target reality may range from a purely imaginary cyberspace to a completely realistic representation of real space and some mix of virtual and real objects occupying these spaces.

A final observation is in order concerning the process of visualizing new realities. These realities are invariably *dynamic*, i.e., changing with time. To portray these realities graphically, then, requires dynamic displays of images that move. This is the subject of *computer animation*, which we explore in more detail below.

Classes of Metarealities

Metarealities may be distinguished and classified according to several characteristics. A systematic classification should take into consideration the following features.

- **Virtual/Real components of the scene** – Realities range from the purely imaginary of video games to the very concrete representations of a real-time chemical plant model.

- **Degree of interactivity/control** – Interactivity is the key that distinguishes metarealities from ordinary simulations. Interactivity may be as simple as the two parameter control (steering wheel and accelerator) of a race car simulation to the complete freedom of unlimited motion and ability to manipulate objects in a virtual scene.

- **Virtual/Real effects of interaction** – Effects range from purely imaginary (e.g., the score of enemy plane kills) to completely real (e.g., the route of a remotely guided land rover on Mars). Virtual interactions modify the databases representing a scene, while real interactions modify the real objects composing the scene.

- **Communication channels** – Almost all metarealities rely on computer graphics as the most effective sensory communication channel. However, more advanced systems have been designed to provide audio signals, olfactory information, and the sense of touch. Increasing the number of sensory channels increases the realism of the virtual scene.

A useful mental image for classifying metarealities is to place them along a virtual/real spectrum such as that shown below.

Let's examine each of these classes of metarealities in a bit more detail.

Virtual Reality

Virtual reality (VR), in its standard form, involves donning data gloves and data goggles that transport you into cyberspace. The data glove contains transducers which generate signals representing the position and orientation of the hand and each finger. The data goggles are relatively high resolution stereo displays mounted in a headset which straps snugly to the user's head. The data goggles also are equipped with transducers that report their position and orientation.

The goggles display some representation of a virtual world populated with virtual objects. Turning the head brings into view new portions of the virtual scene. A symbolic hand image represents the location and orientation of the data glove worn by the user. Motion of the user's hand on which the data glove is worn is reflected by a corresponding motion of the symbolic hand. By moving the data-gloved hand, the user can wander through the 3D cyberspace, grasp and manipulate objects, and even, by symbolic gestures, take off and fly.

Two features characterize true virtual reality systems:

- **Immersion** – The use of gaze-tracking, stereoscopic visualization creates the illusion of being inside the virtual scene.

- **Navigation** – The use of a data glove or other input device to move around within the virtual space.

While computer graphics plays the principle role in VR systems, additional sensory channels increase the illusion of total immersion. The audio channel is relatively easy to add, and progress is being made on adding the sense of touch. The data glove concept has been extended to complete body suits that enable the virtual system to represent the user as a human figure rather than just a disembodied hand.

A practical and widespread example of virtual reality, which most readers have used (but may not have recognized in terms of VR), is the desktop metaphor used in WIMP operating systems. Douglas Englebart first demonstrated this metaphor at the Stanford Research Institute (SRI) in 1968, and it forms the basis for the operating environments of the Macintosh, Windows, and most other modern systems. The power of the desktop metaphor lies in creating the illusion that the screen represents the user's desktop. Papers (documents) may lay on top of other papers and may be shuffled or placed in folders. Unwanted documents are thrown away in the trash can. Hierarchies of folders and documents may be established paralleling those with which the user is familiar. The use of clever graphical icons (documents look like sheets with their type stamped on them; folders look like folders) serves as a constant and intuitive reminder of the organization of the user's filing system in terms of familiar objects.

- Documents ⇒

  Ch.16   Fig.16.1

- Folders ⇒

  CG Book   Courses

The effectiveness of the desktop metaphor becomes apparent in comparisons of the time for training new users of the Mac filing system with that for new users of MS-DOS. The strength of the virtual reality illusion becomes apparent when the user is deprived of extensions such as the mouse. Running MS-DOS as a virtual machine on the Macintosh puts the user in command line mode. The cursor can only be moved by the arrow keys, the mouse is dead, and the user knows it. However, confirmed WIMP users continue to grasp the mouse and attempt direct manipulation —to no avail. The virtual reality term for this sensation of deprivation may appropriately be termed *cybernetic amputation.*

Artificial Reality

The term *artificial reality* was coined by Myron Krueger in 1974 to describe his efforts to combine technology with artistic expression to create a responsive environment.[5] Krueger's experiments in artificial reality began with *GLOWFLOW: An Environmental Art Form*, continued with *META-PLAY* and *PSYCHIC SPACE*, and culminated with *VIDEOPLACE* and its desktop version, *VIDEODESK.*

GLOWFLOW was a computer art project consisting of a light/sound environment that had limited provision for responding to the people within it. The display space consisted of a darkened rectangular gallery with walls containing transparent tubes containing, in turn, phosphorescent particles suspended in water. The tubes contained different colored pigments and were arranged so as to create an optical illusion of a slanted floor.

A Moog synthesizer was used to generate sounds from speakers surrounding the gallery. Hidden light sources activated the phosphors, giving the illusion of objects floating in space and then fading away to nothingness. User input to the system was generated by six pressure-sensitive pads activated by the weight of viewers. The whole system was controlled by a PDP-12 computer.

Krueger reports most interesting results from this experiment in interactive artistic expression.

> *People had amazing reactions to the environment. Communities would form among strangers. Games, clapping, and chanting would arise spontaneously. The room seemed to have moods, sometimes being deathly silent, sometimes raucous and boisterous. Individuals would invent roles for themselves.*[6]

His next experiment was *METAPLAY*, in which the output was an 8 × 10 foot video image consisting of a mixing of video signals from a camera trained on the viewers with that from a camera trained on an Adage Graphic Display Computer, which was coupled to the University's UNIVAC 1108. An unseen operator at the interactive Adage terminal could interact with the image of the audience observers. Members of the audience soon became participants in the graphical scene as their gestures were recognized by the hidden operator and highlighted in the mixed signal image. Participants soon recognized that the visual reality was "intelligent" and began to use their hands as writing instruments to trace lines on the screen.

As a curious coincidence, the author was carrying out his first research in computer graphics on the very same Adage Display Computer during the same period that Krueger was presenting *METAPLAY*. This experiment, funded by the Wisconsin Alumni Research Foundation, used the Adage to represent the 3D momentum vectors from particles created in high-energy physics interactions. This application was designed to study systematic features of the strong nuclear force and was one of the very first demonstrations of scientific visualization.

Krueger's latest work is *VIDEOPLACE* and its desktop implementation, *VIDEODESK*. *VIDEOPLACE* consists of a 16 × 24 foot room with a video screen projected on one wall. The video image is the silhouette of the participant mixed with a video image produced by the computer. Special processors analyze the participant's image to determine edges and identify features such as fingers. Once the computer has some understanding of the participant, it can introduce graphical sprites which romp along the outline of the participant's silhouette, performing apparently intelligent and playful stunts. This implementation, called *CRITTER*, effectively substitutes AI techniques for the intelligent interaction performed by the hidden human operator in *METAPLAY*.

VIDEOPLACE has been exhibited widely in North America, Europe, and Japan at scientific conferences as well as at art exhibits. When not on tour, it is permanently housed at the Connecticut State Museum of Natural History in Storrs.

Krueger's exploration of electronic technology as artistic expression is well documented in his latest book, *Artificial Reality II*. From the broader metareality point of view, his principal contributions are the following. First, he has continuously and strongly emphasized the *responsive* aspect of

human interaction in the artificial reality. That is, Krueger's goal is to elicit an overt, active response from the viewers of his electronic art. By making the electronic medium responsive to viewer input, this goal has been achieved, and new insight has emerged on the nature of human artistic appreciation.

The second contribution of artificial reality, Krueger-style, is to free the explorer of cyberspace from the encumbrance of goggles and gloves. His cyberspace sees and understands the participant through the use of unobtrusive video technology. This medium can be considered as a generalization of the interactive I/O channel, which serves to liberate the traveler in cyberspace.

Finally, Krueger was one of the first to identify the gesture as a legitimate basis for communication with machines. All WIMP systems rely on interpreting the (x,y) location of the cursor at the moment, t=0, of an event. Krueger recognized that the time dependent trajectories of a pointing device, $(x(t),y(t))$, offer a rich medium for communication. In fact, gesture recognition is an essential element of pen-based operating systems.

Mirror Worlds

Of all the metarealities discussed in this chapter, mirror worlds promise the most profound and intriguing possibilities. The concept and implications of mirror worlds are spelled out in nontechnical language in a book of this title by David Gelernter of Yale University.

The subtitle of the book, *The Day Software Puts the Universe in a Shoebox…How it will Happen and What it will Mean*, gives an overview of Gelernter's main thesis. This thesis holds that the technology is now or soon will be available for bringing authentic, real-time models of any institution of interest into the user's workstation. These microcosms will be embedded in your machine and continuously updated to represent the detailed functioning of any organization of interest. Microcosms may represent universities, businesses, hospitals, city government, public school systems, automobile traffic patterns, an airport operation, and so on. In many cases, the databases representing these systems already exist. With the proper environment for injecting agents for examining and reporting this data it can be transformed into a useful mirror world.

The essential feature of mirror worlds, which distinguish them from virtual reality, is that mirror worlds reflect *reality* while virtual reality reflects purely *hypothetical* or *imaginary* constructs. Mirror worlds provide us with the option of monitoring the school board discussion of hiring a new school superintendent, or examining the voting record of your congressperson on the abortion issue. These are real world events that you could observe personally if you chose to attend the school board meeting or deliberations of Congress. Virtual reality, on the other hand, may have provided you with an exciting game of tennis, a challenging exercise in preflight checkout and takeoff of a Boeing 747, or a realistic simulation of open heart surgery.

Mirror worlds might be considered as the ultimate database retrieval system. The intelligent screening and reporting of events from the real world would help all of us deal with the rising flood of information to which we are subjected. Mirror worlds offer a technology for capturing and controlling the chaotic flood of information that threatens to engulf us.

Robotics

While mirror worlds allow us to observe any aspect of society that interests us, robotics allows us to manipulate and change the existing reality. Rather than conventional robots, we are concerned here with remotely controlled robots or, more precisely, *teleoperators*. The design of teleoperators is the subject of remote control engineering, a subject we discuss in detail later in the chapter. The purpose of teleoperators is to act as agents to carry out actions in the physical world under the control of humans who generally are removed from the site of the action.

The motivation for building teleoperators is to perform work in environments which are inhospitable or dangerous for human beings. They originated in the nuclear power industry but have applications in underwater and space exploration, combat zones, and disaster areas such as fires and chemical accidents.

Interactive computer graphics has contributed to teleoperator development by providing better displays for visualizing the action site and through research on interactive devices for manipulating objects in the real world. Many of the devices developed for virtual reality, such as VR goggles and DataGloves are readily adaptable for teleoperators.

Animation

An essential aspect of all metarealities is that they change through time. Whether one is wandering about in cyberspace or probing the processes taking place in a mirror world, the primary visual channel of communication is a *dynamic* graphical image. This involves animation—literally *bringing a scene to life*.

In addition to the important role of animation as the foundation for authentic metarealities, computer animation is displacing conventional animation techniques in television and cinema and expanding its domain in software application. The dazzling—and often annoying—"flying logos" of television are the most visible application of computer animation. While computer animation has contributed significant special effects in movies such as *The Abyss*, *Terminator 2*, and *Beauty and the Beast*, conventional filming techniques still dominate the movie industry. A major milestone in computer animation, however, occurred in 1991 with the announcement of the contract between Walt Disney Studios and Pixar to produce the first feature film based wholly on computer animation.

In the field of computer software, two early products have put simple animation within the grasp of the average user. One is Apple's *Hypercard* that provides for short animation sequences to be embedded in *Hypercard* stacks and activated by the press of a button. The second is *Macromind Director*, a very sophisticated authoring system for animating script and 2D graphics. Many other software packages now offer "tours" or "sampler disks" which incorporate animated sequences in *Hypercard* or *Director* format.

Perhaps the most significant computer animation product yet released is Apple's *QuickTime*. *QuickTime* provides a protocol for manipulating video and animation sequences. Its use of the JPEG image compression standard has overcome the chief obstacle to the widespread use of video and animation information – its huge volume. It is very probable that *QuickTime* will do for dynamic information (video and animation) what *PostScript* did for typographic information. We will discuss the details of *QuickTime* below.

Finally, it should be noted that animation has been "creeping into" design and analysis programs simply as extended features. For instance, NCSA's *Image* and Spyglass' *View* both offer animation options for visualizing the results of supercomputer simulations. We have already presented a series of *Mathematica* images (the drum head displacements) which are best viewed as an animation sequence, and the primary output mode of *Interactive Physics* is animation. The conceptual design program, *Swivel 3D*, offers sophisticated tools for the design of animation sequences.

Let's look at some of these animation tools in more detail.

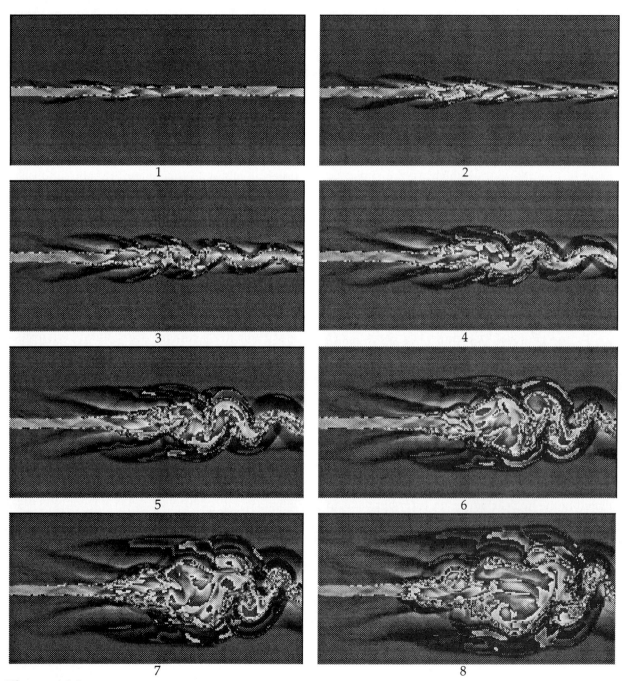

Figure 16.1
Animation sequence representing the onset of turbulence. This simulation represents the nonlinear growth of a Kelvin-Helmholtz kink instability in a Mach 3 supersonic jet.[7] It required two hours of CPU time on the NCSA CRAY X-MP.

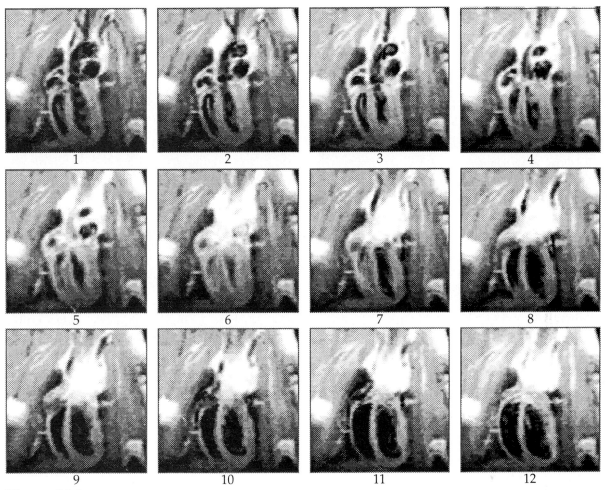

Figure 16.2
Animation sequence of a rat's heart beat.[8] These proton spin echo MRI images of a live rat heart were recorded on a General Electric CSI 2.0T MRI scanner connected to a Macintosh and processed by NIH *Image*, a visualization tool in the public domain.

Animation as a Visualization Tool

Much scientific and engineering research involves the behavior of dynamic systems. The primary objective in many such studies is to observe and understand the time-dependent evolution of complex systems. For these systems, the optimal —and often the only—graphical visualization technique is animation.

Consider the following two examples from the Apple Science CD-ROM visualization project. The first example consists of a series of frames shown in Figure 16.1 illustrating the onset of turbulence when a supersonic jet is excited by a sinusoidal perturbation. This theoretical study required two hours of simulation time on a supercomputer. The animation is pleasing artistically, in addition to its scientific interest, and several frames of the simulation serve as an animated logo for the NCSA *Image* program.

In the second example, we peer into the living heart of a rat and watch it beat. The magnetic resonance images (MRI) measured 256×256 pixels in 8-bit gray scale, with each pixel corresponding to 273 microns in space. Playing back the 18-frame animation, twelve of which are shown in Figure 16.2, produces a very realistic pulse of about 1 Hz on a Macintosh IIcx. While this is slower than the rat's normal 5 Hz pulse rate, it provides an optimal visualization of the inner working of the heart. Again, animation offers the essential tool for visualization.

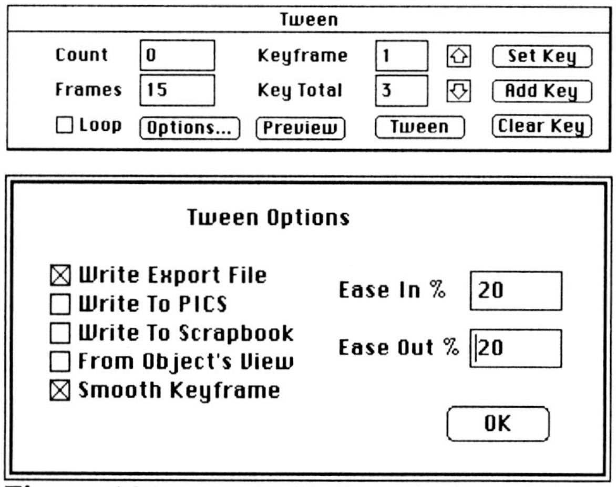

Figure 16.3
Tweening Controls in *Swivel 3D™*. This particular set of parameters indicates that the animation sequence uses three keyframes with 15 interpolated frames between each pair of keyframes and that the smoothing option is active.

These two examples were chosen to illustrate the use of animation in studying theoretical processes in the first case, and experimental graphical data in the second. Both of these processes exhibit a degree of complexity that makes their study by any means other than animation extremely difficult.

Synthetic 3D Animation

A number of valuable tools have been developed to assist the designer in synthesizing animation sequences. Among the most useful of these are the following:

- **Tweening between Keyframes** –
  Keyframes may be considered snapshots of the scene that act as image control points through which the animation must pass as it evolves. The system interpolates *between* the keyframes by computing intermediate frames in the process called *tweening*.

- **Keyframe Smoothing** – The smoothing option fits the trajectories of keyframe objects to Bézier curves. This tends to eliminate the noise introduced by the designer in specifying keyframes, and enhances the realism of the resulting animation. For sharp turns, such as trajectories involving collisions, the smoothing option should be turned off.

- **Ease In/Ease Out** – The inertia of massive objects requires a period of acceleration before a final velocity is achieved. The *ease in/ease out* option simulates this acceleration by varying the time between frames near the beginning and end points of an animation sequence. A closer spacing of frames in these regions of the trajectory enhances the authenticity of a large class of motions. Exceptions, such as impulsive collisions, are handled by turning the *ease in/ease out* option off.

Several programs are available that include these and other animation tools. In Figure 16.3 we show the controls available on the *Open Tween Panel* option of *Swivel 3D™* and its *Options* sub-window.

This system is particularly powerful in providing animation capabilities in 3D space. That is, the model is constructed in 3D space, and key frames are established by manipulating the model to represent the 3D orientation at key moments of the action (*key scenes* might be a better designation than *key frames* for 3D animation). Key frames may be created, edited, added, and deleted from an animation sequence in a manner analogous to manipulating words with a word processor. The *Preview* option allows viewing the animation in "stick figure" form at a rate approaching real time. As indicated in the *Tween Options* window, the user may route the output to individually numbered PICT files corresponding to each frame of the animation or to a single PICS file, an animation standard recognized by other playback systems.

To illustrate the most important animation techniques, consider the problem of creating an animated jogger. This task is accomplished by the following three steps:

1. Create the model.
2. Specify several keyframes.
3. Run tweening.

Let's examine each of these steps in a bit more detail.

1. Create the model

The savvy designer will always ask, "Do I actually have to design the jogger from scratch, or can I use a shortcut?" As libraries of 3D clip art multiply, the answer, in many cases, including ours, is: *Pick an approximate solution from the library and modify it to fit your needs.* We picked *Woodman* from the

Swivel 3D library, amputated his paddle-like hands, and substituted more runner-like clenched fists constructed by picking *Hand* from the 3D library and bending the fingers to form a fist. This solution turned an hour design task into a ten minute graphical editing task.

2. Specify the keyframes

The model was positioned in side view, and the appropriate rotation menu item selected. Then each limb was dragged into the desired starting position (left object in Figure 16.4) with right arm and left leg back. For the first keyframe

Figure 16.4
Three keyframes obtained by rotating arms and legs in *Swivel 3D*.

the *Set Key* button was pressed. Next, a midstride keyframe (center object) was designed, and the *Add Key* button was pushed. Finally, a third keyframe was designed and added as the right-hand side object of Figure 16.4. This figure shows, as a collage, the three keyframes on which the complete animation is based.

3. Run tweening

Once the keyframes are established, the only remaining tasks are to select an output mode and run the tweening option. The *Write Export File* mode was selected first in order to generate images for Figure 16.5. Then the *Write to PICS* mode was selected to generate a file to use in playing back the animation. Since there were three keyframes and fifteen interpolated frames between each pair of keyframes, a total of thirty frames were automatically generated. Because the selected rendering mode specified shading with anti-aliasing, each frame required the better part of a minute to render on a Mac IIcx. The results of every third frame are shown in Figure 16.5.

The important message of this example is the following: *Sophisticated tools enable relatively inexperienced designers to create complex and realistic animations with a minimal investment of time and effort.* While it took the author several hours to explore and master *Swivel 3D's* animation capabilities, an experienced designer could generate animation

sequences like those of Figure 16.5 in a matter of minutes.

MultiMedia

One of the earliest attempts at producing a virtual reality experience was the arcade-style device named *Sensorama* invented by Morton Heilig in 1956.[9] In this device, the user sat on a seat and grasped motorcycle handlebars while viewing a 3D movie of New York traffic seen through stereo-effect lenses. The seat and handlebars vibrated in motorcycle-like fashion, and wind blew on the user's face. The authenticity of the scene was further enhanced by the smell of exhaust fumes and the aroma of pizza emitted to coincide with the appropriate visual environment.

While *Sensorama* was not a commercial success, Heilig's concept that total immersion in virtual reality is best achieved by stimulating the maximum number of senses has become a canon of virtual reality research. The closely related development of multimedia is motivated by a similar concept—human/machine interaction can be improved by opening up more channels of communication. Many of the innovations from multimedia research are directly and immediately applicable to most classes of metarealities.

Consider two channels which have recently become widely available at little or no cost on personal workstations.

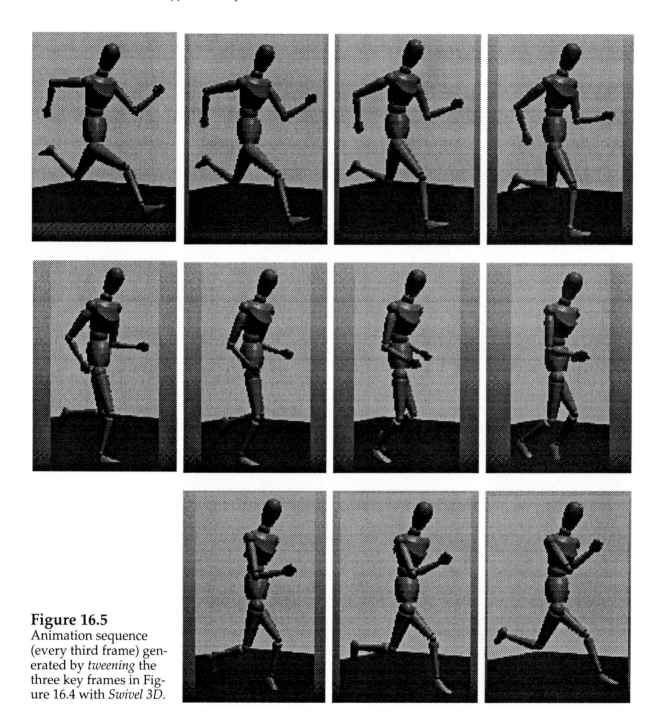

Figure 16.5
Animation sequence (every third frame) generated by *tweening* the three key frames in Figure 16.4 with *Swivel 3D*.

Voice

While understandable, computer-synthesized voice *output* has been available on most machines for many years, only recently has voice *input* become standard. Every Macintosh IIsi and LC comes equipped with an external microphone through which the user may talk to the computer. Short "sound bytes" may be stored in *HyperCard* format and played back at any later time. Major applications programs, like MS-Word 5.0, now support voice annotations. Recorded messages may be embedded anywhere in a word processed document and are indicated by a speaker symbol.

Clicking on the symbol causes the recorded message to be played back. Voice annotations are saved automatically with the MS-Word document and may also be saved in a separate voice annotation library file for use in other applications.

A more sophisticated system, the *Voice Navigator*, interprets the user's vocal commands and executes them. This I/O channel is particularly valuable to the physically handicapped incapable of using the keyboard and mouse. So, while personal computers still may not be able to read lips, they can understand and respond to direct spoken commands like HAL did in the film *2001*.

Video

Television is universally acknowledged as having fundamentally altered society. Personal computers are widely acknowledged as at least having started a similar process. What will happen when these two powerful technologies become integrated?

Until recently, lack of standard protocols and efficient image compression techniques prevented routine integration of video information as a standard data type on personal computers. Consider the horrendous problem posed by the volume of video data. The National Television Standards Committee (NTSC) video format (standard in the U.S.) consists of 640×480 pixel frames displayed at 30 frames/second. Converting an analog video signal into 24-bit digital format produces 30 MB of information *per second*! This would fill a 650 MB CD in 20 seconds and the largest available hard drives in a minute.

The solution to the problem of the huge volume of digital video data is image compression, as discussed in the last chapter. The most widely accepted image compression standard was developed by the Joint Photographic Experts Group (JPEG). The JPEG standard achieves compression ratios of 24:1 with virtually no perceptible degradation of image quality.

The solutions to the both the problem of the lack of standard protocols and the lack of efficient image compression appeared recently under the name *QuickTime*.

QuickTime

Apple published *QuickTime* in 1991 as an architecture for media integration. It is a protocol for compressing, manipulating, and synchronizing full-motion images and sound. *QuickTime* defines a new data type, *dynamic data*, for multimedia information. Dynamic data is a transparent data type equivalent to the *text* and *graphics* transparent data types on the Macintosh. Dynamic data may be cut, copied, and pasted with the same ease as text data and graphical data.

QuickTime serves the same function for audio and video information that *QuickDraw* does for graphical information and that *PostScript* does for page layouts. *QuickTime* provides the time-based framework for recording, playback, and synchronization required for converting video successfully. It is also capable of compression, decompression, and playback of animation sequences. *QuickTime* provides developers with a common set of programming routines and interfaces.

The introduction of a standard protocol for animation and video has resulted in a flood of new hardware and software products for producing and manipulating time-based information. Examples of each of these include the *VideoSpigot* frame grabber card by SuperMac Technology and Adobe *Premiere* movie production program.

Video Image Processing Tools

A number of excellent hardware cards for converting and capturing video images are now on the market. SuperMac's *VideoSpigot* is one of the better ones and was used to generate Figures 16.6, 16.9, and 16.10. Feeding a signal from any video sources to the *VideoSpigot* produces a window like that shown in Figure 16.6. The four controls available along the bottom of the window perform the following operations:

- Record,
- Crop,
- Stop,
- Resize.

The user monitors the *ScreenPlay* video image until a region of interest is detected. To begin recording the desired footage, the circular *Record* button is pressed. The compressed, digital signal is spooled to disk until the square *Stop* button is pressed. The sequence may then be cycled forward and backward to determine if it is appropriate for the task at hand. If so, it is given a name and saved as a *QuickTime* file. Such files then become the raw input data for video image manipulation programs like Adobe *Premiere*.

Premiere serves the same function for dynamic data that *Digital DarkRoom* and *Pixel Paint* do for graphics data. The primary purpose of *Premiere* is to assist the user in producing a video movie by assembling clips. Clips can be still images in *PICT* format, animation sequences in *PICS* format, audio

Figure 16.6
Video image produced by *ScreenPlay* software from the digital video signal generated by the *VideoSpigot* hardware card connected to a VCR playing back a VHS-C video tape of a ski trip to Austria.

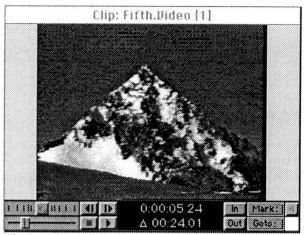

Figure 16.7
Image processing window in Adobe *Premiere*. Video clip taken from a glacier in the Austrian Alps.

files in *SoundEdit* format, or other video movies in *QuickTime* format. Clips are opened in a *Clip Window* like that shown in Figure 16.7. The *Clip Window* provides numerous controls including a duration counter indicating the number of frames in the clip and the current frame count, a jog control to step forward and backward, and *Play* and *Stop* buttons.

In addition to the *Clip Window*, *Premiere* provides the movie editor with a *Project Window*, a *Construction Window*, an *Audio Clip Window*, and a *Special Effects Window*. The *Special Effects Window* lists twenty-four modes, five of which are shown in Figure 16.8, for blending and merging dynamic data clips. Filters for tiling, pointillizing, twirling, waving and zig-zagging allow the movie editor to produce most of the special effects which characterize the "flying logos" of television.

QuickTime Example

To illustrate the application of *QuickTime*, Figure 16.9 shows a sampling of frames from a thirty second video clip captured with *VideoSpigot* and stored on hard disk. The pan sequence from inside a Colorado ski chalet to the mountains outside was recorded on a standard Zenith/JVC camcorder. The VHS-C cassette was then played on a standard VCR whose output served as input to the *VideoSpigot* board mounted in a Mac IIcx. The segment of interest was captured and stored as a dynamic data file on the hard drive and played back by Adobe *Premiere*. An image grabber was

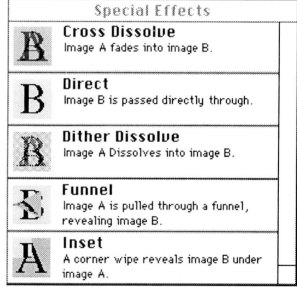

Figure 16.8
Special Effects options available in Adobe Premiere. Shown are five of the library of twenty-four special effects. In addition to these options for blending multiple clips, Premiere provides filters for special effects like posterizing, mosaic, and inversion.

then used to capture sampled images and paste them into the text.

Figure 16.9
Sequence of about every tenth frame captured by the *VideoSpigot* card and stored in *QuickTime* format. Pan shot from inside chalet to the Colorado Rockies.

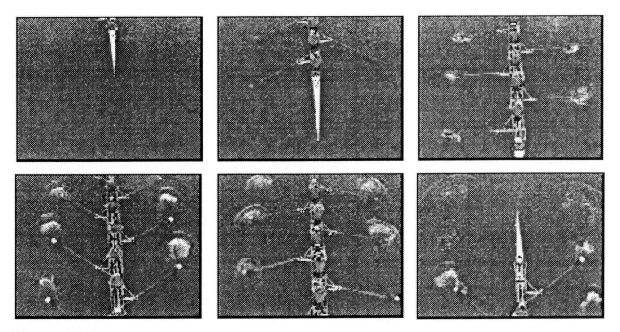

Figure 16.10
Frames from *Rowing Crew* clip art included with Adobe *Premiere*.

Video Clip Art

A wealth of 2D graphic clip art is available to speed the production process of graphic designers.

As we indicate in the next section, libraries of 3D clip art objects are now available for modeling three dimensional scenes. With the advent of the *QuickTime* dynamic data standard, a flood of video clip art libraries is inevitable. As an example of existing video clip art, we show Figure 16.10 representing about every fifth frame of the video clip called *Rowing Crew* sample folder of Adobe *Premiere*.

The conclusion of this section is that new animation and multimedia tools are now available for processing and manipulating dynamic data with the same ease that we expect for textual and graphical data. This development will transform the practice of computer graphics and will contribute significantly to the implementation of various metarealities.

Virtual Reality

Virtual reality has captured the imagination of computer novices and experts alike. Virtually no one who has experienced the full goggle/gloves virtual reality comes away unaffected or less than enthusiastic. Let's look at some of the important aspects of this new technology in more detail before presenting a personal workstation example.

Origins of Virtual Reality

Virtual reality traces its origins to the confluence of three main streams of technology:

- Remote control engineering,

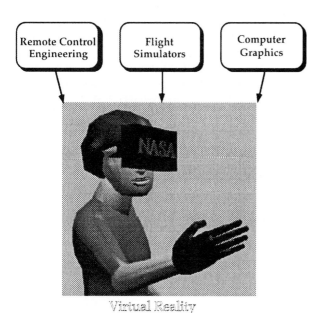

Figure 16.11
Principle technologies on which virtual reality is based.

- Flight simulators,
- Interactive computer graphics.

This integration of technologies is indicated graphically in Figure 16.11.

Remote Control Engineering

In order to work safely with dangerous nuclear materials, a new discipline called *remote control engineering* was developed, primarily at Argonne National Laboratory. The Argonne Remote Manipulator (ARM) consisted of a two-fingered, six-degree-of-freedom system in which a remote "hand" would duplicate the motion of the user's hand. Early versions operated on the basis of pulleys over a several foot thick lead-glass wall through which the operator could watch the response of the slave hand. The author recalls the thrill and satisfaction, during his ANL research associate days, of successfully grasping a remote pen and writing his name with the ARM.

The pulley-based manipulators were soon replaced by selsyn motors which, when combined with video monitors, permitted the manipulation of objects at any distance. The ARM was developed to enable workers to manipulate and machine dangerous materials like plutonium. It allowed chemists to carry out experiments with delicate glassware such as beakers, flasks, and test tubes.

To perform these tasks, it was essential that the ARM provide *sensory feedback*. That is, when the operator applied a one pound grip to the control glove, the remote grasping fingers had to apply a one pound force to the object it was holding. Without this direct tactile feedback, the remote hand would either crush the glassware or let it slip out of its fingers. Both the pulley and selsyn motor technologies provided sensory feedback.

The principal application of remote control engineering in virtual reality is to convert sensory feedback techniques to respond to virtual objects. The first and most successful implementation has been the work of Frederick Brooks and Henry Fuchs of the University of North Carolina.[10] Brooks and his colleagues used an actual ARM in which they replaced the physical remote manipulator hand with a virtual hand that operated in a virtual, molecular space.

The purpose of their *molecular docking* experiment is to assist researchers in molecular structure in determining stable molecular configurations. Test molecules and target molecules are represented both as 3D visual images and by the invisible electric fields they generate. The investigator attempts to combine the test molecule with the target molecule by grasping it with the ARM and trying to fit it into the minimum potential configuration indicated by a minimal reaction force reflected by the ARM. That is, the investigator can actually "feel" where the molecule ought to go for its equilibrium position. The chemical structure of molecules is determined by a complex, 3D distribution of electromagnetic fields. By combining 3D graphics to visualize the geometric structure with tactile feedback to sense the field structure, Brooks' group has created a rich virtual world for investigating and clarifying the structure of matter.

Flight Simulators

The second major building block of virtual reality evolved from flight simulators. *Link trainers* provide a realistic cockpit with instruments duplicating those of real aircraft. The trainer has stubby, cut-off wings and is mounted on a movable platform that can tilt, roll, and vibrate in response to the trainee's commands at the stick and throttle. (After several hours in the University of Illinois Institute of Aviation Link trainers, the author moved on to a real Champion 7FC trainer and was impressed at how similarly the simulator and real aircraft performed.) The authenticity of the flight simulator is the basis for the FAA allowing a significant fraction of pre-solo hours to be logged in a simulator.

More complex aircraft required more complex simulators. The open cockpit of the Link trainer was replaced by a cockpit with television screen windows with images corresponding to the view seen by video cameras mounted on the trainer and viewing a miniature Hollywood style set. Multiple cameras could simulate both front and side views, but only at a relatively high altitude.

In 1968, the computer graphics pioneers Evans and Sutherland developed computer graphics simulations to replace the camera and model trainer. In order to obtain real-time response from their system, Evans and Sutherland developed many of the standard algorithms of modern computer graphics. Their flight simulator scenes represent some of the earliest and most significant achievements in realistic rendering.

Even prior to the screen-mounted flight simulator, Ivan Sutherland had begun work on a head-mounted display, and the first fully functional HMD was demonstrated at the University of Utah in 1970. The HMD has become the symbol of true virtual reality and remains one of the most effective technologies for achieving total immersion of the user in some imaginary cyberspace. The sense of reality is achieved by presenting the user with two small screens, one for each eye, in a helmet strapped to the head. As the user moves her head, the helmet senses the motion and shifts the image presented on the screens to correspond to the view from the direction the helmet is pointing. Even with non-stereoscopic binocular vision (such as the early Sutherland HMD), the visual cueing produced by this head motion produces a powerful sense of presence in the virtual space under observation. With 3D viewing the effect is even more enhanced.

Another major contributor to virtual reality emerged from the field of flight simulators. Thomas Furness designed Darth Vader-like helmets for the Air Force, which combined a detailed digital model of the terrain with forward-looking infrared (FLIR) in the Visually Coupled Airborne Simulator (VCASS) system. Furness is continuing his VR research in civilian applications as director of the Human Interface Technology Laboratory in Seattle.[11]

Interactive Computer Graphics

Interactive computer graphics is the core of any virtual reality system. The realism of the Evans and Sutherland flight simulator was achieved by high quality, realistic images of airports, aircraft carriers, and other aircraft rendered on screens simulating the windows of the trainee's cockpit. Early head-mounted devices built by NASA had resolutions of only 100 × 100 pixels, and more recent ones developed by VPL Research use 300,000 pixels. The technology has included both miniature CRTs and LCDs. Active research is underway by Furness' laboratory to increase the resolution of virtual reality images by projecting them directly on the user's retina by microlaser technology. This system would literally create VR in the mind of the observer if we consider the eye/brain system as the mind.

The major problem faced by computer graphics in virtual reality applications is the unavoidable tradeoff between speed and image quality. As we have seen, even personal workstations are capable of rendering complex, photorealistic images using sophisticated REYES, ray tracing, and radiosity algorithms. However, the task of rendering a single, complex image takes on the order of minutes to hours. Real-time virtual reality requires completely rendered images generated at a rate of at least fifteen, and, preferably, thirty frames per second.

So the continuing compromise is between image complexity and rendering speed. Either one may be achieved to almost any degree, but always at the price of the other. As a result, most of the VR demonstrations at the 1991 SIGGRAPH "coming out" party for virtual reality qualified their users as legally blind. That is, humans with vision limited to the spatial resolution of their VR goggles would be declared legally blind. A critical goal of VR research is to achieve real-time animation on reasonably priced machines. An excellent summary of the state-of-the-art hardware for VR visualization is given by Starks.[12]

The second aspect of interactive computer graphics concerns the mechanism through which the user can interact with the virtual environment. By far the most popular VR input device is the DataGlove manufactured by VPL Research, Inc. This company, founded by VR guru Jaron Lanier, also markets a complete VR body suit and VR goggles. VPL Research teamed up with the toymaker, Mattel, to produce a low-cost version of the DataGlove called the PowerGlove. The under $100 PowerGlove serves as an input device for the popular Nintendo video game, and several million have been sold. The highly precise DataGlove costs about one hundred times as much and, as of early 1992, had an installed base of 500–600 units, about half of which are used in research and development organizations.[13]

Although gloves are the most popular VR input device, other devices offer a natural means for navigating through 3D cyberspace. The six-degree-of-freedom SpaceBall is an example. This device resembles a cue ball mounted on a short joystick and uses strain gages for translating user-applied forces and torques into 3D motions and rotations in virtual space. It has been described as a "3D mouse."

The lowly 2D mouse can, in fact, also be used to navigate in 3D space. The four angular quadrants, beginning with that centered on the y-axis, may be interpreted as "go forward," "turn right," "back up," and "turn left." Combining mouse actions with special keys enables the motions of "rise up," "sink down," "look up," and "look down." As we shall see shortly, this provides a natural, easy-to-learn model for navigation.

Applications of Virtual Reality

Cynical observers may have concluded that VR is, at best, an elegant solution for non-existent prob-

lems, or, at worst, a very expensive video game —systems range from $25K–$1M. What can VR do that can't be done equally well and a lot cheaper with conventional WIMP graphics systems?

Three general areas in which VR techniques offer significant advantages that have resulted in commercial applications include:

- Entertainment,
- Medical and scientific visualization,
- Architectural design.

As more tools for designing virtual reality scenes become available, new applications areas will undoubtedly open up. Let's look at some of the actual implementations in these three areas.

Entertainment

The area of entertainment has provided the test bed for a broad spectrum of virtual reality systems. The principle types of entertainment include virtual travel, advanced video games, and virtual sports.

Virtual Travel

The *Aspen Movie Map* created in 1978 by Scott Fisher and Andrew Lippman of MIT's Architecture Machine Group established a benchmark for future VR efforts.[14] The *Aspen Movie Map* consisted of a random access video disk containing actual images taken by a special camera mounted on top of a car cruising down every street in the lovely town of Aspen, Colorado. In addition to a complete map of the village streets, camera crews entered and filmed the interior of some of Aspen's landmarks, such as the Red Onion restaurant.

The virtual traveler in the *Aspen Movie Map* sits in a room surrounded by actual images of Aspen. By the appropriate gestures he can travel up and down the streets, go around corners, enter appealing buildings, and, in general, go sightseeing through Aspen. The key feature distinguishing virtual travel from passive viewing of travel movies or videotapes is, of course, the active involvement of the virtual traveler in exploring the domain captured in the virtual medium. Virtual travel certainly need not be limited to the tourist attractions of Earth. Clever model-building and the merging of models with real photographs from the space program will enable virtual travel into the outer reaches of space or into the imaginary, fantasy worlds of Hobbits, dungeons, and dragons.

A recent product called the *Virtual Museum*, from Apple Computer Company, incorporates many of the virtual travel concepts of the *Aspen Movie Map*. The *Virtual Museum* allows travelers to stroll down the halls of the Louvre, examining paintings such as the *Mona Lisa* at their leisure, undisturbed by the hassle of crowds. The traveler can explore halls devoted to astronomy, plants, medicine, and the environment, clicking on exhibits to see close-ups and supplementary video clips, animations, and text. The *Virtual Museum* consists of more than a gigabyte of video information compressed into 95 MB of *QuickTime* format.

Advanced Video Games

In 1990, Virtual World Entertainments built a "super arcade" called *BattleTech Center*.[15] It consists of sixteen robot-like BattleMech tanks, each providing its pilot with an awesome arsenal of lasers, particle beams, and missiles. The pilot views the virtual battle field on a 25-inch color screen and has a control panel containing over two dozen controls. The object of the game is to coordinate your attack with your teammates in other BattleMech tanks via radio in order to annihilate the enemy.

BattleTech Center has been a profitable operation since the day it opened and has provided more than 150,000 customers a virtual battlefield experience during the first year of operation. Many *BattleTech* veterans have fought over two hundred virtual battles at $7 a pop.

Fascinating possibilities open up when virtual and real worlds are blended in the spirit of Krueger's *CRITTER*. In France, for instance, a children's television show features real-time computer-generated puppets, controlled by puppeteers wearing data gloves, that interact with human characters in live scenes. Extending these techniques to their ultimate implementation would allow you to interact with such virtual creatures as the water monster in the *Abyss* or the liquid-metal man in *Terminator 2*. And you could choose to play the role of *either* the human or the virtual creature!

Virtual Sports

Several of the most popular sports have been implemented in cyberspace. These include virtual racquetball, virtual golf, and virtual skiing. Consider the advantages: always perfect snow conditions; variable, adaptive terrain to challenge your limits; and no threat of a broken leg.

The complete control of the virtual environment offers some unique possibilities for virtual sports as well as numerous other applications. Assume, for instance, that you want to learn how to juggle. You can turn gravity down to 0.1 g and observe the slower motion resulting from reduced acceleration. With more time to plan your moves, you quickly master the art of keeping four balls in the air. Then you gradually turn gravity up to its nominal value, mastering the required, faster motions at each incremental increase in gravity.

The blending of virtual and real worlds offers unique virtual sports experiences. Autodesk, the maker of *AutoCAD* and a pioneer VR company, markets *Hycycle*, a VR-enhanced stationary bicycle. The virtual cyclist mounts a real stationary cycle and dons a pair of VR goggles. As she pedals along, she passes through a continuous, cartoon countryside. However, as the pedaling speed increases beyond 20 mph, the cyclist takes off and flies over the virtual countryside. With VR, quite literally, everything imaginable becomes possible!

Medical and Scientific Visualization

Virtual reality permits the scientist or doctor to actually "enter" the data under investigation and roam about, looking for interesting patterns or clues as to potential problems. The process of *zooming* up on interesting data in visualization programs such as the Spyglass series is replaced by the investigator *walking up to* the data to see it at close range. If a point is clearly in error, the VR user can simply grasp it with his data glove and put it in the correct position.

Consider the possibilities offered by a *virtual cadaver*. A very accurate 3D model of the human body can be constructed by stacking multiple MRI image slices and interpolating between the slices in the fashion of the program, *Dicer*. By augmenting this 3D image model with tissue-specific information such as color and the physical properties of texture, flexibility, and toughness, a very realistic physical model can be constructed. This virtual cadaver would respond to a virtual scalpel in a manner very similar to the response of a live human body to a real scalpel. In fact, it is very likely that the response of a virtual cadaver would more closely resemble that of a living body than would a real cadaver beset by rigor mortis.

Architectural Design

One of the most practical applications of VR is in architectural design. A real-life example is the design of Sitterson Hall on campus of the University of North Carolina. The VR research team that was to be located in Sitterson Hall built a VR model and conducted tours of the building before it was constructed. The process revealed an unpleasant design feature of the lobby that created a claustrophobic sensation in the VR observers. The designers were given a VR walkthrough and agreed to change the design.

Matsushita Electric Works of Japan has built a VR system which allows customers of major department stores to design their own kitchen, equip it with appliances selected from an appliance object library, and walk through it to see how it looks. Many of these features are available on the personal workstation example we discuss next.

Virtual Reality Application Example

Many of the most significant features of virtual reality are now becoming available in reasonably priced software systems for personal workstations. An outstanding example of VR for a PC is *Virtus WalkThrough*™ by the Virtus Corporation.[16] *Virtus WalkThrough* (*VW*) provides intuitive, mouse-driven navigation through complex, 3D VR models. The most impressive feature of *VW*, however, is the powerful and elegant design environment it offers users for creating their own virtual realities in which to roam. It also provides an option for recording the scenes observed by a traveler wandering through cyberspace in order to play back the journey at a later time.

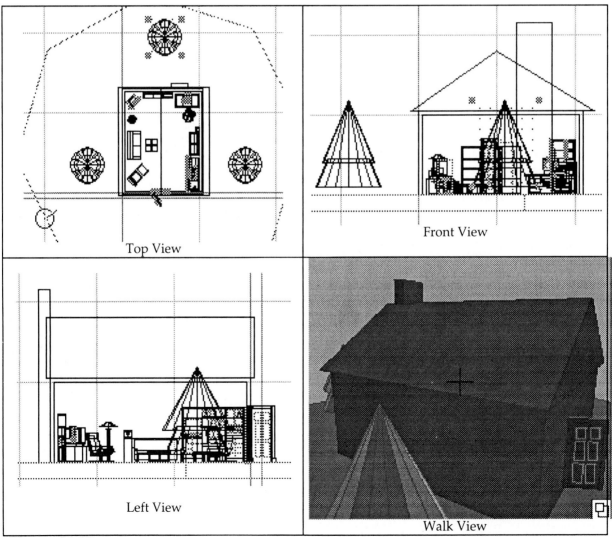

Top View

Front View

Left View

Walk View

Figure 16.12
Four views of the *Office* VR microcosm.

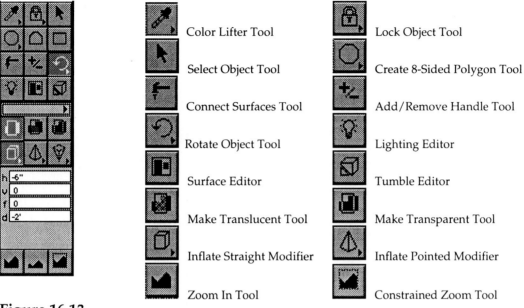

Color Lifter Tool	Lock Object Tool
Select Object Tool	Create 8-Sided Polygon Tool
Connect Surfaces Tool	Add/Remove Handle Tool
Rotate Object Tool	Lighting Editor
Surface Editor	Tumble Editor
Make Translucent Tool	Make Transparent Tool
Inflate Straight Modifier	Inflate Pointed Modifier
Zoom In Tool	Constrained Zoom Tool

Figure 16.13
Design Tools Window in *Virtus WalkThrough.*

Virtus WalkThrough comes with several well-designed virtual worlds and associated tours that the virtual traveler can take with the click of a button. However, for the present example, the author felt compelled to design his own modest virtual world and learn how to navigate through it. What began as a simple office design soon grew into a well-equipped cottage and entertainment room as new design tools were discovered and mastered.

Two very important object lessons emerged from the exercise of preparing this example.

- The value of an intuitive design environment.

- The importance of an extensive object library —3D "Clip art."

The intuitive CAD environment and extensive object library made it possible to learn the whole system and to design the example in just a few hours. A skillful designer could build the model in this example in less than half an hour.

Design Tools

VW presents the VR designer with two viewing modes: a design mode in which objects may be entered and transformed, and a walk mode that shows what the virtual traveler would see. The six

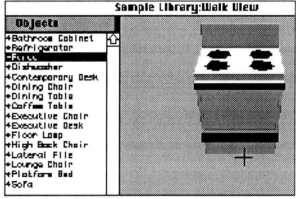

Figure 16.14
Range object selected from *V W Sample Library.* Each library object is presented in the center of a VR microcosm through which the user can walk, looking at the object from various viewpoints.

design mode views, three of which are shown in Figure 16.12, display polygon-based objects in a transparent, wire-frame orthogonal projection. All objects may be selected, dragged to new positions, grouped, duplicated, locked, and edited in any of the design views.

A unique feature of *V W* is the *observer icon*, shown in the lower left-hand corner of the top view. The observer may be selected and dragged to any position in any view and pointed in any direction in the scene. The resulting image seen by the observer is immediately rendered and displayed in the *walk view* shown in the lower right panel.

How was the relatively complex microcosm called *Office* created? *VW* provides a rich array of spatial design tools with which even uninitiated users can rapidly construct coherent virtual models. Several of these tools are shown in Figure 16.13.

The function of most of the tools identified in Figure 16.13 is self evident. Let's clarify a few of them, however. *VW* uses extrusion to generate 3D objects from 2D figures and calls the process *infla-*

tion. To modify straight inflation, it uses variations to achieve pointed and rounded shapes. The *surface editor* is used to modify a whole surface or a portion of a surface and give it properties of translucency or transparency. It is useful in creating doors and windows in architectural designs. Finally, the *tumble editor* is used to select an object and manipulate it in a separate tumble screen without changing its orientation in the original scene. Surfaces or whole objects may be colored or sliced to form new shapes. This is an exceptionally powerful feature of *VW*.

As indicated in earlier chapters, libraries of 3D

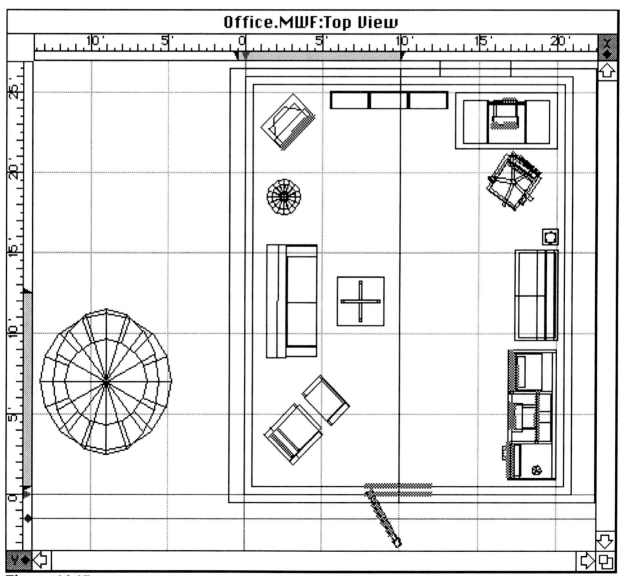

Figure 16.15
Partial Plan view of *Office* created with *Virtus WalkThrough*.

clip art offer a design abstraction tool for creating visually complex scenes with minimal command messages. So, for instance, to design a kitchen we would open the *Sample Library* shown in Figure 16.14 and click on the desired appliance name. Clicking on the *Range* menu item opens a *Walk View* image of the named appliance. Consistent with the VR paradigm, library objects are presented in cyberspace, allowing the user to walk around them and inspect them from all angles before copying them into the VR scene.

In Figure 16.15 we show a detailed top view of the *Office* virtual world. The inner and outer walls, door, gable, roof, chimney, and trees were constructed by standard CAD techniques. The door and inner furnishings were all copied from object libraries.

Figure 16.16 shows the *Walk View* of the cottage interior seen by the observer standing in the doorway. It is taken with a wide-angle, 28 mm lens. (*VW* allows the virtual traveler to adjust the camera lens' focal length from 15 mm to 500 mm.)

Note several features of this image. First, the rendering algorithm uses quite a good lighting/shading model. Second, *VW* uses a convincing transparency model as indicated in the glass-topped coffee table and the glass sculpture case next to the red sofa. The major limitations of the rendering algorithm concern the lack of shadow calculations and the lack of antialiasing (the jaggies are rather pronounced). Also, some hidden plane calculations are not done correctly as is apparent in the rendering of the television screen in the far left corner of the room. However, overall,

Figure 16.16
Rendered image of *Office* interior using 28 mm lens in *Walk View*.

the performance of both the design and rendering algorithms is quite impressive. The image of Figure 16.16 required less than four seconds to render on a Mac IIcx.

Navigation in Cyberspace

Now that we have designed a fairly realistic virtual reality model we should really go on a tour through our personal VR. But how can we without expensive VR goggles and gloves? The answer, of course, is to harness the interactive I/O device available on almost all personal workstations—the mouse.

The mouse/cursor system is intrinsically 2D in nature, with a vertical y-axis and a horizontal x-axis. In the *VW Walk View*, a cross hair is located at the center of the window as origin of the image x-y plane. The +/– y-axis is then interpreted as *Move Forward/Move Backward* and the +/– x-axis as *Turn Right/Turn Left* as shown in Figure 16.17. Additional degrees of freedom are achieved by using the cursor in combinations with function keys. The *Option* key is interpreted as selecting the pan mode (motion in the image plane), and the *Shift* key is interpreted as a pointing mode control as indicated in Figure 16.17.

This navigation protocol is about as intuitive as allowed by a 2D input device. The single cursor control mode—Figure 16.17(a)—is sufficient for moving through most models. In order to fly above the model for an elevated view, the *Option*

key must be employed along with the cursor control. As one would hope, the navigation controls are both linear (i.e., proportional to the distance from the center cross hair) and linearly superimposed (i.e., clicking in the upper right-hand corner of screen (a) will both turn the virtual traveler to the right and move her forward).

Now that we understand how to navigate in a *VW* virtual world, let's go on a tour of the *Office* microcosm. Commentary is given just below each frame of the twelve-frame tour shown in Figure 16.18.

The tour could continue by walking out the door and around the cottage. Several observations are appropriate before we conclude this example. First, due to training and habits acquired in the real world, we tend to want to enter virtual buildings through doorways. However, since virtual reality consists only of numbers in a database and ignores the laws of Coulomb repulsion, nothing prevents us from walking right through the walls of the *Office* cottage as we did through the glass of the entertainment center.

Second, the speed of rendering images of the virtual scene depends on the number of polygons being rendered. Images such as Figure 16.18(11) and images of the exterior of the cottage run at speeds approaching smooth animation. However, rendering complex scenes such as Figure 16.18(12) requires the order of seconds per frame. This time lag is annoying but does not destroy the illusion of reality of the virtual world.

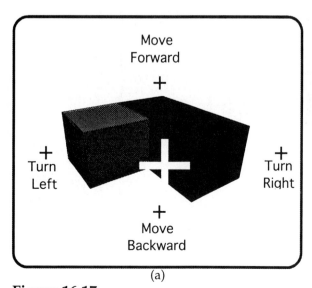

(a)

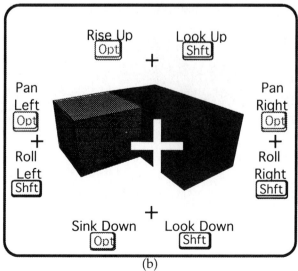

(b)

Figure 16.17
Navigation protocol, using mouse cursor, in *Virtus WalkThrough*.
(a) Single cursor drive control regions, (b) Cursor actions with *Shift* and *Option* keys.

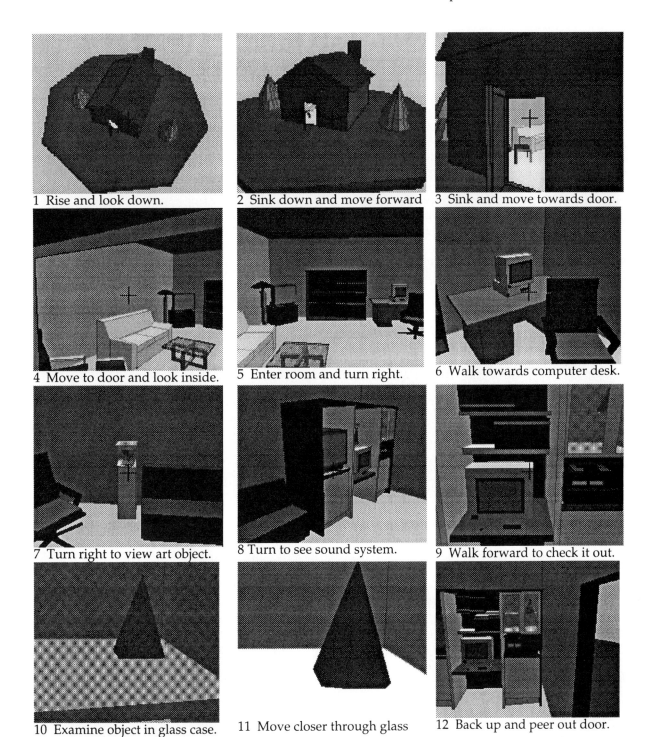

Figure 16.18
Twelve frames from walk through tour of *Office* virtual world.

Finally, *VW* provides a *Record/Playback* option in which the sequence of views experienced by the virtual traveler are recorded as a PICS file. Numerous PICS file players are available for playing back the file as a real-time animation sequence. Thus, tours through virtual reality may be created and reproduced on personal workstations.

Mirror Worlds

The concept of *mirror worlds* is awesome, both in the incredible power users with access to MW will achieve and in the technical problems which must be solved to fully implement the concept. Information is the source of power in the societies of the future,[17] and MW offer not only limitless information but the mechanism for individualized and purposeful processing of information into knowledge. Agents carrying out our designs effectively accomplish the process of converting information into knowledge. Mirror worlds will be not only information rich but knowledgeable. The interaction of humans with knowledgeable systems opens up whole new realms of possibilities.

Figure 16.19 suggests the breadth of human activity for which useful mirror worlds can be created. Each of these areas is the top layer, or "root directory," of a hierarchical database which may extend down through numerous levels. At each level, information is available in a variety of formats, mostly graphical, which allow the user to quickly explore properties of the system at that level or probe more deeply. If, for instance, you are a citizen concerned about your state's tax policy you might bolster your case or relieve your concern by plotting a histogram of the income tax rates of all fifty states, or a scatter plot of states' income tax vs. their sales tax. The government mirror world hierarchy would extend downward through federal agencies, state governments, law enforcement agencies, county, city, village, and precinct governments with relevant numerical,

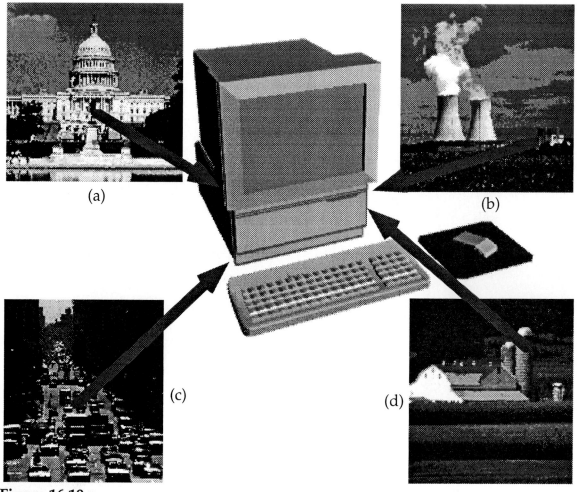

Figure 16.19
Possible Mirror Worlds to capture in your machine. (a) Government, (b) Energy industry, (c) Automobile traffic, and (d) Agriculture.

legal, and personnel data at every level. U.S. Census data, in its properly aggregate form, would be available for examining correlations of any tabulated variable with geographic region, age, sex, or ethnic origin.

Interactive computer graphics will be essential to navigate in a MW. At the higher levels of organizational hierarchies, organizational charts or icons might be used for conveying the "big picture." Clicking on any object within the image will open it, displaying substructures and available options for further exploration. Many of the graphical techniques for navigation through mirror worlds have already been developed and are familiar to users of *HyperCard*. The principle difference between a *HyperCard* stack and a mirror world is that the HyperCard stack, although it may contain animation sequences, is *static* in the sense that it is not routinely updated through a network as a MW would be.

Examples of Mirror Worlds

The war rooms of the Defense Department are probably the closest approximations to the mirror worlds envisioned by Gelernter. However, two more mundane experiences of the author occurred during the writing of this text which illustrate some of the properties of mirror worlds and promise to be much more useful to the average programmer.

First, the delivery of a software package from the mail order warehouse in New Jersey was delayed beyond its expected 24-hour arrival by a snowstorm in the Midwest. A phone call from his University office resulted in the author being informed that, indeed, the package had been shipped and, in fact, received a half hour earlier at his home by someone named "Debbie." This seemed like a mistake since the author's wife teaches and was not at home to accept the package. Finally, it dawned on the author that it was Friday, the day the cleaning person named Debbie visited.

The point of the story is that the software house had a complete, electronically updated mirror world of the delivery system for their products which can pinpoint the location of any of their orders anywhere in the world, including the electronic signature obtained on an electronic clipboard. With the help of their MW, they know more about that aspect of the author's business and the state of his home than he did.

The second example involves what Gelernter has identified as a key component of mirror

worlds – the *hypercomputer*. The key concept is based on the observation that actual duty cycle of most personal computers, workstations, and even many larger computers is essentially *zero*. That is, 99.9999% of the CPU cycles of the machine this text is being written on do no useful work except blink the cursor waiting for the next character to be typed. A hypercomputer would consist of a network of all types of computers to which the various monitoring and query tasks of a mirror world would be assigned. Gelernter notes that many mirror world tasks are intrinsically parallel in nature and readily solved by a network of desktop machines linked by fast fiber optics. He describes an existing hypercomputer coordination language, called *Linda*, written by Craig Kolb of Yale University's Mathematics Department.

Hypercomputers have tremendous potential for computer graphics in general. Rendering of complex, photorealistic images by programs like MacRenderMan requires minutes to hours on standard machines. While this can be done in a multitasking background mode, it is still annoying to have to wait half an hour to complete a rendering task.

Pixar has solved this computer graphics problem with *NetRenderMan*®, a hypercomputer rendering engine built on popular UNIX workstations. MacRenderMan users can select a UNIX rendering host such as a DEC station, Hewlett-Packard 9000 Series, NeXT, IBM RISCStation 6000, Silicon Graphics, and Sun SPARCStation. Rendering performed on the UNIX workstation produces pixel values which are returned directly to the Mac monitor. Depending on the UNIX platform selected, NetRenderMan achieves speed enhancements between five and fifty times that of the native Macintosh.

Another key element in the development of mirror worlds is presently at hand. This is the automation of geographic identification and the simultaneous elimination of geographic constraints on information interchange. Simple, hand-held devices are now available for locating a person or vehicle in 3D to within a few feet anywhere on Earth. Such information is vital for certain mirror worlds. Secondly, wireless modems are now capable of connecting laptop computers located anywhere with networks. Such a system is presently under development in Germany. This system will eliminate the physical constraint of geography from the mirror world and even suggests the concept of "disembodied intelligence."

Challenges to Mirror World Development

The information structures comprising the mirror worlds data bases will be the most complex structures ever invented. Not only must the *static* architecture and contents of a mirror world be specified, but also the monitoring of dynamic processes and the on-line updating of time-dependent data. The complexity introduced by these requirements is unprecedented in the history of software development. In principle, a complete mirror world must be able to report to you "the whole truth about everything" both as it exists at present and as it existed in all earlier times.

To deal with this incredible complexity, Gelernter proposes a series of new techniques and extensions of present techniques. Among these are the following concepts.

Asynchronous Ensembles

Asynchronous software ensembles are collections of information machines (software programs) which may be best understood in object-oriented programming language. Each program of the ensemble is an independent object which may be sent messages to perform various tasks (e.g., scan the school board discussion for the word "tax" or plot the dairy production of Stephenson County, Illinois, vs. Marshall Plan Aid for the period 1947–1953).

Another mental model for asynchronous ensembles is that of a *set of demons*. Demons, as you may recall, are programs within a system which monitor certain conditions and take action whenever the condition is satisfied. Examples of demons within WIMP systems include processes which monitor the mouse position and update the cursor position accordingly and which monitor the mouse button and select the targeted object when it is pressed. Mirror world demons operate asynchronously, rather than sequentially, so that numerous activities can occur simultaneously. They hover in the background waiting for new assignments and carry them out independently of the tasks assigned other demons when they get the message to do so.

Knowledge Plants – The Trellis

For purposes of extracting meaning from the vast quantity of data available to the information machines of a mirror world, Gelernter proposes a vertical array of information machines he calls a *trellis*. The trellis architecture closely resembles that of the *blackboard* which emerged from the research on speech recognition.[18] Raw information enters the trellis from the bottom and gradually percolates to the top, with each level analyzing, organizing, and interpreting it meaning. Machines at each level study the work of machines at a lower level and pass their analysis on to machines at a higher level.

Another useful mental model of trellis knowledge plants is that of an *inference engine* —another AI concept. Each level of the trellis hierarchy takes the conclusions of the lower level and applies the knowledge implicit in the database rules to generate new implications and conclusions. This process continues until the top level is reached, at which point the system announces its conclusion as to the meaning of the input data. The sole purpose of knowledge plants is to generate *topsight*, the broad overview of the meaning implied by input data.

Parallel Processing – The HyperComputer

We have already discussed the basic concept of the hypercomputer – a networked array of desktop, personal computers, workstations, and mainframe computers on which the demons and blackboards reside.

In addition to the hypercomputer possible by networking many individual computers on a network, new parallel processing configurations are appearing for personal computers and workstations. For instance, Inmos produces Transputer chips available in parallel configurations for the IBM PC and Macintosh platforms. Such parallel architecture, personal workstations are capable of more than one hundred MIPS, elevating them to within a factor of ten of supercomputers. Both virtual reality and mirror world calculations are readily decomposed into sets of parallel computations naturally suited to such parallel machines.

Philosophical and Ethical Issues

The philosophical and ethical implications of metarealities are fascinating, profound, and disturbing. They involve the most fundamental questions about the nature of reality and the meaning of human existence. They involve puzzling new issues of ethical behavior between real humans interacting over networks, between virtual humans interacting in cyberspace, between virtual creatures in general, and thus, by implication, between humans and machines. Metarealities also introduce unexplored social and legal issues relating to privacy, security, and commerce. Let's consider a few of these issues in terms of some concrete examples.

Social and Legal Issues

The mirror world of commerce and credit already exists and provides a model for some of the benefits and potential problems posed by metarealities. Consider the following case studies:

Case 1: Commerce and Credit – The author recently purchased a $4000 Gateway 2000 486/33 machine by a simple ten minute phone call. For payment, he offered his Visa, Master Card, or American Express card, and Gateway suggested using the American Express card because this would double the normal warranty.

The author also frequently orders software packages and ASIC cards by phone, pays for them by credit card, and receives them at the front door within twenty-four hours. The point of these examples is that we have recently developed an incredibly powerful and responsive commercial system based entirely on telecommunications and credit. It takes less time and effort to order a video compression card from California or New Jersey than from the local computer store just three miles away. The mirror world of commerce and credit has eliminated geographic space and greatly compressed time. New network services, such as *Prodigy*, are accelerating the pervasiveness of this mirror world.

The potential problems involve the fragile nature of this mirror world. Its success depends, to a great extent, on the honesty and trust of the participants. To date, the system has worked remarkably well. But, because of its fragile nature, abuses will inevitably occur and new legal code will be needed to deal with them.

Case 2: Traffic Law Enforcement – It is now completely feasible technically to develop a *traffic mirror world* that would automate the process of traffic law enforcement and eliminate the problem of auto theft. Miniature transmitters that would broadcast a unique identification number could be installed in every automobile. Using LORAN-C or NavSat technologies, the location of each car could be pinpointed to within fifty feet and its speed reported.

Speeding tickets could then be issued automatically, with fines computed by the time or mileage integral of the excess speed. Auto theft would disappear since stolen cars could be located and the villains apprehended within minutes of the report of the crime. It is difficult to think of any traffic law enforcement problems which could not be cured automatically, or at least greatly reduced, by a traffic mirror world.

Not only would a traffic mirror world solve law enforcement problems, but it would also greatly improve the performance and efficiency of the present traffic network. Analysis of traffic flow patterns, accidents, and congestion could be presented to "intelligent signs" to assist drivers in selecting optimum routes. This would significantly reduce transit time and better utilize the existing infrastructure.

But do we want it? Do we want to be forced to obey speed limits? Do we want a continuous record of our comings and goings? If so, who should have access to it? A traffic mirror world, while technically feasible, is probably socially unacceptable because of the public's unwillingness to accept total disclosure.

Case 3: Public Surveillance – Many banks, filling stations, and twenty-four hour food stores now employ video monitors to reduce the threat of robbery and assist authorities in apprehending perpetrators of robberies. Such video records can be considered as tiny windows on a very much larger mirror world of public activity. As the crime rate persists or grows, the demand for increased public surveillance will increase.

The experience of the airlines in eliminating hijacking through the use of metal detectors is instructive. Most passengers are willing to accept this invasion of their privacy to insure the safety of their flight to the destination of their choice.

How much invasion of privacy are we willing to accept in order to reduce crime and increase our personal safety? Muggings and many other forms of street crime would be reduced by installing and monitoring video cameras on light posts on the corner of each block in high-crime neighborhoods. Assaults on teachers could be reduced by installing video monitors in classrooms.

Video technology provides the tool for building more accurate mirror worlds of public activity. Such mirror worlds will enhance our security and assist in the development of more responsive public policy. But it comes at a terrible price in loss of privacy. This is the ethical dilemma.

Ethical Issues

At the heart of most ethical issues is the question of how human beings ought to relate to one another. That is, most ethical questions are concerned with relationships and interactions. A course on *Ethical Dilemmas Facing Robinson Crusoe in the Pre-Friday Period* would pose a real problem in generating case studies. Metarealities, on the other hand, not only complicate existing relationships between human beings but also open up a whole new domain of interactions between human beings and ethereal virtual creatures. The ethical issues involved challenge some of our most fundamental beliefs in religion, philosophy, and the psychology of personality. These issues have profound implications for public policy and the law.

Let's look at a few of these issues.

Case 1: War Games – The moral dilemmas surrounding war games are posed in even starker terms by the enhanced realism of virtual reality products like *BattleTech*. The issues are not new. Children, both human and animal, have played war games from time immemorial, and arguments can be made for their evolutionary survival value. Just as civilized societies forswear war as an instrument of public policy, civilized families discourage their children from acting out violence.

And yet the matter is not that simple. Some peaceful, primitive societies have evolved institutionalized war games that are ritualistically conducted until someone is seriously injured or killed. It is very difficult to abandon millions of years of genetic programming overnight. In fact, it is not really clear if war games increase or decrease actual antisocial behavior. Some argue that acting out destructive behavior in a non-threatening environment with nonlethal weapons may actually reduce the damage to society from such tendencies.

The realism and intense involvement of those participating in VR war game experiences may, in fact, shed light on the ethical issues of war games. If a causal connection can be established between participation in war games and actual anti-social behavior, it will contribute greatly to resolving this problematic issue. If the correlation is positive, the ethical position will call for eliminating war games. If the correlation is negative, we can conclude that war games provide a channel for sublimating intrinsically violent human behavior. The implications would extend beyond children's arcade games to political and military leaders as well.

Case 2: Sexual Ethics – Both mirror worlds and virtual reality open up questions of sexual ethics that are novel and intriguing and may have long term consequences for society. Consider the issues raised by three existing or potential phenomena.

First, there is the issue of interpersonal relations between people on existing networks. The present network of personal computers, modems, e-mail, and bulletin boards has many of the features of a mirror world in spite of its hazy, incomplete, and non-graphical nature. One example of the new phenomena that emerges from mixing human nature with networking technology was described recently in *The Milwaukee Journal*.[19]

> Throb Net, *one of the largest adult computer bulletin boards in the country, features 20 conferences for those with specific interests, such as dirty jokes, phone sex, sex talk, adult fantasies, gays, swingers, sex toys and sex help. There's even Violet's Bar and Grill for those who want to technologically simulate that scene and "pick up someone" electronically. Violet's has wet T-shirt contests – in words.*
>
> *The other party on the bulletin board may be down the street or thousands of miles away. The parties may be handsome or homely, long-legged beauties or short and plump, bald or beastly, shy or bold. And that's the appeal, users say. Anonymity guaranteed. No touching. No trouble. No consequences. Terminal sex, thanks to technology, in the privacy of your home or office.*

The issues raised by *Throb Net* and similar mirror worlds are tremendously interesting and provocative. They concern fundamental human needs and desires, the nature of personality, and the meaning of human relationships.

Just as problematic are issues raised by virtual reality. One of the first and most impressive virtual reality products for personal computers was the CD-ROM, *Virtual Valerie*. This admittedly X-rated product was described by Jerry Borrell, Editor of MacWorld Magazine, who said, "The graphic environments, navigation, original music, and game-playing aspects make it the most progressive CD-ROM work done to date, bar none."

Ted Nelson, inventor of hypertext and the never-quite-finished *Xanadu*™ project, is credited with inventing the word *teledildonics* to describe simulated sex at a distance. The word was inspired by a patented machine which converts sound into tactile sensations. Howard Rheingold devotes a chapter called "Teledildonics and Beyond" in his book, *Virtual Reality*, to exploring the implications of disembodied sex.

In describing both teledildonics and the *Throb Net* phenomena noted above, Rheingold says:

> *The secondary social effects of technosex are potentially revolutionary. If technology enables you to experience erotic frissons or deep physical, social, emotional communion with another person with no possibility of pregnancy or sexually transmitted disease, what then of conventional morality, and what of the social rituals and cultural codes that exist solely to enforce that morality? Is disembodiment the ultimate sexual revolution and/or the first step toward abandoning our bodies? ...*
>
> *Privacy and identity and intimacy will become tightly coupled into something we don't have a name for yet. ...*

Case 3: Loss of Reality – As more and more time and energy goes into constructing, exploring, and living in virtual worlds, what will happen to the real world? Joseph Weisenbaum long ago decried what he saw as the unhealthy and antisocial fixation that teenage hackers have with their machines.[20] The illusion of reality created by conversations with *Eliza* pale in comparison with the powerful experiences possible with VR. The escapism possible with passive television is nothing compared with that offered in cyberspace. What are the implications?

What will happen to the resorts and tourist industry when exciting travel to any place on Earth, indeed, in the whole Universe, is just a CD-ROM away? Mundane attractions such as the Grand Canyon and Eiffel Tower can't offer the excitement of interacting with good guys, bad guys, and prehistoric creatures possible on every VR tour.

Where will children come from if teledildonics replaces the real thing? Relationships carried on over *Throb Net* give new meaning to the term *meaningful relationship*. Will impressionable young minds sucked into VR become deadened and turn their owners into zombies? Or will they blossom into creative artistic and scientific giants as they leave behind the restrictive constraints and limitations imposed by the real world?

Case 4: Playing God – Humans have a long-standing fascination with miniatures and with construction sets. Recall the joy of playing with doll houses and model railroads. When these got boring, we would turn to building our own houses or cities from Tinker Toys, Leggo sets, or sand on

the beach. This fascination is not limited to children as the collectors of Hummels and the builders of model railroads will attest.

What is the source of this fascination? A large part of it stems from the satisfaction of "playing God" in some microuniverse. Several theological analogies come to mind. First, we act as Creator in building the miniature world of our own design according to our own tastes and whims. Secondly, we act as the source of purpose and meaning in those micro-worlds. The doll baby eats and the toy soldier dies only if we will it to happen. Finally, we are omniscient in our miniature world. Only we know everything that is going on at all times.

These analogies carry over directly and even more forcefully into the virtual realities and mirror worlds of computer science. Every virtual reality is the product of a human creator. Every mirror world allows its owner to be present, in effect, everywhere at the same time and to know everything there is to know about a system. So humans do play the role of God in all of these metarealities.

This conclusion leads to some very interesting results. Just as theologians try to gain insight on the nature of God by studying the nature of Her creation, the nature of the virtual worlds we create will reflect our own values and deepest nature. Perhaps it is significant that *BattleTech Center* was an instant commercial success.

Virtual worlds also offer us an opportunity for probing some of the profound questions of philosophy. Consider, for instance, the troubling theological problem of the existence of evil. If God is good, omnipotent, and the Creator of the Universe, why does evil exist? If we can agree that most evil is a result of human acts of commission or omission, cyberspace can provide us a virtual laboratory to explore this issue.

Cyberspace is the virtual world in which two or more virtual beings can interact. VPL already manufactures RB2 (Reality Built for Two) in which two virtual humans can interact with each other. The virtual laboratory would be populated by a small community of virtual humans. A detailed record of their interactions would be kept by the computer implementing the virtual reality. As situations emerged which produced divisiveness and conflict, the experimenter could play back the scenario and try to pinpoint what, precisely led to the conflict, i.e., what the "seeds of evil" were. Since the virtual beings are acting out the instructions of their human masters, this record might shed light on the nature of human personality and behaviors which have evil consequences.

Conclusions

In this chapter we examine some of the new realities made possible by computer science and the role computer graphics is playing to help visualize these realities. By identifying the term *metareality* and examining classes of metarealities we can better understand what characteristics these visual realities have in common and what features distinguish them from each other. Perhaps the strongest unifying concept in all classes of visual realities is their dynamic, time-dependent nature. The computer graphics implications of this observation focus on animation and video as the key tools for visualizing all of the new realities. Several animation and video examples are illustrated and discussed in detail. The role of *QuickTime* in providing a dynamic data protocol is explored.

Two of the most important metarealities include *virtual reality* and *mirror worlds*. Virtual reality describes a class of techniques in which total immersion and the ability to navigate are central. Virtual reality offers tremendous potential for both the entertainment industry and the field of scientific visualization. We presented a modest example of a personal workstation implementation of a system for building a virtual world and navigating through it.

Mirror worlds describe a somewhat less engrossing but potentially more significant metareality. By building live, authentic models of the real world and giving the observer the ability to probe and interact with it, mirror worlds offer the possibility of gaining topsight and of dealing with the complexity of society. While virtual reality deals with navigation through imaginary worlds, mirror worlds helps us understand and cope with the real world.

The greater the I/O bandwidth of the communication channels between the user and metareality, the more *authentic* the metareality experience becomes. Computer graphics offers the principle medium for delivering metarealities. Many of the most effective computer graphics algorithms have been inspired by the need for fast and convincing VR image rendering. Progress in the emerging field of VR is tied directly to advances in computer graphics. Computer graphics holds the key to visualizing new realities.

Exercises

16.1   The term *metareality* was introduced as an abstraction for the concepts of *alternate realities*, *artificial reality*, *virtual reality*, and *mirror worlds*. What features do these concepts share? These common characteristics are useful in defining metareality.

16.2   Important differences distinguish the various subclasses of metareality. Rank these subclasses in order of the importance of their impact on society, and discuss the differences.

16.3   WIMP operating systems were cited as an example of VR. List arguments supporting this position. In what aspects does the argument break down?

16.4   Myron Krueger's primary concern in building artificial realities is their potential for artistic expression. Assume your thesis project was to create an effective, interactive work of art and that you have access to the latest in modern electronic devices (graphical, acoustic, olfactory, and so on). What would you design?

16.5   One of Krueger's contributions was to recognize the *gesture* as an effective basis for human/machine communication. Suppose your task is to design a gesture-based operating system, using pen input. Describe the command library you would propose and the corresponding gestures for implementing them.

16.6   Both virtual reality and mirror worlds use databases for representing and projecting images of reality. In what important ways do the two approaches differ?

16.7   The discussion classified the teleoperator aspect of robotics as a metareality. What features of teleoperators qualifies them for this classification?

16.8   What application areas, other than those discussed in the book, would you propose for introducing teleoperator-based robotics? What advantages would they have over present techniques?

16.9 It was noted that animation has crept into the examples presented in previous chapters. Describe three such examples and how animation was used.

16.10 Describe three examples, other than those presented, in which animation is absolutely essential to the simulation or application.

16.11 Discuss the advantages object-oriented drawing programs have over bit-mapped painting programs for creating animation.

16.12 Discuss the role of *keyframes* in the *tweening* process. What compromises are inevitably involved? What type of animation is particularly appropriate for tweening? In what cases is it inappropriate?

16.13 Describe how the *ease in/ease out* option of tweening successfully simulates the physical properties of inertia and moment of inertia. In what type of animations does it enhance authenticity and in what cases does it fail?

16.14 Discuss why the three keyframes for the jogger of Figure 16.4 were picked in the configurations shown. Could successful tweening be achieved with fewer keyframes? What arguments favor more keyframes?

16.15 The chief contribution of the Argonne ARM to virtual reality was the mechanism for tactile sensory feed back. Why is this important to VR?

16.16 Describe three application areas, other than molecular docking, in which tactile feedback would be essential to a VR model.

16.17 Flight simulators are technically feasible for almost any vehicle ranging from a bicycle through a NASA space shuttle. Describe what features a motorcycle simulator should have. Describe what features an oil tanker pilot simulator should include. Discuss the role of economics in the development of these two trainers.

16.18 The visual acuity of the eye is defined as the angular separation of two well-illuminated point objects which can just barely be distinguished. Physics textbooks list this as

$\theta_0 \approx 0.03° \approx 5\times10^{-4}$ radians. Assuming a field of view of π steradians, how many pixels are required to match the visual acuity of the eye?

16.19 Assume you wish to navigate through 3D cyberspace but have only a 2D mouse with which to steer. Design a system for mapping mouse commands to 3D motion. (Hint: you may need additional switches in the form of function keys).

16.20 What features distinguished the *Aspen Movie Map* from conventional travelogues of the area? Does the success of this experiment in VR suggest that we will soon see a *New York City Movie Map* and a *Paris Movie Map*? What about a *Chicago Art Institute Map*? Make a reasonable estimate of how many bytes of CD-ROM the latter would require.

16.21 What graphical subroutines and objects would be most valuable for the tool kit of a designer of virtual sports?

16.22 In what sports or skills, besides juggling, could the learning curve be improved by providing the user control over virtual gravity? What other physical quantities, fixed by nature in the real world, could usefully be varied in VR simulations?

16.23 Describe additional medical microworlds, besides the virtual cadaver, which would be valuable for training medical students.

16.24 Most existing CAD systems provide tools for building 3D models but do not make claims of virtual reality. What features would have to be added to these programs to enable virtual reality experiences? Describe how this would be useful for architectural design.

16.25 From the description of Virtus *WalkThrough* it is clear that the program offers some features of virtual reality and lacks others. Discuss one example of each feature and how important you judge it to be for the success of the VR experience.

16.26 The complexity in the VR scene shown in Figure 16.16 was achieved mainly through the use of objects drawn from a library of

3D clip art. Discuss the potential market for such 3D clip art and the natural extensions to 3D "standard scenes" and microworlds.

16.27 Consider the overall design of the hierarchical structure of a complete mirror world. Specify the first three levels of the hierarchical design, in which the top level is labeled "World," the next level "Government," "Industry,"', "Education," and so on. As a design guide, keep in mind the **Rule of Seven:** *Most people cannot deal with more than 7 ± 2 objects at a time.*

16.28 If you were responsible for the GUI to a mirror world, what considerations would you use in the design? Describe some of the visual modes (organizational charts, bulletin boards, 2D cartoons, 3D models, and so on) available for the task and what level of description for which each would be most appropriate.

16.29 Several systems were described which demonstrate aspects of mirror worlds. Discuss three additional systems which can properly be considered mirror worlds.

16.30 Both virtual reality and mirror worlds have the potential for significantly altering how we live our lives and conduct the business of society. Discuss what you believe will be the most important impact of each area. Which area will have the most profound social implications and what are they?

Endnotes

1. Casti, John L., *Alternate Realities – Mathematical Models of Nature and Man*, John Wiley & Sons, New York, NY (1989).
2. Krueger, Myron W., *Artificial Reality II*, Addison-Wesley Publishing Company, Reading, MA (1991).
3. Rheingold, Howard, *Virtual Reality*, Summit Books, New York, NY (1991).
4. Gelernter, David, *Mirror Worlds*, Oxford University Press, New York, NY (1991).
5. Krueger, Myron W., *Artificial Reality*, Addison-Wesley Publishing Company, Reading, MA (1983).
6. Krueger, Myron W., (1991) Op cit, p. 15.
7. Norman, M. L. and Hardee, P.E., "Spatial Stability of the Slab Jet. II. Numerical Simulations," *Astrophysical Journal* **334**, pp. 80–94, (1988).
8. Rampil, I. J., Moseley, M.E., White, D.L., Schmiedl, U., and Brasch, R.C., *Investigative Radiology* **22**, No. 9, pp. 713–721 (1987).
9. Krueger, Myron W., *Op cit*, p.66–67.
10. Brooks, F. P., Jr. Ouh-Young, M., Batter, J. J., and Kilpatrick, P. Jerome, "Project GROPE Haptic Displays for Scientific Visualization," *ACM Computer Graphics* **24**, No. 4, pp. 177–185, August, (1990).
11. Furness, Thomas A., III, "Harnessing Virtual Space," *Society for Information Display Digest*, pp. 4–7 (1988).
12. Starks, Michael, "Stereoscopic Video and the Quest for Virtual Reality," *Beyond the Vision – The Technology, Research, and Business of Virtual Reality*, Proceedings of Virtual Reality '91, pp. 200–225, Meckler Publishing, Westport, CT (1992).
13. Grimes, Jack, "Virtual Reality 91 anticipates future reality," *IEEE Computer Graphics & Applications* **11**, No. 6, pp. 81–83, November (1991).
14. Laurel, Brenda (ed), *The Art of Human-Computer Interface Design*, Addison-Wesley Publishing Company, Inc., pp. 425–426 (1990).
15. Porter, Stephen, "Special Report on Virtual Reality," *Computer Graphics World* **15**, No. 3, pp. 42–43, March (1992).
16. Information of *Virtus WalkThrough*™ is available from:
    Virtus Corporation
    117 Edinburgh South, Suite 204
    Cary, NC 27511
    (919) 467-9700.
17. Feigenbaum, Edward A. and McCorduck, Pamela, *The Fifth Generation – Artificial Intelligence and Japan's Computer Challenge to the World*, Addison-Wesley Publishing Co., Reading, MA (1983).
18. Firebaugh, Morris, *Artificial Intelligence – A Knowledge-Based Approach*, PWS-Kent Publishing Company, pp. 474–478, Boston, MA (1988).
19. Pabst, Georgia, "Throb Net: Fantasies Come to Life on Home Computers," *The Milwaukee Journal*, p. G4, Sunday, March 15 (1992).
20. Weisenbaum, Joseph, *Computing Power and Human Reason*, Freeman, San Francisco, CA (1976).

Appendix A

Vectors and Matrices

by

Yong Y. Auh[§]

In the present appendix, we shall consider basic concepts and methods of vector and matrix algebra. Vectors and matrices are useful in graphics because they enable us to consider complex geometric objects as single objects, refer to them using simple symbols, and perform calculations with these symbols in a very compact form. It is true that any problem which can be solved by vectors or matrices can also be solved without them. However, vector and matrix notations provide the means of representing problems in a conceptually simple manner so that we can visualize the problems and the solutions better.

If we examine how rational numbers are represented and used, we may see how important it is to have a good way to represent mathematical objects for effective calculation. Rational numbers are written by putting the numerator on top of the denominator like "1/3." Once we have this notation, we can easily define rules for rational addition and multiplication. Suppose r_1 and r_2 are rational numbers. Since these are rational numbers, we can represent them as n_1/d_1 and n_2/d_2, respectively. Then, $r_1+r_2 = n_1/d_1 + n_2/d_2 = (n_1{}^*d_2 + n_2{}^*d_1)/d_1{}^*d_2$, and $r_1{}^*r_2 = n_1/d_1 * n_2/d_2 = n_1{}^*n_2 / d_1{}^*d_2$. We have become so used to this notation, we think it's natural. We all forget how many days we spent in grade school to learn this stuff!

Vectors and matrices are very powerful constructs, and they have proven to be quite essential not only in engineering and the sciences, but also in graphics. Once we get used to these concepts and get comfortable with their notations, they will seem to be as "natural" as the fractional notation.

Vectors

When we move an object from one location to another, we can represent the displacement with an arrow or *directed line segment*. This figure shows a translation (displacement without rotation) of a geometric object in a two-dimensional space. The directed line segment shows the distance and direction of movement. This directed line segment geometrically represents the concept of a *vector*. The length of a vector is called its *magnitude*. It is also called the *length* or *Euclidean norm* of the vector. In contrast to vectors which have directions, *scalars* only have magnitudes. Simple numbers representing the length of lines or the area of rectangles are examples of scalars.

Lowercase boldfaced letters such as *a*, *b* are used to refer to vectors in this text. Lowercase letters with arrows on top such as $\vec{a}, \vec{b}$, are also frequently used to designate vectors.

The length of a vector **a** is denoted by $|a|$. Two vectors *a* and *b* are equal if they have the same length and direction, and we use the equal sign for vector equality: *a* = *b*.

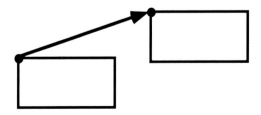

Figure A.1
Translation of a rectangle.

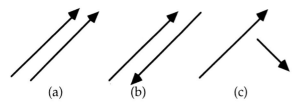

(a)   (b)   (c)

Figure A.2
Equal vectors, (a); vectors with equal magnitude but opposite directions, (b); and vectors with different lengths and directions, (c).

Since the starting point of a vector does not make any difference as far as equality of vectors are concerned, vectors, unlike points, are independent of the choice of coordinate system. When we place a vector in a specific coordinate system, for example, the Cartesian coordinate system in three-dimensional space, we can define components of the vector. Let $P=(x_1, y_1, z_1)$ and $Q=(x_2, y_2, z_2)$ be the initial point and the terminal point, respectively, of a vector a. Then $a_x = x_2 - x_1$, $a_y = y_2 - y_1$, $a_z = z_2 - z_1$ are called the components of the vector a with respect to the coordinate system. Since the length of the vector a is the distance, PQ,

$$|a| = \sqrt{a_x^2 + a_y^2 + a_z^2} .$$

Note that if we choose the origin as the initial point of a vector, then the components are equal to the coordinates of the terminal point. Such a vector is called the *position vector* of the terminal point. Now we can represent vectors algebraically, that is, in terms of their components. Vectors in three-dimensional space are ordered triples of their components. For example, $b = [0, 1, 0]$ repesent represents a vector one unit long pointing in the y direction.

We have special names for some vectors. The vector $[0, 0, 0]$ is called the *zero vector*, 0. Vectors of length 1 are called *unit vectors*. One set of unit vectors of particular interest is the Cartesian set, $\{i, j, k\}$ which are parallel to the x, y, and z axes, respectively. Then we can represent any vector a as

$$a = a_x i + a_y j + a_z k. \qquad [A.1]$$

The vectors i, j, k are mutually *orthogonal* or perpendicular.

Although the geometric interpretation of vectors is useful, algebraic representation has many advantages. The use of coordinate systems and the resolution of vectors into components are very

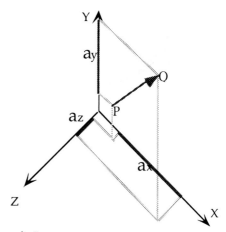

Figure A.3
Three Cartesian components, (a_x, a_y, a_z) of vector, a.

helpful for understanding the significance of vector relations. The behavior of components under coordinate transformations provides a convenient way to manipulate transformations. One of the serious difficulties of the geometric interpretation is that vectors are difficult to visualize in higher dimensional spaces. Can you mentally draw vectors in five-dimensional space?

Vector Addition

We can consider the concept of vector addition as equivalent to moving an object twice. As we saw earlier, we can represent each move as a vector. Thus, vector addition is like moving an object to the terminal point of the second move directly.

Algebraically, this can be expressed (assuming a and b are 3D vectors) as:

$$a + b = [a_x, a_y, a_z] + [b_x, b_y, b_z]$$
$$= [a_x + b_x, a_y + b_y, a_z + b_z] . \qquad [A.2]$$

The equivalent representation in unit vector notation is:

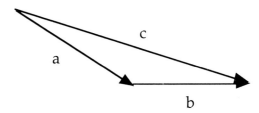

Figure A.4
The vector c is the vector sum of vectors a and b, i.e. $c = a + b$.

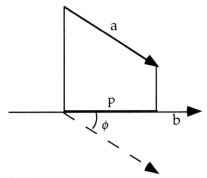

FigureA.5
Interpretation of dot product as projection of one vector on the other.

$$a + b = a_x i + a_y j + a_z k + b_x i + b_y j + b_z k , \quad \text{[A.3]}$$
$$= (a_x + b_x)i + (a_y + b_y)j + (a_z + b_z) k .$$

Scalar Multiplication

Given a vector $a = [a_x, a_y, a_z]$, we can form another vector $[pa_x, pa_y, pa_z]$. *Scalar multiplication* is a multiplication of a scalar by a vector, written as pa. If we define pa component-wise, in other words, multiply the components with p, then we can see that the following statements are true:

The length of pa is $|p| |a|$.
If $a \neq 0$ and $p > 0$, then pa has the same direction as a.
If $a \neq 0$ and $p < 0$, then pa has the opposite direction of a.
$p(a + b) = pa + pb$.
$(p + q)a = pa + qa$, where p,q are both scalars.
$p (qa) = (pq) a$.
$1a = a$.
$0a = 0$.

Vector Multiplication – Dot Product

Now we define a pair of new operations on vectors. Let's start with the *dot product* which is also called *inner product* or *scalar product*. It is defined as

$$a \cdot b = |a| |b| \cos \varnothing \quad \text{[A.4]}$$

where
$\varnothing$ = angle between a and b.

Using the orthogonality relationship of Cartesian unit vectors, $i \cdot i = j \cdot j = k \cdot k = 1$ and $i \cdot j = i \cdot k = j \cdot k = 0$, this can be expressed in the equivalent form:

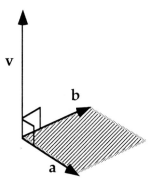

Figure A.6
The cross product, v, of vectors a and b is perpendicular to the plane containing a and b.

$$a \cdot b = (a_x i + a_y j + a_z k) \cdot (b_x i + b_y j + b_z k) ,$$
$$= a_x b_x + a_y b_y + a_z b_z . \quad \text{[A.5]}$$

This form is particularly useful for calculating the dot product of two vectors, given the Cartesian components of each.

Since the length of a vector is scalar, the dot product is also a scalar. Hence the term scalar product. Consider the unit vectors i and j mentioned above. $i \cdot j = |i| |j| \cos (\pi/2) = 0$. It shows that the dot product of orthogonal vectors is 0, and the dot product of parallel vectors is equal to the product of the lengths.

Suppose that a and b are vectors and $\varnothing$ is the angle between them. Then the scalar, p, defined as

$$p = |a| \cos \varnothing \quad \text{[A.6]}$$

is called the *projection* of a in the direction of b as indicated in Figure A.5.

Vector Multiplication – Cross Product

Another useful operation on vectors is the *cross product* (or *vector product*). The cross product of two vectors a and b is written

$$v = a \times b . \quad \text{[A.7]}$$

The relationship of the two vectors and their cross product vector, v, is shown in Figure A.6.

The length of vector v is equal to $|a| |b| \sin \varnothing$ ($\varnothing$ is the angle between a and b) and its direction is perpendicular to both a and b. The triple (a, b, v) form a right-handed system—curling the fingers from a to b points the thumb along v. We can define the vector product in terms of components in a right-handed Cartesian coordinate system as follows: Let $a = [a_x, a_y, a_z]$, and $b = [b_x, b_y, b_z]$. Then the vector product is:

$$a \times b = (a_y b_z - a_z b_y)i + \qquad\text{[A.8]}$$
$$(a_z b_x - a_x b_z)j +$$
$$(a_x b_y - a_y b_x)k .$$

It can be expressed in a more compact form if matrices are used:

$$a \times b = i\begin{bmatrix} a_y & a_z \\ b_y & b_z \end{bmatrix} + j\begin{bmatrix} a_z & a_x \\ b_z & b_x \end{bmatrix} + k\begin{bmatrix} a_x & a_y \\ b_x & b_y \end{bmatrix}$$
$$\text{[A.9]}$$

$$= \begin{bmatrix} i & j & k \\ a_x & a_y & a_z \\ b_x & b_y & b_z \end{bmatrix} . \qquad\text{[A.10]}$$

Geometric Applications of Vectors

We can define lines in terms of vectors. Given a position vector u_0 on a line L, the line can be expressed with the equation $u = u_0 + pv$, where p is a scalar variable and v is a given vector parallel to the line. This is called the *parametric form* of the line.

Likewise, planes can be defined using vectors. Given independent vectors v and w, $v \neq kw$, the equation

$$u = u_0 + pv + qw \qquad\text{[A.11]}$$

defines a plane through position u_0 and parallel to v and w. This is the parametric form for a plane, expressed in terms of scalar parameters, p and q.

Definition of Vector Space

By collecting the basic properties of vectors, we can formally define vector space as follows:

A vector space V over a field S is a mathematical structure <S, V, +, ., -, 0, 1> such that the following equations hold:

$$a + b = b + a$$
$$(u + v) + w = u + (v + w)$$
$$a + 0 = a$$
$$a + (-a) = 0 \qquad\text{[A.12]}$$
$$p(a + b) = pa + pb$$
$$(c+k)a = ca + ka$$
$$c(ka) = (ck)a$$
$$1a = a .$$

Matrices

A *matrix* is a rectangular array of (real or complex) numbers of the form:

$$\begin{bmatrix} a_{11} & a_{12} & \cdots & a_{1j} & \cdots & a_{1n} \\ \cdots & \cdots & \cdots & \cdots & \cdots & \cdots \\ a_{i1} & a_{i2} & \cdots & a_{ij} & \cdots & a_{in} \\ \cdots & \cdots & \cdots & \cdots & \cdots & \cdots \\ a_{m1} & a_{m2} & \cdots & amj & \cdots & a_{mn} \end{bmatrix} \qquad\text{[A.13]}$$

The numbers are called the *elements* of the matrix. The horizontal lines are called *rows* or *row vectors*, and the vertical lines are called *columns* or *column vectors*. A matrix with m rows and n columns is called an $m \times n$ matrix, which is usually read "m by n matrix." The *order* of a matrix is this pair of numbers for the matrix's rows and columns. Bold-faced upper case letters are used as matrix variables. Notations such as $[a_{ij}]$, $[b_{ij}]$ are used to denote matrices as well as $\| a_{ij}\|$, $\| b_{ij}\|$. The first subscript indicates the row and the second subscript the column of the element.

What are matrices for? Like other mathematical concepts, matrices are created to succinctly express some mathematical ideas abstracted from concrete examples so that we can reason about them and apply them to other problems. Consider a linear transformation of a point to another point (for some constant θ):

$$x_1 \cos\theta + x_2 \sin\theta = y_1 \qquad\text{[A.14]}$$
$$-x_1 \sin\theta + x_2 \cos\theta = y_2$$

Given a point, (x_1, x_2), the equations will transform it to give us another point (y_1, y_2). The equations are not independent, unrelated equations. This pair of equations works together to determine (y_1, y_2). So we can postulate an operator, A, or a rule which calculates $Y = (y_1, y_2)$, given a point, $X = (x_1, x_2)$:

$$AX = Y. \qquad\text{[A.15]}$$

We can designate A using the matrix notation:

$$A = \begin{bmatrix} \cos\theta & \sin\theta \\ -\sin\theta & \cos\theta \end{bmatrix} \qquad\text{[A.16]}$$

Later, we will see how the matrix multiplication works.

At this point, it is important to realize that, from an abstract point of view, matrices are a kind of operator which works on vectors or other matrices to produce other vectors or matrices. In the case of linear transformations, each transformation is represented by a matrix, and this matrix maps a vector to another vector. Once we define matrices, we can manipulate them in various ways, e.g., add two matrices together, do scalar multiplication on matrices, and multiply matrices. Before defining these operations, some more terminologies will be introduced.

A matrix which has only one row is called a *row matrix*:

$$[a_{11} \; a_{12} \; a_{13}] \, , \qquad [A.17]$$

and a matrix which has only one column is called a *column matrix*:

$$\begin{bmatrix} b_{11} \\ b_{21} \\ b_{31} \end{bmatrix} . \qquad [A.18]$$

If a matrix has the same number of rows and columns, it is called a *square* matrix. A *diagonal* matrix is a square matrix that is zero everywhere except on its main diagonal, that is, $a_{ij} = 0$ for $i \neq j$. A square matrix is *symmetric* if $a_{ij} = a_{ji}$. Obviously, a diagonal matrix is symmetric. If $a_{ij} = -a_{ji}$ in a square matrix, it is called *skew-symmetric*. A matrix whose diagonal elements are all 1 is called a *unit* matrix.

Matrices are added together by adding corresponding elements. We can't add two matrices if their orders are not the same, i.e., their rows and columns should match. Addition for conformal matrices can be specified as:

$$[a_{ij}] + [b_{ij}] = [a_{ij}+b_{ij}] \qquad [A.19]$$

A matrix can be multiplied by a scalar by multiplying every element in the matrix by that scalar. Thus,

$$k \, [a_{ij}] = [k \, a_{ij}] \qquad [A.20]$$

Given an $m \times n$ matrix, $A = [a_{ij}]$, we can make an $n \times m$ matrix $B = [b_{ij}]$ such that $b_{ij} = a_{ji}$ for each i and j. The matrix B is called the *transpose* of A, or A^T. For instance, if

$$A = \begin{bmatrix} 1 & 2 & 3 \\ 4 & 5 & 6 \end{bmatrix} ,$$

then

$$A^T = \begin{bmatrix} 1 & 4 \\ 2 & 5 \\ 3 & 6 \end{bmatrix} . \qquad [A.21]$$

Matrix Multiplication

We now return to the subject of matrix multiplication. The following represent two linear transformations of points in a 2-dimensional space:

$$\begin{aligned} a_{11}y_1 + a_{12}y_2 &= z_1 \, , \\ a_{21}y_1 + a_{22}y_2 &= z_2 \, , \end{aligned} \qquad [A.22]$$

and

$$\begin{aligned} b_{11}x_1 + b_{12}x_2 &= y_1 \, , \\ b_{21}x_1 + b_{22}x_2 &= y_2 \, . \end{aligned} \qquad [A.23]$$

Since both [A.22] and [A.23] are linear, we would expect that (z_1, z_2) can be obtained directly from (x_1, x_2) by a single linear transformation of the form:

$$\begin{aligned} c_{11}x_1 + c_{12}x_2 &= z_1 \, , \\ c_{21}x_1 + c_{22}x_2 &= z_2 \, . \end{aligned} \qquad [A.24]$$

The coefficients c_{11}, c_{12}, c_{21} and c_{22} can be computed by substituting [A.22] with [A.23]:

$$\begin{aligned} a_{11}(b_{11}x_1 + b_{12}x_2) + a_{12}(b_{21}x_1 + b_{22}x_2) &= z_1 \, , \\ a_{21}(b_{11}x_1 + b_{12}x_2) + a_{22}(b_{21}x_1 + b_{22}x_2) &= z_2 \, . \end{aligned}$$
$$[A.25]$$

From [A.24] and [A.25], we get

$$\begin{aligned} c_{11} &= a_{11}b_{11} + a_{12}b_{21} \, , \\ c_{12} &= a_{11}b_{12} + a_{12}b_{22} \, , \\ c_{21} &= a_{21}b_{11} + a_{22}b_{21} \, , \\ c_{22} &= a_{21}b_{12} + a_{22}b_{22} \, . \end{aligned} \qquad [A.26]$$

So if we represent [A.22], [A.23], and [A.24] as matrices of coefficients, A, B, and C, respectively, we can define the matrix product AB of A and B to be the coefficient matrix C, i.e., $AB = C$.

$$A = \begin{bmatrix} a_{11} & a_{12} \\ a_{21} & a_{22} \end{bmatrix}, \; B = \begin{bmatrix} b_{11} & b_{12} \\ b_{21} & b_{22} \end{bmatrix}, \; C = \begin{bmatrix} c_{11} & c_{12} \\ c_{21} & c_{22} \end{bmatrix}$$
$$[A.27]$$

Well, that's how the matrix multiplication, or matrix product, happened to be defined. Obviously, we can generalize it to cover more than multiplication of 2×2 matrices. If A is an $m \times n$ matrix and B an $n \times p$ matrix, we can define the product AB to be $C = [c_{ij}]$ where

$$c_{ij} = a_{i1}b_{1j} + a_{i2}b_{2j} + \dots + a_{in}b_{nj}$$
$$= \sum_{k=1}^{n} a_{ik}b_{kj} \qquad [\text{A.28}]$$

We can see that c_{ij} is the inner product of the i-th row vector of the first matrix and the j-th column vector of the second matrix. Recall that the inner product operation is defined on vectors of equal lengths. So the matrix product is defined only when the number of columns of the first matrix is the same as the number of rows of the second matrix. For example,

$$\begin{bmatrix} -1 & 2 \\ 3 & 4 \end{bmatrix}\begin{bmatrix} 2 & -1 \\ 4 & 3 \end{bmatrix} = \begin{bmatrix} (-1*2+2*4) & (-1*-1+2*3) \\ (3*2+4*4) & (3*-1+4*3) \end{bmatrix}$$
$$= \begin{bmatrix} 6 & 7 \\ 22 & 9 \end{bmatrix} \qquad [\text{A.29}]$$

and

$$\begin{bmatrix} -1 & 2 \\ 3 & 4 \end{bmatrix}\begin{bmatrix} 2 \\ 4 \end{bmatrix} = \begin{bmatrix} (-1*2+2*4) \\ (3*2+4*4) \end{bmatrix} = \begin{bmatrix} 6 \\ 22 \end{bmatrix} \qquad [\text{A.30}]$$

and

$$\begin{bmatrix} -1 & 2 \end{bmatrix}\begin{bmatrix} 2 & -1 \\ 4 & 3 \end{bmatrix} = \begin{bmatrix} (-1*2+2*4) & (-1*-1+2*3) \end{bmatrix}$$
$$= \begin{bmatrix} 6 & 7 \end{bmatrix}. \qquad [\text{A.31}]$$

Matrix multiplication is not commutative. In other words, AB is not, in general, equal to BA. In fact, BA may be even undefined, while AB is defined. Suppose A is a 2×3 matrix and B a 3×4 matrix. Then AB is a 2×4 matrix, but BA is undefined because the columns of B and the rows of A don't match.

As a special case, consider a matrix multiplication of 2×2 matrix and a 2×1 matrix. What is the order of this matrix product? That should be 2×1.

$$\begin{bmatrix} a_{11} & a_{12} \\ a_{21} & a_{22} \end{bmatrix}\begin{bmatrix} x_1 \\ x_2 \end{bmatrix} = \begin{bmatrix} y_1 \\ y_2 \end{bmatrix}$$

or

$$\begin{bmatrix} x_1 & x_2 \end{bmatrix}\begin{bmatrix} a_{11} & a_{12} \\ a_{21} & a_{22} \end{bmatrix} = \begin{bmatrix} y_1 & y_2 \end{bmatrix}. \qquad [\text{A.32}]$$

So, given a linear transformation T and a vector, the product is a vector, too. T represents a mapping of vectors to vectors (in *vector space*). Given linear transformations, A and B, (AB) represents the combination of the transformations A and B. In case both A and B are square matrices, the product will be also a square matrix of the same order.

The Inverse of a Matrix

The *inverse* of an $n \times n$ matrix, $A = [a_{ij}]$, is an $n \times n$ matrix, A^{-1}, such that

$$AA^{-1} = A^{-1}A = I, \qquad [\text{A.33}]$$

where I is the $n \times n$ unit matrix.

Note that not all square matrices have inverses. Consider the following two cases:

$$A = \begin{bmatrix} 1 & 2 \\ 2 & 1 \end{bmatrix} \quad \text{and} \quad B = \begin{bmatrix} 1 & 2 \\ 1 & 2 \end{bmatrix} \qquad [\text{A.34}]$$

Does A have an inverse? How about B? There is a general way to determine whether a matrix has an inverse or not. Here, however, we just point out that for most geometric transformations, inverses do exist. What this means is that if you do a linear transformation to a geometric object, there is a way to get back to the original object.

Properties of Matrices

The properties of matrix operations can be summarized as follows:

$$A + B = B + A$$
$$A + (B + C) = (A + B) + C$$
$$k(A + B) = kA + kB$$
$$(k + q)A = kA + qA$$
$$k(qA) = (kq)A = q(kA)$$

$$A(BC) = (AB)C$$
$$A(B + C) = AB + AC$$
$$(A + B)C = AC + BC$$
$$A(kB) = k(AB) = (kA)B$$

$$(A + B)^T = A^T + B^T$$
$$(kA)^T = kA^T$$
$$(AB)^T = B^T A^T$$

Exercises

A.1 Find the terminal point based on the given initial point and the initial point components:
  (a) (2, 1, 1)   [1, -1, 1]
  (b) (3, 2, 2)   [-3, 1, 1]

A.2 Let $a = i - j + k$, $b = -i - j$, $c = 2i + k$. Find
  (a) $a + b$ (b) $2(a + (b + c))$
  (c) $|2a - b|$ (d) $|a| - |b|$
  (e) $a \bullet b$ (f) $b \bullet a$

A.3 Find the cosine of the angle between the following vectors, using the definitions [A.4]–[A.6]:
  (a) $a + b$ and c (b) a and $c + b$
  (c) $a \times b$ (d) $b \times a$
  (e) Show that if the diagonals of a rectangle are orthogonal, the rectangle is a square.

A.4 Given the matrices:
$$A = \begin{bmatrix} 2 & -3 \\ 0 & 4 \end{bmatrix}, \quad B = \begin{bmatrix} -5 & 2 \\ 2 & 1 \end{bmatrix}, \quad C = \begin{bmatrix} 0 & 1 & -2 \\ 3 & 0 & 4 \end{bmatrix},$$
compute:
  (a) $A + B$ (b) $B - A$
  (c) $3(A - 2B)$ (d) B^T
  (e) $A - A^T$
  (f) Are $A + A^T$, $A - A^T$, and $B + 2A$ symmetric or skew-symmetric?

A.5 Given the matrices:
$$A = \begin{bmatrix} 4 & 6 & -1 \\ 3 & 0 & 2 \\ 1 & -2 & 5 \end{bmatrix}, \quad B = \begin{bmatrix} 2 & 4 \\ 0 & 1 \\ -1 & 2 \end{bmatrix}, \quad C = \begin{bmatrix} 3 \\ 1 \\ 2 \end{bmatrix},$$
compute the following (if the operation is defined):
  (a) AA (b) BB (c) AB
  (d) BA (e) $A^T B$ (f) $B^T A$
  (g) BC (h) $C^T B$

Endnotes

§   Yong Y. Auh is Project Leader at G. E. Medical Systems in New Berlin, WI.

FIGS
Fundamental Interactive Graphics System

by

Dan Knudson[§]

This appendix is intended to offer a gentle introduction to the *Fundamental Interactive Graphics System – FIGS*. First we discuss the layered architecture by which FIGS achieves device independence. Next, we summarize the model building and viewing philosophy of PHIGS and their implementation in FIGS. Then we list a detailed specification of FIGS routines and calling parameters and conclude with a generic application program illustrating the sequence of calls to FIGS routines.

FIGS Architecture

The *Fundamental Interactive Graphics System* (FIGS) is based on the *Programmer's Hierarchical Interactive Graphics System* and consists of a sub-set of approximately fifty of the most useful PHIGS routines[1]. A primary design objective of PHIGS is to provide a platform independent graphics language for modeling and rendering scenes. This platform independence has been achieved in FIGS by use of a layered approach illustrated in Figure B.1.

The programmer may build applications using standard high-level languages to invoke routines from the FIGS library. The XFIGS layer contains bookkeeping functions used in FIGS but not accessible to the programmer. Both FIGS and XFIGS are written in C, and, therefore, platform independent. All device dependence is isolated in the device driver (DDRIVER) layer. The DDRIVER uses machine-dependent graphics toolkit routines for line drawing, polygon filling, and so on to implement the FIGS library routines.

At the time of this writing, DDRIVERs have been implemented on OS2/Presentation Manager,

Windows, and Macintosh operating system environments. The layered architecture shown in Figure B.1 greatly eases the task of porting FIGS to a new platform. The beauty of graphics languages such as PHIGS and FIGS is that, once the libraries and device drivers have been installed, application program source code can be moved freely from one environment to another with no fear of incompatibility.

Modeling

One of the main contributions of PHIGS was to recognize the importance of hierarchical representation of graphics objects and to introduce data

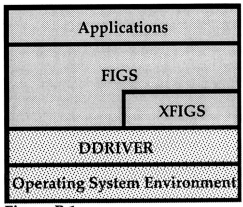

Figure B.1
Layer structure of FIGS applications.

■ = Device independent

▨ = Device dependent

structures to implement this hierarchy. The basic unit of data is the *structure element*, a graphical primitive with optional attributes and applicable transformations. Structure elements may be combined to form *structures* which are stored in the *centralized structure store* (CSS).

Structures and Segments

In FIGS, structures are represented as *segments* which, in turn, are composed of linked lists of *elements*. FIGS provides an extensive library of routines for manipulating the pointers to the lists of elements. Thus, for instance, we can define a cube segment as a hierarchical polyhedron structure composed of primitive polygon elements which are defined as more primitive vertices which, in turn, are defined in terms of elemental 3D points. One method for doing this in Pascal is to set up the 3D points and vertices as constants with the code:

```
cube: array[0..7] of f3DPOINT =
      ((x:2.0; y: 2.0; z:2.0),      (x:2.0; y:-2.0; z:2.0),
      (x:-2.0; y:-2.0; z:2.0),      (x:-2.0; y:2.0; z:2.0),
      (x:2.0; y: 2.0; z:-2.0),      (x:2.0; y:-2.0; z:-2.0),
      (x:-2.0; y:-2.0; z:-2.0),     (x:-2.0; y:2.0; z:-2.0));
      {Eight points defining polygon vertices.}

cubeVertices: array[0..29]of fINT =
      (3, 2, 1, 0, -1,   0, 1, 5, 4, -1,   4, 5, 6, 7, -1,
      7, 6, 2, 3, -1,    7, 3, 0, 4, -1,   5, 1, 2, 6, -1);
      {Indices of vertices for six polygons.}
```

The segment, CUBE_ID, is then defined and entered into the CSS with the following FIGS code:

```
fOpenSegment (CUBE_ID);
    fSetTransformation (@m, REPLACE);
    fPolyhedron (8, @cube, 6, @cubeVertices);
fCloseSegment;
```

Attributes

FIGS provides several routines for specifying the attributes of the graphical objects defined as segments in the CSS. These include such self-evident functions as:

```
fSetLineColor (color);
fSetLineWidthScaleFactor(scale);
fSetEdgeStyle(style); .
```

Transformations

Structures are readily manipulated in 3D space by a complete set of FIGS transformation routines. Included are:

```
fScale(scaleX,scaleY,scaleZ,pMatrix);
fTranslate(tX,tY,tZ,pMatrix);
fRotateX(angle,pMatrix);
{Plus Y and Z equivalents.}
fComposeMatrix(pM1,pM2,pM3);
{To produce M3 = M1 M2.}
```

Structures, as modified by editing their attributes and transformations, are stored as linked lists in the CSS. To display the model, the list of CSS structures is *traversed* and the resulting series of transformed graphical objects *posted* to the workstation screen.

Event Handling

In order to support interaction with the user, FIGS provides the fGetEvent function which recognizes the following six event types:

```
BUTTON1DOWN        BUTTON2DOWN
BUTTON1UP          BUTTON2UP
ASCIICHAR          MOUSEMOVE.
```

It is not a difficult task to use these event primitives for implementing the six *logical input devices* of PHIGS (*locator, pick, choice, valuator, string,* and *stroke*).

Viewing

FIGS supports the standard PHIGS coordinate systems and viewing transformations discussed in some detail in Chapters 7 and 8. Viewing is the process of projecting the posted structures defined in 3D world coordinates onto the 2D device screen. FIGS uses the synthetic camera viewing model described as the fixed world/movable camera mode in Chapter 7. This requires establishing a *view reference coordinate system* (VRC), which involves specifying the camera position (projection reference point), the location of the VRC's origin in world coordinates (view reference point), the direction the camera is pointing (view plane normal vector), and a vector specifying the camera rotation (view up vector).

The geometric information defining the VRC for each view is stored in a FIGS record called fVIEWDATA. In addition, each fVIEWDATA record contains the z-coordinate of the front and back clipping planes required for 3D clipping, a proj-Type parameter specifying parallel or perspective projection, a renderMode parameter specifying wireframe of solid rendering, and the 2D normalized device coordinates defining the viewport location on the screen. A complete specification of the fVIEWDATA record structure is given in the *FIGS Specifications*.

Multiple views may be created by building multiple fVIEWDATA records which are indexed by the parameter, viewID. FIGS provides four routines for creating, manipulating, and projecting views: fComposeView, fQuery View, fDrawView, and fSetRenderMode. The details of their operation and calling sequence is given in the *FIGS Specifications*.

FIGS Specifications

Below we list the complete specification of the FIGS language, indicating the parameters, data structures, routines, and their calling sequences.

```
{*****************************************************************************
   UNIT:     FIGS.PAS

   PURPOSE:  To provide the function prototypes, constants, etc. necessary
             for writing application programs which interface with the
             FIGS graphics library.
   *****************************************************************************}

unit FIGS;
interface
uses WinTypes;

{-----------------------------------------------------------------
                    function return codes
   -----------------------------------------------------------------}

const
  fOK                      = 0;   { function completed normally }
  fERR_NO_SEGMENT_OPEN     = 1;   { a call requiring that a segment be
                                    open was made while no segment was
                                    open (eg. a call to fPolyline,
                                    fSetMarkerStyle, fDeleteElmnt) }
  fERR_INVALID_GDP         = 2;   { invalid general drawing primitive
                                    index }
  fERR_SEGMENT_OPEN        = 3;   { a call requiring that no segment
                                    be open was made while a segment
                                    was open (eg. a call to
                                    fOpenSegment) }
  fERR_ALLOC_MEM_FAILED    = 4;   { attempt to allocate memory
                                    failed at the driver level }
  fERR_SEGMENT_NONEXISTENT = 5;   { attempt to reference a non-existent
                                    segment }
  fERR_INVALID_VIEW        = 6;   { attempt to reference a non-existent
                                    view }
  fERR_SEGMENT_POSTED      = 7;   { attempt to post a segment to a view
                                    which is already posted to that
                                    view }
  fERR_SEGMENT_NOT_POSTED  = 8;   { attempt to unpost a segment from
                                    a view that was not posted }
  fERR_INVALID_LABEL       = 9;   { invalid label }
  fERR_INVALID_ELEMENT     = 10;  { attempt to delete an element was
                                    made when no elements currently in
                                    segment }
```

```
fERR_INVALID_WINDOWHANDLE    = 11; { invalid window handle }
fERR_MAX_NUM_SEGMENT_LINKS   = 12; { maximum number of segment links has
                                     been reached within the driver -
                                     must unpost segment(s) to continue }
fERR_MAX_NUM_SEGMENTS        = 13; { maximum number of segments
                                     (headers) has been reached with the
                                     driver - must delete segment(s) to
                                     continue }
fERR_MAX_NUM_ELMNT_HDRS      = 14; { maximum number of elements
                                     (headers) has been reached in the
                                     driver - must delete element(s) to
                                     continue }
fERR_MAX_NUM_VIEWS           = 15; { maximum number of views reached,
                                     must recompose an existing view }
fERR_INVALID_PARAMETER       = 16; { function called with invalid
                                     parameter }
fERR_CALL_SEGMENT_RECURSION  = 17; { while displaying segments, a segment
                                     tried to call itself (either
                                     directly or indirectly }
fERR_INVALID_SEGMENT_ID      = 18; { invalid segment identifier }
fERR_IGNOREEVENTS            = 19; { fGetEvent called while in
                                     IGNOREEVENTS mode }
fERR_INVALID_FUNC            = 20; { program called function which is
                                     invalid in FIGSGRAPHICS mode }
fERR_FIGS_OPEN               = 21; { fOpenFigs called with FIGS already
                                     open }
fERR_FIGS_CLOSED             = 22; { fCloseFigs called with FIGS already
                                     closed }
fERR_DRIVER                  = 23; { generic FIGS driver error occurred}

{--------------------------------------------------------------------------
                          enumerated constants
--------------------------------------------------------------------------}
const
 PARALLEL          = 0; { projection types - see fVIEWDATA record      }
 PERSPECTIVE       = 1;

 UCBS              = 0; { general drawing primitive types - see        }
 whatever_else     = 1; { fGenlDrawPrim function                       }

 WIREFRAME         = 0; { rendering modes - see fVIEWDATA record       }
 SOLID             = 1;

 REPLACE           = 0; { matrix application modes - see               }
 PRECONCATENATE    = 1; { fSetTransformation function                  }
 POSTCONCATENATE   = 2;

 FIGSONLY          = 0; { FIGS context - see fOpenFigs function        }
 FIGSGRAPHICS      = 1;

 GETEVENTS         = 0; { event modes - see fSetEventMode function     }
 IGNOREEVENTS      = 1;

 BUTTON1DOWN       = 0; { event types - see fEVENT record. Note:       }
 BUTTON2DOWN       = 1; { for 3-button mice, button 3 events will      }
 BUTTON1UP         = 2; { look like button 2 events                    }
 BUTTON2UP         = 3;
 ASCIICHAR         = 4;
 MOUSEMOVE         = 5;

 NORMAL_DRAW       = 0; { drawing modes - see fSetDrawMode function    }
 XOR_DRAW          = 1;
```

```
  SOLID_LINE       = 0;  { line styles - see fSetLineStyle function   }
  DASH_LINE        = 1;
  DOT_LINE         = 2;
  DASHDOT_LINE     = 3;

  SOLID_EDGE       = 0;  { edge styles - see fSetEdgeStyle function   }
  DASH_EDGE        = 1;
  DOT_EDGE         = 2;
  DASHDOT_EDGE     = 3;

  CIRCLE           = 0;  { marker styles - see fSetMarkerStyle function}
  SQUARE           = 1;
  X                = 2;
  CROSS            = 3;
const
  fNULL = 0;

{-----------------------------------------------------------------------
                          FIGS data types
------------------------------------------------------------------------}

type
  fCHAR    = Char;
  fPCHAR   = Pointer;     { note: a "Pointer"-type is a far pointer }

  fBYTE    = Byte;
  fPBYTE   = Pointer;

  fINT     = Integer;
  fPINT    = Pointer;

  fBOOL    = WordBool;
  fPBOOL   = Pointer;

  fLONG    = Longint;
  fPLONG   = Pointer;

  fFLOAT   = Single;
  fPFLOAT  = Pointer;

  fPVOID   = Pointer;

  f4x4MATRIX  = array[0..3,0..3] of fFLOAT;
  fP4x4MATRIX = Pointer;

  f2DPOINT = record
    x: fFLOAT;
    y: fFLOAT;
    end;
  fP2DPOINT = Pointer;

  f3DPOINT = record
    x: fFLOAT;
    y: fFLOAT;
    z: fFLOAT;
    end;
  fP3DPOINT = Pointer;

  f3DVECTOR = record
    x: fFLOAT;
    y: fFLOAT;
    z: fFLOAT;
    end;
```

```
   fP3DVECTOR = Pointer;

   fWINDOWHANDLE = HWnd;

   fEVENT = record          { used by fGetEvent function }
     eventType: fINT;
     view:      fINT;
     mousePos:  f2DPOINT;
     ch:        fCHAR;
     end;
   fPEVENT = Pointer;

   fUCBSDATA = record       { used by fGenlDrawPrim function when UCBS is }
     rowCount:  fINT;       { specified - see fGenlDrawPrim for example  }
     colCount:  fINT;
     stepCount: fINT;
     vertices:  fP3DPOINT;
     end;
   fPUCBSDATA = Pointer;

   fVIEWDATA = record
     winhandle:  fWINDOWHANDLE; { window associated with this view  }
     vrp:        f3DPOINT;      { view reference point - the position of
                                  a view's origin in world coordinates }
     prp:        f3DPOINT;      { projection reference point - the
                                  "eyepoint" (position of user)
                                  relative to the view reference point }
     vpn:        f3DVECTOR;     { view plane normal - the vector (in world
                                  coordinates) normal to the view plane }
     vup:        f3DVECTOR;     { view up vector - the vector (in world
                                  coordinates) determining view's y-axis }
     front:      fFLOAT;        { front clipping plane distance (along
                                  z-axis of viewing coordinate system) }
     back:       fFLOAT;        { back clipping plane distance (along
                                  z-axis of viewing coordinates) }
     ucWinMin:   f2DPOINT;      { lower-left corner of projection "window"
                                  on view plane (z=0), in viewing
                                  coordinates }
     ucWinMax:   f2DPOINT;      { upper-right corner of projection "window"
                                  on view plane (z=0), in viewing
                                  coordinates }
     ndcWinMin:  f2DPOINT;      { lower-left corner of projection "window"
                                  in normalized device coordinates }
     ndcWinMax:  f2DPOINT;      { upper-right corner of projection "window"
                                  in normalized device coordinates }
     renderMode: fINT;          { how to render segments posted to this
                                  view (eg SOLID or WIREFRAME) }
     projType:   fINT;          { projection style for this view (eg.
                                  PARALLEL or PERSPECTIVE) }
     erase:      fBOOL;         { whether to erase view before redrawing
                                  when updating window due to resizing,
                                  bring window to foreground, etc...} 
     end;
   fPVIEWDATA = Pointer;

{-------------------------------------------------------------------------
                        function protoypes
-------------------------------------------------------------------------}

{ FUNCTION: fOpenFigs                                                     }
{                                                                         }
{ INPUTS:   context - describes program context in which FIGS library     }
```

```
{                    will be used                                  }
{                                                                  }
{ RETURNS:   fOK, fERR_FIGS_OPEN, fERR_ALLOC_MEM_FAILED, fERR_DRIVER }
{                                                                  }
{ COMMENTS: fOpenFigs initializes the FIGS graphics library for use }
{           by an application program. This MUST be called prior to }
{           making any other FIGS library calls. The "context"     }
{           parameter can have the following values:               }
{                                                                  }
{               FIGSONLY: the application uses only the FIGS library }
{                         routines and does not utilize any of the  }
{                         platform graphics/windowing capabilities. }
{                         All FIGS functions may be called in this  }
{                         context.                                 }
{                                                                  }
{               FIGSGRAPHICS: the application is using the graphics  }
{                         capabilities provided by FIGS as well     }
{                         as the platform graphics/windowing        }
{                         capabilities. The application should not  }
{                         call the following FIGS functions:        }
{                                                                  }
{                              fCreateWindow                       }
{                              fDestroyWindow                      }
{                              fGetEvent                           }
{                              fSetEventMode                       }
{                              fEraseWindow                        }

function fOpenFigs (context: fINT): fINT;

{ FUNCTION: fCloseFigs                                             }
{                                                                  }
{ INPUTS:    (none)                                               }
{                                                                  }
{ RETURNS:   fOK, fERR_FIGS_CLOSED, fERR_DRIVER                     }
{                                                                  }
{ COMMENTS: fCloseFigs un-initializes the FIGS graphics library    }

function fCloseFigs: fINT;

{ FUNCTION: fPolyline, fPolymarker, fFillArea                      }
{                                                                  }
{ INPUTS:    vertexCount - number of vertices in list              }
{            pVertices - pointer to a list of vertices (f3DPOINTs)  }
{                                                                  }
{ RETURNS:   fOK, fERR_ALLOC_MEM_FAILED, fERR_MAX_NUM_ELMNT_HDRS,    }
{            fERR_NO_SEGMENT_OPEN, fERR_DRIVER                      }
{                                                                  }
{ COMMENTS: fPolyline, fPolymarker, and fFillArea all cause a new   }
{           element to be created at the current element pointer    }
{           position in the current open segment.                  }
{                                                                  }
{           The vertices passed to fFillArea area expected to be    }
{           coplanar, with undefined results if not. It is not      }
{           necessary to specify the starting point twice, as       }
{           fFillArea assumes a connection between the first and     }
{           last points.                                           }
{                                                                  }
{ EXAMPLE:  create a line segment element in the current open segment }
{                                                                  }
{           const                                                  }
{               p: array[0..1] of f3DPOINT = ((x:1;y:1;z:1),       }
```

```
{                                                 (x:2;y:2;z:2));            }
{          begin                                                            }
{             ...                                                           }
{             fPolyline (2, @p);                                            }
{             ...                                                           }
{          end;                                                            }
```

```
function fPolyline   (vertexCount: fINT; pVertices: fP3DPOINT): fINT;
function fPolymarker (vertexCount: fINT; pVertices: fP3DPOINT): fINT;
function fFillArea   (vertexCount: fINT; pVertices: fP3DPOINT): fINT;
```

```
{ FUNCTION: fPolyhedron                                                     }
{                                                                           }
{ INPUTS:    vertexCount - number of vertices in list                       }
{            pVertices - pointer to a list of vertices (f3DPOINTs)          }
{            facetCount - number of polyhedron facets                       }
{            pFacets - pointer to a list of fINTs describing facets         }
{                                                                           }
{ RETURNS:   fOK, fERR_ALLOC_MEM_FAILED, fERR_MAX_NUM_ELMNT_HDRS,           }
{            fERR_NO_SEGMENT_OPEN, fERR_DRIVER                              }
{                                                                           }
{ COMMENTS:  fPolyhedron causes a new element to be created at the          }
{            current element pointer position in the current open           }
{            segment. A facet list has the following structure:            }
{                                                                           }
{              a1 a2...aN  -1  b1 b2...bN  -1  c1 c2...cN  -1 (etc...)       }
{                                                                           }
{            where a1 through aN (also b1-bN, c1-cN) are indices into       }
{            the list of vertices, and where the vertex referenced by       }
{            a1 connects to the vertex referenced by a2, and so on,         }
{            with the vertex referenced by aN connecting to the vertex      }
{            referenced by a1.                                             }
{                                                                           }
{            The -1's in the facet list serve as delimiters between         }
{            each facet definition a1-aN, b1-bN, etc...                     }
{                                                                           }
{            All vertices of a facet are assumed coplanar, and each         }
{            facet must be defined in a counterclockwise order (as          }
{            viewed from the outward facing side of the facet).            }
{                                                                           }
{            The first vertex in the list ("Vertices") ALWAYS has           }
{            an index of 0, the second vertex and index of 1, and           }
{            so on...                                                       }
{                                                                           }
{  EXAMPLE: Create a four sided polyhedron element in the current           }
{            open segment                                                   }
{                                                                           }
{            const                                                          }
{              v: array[0..3] of f3DPOINT = ((x:1;y:0;z:0),                 }
{                                            (x:0;y:1;z:0),                 }
{                                            (x:0;y:0;z:1),                 }
{                                            (x:1;y:0;z:0));                }
{                                                                           }
{              p: array[0..15] of fINT =                                    }
{                        (0, 1, 2, -1,       facet intersecting             }
{                                            x,y,z=0 planes                 }
{                         0, 3, 1, -1,       z=0 plane facet                }
{                         0, 2, 3, -1,       y=0 plane facet                }
{                         1, 3, 2, -1);      x=0 plane facet                }
{            begin                                                          }
{               ...                                                         }
```

```
{                       fPolyhedron (4, @v, 4, @p);                         }
{                       ...                                                 }
{               end;                                                        }

function fPolyhedron (vertexCount: fINT; pVertices: fP3DPOINT;
                      facetCount:  fINT; pFacets:   fPINT): fINT;


{ FUNCTION: fGenlDrawPrim                                                   }
{                                                                          }
{ INPUTS:    gdpType - describes type of generalized drawing primitive     }
{            pGdpData- pointer to the gdp data                             }
{                                                                          }
{ RETURNS:   fOK, fERR_ALLOC_MEM_FAILED, fERR_MAX_NUM_ELMNT_HDRS,          }
{            fERR_NO_SEGMENT_OPEN, fERR_INVALID_GDP, fERR_DRIVER           }
{                                                                          }
{ COMMENTS: fGenlDrawPrim (Genralized Drawing Primitive) causes a          }
{           new type of GDP element to be created at the current           }
{           element pointer position in the current open segment.          }
{           The data pointed at by the "pGdpData" parameter will           }
{           vary according to the "gdpType". At this time, only the        }
{           UCBS (Uniform Cubic B-Spline) patch primitive has been         }
{           implemented.                                                   }
{                                                                          }
{ EXAMPLE:   Create a UCBS element in the current open segment             }
{                                                                          }
{            const                                                         }
{              controlPts: array[0..4,0..3] of f3DPOINT = ...              }
{                                                                          }
{            var                                                           }
{              ucbsData: fUCBSDATA;                                        }
{                                                                          }
{            begin                                                         }
{              ...                                                         }
{              ucbsData.rowCount  := 5;   # of control point array rows    }
{              ucbsData.colCount  := 4;   # of control point array columns }
{              ucbsData.stepCount := 3;   number of intervals to compute   }
{                                              across each 4x4 patch        }
{              ucbsData.vertices  := @ctrlPts;                             }
{                                                                          }
{              fGenlDrawPrim (UCBS, @ucbsData);                            }
{              ...                                                         }
{            end;                                                          }

function fGenlDrawPrim (gdpType: fINT; pGdpData: fPVOID): fINT;


{ FUNCTION: fSetLineColor, fSetIntFillColor, fSetExtFillColor              }
{           fSetMarkerColor, fSetEdgeColor                                 }
{                                                                          }
{ INPUTS:    color - a RGB color of the form $rrggbb                       }
{                                                                          }
{ RETURNS:   fOK, fERR_NO_SEGMENT_OPEN, fERR_MAX_NUM_ELMNT_HDRS            }
{                                                                          }
{ COMMENTS: These functions create a new atttribute element at the         }
{           current element pointer position in the current open           }
{           segment.                                                       }
{                                                                          }
{           fSetLineColor affects all subsequent polyline output for       }
{           the segment being displayed.                                   }
{                                                                          }
{           fSetIntFillColor affects all subsequent polyhedron/fillarea    }
{           inward-facing polygon output for the segment being             }
```

```
{             displayed.                                              }
{                                                                     }
{             fSetExtFillColor affects all subsequent polyhedron/fillarea }
{             outward-facing polygon output for the segment being     }
{             displayed.                                              }
{                                                                     }
{             fSetMarkerColor affects all subsequent polymarker output }
{             for the segment being displayed.                        }
{                                                                     }
{             fSetEdgeColor affects all subsequent polyhedron/fillarea }
{             output (for the segment being displayed).               }
{                                                                     }
{ EXAMPLE:  Create a new line color element in the current open segment }
{                                                                     }
{             begin                                                   }
{               ...                                                   }
{                fSetLineColor ($00ff00);  set line color to bright green }
{               ...                                                   }
{             end;                                                    }
function fSetLineColor    (color: fLONG):  fINT;
function fSetIntFillColor (color: fLONG):  fINT;
function fSetExtFillColor (color: fLONG):  fINT;
function fSetMarkerColor  (color: fLONG):  fINT;
function fSetEdgeColor    (color: fLONG):  fINT;

{ FUNCTION: fSetLineWidthScaleFactor, fSetEdgeWidthScaleFactor,       }
{             fSetMarkerScaleFactor                                   }
{                                                                     }
{ INPUTS:    scale - amount to scale output                           }
{                                                                     }
{ RETURNS:   fOK, fERR_NO_SEGMENT_OPEN, fERR_MAX_NUM_ELMNT_HDRS        }
{                                                                     }
{ COMMENTS: These functions create a new atttribute element at the    }
{             current element pointer position in the current open    }
{             segment.                                                }
function fSetLineWidthScaleFactor (scale: fFLOAT): fINT;
function fSetEdgeWidthScaleFactor (scale: fFLOAT): fINT;
function fSetMarkerScaleFactor    (scale: fFLOAT): fINT;

{ FUNCTION: fSetLineStyle, fSetEdgeStyle, fSetMarkerStyle             }
{                                                                     }
{ INPUTS:    style - specifies line/edge/marker style                 }
{                                                                     }
{ RETURNS:   fOK, fERR_NO_SEGMENT_OPEN, fERR_MAX_NUM_ELMNT_HDRS        }
{                                                                     }
{ COMMENTS: These functions create a new atttribute element at the    }
{             current element pointer position in the current open    }
{             segment.                                                }
{                                                                     }
{             fSetLineStyle affects all subsequent polyline           }
{             output for the segment being displayed.                 }
{                                                                     }
{             fSetEdgeStyle affects all subsequent polygon            }
{             output for the segment being displayed.                 }
{                                                                     }
{             fSetMarkerStyle affects all subsequent polymarker       }
{             output for the segment being displayed.                 }
{                                                                     }
{             Valid line styles are:    SOLID_LINE, DASH_LINE         }
```

```
{                                        DOT_LINE, DASHDOT_LINE            }
{                                                                          }
{            Valid edge styles are:      SOLID_EDGE, DASH_EDGE             }
{                                        DOT_EDGE, DASHDOT_EDGE            }
{                                                                          }
{            Valid marker styles are:  CIRCLE, SQUARE, X, CROSS            }
function fSetLineStyle   (style: fINT): fINT;
function fSetEdgeStyle   (style: fINT): fINT;
function fSetMarkerStyle (style: fINT): fINT;

{ FUNCTION: fSetEdgeVis                                                    }
{                                                                          }
{ INPUTS:    vis - polygon edges visible/invisble (TRUE/FALSE)             }
{                                                                          }
{ RETURNS:   fOK, fERR_NO_SEGMENT_OPEN, fERR_MAX_NUM_ELMNT_HDRS            }
{                                                                          }
{ COMMENTS: fSetEdgeVis creates a new attribute element at the            }
{           current element pointer position in the current open          }
{           segment.                                                       }
{                                                                          }
{           When in WIREFRAME rendering mode, this attribute has no       }
{           effect - polygons will be drawn with visible edges.           }
function fSetEdgeVis (vis : fBOOL): fINT;

{ FUNCTION: fSetDrawMode                                                   }
{                                                                          }
{ INPUTS:    mode - new draw mode (eg. NORNAL_DRAW, XOR_DRAW)              }
{                                                                          }
{ RETURNS:   fOK, fERR_NO_SEGMENT_OPEN, fERR_MAX_NUM_ELMNT_HDRS            }
{                                                                          }
{ COMMENTS: fSetDrawMode creates a new attribute element at the           }
{           current element pointer position in the current open          }
{           segment. All subsequent output (for the segment being         }
{           displayed) is affected.                                        }
{                                                                          }
{           In NORMAL_DRAW mode, output appears on the screen as          }
{           per the appropriate attribute color. In XOR_DRAW mode,        }
{           the output is the result of XOR-ing the appropriate           }
{           attribute color with what already exists on the display.      }
{           The latter mode is useful for "rubber-banding" in             }
{           interactive graphics applications.                            }
function fSetDrawMode (mode : fINT): fINT;

{ FUNCTION: fScale                                                         }
{                                                                          }
{ INPUTS:    scaleX - scale in X value                                     }
{            scaleY - scale in Y value                                     }
{            scaleZ - scale in Z value                                     }
{            pM - pointer to f4x4MATRIX receiving results                  }
{                                                                          }
{ RETURNS:   fOK, fERR_INVALID_PARAMETER                                   }
{                                                                          }
{ COMMENTS: fScale initializes a specified matrix "pM" given              }
{           the scaling values "scaleX," "scaleY," and "scaleZ."          }
function fScale (scaleX: fFLOAT;  scaleY: fFLOAT;
                scaleZ: fFLOAT;  pM:      fP4x4MATRIX): fINT;

{ FUNCTION: fTranslate                                                     }
```

```
{                                                                         }
{ INPUTS:     tX - amount to translate in X                               }
{             tY - amount to translate in Y                               }
{             tZ - amount to translate in Z                               }
{             pM - pointer to f4x4MATRIX receiving results                }
{                                                                         }
{ RETURNS:    fOK, fERR_INVALID_PARAMETER                                 }
{                                                                         }
{ COMMENTS: fTranslate initializes a specified matrix "pM" given          }
{             the translation values "tX," "tY," and "tZ."               }

function fTranslate (tX: fFLOAT;  tY: fFLOAT;
                     tZ: fFLOAT;  pM: fP4x4MATRIX): fINT;

{ FUNCTION: fRotateX, fRotateY, fRotateZ                                  }
{                                                                         }
{ INPUTS:     angle - angle to rotate                                     }
{             pM - pointer to f4x4MATRIX receiving results                }
{                                                                         }
{ RETURNS:    fOK, fERR_INVALID_PARAMETER                                 }
{                                                                         }
{ COMMENTS: fRotateX, fRotateY, and fRotateZ all initialize              }
{             the matrix pointed at by "pM" for a rotation by "angle"    }
{             about the X, Y, and Z axes, respectively.                  }
{                                                                         }
{             Since FIGS using a right-handed system:                    }
{                                                                         }
{               * a positive rotation about the x-axis goes from the     }
{                 positive y-axis to the positive z-axis                 }
{               * a positive rotation about the y-axis goes from the     }
{                 positive z-axis to the positive x-axis                 }
{               * a positive rotation about the z-axis goes from the     }
{                 positive x-axis to the positive y-axis                 }
{                                                                         }
{ EXAMPLE:   initialize a matrix for rotation by 45 degrees about        }
{             the Y-axis                                                  }
{                                                                         }
{             var                                                         }
{               m: f4x4MATRIX;                                            }
{             begin                                                       }
{               ...                                                       }
{               fRotateY (45, @m);                                       }
{               ...                                                       }
{             end;                                                        }

function fRotateX (angle: fFLOAT; pM: fP4x4MATRIX): fINT;
function fRotateY (angle: fFLOAT; pM: fP4x4MATRIX): fINT;
function fRotateZ (angle: fFLOAT; pM: fP4x4MATRIX): fINT;

{ FUNCTION: fComposeMatrix                                                }
{                                                                         }
{ INPUTS:     pM1 - pointer to first matrix                               }
{             pM2 - pointer to second matrix                              }
{             pM3 - pointer to result matrix                              }
{                                                                         }
{ RETURNS:    fOK, fERR_INVALID_PARAMETER                                 }
{                                                                         }
{ COMMENTS: fComposeMatrix performs the following matrix                  }
{             multiplication:                                             }
{                       pM3 = pM1 x pM2                                   }
{                                                                         }
```

```
{          pM3 may point at either the first, the second, or a      }
{          third matrix.                                            }
{                                                                   }
{ EXAMPLE:  Multiply m1 and m2, store results in m1                 }
{                                                                   }
{          var                                                      }
{            m1, m2: f4x4MATRIX:                                    }
{          begin                                                    }
{            ...                                                    }
{            fComposeMatrix (@m1, @m2, @m1);                        }
{            ...                                                    }
{          end;                                                     }
function fComposeMatrix (pM1: fP4x4MATRIX; pM2: fP4x4MATRIX;
                         pM3: fP4x4MATRIX): fINT;

{ FUNCTION: fSetTransformation                                      }
{                                                                   }
{ INPUTS:   pM - a pointer to a f4x4MATRIX containing the           }
{                transformation                                     }
{           mode - order in which to apply transformation when      }
{                displaying segment                                 }
{                                                                   }
{ RETURNS:  fOK, fERR_NO_SEGMENT_OPEN, fERR_INVALID_PARAMETER,      }
{           fERR_MAX_NUM_ELMNT_HDRS, fERR_ALLOC_MEM_FAILED          }
{                                                                   }
{ COMMENTS: fSetTransformation creates a transformation element     }
{           at the current element pointer position in the         }
{           current open segment.  The transformation element      }
{           affects all elements following it.  When segment is     }
{           displayed the "mode" parameter affects the current      }
{           segment transform as follows:                          }
{                                                                   }
{              mode =                                               }
{                                                                   }
{                REPLACE:         currSegXform = newSegXForm        }
{                                                                   }
{                PRECONCATENATE:  currSegXForm = currSegXform x     }
{                                                newSegXForm        }
{                                                                   }
{                POSTCONCATENATE: currSegXForm = newSegXForm  x     }
{                                                currSegXform       }
{                                                                   }
{ EXAMPLE: Create a transformation in the current open segment      }
{                                                                   }
{          var                                                      }
{            m: f4x4MATRIX;                                         }
{          begin                                                    }
{            ...                                                    }
{            fRotateY (45, @m);                 create a 45 degree  }
{                                               y rotation matrix   }
{            fSetTransformation (@m, REPLACE);                      }
{            ...                                                    }
{          end;                                                     }
function fSetTransformation (pM:fP4x4MATRIX; mode: fINT): fINT;

{ FUNCTION: fOpenSegment                                            }
{                                                                   }
{ INPUTS:   segId- segment (identifier) to open                    }
{                                                                   }
```

```
{ RETURNS:    fOK, fERR_SEGMENT_OPEN, fERR_MAX_NUM_SEGMENTS            }
{                                                                      }
{ COMMENTS: fOpenSegment opens an existing segment, or creates         }
{           one if a segment with the identifier "segId" doesn't       }
{           exist.  The element pointer will be set at the last        }
{           element in the segment's element list.                     }

function fOpenSegment (segId: fINT): fINT;

{ FUNCTION: fCloseSegment                                              }
{                                                                      }
{ INPUTS:    (none)                                                    }
{                                                                      }
{ RETURNS:    fOK, fERR_NO_SEGMENT_OPEN                                }
{                                                                      }
{ COMMENTS: fCloseSegment closes the current open segment.             }

function fCloseSegment: fINT;


{ FUNCTION: fDeleteSegment                                             }
{                                                                      }
{ INPUTS:    segId- segment (identifier) to delete                     }
{                                                                      }
{ RETURNS:    fOK, fERR_INVALID_SEGMENT_ID                             }
{                                                                      }
{ COMMENTS: fDeleteSegment deletes the segment (and all the            }
{           elements of the segment) with identifier "segId".          }

function fDeleteSegment (segId: fINT): fINT;

{ FUNCTION: fCallSegment                                               }
{                                                                      }
{ INPUTS:    segId- segment (identifier) to call                       }
{                                                                      }
{ RETURNS:    fOK, fERR_CALL_SEGMENT_RECURSION, fERR_NO_SEGMENT_OPEN,  }
{           fERR_MAX_NUM_ELMNT_HDRS                                    }
{                                                                      }
{ COMMENTS: fCallSegment creates a call segment element  at the        }
{           current element pointer position in the current open       }
{           segment. When the segment is displayed, it will call       }
{           the specified segment, displaying it with the calling      }
{           segment's current transform.                               }

function fCallSegment (segId: fINT): fINT;

{ FUNCTION: fCopySegment                                               }
{                                                                      }
{ INPUTS:    segId- segment (identifier) to copy                       }
{                                                                      }
{ RETURNS:    fOK, fERR_NO_SEGMENT_OPEN, fERR_SEGMENT_NONEXISTENT,     }
{           fERR_MAX_NUM_ELMNT_HDRS, fERR_ALLOC_MEM_FAILED             }
{                                                                      }
{ COMMENTS: fCopySegment copies all the elements of segment            }
{           "segId" into the current open segment at the current       }
{           element pointer position. Element pointer will be set      }
{           to the last element copied.                                }

function fCopySegment (segId: fINT): fINT;

{ FUNCTION: fPostSegment                                               }
{                                                                      }
```

```
{ INPUTS:    segId - segment (identifier) to (un)post            }
{            viewId - view (identifier) to (un)post segment to (or from) }
{            post - post/unpost (TRUE/FALSE)                      }
{                                                                 }
{ RETURNS:   fOK, fERR_SEGMENT_NONEXISTENT, fERR_INVALID_VIEW,    }
{            fERR_SEGMENT_NOT_POSTED, fERR_SEGMENT_POSTED,        }
{            fERR_MAX_NUM_SEGMENT_LINKS                           }
{                                                                 }
{ COMMENTS: fPostSegment posts/unposts segment "segId" to/from    }
{            view "viewId".  If posted, the segment will be drawn  }
{            within the context of the view the next time that     }
{            fDrawView is called.                                  }
function fPostSegment (segId: fINT; viewId: fINT; post: fBOOL): fINT;

{ FUNCTION: fLabel                                                }
{                                                                 }
{ INPUTS:   id - label identifier                                 }
{                                                                 }
{ RETURNS:  fOK, fERR_NO_SEGMENT_OPEN, fERR_MAX_NUM_ELMNT_HDRS    }
{                                                                 }
{ COMMENTS: fLabel creates a label element at the current element }
{            pointer position within the current open segment.    }
function fLabel (id: fINT): fINT;

{ FUNCTION: fMoveElmntPtrToLabel                                  }
{                                                                 }
{ INPUTS:   labl - label to move to                              }
{                                                                 }
{ RETURNS:  fOK, fERR_NO_SEGMENT_OPEN, fERR_INVALID_LABEL         }
{                                                                 }
{ COMMENTS: fMoveElmntPtrToLabel moves the element pointer        }
{            forwards/backwards to the label element "labl." If   }
{            "labl" isn't found, the element pointer does not change. }
function fMoveElmntPtrToLabel (labl: fINT): fINT;

{ FUNCTION: fSetElmntPtr                                          }
{                                                                 }
{ INPUTS:   index - new element pointer position                 }
{                                                                 }
{ RETURNS:  fOK, fERR_NO_SEGMENT_OPEN                             }
{                                                                 }
{ COMMENTS: fSetElementPointer sets the element pointer at the    }
{            given index relative to the first element in the     }
{            segment.  It will point at the last element in the   }
{            segment if index is greater than the number of       }
{            elements currently in the segment.                   }
function fSetElmntPtr (index: fINT): fINT;

{ FUNCTION: fOffsetElmntPtr                                       }
{                                                                 }
{ INPUTS:   offset - amount to offset element pointer             }
{                                                                 }
{ RETURNS:  fOK, fERR_NO_SEGMENT_OPEN                             }
{                                                                 }
{ COMMENTS: fOffetElmntPtr offsets the element pointer relative   }
{            to it's current position.  If the offset is larger than }
{            the actual number of elements in a particular direction, }
{            then the lesser of the two is used for the offset.    }
```

```
function fOffsetElmntPtr (offset: fINT): fINT;

{ FUNCTION: fDeleteElmnt                                                  }
{                                                                         }
{ INPUTS:    (none)                                                       }
{                                                                         }
{ RETURNS:   fOK, fERR_NO_SEGMENT_OPEN, fERR_INVALID_ELEMENT              }
{                                                                         }
{ COMMENTS: fDeleteElmnt deletes the element pointed at by the            }
{           element pointer in the current open segment. Upon             }
{           return, the element pointer will point to the element         }
{           following the deleted one, or, if no element follows,         }
{           the element preceding the deleted one.                        }

function fDeleteElmnt: fINT;

{ FUNCTION: fDeleteElmntsInRange                                          }
{                                                                         }
{ INPUTS:    index1- starting index                                       }
{            index2- ending index                                         }
{                                                                         }
{ RETURNS:   fOK, fERR_NO_SEGMENT_OPEN, fERR_INVALID_LABEL                }
{                                                                         }
{ COMMENTS: fDeleteElmntsInRange deletes the elements between             }
{           index1 and index2 (relative to the start of the              }
{           list), inclusive.  The element pointer will be set            }
{           at the element following index2, or, if no elements           }
{           follow, the element preceding index1.                         }

function fDeleteElmntsInRange (index1: fINT; index2: fINT): fINT;

{ FUNCTION: fDeleteElmntsBetweenLabels                                    }
{                                                                         }
{ INPUTS:    label1 - starting label                                      }
{            label2 - ending label                                        }
{                                                                         }
{ RETURNS:   fOK, fERR_NO_SEGMENT_OPEN, fERR_INVALID_LABEL                }
{                                                                         }
{ COMMENTS: fDeleteElmntsBetweenLabels deletes all elements between,      }
{           but not including, label1 and label2.  Element pointer        }
{           will be set to label2.  If either/both labels don't exist     }
{           no elements are deleted.  If label2 precedes label1 no        }
{           elements are deleted.                                         }

function fDeleteElmntsBetweenLabels (label1: fINT; label2: fINT): fINT;

{ FUNCTION: fComposeView                                                  }
{                                                                         }
{ INPUTS:    viewId - view identifier                                     }
{            pViewData - pointer to an initialized fVIEWDATA record       }
{                                                                         }
{ RETURNS:   fOK, fERR_MAX_NUM_VIEWS                                      }
{                                                                         }
{ COMMENTS: fComposeView creates/composes a view based on the             }
{           fVIEWDATA record pointed at by "pViewData."                   }

function fComposeView (viewId: fINT; pViewData: fPVIEWDATA): fINT;

{ FUNCTION: fQueryView                                                    }
{                                                                         }
{ INPUTS:    viewId - view identifier                                     }
```

```
{            pViewData - pointer to an fVIEWDATA record          }
{                                                                 }
{ RETURNS:   fOK, fERR_INVALID_VIEW, fERR_INVALID_PARAMETER       }
{                                                                 }
{ COMMENTS: fQueryView fills in the fVIEWDATA record pointed at by }
{            "pViewData" with the data corresponding to view "viewId." }

function fQueryView (viewId: fINT; pViewData: fPVIEWDATA): fINT;

{ FUNCTION: fDrawView                                             }
{                                                                 }
{ INPUTS:    viewId - view identfier                              }
{            erase - specifies whether to erase view before drawing }
{                                                                 }
{ RETURNS:   fOK, fERR_INVALID_VIEW, fERR_INVALID_WINDOWHANDLE,   }
{            fERR_DRIVER                                           }
{                                                                 }
{ COMMENTS: fDrawView draws the specified view.                   }

function fDrawView (viewId: fINT; erase: fBOOL): fINT;

{ FUNCTION: fSetViewRenderMode                                    }
{                                                                 }
{ INPUTS:    viewId - view identifier                             }
{            mode - new render mode (eg. WIREFRAME or SOLID)       }
{                                                                 }
{ RETURNS:   fOK, fERR_INVALID_VIEW                               }
{                                                                 }
{ COMMENTS: fSetRenderMode sets the render mode for the specified }
{            view.                                                }

function fSetViewRenderMode (viewId: fINT; mode: fINT): fINT;

{ FUNCTION: fEraseWindow                                          }
{                                                                 }
{ INPUTS:    winhandle - handle of window to erase                }
{                                                                 }
{ RETURNS:   fOK, fERR_INVALID_WINDOWHANDLE                       }
{                                                                 }
{ COMMENTS: fEraseWindow erases the specified window. This function }
{            should not be called in FIGSGRAPHICS context.        }

function fEraseWindow (winhandle: fWINDOWHANDLE): fINT;

{ FUNCTION: fCreateWindow                                         }
{                                                                 }
{ INPUTS:    (none)                                               }
{                                                                 }
{ RETURNS:   a fWINDOWHANDLE if successful, or fNULL if an error occured }
{                                                                 }
{ COMMENTS: fCreateWindow creates a generic window, and returns a }
{            handle to that window. This function should not be called }
{            if in FIGSGRAPHICS context.                          }

function fCreateWindow: fWINDOWHANDLE;

{ FUNCTION: fDestroyWindow                                        }
{                                                                 }
{ INPUTS:    winhandle - handle of window to destroy              }
{                                                                 }
{ RETURNS:   fOK, fERR_INVALID_FUNC, fERR_INVALID_WINDOWHANDLE    }
{                                                                 }
```

```
{ COMMENTS: fDestroyWindow destroys the window referenced by          }
{           "winhandle."  This function should not be called in       }
{           FIGSGRAPHICS context.                                     }

function fDestroyWindow (winhandle: fWINDOWHANDLE): fINT;

{ FUNCTION: fGetEvent                                                 }
{                                                                     }
{ INPUTS:   pEvent - pointer to an fEVENT record                      }
{                                                                     }
{ RETURNS:  fOK, fERR_INVALID_FUNC, fERR_IGNOREEVENTS                 }
{                                                                     }
{ COMMENTS: fGetEvent waits for one of the 6 event types              }
{           (BUTTON1DOWN, BUTTON2DOWN, BUTTON1UP, BUTTON2UP,          }
{           ASCIICHAR, MOUSEMOVE) to occur, fills in the fEVENT       }
{           record pointed at by pEvent, and then returns.            }
{           This function should not be called in FIGSGRAPHICS        }
{           context.                                                  }

function fGetEvent (pEvent: fPEVENT): fINT;

{ FUNCTION: fSetEventMode                                             }
{                                                                     }
{ INPUTS:   mode - new event mode                                     }
{                                                                     }
{ RETURNS:  fOK, fERR_INVALID_FUNC                                    }
{                                                                     }
{ COMMENTS: fSetEventMode sets the current application event mode.    }
{           This function should not be called in FIGSGRAPHICS        }
{           context.                                                  }

function fSetEventMode (mode: fINT): fINT;

{ FUNCTION: fPause                                                    }
{                                                                     }
{ INPUTS:   delay - amount of time to delay                           }
{                                                                     }
{ RETURNS:  fOK, fERR_DRIVER                                          }
{                                                                     }
{ COMMENTS: fPause is a generic delay function.  The delay parameter  }
{           will vary in units according to the platform.            }

function fPause (delay: fLONG): fINT;
```

```
{-----------------------------------------------------------------------
                function DLL entry point definitions (Windows)
-----------------------------------------------------------------------}

implementation

function fOpenFigs;                          external 'FIGS' index 1;
function fCloseFigs;                         external 'FIGS' index 2;
function fPolyline;                          external 'FIGS' index 3;
function fPolymarker;                        external 'FIGS' index 4;
function fFillArea;                          external 'FIGS' index 5;
function fPolyhedron;                        external 'FIGS' index 6;
function fGenlDrawPrim;                      external 'FIGS' index 7;
function fSetLineStyle;                      external 'FIGS' index 8;
function fSetLineWidthScaleFactor;           external 'FIGS' index 9;
function fSetLineColor;                      external 'FIGS' index 10;
function fSetIntFillColor;                   external 'FIGS' index 11;
function fSetExtFillColor;                   external 'FIGS' index 12;
function fSetEdgeVis;                        external 'FIGS' index 13;
function fSetEdgeStyle;                      external 'FIGS' index 14;
function fSetEdgeWidthScaleFactor;           external 'FIGS' index 15;
function fSetEdgeColor;                      external 'FIGS' index 16;
function fSetMarkerStyle;                    external 'FIGS' index 17;
function fSetMarkerScaleFactor;              external 'FIGS' index 18;
function fSetMarkerColor;                    external 'FIGS' index 19;
function fSetDrawMode;                       external 'FIGS' index 20;
function fScale;                             external 'FIGS' index 21;
function fRotateX;                           external 'FIGS' index 22;
function fRotateY;                           external 'FIGS' index 23;
function fRotateZ;                           external 'FIGS' index 24;
function fTranslate;                         external 'FIGS' index 25;
function fComposeMatrix;                     external 'FIGS' index 26;
function fSetTransformation;                 external 'FIGS' index 27;
function fOpenSegment;                       external 'FIGS' index 28;
function fCloseSegment;                      external 'FIGS' index 29;
function fDeleteSegment;                     external 'FIGS' index 30;
function fCallSegment;                       external 'FIGS' index 31;
function fCopySegment;                       external 'FIGS' index 32;
function fPostSegment;                       external 'FIGS' index 33;
function fLabel;                             external 'FIGS' index 34;
function fMoveElmntPtrToLabel;               external 'FIGS' index 35;
function fSetElmntPtr;                       external 'FIGS' index 36;
function fOffsetElmntPtr;                    external 'FIGS' index 37;
function fDeleteElmnt;                       external 'FIGS' index 38;
function fDeleteElmntsInRange;               external 'FIGS' index 39;
function fDeleteElmntsBetweenLabels;         external 'FIGS' index 40;
function fComposeView;                       external 'FIGS' index 41;
function fQueryView;                         external 'FIGS' index 42;
function fDrawView;                          external 'FIGS' index 43;
function fSetViewRenderMode;                 external 'FIGS' index 44;
function fEraseWindow;                       external 'FIGS' index 45;
function fCreateWindow;                      external 'FIGS' index 46;
function fDestroyWindow;                     external 'FIGS' index 47;
function fGetEvent;                          external 'FIGS' index 48;
function fSetEventMode;                      external 'FIGS' index 49;
function fPause;                             external 'FIGS' index 50;

end.
```

Generic FIGS Program Structure

The following program listing outlines the general event-driven control structure appropriate for application programs based on the FIGS graphics language.

Generic FIGS program in Pascal

```pascal
program Generic;

uses WinTypes, WinProcs, FIGS;

procedure WinMain;
var
    hwin: fWINDOWHANDLE;
    event: fEVENT;
begin
    fOpenFigs (FIGSONLY);
    hwin := fCreateWindow;
    fSetEventMode (GETEVENTS);
    fGetEvent (@event);
while event.eventType <> BUTTON2DOWN do
        fGetEvent (@event);
    MessageBeep (0);
    fDestroyWindow (hwin);
    fCloseFigs;
end;

begin
    WinMain;
end.
```

Endnotes

§ Dan Knudson is a software engineer at Microsoft Corporation. This work grew out of a project started during his student days at California State – Long Beach.

1. Howard, T. L. J., Hewitt, W. T., Hubbold, R. J., and Wyrwas, K. M., *A Practical Introduction to PHIGS and PHIGS PLUS*, Addison Wesley Publishing Company, Wokingham, England (1991)

Index